The Professional Practice
of Rehabilitation Counseling

Dennis R. Maki, PhD, LMHC, NCC, ACS, CRC

Dr. Dennis R. Maki is a professor with the Graduate Programs in Rehabilitation and Chair of the Department of Rehabilitation and Counselor Education at The University of Iowa. Dr. Maki has had over 40 years of experience as a rehabilitation counselor, educator, and researcher. His scholarly interests lie in rehabilitation counseling, especially its philosophy, identity, and standards of practice. He has also written in the area of clinical supervision, assessment, graduate rehabilitation counselor education, and cross-cultural issues related to disability and rehabilitation. Dr. Maki has served as a visiting professor at the Universidad de Puerto Rico and the Universidad Autonoma de Yucatan. He spent May 1994 in Africa as a World Rehabilitation Fund Fellow, where he researched traditional medicine and disability. Previously, Dr. Maki taught Vocational Psychology at the IKIP in Jogjakarta, Indonesia. He was invited to Oxford University's 2005 Roundtable on Accommodating the Needs of Persons with Disability. Dr. Maki is a past president of the Council on Rehabilitation Education (CORE), a past president of the American Rehabilitation Counseling Association, as well as a Former CRCC Commissioner. He was selected as the Rehabilitation Educator of the Year by the National Council on Rehabilitation Education. Dr. Maki has been a consistent contributor to the professional literature in our profession and is the coeditor of four texts, *The Professional Practice of Rehabilitation Counseling* (2011), *The Handbook of Rehabilitation Counseling* (2003), *Rehabilitation Counseling: Profession and Practice* (1997), and *Applied Rehabilitation Counseling* (1986), as well as the *Directory of Doctoral Study with Rehabilitation* (1985, 1992, 2000, 2007).

Vilia M. Tarvydas, PhD, LMHC, CRC

Dr. Vilia Tarvydas is a professor of Rehabilitation and Counselor Education and Director of the Institute on Disabilities and Rehabilitation Ethics (I-DARE). She has worked in rehabilitation practice in traumatic brain injury and physical rehabilitation, and as a rehabilitation counselor educator for almost 40 years. Her scholarly works and national and international presentations have concentrated on the areas of ethics, ethical decision-making, and professional governance and standards. She has published extensively in these areas, and aside from this text, she is coauthor of *Counseling Ethics and Decision Making* (2007), a revised third edition of her earlier book, *Ethical and Professional Issues in Counseling*. Dr. Tarvydas has a career-long involvement in counseling professionalization, ethics, and credentialing. She served as Chair of the Iowa Board of Behavioral Science Examiners, and its Disciplinary Committee. She served on the ACA Licensure Committee for many years and more recently served on the Oversight Committee for the joint AASCB/ACA 20/20 Initiative. She also has had extensive experience in counselor certification, having served for 8 years with CRCC as Vice-Chair and Secretary, on the Examination and Research Committee, and as Chair of the Ethics Committee. Dr. Tarvydas is a Past President of three national professional organizations: the National Council on Rehabilitation Education, the American Rehabilitation Counseling Association, and the American Association of State Counseling Boards. She has been a member of the ACA Ethics Committee and the American Occupational Therapy Association's Judicial Council. She was a member of the ACA Taskforce on Revision of the Code of Ethics that produced the 2005 The ACA Code of Ethics. She chaired the groups that developed the 1987 unified Code of Ethics for Professional Rehabilitation Counselors and served on the Task Force that drafted the 2002 CRCC Code of Professional Ethics. Most recently, she was the Chair of the CRCC Task Force on Code Revision that produced the writing of the 2010 Code.

The Professional Practice of Rehabilitation Counseling

Dennis R. Maki, PhD, LMHC, NCC, ACS, CRC
Vilia M. Tarvydas, PhD, LMHC, CRC
Editors

SPRINGER PUBLISHING COMPANY
NEW YORK

Springer Publishing Company, LLC
11 West 42nd Street
New York, NY 10036
www.springerpub.com

Acquisitions Editor: Sheri W. Sussman
Composition: S4Carlisle

ISBN: 978-0-8261-0738-1
E-book ISBN: 978-0-8261-0739-8
Instructor's PowerPoints ISBN: 978-0-8261-0968-2
Instructor's Syllabus ISBN: 978-0-8261-9392-6

Qualified instructors may request supplements by emailing textbook@springerpub.com

11 12 13/ 5 4 3 2 1

The author and the publisher of this Work have made every effort to use sources believed to be reliable to provide information that is accurate and compatible with the standards generally accepted at the time of publication. The author and publisher shall not be liable for any special, consequential, or exemplary damages resulting, in whole or in part, from the readers' use of, or reliance on, the information contained in this book. The publisher has no responsibility for the persistence or accuracy of URLs for external or third-party Internet Web sites referred to in this publication and does not guarantee that any content on such Web sites is, or will remain, accurate or appropriate..

Library of Congress Cataloging-in-Publication Data
The professional practice of rehabilitation counseling / [edited by] Dennis R. Maki, Vilia M. Tarvydas.
    p. cm.
  Includes index.
  ISBN 978-0-8261-0738-1 — ISBN 978-0-8261-0739-8 (ebk)
1. Rehabilitation counseling. I. Maki, Dennis R. II. Tarvydas, Vilia M.
  HD7255.5.P76 2011
  362.4'0486--dc23   2011021918

Printed in the United States of America by Bang Printing

To Dr. T. F. Riggar ...
Professor, mentor, colleague, and friend (1944–2007)

NCRE Presidents

1955–66 Gregory Miller (early years)	1987–88 Bobbie J. Atkins
1967–69 Bob Johnson (CRCE officially begins)	1988–89 Marvin D. Kuehn
	1989–90 William G. Emener
1969–70 Robert Wamken	1990–91 Jeanne Boland Patterson
1970–71 Thomas L. Porter	1991–92 Bud Stude
1971–72 Daniel Sinick	1992–93 Sue Gunn
1972–73 Bob Johnson	1993–94 Tom Evenson
1973–74 Marceline Jaques	1994–95 Susanne Bruyere
1974–75 Joseph A. Szuhay	1995–96 Paul Leung
1975–76 Dan McAlees	1996–97 Carolyn Rollins
1976–77 William H. Graves (CRCE becomes NCRE)	1997–98 Mike Leahy
	1998–99 Kurt Johnson
1977–78 Donald C. Linkowski	1999–2000 Donald W. Dew
1978–79 Glen O. Geist	2000–01 Amos Sales
1979–80 Jack Kite	2001–02 John Benshoff
1980–81 Donald W. Dew	2002–03 Margaret Glenn
1981–82 William M. Jenkins	2003–04 Vilia M. Tarvydas
1982–83 Martha Lentz Walker	2004–05 Jeanne Patterson
1983–84 Ken Reagles	2005–06 Jorge Garcia
1984–85 Ann Meyer	2006–07 David Perry
1985–86 Joe Afanador	2007–08 Linda Holloway
1986–87 Vincent A. Scalia	2008–09 William Downey
	2009–10 David Strauser

NCRA Presidents

1958–59 David E. Young	1962–63 I. W. Leggett
E. J. Buchanan	1963–64 Richard A. Koebler
1959–60 Robert A. Lassiter	1964–65 Gordon D. Smith
1960–61 Harley B. Reger	1965–66 Charles F. Maine
1961–62 LeRoy C. Larsen	1966–67 Richard A. Morris

NCRA Presidents (*cont.*)

1967–68	Daniel C. McAlees	1990–91	Florence Curnutt
1968–69	Edwin J. Chorn	1991–92	Patricia Nunez
1969–70	Alton R. Ray	1992–93	Robert Neuman
1970–71	Mary S. Smith	1993–94	Richard Coelho
1971–72	Michael A. Oliverio	1994–95	Madan Kundu
1972–73	Carl E. Hansen	1995–96	Jack Hackett
1973–74	Thomas K. White	1996–97	Jan La Forge
1974–75	Betty S. Hedgeman	1997–98	Joseph Turpin
1975–76	Anne D. Crumpton	1998–99	John Reno
1976–77	James E. Gray	1999–00	Gregory G. Garske
1977–78	Philip Chase	2000–01	Win Priest
1978–79	Arnold Wolf	2001–2001	Lorie McQuade
1979–80	Joyce Pigg	2002–2003	Chris Reid
1980–81	Robert Hasbrook	2003–2004	Thomas Wilson
1981–82	Lawrence Warnock	2005–2006	Connie McReynolds
1982–83	Henry C. DeVasher, Jr	2006–2007	Jeanne Patterson
1983–84	Martha S. Wolf	2008–2008	Charles Palmer
1985–86	Patricia A. Mundt	2009–2009	Joseph E. Keferl
1986–87	Allen Searles	2010–2010	Penny Willmering
1987–88	Susan Magruder Pollock	2011–2011	Jennipher Wiebold
1988–89	John G. Moline	2012–2012	Elizabeth A. Boland
1989–90	Ethel D. Briggs		

ARCA Presidents

1958–59	Salvatore DiMichael	1969–70	Leonard Miller
1959–60	William Usdane	1970–71	Gregory Miller
1960–61	Abraham Jacobs	1971–72	Richard Thoreson
1961–62	Lloyd Lofquist	1972–73	George Ayers
1962–63	C. H. Patterson	1973–74	Lawrence Feinberg
1963–64	William Gellman	1974–75	George N. Wright
1964–65	Daniel Sinick	1975–76	Tom Porter
1965–66	John McGowan	1976–77	Ray Ehrie
1966–67	John Muthard	1977–78	Bob Johnson
1967–68	Marceline Jaques	1978–79	Frank Touchstone
1968–69	Martin Acker	1979–80	Don Linkowski

ARCA Presidents (*cont.*)

1980–81	Kenneth Reagles	1996–97	Bill Richardson
1981–82	Dan McAlees	1997–98	Vilia Tarvydas
1982–83	Stanford Rubin	1998–99	Donna Falvo
1983–84	Ken Thomas	1999–00	Deborah Ebner
1984–85	Paul McCollum	2000–01	Ellen Fabien
1985–86	Edna Szymanski	2001–02	Susan Bruyere
1986–87	Randy Parker	2002–03	Timothy Janikowski
1987–88	Brian McMahan	2003–04	Betty Hedgeman
1988–89	John Thompson	2004–05	Jan LaForge
1989–90	Ross Lynch	2005–06	Irmo Marini
1990–91	Dennis R. Maki	2006–07	Patricia Nunez
1991–92	Martha Walker	2007–08	Yolanda Edwards
1992–93	Jeanne Patterson	2008–09	Carolyn Rollins
1993–94	John Dolan	2009–10	Frank Lane
1994–95	Linda Shaw	2010–11	Carrie Wilde
1995–96	Michael Leahy		

Contents

Contributors

Catherine A. Anderson, MS, CRC, Assistant Director, Rehabilitation Research and Training Center on Effective Vocational Rehabilitation Service Delivery Practices, Stout Vocational Rehabilitation Institute, University of Wisconsin–Stout, Menomonie, Wisconsin

Mary Barros-Bailey, PhD, CRC, Bilingual Rehabilitation Counselor, Vocational Expert, and Life Care Planner Intermountain Vocational Services, Inc., Boise, Idaho

Norman L. Berven, PhD, Professor, Department of Rehabilitation Psychology and Special Education, University of Wisconsin–Madison, Madison, Wisconsin

Susanne Bruyère, PhD, CRC, Professor of Disability Studies, Director of the Employment and Disability Institute, Associate Dean of Outreach, ILR School, Cornell University, Ithaca, New York

Jennifer L. Burris, MA, Doctoral Student, Department of Special Education and Rehabilitation Counseling, The University of Kentucky, Lexington, Kentucky

Brenda Y. Cartwright, EdD, CRC, NCC, MHC, Associate Professor and Program Director, Department of Kinesiology and Rehabilitation Science, University of Hawaii at Manoa, Honolulu, Hawaii

Fong Chan, PhD, CRC, Professor, Director of Training (PhD Program), Co-Director, Rehabilitation Research and Training Center on Effective Vocational Rehabilitation Service Delivery Practices, Department of Rehabilitation Psychology and Special Education, University of Wisconsin-Madison, Madison, Wisconsin

R. Rocco Cottone, PhD, Professor and Coordinator of Doctoral Programs, Division of Counseling and Family Therapy, University of Missouri–St. Louis, St. Louis, Missouri

Mary O'Connor Drout, PhD, Lecturer, Department of Rehabilitation Psychology and Special Education, University of Wisconsin-Madison, Director, Encore Unlimited, LLC, Stevens Point, Madison, Wisconsin

Mayu Fujikawa, MS, CRC, Doctoral Student, Department of Rehabilitation Psychology and Special Education, University of Wisconsin-Madison, Madison, Wisconsin

Debra A. Harley, PhD, CRC, LPC, Professor and Chair, Department of Special Education and Rehabilitation Counseling, The University of Kentucky, Lexington, Kentucky

Michael T. Hartley, PhD, CRC, Assistant Professor, Department of Disability and Psychoeducational Services, University of Arizona, Tucson, Arizona

James T. Herbert, PhD, CRC, LPC, Professor, Department of Counselor Education, Counseling Psychology, and Rehabilitation Services, Pennsylvania State University, University Park, Pennsylvania

Michael J. Leahy, PhD, LPC, CRC, Professor and Director, Office of Rehabilitation and Disability Studies, Department of Counseling, Educational Psychology and Special Education, Michigan State University, East Lansing, Michigan

William Ming Liu, PhD, Professor, Training Director, Counseling Psychology Program, Department of Psychological and Quantitative Foundations, The University of Iowa, Iowa City, Iowa

Lisa Lopez Levers, PhD, LPCC, LPC, CRC, NCC, Professor, Department of Counseling, Psychology, and Special Education, Duquesne University, Pittsburgh, Pennsylvania

David P. Moxley, PhD, Oklahoma Health Care Authority Medicaid Professor, Anne and Henry Zarrow School of Social Work, University of Oklahoma, Norman, Oklahoma

Veronica Muller, MS, CRC, Doctoral Student, Department of Rehabilitation Psychology and Special Education, University of Wisconsin-Madison, Madison, Wisconsin

Jane E. Myers, PhD, NCC, NCGC, LPC, Professor, Counseling and Educational Development, The University of North Carolina at Greensboro, Greensboro, North Carolina

Margaret A. Nosek, PhD, Executive Director, Center for Research on Women with Disabilities, Professor, Department of Physical Medicine and Rehabilitation, Baylor College of Medicine, Houston, Texas

Deirdre O'Sullivan, PhD, CRC,   Assistant Professor, Department of Counselor Education, Counseling Psychology, and Rehabilitation Services, Pennsylvania State University, University Park, Pennsylvania

Beth Reiter, JD,   Attorney specializing in research and writing on disability law and New York State statutory law Elizabeth A. Reiter, LLC

Theodore P. Remley, Jr., JD, PhD,   Department of Counseling and Human Services, Professor and Batten Endowed Chair, Old Dominion University, Norfolk, Virginia

Amos P. Sales, EdD, CRC,   Professor and Head, Rehabilitation, Department of Disability and Psychoeducational Services, University of Arizona, Tucson, Arizona

Mark A. Stebnicki, PhD, LPC, CRC, CCM,   Professor, Director of Graduate Program in Rehabilitation Counseling, East Carolina University, Greenville, North Carolina

David R. Strauser, PhD,   Associate Professor, Kinesiology and Community Health, University of Illinois at Urbana–Champaign, Champaign, Illinois

Connie Sung, MS,   Doctoral Student, Department of Rehabilitation Psychology and Special Education, University of Wisconsin–Madison, Madison, Wisconsin

Rebecca L. Toporek, PhD,   Associate Professor, Career Counseling Coordinator, Department of Counseling, San Francisco State University, San Francisco, California

Chia-Chiang Wang, MS,   Doctoral Student, Department of Rehabilitation Psychology and Special Education, University of Wisconsin–Madison, Madison, Wisconsin

Alex W. K. Wong, PhD,   Doctoral Student, Kinesiology and Community Health, University of Illinois at Urbana–Champaign, Champaign, Illinois

Foreword

A rehabilitation counselor is a counselor . . .

Through this book, and with these six words, Dennis Maki and Vilia Tarvydas have accomplished what many thought was impossible. They have clearly defined the profession of rehabilitation counseling, contextualized it as a specialty of professional counseling, delimited the scope of practice of rehabilitation counseling consistent with the broader profession, and simultaneously identified what is unique about this specialty. Thus ends a long history of questions and occasional conflict, and thus begins the true actualization of a professional rehabilitation counseling that stands at the forefront in creating sustained positive change in the holistic well being of persons with disabilities.

Leaving behind the uncertainty of professional definition, the authors proceed in this revised and expanded edition of their foundation text to lead, educate, and challenge readers to be the best that we can be in service to others, on behalf of others, steeped in a philosophy of personal empowerment through effective counseling, advocacy for our clients and our profession, and leadership through both advocacy and professional service. They help us know that we are engaged in a most noble profession, one that motivates each of us to become and be our very best. Each student is encouraged to commit to a lifetime of learning, to constantly integrate new knowledge to achieve an ever-better quality of professional service. Each rehabilitation educator is encouraged to model that commitment through continued learning, high-quality research that informs practice, and professional leadership that promotes practitioners as well as the field itself. Each practitioner is similarly encouraged to seek, use, and generate new knowledge to enhance the quality of services to clients.

The authors underscore the evidence-based nature of practice in rehabilitation counseling, citing both the broader generic counseling literature and the specialized literature in rehabilitation counseling and services. They leave nothing out, emphasizing the need for all counselors to constantly enhance our knowledge base and contribute to that knowledge base on behalf of other professionals and the clients we serve. Throughout the book, the science of practice is seamlessly integrated with the art of practice, yet at the core the authors' leave us with one overarching theme: the heart of the field lies in a desire to empower clients to be effective advocates and change agents for themselves, their families, their communities, and society.

The book authors and the many chapter authors collectively model the best in the field. Each has a long history of excellence in teaching, professional service, research, and professional practice. Their sustained leadership and advocacy has been vital to the emergence of rehabilitation counseling as a major counseling specialty. They have worked tirelessly in professional associations (e.g., ACA, NRA, ARCA, NRCA), credentialing bodies (e.g., CORE, CACREP), and with credentialing associations (e.g., CRCC, NBCC) to assure that professionally trained rehabilitation counselors meet the highest standards of the profession, obtain credentials that are widely recognized and meaningful in the marketplace, and obtain jobs that commensurate with their professional preparation and certification.

As you read this book, prepare to be taught by the best. Read carefully, reflect frequently, integrate thoroughly, and continuously ask how this knowledge will help you become an ethical, effective, responsible, and responsive professional counselor, one with a clearly defined specialization in rehabilitation counseling. The tools are waiting to be used. As you read and immerse yourself in the foundations of the field, you will find yourself preparing for a broad scope of practice, consistent with national accreditation and certification standards in professional counseling and rehabilitation counseling. You will emerge from your training into a global marketplace where the need for your services is vital to promoting individual rights and social justice. With the tools provided here, you will be ready to meet the challenges inherent for persons with disabilities seeking to survive and thrive in a changing global society.

On a personal note, I have known the editors, especially Dr. Maki, for most of my 40+ year professional career. When we met, we shared a common bond of knowledge and philosophy, as the writings of George Wright had been seminal readings in each of our rehabilitation counseling master's degree programs. We each were early certificants and held the CRCC (I am proud to hold certificate number 78). As young rehabilitation counselor educators, we shared curriculum materials for teaching, research ideas to support the profession, and professional service roles as advocates for rehabilitation counselors. We also worked together to build the then-newly formed Rho Chi Sigma, the Rehabilitation Counseling and Services Honor Society, serving both as newsletter editors and as presidents, and taking on any other duties that needed to be addressed. In the late 1908s, Rho Chi Sigma merged with Chi Sigma Iota, the Counseling Academic and Professional Honor Society International, in recognition that rehabilitation counseling was a part of the larger profession of counseling.

Though I met Vilia much later, I have had numerous opportunities to be impressed with her effective and consistent advocacy on behalf of our profession. She has devoted countless hours to professional service, helping to lead the profession forward while conducting and publishing high-quality research, and, like her co-editor, training future generations of rehabilitation counselors to meet the needs of persons with disabilities.

Consistent with their years of advocacy and service that I have witnessed and shared over several decades, the authors have prepared this book to serve the needs of the profession, students preparing to enter the profession, and the clients and potential clients we will serve. Royalties will accrue not to the authors but to the American Rehabilitation Counseling Association, for use nationally to support professional and student needs. Kudos to Drs. Maki and Tarvydas for once more devoting their talents to leading the profession toward the possible future.

Jane E. Myers, Professor
Counseling and Educational Development
The University of North Carolina at Greensboro

Acknowledgments

We thank the graduate students who helped us with research and feedback, along with their questions and life stories. We also thank Sheri W. Sussman, our editor at Springer, for encouraging us to write this fourth edition.

The editors and authors would like to acknowledge the Presidents of the National Council on Rehabilitation Education (NCRE), the National Rehabilitation Counseling Association (NRCA), and the American Rehabilitation Counseling Association (ARCA) for their leadership and outstanding contributions to the profession over the years.

We express our gratitude to the countless students whose questions and interests have caused us to remain thoughtful and passionate about the improvement of the practice and professional evolution of rehabilitation counseling. While there are many other persons to whom we should express appreciation, they are too numerous to mention here and we hope we have been gracious enough to personally express our thanks as we have worked with them. However, we do wish to acknowledge the generously given advice and critique of the prior edition of this text offered by Drs. Noel Estrada-Hernandez and Michael Hartley who assisted us in pinpointing specific areas for improvement. The expert work of our doctoral student, MooKyong Jeon, was most valuable in the development of the new instructional supplementary materials to support the book's use in the classroom. Finally, we most especially thank the authors who have generously shared their wisdom and inspired us through their contributions to this text. Many of them have shared the struggles, work, and hopes for improving rehabilitation counseling with us over the years—and for that, all of us in rehabilitation counseling will be forever grateful. A final acknowledgement is to note with gratitude that we have enjoyed a rich professional partnership and personal friendship over the years that have allowed us to develop our ideas and professional passions with the support of a valued colleague.

We hope that readers will respond with excitement to imagining the futures that excellence in professional practice in rehabilitation counseling may bring them, and take to heart the knowledge and wisdom that our authors have sought to impart to them to guide them on this journey.

The Professional Practice
of Rehabilitation Counseling

I

Introduction

1

Rehabilitation Counseling: A Specialty Practice of the Counseling Profession

Dennis R. Maki and Vilia M. Tarvydas

We say seeing is believing but actually, as Santayana pointed out, we are all much better at believing than seeing.

Robert Anton Wilson

For many years, rehabilitation counseling has struggled with development and identity issues that have both excited constructive development and diminished energy and resources that could have better defined its practice. The authors have had the good fortune of entering the field, experiencing the practice of rehabilitation counseling, and providing leadership for some of its professionalization efforts during many fascinating and crucial junctures in the last few decades. We have also had the good fortune of both deeply loving the philosophy and practice of rehabilitation counseling and of forming a productive partnership in our work as rehabilitation counselor educators at the University of Iowa over the last two decades. The ideas and information contained in this text provide a necessary re-structuring of rehabilitation counseling around a clear point of view on its nature and future. This point of view makes a choice in the timeworn debate about whether rehabilitation counseling at its core is essentially counseling or case management. It defines an exciting and transcendent view of the potential future for rehabilitation counselors by firmly focusing on the unique and important partnership its practitioners have with persons with disabilities and yet mindful of the critical grounding we must maintain with the profession of counseling and its standards. Future clients and students seeking to enter the field can derive greater benefit from such clarity of perspective and commitment to one vision that seeks to integrate rehabilitation counseling's practitioners with the strongest potential for excellence in practice and best opportunities in future years.

THE IOWA POINT OF VIEW: REHABILITATION COUNSELING IS A SPECIALTY PRACTICE OF THE COUNSELING PROFESSION

On the face of it, the above statement would appear to be a simple, declarative sentence, and it is our view that we can now make it so. However, the complex evolution of rehabilitation counseling and the growth pains attendant to it would indicate otherwise.

There has been a natural progression from the inception of rehabilitation counseling in legislation to its current recognition as a specialization of the counseling profession. Major changes have occurred in the evolution of rehabilitation counseling over the last several years that will be highlighted in this text. The major and most critical difference distinguishing this text from others in the field is the clear affiliation of the field with the profession of counseling. The professional identity of a rehabilitation counselor as a counselor has wide formal endorsement by the major professional organizations in rehabilitation counseling. This identity has been endorsed by the Council for Accreditation of Counseling and Related Educational Programs (CACREP) and the members of the Rehabilitation Counseling Consortium (RCC) (CORE, CRCC, ARCA, NRCA, NCRE, CARP, IARP, and ADARA). This declaration comes following the adoption of a definition by these major professional rehabilitation counseling organizations consistent with this understanding:

> A rehabilitation counselor is a counselor who possesses the specialized knowledge, skills, and attitudes needed to collaborate in a professional relationship with persons with disabilities to achieve their personal, social, psychological, and vocational goals. (RCC, 2005)

Subsequently, this identity statement and definition have informed the accreditation and certification processes within the field. As a result, professional information placed specifically and clearly within the context of the overall profession of counseling is needed. This text is intended to meet this goal.

With this perspective, it is important that we join the Consortium in making an ongoing commitment to ensure that rehabilitation counselors have access to the credentials to practice and to the employment settings for which they are qualified (CRCC, 2004). The recent knowledge domain study (Leahy, Munzen, Saunders, & Strauser, 2009) in rehabilitation counseling indicated an increased need for pre-service and continuing education in counseling, mental health, and substance abuse. It is our view that these topics have not been sufficiently addressed in rehabilitation counseling texts. The study by Leahy et al. is the most recent in the series of studies used as a basis for both CRCC certification and CORE accreditation standards. Therefore, it is important that our text reflects many of these changes in practice.

Finally, there have been other trends in the field that are incorporated into our text including (a) an increased emphasis in recent years on educating rehabilitation and mental health professionals in empirically based practices, the research bases for them, and learning how to incorporate them into professional practice; (b) the globalization of professional practice in rehabilitation counseling and counseling in general; (c) increased emphasis on mental health counseling knowledge and skills to enter the more specific practice of behavioral health; (d) cultural competencies and social justice perspectives to address the needs of oppressed and disadvantaged persons in a society with a radically shifting ethnic and racial composition; and (e) rising awareness of the critical importance that ethics knowledge and decision-making skills should play in professional preparation.

The "Iowa Point of View" is introduced to readers so that they can have a clear context into which to place the material that will follow. This viewpoint has been developed and successfully utilized by both authors who have been instrumental in growing and operationalizing the scope of practice for rehabilitation counseling throughout the course of our careers. Additionally, our involvement with the leadership of professional organizations and the construction of the curriculum in the Iowa program have been informed by the conviction that counseling is the core profession with which rehabilitation counseling is linked. This book elucidates the knowledge, skills, and attitudes that we believe best serve today's rehabilitation counseling professional in a challenging and exciting career.

The perspective that rehabilitation counseling is a *specialization* within the profession of counseling is in contrast to the traditional approach many other textbooks have taken, that is, rehabilitation counseling is a unique profession. Other texts have portrayed the historic tension between the counseling, case co-ordination/management points of view without taking a position, or avoided the issue entirely by only presenting the case service process. We place rehabilitation counseling firmly within the profession of counseling and include information about the profession of counseling and rehabilitation counseling's relationship to it. Some other points that are important to choices of content for this book are as follows:

- Rehabilitation counselor education and practice should include a "hybrid-ization" of the content in rehabilitation and mental health counseling to best serve the entire range of disabilities common in practice and to reflect a truly holistic and inclusive point of view.
- Rehabilitation counselor education and practice should involve a develop-mental perspective relative to the client's needs throughout the lifespan.
- Rehabilitation counselor education and practice is best conducted from the framework of an ecological, transformative rehabilitation perspective that addresses the person–environment context of disability and seeks to assist individuals with disabilities adapt to the physical and attitudinal environ-ments in which they live, work, learn, and recreate. Simultaneously, it as-sists these environments to accommodate these individuals.
- Rehabilitation counselor education and practice are best conducted from a culturally competent perspective that respects the individual differences, as

well as the commonalities of both the client and the counselor. This view includes both social justice and advocacy perspectives. Rehabilitation counseling must seek a better infusion of the sensibilities and "ways of knowing" about the disability experience within the discipline of disability studies. This field and the study of the various fine arts, social science, and humanities representations of disability and the sensibilities they portray must be taken as serious source material to expand the professional viewpoint that represents the traditional teachings of the field.

We are indebted to the contributions of the past and those scholars who came before us in their thinking. With the evolution of society in our current environment and technology, there is a place for rehabilitation counselors in the delivery of behavioral health services. If they are not included, their absence is a loss of practice opportunities for its professionals. More importantly, it is also a lost opportunity for persons with disabilities to be assisted by individuals who bring advanced knowledge, skills, and attitudes related to disability, and a commitment to advocacy, a disability perspective, and rehabilitation philosophy and practices to their work.

Previously behavioral health practice has been protected by the traditions and regulations of the field of psychology, particularly with respect to the assessment and treatment processes. Historically, these are core regimens of behavioral health practice. Rehabilitation counseling has moved from the medical model of the provider as the expert who looks within the individual as the target of intervention, to a more fully realized, ecological understanding of the role of the environments in which the individual lives, works, learns, and recreates. We are in the best position at this point to synthesize and properly harmonize the disparate elements of the rehabilitation and disability perspectives with those derived from the medical world of behavioral health professions. However, in order to ethically assert our place in the practice of behavioral health, we must have an education and professional preparation program that embraces and integrates all the necessary elements to practice responsibly and with skill and respect. For example, stronger attention to such areas as evidence-based practices and diagnosis and treatment of psychiatric disorders are necessary. Enhanced educational and professional standards that attend to the integration of the traditional and new aspects of our roles would better inform all those who have a stake in the proper definition of rehabilitation counseling practice—regulators, those seeking to enter the practice, colleagues in behavioral health, and the persons and the families of those in need of these services.

The rehabilitation counseling philosophy views clients as decision makers in their own lives. This perspective is predicated on clients making meaning of their lives in their current circumstances. Making meaning requires informed consent; that is, being given accurate and complete information about the choices in a manner that is useful and tailored to the needs of the client. This is essential to the quality of the client's ability to make informed choices. Professional rehabilitation counselors should be educated and prepared to provide such services within their professional and individual scopes of practice. However, the parameters of a profession's scope of practice periodically must be revised to meet the evolving needs of society and the individuals whom it serves. The types of persons served by rehabilitation counselors, their residual assets and limitations that impact their quality of life (QOL), and their successful integration into their responsibilities and communities have substantially expanded over the years. A growing awareness and appreciation of individuals within the context of their culture as well as the advances of technology and a broadening research base of best practice require more intense pre-service preparation and commitment to ongoing continuing education.

This text seeks to highlight some of these critical areas of emerging importance while still providing the most up-to-date information about more traditional aspects of rehabilitation counseling practice. These traditional aspects are more fully realized through their integration and synthesis in the professional practice of counseling. Rehabilitation counseling should be incorporating the emerging trends of counseling into the body of its practice.

FRAMING THE DISCUSSION

The underlying premise of this text is one of *professional identity*; that is, rehabilitation counseling is not a separate and distinct profession with its own accreditation and certification processes. It is a specialty area of practice within the counseling profession. Rehabilitation counselors are counselors. This text is the first text to move beyond the historically contentious debate about the nature of rehabilitation counseling that has cost the field and its clients so much.

As George Wright (1980) pointed out, "counseling is inherent in rehabilitation counseling: this is a nontransferable obligation of the rehabilitation counselor . . . the ultimate professional responsibility for the function of counseling cannot be delegated" (p. 55). Our scope of practice, accreditation standards, and certification requirements support our identity as counselors. With our counseling skills as well as disability and rehabilitation expertise, we also perform functions such as case management, advocacy, and consultation when working with our clients in achieving their individualized goals. The fact that we do more than counsel does not compromise our primary identity as counselors nor does it diminish our other essential functions. To embrace our core identity as counselors is not incompatible with, or disrespectful to, the rehabilitation counselors who choose to work in areas of practice that are not titled counselor or are not primarily counseling in function. It is, in fact, embracing the broadest scope of practice possible.

With the growth in the diversity of clients and settings in which rehabilitation counselors practice, our role has evolved. The functions and competencies of individual practitioners have expanded as well. Counseling skills are an essential component of all activities undertaken by the professional throughout the rehabilitation process. It is the specialized knowledge of disabilities, the disability experience, and the socio-political-environmental factors that impact people with disabilities combined with counseling skills that help differentiate us from social workers, other counselors, and other rehabilitation professionals in today's service environments (Jenkins, Patterson, & Szymanski, 1992; Leahy & Szymanski, 1995).

Our professional identity as counselors has implications for *credentialing*. This text is predicated on creating the most robust practitioner—a licensed mental health or professional counselor with a certification in rehabilitation counseling. In the tradition of the core professions, we advocate for the licensure of the counseling generalist and for certification of the rehabilitation specialist. CORE accredited programs and their graduates have a vested interest in the counselor licensure movement. It is critical to have qualified rehabilitation counselors advocating for language that permits our inclusion in state counseling licensure statutes and regulations.

Both rehabilitation counseling accreditation and certification standards are clearly aligned with its identity as a counseling specialty. CRCC's conjunctive scoring protocol requires an applicant to pass both the counseling and rehabilitation sections of the CRC exam. The 2009–2014 CORE accreditation standards are based on the CRCC knowledge domain validation studies and input from multiple stakeholders. Furthermore, the CORE standards are configured to parallel the first eight general counseling standards of CACREP. These eight parallel curriculum standard areas include the following: C.1 Professional Identity; C.2 Social and Cultural Diversity Issues; C.3 Human Growth and Development; C.4 Employment and Career Development; C.5 Counseling and Consultation; C.6 Group Work; C.7 Assessment; and C.8 Research and Program Evaluation. Two additional areas of specialized rehabilitation counseling standards are C.9 Medical, Functional, Environmental and Psychosocial Aspects of Disability and C.10 Rehabilitation Services and Resources. Without acceptable coursework covering the final two areas and an internship supervised by a CRC, no one can claim the identity of rehabilitation counselor or become a CRC. This strategy requires the accredited master's programs to prepare graduates in both the counseling and rehabilitation competencies.

It is interesting to observe that of all counseling specialties, rehabilitation counselors actually are most clearly aligned with the practice of mental health counseling and are practitioners of mental health counseling. In fact, in the 1970s when the current specialization of mental health counseling initially was being formed, it was a part of ARCA. As the mental health counseling interests became more clearly defined, its proponents sought an interest group within ARCA. When that vehicle did not evolve, they separated and formed the American Mental Health Counseling Association (AMCHA), also a division within the American Counseling Association (ACA). When in the 1980s the Academy of Mental Health Certification was experiencing financial difficulties, it approached the Commission on Rehabilitation Counselor Certification to discuss the possibility of becoming a specialty certification within CRCC, a bid that CRCC did not encourage at that time.

If one thinks objectively about which types of counselors practice most directly with people who have cognitive and emotional disorders, one would have to admit that rehabilitation counselors always have been primary providers of counseling services to persons with mental health disabilities. Rehabilitation counselors have developed advanced expertise in this area and provided innovative treatment models to serve persons with psychiatric disabilities. Witness the evolution of the highly respected psychiatric rehabilitation programs and models such as that developed at Boston University by Dr. Bill Anthony and his colleagues. Anthony is clear that this psychiatric rehabilitation model was based on traditional rehabilitation counseling practices (Anthony, Cohen, & Farkas, 1990). Additionally, rehabilitation counselors have always found it in their mission to work with those persons who experience the greatest stigma and biggest barriers to living their lives with a disability. At this point in our history, persons with psychiatric disorders would certainly be the group most in need of professionals who carry this perspective and have the requisite skills to assist them (Corrigan & Lam, 2007). Therefore, rehabilitation counselors should be practitioners of mental health counseling or psychiatric rehabilitation.

Currently, rehabilitation counselors are being called upon again to work with wounded veterans as they return from Iraq and Afghanistan toward their medical and vocational reintegration. Today's veterans' "signature injuries" are cognitive and emotional injuries calling upon those who serve them to add strong mental health counseling skills to serve those recovering from primarily traumatic brain injuries and psychiatric disorders (Isham et al., 2010). This involvement with returning veterans is also a valued part of the tradition of rehabilitation counseling practice that should spur innovation and further development of relevant areas of expertise.

The credentialing bodies of rehabilitation counseling (CORE and CRCC) have been recognized by the ACA as having parity with CACREP and NBCC (Tarvydas, Leahy, & Zanskas, 2009) by virtue of its unique and robust mission and required skill set. A professional rehabilitation counselor prepared with the core knowledge and competencies in addition to the critical and cutting edge counseling content is a fully and expertly prepared counselor ready to meet the holistic needs of the widest range of contemporary clients and settings.

In addition to the preparation and credentialing standards, the *professional organizations* with which professionals choose to align themselves have historical, philosophical, as well as practical implications. Professional identity is important and a part of this choice. The associations and organizations with which rehabilitation counselors choose to affiliate reflect their professional identities. Each professional must choose from the options available. Some organizations historically had been predicated on the idea that rehabilitation counseling is a separate profession, and others are based on the idea that rehabilitation counseling is a professional specialization of the counseling profession. Since there has been movement toward alignment around the identity of a rehabilitation counselor as professional counselor, rehabilitation counselors should support and become active in an organization that provides this knowledge base and identity, even if they hold additional affiliations to supplement this focus.

In recent years the involvement and stature of rehabilitation counseling organizations in the professional discussions of counseling has been expanded through the participation and affirmation of CORE, CRCC, ARCA, and NRCA in the work of the 20/20 Initiative. The 20/20 Initiative is maintained by the ACA and AASCB to facilitate the unification of the counseling profession, and foster collaborative discussion among the counseling constituency issues of mutual concern. The 20/20 Initiative required all participating organizations to endorse the unified definition of counseling as well as the seven core principles of counseling:

1. Sharing a common professional identity is critical for counselors.
2. Presenting ourselves as a unified profession has multiple benefits.
3. Working together to improve the public perception of counseling and to advocate for professional issues will strengthen the profession.
4. Creating a portability system for licensure will benefit counselors and strengthen the counseling profession.
5. Expanding and promoting our research base is essential to the efficacy of professional counselors and to the public perception of the profession.
6. Focusing on students and prospective students is necessary to ensure the ongoing health of the counseling profession.
7. Promoting client welfare and advocating for the populations we serve is the primary focus of the counseling profession.

It is true that all movements require time for their implications to become clear to all participants. However, it is also true that the decisions that have already been made will drive the future development and agenda of all participants no matter what their individual levels of awareness or endorsement. It is our belief that to be ethical, leaders in academe must prepare their students to have the most robust careers available to them upon graduation. They should be able to access all positions and credentials and work for which they are qualified. These marketplaces and credentials have in the past been restricted from rehabilitation counselors, especially those whose identity and credentials were not in compliance with the counseling marketplace. The historical identity of rehabilitation counselors as vocational rehabilitation counselors prioritized vocational rehabilitation in its identity and credentials, and diverted attention from the capabilities necessary to engage in the full domain of counseling professional practice.

The pre-service curriculum and the educators who design and deliver it set the foundation for their students' identities—be it as counselors, case managers, or job placement professionals. In the earlier years of rehabilitation counseling, educators clearly defined identities around vocational rehabilitation and case management. This focus served a positive purpose for its time, given its historic link to state-federal legislation and service delivery systems. Any system that over-emphasizes the importance of case management services, be it vocational or insurance rehabilitation, also restricts the realization of the full spectrum of the field's competency and services. Therefore, it does not attend to the full range of needs that clients bring to rehabilitation counselors who espouse a holistic model of service and have a title that includes the word counselor. Likewise, those entering the profession who expect to be prepared to become professional counselors may find great confusion and difficulty with their identities. A restricted identity ultimately has not served our practitioners well in the community. Most people say "I'm a rehab counselor" and if asked to be more specific, they may not have a clear, succinct answer to offer their inquirer—thus reflecting the confusion of the field of rehabilitation counseling. We intend to provide a clear answer—"I am a counselor who works with people who have disabilities"—no matter whether the disability is mental illness or some other type of disability.

So we are counselors and we see advantage in alignment with counseling. What does this mean for the design and content of *educational programs*? This text is best understood from the viewpoint that we must continue to perfect the preparation of qualified providers of rehabilitation counseling services. A qualified provider has a graduate degree in rehabilitation counseling or closely related program from an accredited program and is nationally certified and licensed in those states where it is available.

It is important to support a comprehensive rehabilitation career ladder through rehabilitation education from the associate through the doctoral degree. We must acknowledge the critical nature of all points on this career ladder spectrum. Undergraduate preparation programs in disability studies/human relations have an important role in preparing staff at the technician or paraprofessional level. The master's is the core level of education that prepares individuals for professional practice with its affiliated licenses and certification. We endorse the master's preparation as the basis for professional practice and acknowledge the preparatory work of undergraduates and their curricula. Finally, we see the doctoral programs in rehabilitation counselor education as an important element in advancing research, preparing future professionals (capacity building), and providing leadership to the profession of rehabilitation counseling. We acknowledge that all parts of this continuum of preparation are important, but professional practice is seated at the master's level.

OVERVIEW OF BOOK

Intended Audience

This text is intended to be useful to a wide range of readers and can readily serve as a core textbook or resource to explain the history, development, and current practice of rehabilitation counselors within the context of the contemporary profession of counseling. While most clearly useful to counselors-in-training, we think that those rehabilitation counselors at the doctoral level or already in practice who are interested in re-examining the field and understanding its broader positioning and potential will find this text appealing.

Features of the Text

In addition to the refreshed content and updated perspective described in the introduction, several new features have been added to assist both instructors and students in gaining full benefit of this volume. Learning objectives begin each chapter, and discussion questions are provided at the conclusion of the chapter to expand the understanding and relevance of the material covered in the text. Additionally, the appendices that readers of earlier editions of this text had found so helpful are updated and expanded to provide key reference materials of importance. Of particular note is the inclusion of the newly revised CRCC 2010 Code of Professional Ethics for Rehabilitation Counselors.

Sections and Chapters

The Professional Practice of Rehabilitation Counseling consists of 20 chapters that are divided into four sections to emphasize different themes that are important to understanding both the people and types of situations with which rehabilitation counselors work and the specific roles and skill sets that describe professional practice.

Part I: Foundations consists of basic information about the structure and professional practice of rehabilitation counseling. It is here that the evolution and new vision of rehabilitation counseling as a specialty practice of the profession of counseling is introduced. However, this perspective is integrated with the important traditional aspects of the field's history, credentialing structures, disability policy and laws, and a conceptual paradigm to undergird its practice.

Part II: Persons With Disability is a section that is new to this edition of the text. The section serves the important role of introducing the reader to the rehabilitation counselor's most important partner in the counseling process—the person with a disability. The chapters are presented to situate the lives of persons with disabilities by focusing on hierarchically arranged contexts in their lives—moving from individual, to family and intimate relationships, to the disability community, and finally to disability in global context. Care was taken to emphasize the experience, not only the facts, of disability, and to give particular attention to the voices of persons with disabilities themselves through discussion of the disability community/disability rights perspective that is too often superficially treated.

In *Part III: Professional Functions*, we return to a focus on the professional practice of rehabilitation counseling and introduce the specific functions that constitute the work of rehabilitation counseling: assessment, counseling, case management, advocacy, and career development, vocational behavior, and work adjustment of individuals with disabilities. These core functions are masterfully presented by authorities who describe the core elements of each area, but taken together they sketch out the broad parameters of the professional scope of practice in this robust field.

Finally, *Part IV: Professional Competencies* introduces the competencies that provide the types of skills, knowledge, and attitudes that must infuse the practice of rehabilitation counseling because of their pervasive and overarching importance in all aspects of practice. The areas of ethics, ethical decision making, and cultural competency are widely acknowledged as major forces for professionalism and are considered at the outset of the section. The adoption of evidence-based practices and broader issues of research utilization, and increased prominence of technology used in rehabilitation are forces for innovation and critical to maintaining current practice. Fittingly, in the last chapter of this section, clinical supervision is discussed as it performs a critical translational and evaluative role in both the initial education and continual improvement of our professional colleagues.

REFERENCES

Anthony, W. A., Cohen, M., & Farkas, M. (1990). *Psychiatric rehabilitation* (1st ed.). Boston, MA: Boston University, Center for Psychiatric Rehabilitation.

Corrigan, P. W., & Lam, C. (2007). Challenging the structural discrimination of psychiatric disabilities: Lessons learned from the American disability community. *Rehabilitation Education, 21*(1), 53–58.

Isham, G. J. (Chair), Basham, K. K., Busch, A. B., Cassimatis, N. E. G., Moxley, J. H., III., Pincus, H. A., . . . Tarvydas, V. M. (2010). *Provision of mental health services under TRICARE.* Washington, DC: Institute of Medicine, The National Academies Press.

Jenkins, W., Patterson, J. B., & Szymanski, E. M. (1992). Philosophical, historic, and legislative aspects of the rehabilitation counseling profession. In R. M. Parker & E. M. Szymanski (Eds.), *Rehabilitation counseling: Basics and beyond* (2nd ed., pp. 1–41). Austin, TX: Pro-Ed.

Leahy, M. J., Munzen, P., Saunders, J. L., & Strauser, D. (2009). Essential knowledge domains underlying effective rehabilitation counseling practice. *Rehabilitation Counseling Bulletin, 52*(2), 95–106. doi:10.1177/0034355208323646

Leahy, M. J., & Szymanski, E. M. (1995). Rehabilitation counseling: Evolution and current status. *Journal of Counseling and Development, 74,* 163–166.

Rehabilitation Counseling Consortium. (2005). *Rehabilitation counselor and rehabilitation counseling definitions.* Schaumberg, IL: Commission on Rehabilitation Counselor Certification.

Tarvydas, V., Leahy, M. J., & Zanskas, S. A. (2009). Judgment deferred: Reappraisal of rehabilitation counseling movement toward licensure parity. *Rehabilitation Counseling Bulletin, 52,* 85–94. doi:10.1177/0034355208323951

Wright, G. N. (1980). *Total rehabilitation.* Boston, MA: Little, Brown.

II
Foundations

2

Evolution of Counseling and Its Specializations

Theodore P. Remley

LEARNING OBJECTIVES

After reading this chapter, you should be able to:

- Develop an understanding of the broad field of counseling and the role of specializations within that field from the perspective of a rehabilitation counselor.
- Understand the positive role rehabilitation counseling has played in the development of the broader field of counseling.
- Appreciate the benefits of rehabilitation counseling, identifying it as a specialty within the broader field of counseling, and to understand the problems associated with that view as well.
- Review the history of the development of the field of counseling in the United States along with the development of the major specialties that comprise the field of counseling.
- Appreciate the areas in which all counselors work together for the benefit of the counseling profession as a whole.
- Understand the contemporary challenges facing all counselors including standardization of licensure requirements, convincing third-party payers to pay counselors for their services to clients, and to create job classifications for counselors in government and private sector settings.

Preparing to become a professional rehabilitation counselor is an exciting venture that probably raises many questions in the minds of students. Naturally, students preparing to enter a new field within our society want to know where their chosen area of work fits into the complex arena of professions and occupations. Not only do new professionals want to understand the more general question of what the purpose of their work will be and whether their work contributions will be valued by our society, but also they want to know the more practical question of whether good

17

jobs will exist for them once the complete their training and preparation. Emerging professionals also want to know how their work will be perceived by the clients they will serve, by the colleagues they will work with, and by the public in general.

Students preparing to become rehabilitation counselors will be more comfortable in their new professional roles if they develop a thorough understanding of the field they are in the process of entering (Stebnicki, 2009). In order to understand the place of rehabilitation counselors in the United States today, it is helpful to examine the broader field of counseling and to review the evolution of counseling and its various specializations within contemporary American society.

This chapter will consider the status of counseling as a profession within the United States and role of specializations within the counseling field. A brief history of counseling and the various counseling specializations will be presented and milestones in the development of counseling will be identified. The roots of the present-day counseling profession will be traced to the specialization of counseling psychology and an explanation will be offered regarding the separation of counseling from counseling psychology. The development of the three major specializations within counseling (school counseling, rehabilitation counseling, and community mental health counseling) will be summarized. The question of whether counseling has achieved the status of an independent recognized profession in American society will be explored. The lack of cooperation among organizations of specialists within counseling will be addressed. Areas of agreement among specializations in counseling will be addressed including: (a) the unique philosophical foundations of counseling; (b) the successful political agitation of counselors for governmental recognition that has led to counselors being licensed in all states; (c) efforts to create job classifications for counselors; and (d) successes in the area of counselors receiving third-party payments for their services to clients. Views on the relationship between the fields of counseling and rehabilitation counseling will be presented.

THE MANY SPECIALTIES WITHIN COUNSELING

The field of counseling has many specialties. It is not unusual for a field or profession to create specializations. Specialization is necessary in professions that are too broad for every practitioner to be able to provide high-quality services in all areas.

Probably the most significant problem the counseling profession faces today is determining whether the profession will develop a strong identity as one united profession with a common philosophical foundation and knowledge base, or whether the specialties will emerge as the dominant force within counseling (Myers & Sweeney, 2001). If specialties prevail, the general field of counseling has little chance of becoming a unified and societally recognized profession.

The problems associated with specialties within the counseling profession were discussed in a special issue of the *Journal of Counseling and Development* (Myers, 1995b), the primary professional journal of the counseling profession.

In the articles appearing in that issue of the journal, authors discussed the established and emerging counseling specialties. The value of counseling specialties providing focused research and practice in particular areas of counseling was emphasized. In addition, problems associated with specialties within counseling fragmenting the counseling profession were identified and discussed.

Specialties within counseling have been categorized based on the settings where counselors work; the population served by counselors; the approach taken to counseling; and techniques used by counselors. Although the lists of counselor specialists below are not complete, they provide some insight into the complexity of specializations within counseling.

Examples of counselors identified as specialists due to their work setting include the following:

- College counselors
- Employment counselors
- Mental health counselors
- Military counselors
- Offender counselors
- Private practice counselors
- Rehabilitation counselors
- School counselors
- Substance abuse counselors

Examples of counselors identified as specialists because of the population they serve include the following:

- Adolescent counselors
- Bereavement counselors
- Child counselors
- Counselors for persons who are gay, lesbian, bisexual, or transgendered
- Gerontological counselors
- Marriage and family counselors
- Military counselors
- Offender counselors
- Rehabilitation counselors
- Sports counselors
- Substance abuse counselors

Examples of counselors who are identified as specialists because of the approach they take to counseling include the following:

- Career counselors
- Group counselors
- Counselors involved in assessment or evaluation
- Counselors who closely adhere to a particular counseling theory (e.g., existential counselors, behavioral counselors, Gestaltist counselors, and cognitive behavioral counselors)

Examples of counselors who are identified as specialists because they use particular techniques in their counseling include the following:

- Art therapists
- Complementary, alternative, and integrative counselors
- Music therapists
- Native healers
- Play therapists
- Psychodrama counselors
- Sex therapists

The following are examples from the professional literature of articles that provide information regarding some of the many counseling specialties: addictions counseling (Page & Bailey, 1995); gerontological counseling (Myers, 1995a); marriage and family counseling (Smith, Carlson, Stevens-Smith, & Dennison, 1995); mental health counseling (Smith & Robinson, 1995); rehabilitation counseling (Leahy & Szymanski, 1995); and school counseling (Paisley & Borders, 1995).

In considering rehabilitation counselors within the broader context of counseling, rehabilitation counselors could be considered counseling specialists who provide services to persons with disabilities (specialists because of the population they serve) and counseling specialists who work in rehabilitation agencies or settings (specialists because of the setting in which they work). Counselors without the specialized knowledge and skills possessed by rehabilitation counselors would not be effective in a setting in which the counseling of persons with disabilities is the primary focus.

No one practitioner can be proficient in all areas of any particular profession (Abraham, 1978; Kett, 1968; Napoli, 1981). Research, training, and improved practice occur in specialized areas of counseling that have unique needs and issues. Specialists within a complex profession are necessary. Problems arise, however, if specialists within a particular profession believe that their specialties are so different from the general profession that they, in fact, constitute a separate profession. In some cases in which new professions are emerging, specialty groups do attempt to establish themselves as separate professions (Etzioni, 1969). When a specialty presents itself as unique from the overall professional group and takes the position that it is different enough from the overall group that it should be recognized as an entirely separate profession, that position weakens the ability of the overall group to gain needed societal recognition as a profession. To explain this problem, consider a hypothetical scenario in which physicians who are surgeons say that they are really much better prepared and skilled than other physicians, and therefore, they should be licensed separately from general physicians. In order to accomplish their goal of separate societal recognition and licensure, surgeons would have to convince politicians in each state that they are not merely physicians, but a special brand of physicians who possess knowledge and skills beyond those of the typical physician. A position such as that by surgeons would weaken the status of physicians in general in our society, and, in the long run, would weaken the status of surgeons as well.

Counseling was formed as a separate field because counseling specialty groups came together to create the field of counseling. Just as the United States primarily is made of immigrants from other countries and is strong in many ways because of its diversity, the country also must deal with problems that diversity brings. In the same way, counseling has many strengths because of its diversity of specialists. However, in some respects, the growth and recognition of the counseling field as a whole has been inhibited by the focus of counseling specialists on their own particular areas. In some cases they have demanded to be recognized as a profession separate and independent from counseling and have failed to assist the overall field of counseling to achieve societal recognition (Fox, 1994).

A basic aspect of human nature is that people tend to identify with the group they know best and with which they are the most familiar. Members and leaders within the specialty subgroups in counseling have naturally tended to create well-organized entities that represent their specialized interests. It is also clear that counseling is at a critical stage of development (Collison, 2001; Remley & Herlihy, 2010). Either the profession of counseling will find a way through its conflict and will emerge as a unified profession or it will fragment and its various specialties will attempt to establish themselves as separate independent professions.

Rehabilitation counselors, despite being a strong specialty with a history of success in areas such as national certification and graduate program accreditation, have determined that it is in their best interest to support the success of the profession of counseling as a whole, rather than attempt to establish rehabilitation counseling as a separate and distinct profession outside the general profession of counseling (Tarvydas, Leahy, & Zanskas, 2009). The Commission on Rehabilitation Counselor Certification (CRCC, 2010) has identified rehabilitation counselors as *counselors* who possess *specialized knowledge, skills, and attitudes*—words that appear to acknowledge the specialty nature of rehabilitation counseling within the counseling profession. The Council on Rehabilitation Education (CORE) offers the following statement regarding rehabilitation counselors, indicating rehabilitation counselors are specialists within the field of counseling: "Working directly with an individual with a disability or their advocates, a rehabilitation counselor is a special type of professional counselor who helps evaluate and coordinate needed services to assist people with disabilities. . . ." (Council on Rehabilitation Education, 2010).

A BRIEF HISTORY OF COUNSELING AND THE SPECIALIZATIONS WITHIN COUNSELING

Each scholar who has offered a summary of the history of the counseling profession emphasizes different historical developments and reaches different conclusions (Bradley & Cox, 2001; Gibson & Mitchell, 2008; Glosoff, 2009; Hershenson,

Power, & Waldo, 1996; Remley & Herlihy, 2010; Sweeney, 2001). This brief review of how the profession of counseling came into existence particularly examines the role of specialties in the formation of the overall counseling profession.

Emergence of the Independent Field of Counseling

Within the United States, a number of events led to the formation of counseling as a mental health practice separate from and independent of psychology. The following historical transitions led to the creation of the field of counseling: (a) the decision of psychologists to require that specialists within the field of psychology known as counseling psychologists must hold doctoral degrees to enter the field; (b) the development of school counseling programs throughout the country; (c) the introduction of rehabilitation counselors into our society; and (d) the introduction of counselors into community mental health agencies and private practices. These were the four major forces that combined to establish in the United States the current independent profession known as counseling.

Counseling Psychology

If it had not been for events within the profession of psychology that led to the requirement that counseling psychologists in the United States hold doctoral degrees, master's level counselors probably would be known today as master's level counseling psychologists. The counseling profession (which requires a master's degree to enter the profession) basically shares its history with the emergence of counseling psychology as a specialty within the psychology profession (Goodyear, 2000). Early leaders in the specialty of counseling psychology distinguished themselves from other psychologists by declaring that they were interested in the normal, healthy development of human beings, including career choice, rather than focusing primarily on illness and psychopathology. In counseling psychology, the focus was on developmental stages in people's lives and career concerns. World War I and the work of Frank Parsons on career classifications provided the impetus for the development of counseling psychology as a separate specialty within psychology. Parsons created a concept in the United States that citizens should be assisted in selecting careers that would be rewarding and matched to their abilities and interests (Gibson & Mitchell, 2008).

Although the field of psychology has offered doctoral degrees for quite some time, at the beginning of its political movement to become a profession, psychology recognized individuals with master's degrees as professional psychologists. The psychology profession decided in 1949 at the Boulder Conference that only psychologists at the doctoral level would be recognized as professionals (Plante, 2011). The psychology profession, through state licensure boards and professional association polices, decided to continue to recognize all existing psychologists who held master's degrees and allow them to practice, but in the future to allow only individuals who held doctoral degrees in psychology into the profession. Licensure laws in psychology throughout the United States were changed over time to reflect this new political position.

As a result of the psychology profession requiring recognized professionals to hold doctoral degrees, individuals graduating with master's degrees in counseling, counseling psychology, clinical psychology, and other fields of psychology were denied entry into the profession of psychology. Those who took part in the Boulder Conference in 1949 probably expected that universities would discontinue programs that offered master's degrees in counseling and psychology. Or perhaps they thought that if universities did continue to graduate individuals with counseling or psychology master's degrees, master's level practitioners would work as paraprofessionals under the direct supervision of doctoral level psychologists.

However, after 1949, master's degree programs in counseling, rehabilitation counseling, school counseling, and even in counseling psychology and clinical psychology continued to flourish and expand. The master's level graduates of these degree programs assumed positions with professional status and even began to open private practices, not as psychologists, but as counselors.

School Counseling
In 1957, the United States was engaged in what was known as the cold war with Russia. Politicians in the United States feared that because the Russians had exceeded our technology and beat us in the race to space with the launching of the first satellite known as Sputnik, they might overpower the United States politically as well, imposing Russia's brand of communism on our citizens. In response to this fear, Congress created substantial programs to channel young people into technical and scientific careers. Programs funded by the U.S. government included the National Defense Act. This legislatively funded program provided funds to prepare counselors to work in high schools for the purpose of encouraging students to take math and science courses and to pursue scientific career paths. Throughout the United States, universities created summer institutes in which high school teachers were given basic courses that led to their placement in high schools as guidance counselors. In most instances, high school teachers were given two or three courses in guidance or counseling procedures, which then allowed them to be certified as school counselors and assume guidance counselor positions within schools. Because the primary purpose of this effort was to encourage students to take math and science courses, it did not seem necessary for counselors to be prepared beyond the minimal training provided in these summer institutes (Remley & Herlihy, 2010).

Within 10–20 years, school accreditation agencies required that high schools have guidance counselors in order to receive or continue their accreditation. Today, middle and high school accreditation requires that these schools have counselors, and in some areas elementary schools are required to have counselors as well. Almost all states now require that certified school counselors have received the master's degree and have completed specified courses and an internship. For a school counseling program to achieve accredited status from the Council for Accreditation of Counseling and Related Educational Programs (CACREP), the master's degree must include a minimum of 48 semester hours.

Rehabilitation Counseling

As has been outlined earlier in this text, in the 1950s, there was recognition in the United States that citizens with physical and mental disabilities were not being given the help they needed to become productive members of society. As a result, federal legislation was passed that provided counseling and educational resources that were meant to rehabilitate persons with disabilities so that they could function as autonomously as possible.

A major component of this rehabilitation legislation was funding to prepare counselors to help persons evaluate their disabilities, make plans to work, and find satisfactory employment. As a result of this funding, master's degree programs in rehabilitation counseling were developed and existing programs were expanded. State rehabilitation agencies created positions in rehabilitation case management and counseling for the graduates of these programs.

University professors and administrators in rehabilitation counseling provided leadership in the counseling field by being the first group of counselors to establish accreditation of graduate preparation programs through the CORE, and certification of qualified practitioners through the CRCC.

Community Mental Health Counseling

Although counseling master's degree programs in universities throughout the United States originally prepared counselors to practice in K-12 schools and governmental rehabilitation agencies, counselors soon began to find jobs in community agencies. Counselors began to be hired in community mental health centers, substance abuse treatment facilities, hospitals, for programs for individuals with serious mental illnesses, and various other community agencies that hired master's level mental health professionals. In addition, many master's level counselors began to open private practices. Counselors in private practices and in community agencies have most often been referred to as mental health counselors or community counselors.

Counselors offering their services in private practices led to the movement in the United States to license counselors as mental health professionals. A master's level counselor in Virginia was sued by the Virginia Board of Psychology for practicing psychology without a license. With no license to show that the counselor was qualified to provide mental health services, master's level counselors were in a difficult legal situation. As a result, the first statute licensing counselors in the United States was passed in 1976 in Virginia. Thereafter, counselors in Virginia who obtained licenses as professional counselors, that carried with the license the title of Licensed Professional Counselor (LPC), were legally entitled to practice counseling without concern of being accused of practicing psychology without a license. The licensing of counselors has had a significant impact on the development of counseling and its specialties. Credentialing of counselors and specialists within the counseling profession will be summarized later in this chapter.

COUNSELING BECOMES A SEPARATE FIELD

In summary, the dynamics around the movement of the specialty of counseling psychology from entry at the master's degree to requiring a doctoral degree, the emergence of school counseling and requirement that schools employ counselors, the funding of vocational rehabilitation counseling programs, and the movement of counselors into community agencies and private practices led to the creation of counseling as a separate profession in our contemporary society.

IS COUNSELING A PROFESSION?

Most counselors today in the United States would agree that counselors are professionals and that the field of counseling has achieved the status in our society that is afford to professions. However, sociologists who have studied professions and the process required for an occupation to become a profession probably would disagree.

Sociologists and scholars (Abbott, 1988; Caplow, 1966; Etzioni, 1969; Friedson, 1983; Hughes, 1965; Nottingham, 2007; Wilensky, 1964) have identified the essential factors that define what a profession is and the steps a group must take to establish itself as a legitimate, separate, and unique profession. In relation to other professional groups in general and to mental health professional groups in particular, counseling is a relatively new professional entity.

Six criteria for determining professional maturity have been described by Nugent (1981). Members of a mature profession have the following characteristics:

1. They can clearly define their role and have a defined scope of practice.
2. They offer unique services (do something that members of no other profession can do).
3. They have special knowledge and skills (are specifically trained for the profession).
4. They have an explicit code of ethics.
5. They have the legal right to offer the service (have obtained a monopoly, through licensure or certification, over the right to provide the services).
6. They have the ability to monitor the practice of the profession (the profession can police itself).

By considering these traits, conceptualizations, and definitions of a mature profession, it is possible to conclude that the field of counseling fully meets the criteria in some areas and is still struggling to become compliant in others. Certainly counselors have a well-established code of ethics and have achieved societal recognition through state licensure. Areas that are still weak include identifying services that are uniquely offered by counselors, developing a body of knowledge that belongs specifically to counseling and does not borrow so heavily from psychology, and achieving a higher status within society.

The final step in accomplishing the goal of becoming a profession according to Caplow (1966) is prolonged political agitation. Members of the occupational group obtain public sanction to maintain established occupational barriers. Counselors have been involved in substantial political agitation since the first counselor licensure law was passed in Virginia in 1976. That political activity continued as similar licensure laws have been passed in state after state and today, every state has a law that recognizes counselors as a professional group and licenses counselors. In addition, counselors have lobbied state legislators to mandate school counseling programs, to include counselors as providers in health care programs, and to ensure that the professional services of counselors are reimbursed by health care insurance companies. Clearly, Caplow's prolonged political agitation has begun for counselors and is continuing today.

Counselors have been fighting hard and making a number of changes to overcome the deficiencies that have hindered the development of the profession. Some of the changes that have taken place in the last 20–30 years in the field of counseling include the following: The length of most training programs has increased from 30 to 48 or 60 semester hours; efforts have been made to improve the professional status of counselors through credentialing and legislation; laws are continually passed in states granting privileged communication to interactions between counselors and their clients; the body of knowledge is being increased through scholarly publications specifically in counseling, as distinguished from psychology; and counselor licensure laws have brought autonomy from being supervised by others to practice counseling. Evidence suggests that counseling is approaching its goal of becoming a fully recognized profession in the United States.

It is discouraging for graduate students who are preparing to enter any of the specializations within the field to realize that counseling, despite its progress, still has some way to go before achieving recognition on a par with other mental health professions within our society. On the other hand, it is encouraging to note that counseling is making progress toward recognition as a profession at a relatively fast rate when compared to the professionalization efforts in other fields. For example, as late as 1982, scholars within psychology wrote in one of their own profession's journals that they doubted that psychology could validly claim to be a profession (Phillips, 1982). The first law establishing psychologists as independent health practitioners was passed in 1968 in New Jersey (Dorken & Webb, 1980), and there are still some states that do not require a license to practice psychology (in some states, only the title of psychologist is protected, not the practice of psychology). In comparison, the first counselor licensure bill was passed in Virginia in 1976, and already all 50 states and the District of Columbia have passed licensure bills for counselors, even though some counselor licensure bills protect only the title and not the practice of counseling. The strongest state counselor licensure laws (known as *practice laws*) require that individuals in that state hold a license to practice counseling. In some states, the counselor licensure laws (known as *title laws*) require that those individuals who call themselves licensed counselors be licensed, but do not require that all counselors be licensed to practice in that state. The public is not protected by title laws and counselors in states that currently have title laws have the intention of converting those title laws to practice laws in the future.

It is clear that significant progress has been made by counseling toward becoming a societally recognized profession. Although counselors are continuing to work toward full professional status, they currently refer to themselves as professionals and to their field as a profession.

LACK OF COOPERATION AMONG COUNSELING SPECIALTY ORGANIZATIONS

The American Counseling Association (ACA) was formed in 1952 to be an association for all counselors, and at that time, student development professionals in colleges and universities. ACA was formed by four counseling groups (school counselors, career counselors, college counselors and administrators, and counselor educators). The purpose of the group was to provide a unified association for all counselors. Unfortunately, ACA currently operates as more of a federation of associations than it does as a united association that represents all counselors. Many of the divisions of ACA operate independently and have their own professional administrative staff members, separate buildings, and separate conferences. The divisions of ACA, through representatives on the ACA Governing Council, make association policy for the overall association, which has led to a weak national association for counselors.

The division for rehabilitation counselors within ACA, the American Rehabilitation Counseling Association (ARCA), is closely affiliated with ACA. There are numerous other national associations, however, that represent the interests of rehabilitation counselors. As a result, ARCA is not the only voice for the rehabilitation counselors in the United States.

Even though there is a national certifying group that certifies counselors in general (the National Board for Certified Counselors, NBCC) and an organization that accredits counseling preparation programs in several specialty areas (the Council for Accreditation of Counseling and Related Education Programs, CACREP), there are separate specialty counselor certification organizations and counselor preparation program accreditation agencies that do the same thing.

The strongest specialty counselor certification group is the one that certifies rehabilitation counselors, the Commission on the Certification of Rehabilitation Counselors (CCRC), which was established before NBCC came into being. Many other certification organizations exist as well. Examples include the Association for Play Therapy (http://www.a4pt.org) that certifies play therapists and supervisors of play therapists and American Association of Sexuality Educators, Counselors, and Therapists (http://www.aasect.org) that offers certificates for sexuality educators, counselors, therapists, and supervisors.

The strongest and first accreditation group for counseling specialties is also from rehabilitation counseling, the CORE. Again, others exist as well, such as the groups that accredit substance abuse counseling programs: NAADC: The Association for Addictions Professionals' Approved Education Provider Program (http://www.naadac.org); and art therapy programs: The American Art Therapy Association's Educational Program Approval Board (http://www.arttherapy.org). Despite relatively recent attempts to merge some of the specialty certification organizations and specialty preparation accreditation agencies (Tarvydas et al., 2009), it does not appear to be a goal that will be accomplished in the near future.

AREAS IN WHICH COUNSELORS ARE UNITED ACROSS SPECIALTIES

Despite differences among counseling professional associations, certification organizations, and preparation program accrediting agencies, there are a number of areas in which counselors who identify strongly with their specializations are united. All counselors, regardless of specialization, share a philosophy of helping that distinguishes them from other mental health professionals. Counselors also must have licenses to practice in most settings in most states, regardless of their specialty. Finally, counselors with all specializations face some of the same challenges. All counselors must gain public recognition as professionals so they can be hired in agencies. Also, all counselors, regardless of their specialty, must be able to convince the government and insurance companies that they should be paid for the services they render to clients.

Shared Philosophy of Counseling

Counselors have a distinct belief system regarding the best way to help people resolve their emotional and personal issues and problems. This belief system provides the foundation for the professional identity of counselors. According to Remley and Herlihy (2010), counselors across the specialties share the following four beliefs regarding helping others with their mental health concerns:

1. The best perspective for assisting individuals in resolving their emotional and personal issues and problems is the wellness model of mental health.
2. Most of the issues and problems individuals face in life are developmental in nature, and understanding the dynamics of human growth and development is essential to success as a helper.
3. Prevention and early intervention are far superior to remediation in dealing with personal and emotional problems.

4. The goal of counseling is to empower individual clients and client systems to resolve their own problems independently of mental health professionals and to teach them to identify and resolve problems autonomously in the future (p. 26).

The first belief that counselors share is that the wellness model of mental health is the best perspective for helping people (Hermon & Hazler, 1999; McAuliffe & Eriksen, 1999). Myers, Sweeney, and Witmer (2000) have developed a comprehensive model of wellness specific for the field of counseling. The primary model used by other mental health professionals in the United States to address emotional problems has been the medical or illness model, an approach that was created by physicians in caring for persons with physical illnesses.

In the medical model, the physician identifies the illness presented by the patient who is asking for assistance. The first step in helping is the diagnosis of the illness. This illness perspective assumes that the patient is diminished in some significant way. The goal of the physician is to return the patient to the level of functioning enjoyed before the illness occurred. Once the illness has been identified, the physician applies scientific principles to cure the identified illness. If the physician is successful and the illness is cured, the patient is discharged. If another illness negatively affects the patient's well-being, the patient returns to the physician to be cured again.

Psychiatrists who are physicians generally are educated to approach mental health issues utilizing the medical model. Other mental health professionals, including clinical psychologists, psychiatric nurses, and clinical social workers, came into existence when the medical model was prevalent and have their roots in this tradition as well.

Counselors belong to a newer profession with a different tradition. Counselors have adopted the wellness model of mental health as their perspective for helping people. There is evidence that counseling from a wellness perspective is an effective method of helping clients (Myers & Sweeney, 2004; Prochaska, DiClemente, & Norcross, 1992; Tanigoshi, Kontos, & Remley, 2008; Westgate, 1996). In the wellness model, the goal is for each person to achieve positive mental health to the degree possible.

Rehabilitation counselors particularly assess clients' current life situations and help determine which factors are interfering with the goal of reaching their potential. Many persons are limited by physical disabilities or environmental conditions that cannot be changed. Keeping such limitations in mind, rehabilitation counselors assist their clients in becoming as autonomous and successful in their lives as is possible.

A second belief that counselors share is that many personal and emotional issues should be viewed within a developmental perspective. As people progress through life, they meet and must successfully address a number of personal, emotional, and physical challenges. Counselors believe that most of the problems people encounter are developmental in nature, and therefore are a natural part of living.

By studying the developmental stages in life and understanding tasks that all individuals face during their lives, counselors are able to put many problems that clients experience into a perspective that views these problems as developmental, rather than abnormal.

Rehabilitation counselors embrace the concept that there are stages of personal growth that persons with disabilities must address to live their lives successfully. Rehabilitation counselors help persons with disabilities and their family members learn how to live happy and productive lives.

A third philosophical assumption of counselors is the preference for prevention of mental and emotional problems, rather than remediation after problems have become severe (Owens & Kulic, 2001). When prevention is impossible, counselors strive toward early intervention instead of waiting until the problem has reached serious proportions. For rehabilitation counselors, prevention of problems associated with disabilities is a key concern.

A primary tool that counselors use to prevent emotional and mental problems is education. Counselors often practice their profession in the role of teacher, using psychoeducation as a tool. By alerting clients to potential future areas that might cause personal and emotional distress and preparing them to meet such challenges successfully, counselors prevent problems before they arise.

By providing services to individuals when they first become disabled, rehabilitation counselors hope to intervene early and therefore prevent potential problems from escalating. For instance, rehabilitation counselors would prefer to see a client who has recently experienced a debilitating event, rather than counseling that person after a significant time has passed.

The fourth belief that counselors share regarding the helping process is that the goal of counseling is to empower clients to live and function independently (Chronister & McWhirter, 2003; Lynch & Gussel, 1996; Savage, Harley, & Nowak, 2005). Through teaching clients appropriate problem-solving strategies and increasing their self-understanding, counselors believe that clients will not need as much assistance in living their lives in the future. Realizing that individuals often need only transitory help, counselors also try to communicate to clients that asking for and receiving help is not a sign of weakness but instead is often a healthy response to life's problems.

Rehabilitation counselors know that it is quite easy for individuals to become dependent on those who provide help to them. Some systems of mental health care seem to encourage a pattern of lifelong dependence. Rehabilitation counselors recognize this problem and encourage clients to assume responsibility for their lives and learn to live in a manner that allows them self-sufficiency and independence. Although some people may need assistance throughout their lives because of a physical or mental disability, all clients are helped to become as independent as their circumstances will allow. Counselors do not present themselves as experts in mental health who must be consulted when problems arise. Rather, rehabilitation counselors communicate the belief that clients are capable of developing the skills they need for independent living and wellness.

Rehabilitation counselors are comfortable with the overall philosophy of counseling. They believe in wellness as a goal of counseling, rather than remediation of illness. Viewing life's challenges as developmental in nature certainly fits with the tenants of rehabilitation counseling. The concepts of prevention of future problems and early intervention when problems arise also resonate well with the philosophy of assisting persons with disabilities. The empowerment of clients is a component of the philosophy of counseling that came directly from the philosophy of rehabilitation.

Licensing of Counselors and Specialists Within Counseling

It should be clear that it would be impossible for states to license every specialist within counseling separately. The two most widely recognized professions, law and medicine, are not licensed by specialty. Instead, an attorney is licensed by a state to practice law. Licensed attorneys realize they could not possibly practice every aspect of law competently, so they limit their practices to specialty areas in which they are knowledgeable and experienced. Physicians who are licensed by states to practice medicine could legally practice in any area they wish, but they limit their practices to their specialty areas. The same is true for counselors.

From a practical perspective, it is necessary for counselors to be licensed generically. From the list of counseling specialties provided at the beginning of this chapter, it can be seen that it would be necessary for state governments to create 20–40 separate licenses to license every counseling specialist. Exceptions exist to the concept that counselors should be licensed generically. In almost all states, marriage and family therapists, through their professional association, the American Association of Marriage and Family Therapists (AAMFT), have been successful in passing laws that license them separately from counselors in all states except Montana and West Virginia (American Association for Marriage and Family Therapy, 2010). In addition, there are anomalies where a state has licensed a counseling specialty. For example, there is separate license in Louisiana for rehabilitation counselors (http://www.lrcboard.org) and in almost all states, licenses exist separately for substance abuse counselors—including counseling practitioners at levels of education less than a master's degree (http://www.nattc.org/getCertified.asp).

In most states, a license issued by the state is required before a person is allowed to practice counseling in that state. As a result, licensure is an essential issue for counselors within all specializations. The requirement of licensure affects private practice counseling most directly. Most licensure statutes provide for counselors to practice in many settings that are exempt from the licensure requirement. For example, in most states, counselors who practice in local, state, or federal agencies; in nonprofit corporations; or in schools or other educational institutions are exempt from the counselor licensure requirement. Often when professions are first licensed, many exemptions to the licensure requirement are granted. This occurs for the practical reason that agencies that traditionally pay less for professionals' services would not be able to attract and keep employees if they were required to become licensed. When physicians were first licensed by states, those who were employed in a number of settings were exempt from licensure. Over the years, these licensure exemptions were removed for physicians and now almost all physicians, no matter where they practice, must have a state license. The same removal of exemptions for counselor licensure will most likely occur over time.

The American Association of State Counseling Boards (AASCB, 2010) provides a listing of contact information for state licensure boards. All 50 states, the District of Columbia, Puerto Rico, and Guam now have laws that regulate the profession of counseling.

A serious problem for state counselor licensure laws is that states have given a number of titles to counselors who are licensed. The most common title is professional counselor. However, some states use titles such as mental health counselor or clinical counselor. The individuals who proposed the counselor licensing laws in each state decided which title to use. In some cases, titles were chosen to satisfy political compromises that had to be made to obtain legislative support for the bills. Another problem that leads to public confusion is that licensure statutes require from 30 to 60 hours of graduate course work and from 1 to 3 years of post-master's-degree supervision, and they include a variety of requirements that are unique to the state (ACA, 2010b).

These differences in licensure and certification standards reflect a profession that has not been able to establish an agreed-upon set of standards, and then get those standards accepted by political entities throughout the United States. Because of this lack of uniformity, individual counselors who move from state to state often find that they must take additional course work or even earn another master's degree in order to meet the new state's standards. Established professions, such as law, medicine, and even psychology, have been able to establish licensing laws across the United States that are uniform and allow members of their professions to be licensed and practice no matter where they live. Eventually, the licensing and certification laws for counselors will become more uniform, but currently the lack of uniformity causes problems for counselors who relocate. Leaders of AASCB currently are working to resolve problems associated with transferring counselor licenses from one state to another. In addition to portability of licenses across state lines, the lack of uniformity in counseling licensure laws leads the public to question whether the profession of counseling really does have universally accepted standards for the preparation of counselors. This lack of credibility regarding standards leads those who hire counselors or pay for the services of counselors, government officials who consider legislation related to counselors, and other policy makers to question the credibility of counselors and to question whether counseling really is a profession that should be recognized and respected.

Counselors believe that they are qualified to perform a number of professional services for clients, based on their training and expertise. Two areas in which counselors have been challenged by psychologists and other mental health professionals are testing and the diagnosis and treatment of mental and emotional disorders. Some psychologists and social workers claim that they are adequately prepared to perform these professional services and that counselors are not.

There is an economic component to these issues. Counselors who test, diagnose, and treat mental and emotional disorders in their practices often compete in the marketplace with psychologists and social workers. Many health insurance companies and health maintenance organizations (HMOs) require that mental health professionals be qualified to perform these two tasks before they will reimburse their insured for the services of these professionals. Therefore, there is a significant economic advantage for psychologists and social workers to claim that counselors are not qualified in these professional practice areas.

This debate has taken place in the forum of state legislatures in the form of arguments over the language in state statutes that license counselors for practice. In most states, counselors have been successful in inserting language into their licensing statutes that states they are competent and therefore qualified to test, diagnose, and treat mental and emotional disorders. There are some states, however, where these issues are still unresolved.

Job Classifications for Counselors

Positions for counseling professionals exist in many state and federal agencies (Remley & Herlihy, 2010). In some of these agencies, however, no job classification categories have been established for counselors. Rehabilitation counselors have been hired in governmental agencies since the 1950s and job categories usually do exist there for a rehabilitation counselor. However, when rehabilitation counselors and licensed counselors from other specializations have attempted to secure employment in many governmental and large private employment settings, there have been no job classifications for them. As a result, when counselors are hired, their job titles might be psychologist I, social worker I, or mental health technician I. Although being hired into these positions gives counselors jobs and entry into agencies, they may be discriminated against later because promotions might require a license in psychology or social work or a graduate degree in one of those fields.

As a result of this problem, efforts are being made to have job titles established specifically for counselors. Convincing a state or federal agency that job titles or classifications need to be changed is not an easy task. Bureaucracies are very slow to change. Nonetheless, professional associations and leaders within the counseling profession are attempting to address this problem so that counselors will eventually be fully accepted as professionals within these agencies. The U.S. Department of Veterans Affairs (VA) has issued standards that will recognize LPCs as mental health specialists (ACA, 2010a). This positive step by the VA will significantly increase employment opportunities for counselors.

As an example of efforts in the job classification arena, in Louisiana a series of job categories for counselors who work in the state civil service system was created in 2003 (C. Gagnon, personal communication, September 10, 2003). Up until that time, counselors were hired in job categories that limited their ability to receive promotions. Creating these new counselor job categories (which are equivalent to those that existed already for social workers) was completed in a unique manner because of the political and legal environment in that state. The success in this endeavor will have a significant positive impact on all counselors currently working in that state and future counselors who will be hired there.

Third-Party Reimbursement

It is essential for counselors in private practice that their clients be able to access counselors' mental health services as part of the client's health care plan (Palmo, 1999). If clients are participating in HMOs or preferred provider organizations (PPOs), then counselors must be on the list of eligible providers for the clients. If clients are part of an indemnity health care plan, then counselors must be acknowledged as qualified mental health care providers so that clients can be reimbursed for counselor services.

HMOs, PPOs, and health insurance companies can voluntarily acknowledge counselors as qualified mental health care providers, and most do. However, these health care organizations have a legal right to refuse to give their clients access to counselors unless there is legislation to the contrary. This type of legislation, called freedom of choice legislation, requires health care providers to give access to licensed counselors for mental health care if they give access to other mental health care providers such as psychologists or social workers. Many states have passed freedom of choice legislation. In states that have not, counselors are active in trying to get freedom of choice legislation passed (Remley & Herlihy, 2010).

ACA is active in seeking national legislative and regulatory changes that would allow Medicaid recipients, military personnel, and federal employees to receive mental health services from counselors as a part of their health benefits. An important goal is for all Americans to have access to mental health services from counselors, not just from psychiatrists, psychologists, or social workers.

In 2010, a report issued by the Institute of Medicine that is a part of the National Academy of Sciences concluded that counselors should have parity with other mental health providers, such as psychologists and social workers, when providing mental health services to TRICARE recipients. TRICARE is the health care organization that contracts for health care services for members of the U.S. armed services and their families. TRICARE still must act on the recommendations of the report, but it is accomplishments like the positive recommendations in this report that bode well for counselors being recognized in the future as legitimate mental health care providers in the United States.

CONCLUSION

Counseling, like other professions within contemporary American society, has developed as a field that has numerous specializations. Not surprisingly, the existence of specializations within counseling brings strength to the counseling profession and has caused problems as well.

On the strength side, counseling could not be a viable field if specialties did not exist. Counseling is too broad to be understood by all individual practitioners. Out of necessity, counselors must specialize to be competent. Through having specialists within counseling, U.S. citizens have available to them counselors who are well prepared to provide the particular type of counseling services needed.

On the negative side, specialties have led to a fragmentation of the counseling profession at a time when all counselors are being challenged to prove they are well prepared and capable of rendering professional services to clients. Although standing up to political challenges from related mental health professionals such as psychologists and social workers in areas such as licensure, job classifications, and third-party reimbursement, counselors, at the same time, have had to deal with internal turmoil related to concerns of counseling specialists. Failing to agree upon minimum licensure requirements and to accomplish uniformity in counselor statutes throughout the United States has weakened the credibility of counselors in the eyes of policy makers.

Professional associations of counselors are more specialty-focused than unified. There is little hope that all counselors in the near future will support one association that represents all counselors, regardless of specialty. Leaders of counseling specialty groups at this time do not appear to believe that it is in their best interest to work together with other counselors. Instead, counseling specialists support strong separate organizations that represent their specialties and seldom work together for the common good of all counselors. The association that was established to represent all counselors in all specialties, the ACA, has not been successful in bringing all counselors together from the various specializations to work toward common goals.

It does not appear that counselors who represent various specializations will agree in the foreseeable future to unify organizations and agencies that certify counselors and accredit counselor preparation programs. Instead, it appears that specialty counselor certification groups will continue to coexist with the generic counseling certification organization, the NBCC and the generic counseling preparation program accrediting agency, the CACREP. Rehabilitation counselors have a very strong and successful certification organization, the CRCC, and a strong and successful counselor preparation accrediting agency, the CORE.

Despite a poor prognosis for cooperation among counseling specialties in the areas of professional associations, national certification organizations, and counselor preparation accreditation agencies, there is clearly hope for the future for cooperation among counseling specialties in the areas of counselor licensure and acceptance as professionals in society.

Licensure for counselors has been accomplished in all states and jurisdictions in the United States and rehabilitation counselors are, with rare exceptions, fully eligible to obtain state counselor licenses. Much progress is being made in federal, state, and local governments to create job classifications for counselors and to recognize counselors as qualified providers of mental health services.

It appears that the American public knows that counselors exist and value the services they are rendering in their communities. These positive changes are occurring for all counselors and for all specializations within counseling.

Specializations within counseling are here to stay and rehabilitation counseling has been in the past, and will continue to be in the future, a strong counseling specialization. In addition, rehabilitation counselors will benefit from every success the generic field of counseling achieves in the areas of societal recognition and acceptance as professionals.

CONTENT REVIEW QUESTIONS

- How did the broad field of counseling develop within the United States?
- What role do specializations play within the broader field of counseling? What are the benefits of specializations within a profession, and what problems do specializations cause?
- How did the three primary specializations within counseling (school counseling, rehabilitation counseling, and community mental health counseling) develop themselves and then become involved in the development of the overall profession of counseling in the United States?
- How have specialty organizations within counseling failed to work cooperatively?
- In the areas of philosophy of counseling, state licensure, and promoting the counseling profession to the public, how have specialties in counseling contributed to the growth and success of the overall counseling profession?

REFERENCES

Abbott, A. (1988). *The system of professions: An essay on the division of expert labor.* Chicago, IL: University of Chicago Press.

Abraham, S. C. (1978). *The public accounting profession: Problems and prospects.* Lexington, MA: Lexington Books.

American Association for Marriage and Family Therapy. (2010). *The making of the MFT profession: Standards, regulation, and the AAMFT.* Alexandria, VA: Author. Retrieved June 16, 2011, from http://www.aamft.org/iMIS15/AAMFT/Press/FAQs/Content/About_AAMFT/Qualifications.aspx?hkey=7d1341ef-0f95-46a3-9082-6c37fab2dcf6

American Association of State Counseling Boards. (2010). *State counseling boards.* Alexandria, VA: Author. Retrieved September 12, 2010, from http://www.aascb.org/displaycommon.cfm?an=1

American Counseling Association. (2010a). *Department of Veterans Affairs recognizes licensed professional mental health counselors!* Alexandria, VA: Author. Retrieved November 8, 2010, from http://www.counseling.org/PressRoom/NewsReleases.aspx?AGuid=b56bbae2-5083-46ca-9435-0eabea9c4f72

American Counseling Association. (2010b). *Licensure requirements for professional counselors* (2010 ed.). Alexandria, VA: Author.

Bradley, R. W., & Cox, J. A. (2001). Counseling: Evolution of the profession. In D. C. Locke, J. E. Myers, & E. L. Herr (Eds.), *The handbook of counseling* (pp. 27–41). Thousand Oaks, CA: Sage.

Caplow, T. (1966). The sequence of professionalization. In H. M. Vollmer & D. L. Mills (Eds.), *Professionalization* (pp. 19–21). Upper Saddle River, NJ: Prentice-Hall.

Chronister, K. M., & McWhirter, E. H. (2003). Applying social cognitive career theory to the empowerment of battered women. *Journal of Counseling & Development, 81,* 418–425.

Collison, B. B. (2001). Professional associations, standards, and credentials in counseling. In D. C. Locke, J. E. Myers, & E. L. Herr (Eds.), *The handbook of counseling* (pp. 55–68). Thousand Oaks, CA: Sage. Commission on Rehabilitation Counselor Certification. (2010). The importance of the CRC credential. Schaumburg, Il: Author. Retrieved September 12, 2010, from http://www.crccertification.com/pages/employers/16.php

Commission on Rehabilitation Counselor Certification. (2010). *The importance of the CRC credential.* Schaumburg, IL: Author. Retrieved September 12, 2010, from http://www.crccertification.com/pages/employers/16.php

Council on Rehabilitation Education. (2010). *Frequently asked questions.* Schaumburg, IL: Author. Retrieved June 13, 2011, from http://www.core-rehab.org/FAQs.html

Dorken, H., & Webb, J. T. (1980). 1976 third-party reimbursement experience: An interstate comparison by insurance carrier. *American Psychologist, 35,* 355–363.

Etzioni, A. (1969). *The semi-professions and their organization.* New York, NY: The Free Press.

Fox, R. E. (1994). Training professional psychologists for the twenty-first century. *American Psychologist, 49,* 200–206.

Friedson, E. (1983). The theory of professions: State-of-the-art. In R. Dingwall & P. Lewis (Eds.), *The sociology of the professions.* New York, NY: St. Martin's Press.

Gibson, R. L, & Mitchell, M. H. (2008). *Introduction to counseling and guidance* (7th ed.). Upper Saddle River, NJ: Merrill.

Glosoff, H. (2009). The counseling profession: A historical perspective. In D. Capuzzi & D. R. Gross (Eds.), *Introduction to the counseling profession* (5th ed., pp. 1–30). Upper Saddle River, NJ: Merrill.

Goodyear, R. K. (2000). An unwarranted escalation of counselor-counseling psychologist professional conflict: Comments on Weinrach, Lustig, Chan, and Thomas (1998). *Journal of Counseling and Development, 78,* 103–106.

Hermon, D. A., & Hazler, R. J. (1999). Adherence to a wellness model and perceptions of psychological well-being. *Journal of Counseling and Development, 77,* 339–343.

Hershenson, D. B., Power, P. W., & Waldo, M. (1996). *Community counseling: Contemporary theory and practice.* Boston, MA: Ally & Bacon.

Hughes, E. C. (1965). Professions. In K. S. Lynn (Ed.), *The professions in America* (pp. 1–14). Boston, MA: Houghton Mifflin.

Institute of Medicine. (2010). *Provision of mental health counseling services under TRICARE.* Washington, DC: Author. Retrieved September 12, 2010, from http://www.iom.edu/Reports/2010/Provision-of-Mental-Health-Counseling-Services-Under-TRICARE.aspx

Kett, J. F. (1968). *The formation of the American medical profession: The role of institutions, 1780–1860.* New Haven, CT: Yale University Press.

Leahy, M. J., & Szymanski, E. M. (1995). Rehabilitation counseling: Evolution and current status. *Journal of Counseling and Development, 74,* 163–166.

Lynch, R. T., & Gussel, L. (1996). Disclosure and self-advocacy regarding disability-related needs: Strategies to maximize integration in postsecondary education. *Journal of Counseling and Development, 74,* 352–358.

McAuliffe, G. J., & Eriksen, K. P. (1999). Toward a constructivist and developmental identity for the counseling profession: The context-phase-state-style model. *Journal of Counseling and Development, 77,* 267–280.

Myers, J. E. (1995a). From "forgotten and ignored" to standards and certification: Gerontological counseling comes of age. *Journal of Counseling and Development, 74,* 143–149.

Myers, J. E. (1995b). Specialties in counseling: Rich heritage or force for fragmentation? *Journal of Counseling and Development, 74,* 115–116.

Myers, J. E., & Sweeney, T. J. (2001). Specialties in counseling. In D. C. Locke, J. E. Myers, & E. L. Herr (Eds.), *The handbook of counseling* (pp. 43–54). Thousand Oaks, CA: Sage.

Myers, J. E., & Sweeney, T. J. (2004). The indivisible self: An evidence-based model of wellness. *Journal of Individual Psychology, 60,* 234–244.

Myers, J. E., Sweeney, T. J., & Witmer, J. M. (2000). The wheel of wellness counseling for wellness: A holistic model for treatment planning. *Journal of Counseling and Development, 78,* 251–266.

Napoli, D. S. (1981). *Architects of adjustment: The history of the psychological profession in the United States.* Port Washington, NY: Kennikat Press.

Nottingham, C. (2007). The rise of the insecure professionals. *International Review of Social History, 52,* 445–475. doi:10.1017/S0020859007003069.

Nugent, F. (1981). *Professional counseling: An overview.* Pacific Grove, CA: Brooks/Cole.

Owens, P. C., & Kulic, K. R. (2001). What's needed now: Using groups for prevention. *The Journal for Specialists in Group Work, 26,* 205–210.

Page, R. C., & Bailey, J. B. (1995). Addictions counseling certification: An emerging counseling specialty. *Journal of Counseling and Development, 74,* 167–171.

Paisley, P. O., & Borders, L. D. (1995). School counseling: An evolving specialty. *Journal of Counseling and Development, 74,* 150–153.

Palmo, A. J. (1999). The MHC child reaches maturity: Does the child seem short for its age? *Journal of Mental Health Counseling, 21,* 215–228.

Phillips, B. N. (1982). Regulation and control in psychology. *American Psychologist, 37,* 919–926.

Plante, T. G. (2011). *Contemporary clinical psychology* (3rd ed.). Hoboken, NJ: John Wiley & Sons.

Prochaska, J. O., DiClemente, C. C., & Norcross, J. C. (1992). In search of how people change. *American Psychologist, 47,* 1102–1114.

Remley, T. P., Jr., & Herlihy, B. (2010). *Ethical, legal, and professional issues in counseling* (3rd ed.). Upper Saddle River, NJ: Merrill.

Savage, T. A., Harley, D. A., & Nowak, T. M. (2005). Applying social empowerment strategies as tools for self-advocacy in counseling lesbian and gay male clients. *Journal of Counseling and Development, 83,* 131–137.

Smith, H. B., & Robinson, G. P. (1995). Mental health counseling: Past, present, and future. *Journal of Counseling and Development, 75,* 158–162.

Smith, R. L., Carlson, J., Stevens-Smith, P., & Dennison, M. (1995). Marriage and family counseling. *Journal of Counseling and Development, 74,* 154–157.

Stebnicki, M. A. (2009). A call for integral approaches in the professional identity of rehabilitation counseling: Three specialty areas, one profession. *Rehabilitation Counseling Bulletin, 52,* 133–137.

Sweeney, T. J. (2001). Counseling: Historical origins and philosophical roots. In D. C. Locke, J. E. Myers, & E. L. Herr (Eds.), *The handbook of counseling* (pp. 3–26). Thousand Oaks, CA: Sage.

Tanigoshi, H., Kontos, A. P., & Remley, T. P., Jr. (2008). The effectiveness of individual wellness counseling on the wellness of law enforcement officers. *Journal of Counseling & Development, 86,* 64–75.

Tarvydas, V., Leahy, M. J., & Zanskas, S. A. (2009). Judgment deferred: Reappraisal of rehabilitation counseling movement toward licensure parity. *Rehabilitation Counseling Bulletin, 52,* 85–94.

Westgate, C. E. (1996). Spiritual wellness and depression. *Journal of Counseling & Development, 75,* 26–36.

Wilensky, H. L. (1964). The professionalization of everyone. *The American Journal of Sociology, 70,* 137–158.

3

History of Rehabilitation Counseling

Amos P. Sales

LEARNING OBJECTIVES

After reading this chapter, you should learn:

- How the broad field of counseling developed within the United States.
- The role specializations played within the broader field of counseling, the benefits of specializations within a profession, and the problems specializations cause.
- How the three primary specializations within counseling (school counseling, rehabilitation counseling, and community mental-health counseling) developed themselves and then became involved in the development of the overall profession of counseling in the United States.
- How specialty organizations within counseling failed to work cooperatively.
- How, in the areas of philosophy of counseling, state licensure, and promoting the counseling profession to the public, specialties in counseling contributed to the growth and success of the overall counseling profession.

This chapter will describe the birth and evolution of rehabilitation counseling as a unique counseling specialty within our society. With a rich history of professional leadership, rehabilitation counseling had its birth in counseling and has evolved in relation to the impacts of social policies in supportive federal legislation, changing perceptions of and advocacy by its clientele, and effective leadership. The interactive impact of all these areas has resulted in an evolving counseling profession that now more than ever empowers persons with chronic illness and disability to achieve their desired optimal level of overall functioning (Sales, 2007). Rehabilitation counselors are what they are today as a result of their past. Understanding the past can help forge a better future.

The original definition and narrow scope of service of rehabilitation counseling have evolved from its origin as a federally legislated profession (Hershenson, 1998) to a now vibrant profession encompassing new functions for rehabilitation counselors in new settings. The early emphasis in rehabilitation counseling was on counselors as experts, skilled in diagnosis and remediation strategies needed to "restore" individuals with disabilities to their fullest employment potential. Paternalism and "doing for" guided the counseling practice (Sales, 2002). Rehabilitation counseling gradually evolved from this historical paternalism in its practice to a more empowering response to the needs of individuals with disabilities (Sales, 2007).

Readers interested in a more in-depth review of the historical evolution of rehabilitation from paternalism and empowerment should review the works of Groce (1992), IRI (1999), Obermann (1965), Sales (1986, 2002, 2007), and Wright (1980). A much abbreviated review of these works with differing emphasis is presented in this chapter to highlight the historical impact on rehabilitation counseling of (1) counseling, (2) federal legislation, (3) leadership, (4) clientele, and (5) work settings. In this presentation, one can see that these are not isolated areas of impacts. All have intersected with one another to result in rehabilitation counseling as we know it today.

The language used about and references to persons with disabilities are of importance in rehabilitation counseling and continue in our society to perpetuate myths, misconceptions, and negative connotations. Using first person language such as "person with a disability," avoiding use of disability as a noun descriptor, and avoiding outdated terms or words are important considerations for respectful professional practice (Patterson, Szymanski, & Parker, 2005). There are exceptions such as the word "deaf" referring to a physical condition and "Deaf" with upper case D referring to the Deaf culture as preferred by the National Association for the Deaf (2003) and such as "the Blind" as preferred by the major foundations for the Blind. An ongoing debate since 1990s relates to whether references to clientele of rehabilitation counseling should use "client," "consumer," or "customers" (Nosek, 1993; Patterson & Marks, 1992; Thomas, 1993a, 1993b). The majority of counselors in the counseling specialties use "client" and the Rehabilitation Counseling's Code of Professional Ethics for Rehabilitation Counselors (CRCC, 2010) accepts and exclusively uses the term "client." However, Nosek's (1993) argument equating "client" with the historical medical model, with the paternalism of the professional deciding what is best for people with disability and this author's support of an empowerment perspective (Sales, 2007) influence the decision in this chapter to use the term "consumer" except in referenced material.

EVOLUTION OF COUNSELING IN THE UNITED STATES

Rehabilitation counseling evolved in the United States from a rich history of development of theory and practice in counseling. Counseling, representing the fusing of many psychological, philosophical, and practical elements, began in the 19th century with reform movements in the United States, which suggested society had the responsibility to assist its members who were in need and that new humanistic methods should be used (Belkin, 1988). These movements included social workers changing their practice with the poor and destitute, psychiatrists attempting to change the treatment of the mentally ill, and educators practicing more humanistic teaching methods within government-supported universal access to public education (Dewey, 1956; Dykhuizen, 1973; Neukrug, 1994). These movements, along with the testing movement, set the stage for the first comprehensive approaches to vocational guidance, the basis for counseling (Herr & Cramer, 1995). A "psychological" way of viewing the world then evolved from great changes in medicine. Numerous physicians studied causation of mental illness and many discovered the use of hypnosis and attributed emotional problems to unconscious psychological processes (Ehrenwald, 1976). Of these, Freud (Corey, 2005) was the first to develop a theory to explain and treat emotional problems.

The beginning of the 20th century brought the start of systematic vocational guidance and counseling in the United States with Parsons (1939), the founder of guidance in the United States, not only envisioning guidance but also individual counseling in schools. From the turn of the century to the 1930s, a number of federal education acts strengthened vocational guidance and counseling. These included, in 1920, national vocational rehabilitation legislation through the Rehabilitation Act providing vocational guidance and counseling to adults with disabilities and the Wagner O'Day Act of 1932 providing ongoing vocational guidance and placement to all unemployed U.S. citizens through the United States Employment Service.

The emergence of the counseling profession as something other than vocational guidance came during the 1930s when Williamson (1939) developed a comprehensive theory of counseling. Williamson's trait and factor theory modified Parsons's 1909 work into a generic approach to counseling. During the 1930s, the title guidance worker or specialist fell more and more into disfavor. By the early 1940s, terms such as rehabilitation counselor and school counselor were favored.

During the 1930s and 1940s, many humanistic philosophers, psychiatrists, and psychologists fled from Nazism in Europe to the United States and dramatically influenced the field of counseling. Carl Rogers's (1942) initial work, *Counseling and Psychotherapy*, was greatly affected by these humanists and revolutionized the practice of counseling, moving it toward a more humanistic, client-centered, nondirective counseling approach (Neukrug, 1994).

Psychologists, at the end of World War I, offered their services to large numbers of returning soldiers who had psychological problems associated with the war. Long-term psychoanalysis was not practical for these clinicians, so they utilized newer, shorter-term approaches. As these treatment approaches spread, the need for psychological assistants became evident. "These master's level assistants often had degrees in social work but increasingly were individuals with a new degree, a master's degree in counseling, which started as a degree in vocational guidance" (Neukrug, 1994, p. 35).

With increased federal support of social programs in the 1950s and 1960s came a great demand for counselors. Many new approaches in counseling evolved (Gladding, 1996). These included the behavioral approaches of Bandura (1969), Wolpe (1958), and Krumboltz (1966); the rational emotive approach of Ellis (Ellis & Harper, 1961); the relational/behavioral approach of Glasser (1965); the affective Gestalt approach of Perls (1969); the transactional analysis of Berne (1964); and the existential approaches of Arbuckle (1965) and Frankl (1963). This increase in approaches continued into the 1970s and has been identified as related to President Johnson's "Great Society" initiative (Kaplan & Cuciti, 1986). With this expansion came an increased urgency for professionalism. The first guidelines for ethical behavior, certification of counselors, and concern with accreditation of counselor education programs began in this time frame.

Today, professionals who practice counseling will have completed a master's degree level preparation and practice in many specialty areas. Professional preparation is in the various specialties in counseling such as rehabilitation counseling, school counseling, marriage and family counseling, gerontology counseling, substance-abuse counseling, mental-health counseling, and agency or community counseling. All specialties share common course content and accreditation criteria in their professional orientation and education. The content includes individual and group counseling, human growth and development, social and cultural foundations, career and lifestyle development, and assessment and program evaluation. In addition, coursework content and field placements related to the knowledge and skills specific to specialty areas are required (Neukrug, 1994). The core knowledge and skill required in all these specialties relate to individual counseling.

All counseling specialties address the significance of the helping relationship in pursuing the goal of counseling, the enhancement and encouragement of consumer change (Capuzzi & Gross, 2003). The targeted process of counseling varies based on the agency setting, the counselor's personal and professional competence, the counseling approach, and the consumer's personal uniqueness in personality and need for change. The effective process requires the development of a therapeutic relationship, an extended exploration of the consumer's perception of problem(s) and need for change, and the agreement between counselor and consumer on implementation of a treatment plan.

THE REHABILITATION COUNSELING SPECIALTY

Rehabilitation counseling is a unique counseling specialty that has developed in response to the needs of working-age adults with disabilities in our society. It is generally agreed that rehabilitation counselors who help their consumers understand, accept, and resolve their need for change and of problems so that they can lead more satisfied, well-adjusted lives are doing personal counseling. Depending upon the work setting and factors related to caseload and funding, the rehabilitation counselor may engage the consumer first in personal counseling and then career counseling, which focuses on one aspect of a consumer's life, that is the world of work. It is impossible to do career or rehabilitation counseling without doing personal counseling. Rehabilitation counseling builds on personal counseling by focusing on unique issues related to individuals with disabilities. A growing consensus is that rehabilitation counseling is best practiced from an empowering perspective that involves addressing the environmental context of disability and working to improve the physical and social environment in which people with disabilities live and work.

Rehabilitation counseling has all the characteristics of a profession that a specialty in counseling might have. It is a full-time occupation, which has specified education entry requirements, a professional association, a code of ethics, external recognition such as certification or licensure, and a ". . . body of knowledge and . . . an element of control over the conditions of their work" (Rothman, 1998, p. 64). Its early development reflects a rich history of professional leadership. In 1958, this leadership established two professional associations in rehabilitation counseling, the National Rehabilitation Counseling Association (NRCA), a division of the National Rehabilitation Association (NRA), and the American Rehabilitation Counseling Association (ARCA) of the American Counseling Association (ACA). Since 1957, rehabilitation counseling has had an active professional association for its rehabilitation educators, now called the National Council on Rehabilitation Education (NCRE). Rehabilitation counseling was also among the first counseling specialties to establish professional standards for practitioners and a national, nonprofit, independent certification process for counselors. In 1972, it endorsed a national accrediting body, the Council on Rehabilitation Education (CORE), which provides standards for professional master's level graduate rehabilitation counseling programs of study. Also in 1972, NRCA and ARCA supported the development of the Commission on Rehabilitation Counselor Certification (CRCC), a certification body that certifies rehabilitation counselors (Certified Rehabilitation Counselors, CRCs) as meeting established standards of practice at the time of entry into the profession (CRCC, 2003; Graves, 1992). In 1972, NRCA first adopted a Code of Ethics.

While rehabilitation counseling has enjoyed prominence within the history of the counseling profession, its professional associations have created problems of definition regarding which core identity underlies the profession of rehabilitation—counseling or rehabilitation (Tarvydas & Leahy, 1993). Solomone (1996) earlier identified the core identity issue as related to NRCA's view of rehabilitation counselors as case manager/coordinators, and ARCA's view of rehabilitation counselors as counselors, even though both NRCA and ARCA profess counseling as their core function in their by-laws. NCRA's memberships historically were employed within the state federal vocational rehabilitation program. ARCA's membership was and continues to be rehabilitation education faculty, rehabilitation counselors employed in facilities, and rehabilitation researchers. A positive is that these two associations have collaborated to establish the first accreditation process for rehabilitation education programs and the first certification process for counselors. The purpose of CORE accreditation is to both promote excellence in education and protect consumers who will ultimately be recipients of service (CORPA, 1995). There are currently 95 CORE accredited rehabilitation counseling master's degree programs (NCRE Directory, 2009–2010). The CRC certification process (CRCC, 2003) ensures standards of practice in the profession. Current estimates indicate that 16,350 rehabilitation counselors are certified as CRCs with approximately 4,900 currently employed in the state federal vocational rehabilitation program (C. Chapman, personal communication, July 28, 2010).

Attempts have been made to blur the perceived division of rehabilitation counseling perspective between NRCA and ARCA through efforts to combine the two professional organizations into one. To this end, in 1993, NRCA and ARCA formed the Alliance for Rehabilitation Counseling (ARC) as a collaborative structure to possibly merge the two associations. In the late 1990s, the merger efforts targeted a possible unified association and linkage with ACA. This potential merger and the hopes of consolidating rehabilitation counseling as a specialty of counseling have yet to reach fruition. Interestingly, these efforts indirectly resulted in NRCA's exit in 2008 from NRA and the development of a new division in NRA titled the Rehabilitation Counselor and Educators Association (RCEA). This results in there now being three different professional associations representing rehabilitation counseling. On the positive side, NCRA and ARCA have worked closely over the last decade to agree upon a Code of Professional Ethics for Rehabilitation Counselors (CRCC, 2003, 2010) and to collaborate on licensure issues. To address licensure, leadership of NRCA, ARCA, and six other leading organizations in the field of rehabilitation counseling came together in 2005 to form the Rehabilitation Counseling Consortium, a cooperative group to provide a unified voice and needed advocacy for including rehabilitation counseling in counseling licensure language in laws at the state level (ACA, 2005). These organizations included ARCA, Professionals Networking for Excellence in Service Delivery with Individuals who are Deaf or Hard of Hearing (ADARA), the Canadian Association of Rehabilitation Professionals, CORE, CRCC, the International Association of Rehabilitation Professionals, NCRE, and NRCA. State laws now require licensure to practice as counselors in all 50 states.

IMPACT OF LEGISLATION ON REHABILITATION COUNSELING

In the 19th century in the United States, rehabilitation of individuals with disabilities began with private philanthropic and voluntary charitable organizations. These groups pressed for state funding of rehabilitation programs, which did occur in several states prior to the first national Soldier Rehabilitation Act in 1918 and the first civilian rehabilitation legislation, the Vocational Rehabilitation Act of 1920 (Meyers, 1968), being authorized to assist individuals with disabilities to obtain employment. The specialty of rehabilitation counseling traces its roots to this federal legislation that first described and authorized the provision of vocational rehabilitation services. It has been linked to the state-federal public vocational rehabilitation program throughout its history (Hershenson, 1988). The rationale for federal support of services under the Vocational Rehabilitation Act is based on the national need to create employment ". . . equality of opportunity for all citizens . . ." (Garrett, 1969, p. 29). With the result of financial incentive provided by the Rehabilitation Act, the public state-federal vocational rehabilitation program has been established representing all states in the United States. What began as a small temporary program has grown with Rehabilitation Act amendments into an entitlement program, providing a great range of programs and program services to include assessment, guidance, counseling, job search, training, and placement. The public sector has had and continues to have a significant impact on the service emphasis in other areas of the rehabilitation industry. Nationally, about 30% of the CRCs are employed in the state-federal vocational rehabilitation program (C. Chapman, personal communication, July 28, 2010).

In 1935, the Social Security Act established the Vocational Rehabilitation Act's state-federal vocational rehabilitation as a permanent program. Rehabilitation counseling's focus under this legislation continued to be on vocational intervention and guidance of adults with disabilities. The early providers of service held titles such as rehabilitation agents, rehabilitation representatives, or rehabilitation coordinators. Most had a background in education because the first federal administration of state-federal vocational rehabilitation programs was under the Federal Board of Vocational Education with state programs predominantly in state departments of education. Bureaucratic pressure on states to identify a uniform job title began after passage of the 1943 Vocational Rehabilitation Act Amendments. During a national meeting in 1946, administrators of state agencies of vocational rehabilitation agreed "by a show of hands" to adopt the job title of rehabilitation counselor as the preferred title for job classification systems in their home states. Almost all state rehabilitation agencies had adopted this title by 1949 (Cull & Hardy, 1972). The new job title did not change the duties of the rehabilitation counseling position as expert in diagnosis and intervention strategies designed to move the consumer into employment as expeditiously as possible.

Amendments to the Vocational Rehabilitation Act in 1943 provided expansion of the state-federal vocational rehabilitation program to include consumers with more significant disabilities such as those with mental-health and developmental disabilities. This expansion highlighted the need for professional preparation. When the Rehabilitation Act Amendments of 1954 provided grant funding for colleges and universities to professional rehabilitation counselors, there was a lack of consensus and even conflict regarding where the professional preparation training should be housed within universities or what the training should be in terms of content (Sales, 2007).

The 1954 Vocational Rehabilitation Act Amendments also supported facility development and the number of agencies and rehabilitation counseling positions grew tremendously (Menz, Botterbusch, Hagen-Foley, & Johnson, 2003). In response to consumer and professional association impact, the philosophical emphasis of the Rehabilitation Act of 1973 and its later amendments moved counseling services toward consumer involvement and empowerment. The 1986 Rehabilitation Act Amendments stipulated that rehabilitation services to consumers must be delivered by qualified personnel. The 1992 Amendments incorporated the values inherent in the 1990 Americans with Disabilities Act, the "Civil Rights Act" for individuals with disabilities, and stressed "respect for individual dignity, personal responsibility, self-determination, and pursuit of meaningful careers, based on informed choice" [Rehabilitation Act Amendments, Section 2 (c)(1)]. The 1998 Amendments also stated that one purpose of the Act is "to empower individuals with disabilities to maximize employment, economic self-sufficiency, independence and inclusion and integration into society" [Rehabilitation Act, Section 2 (b) (1)]. The 1992 and 1998 Amendments institutionalized not only master's degree preparation but certification as a rehabilitation counselor at the highest national or state level to be employed within the state federal program as a counselor.

In recent decades, the rehabilitation counselor work settings have expanded to include private rehabilitation and insurance rehabilitation, substance-abuse treatment agencies, employee assistance programs, public schools, community rehabilitation programs, hospitals, veterans programs, and colleges and universities.

IMPACT OF LEADERSHIP ON REHABILITATION COUNSELING

Rehabilitation educators have had a major impact on the evolution of rehabilitation counseling. By the 1940s they had established three undergraduate education programs of study for rehabilitation counselors: the New York University Program in 1941 based on an education model, the Ohio State University Program in 1944 based on a social work model, and the Wayne State University Program in 1946 founded on special education. With the 1954 Rehabilitation Act Amendments, grants in support of master's level professional rehabilitation counseling degree programs were funded, providing rehabilitation counseling with the unique distinction of being the only profession established by an act of the U.S. Congress (Wright, 1980). The few master's degree programs in 1954 increased to 25 by 1956 (Miller, 2001).

Wright (1980) concluded that rehabilitation counseling had its roots in psychology and counseling since the first faculty in these programs had basic training and philosophy in these areas. These faculties influenced the development of a psychological counselor model for rehabilitation counseling's sequence of study. The master's level curriculum for rehabilitation counseling was developed by these faculties and directors of state vocational rehabilitation agencies during meetings held at the University of Virginia, Charlottesville, in 1956. These meetings, referred to as the Charlottesville workshops, produced a document titled "Rehabilitation Counselor Preparation" (Hall & Warren, 1956). This document identified a consensus on 24 areas of knowledge and skill to be addressed in the master's degree program, modeled after the then-existing Veterans Administration's psychological counselor requirements. The program of study was, and continues to be, as currently accredited by CORE, a 2-year sequence of study with knowledge and skill development in rehabilitation knowledge, legislation, medical and psychological aspects of disability, assessment, plan development, case management, and counseling skills in vocational and psychosocial adjustment counseling. The counseling process emphasis in this educational sequence of study on an "expert" skilled in problem identification and problem resolution continues today. Szymanski, Parker and Patterson (2005) refer to this as the "paradox" of the rehabilitation counseling profession—how to be an expert but not "counsel" from this perspective.

Through textbooks, early and prominent rehabilitation educators (Bitters, 1979; Cull & Hardy, 1972; Maliken & Rusalem, 1969; McGowan & Porter, 1967) provided support for rehabilitation counseling being a process linked to service delivery in the state federal vocational rehabilitation program. They defined rehabilitation counseling, as does the most popular text currently utilized in master's degree programs in rehabilitation counseling (Rubin & Roessler, 2001), as linked to the counselor skills needed to facilitate a typical state vocational rehabilitation agency process from case finding to closure. This perspective was advocated by NRCA (Mundt, 1986) as late as the mid-1980s and is reflected in the scope of practice of rehabilitation counselors today (CRCC, 2003).

The impact of rehabilitation educators on rehabilitation counseling practice for many of its early years was linked to discussion of the role of the counselor. By the mid-1950s, rehabilitation faculty, like its professional associations NRCA and ARCA, held two distinctly different philosophies regarding the rehabilitation counselor's role. Patterson (1957), in questioning whether "counselor or coordinator" was the correct job title, denounced rehabilitation functions other than counseling as "nonprofessional." Patterson (1958), an early proponent of rehabilitation counseling as a specialty in counseling, argued that the counselor's role was to facilitate consumers' self-responsibility and expertise so that they could develop their own vocational plans. Hamilton (1950) and Johnson (1960) argued that rehabilitation counselors should more realistically be called coordinators. In addition to these two divergent views, others argued for a role that encompassed both counseling and coordination. Anderson (1958) defined the rehabilitation counselor as an expert in influencing consumer decisions regarding choice of vocations (Dawis, England, & Lofquist, 1964). Cubelli (1967) proposed the concept of counselor–rehabilitationist, defined as an enabler devoted to moving consumers in and out of needed rehabilitation services. Cohen, Cote, Galloway, Hedgemen, and Schmones (1971) defined the rehabilitation counselor's role as that of counselor–administrator. Sinick (1977) defined the role as a composite of responsibilities and functions related to consumers' problems. Within the majority of these definitions, once the consumer problem was identified, the counselor had the responsibility to take charge, coordinate, and implement an integrated pattern of services to address the consumer's needs.

The 1990s began descriptions of rehabilitation counselors as mediators, professionals whose multiple roles are used to assist individuals with disabilities maximize their lives within their environments and achieve the best fit through change in the environment, person, or both (Chubon, 1992). This early empowerment perspective is reflected in Hershenson's article (1998) stressing that rehabilitation counselors need one-to-one counseling skills to help consumers attain their goals, and consulting expertise to work with the consumer's family, friends, and employers in redesigning the environment to maximize the consumer's access and opportunity.

A possibly more impactful discussion by educators began in the second half of the 1960s and was related to wide-scale research on the role and function of the rehabilitation counselor. Muthard, Miller, and Barillas (1965) were unable to identify agreement in the field on measures of successful counseling outcomes, due partly to a lack of consensus on professional roles. In 1969, an exhaustive study (Muthard & Salomone, 1969) surveyed perceptions of counselors, supervisors, and administrators of the tasks of the rehabilitation counselor. The findings resulted in a consensus on major categories of job responsibility with counseling and guidance tasks, with face-to-face consumer contact consuming the largest amount of work time (Rubin, Richardson, & Bolton, 1973).

In the 1980s, Rubin et al.'s (1984) review of the five-factor Job Task Inventory (JTI) identified affective counseling as a major part of the rehabilitation counseling role. Leahy, Shapson, and Wright (1987), using the Rehabilitation Skills Inventory, found differences in rehabilitation counseling practice across public, private nonprofit, and private for-profit settings, with personal adjustment counseling and vocational counseling being two of five core areas common to all settings.

Studies conducted in the 1990s helped confirm the effectiveness of rehabilitation counseling as a graduate-degree profession by providing evidence that rehabilitation counselors who had graduate degrees and certification had better counseling outcomes in terms of assisting consumers to achieve employment and independence (Cook & Bolton, 1992; Leahy, Szymanski, & Linkowski, 1993; Szymanski, 1991). This research influenced the major professional association and disability advocacy groups efforts to include in the Rehabilitation Act 1992 Amendments (PL 102–569) to recruit, hire, and re-train "qualified rehabilitation personnel" —language which, through policy implementation in 1998, resulted in rehabilitation counselors in the state-federal vocational rehabilitation system having to meet the highest state or national certification (CRC) requirements for their profession.

Leahy, Chan, and Sanders's (2003) detailed analysis of CRC practices consistently confirms counseling as a core skill no matter what the rehabilitation counseling setting is. The Leahy, Muenzen, Sanders, and Strauser (2009) study suggests increased need for education and training for rehabilitation counselors in general counseling, mental-health counseling, and substance-abuse counseling. These studies have guided the development of criteria for both CRCC certification and CORE accreditation and reinforce the belief that rehabilitation counseling is a specialty of counseling addressing the unique counseling needs of unique clientele. The unique needs of consumers require that multifaceted functions be played out by the counselor but these are dependent upon the ability of the rehabilitation counselor to establish a positive counseling relationship with consumers.

Over the recent decades and in response to the disability rights movement, leadership in rehabilitation education, research, and practice (Bolton & Brookings, 1996; Emener, 1991; Kosciulek, 1998a, 1998b, 1999, 2003a, 2003b; Parker, Szymanski, & Patterson, 2005) began to discuss the need to implement and ensure empowerment concepts and practices within the rehabilitation counseling process. Many (Parker, Hansmann, Thomas, & Thoreson, 2005) see the fundamental goal of rehabilitation counseling to be to empower individuals with disabilities to achieve their highest potential. A few (Kosciulek, 2003a, 2003b; Sales, 2002, 2007; Szymanski & Trueba, 1994) have written about specific counselor competencies or counseling processes needed to empower consumers. These discussions are supportive of defining rehabilitation counseling within an environmental-social approach, which responds more to the empowerment concerns of individuals with disabilities. This approach defines a rehabilitation counselor as one who "assists individuals with disabilities in adapting to the environment, assists environments in accommodating the needs of the individual, and works toward full participation of persons with disabilities in all aspects of society, especially work" (Szymanski, Parker, & Patterson, 2005, p. 3). CORE (Maki, 2005) has adopted the following similar definition of rehabilitation counselor: "A rehabilitation counselor ... possesses the specialized knowledge, skills, and attitudes needed to collaborate in a professional relationship with persons with disabilities to achieve their personal, social, psychological, and vocational goals" (p. 2). The rehabilitation counseling profession should strive toward the following definition: "Rehabilitation counseling is an empowering process wherein a professionally competent counselor, as a partner with the consumer, collaboratively facilitates the consumer's development of the control and power over self and environmental needed to achieve a personal, interpersonal, social, career and independent living goals" (Sales, 2007, p. 181).

IMPACT OF CLIENTELE ON REHABILITATION COUNSELING

The perception and advocacy of rehabilitation counselors' clientele, working-age individuals with disabilities, have historically influenced the emphasis of rehabilitation counseling. As changes in attitudes toward and perceptions of individuals with disabilities in our society have occurred, corresponding changes in the public, the private not-for-profit, and the private rehabilitation programs have occurred. One obvious change in society's perception of individuals with disabilities can be documented in the language used to identify them. The late 19th century references were to the "crippled," "idiotic," and "feebleminded." References in the early 20th century continued to be specific to the disability, the "blind," the "deaf," the "mentally retarded," and so forth. Just after the mid-20th century, more respectful references such as individuals with neurological impairments emphasized first the individual and then the disability. The recent disability movement's value of, and identity with, disability will influence and determine new preferred references for individuals with disabilities.

The historical treatment of individuals with disability from Biblical times through early U.S. history reflects very negative attitudes (Sales, 2002, 2007; Stubbins, 1988). These negative attitudes existed not only in society but in the first rehabilitation services designed to meet the needs of individuals with disabilities. Reflecting the values of the time, these services were designed to create economic good out of the labors of people whose economic potential was limited by disabilities (Sales, 2002, 2007). They were oriented toward helping people with disabilities to earn their own keep by entering the workforce, in either sheltered or competitive employment. This was accomplished through training, rehabilitating, and otherwise altering people with disabilities to fit conditions in the workplace. However, such training was offered only to people perceived to be improvable (Varela, 1983; Wolfensberger, 1969). This strong tendency to select only those with the best prognosis for entry into the workforce characterized vocational rehabilitation from its conception until the 1960s (Berkowitz, 1980). Medical rehabilitation dominated vocational rehabilitation in its early development. The medical perspective of vocational rehabilitation sought to "restore" patients to the fullest levels of physical functioning so that they would be able to compete with and be as close as possible to a normal person. After World War II, people with disabilities, too severe to have been accepted for vocational rehabilitation, became clientele within medical rehabilitation settings. DeJong (1979a, 1979b) indicated that many of the leaders of the disability and independent living movements of the 1960s and 1970s were rehabilitated under what they perceived as a discriminatory medical model and began to manifest a more militant stance against it (Rubin & Roessler, 2001). These leaders formed advocacy groups and organizations such as independent living centers that practiced and advocated the integration of people with disabilities into the mainstream to the maximum extent possible. The advocacy groups, formed by consumers for consumers (DeJong, 1979a, 1979b; Frieden, 1983; Hahn, 1993; Lachat, 1988), are credited with having their principles of self-determination, consumer control, and nondiscrimination codified both in the Rehabilitation Act of 1973 and in its amendments. This consumer movement pressured rehabilitation counseling to move from its focus of counselor control of services, argued for "demedicalization" of services, and emphasized changing the environment, not fixing the person (Hahn, 1993).

As influenced by consumer advocacy, the 1973 Rehabilitation Act endorsed more consumer control over the process by requiring the counselor and consumer to jointly create the Individualized Written Rehabilitation Plan (IWRP) (now Individual Plan of Employment, IPE) for reaching rehabilitation goals. The Act also mandated consumer involvement in state agency policy development. Since 1973, rehabilitation legislation has been based on a foundation of assumed counselor–consumer partnership. The 1978 Rehabilitation Act Amendments provided that individuals with disabilities be guaranteed more substantial involvement in the policies governing their rehabilitation. The 1986 Amendments added support for individual consumer rights and revised the IWRP to include consumers' statements of their own rehabilitation goals. The 1990 Americans with Disabilities Act furthered self-determination by individuals with disabilities by ensuring rights in the areas of employment, transportation, public services, and public accommodations. The 1992 and 1998 Amendments further supported consumer empowerment and self-determination through client-informed choice guarantees and guarantees regarding qualified service. Today, consumer empowerment has become the driving force behind rehabilitation policy and practice.

These acts mandate the fullest possible inclusion of people with disability into U.S. society and participation in vocational rehabilitation services through guarantees of active and informed involvement in decision making within the process. The disability movement and legislation it supports advocate creating change in society and local communities to "reasonably accommodate" people with disabilities. The goal is to create a society that accepts and includes them. Barriers, whether physical or attitudinal, are challenged as discriminatory and harmful.

With emphasis on respect for individual dignity, personal responsibility, self-determination, informed choice, and inclusion, the Rehabilitation Act (1998) is truly empowering. The preamble to the Rehabilitation Act Amendments of 1998 states the one purpose of the Act is "to empower individuals with disabilities to maximize employment, economic self-sufficiency, independence, and inclusion and integration into society" (IRI, 2003).

Many older, disability-related national societies and professions including rehabilitation counseling have had to alter their perceptions to be in tune with this new thinking. Many of the thoughts behind empowerment are not new. What is new is the unity with which individuals with disabilities now expect equal treatment under the law, fair employment practices, equal access, and the right to accessible housing and transportation. This unity has resulted in individuals with disability having an impact on how rehabilitation services designed for them must now be designed with them. Service providers and consumers recognize, now more than ever, that it is the needs of the individual with a disability that must guide rehabilitation services in the state federal program and in the private sector in fulfilling their purpose and obligation to society. What the future brings in relation to rehabilitation counseling will be dependent upon society's evolving perception and leadership response to individuals with disabilities (Sales, 2007).

Impact of Service Delivery Settings

Research (Emener & Rubin, 1980; Matkin, 1982) has suggested that the employment setting is a major determiner in defining and shaping professional identity. As the types of work settings in which rehabilitation counselors practice have increased (Feinberg & McFarlane, 1979; Sales, 1979) and specialty caseloads have developed (Anthony, 1980), increased pressures in identifying responsibilities and related education needs of rehabilitation counselors have occurred. Rehabilitation counselors are employed in distinct areas or sectors within the rehabilitation service system. These are the public, the private, the not-for-profit, and the private for-profit sectors. The public sector refers to agencies funded by state or federal governments from tax dollars. The predominant public-sector agency is the state-federal vocational rehabilitation program. It is funded in each state in the United States through the Rehabilitation Act with state-matched funds and is administered federally by the Rehabilitation Services Administration (RSA), a division of the United States Department of Education's Office of Special Education and Rehabilitation. Its services include personal counseling, career counseling, medical, psychological, and vocational assessments, assistive technology, work modifications and accommodations, job training, education, and placement. Private, not-for-profit agencies are nongovernmental organizations such as Goodwill Industries and the Salvation Army that primarily raise their own funding through a variety of business ventures such as selling donated items, raising money through charitable donations, or receiving fees-for-services from state or other agencies. These usually are private, not-for-profit agencies, with the intent not to make money but to provide services. Private for-profit describes an agency or business, such as in insurance rehabilitation, whose primary purpose is to make money. Insurance rehabilitation had its birth in Workers Compensation legislation, which was enacted at the state level. This legislation held employers responsible to some degree for employee injury or accident on the job and resulted in development of private rehabilitation services as early as 1975. It required mandatory rehabilitation of injured workers, high costs of which led some states to eliminate these laws in the late 1980s. Nonetheless, the private sector, supported by insurance rehabilitation funds, employs the largest number of rehabilitation counselors in the country. Community rehabilitation programs, hospital settings, school settings, employee assistance programs, colleges and universities, substance-abuse treatment agencies, community agencies, and Veterans Administrations are but a few of the additional settings in which rehabilitation counselors practice.

CHALLENGES

Residuals of its past and risks inherent in its uniqueness present challenges to resolve for rehabilitation educators, researchers, and practitioners in order for rehabilitation counseling to attain its fullest potential as a profession. These professionals must strive toward licensure as well as certification standards (ACA, 2005). Leadership must continue efforts to resolve the lack of unity and purpose reflected by now three professional rehabilitation counseling associations. Leadership to develop a truly empowering profession must also be vigilant to avoid the risks inherent in professional power when providing counseling to individuals with disabilities.

Professionalism and professional practice when working with individuals with disabilities, may have unintended consequences (G. Albrecht, 1992; G. L. Albrecht, 1992; Illich, Zola, McKnight, Caplan, & Shaiken, 1977; Skrtic, 1991; Szymanski & Trueba, 1994). By institutionalizing expertise in individuals (Abbott, 1988) and developing and defending their autonomy and monopoly (Rothman, 1998), professions and professionals risk becoming "susceptible to the delusion that their knowledge tradition, and its associate practices and discourses are objective and inherently correct" (Skrtic, 1991, p. 85).

Professional power also is problematic for consumers in several ways. One of these is consumers' perception of a power differential with the counselor and the influence on consumers of counselors carrying out agency mandates (Stubbins, 1988). "Power is the vehicle of castification, which refers to a person's assignment to low status due to disability or other factors. Castification is one of the unintended consequences of the interaction of professionalism with a minority group. It is a form of differential marginalization" (Szymanski et al., 2005, p. 404). "Castification is fundamentally an institutionalized way of exploiting one social group (ethnic, racial, low income, or other minority group), thus reducing this group to the status of a lower caste that cannot enjoy the same rights and obligations possessed by other groups" (Trueba, 1993, p. 30).

The castification problem is compounded by master's level professional preparation programs in rehabilitation counseling, which have a disproportionate emphasis in rehabilitation counseling on individual consumer change and limited or nonexistent coverage of environmental or systems barriers confronting individuals with disabilities (Sales, 2007; Szymanski et al., 2005). Szymanski et al. (2005) concludes castification ". . . may be an inherent characteristic of helping professions . . . that . . . require people who need to be helped. If a helping profession cannot find, classify, and help potential consumers, then it ceases to have purpose as a profession. Paradoxically, the very vehicles of helping may also serve to castify" (p. 405). As Szymanski et al. suggest, this professional castification tendency is more problematic given the "business" emphasis of rehabilitation that as a major industry in the United States, relies on the ability to find and serve "needy" consumers to survive.

How consumers are defined can also be problematic and delimiting in terms of castification (McKnight, 1977; Stubbins, 1991). "The same categories of impairment and functional limitation (constructed mostly by people without disabilities) are used to determine eligibility for services, to prescribe interventions, and, on occasion, to explain failure" (Szymanski & Trueba, 1994, p. 15). Szymanski and Trueba

(1994) highlighted the many difficulties and barriers people with disabilities face as the result of castification processes.

Over the past four decades, consumer advocates (G. Albrecht, 1992; Illich et al., 1977; Novak, 1988) have called attention to rehabilitation counseling's potentially disabling consequences. The rehabilitation counseling process is complex, dynamic, and greatly valued. However, the widely accepted goal of rehabilitation counseling—to empower—is not necessarily the outcome. Rehabilitation counseling's best efforts to help have the subtle potential to be destructive by undermining the personal capabilities and resources of their consumers. Rehabilitation counselors must realize that the strength of the power they possess to help individuals with disabilities improve their own lives is comparable to the potential for unintended harm that can also occur in their counseling relationships. They must consciously and continuously work to ensure positive counseling outcomes (Sales, 2007).

SUMMARY AND PERSPECTIVE

This chapter highlighted the ongoing evolution of rehabilitation counseling as a profession and the various sources transforming the practice of rehabilitation counseling to an emphasis on empowerment. This evolution was highlighted through a discussion of historical influence on rehabilitation counseling of counseling, federal legislation, consumers, leaders, and service delivery settings. This discussion documents the continuing need to transform the practice of rehabilitation counseling through an emphasis on empowerment. Rehabilitation counseling, as it exists in the United States today, is a result of dozens of interrelated historical movements, events, organizations, academic disciplines, and professional fields.

Rehabilitation counseling reflects society's beliefs about, and perception of, individuals with disability at any given time. Its origins reflected "doing for" individuals with disability. This had the side effects of making consumers, who have the least power in our society, feel even less powerful and more unable to guide their own lives as rehabilitation counselors made decisions for them. Fortunately, the historical transition in rehabilitation counseling, from an emphasis on paternalism in its medical model to a counseling process model striving toward empowerment (Sales, 2002, 2007), has evolved as social attitudes toward disability within our society have improved. Rehabilitation counseling has made major progress toward empowerment in practice, but challenges remain to be resolved to ensure all counseling contacts are empowering.

Rehabilitation counseling practice continually must be vigilant to help consumers find ways to exercise more control over their lives. A rehabilitation counseling empowerment perspective views consumers as competent and capable of identifying their own problems and making their own decisions (Cowger, 1994; Omvig, 2002). It also views consumers as partners and allies and not passive recipients in the counseling process, and views the counselor as a collaborative resource to teach consumers problem-solving and decision-making skills. The rehabilitation counselor, within the counseling process, should encourage active decision making, encourage and promote consumer participation, and continually send messages to consumers that they are capable, competent, and able to make sound decisions (IRI, 2003).

The counseling specialty, rehabilitation counseling, has a history of impact and a future of promise. Its history is the impact of its leadership, its clientele, and its service mandates. What the future brings depends upon future leadership and their ability to build on the impact of the past. Without familiarity with the historical developments, which have molded and shaped the profession of rehabilitation counseling, professionals will lack the awareness and sensitivity needed to understand how these developments, positive or negative, influence current and future counseling practice. Rehabilitation counseling practitioners who do not have knowledge of the past will not be prepared to effectively meet the challenges of the future.

CONTENT REVIEW QUESTIONS

- What are the characteristics of a profession as identified within the chapter?
- What is the rationale provided within the chapter for rehabilitation counseling being a specialty in counseling?
- Why is rehabilitation counseling often referred to as a federally legislated profession?
- What changes in rehabilitation counseling practice are reflected in the chapter's emphasis on change from paternalism to empowerment?
- What differences does the author refer to in relation to the profession having a "duality" of definition and purpose?
- What are current challenges to the profession of rehabilitation counseling?

REFERENCES

Abbott, A. (1988). *The system of professions: An essay on the division of expert labor.* Chicago, IL: University of Chicago Press.

Albrecht, G. (1992). *The disability business: Rehabilitation in America.* London, UK: Sage.

Albrecht, G. L. (1992). The social meaning of impairment and interpretation of disability. In G. I. Albrecht (Ed.), *The disability business: Rehabilitation in America* (pp. 67–90). Newbury Park, CA: Sage.

American Counseling Association. (2005, July). *Rehabilitation counseling consortium.* Counseling Today, Alexandria, VA: Author.

Anderson, R. P. (1958). The rehabilitation counselor as counselor. *Journal of Rehabilitation,* 24(2), 4–5.

Anthony, W. (1980). A rehabilitation model for rehabilitating the psychiatrically disabled. *Rehabilitation Counseling Bulletin,* 24, 6–21.

Arbuckle, D. S. (1965). *Counseling: Philosophy, theory and practice.* Boston, MA: Allyn & Bacon.
Bandura, A. (1969). *Principles of behavior modification.* New York, NY: Holt, Rinehart, & Winston.
Belkin, G. S. (1988). *Introduction to counseling* (3rd ed.). Dubuque, IA: William C. Brown.
Berkowitz, E. D. (1980). *Rehabilitation: The federal government's response to disability 1935–1954.* New York, NY: Arno Press.
Berne, E. (1964). *Games people play.* New York, NY: Simon and Schuster.
Bitters, J. (1979). *Introduction to rehabilitation.* St. Louis, MO: C.V. Mosby.
Bolton, B., & Brookings, J. (1996). Development of a multifaceted definition of empowerment. *Rehabilitation Counseling Bulletin, 39*(4), 256–264.
Capuzzi, D., & Gross, D. R. (2003). *Counseling and psychotherapy: Theory and intervention.* (3rd ed.). Upper Saddle River, NJ: Pearson Education.
Chubon, C. (1992). Defining rehabilitation from a systems perspective: Critical implications. *Journal of Applied Rehabilitation Counseling, 23*(1), 27–32.
Cohen, M., Cote, R., Galloway, F., Hedgeman, B., & Schmones, T. (1971). *The role and function of the counselor.* A paper of a committee of the Northeast Rehabilitation Counseling Association.
Commission on Recognition of Postsecondary Accreditation. (1995). *The COPA handbook.* Washington, DC: Author.
Commission on Rehabilitation Counselor Certification. (2001). *Code of professional ethics for rehabilitation counselors.* Rolling Meadows, IL: Author.
Commission on Rehabilitation Counselor Certification. (2003). *Scope of practice for rehabilitation counseling.* Rolling Meadows, IL: Author.
Commission on Rehabilitation Counselor Certification. (2010). *Code of professional ethics for rehabilitation counselors.* Rolling Meadows, IL: Author.
Cook, D. W., & Bolton, B. (1992). Rehabilitation counselor education and case performance: An independent replication. *Rehabilitation Counseling Bulletin, 36,* 37–43.
Corey, G. (2005). *Theory and practice of counseling and psychotherapy* (7th ed.). Pacific Grove, CA: Brooks/Cole.
Cowger, C. D. (1994). Assessing client strengths: Clinical assessment for client empowerment. *Social Work, 39*(3), 262–269.
Cubelli, G. E. (1967). Longitudinal Rehabilitation: Implications for rehabilitation counseling. Professional Bulletin, National Rehabilitation Association, 7(6), 1–5.
Cull, J. G., & Hardy, R. E. (1972). *Vocational rehabilitation: Profession and process.* Springfield, IL: Charles C. Thomas.
Dawis, R. V., England, G. W., & Lofquist, L. H. (1964). *A theory of work adjustment.* Minneapolis, MN: University of Minnesota, Regional Rehabilitation Research Institute.
DeJong, G. (1979a). Independent living: From social movement to analytical paradigm. *Archives of Physical Medicine and Rehabilitation, 60,* 435–446.
DeJong, G. (1979b). *The movement for independent living: Origins, ideology, and implications for disability research.* East Lansing, MI: Michigan State University, Center for International Rehabilitation.
Dewey, J. (1956). *School and society.* Chicago, IL: University of Chicago Press (originally published in 1900).
Dykhuizen, G. (1973). *The life and mind of John Dewey.* Carbondale, IL: Southern Illinois.
Ehrenwald, J. (Ed.). (1976). *The history of psychotherapy: From healing magic to encounter.* New York, NY: Aronson.
Ellis, A., & Harper, R. A. (1961). *A guide to rational living.* Englewood Cliffs, NJ: Prentice Hall.
Emener, W. (1991). Empowerment in rehabilitation: An empowerment philosophy for rehabilitation in the 20th century. *Journal of Rehabilitation, 57*(4), 7–13.

Emener, W. G., & Rubin, S. E. (1980). Rehabilitation counselor roles and functions and sources of role strain. *Journal of Rehabilitation Counseling, 11,* 57–69.
Feinberg, L. B., & McFarlane, F. (1979). Setting-based factors in rehabilitation counselor role variability. *Journal of Rehabilitation Counseling, 12*(2), 65–68.
Frankl, E. V. (1963). *Man's search for meaning.* Boston, MA: Beacon.
Frieden, L. (1983). Understanding alternative program models. In N. Crewe & I. Zola (Eds.), *Independent living for physically disabled people.* San Francisco, CA: Jossey-Bass.
Garrett, J. F. (1969). Historical background. In D. Malikin & H. Rusalem (Eds.), *Vocational rehabilitation of the disabled* (pp. 29–38). New York, NY: New York University Press.
Gladding, S. (1996). *Counseling: A comprehensive profession* (3rd ed.). Englewood Cliffs, NJ: Merrill.
Glasser, W. (1965). *Reality therapy: A new approach to psychiatry.* New York, NY: Harper & Row.
Graves, W. H. (1992). Participatory research: A partnership among individuals with disabilities, rehabilitation professionals, and rehabilitation researchers. *Rehabilitation Education, 6,* 221–224.
Groce, N. (1992). *The U.S. Role in International Disability Activities: A history and a look towards the future.* New York, NY: Rehabilitation International.
Hahn, H. (1993). The political implications of disability definitions and data. *Journal of Disability Policy Studies, 4,* 41–52.
Hall, J. H., & Warren, S. L. (Eds.). (1956). *Rehabilitation counselor education.* Washington, DC: National Rehabilitation Association and National Vocational Guidance Association.
Hamilton, K. W. (1950). *Counseling the handicapped in the rehabilitation process.* New York, NY: Ronald Press.
Herr, E. L., & Cramer, S. H. (1995). *Career guidance and counseling through the life span: Systematic approaches* (5th ed.). Reading, MA: Addison-Wesley.
Hershenson, D. B. (1998). Along for the ride: The evolution of rehabilitation counselor education. *Rehabilitation Counselor Bulletin, 31,* 204–217.
Illich, I., Zola, I. K., McKnight, J., Caplan, J., & Shaiken, H. (1977). *Disabling professions.* London, UK: Marion Boyars.
Institute on Rehabilitation Issues. (1999). *Achieving employment outcomes through VR counselors who meet the comprehensive system of personnel development requirements.* Fayetteville, AR: University of Arkansas, Department of Rehabilitation, Human Resources and Communication Disorders, Region 6 Rehabilitation Continuing Education Center.
Institute on Rehabilitation Issues. (2003). *Promoting consumer empowerment through professional counseling.* Fayetteville, AR: University of Arkansas, Department of Rehabilitation, Human Resources and Communication Disorders, Region 6 Rehabilitation Continuing Education Center.
Johnson, L. T. (1960). The counselor as others see him. In C. H. Patterson (Ed.), *Readings in rehabilitation counseling* (pp. 41–43). Champaign, IL: Stipes Publishing.
Kaplan, M., & Cuciti, P. L. (Eds.). (1986). *The Great Society and its legacy: Twenty years of U.S. social policy.* Durham, NC: Duke University Press.
Kosciulek, J. F. (1998a). Empowering the life choices of people with disabilities through career counseling. In N. C. Gysbers, M. J. Heppner, & J. A. Johnston (Eds.), *Career counseling: Process, issues, and techniques* (pp. 109–122). Boston, MA: Allyn & Bacon.
Kosciulek, J. F. (1998b, March). *Relationship between consumer-direction, community integration, and empowerment.* Paper presented at the American Counseling Association World Conference, Indianapolis, IN.
Kosciulek, J. F. (1999). The consumer-directed theory of empowerment. *Rehabilitation Counseling Bulletin, 42*(3), 196–214
Kosciulek, J. F. (2003a). Rehabilitation counseling with individuals with disabilities: An empowerment framework. *Rehabilitation Education, 17*(4), 207–214.

Kosciulek, J. F. (2003b). Empowering people with disabilities through career counseling. In N. C. Gysbers, M. J. Heppner, & J. A. Johnston (Eds.), *Career counseling: Process, issues, and techniques* (2nd ed., pp. 139–153). Boston, MA: Allyn & Bacon.

Krumboltz, J. (Ed.). (1966). *Revolution in counseling*. Boston, MA: Houghton Mifflin.

Lachat, M. A. (1988). *The independent living service model: Historical roots, core elements, and current practice*. Hampton, NH: Center for Resource Management.

Leahy, M. M., Shapson, P., & Wright, G. (1987). Rehabilitation practitioner competencies by role and setting. *Rehabilitation Counseling Bulletin, 31*, 119–130.

Leahy, M. J., Chan, F., & Sanders, J. L. (2003). Job functions and knowledge requirements of certified rehabilitation counselors in the 21st century. *Rehabilitation Counseling Bulletin, 46*(2), 66–81.

Leahy, M. J., Muenzen, P., Sanders, J. L., & Strauser, D. (2009). Essential knowledge domains underlying effective rehabilitation counseling practice. *Rehabilitation Counseling Bulletin, 52*(2), 95–106.

Leahy, M. J., Szymanski, E. M., & Linkowski, D. (1993). Knowledge importance in rehabilitation counseling. *Rehabilitation Counseling Bulletin, 37*(2), 95–106.

Maki, D. R. (2005, February). CORE president's report. *CORE NEWS, 14*(1). Retrieved August 28, 2005, from http://www.core-rehab.org

Maliken, D., & Rusalem, H. (1969). *Vocational rehabilitation of the disabled: An overview*. New York, NY: New York University Press.

Matkin, R. E. (1982). Rehabilitation services offered in the private sector: A pilot investigation. *Journal of Rehabilitation, 48*(4), 31–33.

McGowan, J. F., & Porter, T. L. (1967). *An introduction to the vocational rehabilitation process*. Washington, DC: Superintendent of Documents, Government Printing Office.

McKnight, J. (1977). Professionalized service and disabling help. In I. Illich, I. Zola, J. McKnight, J. Caplan, & H. Shaiken (Eds.), Disabling Professions (pp 69–71). London: Marion Boyars.

Menz, F. E., Botterbusch, K., Hage-Foley, D., & Johnson, P. T. (2003, April 7). *Achieving quality outcomes through community based programs: The results are in*. Paper presented at the 2003 NISH National Training Conference, Denver, CO.

Meyers, J. K. (1968). The prophetic mission of rehabilitation: Curse or blessing. *Journal of Rehabilitation, 34*(1), 23–33.

Miller, G. A. (2001). 1955–56 Early years. In G. A. Etzbach & M. D. Kuehn (Eds.), A history of the National Council on Rehabilitation Education. Logan, UT: Author.

Mundt, P. (1986). The National Rehabilitation Counseling Association. *Journal of Rehabilitation, 52*(3), 51–53.

Muthard, J. E., Miller, L. A., & Barrillas, M. (1965) A time study of vocational rehabilitation counselors. *Rehabilitation Counseling Bulletin, 9*, 53–60.

Muthard, J. E., & Salomone, P. R. (1969). The roles and functions of the Rehabilitation counselor (Special Issue). *Rehabilitation Counseling Bulletin, 13*, 81–168.

National Association of the Deaf. (2003). What is wrong with the use these terms: "Deaf-Mute," "deaf and dumb" or "hearing-impaired"? Retrieved June 19, 2011, from http://www.nad.org/print/issues/american-sign-language/community- . . .

National Council on Rehabilitation Education 2009–2010 Directory, Fresno, CA: Author.

National Rehabilitation Counseling Association. (1958). *Constitution of the National Rehabilitation Counseling Association*. Ashville, NC: Author.

Neukrug, E. (1994). *Theory, practice and trends in human services: An overview of an emerging profession*. Pacific Grove, CA: Brooks/Cole.

Nosek, M. A. (1993). A response to Kenneth R. Thomas' commentary: Some observations of the use of the word "consumer." *Journal of Rehabilitation, 59*(2), 9–18.

Novak, A. R. (1988). A perspective on the present and notes for new directions. In L. W Heal, J. I. Haney, & A. R. Novak Amado (Eds.), *Integration of developmentally disabled individuals into the community* (2nd ed., pp. 299–305). Baltimore, MD: Brookes.

Obermann, C. E. (1965). *A history of vocational rehabilitation in America* (p. 254). Minneapolis, MN: T.S. Denison.

Omvig, J. H. (2002). The nature of empowerment. In J. H. Omvig's (Ed.), *Freedom for the blind: The secret is empowerment.* University of Arkansas: Region VI Rehabilitation Continuing Education program.

Parker, R. M., Hansmann, S., Thomas, K., & Thoreson, R. W. (2005). Rehabilitation counseling Theories. In R. M. Parker, E. D. Szymanski, & J. P. Patterson (Eds.), *Rehabilitation counseling basics and beyond* (4th ed.). Austin, TX: Pro-Ed.

Parker, R. M., Szymanski, E. M., & Patterson, J. B. (Eds.). (2005). *Rehabilitation counseling: Basics and beyond* (4th ed.). Austin, TX: Pro. Ed.

Parsons, F. (1939). *Choosing a vocation* (reprint of 1909 original version). Garrett Park, MD: Garrett Park.

Patterson, C. H. (1957). Counselor or coordinator? *Journal of Rehabilitation, 25*(2), 9–10, 27–28.

Patterson, C. H. (1958). The counselor's responsibility in rehabilitation. *Journal of Rehabilitation, 24*(2), 7–11.

Patterson, J. B., & Marks, C. (1992). The client as a customer: Achieving service quality and consumer satisfaction in Rehabilitation. *Journal of Rehabilitation, 55*(4), 16–23.

Patterson, J. B., Szymanski, E. M., & Parker, R. M. (2005). Rehabilitation counseling: The profession. In R. M. Parker, E. M. Szymanski, & J. B. Patterson (Eds.), *Rehabilitation counseling: Basics and beyond* (4th ed.). Austin, TX: ProEd.

Perls, E. (1969). *Gestalt therapy verbatim.* Moab, UT: Real People Press.

Rogers, C. R. (1942). *Counseling and psychotherapy.* Boston, MA: Houghton Mifflin.

Rothman, R. A. (1998). *Working: Sociological perspectives* (2nd ed.). Upper Saddle River, NJ: Prentice Hall.

Rubin, S. E., Matkin, R. E., Ashley, J., Beardsley, M. M., May, V. R., Onstott, K., . . . Puckett, F. (1984). Roles and functions of certified counselors (Special issue). *Rehabilitation Counseling Bulletin, 27,* 199–224.

Rubin, S. E., Richardson, B. K., & Bolton, B. (1973). *Empirically derived rehabilitation counselor sub-groups and their biographical correlates.* Arkansas Studies in Vocational Rehabilitation: Series 1. Monograph VI, Fayetteville: University of Arkansas, Arkansas Rehabilitation Research and Training Center.

Rubin, S. E., & Roessler, R. T. (2001). *Foundations of the VR process* (5th ed.). Austin, TX: ProEd.

Sales, A. (1979) Rehabilitation counseling in the private sector: Implications for graduate education. *Journal of Rehabilitation, 45*(3), 59–61.

Sales, A. (2007). *Rehabilitation counseling: An empowerment perspective.* Austin, TX: Pro-Ed.

Sales, A. P. (Ed.). (1986). History of the National Rehabilitation Association (Special Issue). *Journal of Rehabilitation, 52*(3).

Sales, A. P. (Ed.). (2002, 2007). History of rehabilitation movement: Paternalism to empowerment. In J. D. Andrew, C. W. Faubian (Eds.), *Rehabilitation services: An introduction for the human services professional* (pp. 1–41). Osage Beach, MO: Aspen Professional Services.

Salomone, P. (1996). Career counseling and job placement: Theory and practice. In E. M. Szymanski & R. M. Parker, (Eds.), Work and disability: Issues and strategies in career development and job placement (pp. 365–420). Austin, TX: Pro-Ed.

Sinick, D. (1977). Can vocational counselors change society? *Vocational Guidance Quarterly, 25*(3), 245–251.

Skrtic, T. M. (1991). *Behind special education: A critical analysis of professional culture and school organization.* Denver, CO: Love.

Stubbins, J. (1988). The politics of disability. In H. E. Yuker (Ed.), *Attitudes toward persons with disabilities* (pp. 22–32). New York, NY: Springer.

Stubbins, J. (1991). The interdisciplinary status of rehabilitation psychology. In R. P Marinelli & A. E. Dell Orto (Eds.), *The psychological and social impact of disability* (3rd ed., pp. 9–17). New York, NY: Springer.

Szymanski, E. M. (1991). The relationship of level of rehabilitation counselor education to rehabilitation client outcome in the Wisconsin Division of Vocational Rehabilitation. *Rehabilitation Counseling Bulletin, 35,* 23–37.

Szymanski, E. M., Parker, R. M., & Patterson, J. B. (2005). Beyond the basics: Sociopolitical context of rehabilitation counseling practice. In R. M. Parker, E. M. Szymanski, & J. B. Patterson (Eds.), *Rehabilitation counseling: Basics and beyond* (4th ed., pp. 395–412). Austin, TX: Pro-Ed.

Szymanski, E. M., & Trueba, H. T. (1994). Castification of people with disabilities: Potential disempowering aspects of classification in disability services. *Journal of Rehabilitation, 60*(3), 12–20.

Tarvydas, V., & Leahy, M. (1993). National Council on Rehabilitation Education listserv email communications, June–August, 2005.

Thomas, K. R. (1993a). Commentary: Jones observations on the use of the word "consumer." *Journal of Rehabilitation, 59*(2), 6–8.

Thomas, K. R. (1993b). Consumerism vs. Clientism: A reply to Nosek. *Journal of Rehabilitation, 59*(2), 11–12.

Trueba, H. T. (1993). Castification in multicultural America. In H. T. Trueba, C. Rodriguez, Y. Zou, & J. Cintron (Eds.), *Healing multicultural America: Mexican immigrants rise to power in rural California* (pp. 29–57). Philadelphia, PA: Falmer.

Valera, R. A. (1983). Changing social attitudes and legislation regarding disability. In N. M. Crewe & I. K. Zola (Eds.), *Independent living for physically disabled people* (pp. 28–48). San Francisco, CA: Jossey-Bass.

Vocational Rehabilitation Act Amendments of 1943, PL 78, Stat. 113.

Vocational Rehabilitation Act Amendments of 1954, PL 93, Stat. 565.

Vocational Rehabilitation Act Amendments of 1973, 87 Stat. 355, 29 U.S.C. 701 et seg.

Vocational Rehabilitation Act Amendments of 1992, 106 Stat. 4344, Section 2(c) (1).

Williamson, E. G. (1939). *How to counsel students.* New York, NY: McGraw Hill.

Wolfensberger, W. (1969). The origin and nature of our instructional models. In R. B. Kugel & W. Wolfensberger (Eds.), *Changing patterns in residential services for the mentally retarded* (pp. 59–72). Washington, DC: President's Committee on Mental Retardation.

Wolpe, J. (1958). *Psychotherapy by reciprocal inhibition.* Stanford, CA: Stanford University Press.

Workforce Investment Act of 1998, Vocational Rehabilitation Act Amendments Title IV, 29 U.S.C. 1320 et seg., Section (b) (1).

Wright, G. (1980). *Total rehabilitation.* Boston, MA: Little, Brown & Company.

4

Disability Policy and Law

Susanne Bruyère and Beth Reiter

LEARNING OBJECTIVES

After reading this chapter, you should be able to:

- Recognize the array of laws which govern and impact the provision of vocational rehabilitation services.
- Understand the specific provisions of the laws related to improved employment outcomes for persons with disabilities.
- Consider the implications of this legislation for vocational rehabilitation counseling, practice, training, and research.

INTRODUCTION

Although counseling is focused on the one-on-one relationship between the counselor and the client, these services are provided within a context of state and national legislation and regulation that can have a significant influence. As well as being motivators for both service provider and recipient, service availability and outcomes are governed and influenced by a myriad of individual intersecting laws. The purpose of this chapter is to identify a selection of these laws, discuss their provisions and why these might be of interest to counselors, particularly those providing services to people with disabilities, and discuss implications for the counseling profession, specifically the specialization of rehabilitation counseling. Employment is the focus in this chapter, as work is a means to economic and social independence, as well as to enhanced personal self-confidence and community participation. Access to employment for people with disabilities is a significant key to building a more inclusive society, one that not only contributes to an individual's economic self-sufficiency, but also enables that individual to have a higher quality of life and resulting enhanced overall life satisfaction.

Because improved employment outcomes are a primary focus of rehabilitation counseling, this chapter concentrates on laws that support and intersect with employment for people with disabilities. This is a worthy focus, as persons with disabilities, the target population, remain significantly disadvantaged in the employment arena. They experience half the employment participation rates of those without disabilities. In 2008, an estimated 39.5% of noninstitutionalized working age (21–64) people with a disability regardless of gender, race, ethnicity, or education level were employed compared to 79.9% of those without disabilities. This disparity translates to significant economic disparities. The median annual household income of Americans with a disability was $39,600, compared to $61,200 for households that do not have any person with disability. The lower median household income translates to a significantly higher percentage of people with disabilities in the United States living below the poverty line (25.3% compared to 9.6% of those without disabilities) (Erickson, Lee, & von Schrader, 2010).

The following laws have been selected for inclusion, description, and discussion in this chapter: Rehabilitation Act of 1973, the Americans with Disabilities Act (ADA) of 1990, the Family and Medical Leave Act (FMLA), the Uniformed Services Employment and Reemployment Rights Act (USERRA), the Workforce Investment Act (WIA), the Ticket to Work and Work Incentives Improvement Act (TWWIIA), workers' compensation laws, the Health Insurance Portability and Accountability Act (HIPAA), and the Genetic Information Nondiscrimination Act (GINA). These nine laws span over 35 years of history, including some that are very recent. Readers will learn about: definitions of disability, workplace disability nondiscrimination requirements, disclosure of disability and confidentiality issues in the employment process, unique employment protections afforded veterans with disabilities, service delivery systems, and emerging issues such as genetic testing.

OVERVIEW OF SELECT RELEVANT DISABILITY LAWS

Rehabilitation Act of 1973

Vocational Rehabilitation
Title I of the Rehabilitation Act deals with the state-federal vocational rehabilitation (VR) system that provides employment support to individuals with disabilities. The goal of this federal law is to assist states with the operation of "comprehensive, coordinated, effective, efficient, and accountable" vocational rehabilitation programs. These involve both public- and private-sector services, including: vocational assessment, career counseling, job training, job development and placement, assistive technology, supported employment, and follow-along services. In the event that state resources are not

sufficient to serve all eligible parties, the Rehabilitation Act mandates that states first provide services to those individuals with the most significant disabilities.

Under the law, all individuals with disabilities are presumed to be employable, and thus the goal of all rehabilitation services is to improve the ability of each individual to become employed. Placement in an integrated employment setting at a prevailing wage rate for at least 90 days is a successful final outcome, but other outcomes such as becoming a homemaker or unpaid family worker may be the vocational outcome for those individuals who simply cannot seek competitive employment.

Every year, the state and federal VR program serves approximately 1.2 million individuals with disabilities and places nearly 250,000 consumers into competitive employment (Council of State Administrators of Vocational Rehabilitation, n.d.). The funding for the VR service delivery system was over $2.8 billion in 2009 (National Rehabilitation Association, 2008) and in 2009, the American Recovery and Reinvestment Act of 2009 appropriated $540 million for grants to state VR programs (U.S. Department of Education, 2009). The laws specifically affecting other aspects of vocational rehabilitation will be discussed in later sections of this chapter.

Employment Discrimination

Title V of the Rehabilitation Act of 1973 is the precursor to modern disability law as codified in the ADA (Rubin & Roessler, 2001). However, its application is limited, only to federal employers. Federal employers included less than 10% of all American employers in the years leading up to 1990 (Olsheski & Schelat, 2003), and only 200,000 of the 34 million people who entered the workforce between 1970 and 1990 reported having disabilities (Bowe, 1990). Therefore, the application of Title V of this act was much too narrow to support the integration of individuals with disabilities into the workplace on a widespread basis. The most laudable contribution of the Rehabilitation Act is that it laid the groundwork for the passage of the ADA. Because the prohibitions against discrimination in the Rehabilitation Act so closely resemble those in the ADA, they will be discussed in the next section.

Americans With Disabilities Act of 1990

The ADA is the seminal piece of federal legislation addressing disability in the workplace. When passing the ADA in 1990, the U.S. Congress called attention to the fact that approximately 43 million Americans had one or more physical or mental disabilities, a number that was expected only to escalate as the age of the U.S. population continued to increase (42 U.S.C. § 12101). The ADA reached out to those millions of Americans working in nonfederal employment and extended to them the protections enjoyed by federal employees.

What Is a Disability?

Title I of the ADA provides that no covered employer shall discriminate against a qualified individual with a disability on the basis of his or her disability with respect to job application procedures, hiring, advancement, compensation, job training, or other privileges of employment. The definition of disability in ADA mirrors that contained in the Rehabilitation Act: "(1) a physical or mental impairment that substantially limits one or more of the major life activities of such individual, (2) a record of such an impairment, or (3) being regarded as having such an impairment" (42 U.S.C. § 12102[1]).

Regarding the phrase "major life activities," the ADA specifically includes functions such as caring for oneself, performing manual tasks, walking, seeing, hearing, breathing, speaking, learning, reading, concentrating, communicating, and thinking. A major life activity also includes the operation of a major bodily function, such as the functions of the immune system, normal cell growth, and the functions of the respiratory, circulatory, endocrine, or neurological systems—to name a few examples (42 U.S.C. § 12102).

In order for an impairment to qualify as an ADA disability, it must substantially limit a major life activity or bodily function, meaning that the individual is unable to perform—or is significantly limited in the ability to perform—the function or activity as compared with an average person in the general population. One cannot consider mitigating measures when determining whether an impairment substantially limits a major life activity. Thus, an individual who ameliorates the effects of his or her impairment with medication, and as a result experiences few symptoms of the impairment while taking the medication, would nevertheless have an ADA disability if, among other things, the impairment substantially limits a major life activity or bodily function in its unmitigated state.

Determining Who Is Qualified to Work

In addition to having a disability as defined above, individuals must be "otherwise qualified" for the position in question—with or without reasonable accommodation. If an applicant or employee cannot perform an essential function of the job, even with reasonable accommodation, then the ADA does not apply and the individual in question is not protected against discrimination. In other words, the ADA does not obligate employers to hire, promote, or provide any other privilege of employment to an individual who simply cannot perform the essential functions of the job. On the other hand, this requirement protects the employee or applicant against an employer who might otherwise screen out individuals with disabilities based on stereotypes regarding that individual's abilities. Ideally, if employers base their employment decisions upon the essential functions of the job rather than marginalized ones, they should be able to determine whether or not an individual is truly qualified for the position at issue.

Essential functions are those that are not marginal tasks. A job function may be essential if: (1) the position exists solely for the performance of such function,

(2) there are a limited number of employees available among whom the job function can be distributed and shared, or (3) the function is highly specialized and the employee was hired specifically because of his or her expertise.

Reasonable Accommodation

Provided that an individual who is otherwise qualified for a position has a mental or physical impairment that substantially limits a major life activity, then the ADA obligates the employer to reasonably accommodate him or her (42 U.S.C. § 12112). An employer therefore engages in unlawful discrimination if: (1) the employer fails to provide reasonable accommodation to a qualified individual with a disability, and (2) that failure denies the applicant or employee an employment opportunity.

A reasonable accommodation is any modification or adjustment to a job, employment practice, or work environment that makes it possible for a qualified individual with a disability to participate in the job application process, perform the essential functions of a job, and/or enjoy benefits and privileges of employment equal to those enjoyed by similarly situated employees without disabilities (U.S. Equal Employment Opportunity Commission [EEOC], 2002). Examples of reasonable accommodations include restructuring of the job, modifying the workspace, modifying work schedules or instituting flexible work schedules, providing adaptive or assistive equipment, and modifying the job application process or company policies.

Generally, the burden lies on the applicant or employee to notify the employer of the need for accommodation, whether in writing or in the course of conversation. In some circumstances, however, the employer should initiate the process of determining a reasonable accommodation. Specifically, employers should inquire whether an accommodation is necessary when they know that the employee's or applicant's disability exists, and know or have reason to know that the disability is causing problems in the workplace and that it also is preventing the employee or applicant from requesting any accommodation.

Undue Hardship

The duty of an employer to provide reasonable accommodation is limited by the doctrine of "undue hardship," which means significant difficulty or expense to the employer (42 U.S.C. § 12112). When determining whether a proposed accommodation would constitute an undue hardship, the employer examines factors such as its financial resources, its size, and the impact that the proposed accommodation would have upon the operation of the facility. As one might imagine, employers often identify cost as the source of undue hardship (Olsheski & Schelat, 2003, p. 64). When this is the case, the employer should grant the employee or applicant the option of contributing the burdensome portion of that accommodation cost. This arrangement preserves the employment opportunity for the employee or applicant while bringing the employer's cost of accommodation within a reasonable price range.

Input from rehabilitation counseling professionals can be an integral part of the accommodation process. "The most successful accommodations are not developed when the employer operates independently of all others. Rather, they tend to be the product of the efforts of many individuals, including supervisors, union officials, health care workers, rehabilitation counseling professionals, occupational therapists, physical therapists, and ergonomists, among others" (Olsheski & Schelat, 2003, p. 65). Ideally, the accommodation process is one of give and take among the employer, the employee or applicant, and the relevant professionals. If there is more than one potential reasonable accommodation, the employer may select which one to implement.

Direct Threat

The ADA does allow an employer to exclude from employment any individual who poses a "direct threat" to workplace safety or to health (42 U.S.C. § 12113[b]). A direct threat is a significant, as opposed to slightly increased, risk of substantial harm to the health or safety of the individual or others that cannot be eliminated or reduced by reasonable accommodation (U.S. EEOC, 1997). This determination depends upon an assessment of the present ability of the employee or applicant to perform job functions, taking into account reasonable medical opinion based upon the best available medical knowledge or other objective evidence. The employer should consider the following factors and apply them equally to all employees and applicants, regardless of disability, when determining the presence of a direct threat: (1) the duration of the risk, (2) the nature and severity of the potential harm, (3) the likelihood that the potential harm will occur, and (4) the imminence of the potential harm (U.S. EEOC, 1997).

Medical Testing

The ADA limits the use of pre- and post-employment medical examinations and inquiries as an additional means of preventing employers from basing employment decisions upon disability-related stereotypes (42 U.S.C. § 12111). During the initial application stage, an employer may ask any applicant about his or her professional qualifications for the job and/or ability to perform the essential functions of the job, but may not ask any questions regarding the applicant's health, medical history, or history of workers' compensation claims (Rubin & Roessler, 2001). Therefore, questions with respect to, for example, the number of days an applicant was absent in a prior job due to illness or whether the applicant is taking any prescription medication would be prohibited. In addition, no medical examination of any kind is allowed during the pre-employment stage. Examinations that are not medical, per se, such as the measurement of an applicant's performance of relevant physical criteria would be allowed, however, provided that medical measurements such as blood pressure and heart rate are not obtained during or after such test (Rubin & Roessler, 2001).

Once the employer has extended an offer of employment to the applicant; however, it may condition such offer upon a medical exam or responses to medical inquiries, provided that such exams or inquiries are required for all entering candidates in that job category. If the employer screens out an applicant due to the presence of a disability, it must show that such decision was "job-related and consistent with business necessity" (42 U.S.C. § 12112 [d]). The ADA provides that employers must keep any employee medical information or medical histories that it receives in separate medical files and treat all such information as a confidential medical record (42 U.S.C. § 12112; U.S. EEOC, *Facts about the Americans with Disabilities Act*, n.d.). More than 10 million workers sign authorizations every year, before the commencement of their employment, for the release of medical records (Rothstein & Talbott, 2007).

Corresponding state disability law. While Title I of the ADA applies only to employers having 15 or more employees, disability nondiscrimination legislation enacted by states may be more expansive. For example, New York (N.Y. Exec. Law § 292), California (Cal. Gov. Code § 12926), and other states have passed disability nondiscrimination legislation applicable to employers having fewer than 15 employees. Therefore, individuals who would be unable to file a claim against an employer under the ADA due to the small size of the employer's business should determine whether their claim is nevertheless viable under state law.

Accommodating Individuals With Psychiatric Disabilities

The prevalence of mental disorder in the United States is quite high—in any given year, one in five Americans is affected by a mental disorder (Jans, Stoddard, & Kraus, 2004). The labor force participation rate of individuals with mental illness has consistently lagged behind not only that of employees without disabilities, but also that of all employees with a disability in general. According to the analysis of the 2002 National Health Interview Survey (NHIS) data, the employment rate of persons aged 25–61 with mental illness was 37.1%—lower than that of persons with physical impairments (43.8%) and those with sensory impairments (58.6%). For comparison, the employment rate of people with "any disability" was 47.3%, while the rate for people without any disability was 83.3% (Harris, Hendershot, & Stapleton, 2005). Not surprisingly, the workplace accommodation of individuals with psychiatric disabilities presents unique issues and leads to unique problems that merit separate discussion.

The ADA accommodation process encourages employers and employees to share information with each another. The employer has the right to request information regarding the nature of that disability so that it may make an informed decision regarding the accommodation request. Because a psychiatric disability is not necessarily an obvious one, the employer may need to ask more questions and/or require reasonable documentation in order to determine an appropriate accommodation. Employees are encouraged to communicate with their employer in order to assist them in selecting the most effective accommodation. These forces, which strongly favor the disclosure of information regarding a psychiatric disability, run counter to an opposing force—the stigma of having a psychiatric disability. That stigma could cause the employer to assume, often incorrectly, that the individual with a psychiatric disability poses a significant risk to the health and safety of other individuals in the workplace, due in part to stereotypical beliefs about the association of psychiatric disability and violent behavior (Rubin & Roessler, 2001). In such a scenario, the employer would improperly consider himself or herself to be exempt from providing any reasonable accommodation due to the "direct threat" exclusion.

Faced with the stigma of psychiatric disability, some rehabilitation counseling professionals have advised clients against disclosing prior hospitalizations to employers (Campbell, 1994). This would foreclose an employee from obtaining any ADA accommodation, however, because employers need not provide any accommodation for individuals with disabilities of which the employer is unaware (42 U.S.C. § 12112).

In contrast, the ADA confidentiality provisions forestall employers from sharing any information regarding an employee's psychiatric condition with fellow workers. If coworkers question the employer about an individual with a psychiatric disability, employers may not disclose that they are providing a reasonable accommodation to any particular individual, and they should state instead that they are "acting for legitimate business reasons or in compliance with federal law" (U.S. EEOC, 1997). In that respect, an employee need not be concerned that the opinion of his or her coworkers will be influenced by knowledge of his or her psychiatric condition.

Family and Medical Leave Act

The FMLA (29 U.S.C. §§ 2601–2654), which went into effect in 1993, allows eligible employees up to 12 weeks of leave for family or medical reasons during any 12-month period. Its purpose is different from that of the ADA in that the FMLA seeks to provide reasonable leave opportunities for all eligible employees, rather than focusing on creating equal employment opportunities for qualified employees (Lipnic & DeCamp, 2007). An employee may have a condition, however, that qualifies him or her for FMLA leave, and leave may be a reasonable accommodation under the ADA. As such, rehabilitation counseling professionals must strive to understand both the manner in which these two statutes overlap and the manner in which they appear, at times, to conflict.

The FMLA applies to fewer employers than the ADA—those employers with 50 or more employees rather than 15 or more. It specifically allows 12 weeks of unpaid leave for any one or more of the following reasons: the birth of a child; the care of a newborn child; the placement of a child with the employee through adoption or foster care and the care of such child; the care of the employee's spouse, son, daughter, or parent with a serious health condition; or a serious health condition of the employee that causes the employee to be incapable of performing one or more of the essential functions of his or her job. The FMLA also allows 26 weeks of unpaid leave for employee's next of kin who is a member of the Armed Forces (including the National Guard or Reserves) or, in some cases, a veteran who is undergoing medical treatment, recuperation, or therapy; is otherwise in outpatient status; or is otherwise on the temporary disability retired list for a serious injury or illness.

FMLA serious health conditions are illnesses, injuries, impairments, or physical or mental conditions that involve inpatient care or continuing treatment by a health care provider. FMLA serious health conditions and ADA disabilities are not mutually exclusive categories. If an employee must visit a doctor twice and stay out of work for 4 days due to an illness, the FMLA applies (Postol, 2002). By contrast, a condition must normally be long term and substantially limiting with respect to a major life activity to constitute an ADA disability (Postol, 2002). While under the ADA an employer has no obligation to provide an accommodation if it would impose an "undue burden," such is not the case with FMLA leave.

An employer who desires to know the medical reason behind the requested leave may, in accordance with the FMLA, request certification of the employee's "serious health condition" by means of a FMLA certification form (U.S. Department of Labor, 2009). This form seeks information pertaining solely to the health condition that is the basis for the leave request. ADA medical inquiries are limited by a different standard—that is, the inquiry be job related and consistent with business necessity. The EEOC has noted that an employer medical inquiry using the FMLA certification form will not violate the ADA medical inquiry standard (U.S. EEOC, 2000). Regardless, a more recent study has revealed employer problems in this area, as some employers grant FMLA requests that they deem to be of "questionable" reliability without additional inquiry out of fear of violating employee rights under the ADA (Lipnic & DeCamp, 2007).

Many issues also have arisen with respect to the option of light duty work. Under the FMLA, an employer may offer light duty work as an option in lieu of or in addition to leave, but may not compel the employee to select light duty work. Some employers may perceive this as an obstacle to the employee's return to work. If the employee selects a light duty option, the time spent doing that work does not count against his or her FLMA leave entitlement (Lipnic & DeCamp, 2007). On the other hand, under the ADA, an employer may offer light duty work as a reasonable accommodation for an injured worker who is returning to work. Any employee who accepts such accommodation, and who also possesses rights under the FMLA with respect to a serious health condition, reserves the FMLA right to be restored to the same or an equivalent position to that which he held at the commencement of the leave period.

Uniformed Services Employment and Reemployment Rights Act

Veterans have enjoyed reemployment rights since the creation of the Selective Training and Service Act of 1940. In 1994, however, the U.S. Congress passed the USERRA, which is now the principal statute dealing with the employment and reemployment of members of the uniformed services (38 U.S.C. § 4301–4334). Although many provisions of USERRA are similar to those that were included in the 1940 law (Quinn, 2005), USERRA provides broader coverage in order to encourage noncareer service in the military by minimizing disadvantages to civilian careers, minimizing the disruption of the lives of service members and their employers' businesses by facilitating prompt job reinstatement, and reducing discrimination on the basis of service in the military (38 U.S.C. § 4301[a]).

More specifically, USERRA requires that employers must provide employees time off from work for active military duty, prohibits employers from discriminating against employees or applicants based upon military service, and provides that employers must reinstate their employees returning from up to 5 years of leave for service in the uniformed services—subject to certain limitations. Employers must also restore all benefits to their returning service members, treating time spent on leave as time worked. Finally, employers cannot fire returning service members without good cause for up to 1 year after their return from active duty.

USERRA is applicable to every employer, whether private or public. Even foreign businesses incorporated abroad must comply with USERRA if a U.S. employer controls the foreign business. With respect to veterans, those who separate from a uniformed service under other than honorable conditions will not be eligible for USERRA privileges and protections.

As of August 2009, 2.8 million veterans reported having a service-related disability (U.S. Department of Labor, 2010). This number represents approximately 13% of the total number of veterans as of that date (U.S. Department of Labor, 2010). Despite legislative efforts to support and promote the employment and reemployment of American veterans via USERRA, veterans have experienced unemployment rates close to those of non-veterans in recent years (U.S. Department of Labor, 2010). This may be due, in part, to the inadequate knowledge of USERRA on the part of the employers, the employees, or both (U.S. General Accounting Office [GAO], 2005). Rehabilitation counseling professionals should be aware of the expansive protections available to veterans under USERRA in order to best advise clients and employers regarding the rights of veterans with disabilities.

Workforce Investment Act

The WIA (105 P.L. 220, 112 Stat. 936 [1998]) is a continuation and improvement of the vocational rehabilitation service portion of the Rehabilitation Act. The goal of WIA was to require states to coordinate most federally funded employment and training services, including those in Title V of the Rehabilitation Act, into a single, comprehensive, "One-Stop" system (U.S. GAO, 2003), thereby creating a new and improved workforce investment system. WIA was designed to streamline the old system, in which parties sought services from a variety of sources in what could be a costly and confusing process (Hager & Sheldon, 2001). Instead, WIA designates about 17 categories of programs that are mandatory partners with the One-Stop Program, including Veterans Employment and Training Services, adult literacy programs, HUD-administered employment and training, and Department of Labor (DOL) employment training for migrant workers, Native Americans, youths, and dislocated workers.

Any person who can demonstrate a physical, mental, or learning disability that creates a substantial impediment to his or her ability to work is eligible for WIA services. People who are qualified to receive social security income or social security disability insurance (SSDI) are presumed to be eligible, provided that they are seeking WIA services for the purpose of obtaining employment (Hager & Sheldon, 2001). Similar to requirements under the Rehabilitation Act, if VR agency resources are inadequate to serve every individual seeking employment, it must provide services according to an order of selection.

The role of the VR agency is to assist individuals with disabilities in making informed choices with respect to their desired employment outcomes and the services necessary to achieve such goal. VR agencies assist eligible individuals in developing a written Individualized Plan for Employment (IPE).

A VR agency may deny services to any individual that it deems cannot benefit from them. WIA mandates a presumption that individuals with disabilities are capable of employment, but a VR agency may rebut that presumption if it shows by clear and convincing evidence that the individual cannot benefit from services. To this point, the VR agency must provide the individual with trial work experiences of "sufficient variety and over a sufficient length of time to determine" whether the individual may benefit from services (29 U.S.C. § 722[a][2][B]).

WIA faced challenges in achieving the complete integration of the workforce investment systems that existed prior to WIA (under the Rehabilitation Act) and the One-Stop system. For example, both systems continue to maintain separate administrations, and in some states, the systems are located in completely separate state agencies (Bruyère, Van Looy, & Golden, 2010). Part of the challenge arises from the fact that WIA is integrating VR—a specialized field—into the broader workforce development system. In 2002, the Social Security Administration (SSA) and the DOL jointly launched a Disability Program Navigator position in response to these challenges; the purpose of which is to have the Navigator serve as a resource person ready to assist individuals with disabilities in their effort to receive appropriate VR services (http://www.doleta.gov/disability/new_dpn_grants.cfm).

Ticket to Work and Work Incentives Improvement Act (TWWIIA)

The TWWIIA (106 P.L. 170, 113 Stat. 1860), enacted in 1999, was designed to provide beneficiaries and recipients of supplemental security income (SSI), SSDI, or both—the incentives and supports that they need to prepare for, attach to, or advance in work. It also expanded options for continuing health care coverage for benefiting recipients' transition to work and eliminating the disincentive to work for recipients of SSI or SSDI cash benefits that arose when such individuals lost their eligibility to receive benefits due to participation in work activities (*http:// www.ssa.gov/work/aboutticket.html*).

The Ticket to Work and Self-sufficiency Program, found in Subtitle A of Title I of the TWWIIA, replaced SSA's existing vocational rehabilitation system with an outcomes-based, market-driven program. It created a system in which all eligible beneficiaries receive a Ticket to Work—a voucher that the beneficiary may deposit with a service provider (otherwise known as an "Employment Network" [EN]) in order to receive employment services, which may include case management, work incentives planning, supported employment, career planning, career plan development, vocational assessment, job training, and other services like those available under state and federal VR programs discussed earlier (42 U.S.C. § 1320b-19[e][5]).

The Ticket Program is purely voluntary on the part of the beneficiary. He or she may decide whether to use the Ticket, may select a desirable EN from among an array of choices, and may at any time retrieve the Ticket from the EN if he or she feels that the EN's employment services are not adequate.

Service providers, either private or public organizations, that provide employment support services to assist a SSA beneficiary or recipient in preparing for, obtaining, or remaining at work may elect to become ENs. A state VR agency may be part of numerous ENs in any given state, but the statute requires each EN to be part of an agreement with a VR before referring a beneficiary to the designated state VR agency. ENs may also choose the preferred system of payment for services, either: (1) outcome payments for those months in which the beneficiaries do not receive benefits due to work activity (up to 60 months) or (2) reduced outcome payments in addition to payments for helping the beneficiary to achieve certain employment milestones. VRs have the additional option of electing to receive payment under a cost-reimbursement option.

Initial studies of the success of the Ticket Program following its initial rollout revealed low participation rates among potential beneficiaries due to an inadequate and inefficient payment system and the lack of adequate marketing, incentive, technical assistance, and training (Ticket to Work and Work Incentives Advisory Panel, 2004). In response to these findings, SSA revised the Ticket Program regulations with the goal of improving Program participation rates. The revisions took effect in late 2008, and their effects are not yet known (Stapleton et al., 2008).

Workers' Compensation

Workers' compensation programs, which exist in each of the 50 states, the District of Columbia, and the U.S. territories, provide protections for employers and employees with respect to work-related injuries. Additional related federal laws are the Federal Coal Mine Health and Safety Act, the Longshore and Harbor Workers' Compensation Act, and the Federal Employers' Liability Act. Rehabilitation counseling professionals will regularly interact with these laws as they impact the return-to-work process for most individuals with disabilities.

Prior to the development of workers' compensation laws, employees had little recourse against employers in the event of a work-related injury, and many faced destitution resulting from occupational injuries or diseases. On the other hand, with respect to the few cases in which injured employees succeeded in suing their employers for negligence, employers faced the prospect of being ordered to pay injured employees large sums, and were thus subjected to unpredictable financial risk.

Workers' compensation remedies these two problems. First, it created a "no-fault approach" to occupational injury and disease, in which a worker would be eligible for disability benefits if he or she could show that the injury or disease was work related. Second, workers' compensation statutes limited employer liability by insulating them from negligence suits, provided that the employers paid for the no-fault workers' compensation benefits prescribed by statute (Spieler & Burton, 1998). The benefits available under workers' compensation law include medical care, disability payments, rehabilitation services, survivor benefits, and funeral expenses. In addition, benefits for temporary incapacity, scarring, and permanent impairment of specific body parts are typically included. The job and benefit protections available under the FMLA and, to an extent, under the ADA are not available under workers' compensation law.

Initially, workers' compensation laws did not focus upon returning injured workers to the workplace. A remarkable shift in workers' compensation law occurred during the later half of the 20th century. These changes brought an increased focus upon disability management and return-to-work options, and thus brought the goals of workers' compensation more closely in line with those of state and federal disability discrimination law (Spieler & Burton, 1998). The distinctive philosophies underlying workers' compensation and disability discrimination law give rise to somewhat conflicting perspectives of individuals with disabilities and their interaction with the workplace. While the ADA focuses on the removal of barriers to employment through accommodations in the workplace, workers' compensation views impairments as causing work limitations. Thus, workers' compensation laws may require an employee to emphasize the limitations caused by his or her disability in order to be eligible for benefits, but those very statements may, at the same time, be detrimental to an ADA accommodation request (Geaney, 2004).

Rehabilitation counseling professionals may better assist individuals with disabilities and their employers if they possess a solid understanding of workers' compensation laws and the manner in which they interact with ADA and FMLA protections. Specific areas of concern include: (1) whether an injured worker also qualifies as having an ADA disability or has a serious medical condition under the FMLA, (2) how the ADA rules regarding medical inquiries impact an applicant with a history of occupational injury or disease, (3) whether an employee with a history of occupational injury or disease poses a direct threat to himself or herself or coworkers under the ADA, (4) ADA accommodations available to individuals injured in the workplace, including the development of light-duty positions, and (5) the impact of exclusive remedy provisions under workers' compensation laws upon an employee's rights under other disability statutes (U.S. EEOC, 1996). Although an employer bears the ultimate responsibility of determining whether an employee is ready to return to work, the employer may seek the advice of a rehabilitation counselor or other specialist in order to understand an employee's specific functional limitations or abilities when returning to work.

Health Insurance Portability and Accountability Act

The HIPAA (42 U.S.C. §§ 1320d–1320d-8) governs disclosure of medical information by covered entities. A covered entity is a health plan, health care provider, or health care clearinghouse. Based upon this definition, employers generally do not qualify as covered entities under HIPAA. Thus, HIPAA rules would not apply to any "return to work notes—medical information provided to substantiate requests for employee benefits such as short-term disability, long-term disability, FMLA requirements, job accommodation requests, or medical information for compliance with ADA" (DiBenedetto, 2005). The confidentiality of the medical information in such records would remain protected, however, by the confidentiality rules contained within the ADA and FMLA, as previously mentioned.

The greater impact of HIPAA upon the practice of rehabilitation counseling, however, involves the situation in which an occupational health provider qualifies as a health care provider or business affiliate under HIPAA. The regulations implementing HIPAA broadly define health care provider as one who "furnishes, bills, or is paid for health care in the normal course of business" (45 C.F.R. 160.103). Health care

> means care, services, or supplies related to the health of an individual. Health care includes, but is not limited to, the following: (1) Preventive, diagnostic, therapeutic, rehabilitative, maintenance, or palliative care, and counseling, service, assessment, or procedure with respect to the physical or mental condition, or functional status, of an individual or that affects the structure or function of the body and (2) Sale or dispensing of a drug, device, equipment, or other item in accordance with a prescription. (45 C.F.R. 160.103)

All covered entities must comply with HIPAA's Privacy Rule (Standards of Privacy for Individually Identifiable Health Information, 45 C.F.R. Part 160 and Subparts A and E of Part 164) in order to safeguard individually identifiable medical information (referred to as "protected health information" or "PHI") that it handles or transmits. Generally, the covered entity may provide PHI to the individual to whom it belongs and may use such information for its own treatment, payment, and health care operations. Otherwise, covered entities may use the PHI only as required by law or with the written authorization of the individual to whom it belongs.

HIPAA further requires that covered entities tailor their uses and disclosures of PHI, other than those to the subject individual or with his or her authorization, so that it uses or discloses only the minimum amount of information necessary to meet the purpose of that use or disclosure (45 C.F.R. 164.502).

Interestingly, the Privacy Rule contains a direct reference to psychotherapy notes, which it defines as:

> notes recorded (in any medium) by a health care provider who is a mental health professional documenting or analyzing the contents of conversation during a private counseling session or a group, joint, or family counseling session and that are separated from the rest of the individual's medical record. Psychotherapy notes exclude medication prescription and monitoring, counseling session start and stop times, the modalities and frequencies of treatment furnished, results of clinical tests, and any summary of the following items: Diagnosis, functional status, the treatment plan, symptoms, prognosis, and progress to date. (45 C.F.R. 160.501)

The Privacy Rule provides that covered entities must obtain the subject individual's permission to use or disclose psychotherapy notes except when using such notes for the treatment of that individual or for other specified circumstances generally pertaining to the training of the covered entity, the need to protect the health or safety of that individual or others in the community, or where necessitated by law (45 C.F.R. 160.508[a][2]).

HIPAA also contains a Security Rule (Security Standards for the Protection of Electronic Protected Health Information, 45 C.F.R. Part 160 and Subparts A and C of Part 164), which sets forth the standards to which covered entities must adhere in order to maintain the confidentiality and integrity of PHI that is stored or transferred electronically. After a covered entity identifies any potential risks to its PHI, it must then adopt appropriate administrative, physical, and technical safeguards.

Business associates also are drawn within the umbrella of HIPAA legislation. HIPAA defines a business associate as a person or entity that provides services to a covered entity or performs functions or activities for a covered entity that involve the use or disclosure of PHI (45 C.F.R. 160.103). The concept of a business associate was developed to prevent covered entities from shirking their responsibilities under HIPAA by simply outsourcing certain aspects of their businesses to non-covered entities. Under the HIPAA Privacy Rule, covered entities may release certain PHI to a business associate only if they obtain the business associate's written assurance that it will safeguard the PHI and assist the covered entity in complying with the Privacy Rule (45 C.F.R. 164.502[e]).

Most recently, the Health Information Technology for Economic and Clinical Health (HITECH) Act (42 U.S.C. § 17921 et seq.) updates HIPAA obligations by requiring both business associates and covered entities to notify an individual if the confidentiality or integrity of his or her PHI has been compromised. The HITECH Act also extends the application of many of the HIPAA privacy and security regulations that originally applied only to covered entities to business associates as well. As of the date of this publication, although the Office of Civil Rights (OCR) of the U.S. Department of Health and Human Services had not yet enacted the final rules implementing the HITECH Act, the interim rules were in full force and effect.

In conclusion, any individual planning to practice in the area of rehabilitation counseling or counseling in general must become educated regarding HIPAA in order to determine the extent to which he or she must comply with its rules and regulations. For those who are unsure whether they fall within the scope of HIPAA, they may certainly choose, nevertheless, to voluntarily implement the practices described in the Privacy Rule and the Security Rule as a means of protecting the privacy of their clients and maintaining the confidentiality of information to which they have access.

Genetic Information Nondiscrimination Act

Enacted in 2008, the GINA prohibits employers from discharging, refusing to hire, or making other decisions related to the terms and privileges of employment based upon an employee's genetic information (42 U.S.C. § 200ff-1). GINA also bars employers from using genetic information to classify employees in such a way as to decrease their employment opportunities or to otherwise negatively affect their employment status. GINA was passed in response to mounting fears among Americans that employers could discriminate against them based upon the improper use of genetic information. Such fears inhibited the use of genetic testing and raised issues regarding the viability of finding willing subjects for future genetic research (Appelbaum, 2010).

The definition of genetic information in GINA is broad enough that it covers genetic tests performed both upon an employee/applicant and upon his or her family members because the test results of family members could adversely affect the employee/applicant's risk status. In the absence of a formal genetic test, a family medical history may, in and of itself, constitute genetic information if it reveals the presence of genetically linked diseases among family members. Medical providers and health professionals should therefore omit both types of information when responding to an employer's request for medical information or documentation.

Regardless of efforts by health professionals to redact or omit genetic information contained in records that are being provided to employers, family medical information may be interspersed throughout the records and therefore be challenging to completely remove ("Are you compliant with genetic screening law?", 2010). Questions abound regarding whether medical providers and health professionals have "the time, inclination, or even ability to carefully redact genetic information from patient records," particularly with the increasing prevalence of electronic health record systems (Hoffman, 2010). Even assuming that medical providers and health professionals do have adequate time and ability to redact genetic information from records, it may be best for medical professionals to heed the recent warning of Marcia Scott, MD, affiliated with the Department of Psychiatry at Harvard Medical School—"because a family history is a necessary part of any evaluation, we all need to be aware that the pen and computer have become dangerous instruments" (Scott, 2010). When questions regarding genetic testing arise, health professionals should ensure that their patients/clients are aware of GINA and understand its protections (Appelbaum, 2010).

There is no overlap in coverage between GINA and the FMLA. Instead, GINA specifically excludes from its coverage any family medical history that an employer requests or requires in order to comply with the FMLA.

IMPLICATIONS FOR COUNSELING PRACTICE

The purpose of this chapter is to provide a broad overview of select pieces of legislation that impact employment of people with disabilities either through creation and implementation of employment services for people with disabilities or through protection of their employment rights. In the remainder of this chapter the implications of these laws for rehabilitation and general counseling practice, training, and research are discussed.

The laws described here have implications for counseling practice in that they govern the provision of vocational rehabilitation services and provide protections against workplace discrimination for both applicants and employees with disabilities. Counseling professionals providing employment services to people with disabilities should know that these laws exist, be very familiar with the services they make available, and be knowledgeable about the rights and protections that people with disabilities are afforded in the employment process.

Many rehabilitation counseling professionals work within the state VR service delivery system governed by the Rehabilitation Act, and so are likely knowledgeable about these services. However, for those whose employment setting is outside this system, being knowledgeable about available services for referral purposes is imperative, as is knowledge of the interface with other workforce development systems afforded by the WIA. Similarly, for those providing services to Social Security recipients, veterans, or those impacted by an occupational injury, awareness of TWWIIA, USERRA, and workers compensation laws is a necessity. Without this knowledge, counselors will not be able to direct their clients to the services for which they are eligible, or guide their vocational choices in light of available benefits that may impact decisions about income-earning capacity and benefits eligibility.

Support of employment disability nondiscrimination policy and practice is a part of every rehabilitation counseling professional's role. The opportunity to execute this responsibility comes daily, in moving people toward the employment application process and in coaching them in ways to maximize their employment retention and advancement. To do so effectively, it is necessary that practitioners are knowledgeable about the protections against discrimination and the requirements of accommodations (including leaves) provided by the ADA, FMLA, workers' compensation laws, and newly emerging laws such as GINA. Coaching on disclosure issues can also be informed by knowledge of the confidentiality requirements of these laws, as well as the related provisions afforded by HIPPA. These issues may be even more complex to navigate for those with psychiatric disabilities, where disclosure can be a particularly challenging issue, so that heightened attention to the implications for this population is imperative.

COUNSELING PROFESSIONAL EDUCATION

The importance of having knowledge of these laws for effective rehabilitation counseling service delivery has been discussed. Therefore it is imperative that information about these laws must be an expected part of core coursework requirements in counselor preparation. Perhaps not as obvious, however, are the implications of this knowledge for the preparation of counselors in fulfilling their professional roles as workplace educators and policy advocates. Not only rehabilitation clients, but the employers who hire them, as well as policy makers at the local and state level, must be informed about the provisions for employment disability nondiscrimination, confidentiality of medical information, access to employment services, application process and workplace accommodation, and other rights that these laws provide. Rehabilitation counseling professionals have a role to play in this community education process. Only if they are informed, as part of their pre-service and post-graduate educational processes, about the laws and roles they can play will these outcomes be realized in their professional practices.

NEEDED RELATED RESEARCH

Finally, there is a significant need for rehabilitation counseling researchers to become partners in the policy formulation and evaluation processes. All too often, this discipline is all but absent from the policy discourse when such laws are being formulated. Rehabilitation counselors' disciplinary preparation and field-based practice experiences make them exceedingly valuable potential allies in this process, as well as in the evaluation of these laws once implemented. Their educational processes should have students informed to be able to maximally utilize these laws to support effective rehabilitation counseling service delivery. They also must convey in this educational process the responsibility that future rehabilitation counseling practitioners have to be on-the-ground policy advocates and policy analysts.

As discussed in the overview of particular laws, in many cases the impact of these laws on increasing employment outcomes for people with disabilities is as yet unknown or unclear. Rehabilitation counseling researchers are needed who are able to work alongside economists, policy analysts, and others in determining the impact of WIA, TWWIIA, and workers' compensation legislation in improving initial hiring and the return to work for persons with disabilities. Similarly, rehabilitation counselors should be applying their unique analytical lens in determining whether employment disability nondiscrimination and accommodation provisions are currently designed in a way to minimize marginalization and maximize inclusion. It is a tremendous opportunity for these specialized professionals to contribute in the policy arena.

CONTENT REVIEW QUESTIONS

- How does the Vocational Rehabilitation Act of 1973 as amended assist states with the operation of comprehensive coordinated and effective vocational rehabilitation services?
- What are the specific provisions of the Americans with Disabilities Act of 1990 (ADA) as they relate to employer requirements to make reasonable accommodation for an applicant or employee with a disability?
- How might the requirements of the ADA and the Family Medical Leave Act (FMLA) intersect?
- Why should rehabilitation professions be familiar with the provisions of the Uniformed Services Employment and Reemployment Rights Act (USERRA)?
- What might be the strengths and weaknesses of the provision of services to people with disabilities through the workforce development system provided for under the Workforce Investment Act (WIA)?
- Which challenges to employment faced by Social Security beneficiaries was the Ticket to Work and Work Incentives Improvement Act (TWWIIA) designed to address?
- How might the ADA and the provisions of state workers' compensation laws intersect?
- What are the rehabilitation counseling practice implications for the Health Insurance Portability and Accountability Act (HIPAA) and the Genetic Information Nondiscrimination Act (GINA)?

ACKNOWLEDGMENTS

The authors were supported in preparation of this manuscript by a grant from the U.S. Department of Education National Institute of Disability and Rehabilitation Research to the Employment and Disability Institute at Cornell University ILR School for a Rehabilitation Research and Training Center (RRTC) on *Employment Policy for Persons with Disabilities* (Grant No. H133B040013), Susanne M. Bruyère, Project Director.

The authors would like to acknowledge the editorial assistance of Sara Van Looy, Administrative/Research Assistant with the Employment and Disability Institute at Cornell University.

REFERENCES

Appelbaum, P. S. (2010). Law & psychiatry: Genetic discrimination in mental disorders: The impact of the Genetic Information Nondiscrimination Act. *Psychiatric Services, 61,* 338–340.

Are you compliant with genetic screening law? (2010, May 1). *Occupational health management.* Retrieved from Academic Onefile, Gale Document No. A226579431.

Bowe, F. (1990). Into the private sector: Rights and people with disabilities. *Journal of Disability Policy Studies, 1*(1), 89–101.

Bruyère, S., Van Looy, S., & Golden, T. (2010). Legislation and rehabilitation professionals. In S. Flanagan, H. Zaretsky, & A. Moroz (Eds.), *Medical aspects of disability: A handbook for the rehabilitation professional* (4th ed., pp. 669–686). New York, NY: Springer.

Campbell, J. (1994). Unintended consequences in public policy: Persons with psychiatric disabilities and the Americans with Disabilities Act. *Policy Studies Journal, 22,* 133.

Council of State Administrators of Vocational Rehabilitation. (n.d). *Public vocational rehabilitation program fact sheet.* Retrieved July 22, 2009, from http://www.rehabnetwork.org/press_room/vr_fact_sheet.htm

DiBenedetto, D. V. (2005). HIPAA not always is applicable to occ-health. *Occupational Health Management.* Retrieved from Academic Onefile.

Erickson, W., Lee, C., & von Schrader, S. (2010). *2008 Disability status report: The United States.* Ithaca, NY: Cornell University Rehabilitation Research and Training Center on Disability Demographics and Statistics.

Geaney, J. (2004). The relationship of workers' compensation to the Americans with Disabilities Act and Family and Medical Leave Act. *Clinics in Occupational and Environmental Medicine, 4,* 273–293.

Hager, R. M., & Sheldon, J. R. (2001). *State and federal vocational rehabilitation programs: Services and supports to assist individuals with disabilities in preparing for, attaching to, and advancing in employment.* Retrieved from http://digitalcommons.ilr.cornell.edu/cgi/viewcontent.cgi?article=1218&context=edicollect

Harris, B. H., Hendershot, G., & Stapleton, D. C. (2005, October). *A guide to disability statistics from the National Health Interview Survey. Rehabilitation research and training center on disability demographics and statistics.* Ithaca, NY: Cornell University. Retrieved from http://digitalcommons.ilr.cornell.edu/edicollect/186/

Hoffman, S. (2010). Employing E-health: The impact of electronic health records on the workplace. *Kansas Journal of Law & Public Policy, 19,* 409.

Jans, L., Stoddard, S., & Kraus, L. (2004). *Chartbook on mental health and disability in the United States. An InfoUse report.* Washington, DC: United States Department of Education, National Institute on Disability and Rehabilitation Research. Retrieved from http://www.infouse.com/disabilitydata/mentalhealth/

Lipnic, V. A., & DeCamp, P. (2007). *Family and medical leave Act regulations: A report on the Department of Labor's request for information.* Washington, DC: United States Department of Labor. Retrieved from http://digitalcommons.ilr.cornell.edu/key_workplace/315/

National Rehabilitation Association. (2008). *The president's 2009 federal budget.* Retrieved from http://nationalrehab.org/index.php?option=com_content&task=view&id=83&Itemid=2

Olsheski, J., & Schelat, R. (2003). Reasonable job accommodations for people with psychiatric disabilities. In D. Moxley & J. Finch (Eds.), *Sourcebook of rehabilitation and mental health practice* (pp. 61–76). New York, NY: Kluwer Academic Publishers.

Postol, L. (2002). Sailing the employment law Bermuda Triangle. *The Labor Lawyer, 18,* 165–192.

Quinn, M. (2005). Uniformed Services Employment and Reemployment Rights Act (USERRA)—broad in protections, inadequate in scope. *University of Pennsylvania Journal of Labor & Employment, 8,* 237.

Rothstein, M. A., & Talbott, M. K. (2007). Compelled authorizations for disclosure of health records: Magnitude and implications. *American Journal of Bioethics, 7,* 38–40.

Rubin, S. E., & Roessler, R. T. (Eds.). (2001). *Foundations of the vocational rehabilitation process.* Austin, TX: Pro-ed.

Scott, M. (2010). Letter: Family history and GINA. *Psychiatric Services, 61,* 634.

Spieler, E. A., & Burton, J. F. (1998). Compensation for disabled workers: Workers' compensation. In T. Thomason, J. Burton, & D. Hyatt (Eds.), *New approaches to disability in the workplace* (pp. 205–244). Madison, WI: Industrial Relations Research Association.

Stapleton, D., Livermore, G., Thornton, C., O'Day, B., Weathers, R., Harrison, K., ... Wright, D. (2008, September). *Ticket to work at the crossroads: A solid foundation with an uncertain future.* Report submitted to the Social Security Administration Office of Disability and Income Support Programs. Washington, DC: Mathematica Policy Research Institute. Retrieved September 23, 2010, from http://mathematicampr.com/publications/PDFs/disability/tickettowork_ppt_0409.pdf

Ticket to Work and Work Incentives Advisory Panel. (2004). *The crisis in EN participation—A blueprint for action.* Washington, DC: Social Security Administration. Retrieved from http://ssa.gov/work/panel/panel_documents/pdf_versions/CrisisEnParticipation.pdf

U.S. Department of Education. (2009). *American Recovery and Reinvestment Act of 2009: Vocational rehabilitation recovery funds.* Retrieved from http://www.ed.gov/policy/gen/leg/recovery/factsheet/vr.html

U.S. Department of Labor. (2009). *Frequently asked questions and answers about the revisions to the Family and Medical Leave Act.* Washington, DC: Author. Retrieved September 23, 2010, from http://www.dol.gov/whd/fmla/finalrule/NonMilitaryFAQs.pdf

U.S. Department of Labor. (2010). *Bureau of labor statistics, economic news release: Employment situation of veterans—2009.* Retrieved from: http://www.bls.gov/news.release/vet.nr0.htm

U.S. Equal Employment Opportunity Commission. (n.d.). *Facts about the Americans with Disabilities Act.* Retrieved September 20, 2010, from http://www.eeoc.gov/facts/fs-ada.html

U.S. Equal Employment Opportunity Commission. (1996). *EEOC enforcement guidance: Workers' compensation and the ADA.* (No. 915.002).

U.S. Equal Employment Opportunity Commission. (1997, March 25). *Enforcement guidance on the Americans with Disabilities Act and psychiatric disabilities* (No. 915.002).

U.S. Equal Employment Opportunity Commission. (2000, July 27). *Enforcement guidance: Disability-related inquiries and medical examinations of employees under the Americans with Disabilities Act* (No. 915.002).

U.S. Equal Employment Opportunity Commission. (2002). *Enforcement guidance on reasonable accommodation and undue hardship under the Americans with Disabilities Act.* Retrieved from http:eeoc.gov/policy/docs/accommodation.html#privileges

U.S. General Accounting Office. (2003). *Workforce Investment Act: One-stop centers implemented strategies to strengthen services and partnerships, but more research and information sharing is needed.* Retrieved from the GAO Web site: http://www.gao.gov/new.items/d03725.pdf

U.S. General Accounting Office. (2005). *Military personnel: Federal management of service member employment rights can be further improved.* Retrieved from the GAO Web site: http://www.gao.gov/new.items/d0660.pdf

5

Concepts and Paradigms in Rehabilitation Counseling

Dennis R. Maki

LEARNING OBJECTIVES

After reading this chapter, you should be able to:

- Define the key concepts and paradigms of rehabilitation and rehabilitation counseling.
- Discuss the philosophy and process of rehabilitation counseling.
- Summarize and apply models relevant to the professional practice of rehabilitation counseling.
- Understand the process of professional counselor development.

It is essential to begin a study of rehabilitation counseling with shared definitions and fundamental concepts. With such knowledge, it is possible to understand how these concepts translate into the paradigms and models of professional practice. These paradigms and models then provide a systematic framework to understand the professional practice of the rehabilitation counselor.

Rehabilitation is a robust concept used in diverse contexts referring to the restoration of persons, places, or things. In each of these contexts, there is the connotation of a return to a state of health or useful and constructive activity. As a concept, *rehabilitation counseling* is not as robust, or is it as generally understood. However, this concept is used to refer to a specialty practice area of the counseling profession and to a scope of practice within the health care and human service delivery systems.

Definitions for the following terms and concepts are provided and also an infrastructure for this and subsequent discussions. Therefore, it is important to first understand each definition independently and then to further consider each definition in relation to the others. This process will result in a better understanding of the direct, though complex, relationships linking the terms and underscoring the importance of a shared language.

- Rehabilitation is defined as "a holistic and integrated program of medical, physical, psychosocial, and vocational interventions that empower a person with disability to achieve a personally fulfilling, socially meaningful, and functionally effective interaction with the world" (Banja, 1990, p. 615).
- Counseling is defined as "a professional relationship that empowers diverse individuals, families, and groups to accomplish mental health, wellness, education, and career goals" (ACA, 2010).
- Rehabilitation counseling is defined as a practice that "assists persons with disabilities in adapting to the environment, assists environments in accommodating the needs of the individual, and works toward full participation of persons with disabilities in all aspects of society, especially work" (Szymanski, 1985, p. 3).
- Rehabilitation within the context of the rehabilitation counseling process is defined as "a comprehensive sequence of services, mutually planned by the client and rehabilitation counselor, to maximize employability, independence, integration, and participation of persons with disabilities in the workplace and the community" (Jenkins, Patterson, & Szymanski, 1992, p. 2).
- Rehabilitation counseling as a *scope of practice* is defined as "a systematic process, which assists persons with physical, mental, developmental, cognitive, and emotional disabilities to achieve their personal, career, and independent living goals in the most integrated setting possible through the application of the counseling process. The counseling process involves communication, goal setting, and beneficial growth or change through self-advocacy, psychological, vocational, social, and behavioral interventions. The specific techniques and modalities utilized in the rehabilitation counseling process may include, but are not restricted to:
  - Assessment and appraisal
  - Diagnosis and treatment planning
  - Career (vocational) planning
  - Individual and group counseling treatment interventions
  - Case management, referral, and service coordination
  - Program evaluation and research
  - Interventions to remove environmental, employment, and attitudinal barriers
  - Consultation services
  - Job analysis, job development, and placement services, including assistance with reasonable accommodations
  - Provision of consultation about and access to rehabilitation technology" (CRCC, 1994, pp. 1–2).

A rehabilitation counselor is defined as "a counselor who possesses the specialized knowledge, skills, and attitudes needed to collaborate in a professional relationship with people who have disabilities to achieve their personal, social, psychological, and vocational goals" (Rehabilitation Counseling Consortium [RCC], 2005).

The concepts and paradigms critical to developing an understanding of the elements and contexts of the professional practice of rehabilitation counseling are provided throughout this text. Definitions of key terms contained in the Scope of Practice Statement are found in Appendix B. Also, acronyms commonly used in rehabilitation constitute a shared language used among professionals and are found in Appendix A.

REHABILITATION PHILOSOPHY

The philosophy of rehabilitation counseling is based on a belief in the dignity and worth of all people. It values independence, integration, and the inclusion of people with and without disabilities in those environments in which they live, learn, work, and recreate. Rehabilitation counseling embodies the philosophy that, whenever possible, persons with disability should be integrated into the least restrictive environments possible. Inherent in this philosophy is a commitment to equalizing the opportunities for persons with disabilities to participate in all rights and privileges available to all people, and to providing a sense of equal justice based on a model of accommodation. In addition, the philosophy contains a commitment to supporting persons with disabilities in advocacy activities in order to enable them to achieve independence and thereby further empower themselves.

Within this philosophy there is a commitment to models of service delivery that emphasize integrated, comprehensive services that are mutually planned by the client and the rehabilitation counselor. The philosophy of rehabilitation counseling requires informed choice and empowerment. This emphasis serves to define the philosophy of rehabilitation counseling as one that is *existential*. That is, as people seek to make meaning out of their lives and become more self-aware, they take on increased responsibility and ownership of their choices and behaviors in the face of an uncertain future. Full consideration must be given to the individual's right to success as well as failure as potential outcomes involved with choice, growth, and risk.

Embedded within this philosophy is the principle of *informed consent*. Informed consent has two central aspects. The first is disclosure and awareness of all pertinent information the client needs to make a decision. The second aspect is possessing free consent to engage in an activity or intervention without coercion. Underlying the requirement of informed consent is the view of the client as an autonomous being who is able to direct his or her own life (Welfel, 2002). The philosophy of rehabilitation counseling embraces a person's right to choose his or her relationships and goals. This philosophy of rehabilitation has been clearly articulated as part of the Underlying Values section of the Scope of Practice Statement (Appendix B).

Contemporary rehabilitation counseling philosophy also is reflected in several paradigm shifts. These shifts include a movement from an individual problem-solving approach to an ecological solution-focused approach, from institutionalization to community participation, from charity to civil rights, from segregated vocational training models to community-integrated or community-supported employment and independent living models, and from a medical model with an illness and pathology focus to a wellness model focusing on development and life stages. Maki and Murray (1995) provide a more complete discussion of the philosophy of rehabilitation. This reference and its source documents, as well as the discussion found therein, provide an excellent resource for further exploration of this topic.

The philosophy of rehabilitation counseling is solution focused and stresses the assets of the person and the resources of his or her environment. Individuals are conceptualized as interacting within multiple contexts of life, especially within the contexts of their family and culture. The focus is on adaptation and accommodation from an ecological perspective that is directed toward achieving a meaningful quality of life (QOL) for the person with a disability. Disability and the philosophy of rehabilitation are different in various cultures. Therefore, each of these concepts must be defined and understood within their cultural contexts.

PERSONS WITH DISABILITIES

The philosophy of rehabilitation counseling begins with a belief in the dignity and worth of all people. The terms and languages used in professional practice must reflect and reinforce this belief as well. Professionals use different terms when referring to those individuals seeking their services. Medical professionals refer to their "patients" and educators to their "students," whereas legal and mental health professionals refer to their "clients." Traditionally, the term *client* has predominated in rehabilitation counseling and its practice. However, the term *consumer* has been advocated for as a preference among some persons within disability communities as a term believed to reflect a more empowered status for persons with disability relative to their service delivery systems and professionals. The terminology used may be a sensitive issue for some persons. It is always appropriate to ask each person about his or her preferred terminology. The term "client" will be used primarily throughout this text when referring to persons who seek or receive rehabilitation counseling services.

In addition to the terms used in spoken reference to persons with disability, it is important to be aware of, and to comply with, similar principles concerning written communication. The *Publication Manual of the American Psychological Association* (2010) provides the standard reference style guidelines for the field.

Consistent with the conceptual and philosophical framework of rehabilitation counseling professional practice, use of the term "disability" should occur only to describe an attribute of a person, and *handicap* to describe the experienced result of the limitations, such as the attitudinal, legal, and architectural barriers. It is important to note that *disability* and *handicap* are not synonymous. In addition, the terms "challenged" and "special" are often considered euphemistic and should be used only if the person served by the rehabilitation counselor prefers them.

As professionals working with persons with and without disabilities, rehabilitation counselors must communicate clearly and respectfully. An open discussion with the person with whom the counselor is working usually provides a forum for selecting language to be used subsequently with each individual. The language chosen communicates a philosophical and attitudinal orientation at both a personal and a professional level. It is important to reiterate that the language used to describe a person involved in rehabilitation counseling services is a critical consideration for the professional.

DEFINITIONS OF DISABILITY

The rehabilitation counselor must be sensitive to the existence of various definitions of disability, their varied uses, and the relationship among them. In addition to culturally based definitions, these definitions are used to define eligibility for programs and services. For example, for a person to be protected by the Americans with Disabilities Act (ADA, 1990), the law specifically defines an individual with a disability as a person who: (1) has a physical or mental impairment that substantially limits one or more of the major life activities of that person, (2) has a record of such an impairment, or (3) is regarded as having such an impairment. Major life activities include caring for oneself, performing manual tasks, walking, seeing, hearing, breathing, learning, and working.

On January 1, 2009, the Americans with Disabilities Act Amendments Act of 2008 (ADAAA) took effect. The ADAAA retains the "three-prong" definition of disability as set out in the ADA of 1990, but requires a broader interpretation of the statutory terms. Most important to rehabilitation counselors is the expansion of the definition of "major life activities" to include "functions of the immune system, normal cell growth, digestive, bowel, bladder, neurological, brain, respiratory, circulatory, endocrine, and reproductive functions" (ADAAA, 2008), which would allow a person diagnosed with cancer, for example, to be covered under the law. In addition, the ADAAA states conditions that are episodic or relapsing and remitting in nature (e.g., multiple sclerosis) that do substantially limit a major life activity when active must be considered disabling conditions.

Other changes to the definition of disability under the ADAAA are that a condition need only substantially limit one major life activity to be considered a disability. In addition, mitigating measures, with the exception of "ordinary eyeglasses and contact lenses" (ADAAA, 2008) will not be considered when determining whether or not a condition substantially limits a major life activity, and, to be covered under the "regarded as" prong, an applicant or employee no longer needs to demonstrate that the employer perceived him/her as substantially limited in a major life activity. Rather, the ADAAA states that a potential or current employee is "regarded as" having a disability if he/she is subject to an action by an employer that is prohibited under the ADA (e.g., not hired) due to a condition that is not minor or transitory in nature. However, individuals covered only under the "regarded as" prong are not entitled to reasonable accommodation or modifications.

The Social Security Administration adheres to a different definition of disability. Disability under Social Security is based on an individual's inability to work. Income payments are for persons with total, long-term disability only; no benefits are paid to those with partial or short-term disability. Individuals are considered "disabled" under Social Security rules if unable to do the work they did before illness or injury, and if Social Security decides they cannot adjust to other work given their disabling condition(s). The disability must be expected to last at least 1 year, or to result in death. The different definitions of disability espoused by the ADA and the Social Security Administration have created some compatibility issues that have not been resolved. Persons who have been found to be "disabled" under Social Security rules have been found unable to do work of any type. Qualified persons with disabilities under the ADA must be capable of doing work, with or without accommodations. The intent of the rules of each program was not to be mutually exclusive, or to disqualify an individual from accessing either or both programs.

The Rehabilitation Services Administration states that to be eligible to receive vocational rehabilitation (VR) services through the state-federal partnership programs, an individual must have a disability that affects their ability to work, be able to get and keep a job after receiving services and must need rehabilitation services in order to get and keep a job. Information is gathered under the authority of the Rehabilitation Act of 1973, as amended (Public Law 93–112). In addition to eligibility, this information, which must be provided by a medical professional to document disability, is used to determine the category of severity and, if appropriate, to help develop and carry out a plan of services to enable the person to reach a suitable vocational goal. This goal is indicated in the individual plan for employment (IPE).

PARADIGMS OF REHABILITATION PRACTICE

A conceptual model described by Hershenson (1996) provides a rationale for distinguishing rehabilitation counseling from the other helping disciplines involved in rehabilitation such as medicine or psychology. This system of categories considers rehabilitation from the perspective of primary, secondary, and tertiary prevention of disability:

■ *Primary prevention* is characterized by the provision of interventions directed toward preventing the onset of disease or disability. Professionals from such fields as public health and occupational health and safety have traditionally provided primary prevention.

■ *Secondary prevention* is characterized by the provision of interventions directed toward preventing or, when that is not possible, limiting the effects of the disease or disability in persons when primary prevention has failed. Professionals from medicine, psychology, and similar curative fields have traditionally provided this level of prevention.

■ *Tertiary prevention* is characterized by activities directed toward preventing long-term residual conditions from having any greater disabling effects than necessary, once the secondary prevention fields have done all they can do to cure or limit the disease/disabling process. Professionals from rehabilitation counseling and allied fields have traditionally provided tertiary prevention.

Hershenson (1996) described how the attention given to the individual and the environment differs at each level. Primary prevention, for example, is heavily weighted toward the environment (e.g., drinking-water supply, worksite safety, and automobile seat belts) and considers individuals only insofar as that environment affects them. Secondary prevention is heavily weighted toward the individual (e.g., curing or limiting the pathology that exists within the individual) and examines the environment only insofar as it facilitates or impedes the curative process within the individual. Tertiary prevention differs from the other two categories of prevention in that it requires an equally balanced focus on both the environment and the individual. This dual focus is necessary because disability may stem as much from environmental barriers as from individual limitations.

The paradigms derived from the three categories of prevention provide a basis for understanding and distinguishing the roles of the multiple disciplines that are part of the interdisciplinary rehabilitation process. Each level is represented by a discipline such as public health, medicine/psychology, and rehabilitation counseling. Each discipline and each level is different from the other in its basic science, focus, strategy for intervention, and goals. All disciplines have a unique and important contribution to make in the rehabilitation endeavor.

PARADIGMS FOR REHABILITATION COUNSELING

For intentional, systematic practice to occur, it is critical that rehabilitation counselors have a conceptual model or paradigm to guide their work. It has been suggested that rehabilitation counselors have at least three orientations from which to conceptualize their teaching, research, and practice. These paradigms include the *psychomedical model*, the *systems model*, and the *ecological model* (Cottone & Emener, 1990). Each of these orientations has merit and distinguishes itself by the relative emphasis it places on the person, the environment, and the relationship between the two. After a brief discussion of the psychomedical and systems model, a more detailed description of the ecological model will be presented.

The Psychomedical Model

The psychomedical model looks within the individual for a diagnosis of the problem, placing the person in a "one-down position" relative to the expert, typically a physician. From this perspective, the person with a disability is considered a patient. The psychomedical model represents a biomedical orientation toward the scientific representation of the person's condition and uses diagnostic categories to administratively classify and subsequently treat the underlying cause of a person's disability. This approach is valuable for understanding the medical and allied health professional's contribution to the rehabilitation team. It underlies the restorative services offered in rehabilitation and is related to the secondary prevention model referred to previously when the counselor is providing diagnosis and treatment planning.

The Systems Model

Cottone and Cottone (1986) provided yet another perspective for conceptualizing rehabilitation counseling practice, that is, the systems approach. This perspective suggests that neither the person nor the environment is the unit of analysis. The unit of analysis is, in fact, the relationship between the two. This perspective suggests that to focus on either the individual (psychomedical) or the individual–environment transaction (ecological) is inadequate as the inherent nature of rehabilitation is systemic and the impact of disability affects all persons with a relationship to the person and in the varied environments involved. This perspective argues for the inclusion of family counseling and systems training in the curriculum for the development of the rehabilitation counselor.

The Ecological Model

The ecological model of rehabilitation counseling proposed herein reflects a tertiary prevention model with equal consideration being given to the person and the environment (Figure 5.1). Cottone and Emener (1990) suggested that such an approach represents an alternative to the psychomedical and systemic models. Historically, the ecological perspective of rehabilitation has emerged from a trait–factor tradition, which measures traits within the individual as well as factors within the environment. An evaluation is then made to determine the extent of match or congruence between the traits and the factors. Decisions about the probable success of a person placed in a vocational, independent living, or other environment would then be made based on this information. This model is consistent with an existential philosophy as empowered clients make meaning out of their experiences. They take responsibility and ownership of their decisions given their increased awareness about their strengths and the demands of the options they are considering.

FIGURE 5.1

A Transactional Approach Seeking Correspondence Between an Individual's Maximum and Typical Behaviors With the Criterion Requirements and the Reinforcers and Demands Present in the Environment. The Rehabilitation Counselor's Four Essential Functions Are Indicated Within This Model.

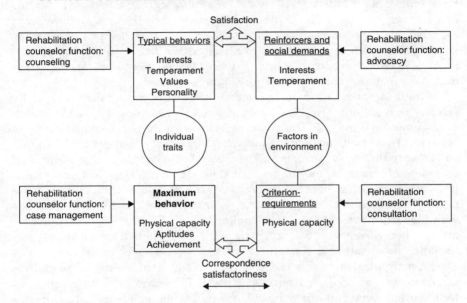

The Minnesota Theory of Work Adjustment (Dawis, 1996; Lofquist & Dawis, 1969) has provided an empirically valid version of the trait–factor model for VR practice. Maki, McCracken, Pape, and Scofield (1979) suggested that an ecological perspective with a developmental orientation transformed a trait–factor approach into a viable theoretical framework for rehabilitation. Kosciulek (1993) supported the continuing validity of this approach to contemporary practice, a position with which Lofquist and Dawis (2002) agreed, describing a person–environment-correspondence theory.

The ecological model, in consideration of individual traits and environmental factors, provides a conceptual infrastructure for the professional practice of rehabilitation counseling. It is assumed that the conceptual discussion that follows would apply to persons with or without disability. In addition, the model can be applied to tasks and environments other than vocational. In those instances, individual traits would be compared to the environmental factors or the task criterion requirements and the reinforcers available in the selected environment, such as independent living, education, and recreation. Both traits and factors can be measured or assigned numbers to indicate the extent to which each is present in the individual and the environment. To better understand this model, it is described in the following.

Traits refer to the underlying characteristics that exist in people. Traits account for the observed behavioral consistencies within people and for the stable and enduring differences among people. All people are assumed to possess the same traits, but in differing amounts. Cronbach (1990) has differentiated between those traits that are indicators of *typical performance* and those that are indicators of *maximum performance*. In the process of measuring the traits of an individual, the rehabilitation counselor must infer their presence from samples of behavior, as traits cannot generally be measured directly other than physical traits such as range of motion. The particular traits that the rehabilitation counselor decides to evaluate will depend upon the purpose of the assessment.

Traits indicative of typical performance describe how a person typically behaves in situations. The behavioral consistency principle is applied here with the assumption being made that past performance is the best indicator of future behavior. These traits include the individual's interests, temperaments, values, and other indicators of personality. The typical behaviors are evaluated through interview, observation, and the occasional use of inventories. Evaluating these traits and comparing their correspondence with potential environments facilitates making more accurate predictions regarding a client's probable *satisfaction* with the factors present in various environments. The rehabilitation counselor may predict with enhanced accuracy the person's likelihood to remain in a particular environment by evaluating this satisfaction. The factors against which a person's typical behavior traits are evaluated include environmental reinforcers such as salary, advancement possibilities, and position prestige, as well as other social and interpersonal factors. Therefore, it is critical to identify the client's needs, interests, and personality, as well as the reinforcers and the social/interpersonal factors that are present in environments under consideration. The extent to which factors meet specific needs will provide important data to the client for decision making.

Traits indicative of maximum performance describe a person's capacities and capabilities. These traits include physical capacity, aptitude and achievement, and other indicators of ability. The maximum behaviors are evaluated through testing, observation, and interviews. Evaluating these traits facilitates making more accurate predictions regarding the *satisfactoriness* of a person's capacity to perform the essential functions and tasks required in education, employment, independent living, and other major life activities. The matching or congruence between the client's performance and the job or task has been described as the level of satisfactoriness. The factors against which a person's maximum behavior traits are evaluated include the environment's essential and marginal functions including the physical, educational, and skill demands.

Based on the current trends in empowerment and informed choice (Hagen-Foley, Rosenthal, & Thomas, 2005), besides an objective measurement of clients' traits and environmental factors, counselors also need to pay attention to persons' subjective understandings of their internal as well as external worlds. For example, the concept of contextual self-understanding sheds light on the importance of assisting people with disabilities in understanding themselves with regard to the opportunities, which are provided by environments to fully exert their existing capabilities (Breeding, 2008). From this perspective, the promotion of the clients' self-efficacy as well as locus of control should be considered by a counselor in addition to their individuals' personal traits. The enhancement of subjective understanding only increases people with disabilities' confidence about their choices, and also helps counselors make a more accurate hypothesis about clients' possible satisfaction and satisfactoriness.

In evaluating persons' traits, equal consideration must be made for what they want to do (typical behavior) and what they are capable of doing (maximum behaviors). Therefore, it is critical to consider persons' interests and the environment's ability to meet these needs, as well as their ability to do the essential functions in the environment in order to enhance their tenure in a given life domain. An ongoing emphasis on the client's self-exploration (i.e., contextual self-understanding and self-perceptions toward barriers) can further impact a successful outcome from this ecological perspective. Although in some instances referral to psychologists and other professionals may be involved in this rehabilitation assessment and information gathering process, it is possible that rehabilitation counselors themselves would secure this information through interview, observation, and the occasional use of inventories. The question of who secures what information is a matter of each individual professional's scope of practice, and the available resources that define the functions performed by the staff in a particular human service or rehabilitation system.

The ecological model of rehabilitation counseling presented in the preceding considers the person and his or her potential environments from a trait–factor perspective. This model is a cognitive map to guide the client in making decisions and choices about his or her external world such as what type of work to do, where to live, learn, and recreate. This model does not give consideration to the person's internal world and psychosocial adaptation process in relation to these environments. This is critical to understanding the decisions made and the corresponding meaning they have from the person's perspective. A social learning model acknowledging the reciprocal impact between both the person's adaptation and their environments' accommodations is presented in the ecological adaptation model. This model is presented in the following to provide insight into the person and the people in his or her environments as they process the meaning of his or her interactions.

Ecological Adaptation Model

The ecological model of rehabilitation counseling provides a framework for professional practice and client decision making. However, this trait factor approach does not address the psychosocial adaptation of persons with their disabilities. It is important that the rehabilitation counselor also have a framework to consider the psychosocial impact of disability. The ecological adaptation model (Figure 5.2) provides such a framework and, when considered with the

FIGURE 5.2
The Ecological Adaptation Model for Understanding the Psychosocial Adaptation of Persons With Disability

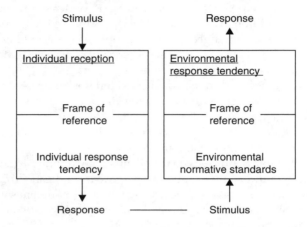

ecological model of rehabilitation counseling, a comprehensive paradigm for understanding the profession and process of rehabilitation counseling emerges. This model highlights the importance of not only assessing traits and factors, but also the transactions that dynamically describe the interactive nature of person(s) and their environment(s).

The ecological adaptation model is informed by a social learning orientation respectful of the reciprocal nature of both persons and their environments. Scofield, Pape, McCracken, and Maki (1980) described the ecological adaptation model, which conceptualizes this reciprocal relationship in describing: (1) the nature of the individual with a disability as he or she interacts and, to various degrees, *adapts to* various environments, and (2) the simultaneous ability of environments to *accommodate* persons with disability. It is suggested that *adaptation* as a dynamic concept, describing the extent to which a person accepts disability as one of his or her many characteristics, is a preferred concept to *adjustment*, because it infers a more enduring, static, and categorical description when referring to a person's acceptance of disability.

This ecological adaptation model provides a framework for assessing the normative standards, frames of reference, and response tendencies of environments and persons within these environments at various levels of intimacy to the person with a disability. The *environmental normative standards* include the cultural values, community moral code, as well as those policies and laws that set the standards for acceptable behavior in the environment. Persons within the environment develop *frames of reference* based on the normative standards by which they interpret the behavior of others. The model suggests that *environmental response tendencies* are based on frames of reference with regard to a person with disability's capacity to meet the normative standards. The extent to which a person with disability deviates from these standards, as interpreted in the frame of reference, predisposes persons in that environment to respond to the person with disability in ways compatible with the standards. One such response tendency is *attitude*, defined as learned predisposition to respond in an evaluative manner, which is especially critical to assess considering the potential impact. This model acknowledges that only verbal or nonverbal responses by the environment, that is, those messages and behaviors that are actually exhibited and observable, serve as stimuli to the person.

In addition to the environment, the model also requires assessment of the individual. Specifically needing to be assessed are the person with disability's capacity to receive overt and covert messages provided by the environment, the *person's frame of reference* including self-concept and self-efficacy as a way to understand how meaning is made out of the messages received, and the *person's response tendencies*, or typical interaction style in response to particular persons, environments, and the messages they send. Disability may interfere with the person's ability to see or hear messages, cognitively make meaning from the messages, or establish response tendencies relative to the person's acceptance or not of disability. The manifestation of the response tendency is the actual *behavior or message* emitted by the person. These then serve as stimuli and send a message to the environment that will either reinforce the normative standards or act as a catalyst for changing those standards that are inaccurate or inappropriate.

The ecological adaptation model perspective also provides rehabilitation counselors with a systematic framework to organize and conceptualize the complexities of their work with individuals with disabilities in relation to those significant persons and environments in which they live, work, and recreate. This model can be considered in conjunction with self-efficacy theory. Perceived self-efficacy is concerned with the person's beliefs in his or her ability to influence events that affect their lives. This core belief is the foundation of human motivation, performance accomplishments, and emotional well-being. Unless people believe that they can produce desired effects by their actions, they have little incentive to undertake activities or to persevere in the face of difficulties. Whatever other factors may serve as guides and motivators, they are rooted in the core belief that people can make a difference by their actions. Self-efficacy is concerned with personal self-judgments that influence the environments that people choose, the activities in which they engage, and the effort and persistence they demonstrate at a task in the face of obstacles.

The theory provides an overall framework to conceptualize why some clients are successful in rehabilitation efforts and others are not. It also addresses how counselors can most effectively help clients maximize rehabilitation potential. Brodwin and Brodwin (1992) described the usefulness to the field of rehabilitation of Bandura's work (1982) on self-efficacy. They suggest that this growing body of research related to individual response tendencies supports the hypothesis that self-efficacy beliefs are cognitive mediators of assured, purposeful, and persistent behavior. These are behaviors that need to be developed and/or increased in persons with disabilities if they are to receive maximum benefit from the various rehabilitation systems.

Rehabilitation potential as defined by these same authors consists of three characteristics: (1) attaining increased functioning in the direction of maximum physical and emotional growth, (2) having a sense of well-being, and (3) facilitating development of a personally satisfying level of independence. These authors note that different rehabilitation systems (e.g., worker's compensation, long-term disability, social security, state VR, and independent living) define a client's rehabilitation potential within the context of their specific organization's parameters. Crimando and Riggar (1991) stressed that counselors need to be aware of the differing requirements of each rehabilitation system providing services.

THE REHABILITATION CONCEPT

Once rehabilitation counselors has a clear respect for and understanding of the philosophy of rehabilitation, the concept of disability, their own role and scope of practice, as well as a systematic paradigm to guide their professional practice, it is possible to revisit and further describe the rehabilitation concept. Maki (1986) operationalized the rehabilitation philosophy, defining the rehabilitation concept in terms of a comprehensive, individualized process, prescriptive in nature and directed toward the development or restoration of functional independence and a QOL. Traditionally, rehabilitation defines functional independence in terms of economic self-sufficiency, while independent living rehabilitation defines it in terms of community integration and autonomous living. Both vocational and independent living rehabilitation programs increasingly include QOL indices in their definitions of successful outcome. Condelucci (1995) extended this concept to embrace "interdependence" as a new plan of action for reestablishing the individual with the community and enhancing personal lives through a sense of similarity, rather than difference.

The following statements represent the key elements in understanding the concept of rehabilitation:

■ *It is comprehensive in scope and holistic in nature.* The rehabilitation process is an orderly sequence of activities related to the needs of the individual. Although comprehensive services will differ from client to client, certain basic dimensions are relevant to understanding the total person. The most significant dimensions of the person, which need consideration, include the medical, psychological, personal-social, cultural, educational, vocational, as well as the spiritual. To understand the client or provide services relating to only one dimension of the person's life functioning without considering the other aspects and their interdependency would be ineffective and could result in the ultimate failure of the rehabilitation effort. Thus, effective rehabilitation often demands the coordinated efforts of a multidisciplinary, interdisciplinary, or transdisciplinary team. The rehabilitation counselor is an integral member of these teams.

■ *It is an individualized process.* Each person is unique in terms of his or her skills, residual capacities, functional limitations, resources, and personality. The manifestations of disability present themselves differently in each individual, with varying meanings and implications for rehabilitation depending on the environmental and cultural context. Rehabilitation is considered a process based on the needs and assets of each individual client. Rehabilitation counselors continually must be aware of the pitfalls of labeling and stereotyping. Various authors (Feist-Price, 1995; Nathanson, 1979) have noted that counseling professionals are not immune to bias or prejudice regarding disability and must be aware of their own attitudes and expectations.

■ *It is prescriptive in nature.* That is to say, a prescriptive course of action is developed with each individual. The type and amount of services provided are based on the needs and resources of the individual. The services are selected that will remove, reduce, or compensate for the functional and societal limitations of the individual so that he or she can achieve the goals established in the individualized plan. Environmental accommodations and modifications must be considered, as well as client development and adaptation.

■ *It functions to develop or restore.* Habilitation is the term denoting the development or acquisition of skills and functions previously not attained. This term is used commonly to refer to the service of persons with disabilities who, due to lack of training or experience, are initially developing their functional independence. Habilitation refers to an initial learning of skills and roles that allow an individual to function in society. Rehabilitation refers to the restoration or reacquisition of skills and functions lost through injury, disease, or trauma. The term "rehabilitation" is used here as well as throughout the text to describe either process resulting in functional independence.

■ *Its goal is functional independence and a quality of life.* Functional independence is the capacity of individuals to take care of their affairs to the extent that they are capable. Functional independence is a broad goal; subsumed under the goal are economic self-sufficiency as well as personal, social, and community living skills (Morris, 1973). It also reflects the individualized nature of the definition of success and functioning. Functional independence considers the total individual in all his or her environments.

A QOL perspective on rehabilitation counseling integrates competing program goals such as client independence or employment into a higher-order and multi-dimensional rehabilitation outcome. Counselors committed to a QOL orientation work from a wellness and holistic position that addresses both the development and the adaptation of the individual and the environments where the person lives, learns, works, and recreates. QOL is directly applicable to the long-standing question of how to define successful outcomes in rehabilitation. Rehabilitation professionals often disagree as to whether the primary goal of rehabilitation is promoting client independence or vocational placement. QOL offers a higher-order goal that subsumes both independence and employment as legitimate outcomes (Roessler, 1990).

THE REHABILITATION PROCESS

Historically, persons with disabilities have received services through a delivery system containing the following ordered components: intake, assessment, services, and outcomes. This generic model accommodates the interdisciplinary nature of rehabilitation. A model presented by Maki et al. (1979) provides a framework for describing this rehabilitation process.

The client's entry into the rehabilitation service delivery system typically begins with *intake*. Here, administrative decisions are made regarding the client's eligibility for services based on predetermined criteria, such as age, qualifying disability, location of primary residence, or financial status. If the client is determined to be ineligible or does not qualify for the program, there is an appeal process available to the client such as the Client Assistance Program (CAP) in the state-federal VR program. If the client is determined to be eligible, the client begins an individualized *assessment*. Accurate and effective assessment is a prerequisite to successful rehabilitation planning. When working in settings that serve persons with psychiatric disabilities or provide mental health services, this process may include a mental status evaluation and/or a clinical diagnostic interview in the development of an appropriate diagnosis that will be the foundation of an individualized treatment plan. Assessment is designed to establish a plan based on the client's current level of functioning, the goal(s) of rehabilitation, and what services are required to achieve the goal(s).

The client and rehabilitation counselor work together in assessment and plan development using the skills of problem solving and resource analysis. Included in the plan are the necessary *services* to assist the client in attaining the specified outcomes, along with a listing of who will provide these services and a timeline for completion or review. The counselor and client must mutually establish the goals to be accomplished within the parameters of the practice setting. The practice setting will also affect the range of functions and tasks that are to be performed by the rehabilitation counselor.

The rehabilitation counselor performs *four essential functions* in the delivery of services to persons with disability. These functions are counseling and case management in working with the client and consultation and advocacy in working with others and the environments impacting the person. Services are selected, which will allow the client to achieve the goals such as to acquire skills and behaviors appropriate for the designed outcomes.

Services provided to the individual by the rehabilitation counselor are generally either in the area of *case management* or *counseling services*. Case management has been defined by Moxley (1989) as a client-level strategy for promoting the coordination of human services. He refers to a case manager as "a designated person (or team) who organizes, coordinates, and sustains network of formal and informal supports and activities designed to optimize the well-being and functioning of people with multiple needs" (p. 17). The case manager identifies appropriate providers and facilities while ensuring that the resources are being used in a timely and cost-effective manner. Mullahy (1995) refers to case management as "a collaborative process which assesses, plans, implements, coordinates, monitors, and evaluates the options and services to meet an individual's health needs, using communication and available resources to promote quality, cost-effective outcomes" (p. 9).

Two typical areas for which case management services are provided by the rehabilitation counselor are education and restoration services. Education is usually a service for clients who lack the skills or knowledge necessary to reach their long- or short-term goal(s) and the objectives outlined in their individual rehabilitation plans. Education may be formal or informal and generally lies outside the scope of practice of the rehabilitation counselor. Restoration services are usually prescribed when the counselor sees that there is a need for enhancing the physical functioning of an individual; prosthetics, work hardening programs, or speech therapy are examples of these services. As with education, these services are often coordinated or managed by the rehabilitation counselor, as they lie outside his or her scope of practice.

Counseling is a therapeutic or psychoeducational service. This service is provided by the rehabilitation counselor within the relationship with the client and parameters of the agency, organization, or facility in which a particular counselor functions. In the performance of this function, the rehabilitation counselor selects evidence-based practices and an individual, group, or family counseling theory to guide this aspect of his or her practice. No matter where or what other functions and responsibilities are engaged in by the rehabilitation counselor, counseling is the central function that is provided continuously throughout the rehabilitation process. G. N. Wright (1980) stated that counseling is:

> a nontransferable obligation of the rehabilitation counselor. Consultant and rehabilitation services of other kinds may or should be purchased, but the ultimate professional responsibility for the function of counseling cannot be delegated. Professional counseling is indispensable to the proper selection, provision, and utilization of the other rehabilitation services. (p. 55)

Services provided by the rehabilitation counselor directed toward the environment are *consultation* and *advocacy* when those environments and persons in them are relevant to the success of the client's plan. Moxley (1989) describes both these functions as environmental interventions and indirect services as they do not involve direct contact with the client. As such, they involve activities and interventions that are implemented with persons and systems external to the client. These activities serve as a means to achieve the plan, build the capacities of the systems to respond to the needs of the client, and provide access to resources (Steinberg & Carter, 1983).

Lynch, Habeck, and Sebastian (1997) discussed the key skills, knowledge, and ethical and professional issues relevant to consultation by rehabilitation counselors. The following discussion of consultation is based on their work. Brown, Pryzwansky, and Schulte (1995) conceptualize consultation as an indirect service provided to a consultee. This service may be *formal* with a contract or more *informal* in nature. Consultation is frequently interdisciplinary with the consultant either being *internal* to the organization or *external* from it. External consultants are, more often, readily viewed as experts but may lack important background information that would be more accessible to an internal consultant.

Consultation may occur as *expert consultation* or *process consultation*. Kurpius, Fuqua, and Rozecki (1993) distinguish these two forms of consultations. In expert consultation, the consultant is responsible for the design, implementation, and success of the intervention. In process consultation, the consultant works in active partnership with the consultee to design and implement change. Here the success of the intervention is shared between the consultant and the consultee.

Consultation may focus on primary, secondary, or tertiary prevention. Each of these foci may be targeted to individuals, groups, organizations, or communities. *Primary prevention consultation* focuses on such areas as enhanced communication, decision making, and coping. *Secondary prevention consultation* would occur in areas such as job-enrichment programs or remediation of learning disabilities. *Tertiary prevention* would focus on reducing the impact of functional limitations (Brown et al., 1995).

Advocacy is the action a counselor takes in assisting clients to achieve their goals through participating in their environments. Advocacy has a role in the other functions: counseling, case management, and consultation. Teaching clients to become self-advocates is possibly the most important aspect of this process. In all cases, changing environments for growth and development is the goal. Sosin and Caulum (1983) argue that advocacy involves the use of influence or confrontation to get a third party to make a decision regarding the welfare of the client who has less power than the decision maker. The rehabilitation counselor in this way represents the client to the decision makers.

The final component of the service delivery system is *outcome*. During this stage, placement and follow-up occur. The rehabilitation counselor may perform these activities or the client may be referred to a professional who specializes in these functions. In addition to the state-federal VR program's employment criterion of success (i.e., Status 26 or successfully placed in a job for 90 days), other outcomes related to independent living and QOL are valued criteria of success in contemporary rehabilitation practice. In mental health or psychiatric rehabilitation settings, more specific measures such as continuing improvement in mental health as measured on the Beck Depression Scale or maintaining community living status would represent outcomes of success.

Counselors are both direct and indirect service providers, and the manner in which they manage their time and activities contributes significantly to the efficiency and effectiveness of the rehabilitation process.

PROFESSIONAL COUNSELOR DEVELOPMENT

Any discussion of the development of professional competence begins with consideration of those individuals who have self-selected themselves for a career in rehabilitation counseling, and have been selected to study or provide services to persons whose rehabilitation would be the focus of such a professional. Competence is the sum total of knowledge, skills, and attitudes considered necessary by the professional standards and community sanctions, values, and expectations within the context of its social, political, and cultural mores (Figure 5.3).

Individuals who choose to engage in the rehabilitation counselor role must be vigilant in their commitment to self-awareness, and reflect on their beliefs, motives, needs, and competencies within themselves first. It requires an honest and ongoing process of self-assessment and self-understanding about how they are alike and different in relation to other persons. This self-evaluation is a key first step in the adoption or induction into any role as either the provider or the recipient. The following dimensions of self-assessment/definition are representative of those critical aspects of the self that need articulation: age, gender, learning style, socioeconomic status, sexual orientation, life style, developmental life stage/tasks, disability status, ethnic/cultural identity, occupation, and values, beliefs, and attitudes toward the role being considered. By definition, this introspection is self-focused and phenomenological. From this awareness

FIGURE 5.3
The Structured Developmental Model (SDM) Is a Robust and Relevant Paradigm to Understand Counselor Development and Clinical Supervision

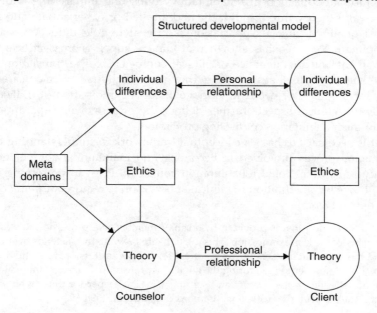

perspective, consideration of others as individuals and the roles they may be engaged in, such as supervisor or client, is prerequisite to ethical practice. This stance is also a prerequisite for the person to adopt and practice the various roles they are called upon to play such as parent, child, student, professional, or client, or some combination thereof.

In consideration of the role of an individual as a professional rehabilitation counselor, it is important first to understand and be aware of his or her own personhood. Given this basis, it is then possible to select and systematically practice as a professional through an adopted theory of practice that is compatible with a personal belief system that the individual integrates into his or her role as counselor. That is to say, a professional counselor engages in an ethical and defined relationship based on the articulated philosophy and theory that guides the content and process of his or her work.

Specifically, the role and responsibilities of the counselor and the reciprocal role and responsibilities of the person seeking his or her services (client, patient, or consumer) are, by design, established through the adoption of a theory or paradigm of practice appropriate to the profession and reflected in the mission and staffing patterns of their agency. The person-to-person professional relationship between counselor and client is a social interaction, but it has an ethical and theoretical dimension. This ethical and theoretical dimension differentiates it from a purely social relationship between counselor and client, such as a friendship or peer-counseling relationship. These latter relationships occur on a person-to-person level without the theoretical or ethical constructions invoked in a professional relationship between two individuals engaged in intentional role-defined interactions.

Graduate education in rehabilitation counseling imparts the knowledge of ethics and theory through didactic and applied or experiential coursework, whereas qualified clinical supervision is critical to role induction and skill development. Research has shown that clinical supervision is critical to the development and maintenance of clinical competence. The translation of the natural helping skills that may have drawn an individual to seek a career as a professional counselor needs to be developed. A combination of didactic and experiential/clinical aspects further defines the professional preparation standards of the rehabilitation counseling profession.

It is necessary to have a conceptual framework for understanding the developmental process involved in becoming and maintaining competence and integrity as a professional rehabilitation counselor. Prior to presenting such a model, however, a definition of clinical supervision is required. *Clinical supervision* is defined as:

> An intervention that is provided by a senior member of a profession to a junior member of the same profession. This relationship is evaluative, extends over time, and has the simultaneous purposes of enhancing the professional functioning of the junior member(s) monitoring the quality of professional services offered to the clients, she, he, or they see(s), and serving as a gatekeeper for those who are to enter the particularly profession. (Bernard & Goodyear, 1998, p. 4)

Clinical supervision is a distinct intervention that requires a trained supervisor. Thus, specialized education in the area of clinical supervision is essential, and such supervision is critical at the preservice level. It is equally as necessary at the continuing education and professional practice levels. Not to engage in appropriate clinical supervision does a disservice to the counselor and potentially places the client at risk.

Maki and Delworth (1995) have proposed the SDM as a robust and relevant paradigm to understand counselor development. The SDM refines the integrated developmental model (IDM) proposed by Stoltenberg and Delworth (1987), through an organization of the eight domains that reflect counseling practice. Stoltenberg and Delworth assumed that progression from a Level-1 counselor to a Level-3 (integrated) counselor proceeds in a relatively systematic manner through eight domains or areas of professional competence. The SDM categorizes these domains into two main categories: (1) three primary domains and (2) five process domains. The *primary domains*, essential for every counselor, are sensitive to individual differences, theoretical orientation, and professional ethics. These first three domains serve as metadomains (Figure 5.3) and will continue to be addressed as counselor's work through the levels as well as through each of the remaining five process domains.

The five *process domains* parallel the functions of the rehabilitation counselor and are presented in the traditional sequence of case service delivery as follows: (1) interpersonal assessment, which uses the counseling relationship to evaluate the social skills, personality characteristics, and interaction style of the client, (2) individual client assessment in his or her environment, which focuses on the person and the functional impact of disability and incorporates psychometric procedures and medical consultation, (3) case conceptualization, which requires the integration of interpersonal assessment and individual client assessment data to generate a working image of the client as a whole person, (4) treatment goals and plans, and (5) intervention strategies. Each of these process domains contains specific knowledge and skills that are interrelated and become integrated as the counselor reaches the fourth and final level proposed by this model, Level-3 Integrated. The model presented herein provides the supervisor with a format to achieve the goals of clinical supervision: enhancing the therapeutic competence of the counselor while simultaneously monitoring the client's welfare.

The following is a brief description outlining a model developmental sequence defining the levels referred previously. The developmental model assumes that counselors-in-training progress through four levels while learning to function clinically. According to Stoltenberg and Delworth's (1987) IDM, as individuals progress across these levels, change occurs in a continuous manner with regard to the following: *self and other awareness, motivation*, and *autonomy*. As the individual moves through the levels, increased competence in each domain can be observed.

At *Level 1*, counselors are both highly dependent on their supervisor and highly motivated to learn. They are concerned with their counseling performance to such an extent that they seem largely self-focused on their own behavior instead of their clients. Counselors at this level are also influenced by their supervisor's method or technique and will most likely function from an imitative or recipe-oriented approach to counseling. The supervisor is a teacher at this level.

At *Level 2*, the counselor is less method bound, more client focused, and concerned with investing his or her own personality style into the counseling work. Counselors begin to experience in greater depth the emotional and cognitive states of the client. Developing insight and differentiating personal reactions from client realities are recurrent struggles during this level. This dynamic may result in the counselor's vacillating motivational level. Because of the increase in skill base, Level-2 counselors also seem to vacillate between the need for supervision and autonomy.

Level-3, counselors are more likely to assume a collegial relationship with their supervisor and other professionals. At this level, the counselor is able to ask for what they need without feeling inadequate or that his or her competency will be called into question through such requests. Supervision becomes consultative in nature and counselor initiated. The Level-3 counselor also tends to have developed the ability to be empathetic with clients and to have a simultaneous sense of self-awareness, which allows for clear, professional boundaries. Having developed a balanced sense of personal and professional identity usually reflects itself in a fairly stable level of motivation.

The goal of an accredited rehabilitation counselor education program is to provide the preservice foundation for the counselor to become a Level-3 integrated professional who is able to function independently. It is believed that this level can occur with supervised experience and continuing education after graduation.

SUMMARY

This chapter introduced the concepts and paradigms essential to understanding the professional practice of rehabilitation counseling. Key definitions and conceptual frameworks, as well as the scope of practice were introduced. In a manner consistent with the holistic nature of rehabilitation counseling, this chapter addressed the philosophy of rehabilitation and its attendant components, the concept of disability, various paradigms of both rehabilitation practice and rehabilitation counseling, the sequential process involved, and the centrality of the person with a disability throughout the rehabilitation counseling professional practice.

The ecological model of rehabilitation counseling and the ecological adaptation model were described to provide frameworks for effective and intentional practice. The four essential functions of the rehabilitation counselor were presented in this process. These functions are counseling and case management in working with the client and consultation and advocacy in working with the client's significant others and the environments impacting the person. Issues related to appropriate and respectful language and terminology were emphasized, along with a discussion of the importance of rehabilitation outcomes, including QOL.

Professional preparation of rehabilitation counselors also was presented to address the critical importance of adequate and ethical rehabilitation counselor education and supervision that ultimately serves to guide professional practice. It is important to recognize not only the centrality of the person with a disability throughout this rehabilitation process, but also the integrative and reciprocal nature inherent in this process. The rehabilitation counselor becomes a key component in the environment of the person with a disability once services commence, and the domains discussed in the SDM serve to enhance both the development of the rehabilitation counselor as a professional and the quality of services provided to those who seek rehabilitation services from qualified professionals.

CONTENT REVIEW QUESTIONS

- What is a rehabilitation counselor?
- Discuss the philosophy of rehabilitation counseling and the concept of rehabilitation.
- Describe the ecological model of rehabilitation counseling as a framework for professional practice.
- Describe the ecological adaptation model as a model for understanding psychosocial adaptation. Differentiate this model from the ecological model of rehabilitation counseling.
- What are the four functions of the rehabilitation counselor? Discuss them in the context of the process of rehabilitation.
- What are the primary and process domains of the SDM? What are the main characteristics of each across the levels of counselor development?

REFERENCES

American Counseling Association. (2010). *20/20: A vision for the future of counseling.* Retrieved July 28, 2010, from http://www.counseling.org/20-20/index.aspx

American Psychological Association. (2010). *Publication manual of the American Psychological Association* (6th ed.). Washington, DC: Author.

Americans with Disabilities Act of 1990, 42 U.S.C.A. Sec. § 12101.

Americans with Disabilities Amendments Act of 2008, Pub. L. 110–325, 122 Stat. 3553 (2008).

Bandura, A. (1982). Self-efficacy mechanism in human agency. *American Psychologist, 37,* 122–147.

Banja, J. (1990). Rehabilitation and empowerment. *Archives of Physical Medicine and Rehabilitation, 7*(1), 614–615.

Bernard, J. M., & Goodyear, R. K. (1998). *Fundamentals of clinical supervision* (2nd ed.). Needham Heights, MA: Allyn and Bacon.

Breeding, R. R. (2008). Empowerment as a function of contextual self-understanding. *Rehabilitation Counseling Bulletin, 51*(2), 96–106.

Brodwin, M., & Brodwin, S. (1992). Rehabilitation: A case study approach. In M. Brodwin, F. Tellez, & S. Brodwin (Eds.), *Medical, psychological and vocational aspects of disability* (pp. 1–19). Athens, GA: Elliott & Fitzpatrick.

Brown, D., Pryzwansky, W. B., & Schulte, A. C. (1995). *Psychological consultation: Introduction to theory and practice* (3rd ed.). Boston, MA: Allyn & Bacon.

Commission on Rehabilitation Counselor Certification. (1994). *CRCC Certification Guide.* Rolling Meadows, IL: Author.

Condelucci, A. (1995). *Interdependence: The route to community.* Youngsville, NC: Lash & Associates.

Cottone, R., & Cottone, L. (1986). A systematic analysis of vocational evaluation in the state-federal rehabilitation system. *Vocational Evaluation and Work Adjustment Bulletin, 19*(2), 47–54.

Cottone, R., & Emener, W. (1990). The psychomedical paradigm of vocational rehabilitation and its alternatives. *Rehabilitation Counseling Bulletin, 34,* 91–102.

Crimando, W., & Riggar, T. F. (Eds.). (1991). *Utilizing community resources.* Delray Beach, FL: St. Lucie Press.

Cronbach, L. J. (1990). *Essentials of psychological testing* (5th ed.). New York, NY: HarperCollins.

Dawis, R. (1996).The theory of work adjustment and person-environment correspondence counseling. In D. Brown, L. Brooks, & Associates (Eds.), *Career choice and development* (3rd ed., pp. 75–120). San Francisco, CA: Jossey-Bass.

Feist-Price, S. (1995). African Americans with disabilities and equity in vocational rehabilitation services: One state's review. *Rehabilitation Counseling Bulletin, 39,* 119–129.

Hagen-Foley, D. L., Rosenthal, D. A., & Thomas, D. F. (2005). Informed consumer choice in community rehabilitation programs. *Rehabilitation Counseling Bulletin, 48*(2), 110–117.

Hershenson, D. (1996). A theoretical model for rehabilitation counseling. *Rehabilitation Counseling Bulletin, 33,* 268–278.

Jenkins, W., Patterson, J. B., & Szymanski, E. M. (1992). Philosophical, historic, and legislative aspects of the rehabilitation counseling profession. In R. M. Parker & E. M. Szymanski (Eds.), *Rehabilitation counseling: Basics and beyond* (3rd ed., pp. 1–41). Austin, TX: Pro-Ed.

Kosciulek, J. (1993). Advances in trait-and-factor theory: A person × environment fit approach to rehabilitation counseling. *Journal of Applied Rehabilitation Counseling, 24*(2), 11–14.

Kurpius, D. J., Fuqua, D. R., & Rozecki, T. (1993). The consulting process: A multidimensional approach. *Journal of Counseling and Development, 71,* 601–606.

Lofquist, L. H., & Dawis, R. V. (1969). *Adjustment to work: A psychological view of man's problems in a work-oriented society.* New York, NY: Appleton-Century-Crofts.

Lofquist, L. H., & Dawis, R. V. (2002). Person-environment-correspondence theory. In D. Brown (Ed.), *Career choice and development* (4th ed.). San Francisco, CA: Jossey-Bass.

Lynch, R., & Martin, T. (1982). Rehabilitation counseling: A training needs survey. *Journal of Rehabilitation, 48,* 51–52, 73.

Maki, D. R. (1986). Foundations of applied rehabilitation counseling. In T. F. Riggar, D. Maki, & A. Wolf (Eds.), *Applied rehabilitation counseling* (pp. 3–11). New York, NY: Springer Publishing.

Maki, D. R., & Delworth, U. (1995). Clinical supervision: A definition and model for the rehabilitation counseling profession. *Rehabilitation Counseling Bulletin, 38,* 282–293.

Maki, D. R., McCracken, N., Pape, D. A., & Scofield, M. E. (1979). A systems approach to vocational assessment. *Journal of Rehabilitation, 45*(1), 48–51.

Maki, D. R., & Murray, G. (1995). Philosophy of rehabilitation. In A. Dell Orto & R. Marinelli (Eds.), *Encyclopedia of disability and rehabilitation* (pp. 555–561). New York, NY: Macmillan.

Morris, K. (1973). Welfare reform 1973: The social services dimension. *Science, 81*, 515–522.

Moxley, D. P. (1989). *The practice of case management.* Newberry Park, CA: Sage.

Mullahy, C. M. (1995). *The case manager's handbook.* Gaithersburg, MD: Aspen.

Nathanson, R. (1979). Counseling persons with disabilities: Are the feelings, thoughts, and behaviors of helping professionals helpful? *Personnel and Guidance Journal, 58,* 233–237.

Rehabilitation Counseling Consortium. (2005). *Rehabilitation counselor and Rehabilitation counseling definitions.* Schaumburg, IL: Commission on Rehabilitation Counselor Certification.

Roessler, R. (1990). A quality of life perspective on rehabilitation counseling. *Rehabilitation Counseling Bulletin, 34*(2), 82–90.

Scofield, M., Pape, D., McCracken, N., & Maki, D. (1980). An ecological model for promoting acceptance of disability. *Journal of Applied Rehabilitation Counseling, 11*(4), 183–187.

Sosin, M., & Caulum, S. (1983). Advocacy: A conceptualization for social work practice. *Social Work, 28*(1), 12–17.

Steinburg, R. M., & Carter, G. W. (1983). *Case management and the elderly.* Lexington, MA: Brooks.

Stoltenberg, C., & Delworth, U. (1987). *Supervising counselors and therapists.* San Francisco, CA: Jossey-Bass.

Szymanski, E. M. (1985). Rehabilitation counseling: A profession with a vision, an identity, and a future. *Rehabilitation Counseling Bulletin, 29*(1), 2–5.

U.S. Equal Employment Commission. (2009). *Notice concerning the Americans with Disabilities Act (ADA) Amendments Act of 2008.* Retrieved from http://www.eeoc.gov/laws/statutes/adaaa_notice.cfm

Welfel, E. R. (2002). *Ethics in counseling and psychotherapy: Standards, research, and emerging issues* (2nd ed.). Pacific Grove, CA: Brooks/Cole.

Wright, G. N. (1980). *Total rehabilitation.* Boston, MA: Little, Brown.

III

Persons With Disabilities

6

The Person With a Disability

Margaret A. Nosek

LEARNING OBJECTIVES

After reading this chapter, you should be able to:

1. Recognize life as a process of constant change and adjustment for people with disabilities.
2. Understand differences between medical models of disability and psychosocial models of disability.
3. Identify environmental and psychosocial influences on relationships of individuals with disabilities.
4. Explain how persons with disabilities can achieve and maintain optical health and functioning.
5. Recognize the current health care systems in the United States and review alternative ways to improve weaknesses of the health care system.

Through the eyes of the individual, disability looks quite different from what has been taught in most textbooks. First, the traditional model for the academic understanding of disability has been medical and not psychosocial. Second, if you have had personal experience with disability yourself or in a close family member, you know that it is dynamic in nature and holistic in a way that is difficult to understand if your understanding of disability is from a distance. Third, the notion of coping has traditionally been regarded as a positive strategy, whereas for people with disabilities it could be both positive and negative. Fourth, the effect of disability on relationships is personal and intimate, and the adoption of legal rights for a positive attitude is often difficult to obtain or maintain. Fifth, individuals' efforts to maintain health and wellness in the context of disability do not always mean complying with medical advice. Sixth, public policies related to health care and social services, more often than not, reflect the arcane image of disability that is fueling the current rebellion. These are just a few of the topics that will be discussed in this chapter in an attempt to convey to rehabilitation counselors what it means to live with disability.

Disability is a universal phenomenon and few people recognize it as such. As an exercise, try to think of one person you know who does *not* have a disability. A career-changing memory comes to my mind. In the early 1980s, as I was working for my mentor, the father of the American with Disabilities Act, Justin W. Dart, Jr., I helped him organize one of his famous parties as a lakeside fundraiser for the Austin (Texas) Resource Center for Independent Living. At the end of the event he asked everyone present who had a disability to gather in one area for a group photo. Those with obvious disabilities, such as wheelchair users like Justin and myself were the first to move toward the designated spot near the lake. Everyone else looked around rather awkwardly before another brave few walked over. Then the cat calls started—"Hey Bill, you have diabetes, don't you?" "Maria, I was in the same class as you and I know you got some tutoring because you still couldn't write in the fifth grade!" "Those glasses are mighty thick, Lupe." Eventually, everyone was over by the lake!

It would be surprising if you could think of anyone who does not have some type of chronic or disabling condition. We live in times that seem designed to produce disability—from accidents (industrial, traffic, or sports), pollution, never-ending wars, or unaffordable health insurance. Disability can come into a life at any point and by any means. We now understand the genetic origins of some congenital conditions that may manifest at birth or not until later in life, such as my disability, spinal muscular atrophy. Problems with pregnancy, prenatal care, or the birthing process result more and more in babies with intellectual impairment, cerebral palsy, or other severe malformations of multiple organs, yet these children are able to survive thanks to advances in neonatal care and technology. Despite all the safety inventions and increased awareness, human beings seem to thrive on risk. This tendency combined with the weakening of industrial safety standards has led to an increasing rate of disability from work-related injury, such as back problems, spinal cord injury, brain injury, and amputations. Arthritis and fibromyalgia are just two conditions that have a gradual onset in early or mid-adulthood, often associated with environmental and lifestyle factors, and affect women more than men. Lifestyle factors also can result in hearing and vision impairment, for example, listening to loud music especially through earphones or staring at a computer screen for untold hours. And finally, mental illness, which is one of the most common and yet mostly invisible disabilities, is often incapacitating for individuals and families. Although many types of mental illness, such as schizophrenia and severe depression, result from chemical imbalances in the brain, other types can be associated with a lifestyle of excess use of alcohol and drugs (both prescribed and otherwise), an inability to deal with rapid social change, disruption of support systems, and, most of all, stress.

No matter how or when disability has its onset, the impact is life altering. It can affect individuals in all four dimensions of health—biological, psychological, social, and spiritual—to varying degrees depending upon environmental and lifestyle factors and how well medical care and support systems align to match the individual's needs. The following two examples will illustrate this fact more clearly.

Gerald had worked as the manager of a small chain of restaurants for 12 years since graduating from high school. Driving home after closing up late one evening with more than the usual exhaustion, he failed to see an 18-wheel truck that had stalled around a bend in the road. The impact crushed both of his legs. After 5 months in the hospital and numerous surgeries he was sent home with both legs amputated, one above the knee and one below the knee, chronic back pain, and a bill of more than $100,000 that his insurance did not cover. The pain medications left him in a constantly groggy and irritable state that eventually became clinical depression. He had no desire to return to work and was eventually told by the restaurant owner that he should apply for social security disability insurance (SSDI). However, his application was rejected. He started to drink and that put even more stress on his wife. She filed for divorce and was granted custody of their two young children and possession of their house. Gerald became homeless. After many months on the street he discovered a resourcefulness that he did not know he had, inventing a cooking pot out of discarded cans and a way to arrange cardboard boxes to maximize warmth during the winter. He was able to survive and even found joy in teaching some of the other homeless people how to use his inventions. A street medicine doctor from the homeless clinic got to know him and invited him to serve on its board of directors. This was a turning point for Gerald that eventually led to full-time employment as a counselor at the clinic.

Laurel's experience with disability came on gradually. As a flight attendant for a major airline she found it harder and harder to read the passenger manifest even with over-the-counter reading glasses. She finally made an appointment with an ophthalmologist through her health maintenance organization and found that she had a degenerative, incurable eye disease called retinitis pigmentosa. She was devastated by this news and was afraid to share it with her employer and family. When she finally got up the nerve, she was surprised to see that her supervisor at the airline was able to refer her to many different resources both within the company and in their home-base community. The first person with whom she talked was the company's coordinator for the Americans with Disabilities Act, who had also been trained as a rehabilitation counselor. He told her about the company's policy of retraining employees with degenerative conditions for new positions that would take advantage of their other skills, before they were totally unable to deal with their current job. He also linked her up with a support group of people with visual impairments. The depression and fear she had been experiencing gradually diminished and she gained confidence and strength from the new friends she made in the support group. She is now working as branch manager in the reservations department of the airline and accesses her computer using a screen reading device with audio output that the company provided.

These personal stories show that although disability poses challenges in all dimensions of health and well-being, its effect on productivity and quality of life (QOL) is determined mostly by attitudes, and the availability and adaptability of environmental resources. In the example of Gerald, the health care system repaired his body but devastated his personal and financial life. At every turn he found dead ends and no one helped. The one supportive resource that opened for him was the key to regaining his self-esteem and status in the community. Laurel was much luckier in beginning her career with an extraordinarily progressive company that had a high level of awareness and understanding about tapping the potential of people with disabilities by offering them flexibility and supportive resources. These two examples illustrate extremes of how individuals and society can respond to disability, and they correspond to two very different paradigms referred to as the medical and the psychosocial models of disability.

MEDICAL VERSUS PSYCHOSOCIAL MODELS OF DISABILITY

An entire issue of the medical journal *The Lancet* in 2009 was dedicated to discussing the medical model of disability, which emphasizes an individual's physical or mental deficit, and the social model of disability, which highlights the barriers and prejudices that exclude people with disabilities from fully engaging in society and accessing appropriate health care ("Disability: Beyond the medical model," 2009). Most of us who live with disabilities suffer (and I use that word advisedly) not nearly as much from the disability itself as from millennia of negative perceptions surrounding it. The history of people with disabilities and society's response to them has been documented by several prominent historians who themselves had disabilities, among them are Paul K. Longmore (2003), Harlan Hahn (Hahn & Belt, 2004), and Hugh Gallagher (1995). All cite examples throughout Western history of disability as a sign of sin and suffering, being outcast, the object of pity, and most of all repulsion and fear. It was perceived as a great step forward when an attitude of charitable giving and protection toward people with mental and physical impairments was adopted in the Industrial Age. From this spectrum of attitudes that either put us high on a pedestal or stomped us beneath society's collective feet emerged the *medical model*. This paradigm established disability as source of the problem that resides within the individual; a deficiency or abnormality, a negative that must, by any means, be eliminated, neutralized, or at least hidden from view. The starting point is when disability is diagnosed and labeled, and then becomes the focus of attention. The primary remedy for this problem is cure or normalization, most often delivered from the hands of a medical or educational professional. It follows that segregation and specialized attention are the most efficient and, therefore, the best means for delivering curative therapies and programs. The industry of rehabilitation services that arose from this paradigm included long-term rehabilitation centers in remote locations (e.g., Warm Springs, Georgia, and Gonzalez, Texas) and vocational training centers that focus on preparing people for placement in sheltered workshops (e.g., Goodwill Industries and the Salvation Army). Parallel with this development were efforts emerging from the wars of the early 20th century. Mentally and physically injured soldiers were given government funds, state-of-the-art medical treatment, prosthetic devices, and work training, so that they could return to society as productive citizens.

In the 1960s, a new paradigm of disability emerged called the *social model* (DeJong, 1979; Oliver, 1990; Union of the Physically Impaired Against Segregation, 1976). The social model regards disability as a difference within the range of human variation. Conditions causing impairments are in themselves neutral, but lead to disabilities when there is a dysfunctional interaction between the individual and society, or the environments that societies create. The source of the problem, therefore, resides in society, not within the individual, and it is the society's responsibility to become more inclusive and accommodating toward people with emotional, cognitive, physical, or sensory impairments. The agent of remedy is anyone who seeks to improve the response of society (e.g., families, friends, educators, employers, public services providers, or health care professionals) to the ordinary and extraordinary needs of people with disabilities. In the social model, individuals are valued for their humanity and potential to be threads in the fabric of society, and the differences they bring to their sphere of influence are valued as a source of enrichment.

When disability enters an individual's life, whether by gradual onset, sudden onset, or through the normal processes of aging, there is a point of decision about whether to follow and internalize the medical paradigm or social paradigm. Too often, the only information available to individuals and their families, friends, teachers, clergy, and health care providers is the traditional negative, isolationist medical model that places the "blame" on the individual. Negative messages are pervasive—"You shouldn't have been driving/drinking/playing/living so dangerously," "Don't expect to be able to work/love/have sex/do what you used to do anymore," "You should have listened to me when I told you a long time ago to go see a doctor/get some help/try harder." All these messages put responsibility on the individual for both causing and curing the condition. They also diminish any sense of responsibility on the part of the observer to change or address effective solutions to problems that may arise. By preserving distance, with the observer above and the disabled individual below, these attitudes do little more than perpetuate the archaic stigma and failure traditionally associated with disability.

The more current and progressive attitude toward disability, as illustrated in Laurel's example, accepts and deals with new limitations in function by spreading responsibility between the individual and everyone and everything within their circle. A willingness to change and try new approaches to maintaining or even improving their way of doing things that matter characterizes the more positive and productive attitude toward disability. Amazing progress has been made not only in medicine to minimize the effects of disabling conditions, but also in the education of rehabilitation professionals, including psychologists, physical therapists, occupational therapists, and rehabilitation counselors, on how to use techniques that will help individuals adopt a positive attitude, learn the skills they need to maintain their roles in society, and preserve the relationships that offer them support and QOL.

DISABILITY AS DYNAMIC AND HOLISTIC

Living with disability is a process of constant change and constant adjustment, a process that is difficult to measure and categorize. There exists a dynamic tension between the response to disability by the person, and the response to a person's disability by an external observer (Schwartz, Andresen, Nosek, & Krahn, 2007). Albrecht and Devlieger (1999) described a "disability paradox" and addressed the question: "Why do many people with serious and persistent disabilities report that they experience a good or excellent QOL when to most external observers these people seem to live an undesirable daily existence?" (p. 977). In recognizing this phenomenon, Albrecht and Devlieger initiated a dialogue that raises central questions including: (1) What constitutes QOL and health-related quality of life (HRQOL)? (2) Whose perceptions are most important in measuring HRQOL? (3) What appraisal framework influences those perceptions? (4) How do those perceptions vary over time and circumstances?

For example, the experience of spinal cord injury by a person we will refer to as Juanita will help clarify this dynamic and holistic approach to disability. At the age of 18, a motor vehicle collision left her with complete C6 and C7 tetraplegia. Juanita spent 2 months in comprehensive medical rehabilitation center where she regained mobility by using a motorized wheelchair and strength in her arms as she learned how to transfer using a transfer board and to access a keyboard by using a pointing device attached to her hand and forearm. After discharge, she experienced more difficulty with psychological adjustment than with physical functioning and found significant changes in how her family and friends responded to her and, indeed, how she viewed herself. Most difficult was reestablishing her relationship with her boyfriend. Realizing that he could never be able to regard her as anything but pitiable, she broke off their relationship. Juanita entered college as planned, and, despite having to learn the limits of her physical abilities and energy, she graduated, married, and secured a well-paying job. After the birth of her first child, she took some time off but returned to full-time employment after becoming comfortable with the adaptations that facilitated motherhood. Life was good for the following two decades, but then her self-image and understanding of her roles were challenged once again as symptoms of aging appeared. She was more likely to experience pressure ulcers than earlier in her life. For 4 months, she had to go on short-term disability leave from her work for surgery, and then to rebuild her strength and stamina. Because work plus homemaking had become more exhausting, she began considering the possibility of early retirement or applying for long-term disability benefits. The possible effects of her decision on her health and functioning and on the well-being of her family and their economic stability were distressing.

From a rehabilitation perspective, five distinct phases of life are discernable for Juanita: preinjury, immediate postinjury, intermediate postinjury, long-term postinjury, and aging. Before her injury she had strong relationships with and support from her parents, a positive self-image, and good grades; she was very active in her circle of friends and her community and had a lot of hope for the future. Immediate postinjury was dominated by dealing with the physical trauma and fears about the future. Everything about her physical body, from the way she moved to the way she had to care for it, had changed. Although the social workers at the rehabilitation hospital wanted to talk with her about sexuality, she was more interested in figuring out how she was going to help her boyfriend adjust to her new physical limitations and then get on with her life plan. The phase when she saw significant return of physical and psychosocial functioning for independence in her daily activities was intermediate postinjury, in which Juanita adjusted to these changes and prepared for her future. She recognized and accepted the fact that although she did things differently from others, she still fulfilled the roles of wage earner, wife, mother, and friend, and she cherished her ability to contribute to her family and society. Long-term postinjury was a period of relative stability, but the onset of aging symptoms initiated a new phase of change and adjustment. Some of her initial fears returned as she experienced menopause and had to make adjustments to more changes in her body. Comparing measures of HRQOL in each of these phases of Juanita's life could well be more like comparing measures of five different people. This constant change in physical and general life circumstances is even more dynamic for people with disabilities compared to most of their peers in the general population, and demands a corresponding change in the psychological and social processes that enable them to maintain positive self-esteem and fulfillment of their roles in family and community.

This process of continual reassessment and adjustment is called *response shift*. The most severe disabling conditions, such as blindness, stroke, neuromuscular disorders, amputation, traumatic brain injury, Parkinson's disease, or high-level spinal cord injury, are often referred to by others with terms like suffering, tragedy, catastrophe, and the end of life worth living. This outlook rarely reflects the perception of the individual experiencing such conditions. Those who hold negative and limiting attitudes toward disability often exert an undue influence and render a disservice to the individual by forcing them to internalize these perceptions. The degree to which individuals and families have developed the capacity to adjust to any new circumstances will determine how they respond to disability.

COPING AS POSITIVE AND NEGATIVE

Coping refers to how we respond to adversity and to the distress that results (Carver & Connor-Smith, 2010). In the early days of rehabilitation counselor training, coping was generally regarded as a positive phenomenon, synonymous with accommodating, adjusting, continuing the battle, pulling yourself up, managing, and other concepts from the rugged West. Research over the past 20 years has expanded this limited understanding by illuminating an equally important negative side to coping such that it is now divided into strategies or styles. How we cope can depend on many factors, including age, gender, personality, experience, intellectual ability, cognitive style, severity of the stress, and how much time has passed since the stressful event (Carver & Connor-Smith, 2010).

Coping styles have been categorized in many different ways according to the focus and the method used, for example, problem focused or emotion focused (Lazarus & Folkman, 1984), engagement versus disengagement (Roth & Cohen, 1986), cognition or behavior (Moos & Billings, 1982), and internalizing or externalizing (Lengua & Stormshak, 2000). According to Moos and Holahan (2003, p. 1391), these are often combined into four categories:

> Cognitive approach coping includes strategies such as logical analysis and positive reappraisal. These coping skills encompass paying attention to one aspect of the situation at a time, drawing on past experiences, mentally rehearsing alternative actions and their probable consequences, and accepting the reality of a situation but restructuring it to find something favorable. Behavioral approach coping includes strategies such as seeking guidance and support, and taking concrete action to deal directly with a situation or its aftermath. Cognitive avoidance coping comprises responses aimed at denying or minimizing the seriousness of a situation or its consequences, as well as accepting a situation as it is and deciding that the basic circumstances cannot be altered. Behavioral avoidance coping covers seeking alternative rewards; that is, trying to replace the losses involved in certain crises by becoming involved in new activities and creating alternate sources of satisfaction. It also includes strategies such as openly venting one's feelings of anger and frustration and behavior that may temporarily reduce tension, such as acting impulsively and doing something risky.

Hanoch Livneh has produced a body of literature on coping and disability in which he refers to five psychosocial reactions: anxiety, depression, anger, denial, and positive adjustment (Livneh & Antonak, 1997; Livneh & Martz, 2007). Anxiety reflects a negative regard for the past and fear of the future. A depressive orientation focuses on personal loss and failures, and is characterized by pessimism, hopelessness, and helplessness. Anger can be expressed within a wide range of social contexts. Feelings of frustration, perceptions of being mistreated, discounted, or invalidated as a person, and observational learning of aggressive acts have been found to be at the root of aggressive behaviors. Denial typically is viewed as either a conscious or an unconscious act of loosely linked efforts to mitigate distressing thoughts that remind the person of his or her condition, its long-term implications, emotional vulnerability, uncertain future, and even accelerated mortality. Positive adjustment is cognitive acceptance marked by increased insight into one's strength and limitations (Martz, 2004).

The literature has very little to teach us, however, about coping with other aspects of the disability experience beyond personal adjustment. Institutionalized social exclusion, discrimination, stigma, and devaluation are part of the disability reality, as is the social tendency to look the other way when people with disabilities are subjected to emotional, physical, sexual, or disability-related abuse. How individuals transcend these negative social tendencies to acquire positive, well-balanced self-images is not addressed in the literature on coping. Because most studies have been conducted on people with traumatic or adult onset disabilities, we know little about how coping styles develop for those who grow up knowing only a self-determined sense of "normal." Denial is regarded by some as a maladaptive way of dealing with disability, and yet many people with disabilities use denial as a way to survive. Only by ignoring chronic pain, for example, or choosing to suppress acknowledgment of their distinctive appearance or manner of functioning are some people with disabilities able to maintain their sense of coherence and wholeness.

The grassroots independent living movement (see Hartley's discussion of the independent living movement in Chapter 9) has brought to light the importance of peer role modeling and peer counseling, borrowed from its predecessors in the feminist and the civil rights movements. By talking with others who face similar or even greater disability-related barriers and psychosocial challenges, individuals can gain confidence and new ideas about coping strategies, daily functioning, self-image, and more effective ways of relating to other people and the world around them.

EFFECT OF DISABILITY ON RELATIONSHIPS

People with disabilities often have more difficulty in finding partners and forming personal relationships leading to intimacy than people without disabilities. Chronic illness and disability tend to remove individuals from "accustomed personal, social, and sexual interactions, changing the entire life pattern. . . . Feelings of self-worth and attractiveness are threatened at a time when need for intimacy and belonging is greatest, causing a sense of loneliness and isolation" (Glass & Padrone, 1978, p. 44). The whole approach to sexuality and disability has been a victim of the medical model discussed earlier, with the emphasis on "performing," a distinctly male phenomenon, and little attention paid to the development of relationships or sexual satisfaction (Tepper, 2000). Although the medical model limited sexuality and disability to issues of mechanics, social stigma has made it taboo. For women especially, eugenics has added the notion of "should not" to assumptions of "cannot" when it comes to pregnancy (Rintala et al., 1997; Waxman, 1994).

Psychosocial factors such as self-concept, self-esteem, desirability as a sexual partner, emotional status, independence, and social skills occasionally are discussed in relation to sexuality, but seldom studied empirically. One notable exception (Rintala et al., 1997) compared women with physical disabilities to women without disabilities and found that women with disabilities were less satisfied with their dating frequency, perceived more constraints on attracting dating partners, and perceived more societal and personal barriers to dating. In addition, women whose disabilities occurred before their first date were older at the time of their first date than women who were either not disabled or disabled after their first date. Higher self-esteem was associated with more satisfaction with dating. Within the last decade "our understanding of individual sexuality has broadened such that we can acknowledge that one's sexual development is a multidimensional process and includes the basic needs of being liked and accepted, displaying and receiving affection, feeling valued and attractive, and sharing thoughts and feelings" (Esmail, Darry, Walter, & Knupp, 2010, p. 1149).

Expectations and opportunities have a lot to do with social and sexual development and opportunities, on both the positive and the negative sides. Children growing up with disabling conditions are often excluded from the mainstream school environment despite legislation prohibiting this except in the most severe cases, which makes them disadvantaged in learning about social role expectations and the rules of social engagement. Overprotective attitudes of family and medical professionals that can take the form of excessive assistance, recommendations to avoid activities, constant vigilance, constant reminders of self-care, and being overly deferential also serve to limit the exposure of children and adolescents with disabilities to normalized social expectations and can result in significantly lower happiness, self-esteem, perceived popularity, self-consciousness, and higher levels of anxiety (Blum, Resnick, Nelson, & St. Germaine, 1991). These sociocultural barriers can be more disabling than the impairment itself. It would be nice to be able to say that among people with disabilities, those who are expected to marry will marry. However, no studies have been conducted on the positive aspects of social expectations.

We know that disparities exist in opportunities for dating and rates of marriage from studies of specific disability samples and subpopulations, but population-based statistics are very difficult to find. One study examined data from the 1994–1995 national health interview survey and found a significant difference in rates of marriage among women with no functional limitations (63%), women with one or two functional limitations (55%), and women with three or more functional limitations (48%) even after adjusting for age (Chevarley, Thierry, Gill, Ryerson, & Nosek, 2006). It is generally understood that more men than women abandon marriages when their spouse becomes ill or disabled (Sandowski, 1989). Men are more likely than women to have their spouses meet their needs for personal assistance whether disability has its onset before or after the intimate relationship has been established, a consequence of the caregiving role generally ascribed to women.

Opportunities to have an active dating life are limited by environmental barriers as much as psychosocial barriers. The classic notion of going out to eat with a significant other, for example, requires accessible transportation and affordable restaurants, two precious commodities for many people with disabilities (Taylor, Krane, & Orkis, 2010). Privacy is often at odds with the need for personal assistance (Earle, 1999). Internalized stereotypes of asexuality make some people with disabilities suspicious of why anyone would be attracted to them (Rintala et al., 1997). There is also the issue of having to explain, especially about assistive devices (Rintala et al., 1997) or when the disabling condition is not visible (Esmail et al., 2010).

Ending unhealthy relationships often is very difficult for people with disabilities. One woman who used a wheelchair spoke about her abusive partner by saying, "I think that was one reason why it sort of kept going or held on for so long was that even though I was trying to let it go, there was a large part of me that was saying, even though this is bad, this is all you have, the feeling that I wasn't good enough to get anybody else ever. This was my one and only shot." There are many ways that people with disabilities experience abuse— through emotional manipulation and belittlement, physical maltreatment, forced sexual activity, and withholding necessary equipment, medications, and assistance (Nosek, Foley, Hughes, & Howland, 2001). Compared to women without disabilities, women with disabilities are more likely to experience physical and sexual violence (Brownridge, 2006; Martin et al., 2006; Powers et al., 2002; Smith, 2008), increased severity of violence (Brownridge, 2006; Nannini, 2006; Nosek, Howland, & Hughes, 2001), multiple forms of violence (Curry, Powers, Oschwald, & Saxton, 2004; Martin et al., 2006; Nosek et al., 2001), and longer duration of violence (Nosek et al., 2001). Although not as well studied as violence against women with disabilities, violence against men with disabilities has been shown to be a serious problem (Cohen, Forte, DuMont, Hyman, & Romans, 2006; Marchetti & McCartney, 1990; Powers et al., 2008; Saxton et al., 2006). There is an emerging body of literature on interventions to help people with disabilities learn to identify abuse and plan for their safety (Powers, Hughes, & Lund, 2009).

Thankfully, with the emergence of the Internet as a communication, educational, and networking tool, resources are expanding rapidly for people with disabilities and the professionals who serve them to learn about healthy sexuality (e.g., http://www.disaboom.com/marriage-and-disability and http://www.sexualhealth.com/channel/view/disability-illness/).

HEALTH AND WELLNESS IN THE CONTEXT OF DISABILITY

The notion that people with disabilities could achieve optimal health, in all of its physical, psychological, and social dimensions, is relatively new in wellness research. This realization gained momentum with the rise of the independent living movement in the mid-1970s, in which people with disabilities demanded acknowledgment of their civil rights and expected to exert control over their lives. Although still far behind the search for cures, the health of people with disabilities is a topic of growing interest and it is beginning to be the focus of federal research funds. As a result, we now have an embryonic body of literature and the beginnings of discussions about how disability puts to the test wellness theory, research, and practice (Nosek, 2005).

Health and wellness in the context of disability has many unique aspects that are not generally known or understood by medical or mental health professionals. These unique aspects interrelate in a complex web of factors that affect the ability of individuals with disabilities to achieve and maintain optimal health and functioning. Consider the case of a 54-year-old woman named Melinda who had polio as a child and functions with a motorized wheelchair and a variety of adaptive devices. For all of her work life she has never had the opportunity to use the bathroom during the work day. She lives in an apartment complex that has a shared attendant program, but the attendants are not allowed to leave the premises to provide services. Even if she had not been raised with the expectation that she should be totally self-sufficient, or at least give the appearance of such, and even if she could find someone at the hospital where she works to help her at lunchtime, her wheelchair is too large to fit into the stalls of the public restrooms there. As a result, she has had to train her bladder to retain substantial amounts of urine and restrict her fluid intake to a minimum. Although this solution was uncomfortable, it was not a serious problem until recently. She now gets frequent urinary tract infections and is beginning to have some incontinence. Melinda's internist has no idea how she could change her living and working situation to be more conducive to health, so she prescribed antibiotics to get her through until the next occurrence.

The presentation of this real-life scenario could go on to include the effect of her managed care plan on getting needed prescriptions from her primary care physician, the restrictions it places on seeing specialists, the limitations it forces on her behaviors and planned activities, the impact this problem has on her self-image, the complicating effects that adaptive equipment (wheelchair, seat cushion) or the lack thereof (including an effective female urinal) has on the problem, and the numerous other health problems that stem from frequent urinary tract infections (e.g., yeast infections, antibiotic resistance, skin breakdowns, and lowered immunity to other bacterial and viral infections). The solution to this individual's health problems would require massive changes in policies governing the financing and delivery of health care services, rehabilitation services, social support services, and the research and development of adaptive equipment. Her health might also be improved if disability- and gender-sensitive health promotion education and intervention programs were available to her, perhaps something with peer interaction and information about her potential to improve her health. And so the litmus test for wellness theory, research, and practice becomes the question of how effectively it meets the needs of people with disabilities.

People with disabilities face the effects of the increased risk of developing health conditions that often accompany disability, the stresses that result from living in a society that imposes many limitations and stereotypes on persons with disabilities, and the pervasive environmental barriers that restrict socialization and participation in the community. Nevertheless some people with physical disabilities live in a state of vibrant health and, moreover, are able to maintain equilibrium whenever threats to their well-being arise.

Understanding that the process of living with disability carries with it a plethora of risks for additional health problems makes it difficult to imagine how a person with a disability could achieve and maintain wellness. To make sense of this, we must hold all preconceptions at bay and examine disability as one component of the context within which we all live. *It is largely society and our environment that make disability a disadvantage.* Consider the three-legged cat, functional in every way and even content, that is, an object of pity only in the eyes of some humans. Even with progressively disabling conditions, achieving and maintaining wellness is associated most closely with resilience, perseverance, and creative problem solving, among other survival traits. The investigation of wellness in the context of disability, therefore, demands an understanding of the ingredients in this complex recipe.

We talk about a *model of health and wellness* that includes (1) physical or biological health, including general health status, body mass index, vitality, pain, functional limitations, chronic conditions, and secondary conditions, (2) psychological health, including general mental health, life satisfaction, perceived well-being, and self-esteem, (3) social health, including intimacy, social connectedness, social functioning, and social integration, and (4) spiritual health, including transcendence, meaning or purpose in life, optimism, and self-understanding (Nosek, 2005).

At the foundation of this model lies the intricate web of *contextual factors* that can have a very different configuration for people with disabilities. The contextual factors that are of interest in our research are either internal to the individual or external in the environment and cannot be easily changed, but some of them can be modified through management strategies. These factors include health history, disability characteristics, demographics, relationships, values and beliefs, life experiences, and environmental resources. The category of environmental resources encompasses many aspects of the micro-, meso-, exo-, and macro-systems in which people with disabilities live, including access to financial resources; education level; the built and natural environments; technology; information from the print and broadcast media and the Internet; instrumental social support and services; and access to health care services.

It is the challenge of each individual to adopt health-promoting behaviors to the extent their disability allows. Here, too, perceptions and stereotypes play an important role. Just because someone has significant impairment in their ability to walk does not mean that they cannot exercise. Whether or not an individual has a disability, behaviors such as smoking, excessive drinking of alcohol, and use of illegal drugs and other substances are self-destructive activities. Physical inactivity and obesity are quite prevalent among people with all types of disabilities, and often have more negative effects on their health than for people in the general population. Unfortunately, little is known about the types of activity and diet that would be most beneficial for people with specific types of disabilities. Adopting health-promoting behaviors also includes behaviors that specifically relate to disability management, such as medication management, personal assistance management, prevention of secondary conditions, and maintenance of assistive devices.

Maintaining health and wellness for individuals with any type of disabling condition is a complex balancing act affecting every dimension of living. It is no wonder then that stress and exhaustion can result from trying to maintain this balance, leaving little energy left over to hold down a paid job or be involved in family and community activities. Another Catch-22 situation that many people with disabilities face is the policy and political decision the United States has taken to link work and access to health care insurance, a decision that has left people with disabilities victims of work disincentives and health care apartheid (Nosek, 2010).

HEALTH CARE REFORM

There are essentially two ways to access to health care in the United States. The first is by having private health insurance purchased from a for-profit health insurance company by your employer, yourself, or a family member. The second is by being eligible for Medicare or government-funded programs, most commonly Medicaid, the Veterans Health Administration, or the Indian Health Service. Eligibility for Medicare is automatic when you turn age 65 without regard to your income or work status, and there is no waiting period for receiving this benefit. If you are under age 65 and have worked and accumulated sufficient points in the Social Security system before you develop or acquire a disabling condition that prevents you from working, you can apply for SSDI, which includes Medicare. This process, however, demands that you have unequivocal medical evidence that you are too disabled to work. It may take years of submitting and resubmitting paperwork, and many people are forced to hire a lawyer to navigate the system of disability determination on their behalf. Once eligibility is obtained there is a 2-year waiting period before you have access to health care insurance through Medicare.

Access to health care is automatically available for veterans through the Veterans Health Administration and for members or descendants of a federally recognized American Indian or Alaska Native Tribe through the Indian Health Service. Eligibility for supplemental security income (SSI) and Medicaid, however, is totally dependent upon income. Each state determines income eligibility as a percentage (in most states 133%) of the federal poverty limit (Centers for

Medicare and Medicaid Services, 2010a), which is based on a formula established by the U.S. Department of Health and Human Services that combines the amount of income received and the number of people who are supported by that income. For an individual with no dependents, the 2010 poverty level was $10,830 per year or $902.50 per month; for a family of four it was $22,050 per year or $1,837.50 per month (limits are higher for Alaska, Hawaii, and DC) (Centers for Medicare and Medicaid Services, 2010b). The eligible income level for Medicaid in most states in 2010 was $1,200.33 per month for an individual and $2,443.88 per month for a family of four. There are also limits on the amount of resources that are available to the individual, such as bank accounts, real property, or other items that can be sold for cash (Centers for Medicare and Medicaid Services, 2010a). Medicaid benefits are only available to those who are U.S. citizens or lawfully admitted immigrants.

In addition to having limited income, individuals can be eligible for Medicaid if they are blind, children or adults with other disabilities or serious chronic health conditions, women who are pregnant, or people over age 65. Eligibility for Medicaid by an adult or child also brings with it eligibility for food stamps, housing assistance, personal assistance (attendant care) services, and other benefit programs that vary by state. For children growing up with health care coverage and other eligibilities through Medicaid, the burden is heavy to achieve an independent lifestyle or obtain work yielding an income and access to health insurance that would be sufficient to offset the monetary value of these benefits. This is referred to as the work disincentive.

The U.S. Congress attempted to remove some of these work disincentives by enacting the Ticket to Work and Work Incentives Improvement Act in 1999. Under this law, individuals who receive SSI or SSDI develop a plan to achieve self-sufficiency that can involve receiving vocational training, advanced education, or a trial work period during which they can maintain their benefits and access to health care coverage. At the end of their training or trial work period cash benefits are terminated and eligibility for Medicaid or Medicare ends. If a plan to achieve self-sufficiency is not successful, individuals may continue to earn a small amount of money (less than $100 per month in most states) and still received SSI and Medicaid coverage, or up to $800 a month and still receive SSDI and Medicare coverage.

Once these Medicaid-eligible children with disabilities reach adulthood they risk losing all of their benefits if they marry because their spouse's income and resources are considered in determining their continued eligibility. This is referred to as the marriage penalty. Parents can also jeopardize the Medicaid eligibility of their adult children with disabilities by writing them into their will without certain safeguards. They can establish some degree of security for their Medicaid-eligible child only by setting up a tightly regulated trust fund for any inherited funds or property.

The unfortunate truth about Medicaid-funded health care is that it is most often substandard. Reimbursement rates for medical providers are extremely low, causing the majority to refuse services to people who have Medicaid coverage. Only a little more than half of physicians (53%) reported that their practices were accepting all or most new Medicaid patients in 2008 (Boukus, Cassil, & O'Malley, 2009). Waiting times are extraordinarily long for getting an appointment with a provider who accepts Medicaid or with a county-funded community clinic or hospital, often coming well after initial symptoms have escalated into a serious illness. For this reason, many people with disabilities seek care for otherwise preventable conditions in the emergency room of a county hospital where service is guaranteed and more immediate, though much more expensive for taxpayers than if they had timely access to a primary care provider.

The Patient Protection and Affordable Care Act of 2010 (ACA) requires states to expand their Medicaid program by 2014 to include people with incomes that are a greater percentage above the federal poverty limit (U.S. Department of Health and Human Services, 2010). The unfolding political drama surrounding this act has some states threatening to withdraw from the Medicaid program completely. Unknown to many members of the public is the fact that in most states Medicaid is funded 60% by the federal government and 40% by the state, and that the majority of these funds go toward maintaining older and younger people with disabilities in nursing homes. By withdrawing from the Medicaid program states would, in effect, be losing a substantial amount of federal matching money, thereby increasing the tax burden on its own citizens.

Medicaid programs prevent indigent individuals and families from being totally without access to health care services, but they come at the price of individual freedom. Their strict income and resource eligibility requirements force people to maintain a state of impoverishment and reduce the incentive for finding work. The health care available with Medicaid coverage does not match the quality available with private health insurance in terms of choice of provider and waiting times for service. Medicaid-eligible individuals are limited in their freedom to marry or accept gifts from family without risk of losing critical life-sustaining services. In most states it is difficult to obtain Medicaid-funded home-based services, creating the constant threat of institutionalization for many people with disabilities or age-related functional limitations.

An organization of activist people with disabilities called ADAPT (www.adapt.org) is dedicated to creating a priority on home-based services over institutionalization for people with disabilities. Through its nationwide advocacy, the Community Living Assistance Services and Supports Act has been introduced to Congress and included in the Patient Protection and Affordable Care Act as the Title VIII (Community Living Assistance Services and Supports Act, Title VIII of the Patient Protection and Affordable Care Act, 2010). This is a consumer-funded provision, whereby a designated amount determined by age is deducted monthly from an individual's paycheck. After an investment period of 5 years, funds can be deducted up to $75 per day when a disability-related need for in-home services arises. The provision is not available for those who are not working.

In the current economic climate with the skyrocketing costs of health care, more and more employers are eliminating health care benefits. This decline in coverage, combined with high unemployment rates, is creating a rapidly growing population of working-age people who are uninsured. The price of health care insurance in the individual market is generally unafford-able. Many people with disabling conditions also fall into this category if they are too disabled to work but not disabled enough to qualify for Medicaid or Medicare. For people with preexisting conditions, states have established high-risk pools that offer coverage at a high price with limited benefits. It is, sadly, a no-win situation.

Efforts are underway by activists in Physicians for a National Health Program (www.PNHP.org) and Health Care Now (www.healthcare-now.org) to achieve more comprehensive health care reform. The Affordable Care Act, though opening new opportunities for coverage for some, essentially rein-forces the existing system of high-priced health care insurance offered by for-profit corporations to those who are working or have the resources to pur-chase their own coverage. It relies on Medicaid and other government subsi-dies to provide what is generally regarded as substandard care for those who have significantly limited income and resources. In the rest of the industrial-ized world, single-payer health care systems predominate, in which necessary care is available to everyone with minimal or no out-of-pocket expenses. The "single-payer" in these cases is either the government or a nonprofit insur-ance company. By expanding the risk pool to include everyone regardless of their age, health status, or work status, these systems are able to reduce health care costs while ensuring access to everyone. The profit motive in the United States has unfortunately taken priority over health care freedom for everyone.

CONCLUSIONS

Living with disability is complicated and can be overwhelming. Rehabilitation counselors can also feel overwhelmed by the complex systems that have been set up to help people with disabilities achieve optimal health and social integration. At some point everyone has to make the decision to keep up the fight, accept things as they are, or succumb to defeat. There will be days when all three of these can be experienced simultaneously. Many of us who work in the field of rehabilitation and also experience disability personally in our daily lives know that the fight can be positive, acceptance can be a victory, and defeat must be reframed so that it is consistent with striving for wholeness. By understanding that complexity can also bring richness and opportunity, we can gain strength to continue working toward positive change in our personal lives and in the context within which we live.

<hr>

CONTENT REVIEW QUESTIONS

- Explain the difference between the medical and psychosocial models of disability.
- What are the limitations of current studies about coping with disability experience? How can these limitations be improved?
- Identify significant psychosocial and environmental barriers that limit opportunities of individuals with disabilities to have an active dating life.
- What is meant by contextual factors? How can contextual factors be used in understanding of health and wellness of persons with disabilities?
- What are the limitations of public health care system? Explain societal efforts to improve the system.
- What are the major changes and challenges that persons living with disabilities may experience?

<hr>

REFERENCES

Albrecht, G. L., & Devlieger, P. J. (1999). The disability paradox: High quality of life against all odds. *Social Science & Medicine, 48,* 977–988.

Blum, R. W., Resnick, M. D., Nelson, R., & St. Germaine, A. (1991). Family and peer issues among adolescents with spina bifida and cerebral palsy. *Pediatrics, 20,* 280–285.

Boukus, E., Cassil, A., & O'Malley, A. S. (2009). *A snapshot of U.S. physicians: Key findings from the 2008 health tracking study physician survey.* Center for Studying Health System Change Data Bulletin No. 35. Washington, DC: Center for Studying Health System Change. Retrieved January 8, 2010, from http://www.hschange.com/CONTENT/1078/#top

Brownridge, D. A. (2006). Partner violence against women with disabilities: Prevalence, risk, and explanations. *Violence Against Women, 12,* 805–822.

Carver, C. S., & Connor-Smith, J. (2010). Personality and coping. *Annual Review Psychology, 61,* 679–704.

Centers for Medicare and Medicaid Services. (2010a). *Medicaid eligibility.* Retrieved December 13, 2010, from http://www.cms.gov/medicaideligibility/

Centers for Medicare and Medicaid Services. (2010b). *2010 Poverty guidelines.* Retrieved December 13, 2010, from https://www.cms.gov/MedicaidEligibility/downloads/POV10Combo.pdf

Chevarley, F., Thierry, J. M., Gill, C. J., Ryerson, A. B., & Nosek, M. A. (2006). Health, preventive health care, and health care access among women with disabilities in the 1994–1995 National Health Interview Survey. *Women's Health Issues, 16*(6), 297–312.

Cohen, M. M., Forte, T., DuMont, J., Hyman, I., & Romans, S. (2006). Adding insult to injury: Intimate partner violence among women and men reporting activity limitations. *Annals of Epidemiology, 16,* 644–651.

Community Living Assistance Services and Supports Act, Title VIII of the Patient Protection and Affordable Care Act, Pub. L No. 111–148, 124 Stat. 119 C.F.R. (2010).

Curry, M. A., Powers, L. E., Oschwald, M., & Saxton, M. (2004). Development and testing of an abuse screening tool for women with disabilities. *Journal of Aggression, Maltreatment and Trauma, 8*(4), 123–141.

DeJong, G. (1979). Independent living: From social movement to analytic paradigm. *Archives of Physical Medicine and Rehabilitation, 60,* 435–446.

Disability: Beyond the medical model. (2009). *The Lancet, 374*(9704), 1793.

Earle, S. (1999). Facilitated sex and the concept of sexual need: Disabled students and their personal assistants. *Disability & Society, 14,* 309–323.

Esmail, S., Darry, K., Walter, A., & Knupp, H. (2010). Attitudes and perceptions towards disability and sexuality. *Disability & Rehabilitation, 32*(14), 1148–1155.

Gallagher, H. G. (1995). *By trust betrayed: Patients, physicians, and the license to kill in the third Reich.* St. Petersburg, FL: Vandamere Press.

Glass, D. D., & Padrone, F. J. (1978). Sexual adjustment in the handicapped. *Journal of Rehabilitation, 44*(1), 43.

Hahn, H. D., & Belt, T. L. (2004). Disability identity and attitudes toward cure in a sample of disabled activists. *Journal of Health and Social Behaviour, 45*(4), 453–464.

Lazarus, R. S., & Folkman, S. (1984). *Stress, appraisal, and coping.* New York, NY: Springer.

Lengua, L. J., & Stormshak, E. A. (2000). Gender, gender roles, and personality: Gender differences in the prediction of coping and psychological symptoms. *Sex Roles, 43*(11/12), 787–820.

Livneh, H., & Antonak, R. F. (1997). *Psychosocial adaptation to chronic illness and disability.* Gaithersburg, MD: Aspen.

Livneh, H., & Martz, E. (2007). Reactions to diabetes and their relationship to time orientation. *International Journal of Rehabilitation Research, 30*(2), 127–136.

Longmore, P. K. (2003). *Why I burned my book and other essays on disability.* Philadelphia, PA: Temple University Press.

Marchetti, A. G., & McCartney, J. R. (1990). Abuse of persons with mental retardation: Characteristics of the abused, the abusers, and the informers. *Mental Retardation, 28*(6), 367–371.

Martin, S. L., Ray, N., Sotres-Alvarez, D., Kupper, L. L., Moracco, K. E., Dickens, P. A., . . . Gizlice, Z. (2006). Physical and sexual assault of women with disabilities. *Violence Against Women, 12,* 823–837.

Martz, E. (2004). Reactions of adaptation to disability as predictors of future time orientation among individuals with spinal cord injuries. *Rehabilitation Counseling Bulletin, 47,* 86–95.

Moos, R. H., & Billings, A. G. (1982). Conceptualizing and measuring coping resources and processes. In L. Goldberg & S. Breznitz (Eds.), *Handbook of stress: Theoretical and clinical aspects* (pp. 212–230). New York, NY: The Free Press.

Moos, R. H., & Holahan, C. J. (2003). Dispositional and contextual perspectives on coping: Toward an integrative framework. *Journal of Clinical Psychology, 59,* 1387–1403.

Nannini, A. (2006). Sexual assault patterns among women with and without disabilities seeking survivor services. *Women's Health Issues, 16*(6), 372–379.

Nosek, M. A. (2005). Wellness in the context of disability. In J. Myers & T. Sweeney (Eds.), *Wellness in counseling: Theory, research, and practice.* Alexandria, VA: American Counseling Association.

Nosek, M. A. (2010). Healthcare apartheid and quality of life for people with disabilities. *Quality of Life Research, 19*(4), 609–610.

Nosek, M. A., Foley, C. C., Hughes, R. B., & Howland, C. A. (2001). Vulnerabilities for abuse among women with disabilities. *Sexuality and Disability, 19*(3), 177–190.

Nosek, M. A., Howland, C. A., & Hughes, R. B. (2001). The investigation of abuse and women with disabilities: Going beyond assumptions. *Violence Against Women, 7*(4), 477–499.

Oliver, M. (1990). *The individual and social models of disability.* Paper presented at Joint Workshop of the living options group and the research unit of the Royal College of Physicians on people with Established Locomotor Disabilities in hospitals. Retrieved November 21, 2010, from http://www.leeds.ac.uk/disability-studies/archiveuk/Oliver/in%20soc%20dis.pdf

Patient Protection and Affordable Care Act, Pub. L. No. 111–148, 124 Stat. 119 C.F.R. (2010).

Powers, L. E., Curry, M. A., McNeff, E., Saxton, M., Powers, J., & Oschwald, M. M. (2008). End the silence: A survey of the abuse experiences of men with disabilities. *Journal of Rehabilitation, 7*(4), 41–53.

Powers, L. E., Curry, M. A., Oschwald, M., Maley, S., Saxton, M., & Eckels, K. (2002). Barriers and strategies in addressing abuse: A survey of disabled women's experiences. *The Journal of Rehabilitation, 68*(1), 4–13.

Powers, L. E., Hughes, R. B., & Lund, E. M. (2009). *Interpersonal violence and women with disabilities: A research update.* Harrisburg, PA: VAWnet, a project of the National Resource Center on Domestic Violence/Pennsylvania Coalition Against Domestic Violence. Retrieved September 23, 2009, from http://www.vawnet.org

Rintala, D. H., Howland, C. A., Nosek, M. A., Bennett, J. L., Young, M. E., Foley, C. C., et al. (1997). Dating issues for women with physical disabilities. *Sexuality and Disability, 15*(4), 219–242.

Roth, S., & Cohen, L. J. (1986). Approach, avoidance, and coping with stress. *American Psychologist, 41,* 813–819.

Sandowski, C. L. (1989). *Sexual concerns when illness or disability strikes.* Springfield, IL: Charles C. Thomas.

Saxton, M., McNeff, E., Powers, L. E., Curry, M. A., Limont, M., & Benson, J. (2006). We are all little John Waynes: A study of disabled men's experiences of abuse by personal assistants. *The Journal of Rehabilitation, 72*(4), 3–13.

Schwartz, C. E., Andresen, E. M., Nosek, M. A., & Krahn, G. L. (2007). Response shift theory: Important implications for measuring quality of life in people with disability. *Archives of Physical Medicine and Rehabilitation, 88*(4), 529–536.

Smith, D. L. (2008). Disability, gender and intimate partner violence: Relationships from the behavioral risk factor surveillance system. *Sexuality and Disability, 26*(1), 15–28.

Taylor, H., Krane, D., & Orkis, K. (2010). *The ADA, 20 years later: Kessler foundation/NOD survey of Americans with disabilities.* New York, NY: Harris Interactive.

Tepper, M. S. (2000). Sexuality and disability: The missing discourse of pleasure. *Sexuality and Disability, 18,* 283–290.

Ticket to Work and Work Incentives Improvement Act, Pub. L No. 106–170, 113 Stat. 1860–1951 C.F.R. (1999).

Union of the Physically Impaired Against Segregation. (1976). *Fundamental principles of disability.* London, UK: UPIAS.

U.S. Department of Health and Human Services. (2010). *People with disabilities have more affordable options for health coverage.* Retrieved December 13, 2010, from http://www.healthcare.gov/foryou/disabilities/

Waxman, B. F. (1994). Up against eugenics: Disabled women's challenge to receive reproductive health services. *Sexuality and Disability, 12*(2), 155–171.

7

Family and Relationship Issues

R. Rocco Cottone

LEARNING OBJECTIVES

After reading this chapter, you should be able to:

- Provide a historical backdrop related to the psychomedical framework of traditional vocational rehabilitation (VR) as compared to the emerging systemic-relational view of the rehabilitation process.
- Recognize the influence of relationships on the rehabilitation process, on the client, and within the family or social system of significance.
- Present a perspective of clients as embedded within the network of relationships and the rehabilitation counselor as a social agent interfacing client and rehabilitation systems.
- Reconceptualize the rehabilitation process as a social process.
- Describe the role and influence of the family system in rehabilitation.
- Describe the adaptation process of families addressing disabilities.
- Outline the effect of disability on the family and on caregivers.
- Address family members' roles and possible disruption of family routines during the rehabilitation process.
- Describe family dynamics related to job placement or community living.
- Argue the role of the rehabilitation counselor is that of family advocate who encourages rehabilitation counseling training in family therapy and social systems theory.
- Address educational and competency issues of rehabilitation counselors related to family intervention.

Rehabilitation counseling is a counseling specialty closely and historically aligned with the psychomedical paradigm of mental health services (Cottone & Emener, 1990). The psychomedical paradigm of mental health services is a framework for conceptualizing client problems. It is also a framework for identification and implementation of methods of problem solving. The focus of the psychomedical paradigm is the individual person—the person with a diagnosed medical condition. The individual is viewed as an independent focus of treatment (Cottone & Emener, 1990). Prior to the late 1970s and early 1980s, rehabilitation counselors focused on individual clients, serving them outside of family or other larger influential social systems. Clients were viewed as individuals (somewhat isolated from their social contexts) with problems that derived from their physical and mental conditions. Disability was first and foremost a matter of limitations deriving from a medical problem. There was a little emphasis placed on identifying or treating social factors that affected a client's adaptation.

Because, historically, rehabilitation counseling was closely associated with vocational issues, many of the early rehabilitation assessment and intervention methods were consistent with the vocational trait-factor movement (Kosciulek, 1993; Kosciulek & DeVinney, 2004), an approach that emphasized methods for fitting the peg (client) into the best hole (job). The trait-factor approach dates back to Parsons (1909) and the vocational choice movement. Trait-factorism held that a client could be viewed as having characteristics (in a classic psychological and physical sense) and that matching the client's positive and negative characteristics to a job and a work context was the best and easiest way to find a place for the client to work and to earn a living. Clients could thereby become productive members of society.

Rehabilitation counseling, based on trait-factor philosophy and grounded in the psychomedical paradigm, was a conglomeration of methods that were used to assess and to treat clients. Vocational assessment, for example, focused on identifying traits. Psychological traits (such as intelligence, aptitudes, and interests) and physical skills (such as finger dexterity, speed of processing, physical mobility, and strength) were identified, assessed, and matched to jobs in the marketplace. In the late 1970s and early 1980s, some theoreticians began to identify and to challenge the trait-factor or psychomedical framework, arguing that such a framework was less than ideal for addressing issues associated with disability. Notably, the psychosocial movement in rehabilitation, as best represented by the work of Wright (1983) and Stubbins (1977), began to recognize and to conceptualize the social (along with the psychological) aspects of disability. Stubbins (1984) further challenged the status quo, as he was the first to argue for a more social systemic understanding of disability. Stubbins argued for expanding the definition of VR to include "social systems factors" (p. 375).

Soon after the call by Stubbins (1984) for a systemic understanding of the rehabilitation process, the first comprehensive theory of VR was developed to challenge the historical psychomedical framework of rehabilitation counseling. Cottone (1987) developed his "systemic theory of vocational rehabilitation." The impetus for the theory's development was the recognition that family issues were influential in the success of rehabilitation efforts, and they were largely ignored in rehabilitation programming. In those days, the individual written rehabilitation plan, used in the state-federal program, had no place to address family-relevant issues. Cottone, a rehabilitation counselor with training in family therapy, began to realize that family involvement (when possible) was crucial to rehabilitation success, and that family factors were related to or could be predictive of rehabilitation outcomes (Cottone, Handelsman, & Walters, 1986). Other authors and theorists also expressed the need to address family issues in rehabilitation (e.g., Power & Dell Orto, 1986). The client's family system began to be viewed as a network of relationships that was influential on the rehabilitation process. Cottone also took the position that the rehabilitation system could be conceptualized as a network of relationships, and that counselors could be viewed as social agents that were conduits for the larger social factors addressed at the interface between the counselor and the client being served in the state-federal system (or any rehabilitation service delivery system). From a purely relational viewpoint, the counselor–client relationship was crucial, because it represented a linkage of two systems—the client's system and the rehabilitation service delivery system. Rehabilitation outcomes could then be viewed as predictable based on the ease of interface of involved systems (Cottone, 1987; Cottone & Cottone, 1986; Cottone, Grelle, & Wilson, 1988). If a client came from a supportive family, showed social capacity, and could communicate in a healthy way, there was likely a place that could be found for that person to work, regardless of skills or abilities. On the other hand, a client connected to an unhealthy family or other system (e.g., the drug culture), showing poor social skills (e.g., poor grooming and unusual interaction), and poor communication skills would likely be expelled from the rehabilitation program, even if the client had some work-related skill (Cottone & Cottone, 1986; Cottone et al., 1988). Expulsion from the program occurred typically as case closure as a poor risk, or the client was put through a number of remediating measures (evaluation or personal adjustment programs) that acted more like screening programs than rehabilitation interventions (Cottone & Cottone, 1986; Cottone et al., 1988). Those clients who survived screening were able to show some social capacity; those who did not fit socially (e.g., those who broke the rules) were clearly identified and prevented from receiving further services. It could be argued that too little rehabilitation and remediation and too much screening were occurring. Cottone et al. (1988) concluded:

> At least on cases where clients are disabled by nonphysical disabilities of an emotional, intellectual, or behavioral nature, vocational evaluators seem to be making judgments about client readiness for competitive employment or job training based primarily on incidental data of a social/interpersonal nature. Psychological evidence, allegedly gathered for employability decision making, appears to play a lesser role. The results of this study bring into question the nature of the vocational evaluation process as presently conceived within a psychomedical framework. (p. 50)

In effect, the state-federal VR system could be viewed as a social mechanism for screening the socially deviant from entry into the work world.

Reconceptualizing the rehabilitation process as a social process requires rehabilitation professionals to at least acknowledge the influence of family and other relevant social systems on rehabilitation outcomes. Even if rehabilitation counselors do not adopt a purely social perspective as recommended by Cottone's (1987) "systemic theory of vocational rehabilitation," they must acknowledge the influence of relational systems on the outcomes of rehabilitation programming, or they will blindly provide services always identifying failure as an individual client problem (e.g., poor motivation). Consider that a client who appears poorly motivated in the rehabilitation system might be the most motivated drug pusher on the street. Motivation, from a relational standpoint, is always viewed in context.

For those clients who have intact family systems, family relationships and family dynamics will play a major role in the rehabilitation process and rehabilitation outcomes. Adaptation to disability is not just an individual issue. Families, too, adjust to disability, and the dynamics of the family may be significantly influenced by the presence of a mental or physical condition or some combination of conditions that affect family members as well as the individual with the disability. This chapter fully acknowledges the influence of relational factors in the rehabilitation process, but focuses primarily on the effect of disability from the perspective of the family. Adaptation to both disability and the rehabilitation process will also be addressed.

THE FAMILY AS A SYSTEM

A system is a network of relationships—a "set of elements standing in interaction" (Bertalanffy, 1968). Relationships (the interaction between people) is the focus of systems theory (Cottone, 1992). A system of three people is three relationships. A system of four people is six relationships (see Figure 7.1) and a system of five people is 10 relationships (see Figure 7.2).

FIGURE 7.1
A System of Four People Is Six Relationships—Each Line Represents a Relationship; Each Circle Represents a Person

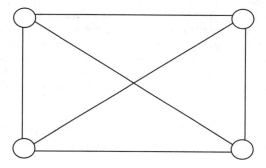

FIGURE 7.2
A System of Five People Is 10 Relationships—Each Line Represents a Relationship; Each Circle Represents a Person

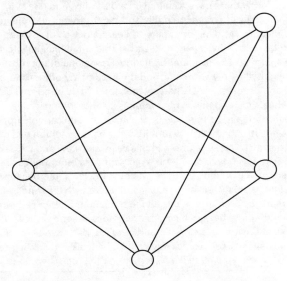

The relationships are viewed as the crucial elements in a system. For a family of four with one individual with a disability, each member is in relationship with each other. Each relationship is influenced by the disability. Although all family members experience the presence of the disability in the family through relationships, in some families parents may be the primary caregivers. In families with an absent parent, siblings may be significantly involved in daily activities with family members with disabilities. Spouses or partners of adults with disabilities are often involved. The interaction among family or household members around the disability is important to note, as the family not only has a history of adjustment dynamically to the presence of the disability, but also will have to adjust to changes in the family routine around the client's rehabilitation.

FAMILY ADAPTATION TO DISABILITY

The Importance of Family

If there is an intact family system (whether the family is nuclear, extended, biological, blended, or culturally defined), and the family is involved with the individual with a disability, then most likely there has been significant family adaptation to the disability itself. Some disabilities are congenital (e.g., inherited conditions evident at birth) and they have been with the family since the beginning of the individual's life with a disability. Other disabilities are acquired,

TABLE 7.1
A Personal Experience

The reader should know that I have a child with a disability, and I have experienced family adjustment to disability in my own family and by observing the adjustments of my clients to their concerns. My son, Torre, now 14 years old, was diagnosed at age 2 with Duchenne muscular dystrophy, a genetic disorder that is fatal, usually taking young boys before the age of 20. The moment of diagnosis was one of the most powerful moments affecting my life, my wife's life, and the lives of my other children. Torre's condition is genetic and progressive. He had several early years of normal development. Now he is in a wheelchair and needs near total assistance with most daily activities. He can still feed himself and has full use of his hands, but he cannot support his own weight and he is not strong enough to turn in bed. As his condition has progressed, the family has had to adjust. The adjustment in this case was slow and followed the course of the disease. Each of us has had to learn to accommodate our needs to ensure that Torre's needs were met. It sounds burdensome at some level, but because Torre is a lovable and loved child, in many ways it is a pleasure to be with him and to assist him. My wife and I have made a commitment to provide him and the other children with a rich and full life. Although there has been commitment to someone we love, it is also clear that sometimes relationships are strained and our lifestyles have been affected. Since Torre's diagnosis, I have worked extensively with individuals and families facing muscular dystrophy, and for those families that stay together, the process appears similar.

such as those that result from trauma (e.g., physical injury and traumatic brain injury). Some are developmental or reveal themselves at different stages (e.g., intellectual impairment). Some are progressive, which means that they are typically inherited but they worsen with time, where the individual may have had some normal developmental period (e.g., certain muscular dystrophies, arthritis, and dementia). Regardless of the type or onset of a condition, the intact family system must adjust. Family members must adapt to the disease process (if there is one) and to the personal limitations that exist or develop over time (see Table 7.1).

Family Challenges

Unfortunately, all families do not stay together. Sometimes parents of children with disabilities divorce or abandon their children. Divorce rates among parents of children with disabilities have been estimated (often unreliably) as high as 80%. This creates a complicated circumstance for remaining caregivers, as their share of the "load" increases with the lower number of committed caregivers. Generally, the percentage of children with disabilities in single parent households exceeds the percentage of children without disabilities. Regardless of the presence and commitment of one or both parents, or of spouses or partners of individuals with disabilities, families of individuals with disabilities need help. Extended family members sometimes become involved. Sometimes, loving friends make special efforts to assist families in need. Reporting in a 1996 published survey, Burke (2008) indicated that "[t]he need for help and assistance in the families surveyed was overwhelming; over 60 percent of families indicated this need" (p. 48). Siblings often take a caregiver role, as Burke indicated that parents reported that siblings of a child with a disability were involved directly in care 75% of the time (one study reported involvement as high as 80%). Some families are able to afford assistance or to obtain government assistance to hire others to care for, to watch over, or to supervise the individual with the disability. The greater the network of support, the greater the likelihood that the individual with the disability will find meaning in life and will seek and cooperate with means of rehabilitation. And even with support, families of individuals with disabilities face similar challenges. Case-Smith (2007) reported that parenting a child with a chronic medical condition was associated with several challenges, including: (a) managing and scheduling caregiver responsibilities, (b) feeling the burden of "always having to be there," (c) experiencing negative effects on the caregiver's outside career trajectory/plans, (d) addressing compromises in dealing with external service providers (schools, pharmacies, insurance companies, and resource and rehabilitation agencies), (e) maintaining a social life outside the home, and (f) maintaining a self-identity.

Family Caregivers

Committed parents tend to be incredible caregivers—often sacrificing their own needs for the needs of their children. But it is also the case when the disability is acquired in adulthood that spouses and loving partners often accept the caregiver role. With serious disabilities, totally debilitating conditions such as amyotrophic lateral sclerosis or Huntington's disease (fatal disorders with serious downward health trajectories sometimes with death looming within a matter of years), or for conditions that permanently negatively affect a family member (e.g., brain damage and quadriplegia), the toll on caregivers can be serious. Debilitating progressive diseases or serious permanent loss of function are some of the most difficult situations for families to face. Caregivers in these circumstances appear to go through some predictable stages. First, upon diagnosis of the loved one, there is a sincere commitment to the love and care of the affected individual. Caregivers embrace the client and they formally commit to be there for the client, no matter what is faced. This is the "commitment stage." The second stage is the "resource identification stage," as the caregiver and family members collect resources (both personal and other resources) in order to make a difficult situation tolerable. There is much activity in this stage as the caregiver begins to identify resources, other helpers, family supports, community and church assistance, support from associations of others faced with similar circumstances, and financial supports (in the form of government assistance for rehabilitation or disability benefits). The third stage is "the plateau" stage, where often well-intended others begin to withdraw support and caregivers begin to face daily routines with limited assistance and limited or depleted resources. The fourth stage is the "exhaustion" stage. At this stage, caregivers begin to recognize that they cannot do it all—that they are overwhelmed even with the support they receive from others. They begin to feel neglected themselves and feel that their own needs are not being met. Anger may begin to set in, and they begin to ask, "Why?" They are often faced with their own career stressors, management of a home or other family members, household issues, financial issues, and lack of sleep. The fifth stage is the "confusion" stage. Caregivers actually find themselves wishing it were over, which is frightening to them, because in some cases that would mean that their loved one would be gone. They cannot see the end. They feel a sense of hopelessness. They also feel the competing interest of self and loved one. They begin to feel real loss in their own lives, while at the same time recognizing the loss experienced by the loved one. They are torn and do not feel that they have a way out. The sixth stage is the "recommitment" stage. This typically comes near the end of the life of the affected individual, at a point of near permanent stabilization, or at the end of the caregiver's formal commitment. Caregivers appear to rally at this stage, drawing on all their remaining resources as they recommit to the care and well-being of the individual with the disability. They are then committed until the end. Counseling through this process is crucial, as both the medically affected individual and the caregiver face very serious social, physical, and psychological challenges.

If clients are lucky enough to stabilize and to have the capacity to work or to live independently, then family members and caregivers will face a transition when rehabilitation services become available.

FAMILY ADAPTATION TO THE REHABILITATION PROCESS

Routines in families with an individual with a disability appear to be fairly structured. Roles also appear to emerge over time and with experience. Consider transportation as an example. An individual in a wheelchair may be pushed by one member to a vehicle, then assisted by another to enter the car or to operate a lift or ramp, and then secured in the vehicle by another family member. So something as typical as transportation often calls for a clear separation of roles and responsibilities in family accommodation to the unique requirements of transporting an individual in a wheelchair. Family members tend to fall into these roles as the family learns efficiently to address the limitations of the individual with the disability. These roles tend to crystallize and, at best, make life a little more predictable and orderly. At worst, the roles may become rigid and unyielding. Rehabilitation efforts always call for change, and family routines typically will be disrupted.

When a counselor develops a rehabilitation plan with a client, it is always wise to explore how the client's routine will change, and how family members will be required to adjust. The more resistant the family members are to change, the more likely that rehabilitation efforts will fail. For example, requiring a client to attend a workshop for training, when in the past the family's routine was established around the client staying at home, is a major change. In this case, the family members will have to adjust to what can be a burdensome task in adhering to a new schedule. In family systems theory, a change in routine may be interpreted as a disruption in the family "homeostasis," the dynamic equilibrium of family interactions around the routines that have been well established in the home (Goldenberg & Goldenberg, 2008). Technically, it disrupts the homeostatic "set-point," the rules for family operation, just like leaving the door open on a very hot day disrupts the temperature in an air-conditioned home with a set point of 72°F. Disruption of a routine is equivalent to pushing the family to establish new family rules and requiring new family roles to emerge around the new rules. Classic systems theory teaches that family homeostasis tends toward stability, not change; there are often relationship dynamics that tend to work to reestablish the equilibrium (Bertalanffy, 1968). Counselors must be alert to such factors and they must not simply identify the client as "the culprit" if problems arise related to issues such as attendance, punctuality, and full engagement in the rehabilitation process. The client's apparent "resistance" may be the evidence of systemic dynamics designed to reassert the family's homeostatic process—to reestablish or maintain the old and once functional rules and roles.

FAMILY ADAPTATION TO JOB PLACEMENT AND COMMUNITY LIVING

Dosa, White, and Schuyler (2007) stated that "in 2004, employment rates for the 14 million U.S. adults who have a disability (7.9% of adults age 18–64) were substantially lower than for adults who do not have a disability (19% versus 77%)" (p. 615). Dosa et al. went on to report a poverty rate of 28% for individuals with disabilities, versus 9% for individuals without disabilities. Certainly, VR professionals have a very important role in assisting individuals with disabilities in job training, development, and placement.

The family is an economic unit, and for those individuals with disabilities in a position to support (or to help to support) a family, employment is very important. In many cases, the moment of first meaningful employment, or a return to meaningful employment, will be welcomed by family members, especially when the family has been deprived of adequate resources, perhaps due to the disability. Therefore, motivated work-capable clients in a healthy support system will tend to appreciate work opportunity, as gainful employment may mean establishment (or a return) to a better family life. Work may also prove to be personally fulfilling for the individual with the disability and lead to increased social connections, as in American society, workers are valued as productive members of society. For such clients it will appear that the family is rallying around final rehabilitation efforts, and job placement and retention will be cause for celebration.

For individuals who do not appear motivated to find employment, even after extensive rehabilitation programming, it is incumbent upon the rehabilitation counselor to assess the systemic dynamics that may be affecting what appears to be the client's poor "motivation." Motivation, from a systemic perspective, is a reflection of activity within the social matrix; it is not inside the personality of the client. It is too easy to simply label a client as unmotivated and to close a demanding rehabilitation case. Often there are social factors, family dynamics, or otherwise, which may be pivotal to successful job placement and job retention. For example, the family may be losing Social Security benefits (either supplemental Security Income [SSI] or Social Security Disability Insurance [SSDI]), which may significantly affect the financial stability of the household, or temporary benefits may be lost (e.g., worker's compensation). The employment of one family member may adversely affect the employment or routines of another family member, for example, when the family has limited means of transportation and vehicle sharing is required. Alternatively, the absence of the individual with a disability in the home may create a void in the lives of those who have been actively involved in caregiving in the home, creating some role confusion. All these factors may be influential at the point of job placement. When family dynamics appear to interfere with the final stages of job placement, then the astute counselor must be willing to analyze possible relational pressures and to address those concerns in a way that will facilitate the final stages of worker placement.

It is often surprising to early career rehabilitation professionals when everything looks positive for employment after an otherwise successful rehabilitation program, and then something happens at the end of a rehabilitation program that appears to sabotage the job placement effort. Those kinds of experiences, especially when families are involved, may speak to the failure of the rehabilitation counselor to take into account, address, or ameliorate systemic dynamics inconsistent with successful rehabilitation and employment of the individual with the disability.

Similar dynamics may operate when community living is a goal. Removal of the client from the household of a family of origin will significantly affect relationships in the household. Counselors must be alert to family dynamics when household members appear to resist a client's independence. Just like the empty nest syndrome that most couples experience when the last child leaves the household, families with an individual with a disability experience a change in routine and roles when a formerly dependent person is transitioned to a new living or working situation. It is important for rehabilitation counselors to be sensitive and responsive. Rehabilitation counselors can help ensure smooth transitions, and their role as family counselors or family advocates is never clearer than at these times.

COUNSELING FAMILIES OF INDIVIDUALS WITH DISABILITIES

Is there a valuable role for rehabilitation counselors as family therapists for families of individuals with disabilities? Generally, family health and adaptation have played secondary roles in the rehabilitation process, as the focus, consistent with the psychomedical paradigm, has been the well-being and adaptation of the person with the disability. But rehabilitation counselors are mental health professionals, and to ignore or to neglect the needs of the family is to view the client in isolation, potentially at the expense of rehabilitation goals or to the detriment of family members closely involved with the client.

Kosciulek (2004) has argued that the impact of disability is "at least as great for families as for the affected person, and family members are often more distressed than the person with the disability" (p. 264). He further stated, "Family members themselves are a high-risk group for physical, emotional, and social difficulties. Families require help in their own right and not only as a by-product of the counseling or rehabilitation process with the family member with the disability" (p. 264). But how much help can rehabilitation counselors offer? Most rehabilitation counselors do not have adequate training to do marital and family therapy. It takes more than a course on systems theory and a course on family counseling to work competently and ethically with families. Counselors who have an interest in focusing on family issues must seek additional comprehensive training through coursework, continuing education, and supervised experience under the watchful eye of a trained family therapist. This is asking much, because it almost constitutes additional specialty training for already highly trained specialists in counseling.

Short of cross-training to a second specialty, it is incumbent on the rehabilitation counseling generalist to acquaint himself/herself with the systemic paradigm of mental health services. The systemic paradigm focuses exclusively on defining the nature of problems and solutions as imbedded in relationships. It is, at its extreme, mutually exclusive to the psychomedical paradigm at the foundation of rehabilitation programs, which focuses on the individual client and individual stakeholders in the rehabilitation process. You cannot see people and focus on relationships at the same time. It is like the classic Gestalt diagram of the vase and the two twin faces—you see the vase if you focus on the middle of the diagram, but you see the twins if you look to one side (see Figure 7.3).

Systems theory focuses on the middle between two people (like looking at the vase). It does not focus on people—their traits, abilities, interests, or skills. It looks at each person as fitting within some context. "Good fit" means finding a special place within some social network; "bad fit" means the person will appear out-of-sync with other individuals within a social network. Counselors ideally facilitate good fit for the client in some healthy social context. The systemic framework requires counselors to be mindful of how relationships affect mental health and especially the specific behaviors of the client within the family and larger systemic contexts. It helps counselors to see the big picture.

One way that rehabilitation counselors can begin to acquaint themselves with relational influences on the rehabilitation process is first to acknowledge the influence of relationships on their own adaptation. This is usually fairly easy, because most counselors will readily admit that the times they have felt most unhealthy mentally were the times that they were enmeshed in relationships that were unhealthy. If one is in a healthy loving network, it is easy to feel and act comfortably. Recognizing this fact is an easy first step. Then, it is important for the rehabilitation counselors to acquaint themselves with some literature on family adaptation and/or stress when faced with a member with a disability.

Some theorists have likened the family reaction to the diagnosis of a child with a disability to the bereavement process (e.g., Cobb & Warner, 1999). After

FIGURE 7.3
The Gestalt Diagram—Two Twins Facing Each Other Versus a Vase

the initial shock of the diagnosis, families may go through a period of denial, anger, and bargaining until some level of coping is achieved. The message in such analyses is that the adaptation process is not easy.

Related to connecting theory to practice, Kosciulek, McCubbin, and McCubbin's "Resiliency Model of Family Stress, Adjustment, and Adaptation" (Kosciulek et al., 1993) is a good place for rehabilitation counselors to start. This model is built on prior works that addressed: "(a) Illness and disability as potential family stressors, (b) family resistance resources (e.g., economic, psychological), (c) the family's appraisal of a disability, and (d) coping patterns designed to protect the family from breakdown and facilitate adjustment to disability" (Kosciulek, 2004, p. 265). By recognizing family reactions to disability, rehabilitation counselors can begin to conceptualize means to address such stress in a way that facilitates the family's adaptation to the rehabilitation process. Although rehabilitation may represent hope to families that their loved ones will achieve some level of independence, it still represents change. Where there is relationship change, all parties connected to the web of involved relations are affected, for better or for worse. The more resistance that is met by rehabilitation efforts within families, the more likely there will be dramatic adjustments necessary to accommodate changes; in those cases, family intervention would be important.

If a rehabilitation counselor is not trained to provide family therapy interventions, then it is incumbent on the rehabilitation counselor to refer families to appropriately trained professionals who will understand and work within the context of the rehabilitation programs. Many not-for-profit agencies provide family counseling services for little or no charge, and sometimes there are special considerations given to families with a member affected by a disabling condition. Knowing and developing family treatment resources should be a normal part of any rehabilitation counselor's job when family issues are addressed in the rehabilitation process.

Typically, family therapy occurs with all household members present (or as many as will participate). Usually, it is acceptable to have up to five or six family members in a session. More than five or six participants become unwieldy and may challenge even the most skilled family therapist (because there 10 relationships interacting in a family of five). So maintaining some control of the sessions becomes difficult when more relationships are present in the session.

Family counselors typically will analyze the relationship dynamics during sessions, viewing problems primarily within their social contexts (Goldenberg & Goldenberg, 2008; Nichols, 2006). They tend to be less interested in the individual behaviors, traits, or abilities of clients, and more interested in interactional patterns that have developed around specific family activities. Family therapists have many names for the patterns of interaction observed during sessions, such as "enmeshed," "disengaged," "symmetrical," "escalating," and "complementary" relationships. Each pattern has predictable consequences for individuals involved in the pattern. The intention of family counseling for rehabilitation clients typically is to strengthen family relationships and interactions that are supportive or facilitative of the natural transition experienced by successful rehabilitation clients.

Classic systems interventions always involve at least two people. Consider a family where parents have had to be extensively involved in their child's care. The child now is a young adult and is participating in a rehabilitation program. Thus, a family counselor might address how a mother and father of a young adult rehabilitation client might spend their time together or alone (in a healthy way) while the rehabilitation client is outside the home involved in rehabilitation programs. In this case, the intent would be to strengthen the marital bond, so that one or both parents do not become or remain enmeshed with the adult child rehabilitation client, potentially in a way that may interfere with the rehabilitation program. The astute family counselor, then, is always addressing relational dynamics and will intervene where it might seem tangential to the classically psychomedically trained counselor.

There are a number of family therapy theories or approaches that may be used by a trained family therapist (see Gladding, 2007; Goldenberg & Goldenberg, 2008). Entire college graduate courses are offered surveying the well-known family therapy approaches of people like Virginia Satir, Murray Bowen, Carl Whitaker, Salvador Minuchin, Jay Haley, Nathan Ackerman, and others. Rehabilitation counselors should at least acquaint themselves with the major family therapy theorists so that they may speak and act intelligently on these matters when working closely with a family therapist. In fact, the Council on Rehabilitation Education (CORE) and the Council on the Accreditation of Counseling and Related Educational Programs (CACREP) standards for accreditation of educational programs for counselors require some basic introduction to family dynamics and interventions.

Ideally, family therapy will be viewed as a support for rehabilitation efforts. It may be adjunctive, but the effects may be very positive in those cases where there is active family involvement in the lives of family members with disabilities. From a purist systems perspective, involving family in the rehabilitation process is crucial to rehabilitation success and to the long-term healthy adaptation of clients.

Identifying a qualified family therapist is as easy as assessing their credentials. Those who are trained typically in counselor education programs will likely affiliate with the International Association for Marriage and Family Counseling (IAMFC), which is a division of the American Counseling Association (ACA). The IAMFC has actively pursued establishment of a viable, credible, and valuable credential in family therapy, and members of the IAMFC have established the National Credentialing Academy (NCA) for Certified Family Therapists (CFTs). The NCA has established standard coursework and experience requirement for mental health professionals to qualify as a CFT. Rehabilitation counselors interested in seeking training in family counseling would be well served to contact the NCA for information and standards for certification. The older more established American Association for Marital and Family Therapy (AAMFT) has set requirements for what they define as "clinical membership," which constitutes a certification of sorts. The AAMFT's standards are high, and there has been some tension between the AAMFT and the ACA, as the AAMFT has abandoned the use of the title "counselor," and some AAMFT members have argued that counseling and family therapy are separate professions. (The ACA has taken the position that marriage and family counseling is a counseling "specialty.") So, in a sense, there are two professional organizations vying for the allegiance of those who would identify themselves as marriage and family counselors/therapists. Regardless, if a family counselor is a CFT or a clinical member of the AAMFT, it is likely that he or she has met stringent training and supervision requirements in the areas of couples, marital, and family treatment.

CONCLUSION

This chapter has addressed relationship and family issues in rehabilitation counseling. Although rehabilitation counseling theory and practice has been closely and historically aligned with the psychomedical paradigm of mental health services, rehabilitation theoreticians and practitioners are now recognizing the influence of relationships on the rehabilitation process. The influence of relationships in rehabilitation may be reflective of the rehabilitation system itself, and the role the rehabilitation system plays within the larger free enterprise system in American society. It may also reflect the influence of intact family systems that may directly influence the behavior of clients being served by rehabilitation systems. A "systemic theory of vocational rehabilitation," the first comprehensive and coherent theory of VR to challenge the traditional rehabilitation model, addresses the relationship interface of clients and rehabilitation systems in conceptualizing and providing rehabilitation services and programs. The systemic perspective represents a call for recognition of relationship influences on the behavior of clients and professionals. It may act as an impetus for rehabilitation counselors to educate themselves on the relational way of viewing clients in the context of rehabilitation programs.

For clients with intact families, recognition of the influence of the family on the individual with a disability is important. Also, rehabilitation counselors must be sensitive to the adjustment of the family to: (a) the disability, (b) rehabilitation efforts, and (c) to job placement and community living. Some families may be more resilient facing disability; others may struggle. Some families adjust more easily to rehabilitation programs and goals; others may be resistant. By understanding family dynamics and the challenges faced by family members, rehabilitation counselors may be able to conceptualize the social and systems factors that may potentially affect rehabilitation outcomes, including job placement.

Rehabilitation counselors should be educated about social systems theory and family therapy. Although cross-training in family therapy would be ideal, rehabilitation counselors must at least be willing to obtain continuing education and appropriate training to identify relationship factors impinging the rehabilitation process. In cases where family or other relationship factors negatively affect the client, rehabilitation counselors must be able to intervene or to seek, to recommend, or to engage appropriate family relationship treatment. Both the families and the individuals with disabilities deserve no less.

CONTENT REVIEW QUESTIONS

- How does social systems theory reconceptualize the rehabilitation process?
- What is the family role in the rehabilitation process?
- What is the role of the rehabilitation counselor addressing family issues during the rehabilitation process?
- How is the family affected by the rehabilitation process?
- How is the rehabilitation process affected by family dynamics?

REFERENCES

Bertalanffy, L. von (1968). *General systems theory*. New York, NY: George Braziller.
Burke, P. (2008). *Disability and impairment: Working with children and families*. Philadelphia, PA: Jessica Kingsley Publishers.

Case-Smith, J. (2007). Parenting a child with a chronic medical condition. In A. E. Dell Orto & P. W. Power (Eds.), *The psychological and social impact of illness and disability* (pp. 310–328). New York, NY: Springer.

Cobb, H. C., & Warner, P. (1999). Counseling and psychotherapy with children and adolescents with disabilities. In H. T. Prout & D. T. Brown (Eds.), *Counseling and psychotherapy with children and adolescents: Theory and practice for school and clinical settings* (pp. 401–426). New York, NY: John Wiley & Sons.

Cottone, R. R. (1987). A systemic theory of vocational rehabilitation. *Rehabilitation Counseling Bulletin, 30,* 167–176.

Cottone, R. R. (1992). *Theories and paradigms of counseling and psychotherapy.* Needham Heights, MA: Allyn & Bacon.

Cottone, R. R., & Cottone, L. P. (1986). A systemic analysis of vocational evaluation in the state-federal rehabilitation system. *Vocational Evaluation and Work Adjustment Bulletin, 19,* 47–54.

Cottone, R. R., & Emener, W. G. (1990). The psychomedical paradigm of vocational rehabilitation and its alternatives. *Rehabilitation Counseling Bulletin, 34,* 91–102.

Cottone, R. R., Grelle, M., & Wilson, W. C. (1988). The accuracy of systemic versus psychological evidence in judging vocational evaluator recommendations: A preliminary test of a systemic theory of vocational rehabilitation. *Journal of Rehabilitation, 54,* 45–52.

Cottone, R. R., Handelsman, M. M., & Walters, N. (1986). Understanding the influence of family systems on the rehabilitation process. *Journal of Applied Rehabilitation Counseling, 17,* 37–40.

Dosa, N. P., White, P. H., & Schuyler, V. (2007). Future expectations: Transition from adolescence to adulthood. In M. L. Batshaw, L. Pellegrino, & N. J. Roizen (Eds.), *Children with disabilities* (pp. 613–622). Baltimore, MD: Paul H. Brookes Publishing.

Gladding, S. T. (2007). *Family therapy: History, theory, and practice* (4th ed.). Upper Saddle River, NJ: Pearson/Merrill Prentice Hall.

Goldenberg, H., & Goldenberg, I. (2008). *Family therapy: An overview* (7th ed.). Belmont, CA: Thomson Brooks/Cole.

Kosciulek, J. F. (1993). Advances in trait-and-factor theory: A person X environment fit approach to rehabilitation counseling. *Journal of Applied Rehabilitation Counseling, 24*(2), 11–14.

Kosciulek, J. F. (2004). Family counseling. In F. Chan, N. L. Berven, & K. R. Thomas (Eds.), *Counseling theories and techniques for rehabilitation health professionals* (pp. 264–281). New York, NY: Springer.

Kosciulek, J. F., & DeVinney, D. J. (2004). The trait-factor approach. In F. Chan, N. L. Berven, & K. R. Thomas (Eds.), *Counseling theories and techniques for rehabilitation health professionals* (pp. 211–223). New York, NY: Springer.

Kosciulek, J. F., McCubbin, M. A., & McCubbin, H. I. (1993). A theoretical framework for family adaptation to head injury. *Journal of Rehabilitation, 59*(3), 40–45.

Nichols, M. P. (2006). *Family therapy: Concepts and methods.* Boston, MA: Pearson/Allyn & Bacon.

Parsons, F. (1909). *Choosing a vocation.* Boston, MA: Houghton-Mifflin.

Power, P. W., & Dell Orto, A. E. (1986). Families, illness and disability: The roles of the rehabilitation counselor. *Journal of Applied Rehabilitation Counseling, 17*(2), 41–44.

Stubbins, J. (Ed.). (1977). *Social and psychological aspects of disability.* Austin, TX: Pro-ed.

Stubbins, J. (1984). Vocational rehabilitation as social science. *Rehabilitation Literature, 45,* 375–380.

Wright, B. A. (1983). *Physical disability—A psychosocial approach.* New York, NY: Harper & Row.

8

The Disability Rights Community

Michael T. Hartley

LEARNING OBJECTIVES

After reading this chapter, you should be able to:

- Review the history of the independent living movement, disability studies, and disability culture.
- Understand the fight for disability rights within the context of a larger cultural movement.
- Identify the core tenets of the independent living movement and corresponding services provided by centers of independent living.
- Consider the emergence of the academic field of disability studies as a sociopolitical critique of the dominant cultural discourse of disability.
- Review the evolution of disability culture as championing complex identities of people with disabilities.

Rehabilitation counselors work with "persons with physical, mental, developmental, cognitive, and emotional disabilities to achieve their personal, career, and independent living goals in the most integrated setting possible" (Commission on Rehabilitation Counselor Certification [CRCC], 2010, p. 1). Rehabilitation counseling is thus based on a person-environment fit (Maki & Riggar, 2004; Parker, Szymanski, & Patterson, 2005; Rubin & Roessler, 2008), and a successful rehabilitation outcome is not the result of working with the individual alone, but rather of understanding the reciprocal interaction between the individual and his/her environment (Hershenson, 1998; Kosciulek, 1993; Lofquist & Dawis, 1969; Maki, McCracken, Pape, & Scofield, 1979). Rehabilitation counseling as a field has been somewhat resistant to the Disability Rights community (Carluccio & Patterson, 2001; Hahn, 1991; Nosek, 1988), and this has undermined the development of strategies for addressing perennial issues related to long-term health care and disability (Braddock & Parish, 2001).

In rehabilitation counseling practice, there are three models that construct disability from three different points of view: (a) the bio-medical or disease model, (b) the functional limitations or economic model, and (c) the sociopolitical or minority model, also known as the social model (Smart, 2001, 2004), which is espoused by the Disability Rights community (Shakespeare & Watson, 1997). Unfortunately, the social model of disability has been inadequately applied in rehabilitation practice (Carluccio & Patterson, 2001; Hahn, 1991; Nosek, 1988) despite the benefits it offers, such as the political, social, cultural, and historical understandings of disability (Albrecht, Seelman, & Bury, 2001; Davis, 2006; Longmore, 2003). The Disability Rights community provides the lens through which we can understand how the experience of disability is influenced by environmental factors. Thus, understanding the Disability Rights community is critical for rehabilitation counseling professionals.

From a sociological perspective, a community is a group of people who have common goals and cooperate as a group to achieve these goals (Frazer, 1999; Hoggett, 1997). There may be conflict between various factions of people within the community, but the community is linked by a common cause (Frazer, 1999; Hoggett, 1997). The Disability Rights community is an assemblage of diverse disability-specific groups with parallel histories that have coalesced into a larger "sense of disability as collectively shared status and experience" (Longmore & Umansky, 2001, pp. 4–5), but the Disability Rights community has never been homogeneous or monolithic (Barnartt & Scotch, 2001; Longmore, 2003; Longmore & Umansky, 2001; Scotch, 1988). Viewed through the social model lens, the histories of disability-specific groups are distinct yet similarly characterized by experiences of cultural devaluation (Longmore, 2003; Longmore & Umansky, 2001; Scotch, 1988).

Disability activism has existed for centuries; however, until recently, there was never a broad-based Disability Rights community, but rather, "disability groups typically formed around disability-specific categories," often competing for scarce material resources (Longmore, 2003, p. 109). For instance, since the 18th century, the Deaf community has campaigned to protect sign as an authentic language, seeking political and economic support for signing schools in Europe and America, including Gallaudet University (Baynton, 1996; Lane, 1984). Further, as early as the 1940s, the Blind community rallied to form a political lobby in the United States (Koestler, 1975; Matson, 1990). Countless other disability-specific groups, such as individuals with physical disabilities (Byrom, 2001; Longmore & Goldberger, 2003), cognitive and learning disabilities (Noll & Trent, 2004; Trent, 1994), and psychiatric disabilities (Beers, 1908; Porter, 1989) have fought long and hard for inclusion in education, employment, and community living. Finally, in the 1970s, a broad cross-section of the population of people with disabilities formed a politicized identity in the United States (Barnartt & Scotch, 2001; Campbell & Oliver, 1996; Charlton, 1998; Longmore, 2003; Oliver, 1990; Shapiro, 1994; Switzer, 2003).

Perhaps one of the most important moments was April 5, 1977 (Longmore, 2003; Shapiro, 1994), when the American Coalition of Citizens with Disabilities

(ACCD) organized simultaneous protests in nine cities across the United States, including Denver, New York, and San Francisco, to demand implementation of Section 504 of the 1973 Rehabilitation Act (Barnartt & Scotch, 2001; Longmore, 2003). Many have noted that it was during these protests that cross-disability identification first emerged, representing a critical transformation in the consciousness of people with disabilities (Barnartt, 1996; Charlton, 1998; Longmore, 2003, 1995). Longmore (2003), quoting San Francisco-activist Mary Jane Owen, noted that "People went into that building with some kind of idealism, but they didn't have much knowledge of other disabilities. Up to that point, we had blind organizations, organizations for deaf people, for wheelchair users, for people with spina bifida, or people with mental retardation" (p. 110).

As with other social justice movements, such as the women's movement and the gay and lesbian movement, the fight for equal employment, greater political participation, and better community services represented the platform for a larger cultural movement (Campbell & Oliver, 1996; Charlton, 1998; Davis, 2006; Longmore, 2003; Oliver, 1990). The emergence of a universalistic approach to Disability Rights was more significant than the passage of disability civil rights legislation, including Section 504 of the Rehabilitation Act Amendments of 1973 and the Americans with Disabilities Act of 1990 (Barnartt & Scotch, 2001; Charlton, 1998; Longmore, 2003; Shapiro, 1994; Switzer, 2003). Of course, disability-specific organizations, political interests, and agendas have remained (Longmore, 2003); yet, since the 1970s there has been a collective view, expressing that individuals with disabilities should have a say in health care policies and practices, best captured by Charlton (1998) in the phrase: "Nothing about us, without us" (p. 3).

Rehabilitation counselors need to understand the rich history of the Disability Rights community to become effective practitioners. Indeed, even well-intentioned rehabilitation professionals can inadvertently contribute to the perceptions of people with disabilities as diseased, broken, and in need of fixing without an understanding of this perspective, as embraced by the Disability Rights community (Baker, 2009; Bricher, 2000; Conyers, 2003; Donaghue, 2003; Illich, Zola, McKnight, Caplan, & Shaiken, 2005). Understanding the Disability Rights community will prepare practitioners to situate disability within sociopolitical contexts and thus be more empathetic and respectful of people with disabilities (Conyers, 2003). This chapter discusses some of the complexities of the Disability Rights community, including the emergence of the independent living movement, disability studies, and disability culture, in order to prepare practitioners to locate rehabilitation within the broader experience of disability.

INDEPENDENT LIVING MOVEMENT

Independent living, as a concept, emerged out of the 1959 deinstitutionalization movement, in which millions of individuals with disabilities were released from institutions (DeJong, 1979; Longmore, 2003; Nosek, Zhu, & Howland,

1992; Switzer, 2003). However, it was not until the late 1960s, and the social and political activism of students with physical disabilities in Berkeley, California, that the Rehabilitation Services Administration (RSA) funded the first center of independent living (using the acronym CIL or ILC) (DeJong, 1979; Noseket al., 1992; Switzer, 2003). Forced to live in a hospital infirmary because there was no accessible student housing, these students demanded inclusion in mainstream university life (Shapiro, 1994; Switzer, 2003). Initially funded to serve college students, CILs quickly shifted to serving nonstudents, and centers were created in large urban environments such as Boston and Houston (DeJong, 1979; Longmore, 2003; Switzer, 2003). Designed by activists, CILs were an important training ground for political and social activism, including participation in the April 5, 1977, protests demanding implementation of the Rehabilitation Act Amendments of 1973 (Longmore, 2003; Switzer, 2003). However, in the 1980s, in response to conservative political threats to withdraw funding, CILs began to emphasize individual services over large-scale activism (Longmore, 2003; Varela, 2001). As a consequence, those who believed that large-scale activism was the way to create societal change left CILs and formed groups that were not dependent on governmental funding, such as the American Disabled for Adaptive Public Transportation (ADAPT) (Johnson, 2003; Longmore, 2003; Scotch, 1988). In the 1980s, with the exodus of many activists and increased government oversight, CILs were increasingly run by professionals without disabilities (Longmore, 2003; Nosek et al., 1992). In response to complaints from the disability rights community, the 1986 Amendments to the Rehabilitation Act of 1973 required that 51% of CIL staff and board of directors consist of people with disabilities (Longmore, 2003; Nosek et al., 1989, 1992). Today, CILs must be run by people with disabilities and as a result, many CILs have returned to social and political activism while also providing individual services (Longmore, 2003).

A basic premise of CILs is that people with disabilities are experts on living with their disabilities (Crewe & Zola, 2001; DeJong, 1979; Nosek et al., 1992; Switzer, 2003). Unlike other rehabilitation services, CILs are run by people with disabilities who themselves have been successful in establishing independent lives (DeJong, 1979; Nosek et al., 1989, 1992; Switzer, 2003). Most traditional rehabilitation programs were built on the medical model of service delivery; CILs were the first to use the social model of disability to help individuals with disabilities achieve and maintain independent lifestyles (Crewe & Zola, 2001; DeJong, 1979; Nosek et al., 1989, 1992). Thus, CILs were revolutionary in defining disability as primarily a social (rather than a medical) issue, and are a unique and important development in service delivery (DeJong, 1979; Longmore, 2003; Nosek et al., 1992; Switzer, 2003).

CILs provide information and referral for accessible housing, transportation, and community services, such as personal care assistants and sign language interpreters (Frieden, 2001; Richards & Smith, n.d.;). Further, using a peer-based self-help model, they provide counseling and independent skill training to help people with disabilities become more independent (Cole, 2001; Saxton, 2001; Shreve, 1991). Finally, CILs provide advocacy, which is "eliminating or diminishing institutional and cultural barriers" (Liu & Toporek, 2004, p. 192). Distinct from other CIL services, rather than providing direct services to the individual, advocacy confronts inaccessible environments and negative social attitudes toward disability, which from a social model perspective serves to "exaggerate disability and even construct disability" (Smart, 2004, p. 42). CILs provide two types of advocacy: individual and large-scale social and political advocacy (Richards & Smith, n.d.). Individual advocacy supports the self-determination of individuals to obtain necessary support services from other community agencies, such as state and federal vocational rehabilitation (Zola, 2001). Social and political advocacy is broader, advocating, for instance, for accessible housing and transportation in society to help a wide range of people with disabilities (Valera, 2001). Although all CILs in the United States are legally mandated to provide all these services, not all CILs have the same resources. Each one is unique in terms of funding, staff, and the local communities served (Frieden, 2001; Nosek et al., 1992). In addition, different services may be more or less important in different communities, and CILs are designed to be responsive to the needs of local communities. For instance, rural communities often struggle with lack of transportation, and as a result, rural CILs may be particularly focused on providing accessible transportation (Schwab, 2001). Further, with the 1999 Olmstead Supreme Court decision supporting the right of individuals with disabilities to live in the least restrictive environments, there are state and federal funds to assist individuals with disabilities to transition out of institutional care facilities and into the community (Iowa Real Choices Program, 2009). Imbedded within local communities, CILs are a critical resource to support the local needs of people with disabilities to live independently.

There are great benefits to CILs. Perhaps the most significant benefit of CILs is that they can help individuals with disabilities understand how the experience of disability is influenced by environmental factors (Crewe & Zola, 2001; DeJong, 1979; Nosek et al., 1992). With increasingly high caseloads and limited resources, many rehabilitation counselors do not have the time or resources to work with clients to explore the effects of environmental factors on their experience of disability. CILs offer individuals with disabilities a place to share their experiences and realize that they are not alone (Zola, 2001). Like self-help movements, CILs provide a safe haven for individuals with disabilities to express themselves (Saxton, 2001; Shreve, 1991). Further, CILs have been a powerful voice in confronting inaccessible environments and negative social attitudes toward disability. Rehabilitation professionals share the value that CILs place on individuals with disabilities living independently in the community, and advocacy continues to be a core value of the rehabilitation counseling profession (CRCC, 2010). Rehabilitation counselors who may have personal experience with disability and share a passion for sociopolitical advocacy often pursue careers with CILs. Similar to other rehabilitation work settings, interested rehabilitation counselors should consult relevant CIL professional organizations, such as the National Council on Independent Living (2010) and the Association of Programs for Rural Independent Living.

DISABILITY STUDIES

Although the independent living movement has greatly informed the Disability Rights community, it is also important to understand the field of disability studies, which offers a sociopolitical critique of the dominant cultural discourse of disability (Albrecht et al., 2001; Barnes, Oliver, & Barton, 2002; Davis, 2002, 2006; Linton, 1998). As an academic field of inquiry, the field of disability studies has come a long way in a short time (Cushing & Smith, 2009; Davis, 2006). Prior to the 1980s, "academic interest in disability was confined almost exclusively to conventional, individualistic medical explanations" (Barnes et al., 2002, p. 3). Initially based in the United Kingdom, by the 1980s disability studies courses were being taught in the United States, and the first American disability studies journal, *Disability Studies Quarterly*, was published by the Society for Disability Studies (Barnes et al., 2002; Davis, 2006). The initial disability studies movement was rooted in the social sciences, especially sociology; however, in the late 1980s, there was a shift toward a humanities approach of cultural reevaluation (Barnes et al., 2002; Davis, 2002, 2006; Linton, 1998). Going beyond a critique of the social forces of oppression that shaped the lives of people with disabilities, the goal became to assemble a collective body of knowledge that "places disability in a political, social, and cultural context, that theorizes and historicizes deafness or blindness or disability in similarly complex ways to the way race, class, and gender have been theorized" (Davis, 2006, p. xvi).

A number of disability studies programs and courses wereexploded in the 1990s and 2000s (Barnes et al., 2002; Cushing & Smith, 2009; Davis, 2006; Linton, 1998). Yet many of the courses and degrees remained in the social sciences and allied health fields, though this was incongruent with the social model of disability (Cushing & Smith, 2009; Linton, 1998). While some argued that health care professionals were listening to a disability studies perspective, others were concerned that the field was being diluted and influenced by medical perspectives (Cushing & Smith, 2009; Linton, 1998). To distinguish disability studies programs rooted in the social model of disability, rehabilitation counselors should be able to recognize humanities-based language, curriculum, and worldview; a social model paradigm will emphasize power relations and subjectivity. For instance, as with other cultural identity studies, a second wave of disability studies scholars moved to postmodern theories, allowing for the complexity of multiple and shifting identities and differentiating the experiences of disabilities for men and women, middle-class White and nondominant minority communities, and heterosexual and lesbian, gay, bisexual, and transgender people (Davis, 2002, 2006; McRuer, 2006; Siebers, 2008; Snyder & Mitchell, 2006). Davis (2006) wrote,

"It is still very possible to articulate what disabilities studies is and does, and who is a person with disabilities, but it is equally possible to interrogate the presumptions" (p. xvii). Despite these complexities, the basic tenets of disability studies extend from and contribute to the Disability Rights community.

The primary mission of disability studies is to examine the meaning of disability through an analysis of the experiences of people with disabilities in social, political, and cultural contexts (Barnes et al., 2002; Davis, 2002, 2006; Gill, 1995; Linton, 1998). Informed by the social model of disability, disability studies challenges the notion of disability as primarily a medical category studied and treated by specialists in fields such as rehabilitation counseling that often reinforce the positioning of people with disabilities as abnormal (Davis, 2002, 2006; Linton, 1998). Similar to other cultural studies, disability studies advances a critique of language use that depends upon defining some groups of people as normal contrasted against the abnormal. This pattern establishes how people with disabilities are defined as different or "othered." Relatedly, the term "essentialized" refers to discourse practices that reduce a group of people who are different into a single salient trait rather than viewing the full complexity of an individual and his/her life.

There are three important aspects of the positioning of people with disabilities as abnormal. First, at the root of reframing disability is the use of language (Davis, 2002, 2006; Linton, 1998). Disability studies recognizes the underlying messages conveyed through language as a discourse system and thus shifts from medical discourse to discourses on disability as a social, political, intellectual, and ideological issue (Davis, 2002, 2006; Linton, 1998). Second, popular media have reinforced disability stereotypes, which have described people with disabilities as "pitiable and pathetic, objects of violence, sinister and evil, a curiosity, super-cripple, objects of ridicule, their own worst enemy, a burden, sexually abnormal, incapable of participating fully in community life, and normal life" (Barnes & Mercer, 2001, p. 519). Disability studies scholars critique the effects of popular media on the perception of disability and point to positive images of disability in the culture (Longmore, 2003). Third, influenced by postmodern theorists, the underlying cultural narratives of what it means to have a disability are being reexamined (McRuer, 2006; Siebers, 2008; Tremain, 2006). For instance, in response to high-profile cases of assisted suicide, the group Not Dead Yet on their blog has questioned the dominant cultural narrative of who has worth in our society (Johnson, 2003; Longmore, 2003). Rather than transforming society through protests and legislation, disability studies seeks to change society through critical analysis of meanings that are taken for granted. Disability studies scholars argue that the ways in which disability is used in areas such as genetic testing and euthanasia provide a lens to see how disability is understood in popular culture and to change how disability is treated in health care and rehabilitation policies.

Rehabilitation counselors can benefit from the disability studies critique of disability as a disease or ailment (Albrecht et al., 2001; Barnes et al., 2002; Davis, 2002, 2006; Linton, 1998). In particular, rehabilitation professionals should critically reflect on the experiences of people with disabilities and promote the social model of disability in medically based and other rehabilitation settings (Baker, 2009; Bricher, 2000; Conyers, 2003; Donaghue, 2003). Rehabilitation counselors work with people in sites like nursing homes, assisted living, and other institutions. As frontline service providers, these rehabilitation counselors can have a major impact on how agency policies and practices are implemented. The medical model of disability makes it difficult to communicate with clients and therefore makes doing jobs in health care more challenging (Baker, 2009; Bricher, 2000; Conyers, 2003; Donoghue, 2003). For instance, a client is likely to become suspicious and resentful if a rehabilitation practitioner focuses on the medical aspects of disability, while ignoring the client's social and emotional experience (Baker, 2009; Bricher, 2000; Conyers, 2003; Donoghue, 2003). What's more, although the functional limitations or economic model of disability acknowledges that environmental prejudice and discrimination may limit an individual's work and life experiences, "in reality, societal prejudice is rarely considered" (Smart, 2004, p. 39). Rather, the traditional focus of the functional limitations model of disability is to enhance an individual's functioning through skill development and assistive technology. When the environment is considered, interventions may address accessibility, but rarely do interventions target social policies and practices that discriminate against individuals with disabilities. Rehabilitation practitioners, who understand the social model of disability, will be more capable of understanding the social experience of disability. The development of a therapeutic relationship and working alliance are critical to rehabilitation practice (Lustig, Strauser, Rice, & Rucker, 2002); a rehabilitation counselor who understands disability studies will be better able to communicate and situate an individual's experiences, values, and attitudes in social, political, and cultural contexts.

DISABILITY CULTURE

Stemming from the sociopolitical critique of disability studies and the services and philosophies of the independent living movement, disability culture is best understood as a social movement that champions "a sense of common identity and interests that unite disabled people and separate them from their nondisabled counterparts" (Barnes & Mercer, 2001, p. 522). Beginning in the late 1980s, advocates of disability culture pointed to the need for a politicized identity for people with disabilities that resisted marginalizing narratives of the dominant culture (Barnes & Mercer, 2001; Brannon, 1995, 2001; Gill, 1995; Hirsch, 1995; Johnson, 1987; Longmore, 1995). With the disability studies shift toward the humanities, disability culture was a response to the widespread cultural devaluation of people with disabilities (Brannon, 1995; Brown, 2001; Gill, 1995; Hirsch, 1995; Johnson, 1987; Longmore, 1995). For instance, during the 19th and 20th centuries, U.S. legislation, commonly known as the "Ugly Laws," restricted the public appearance of individuals with physical disabilities because they were considered offensive and frightening (Schweik, 2008). In the 1930s,

fathers who killed adolescent children with severe physical and intellectual disabilities were not punished because it was considered merciful (Brockley, 2001).
Challenging social policies and practices that marginalize people with disabilities,
disability culture is a "lived interrogation" of the idea that disability is primarily
a medical condition. In contrast to the eugenics view that people with disabilities were biologically inferior (Block, Balcazar, & Keys, 2001), disability studies
emerged as a celebration of the lived experience of disability as uniquely beautiful and shaped by a person's particular social and cultural identity (Barnes &
Mercer, 2001; Conyers, 2003; Ingtad & Whyte, 1995; Snyder & Mitchell, 2006).
Perhaps most importantly, disability culture is a social movement intended to
unite a broad crosssection of people with disabilities (Gill, 1995). As part of the
Disability Rights community, disability culture is not about a single disability-
specific group, but rather a larger, universalistic approach to disability as a cultural identity.

Defining disability culture is difficult. Not even the Disability Rights community has agreed on a common language or description of acculturation (Peters,
2000). Embodied in art, music, literature, and other expressions, disability culture
celebrates the ways in which people with disabilities view themselves (Brown,
1995, 2001). For instance, Golfus, a filmmaker, made the documentary *When Billy
Broke His Head* (1995) and chronicled his experiences after a traumatic brain injury.
Sometimes shown in master's-level rehabilitation counseling courses, the most
striking part of the documentary is the way in which Golfus situates rehabilitation in the larger experience of his disability and the perspectives of the Disability
Rights community. Rehabilitation professionals who watch the film often express
frustration with how Golfus portrays the rehabilitation system as ineffectual and
removed from the lived experience of disability. Another well-known story is that
of Christy Brown, an Irish author, painter, and poet who had severe cerebral palsy.
Brown's autobiography *My Left Foot* (1954), is a complex portrayal of a very tal-
ented individual with multiple identities intersecting with class, religion, gender,
and sexuality in the mid-20th century. In a review of the film, Longmore (2003)
noted that Christy Brown's story is important because it is not an "essentialized"
depiction of an individual with a disability as tragic or heroic, but captures the
larger theme of people with disabilities who "fight bias and battle for control of
their lives and insist that they will make their mark on the world" (p. 130). Many
famous authors, including John Milton, James Joyce, and John Keats, have experienced disability (Davis, 2006). Today, artists use disability as a lens through which
to express themselves in art, music, and theater in ways beyond "essentialized"
portrayals as victims or villains (Lewis, 2006). A relatively recent and well-known
illustration of the lived experience of disability is the television series *Big People,
Little World* that began in 2005 and followed life in the family of little people (TLC,
2010). The series shares the perspectives of parents Matt and Amy Roloff and
their four children who are determined to succeed even though the world is not
always accessible or welcoming (TLC, 2010). Compared to the disability studies
emphasis on intellectual arguments, disability culture is premised on the notion

that the way to change society is through the expression of the lived experience of disability through art, music, and literature (Brown, 1995, 2001).

Disability culture offers a critical perspective for rehabilitation practitioners, who often work with people who have recently acquired a disability. For instance, an individual with a recent quadriplegic spinal cord injury who watched the Academy Award winning movie *Million Dollar Baby* (Eastwood, 2004) may mistakenly believe it will be impossible to live a fulfilling life with a severe spinal cord injury and a mercy killing is preferable. Extending from the 1930s theme of mercy killings, there are still dominant cultural messages regarding quality of life and disability. Thus, an individual with a recent injury, without an understanding of disability culture, may internalize messages of disability as tragic. Disability culture responds to these negative societal messages by examining the complex identities of disability that intersect with gender, race, and sexuality, and by promoting the idea that an individual with a severe disability can live a fulfilling life. Therefore, in order to work with clients with severe disabilities, rehabilitation counselors must understand disability as a complex lived experience that is embodied in the disability culture movement (Barnes & Mercer, 2001; Conyers, 2003; Ingtad & Whyte, 1995; Snyder & Mitchell, 2006). An understanding of disability culture will lead to an approach to disability that questions the misrepresentation of disability in the dominant culture and encourages individuals to recognize the social and emotional experience of disability. Without an understanding of the social model, as embraced by the disability culture movement, rehabilitation practitioners can inadvertently contribute to the perceptions of people with disabilities as diseased, broken, and in need of fixing (Baker, 2009; Bricher, 2000; Conyers, 2003; Donaghue, 2003; Illich et al., 2005). Thus, it is particularly important for rehabilitation counselors to be exposed to disability culture.

ONGOING CONSIDERATIONS

As in other specialized health fields, the medical model of disability has traditionally been the central focus of rehabilitation research and policy decisions. As a consequence, many in the Disability Rights community have viewed this knowledge base as "oppressive" (Bricher, 2000, p. 781). Today the rehabilitation counseling literature is increasingly influenced by the social model of disability (Armstrong & Fitzgerald, 1996; Carluccio & Patterson, 2001; Conyers, 2003; Kosciulek, 1999, 2000; McCarthy, 2003; McMahon & Shaw, 1999; Middleton, Rollins, & Harley, 1999; Szymanski, Parker, & Patterson, 2005), and the growing body of literature that moves away from the traditional medical model and toward the social model is a positive response to the disability rights community. However, if rehabilitation professionals are to incorporate the social model, a further dialogue is needed between rehabilitation counselors and the disability rights community. In developing such a dialogue, several ongoing issues need to be addressed.

First, to collaborate with the Disability Rights community, rehabilitation professionals need to understand that language is never value-neutral, but rather represents an approach to understanding disability. The field of rehabilitation considers person-first language to be respectful because it highlights the individual rather than the medical condition (Parker et al., 2005). However, there are many less overt ways in which language can marginalize people. For instance, individuals with disabilities have high rates of unemployment and poverty (Lustig & Strauser, 2007), and to attribute the cause of high unemployment to medical conditions is to fail to see the larger cultural problems. For example, individuals with severe psychiatric disabilities have unemployment rates as high as 80% to 90% (Crowther, Marshall, Bond, & Huxley, 2001; Goldberg et al., 2001; Nobel, Honberg, Hall, & Flynn, 2001). Without an understanding of the social model, rehabilitation practitioners may mistakenly conclude that the main reason is their psychiatric symptoms. However, research has shown that a major reason for the high unemployment rate is the stigma of mental illness: Terms such as "unstable" and "volatile" have perpetuated the myth that employing workers with psychiatric disabilities is dangerous (Diksa & Rogers, 1996; Hazer & Bedell, 2000; Weber, Davis, & Sebastian, 2002). Surveys indicate that 50% of U.S. employers are reluctant to hire someone currently undergoing psychiatric treatment, and 70% are reluctant to hire someone currently taking antipsychotic medication (Scheid, 1999). Even after gaining employment, disclosure of a psychiatric disability can seriously limit a person's career advancement (Stuart, 2006). Workers who return to their jobs after a psychiatric leave of absence report being receiving negative comments from colleagues who had previously been supportive and friendly (Wahl, 1999). Individuals with physical disabilities also are discriminated against, and employer fears of expensive accommodations and insurance claims contribute to unemployment rates of 60% to 70% (Stapleton, O'Day, & Livermore, 2005; Wilson-Kovacs, Ryan, Haslam, & Rabinovich, 2008). Besides unemployment, even career advancement can be difficult (Wilson-Kovacs et al., 2008). For instance, in a qualitative study one individual who had his eyesight and hearing affected by a genetic illness noted that senior management viewed him as having "half the capacity" and not up to challenging assignments associated with promotion (cited in Wilson-Kovacs et al., 2008, p. 709). In addition, discrimination occurs in every facet of life. In fact, people with disabilities face more barriers to housing and therefore have less access to community living options. Perhaps the most obvious barrier is that over 90% of U.S. homes are inaccessible to people with physical disabilities (Smith, Rayer, & Smith, 2008; Steinfeld, Levine, & Shea, 1998).

Thus, effective rehabilitation needs to address not only medical symptoms, but also the social problems of stigma and discrimination, and treatment models need to include the perspectives of individuals with disabilities in developing strategies for addressing discrimination. As frontline service providers, rehabilitation counselors work directly with individuals with disabilities, and it is essential that these professionals contextualize the difficulties in obtaining and maintaining employment and independent living often experienced by individuals with disabilities. Choice of language reflects the larger approach to rehabilitation, and in order to establish therapeutic relationships with individuals with disabilities, rehabilitation professionals need to move beyond simply adopting person-first language and consider underlying messages conveyed through language and the consequences to which each leads. The Disability Rights community is suspicious of overly medicalized or "essentialized" language depicting disability.

The epistemological knowledge base of rehabilitation practice, including rehabilitation research and policy development, is another area where critical analysis should occur. Although practitioners typically do not conduct research, there is a need to understand fundamental concerns regarding the construction of rehabilitation knowledge. Specifically, there is concern that traditional rehabilitation knowledge was constructed from a medical model approach to disability (Bricher, 2000). From a Disability Rights perspective, most of this research has been conducted *on* rather than *with* people with disabilities (Barnes, 1996; Oliver, 1992; Shakespeare, 1996). Further, most rehabilitation research has looked for a cure to eradicate disability, and few studies have explored the experience of disability from the perspective of the Disability Rights community (Barnes, 1996; Oliver, 1992; Shakespeare, 1996). Research influences health care policies and practices, and the Disability Rights community is rightfully wary of research on disability conducted without input from people with disabilities (Barnes, 1996; Oliver, 1992; Shakespeare, 1996). Noted by Charlton (1998), without input from individuals with disabilities, research on disability violates the notion of "nothing about us, without us" (p. 3). Rehabilitation researchers have responded to this concern, and participatory action research is growing in importance (Bruyere, 1993; Walker, 1993; White, 2002). The goal of participatory action research is to enhance the relevance of research to the lives of people with disabilities by including people with disabilities in all aspects of the research process, beginning with the generation of research questions (Bruyere, 1993; Walker, 1993; White, 2002). Thus, when working with people with disabilities, practitioners should be aware that from a Disability Rights community perspective, much of the knowledge base of rehabilitation counseling is questionable. Participatory action research is likely to lead to more collaboration; however, there will always be conflict between proponents of the medical model and the social model. As a result, rehabilitation counseling professionals without disabilities may find it "difficult to find a rightful place in relation to research with disabled people and the social model" and struggle to find a comfortable role in discussing traditional rehabilitation knowledge and research with individuals with disabilities (Bircher, 2000, p. 782). Perhaps it is most important for rehabilitation counselors to recognize disabilities as a social and emotional experience, not a medical issue that needs to be solved or prevented to engage in a dialogue with the Disability Rights community (Baker, 2009; Barnes, 1996; Conyers, 2003; Donoghue, 2003). Critically examining how knowledge is constructed is an important part of developing a climate of respect and reciprocity with the Disability Rights community.

Finally, rehabilitation counselors can collaborate with national nonprofit organizations that address disability-specific concerns. Although many disability-specific groups, such United Cerebral Palsy (2010), ARC (2010), and National Alliance on Mental Illness (2010) originated from a medical model of disability perspective that looked to eradicate disability by finding a cure, these organizations are shifting toward the social model of disability perspective when people with disabilities assume leadership roles (Valera, 2001). Rehabilitation counselors can serve as an important link between national nonprofit organizations and the Disability Rights community, bridging the gap between the medical and social model perspectives.

CONCLUSION

There is a clear need for interdisciplinary dialogue between disability studies and specialized professional fields such as rehabilitation counseling. With that said, collaboration is likely to be difficult because the two fields are so divergent in their missions and approaches to disability. The three models of disability (bio-medical model, functional limitations model, and social model) are the best places for dialogue. With advances in gene therapy, biotechnology, neuroscience research, and assisted suicide (Braddock & Parish, 2001), none of the three models alone is complex enough to arrive at workable solutions to all issues experienced in rehabilitation counseling. Therefore, instead of viewing the three models as isolated constructs, our fields might recognize the relationships among the models as they inform rehabilitation practice. Finally, rather than forming opinions in a vacuum, rehabilitation counselors need to learn to listen to the Disability Rights community. For instance, how might the Disabilities Rights perspective influence the education of rehabilitation practitioners? How might the Disability Rights perspective view current rehabilitation policies and practices? How might collaborations between our fields lead to workable solutions to issues of health care and disability?

CONTENT REVIEW QUESTIONS

■ With respect to the disability rights movement, what is meant by the phrase coined by Charlton (1998) "nothing about us, without us?"
■ What are the principles of the independent living movement?
■ What are three important domains for the critique of the dominant perspectives of disability?
■ What is the significance of Disability Culture?

■ What are the benefits of understanding the Disability Rights community prior to working as a rehabilitation counselor?
■ What are two important considerations for respectful communication between rehabilitation professionals and Disability Rights community members?

REFERENCES

Albrecht, G. L., Seelman, K. D., & Bury, M. (2001). Introduction: The formation of disability studies. In G. L. Albrecht, K. D. Seelman, & M. Bury (Eds.), *Handbook of disability studies* (pp. 1–10). Thousand Oaks, CA: Sage Publications.

Americans with Disabilities Act. (1990). 42 U.S.C. Section 12101 et seq. (July 26, 1990).

ARC. (2010). *The ARC*. Retrieved from http://www.thearc.org/page.aspx?pid=183

Armstrong, M. J., & Fitzgerald, M. H. (1996).Culture and disability studies: An anthropological perspective. *Rehabilitation Education, 10,* 247–304.

Association of Programs for Rural Independent Living. (2010). *The united voice of independent living in rural America*. Retrieved from http://www.april-rural.org/

Baker, D. (2009). Bridging the deficiency divide: Expressions of non-deficiency models of disability in health care. *Disability Studies Quarterly, 29,* 6–12.

Barnartt, S. (1996). Disability culture or disability consciousness? *Journal of Disability Policy Studies, 7,* 1–19.

Barnartt, S., & Scotch, R. (2001). *Disability protests: Contentious politics 1970–1999*. Washington, DC: Gallaudet Press.

Barnes, C. (1996). Disability and the myth of the independent researcher. *Disability & Society, 7,* 115–124.

Barnes, C., & Mercer, G. (2001). Disability culture. In G. L. Albrecht, K. D. Seelman, & M. Bury (Eds.), *Handbook of disability studies* (pp. 515–534). Thousand Oaks, CA: Sage Publications.

Barnes, C., Oliver, M., & Barton, L. (2002).*Disability studies today*. Malden, MA: Blackwell Publishers.

Baynton, D. (1996). *Forbidden signs*. Chicago, IL: University of Chicago Press.

Beers, C. W. (1908). *A mind that found itself*. New York, NY: Doubleday and Company.

Block, P., Balcazar, F., & Keys, C. (2001). From pathology to power: Rethinking race, poverty, and disability. *Journal of Disability Policy Studies,12,* 18–39.

Braddock, D. L., & Parish, S. L. (2001). An institutional history of disability. In G. L. Albrecht, K. D. Seelman, & M. Bury (Eds.), *Handbook of disability studies* (pp. 1–10). Thousand Oaks, CA: Sage Publications.

Brannon, R. (1995). The use of the concept of disability culture: A historian's view.*Disability Studies Quarterly, 15,* 3–15.

Bricher, G. (2000). Disabled people, health professionals and the social model of disability: Can there be such a relationship? *Disability & Society, 15,* 781–793. doi: 10.1080/09687590050119929

Brockley, J. A. (2001). Martyred mothers and merciful fathers: Exploring disability and motherhood in the lives of Jerome Greenfield and Raymond Repouille. In P. Longmore & L. Umansky (Eds.), *The new disability history: American perspectives* (pp. 268–292). New York, NY: The New York University Press.

Brown, C. (1954). *My left foot*. London, England: Secker & Warburg.

Brown, S. E. (2001). Editorial: What is disability culture? *Independent Living Institute Newsletter 2001–12.* Retrieved June 25, 2010, from http:www.independentliving.org/newsletter/12-01.html

Bruyere, S. M. (1993). Participatory action research: Overview and implications for family members of persons with disabilities. *Journal of Vocational Rehabilitation, 3,* 62–68.

Byrom, B. (2001). A pupil and a patient. In P. Longmore & L. Umansky (Eds.), *The new disability history: American perspectives* (pp. 133–156). New York, NY: The New York University Press.

Campbell, J., & Oliver, M. (1996). *Disability politics.* London, England: Routledge Press.

Carluccio, L. W., & Patterson, J. (2001). Promoting independent living in the rehabilitation curriculum. *Rehabilitation Education, 15,* 409–419.

Charlton, J. (1998). *Nothing about us without us.* Berkeley, CA: University of California Press.

Cole, J. A. (2001). Developing new self-images and interdependence. In N. M. Crewe & I. K. Zola (Eds.), *Independent living for physically disabled people* (pp. 187–204). San Jose, CA: People with Disabilities Press.

Commission on Rehabilitation Counselor Certification. (2010). *Rehabilitation counseling.* Retrieved from http://www.crccertification.com/pages/rehabilitation_counseling/30.php

Conyers, L. M. (2003). Disability culture. *Rehabilitation Education, 3,* 139–154.

Crewe, N. M., & Zola, I. K. (Eds.).(2001). *Independent living for physically disabled people.* San Jose, CA: People with Disabilities Press.

Crowther, R. E., Marshall, M., Bond, G. R., & Huxley, P. (2001). Helping people with severe mental illness to obtain work: Systematic review. *British Medical Journal, 322,* 204–208.

Cushing, P., & Smith, T. (2009). A multinational review of English-language disability studies degrees and courses. *Disability Studies Quarterly, 29,* 11–22.

Davis, L. J. (2002). *Bending over backwards.* New York, NY: The University Press.

Davis, L. J. (Ed.). (2006). *The disability studies reader* (2nd ed.). New York, NY: Routledge.

DeJong, G. (1979). Independent living: From social movement to analytic paradigm. *Archives of Physical Medicine and Rehabilitation, 60,* 435–446.

Diksa, E., & Rogers, E. S. (1996). Employer concerns about hiring persons with psychiatric disability. *Rehabilitation Counseling Bulletin, 40,* 31–44

Donoghue, C. (2003). Challenging the authority of the medical definition of disability: An analysis of the resistance to the social constructionist paradigm. *Disability & Society, 18,* 199. doi:10.1080/0968759032000052833.

Eastwood, C. (Director). (2004). *Million dollar baby [Motion picture].* Burbank, CA: Warner Bros. Pictures.

Frazer, E. (1999). *The problem of communitarian politics: Unity and conflict.* Oxford, England: Oxford University Press.

Frieden, L. (2001). Understanding alternative program models. In N. M. Crewe & I. K. Zola (Eds.), *Independent living for physically disabled people* (pp. 62–72). San Jose, CA: People with Disabilities Press.

Gill, C. J. (1995). A psychological view of disability culture. *Disability Studies Quarterly, 15,* 16–19.

Goldberg, R. W., Lucksted, A., McNary, S., Gold, J. M., Dixon, L., & Lehman, A. (2001). Correlates of long-term unemployment amount inner-city adults with serious and persistent mental illness. *Psychiatric Services, 52,* 101–103.

Golfus, B., & Simpson, D. (1995). *When Billy broke his head and other tales of wonder.* St. Paul, MN: Independent Television Series.

Hahn, H. (1991). Theories and values: Ethics and contrasting perspectives on disability. In R. P. Marinelli & A. E. Dell Orto (Eds.), *The psychological and social impact of disability* (pp. 18–22). New York, NY: Springer Publishing Company.

Hazer, J. T., & Bedell, K. V. (2000).Effects of seeking accommodation and disability on preemployment evaluations.*Journal of Applied Social Psychology, 30,* 1201–1223. doi:10.1111/j.1559-1816.2000.tb02517.x

Hershenson, D. B. (1998).Systematic, ecological model for rehabilitation counseling. *Rehabilitation Counseling Bulletin, 42,* 40–50.

Hirsch, K. (1995). Culture and disability: The role of oral history. *Oral History Review, 22,* 1–27.

Hoggett, P. (1997). *Contested communities: Experiences, struggles, policies.* Bristol, England: Policy Press.

Illich, I., Zola, I. K., McKnight, J., Caplan, J., & Shaiken, H. (2005). *Disabling professions.* London, England: Marion Boyers Publishers LTD.

Ingstad, B., & Whyte, S. R. (Eds.). (1995). *Disability and culture.* Los Angeles, CA: The University of California Press.

Iowa Real Choices Program. (2009). *Olmstead—real choices for Iowa.* Retrieved from http://www.olmsteadrealchoicesia.org/

Johnson, M. (1987). Emotion and pride: The search for a disability culture. *Disability Rag (January/February),* 1–27.

Johnson, M. (2003). *Make them go away.* Louisville, KY: The Avocado Press.

Koestler, F. A. (1975). *The unseen minority.* New York, NY: American Foundation of the Blind.

Kosciulek, J. (1993). Advances in trait- and-factor theory: A person x environment fit approach to rehabilitation counseling. *Journal of Applied Rehabilitation Counseling, 24,* 11–14.

Kosciulek, J. (1999). The consumer directed theory of empowerment. *Rehabilitation Counseling Bulletin, 42,* 196–213.

Kosciulek, J. (2000). Implications of consumer direction for disability policy development and rehabilitation service delivery. *Journal of Disability Policy Studies, 11,* 82–89.

Lane, H. (1984). *When the mind hears.* New York, NY: Random House.

Lewis, V. A. (2006). *Beyond victims and villains: Contemporary plays by disabled playwrights.* New York, NY: Theatre Communication Group.

Linton, S. (1998). *Claiming disability, knowledge and identity.* New York, NY: The New York University Press.

Liu, W. M., & Toporek, R. L. (2004). Advocacy. In T. F. Riggar & D. R. Maki (Eds.), *Handbook of rehabilitation counseling* (pp. 188–198). New York, NY: Springer Publishing.

Lofquist, L. H., & Dawis, R. V. (1969). *Adjustment to work: A psychological view of man's problems in a work-orientated society.* New York, NY: Appleton-Century-Crofts.

Longmore, P., & Goldberger, E. (2003). The league of physically handicapped and the great depression. In P. Longmore (Ed.), *Why I burned my book and other essays on disability* (pp. 53–101). Philadelphia, PA: Temple University Press.

Longmore, P., & Umansky, L. (Eds.). (2001). *The new disability history.* New York, NY: The New York University Press.

Longmore, P. K. (1995). The second phase: From disability rights to disability culture. *Disability Rag (September/October),* 4–11.

Longmore, P. K. (2003). *Why I burned my book and other essays on disability.* Philadelphia, PA: Temple University Press.

Lustig, D., & Strauser, D. (2007). Causal relationships between poverty and disability. *Rehabilitation Counseling Bulletin, 50,* 194–202.

Lustig, D. C., Strauser, D. R., Rice, N. D., & Rucker, T. F. (2002). The relationship between working alliance and rehabilitation outcomes.*Rehabilitation Counseling Bulletin, 46,* 25–33.

Maki, D. R., McCracken, N., Pape, D., & Scofield, M. E. (1979). A systems approach to vocational assessment. *Journal of Rehabilitation, 45,* 48–51.

Maki, D. R., & Riggar, T. F. (2004). Concepts and paradigms. In T. F. Riggar & D. R. Maki (Eds.), *Handbook of rehabilitation counseling* (pp. 1–24). New York, NY: Springer Publishing.

Matson, F. (1990). *Walking alone and marching together.* Baltimore, MD: National Federation of the Blind.

McCarthy, H. (2003). The disability rights movement: Experiences and perspectives of selected leaders in the disability community. *Rehabilitation Counseling Bulletin, 46,* 209–223.

McMahon, B. T., & Shaw, L. (Eds.). (1999). *Enabling lives: Biographies of six prominent Americans with disabilities.* New York, NY: CRC Press.

McRuer, R. (2006). *Crip theory: Cultural signs of queerness and disability.* New York, NY: The New York University Press.

Middleton, R. A., Rollins, C. W., & Harley, D. A. (1999). The historical and political context of the civil rights of persons with disabilities: A multicultural perspective for counselors. *Journal of Multicultural Counseling and Development, 27,* 105–120.

National Alliance on Mental Illness. (2010). *National alliance on mental illness.* Retrieved from http://www.nami.org/

National Council on Independent Living (2010). *National council on independent living.* Retrieved from http://www.ncil.org/

Nobel, J. H., Honberg, R. S., Hall, L. L., & Flynn, L. M. (2001). A legacy of failure: The inability of the federal-state vocational rehabilitation system to serve people with severe mental illness. Retrieved from National Alliance for the Mentally Ill website, http://www.nami.org/Content/ContentGroups/E-News/20013/January_20012/Vocational_Rehabilitation_Report__A_Legacy_Of_Failure.htm

Noll, S., & Trent, J. (Eds.). (2004). *Mental retardation in America: A historical reader.* New York, NY: The New York University Press.

Nosek, M. (1988). Independent living and rehabilitation counseling. In S. Rubin & N. Rubin (Eds.). *Contemporary challenges to the rehabilitation counseling profession* (pp. 45–60). Baltimore, MD: Paul H. Brookes.

Nosek, M. A., Zhu, Y., & Howland, C. (1992). The evolution of independent living programs. *Rehabilitation Counseling Bulletin, 35,* 174–179.

Not Dead Yet. (n.d.). Retrieved July 2010 from Not Dead Yet Blogspot: http://notdeadyetnewscommentary.blogspot.com/

Oliver, M. (1990). *The Politics of disablement.* London, England: Macmillan Press.

Oliver, M. (1992). Changing the social relations of research production. *Disability, Handicap, and Society, 7,* 101–114.

Parker, R., Szymanski, E., & Patterson, J. (Eds.). (2005). *Rehabilitation counseling: Basics and beyond* (4th ed.). Austin, TX: Pro-Ed.

Peters, S. (2000). Is there a disability culture? A syncretisation of three possible worldviews. *Disability & Society, 15,* 583–601. doi:10.1080/09687590050058170

Porter, R. (1989). *A social history of madness.* New York, NY: Dutton.

Richards, L., & Smith, Q. (n.d.). An orientation to independent living centers. *ILRU field work: A national technical assistance project for independent living* (pp. 1–6). Developed as part of the National Technical Assistance Project for Independent Living. Houston, TX: ILRU Research & Training Center on Independent Living at TIRR. Retrieved from http://www.ilru.org

Rubin, S., & Roessler, R. (2008). *Foundations of the vocational rehabilitation process.* Austin, TX: PRO-ED.

Saxton, M. (2001). Peer counseling. In N. M. Crewe & I. K. Zola (Eds.), *Independent living for physically disabled people* (pp. 171–186). San Jose, CA: People with Disabilities Press.

Scheid, T. L. (1999). Employment of individuals with mental disabilities: Business response to the ADA challenge. *Behavior Science and the Law, 17,* 73–91.

Schwab, L. (2001). Developing programs in rural areas. In N. M. Crewe & I. K. Zola (Eds.), *Independent living for physically disabled people* (pp. 73–87). San Jose, CA: People with Disabilities Press.

Schweik, S. M. (2008). *The ugly laws*. New York, NY: The New York University Press.

Scotch, R. K. (1988). Disability as the basis of a social movement: Advocacy and the politics of definition. *Journal of Social Issues, 44*, 159–172.

Shakespeare, T. (1996). Rules of engagement: Doing disability research. *Disability & Society, 11*, 115–119.

Shakespeare, T., & Watson, N. (1997). Defending the social model. *Disability & Society, 12*, 293–300.

Shapiro, J. P. (1994). *No pity*. New York, NY: Three Rivers Press.

Shreve, M. (1991). *Peer counseling in independent living centers* (pp. 1–29). Houston, TX: ILRU Program. Retrieved January 31, 2006, from www.ilru.org

Siebers, T. (2008). *Disability theory*. Ann Arbor, MI: University of Michigan Press.

Smart, J. (2001). *Disability, society, and the individual*. Gaithersburg, MD: Aspen Press.

Smart, J. (2004). Models of disability. In T. Riggar & D. Maki (Eds.), *Handbook of rehabilitation counseling* (pp. 25–49). New York, NY: Springer Publishing.

Smith, S. K., Rayer, S., & Smith, E. A. (2008). Aging and disability: Implications for the housing industry and housing policy in the U.S. *Journal of American Planning Association, 74*, 289–306. doi:10.1080/101944360802197132

Snyder, S. L., & Mitchell, D. T. (2006). *Cultural locations of disability*. Chicago, IL: The University of Chicago Press.

Stapleton, D. C., O'Day, B., & Livermore, G. A. (2005, July). *Dismantling the poverty trap: Disability policy for the 21st Century*. Washington, DC: Cornell Institute for Policy Research, Rehabilitation Research and Training Center. Retrieved from http://digitalcommons.ilr.cornell.edu/edicollect/124/

Steinfeld, E., Levine, D. R., & Shea, S. M. (1998).Home modifications and the fair housing laws. *Technology & Disability, 8,* 15–35.

Stuart, H. (2006). Mental illness and employment discrimination. *Current Opinion in Psychiatry, 19*, 522–526. doi:10.1097/01.yco.0000238482.27270.5d

Switzer, J. V. (2003). *Disability rights*. Washington, DC: Georgetown University Press.

Szymanski, E., Parker, R., & Patterson, J. (2005). Beyond the basics: Sociopolitical context of rehabilitation counseling practice. In R. Parker, E. Szymanski, & J. Patterson (Eds.), *Rehabilitation counseling: Basics and beyond* (4th ed., pp. 395–412). Austin, TX: Pro-Ed.

TLC. (2010). *Big people, little world*. Retrieved from http://tlc.discovery.com/tv/little-people-big-world/

Tremain, S. (Ed.). (2006). *Foucault and the government of disability*. Ann Arbor, MI: University of Michigan Press.

Trent, J. W. (1994). *Inventing the feeble mind*. Berkeley, CA: University of California Press.

United Cerebral Palsy. (2010). *United cerebral palsy*. Retrieved from http://www.ucp.org/

Valera, R. A. (2001). Changing social attitudes and legislation regarding disability. In N. M. Crewe & I. K. Zola (Eds.), *Independent living for physically disabled people* (pp. 28–48). San Jose, CA: People with Disabilities Press.

Wahl, O. F. (1999). *Telling is risky business*. Piscataway, NJ: Rutgers University Press.

Walker, M. L. (1993). Participatory action research. *Rehabilitation Counseling Bulletin, 37,* 2–5.

Weber, P. S., Davis, E., & Sebastian, R. J. (2002). Mental health and the ADA. *Employee Responsibilities and Rights Journal, 14,* 45–55.

White, G. W. (2002). Consumer participation in disability research: The golden rule as a guide for ethical practice. *Rehabilitation Psychology, 47*, 438–446. doi:10.1037//0090-5550.47.4.438

Wilson-Kovacs, D., Ryan, M. K., Haslam, S. A., & Rabinovich, A. (2008). Just because you can get a wheelchair in the building doesn't necessarily mean that you can still participate. *Disability & Society, 23*, 705–717. doi:10.1080/09687590802469198

Zola, I. K. (2001). Developing new self-images and interdependence. In N. M. Crewe & I. K. Zola (Eds.), *Independent living for physically disabled people* (pp. 49–59). San Jose, CA: People with Disabilities Press.

9

Disability Issues in a Global Context

Lisa Lopez Levers

LEARNING OBJECTIVES

After reading this chapter, you should be able to:

- Define disability in an international context.
- Compare and contrast global disability issues with these same issues in a North American context and also between high-resource and low-resource countries.
- Understand the scope of rehabilitation counseling in an international context.
- Learn about the work of relevant disability-related international organizations.
- Identify some of the global epidemiological implications of disability.
- Identify some of the concerns regarding the lack of data related to global disability issues.
- Enhance awareness of current global contextual factors and other issues affecting disability such as culture, poverty, trauma, crisis, large-scale disaster, HIV and AIDS, and psychosocial issues across the lifespan.
- Learn about some of the useful practices employed internationally to assist people with disabilities.
- Identify additional resources for promoting better understanding of disability and rehabilitation in an international context.

The purpose of this chapter is to discuss and illuminate the role of rehabilitation counselors (RCs) within an international context. In order to do this, it is important to understand relevant worldwide issues concerning disability, disability policy, and disability classification systems, as these compare and contrast with disability-related issues in North America. In this chapter, the reader is introduced to relevant disability demographics, constructs, and resources that relate to global perspectives of disability issues and the role of RCs.

INTRODUCTION

The World Health Organization (WHO) (2010c) estimates that approximately 10% of the world's population, or about 650 million people, live with some form of disability. WHO further indicates that "This figure is increasing through population growth, medical advances, and the ageing [*sic*] process" (WHO, cited in UNICEF, n.d., Overview, para. 2). About 80% of all persons with disabilities (PWDs) reside in low-resource countries. The relationship between disability and poverty has become clear, and disability is considered both a cause and a consequence of poverty (Mitra, 2004, 2005). Therefore, it is important to check assumptions regarding North American-based and other industrial economies-based disability services and RC roles against the low-resource reality in which the majority of PWDs live. According to the *Lancet* (Editorial, 2009), this majority of the world's PWDs who live in low-income countries has "little or no access to basic health services, including rehabilitation facilities" (p. 1793). It therefore becomes essential to focus discussion on non-Western or developing, as well as Western or developed, systems of rehabilitation when addressing international disability concerns (DePoy & Gilson, 2011).

Well-established social safety mechanisms for PWDs exist in many high-resource countries; for example, Sweden, England, and Canada arguably have some of the strongest disability-related systems in the world (Levers, Magweva, & Mufema, 2010). Although popular belief would suggest that the United States has a comparable disability-related system, recent evidence of the quality versus cost of medical care in the United States (e.g., Agency for Healthcare Research and Quality [AHRQ], 2009b; Bureau of Labor Education, 2001; Kaiser Family Foundation, 2010), health inequity (e.g., AHRQ, 2009a) and still-prevalent negative perceptions about PWDs (e.g., Martz, Strohmer, Fitzgerald, Daniel, & Arm, 2006) perhaps calls this into question. The major point, though, is that higher-resource countries tend to have already-embedded social safety nets (SSNs) for PWDs, and rehabilitation services typically are delivered by relatively well-trained personnel. However, this is not necessarily the case in middle- and low-resource countries.

Throughout the world, PWDs who live in poverty struggle with daily life activities without the advantage of any state-sponsored assistance; in most low-resource areas, service provision by a master's-level RC simply is not financially feasible. This is not to say that services are completely absent or that no one assumes the functions of rehabilitation counseling; however, the greater picture looks very different outside the protective structures of the SSNs that have been established in higher-resource societies. This chapter, then, focuses on the relevant discrepancies between high- and low-resource conditions, as these relate to disability issues and rehabilitation counseling in a global context, by discussing and illuminating the following areas: (1) definitions and scope, (2) trends in the relevant international literatures, and (3) useful practices. These discussions are followed by a conclusion section that summarizes the key points of the chapter and offers recommendations for consideration of future actions by RCs in reference to international disability issues.

DEFINING DISABILITY AND THE SCOPE OF REHABILITATION COUNSELING IN AN INTERNATIONAL CONTEXT

Just as the Rehabilitation Act of 1973, the Rehabilitation Act Amendments of 1998, and the Americans with Disabilities Act of 1990 represent hallmark legislative efforts in the United States and offer benchmark definitions of relevant health-related and disability issues. There are a number of documents that are somewhat parallel, in terms of their international cache. These include the following globally relevant documents: the UN Convention on the Rights of Persons with Disabilities (CRPD, 2006); the WHO *International Classification of Disease*, 10th Edition (ICD-10, 2007a); the WHO's *International Classification of Functioning, Disability and Health* (ICF, 2001); and, the WHO's *Children and Youth Version of the International Classification of Functioning, Disability and Health* (ICF-CY, 2007). It is important to note here that although the United Nations Millennium Declaration, commonly referred to as the Millennium Development Goals (MDG) (United Nations [UN], 2000), is an important document related to international health goals, it has been criticized widely for ignoring the health needs of PWDs (e.g., Editorial, 2009; Levers et al., 2010).

The governments of many countries have demonstrated the political will to improve the lives of PWDs by taking action and signing important conventions such as the CRPD; however, the fiduciary power to follow through is not always available and includes the attainability of human as well as material resources. In addition, the struggle for human rights has been trying at times for PWDs, when the security nets for which they have advocated do not materialize to meet concrete needs. For example, in a recent evaluation of the effects of poverty on PWDs in a southern African country (Levers et al., 2010, p. 119), consumers of services indicated that "rights do not provide the immediate solution to problems of poverty such as lack of food ... [arguing] that 'we do not eat rights.'" Yet in spite of obvious challenges, the important documents mentioned in the preceding offer aspirations for strategic planning and provide frameworks for setting goals that hopefully will contribute to legislative and policy change that eventually can have a real impact on the quality of living for PWDs worldwide.

According to the UN (n.d., Overview section, para. 12), comparative examinations of disability-related legislation indicate that "only 45 countries have anti-discrimination and other disability-specific laws," thereby highlighting the urgent need to advocate for disability-friendly policies worldwide. These important issues relate directly to: (1) theoretical perspectives on disability, (2) definitions of disability, and (3) the role of RCs, which are all discussed more fully in the following subsections.

Theoretical Perspectives on Disability

As mirrored by developments in North America, the international theoretical perspective on disability has shifted from a purely medical model, to one with a greater social systems emphasis, that is, to a bio-psychosocial or ecological model. This shift is so widely accepted that a special issue of the British-based *Lancet*, one of the world's leading medical journals, was dedicated to the topic of disability, and the title of the special issue was "Disability: Beyond the Medical Model" (*Lancet*, 2009, p. 1793).

A second shift in theoretical perspective regards the issue of disability and cultural meaning, and many international organizations have begun to address this by reevaluating base-line definitions of disability. One example rests with WHO's nosologies of disability. In its earlier text, the *International Classification of Impairments, Disabilities and Handicaps* (ICIDH) (WHO, 1980), WHO classified disabilities from a more or less restrictive biomedical or disease-model perspective. However, the need eventually emerged for a more contextual consideration of disability and the community-based inclusion of people with disabilities, thus leading to the development of related guidelines. In its more recent text, the *International Classification of Functioning, Disability and Health* (WHO, 2001), WHO has engaged in a process of refining definitions of disability to reflect a bio-psychosocial or ecological model, thereby having greater personal and international utility and applicability. In a review of the literature that was conducted 3 years after the publication of the ICF, Bruyère, VanLooy, and Peterson (2005) summarized discussions that reflect both support for and reservations about the ICF's most recent conceptualization of disability. However, the ICF is considered by most as offering a holistic approach to disability, one that is applicable to a diversity of disability issues (e.g., Berg et al., 2009; Oltman, Neises, Scheible, Mehrtens, & Grüneberg, 2008; Pollard, Dixon, Dieppe, & Johnston, 2009; Steiner et al., 2002; Weigl, Cieza, Kostanjsek, Kirschneck, & Stucki, 2006).

How disability is defined becomes extremely important, because officially sanctioned definitions, in turn, determine eligibility of PWDs for social protection programs or SSNs. For example, impairment-oriented definitions, largely used in developing countries, tend to underreport the prevalence of disability and inadvertently exclude PWDs from eligibility for social protection services (Levers, Magweva, Maundeni, & Mpofu, 2008). Conversely, definitions of disability are more inclusive when based on activity and participation limitations, thus resulting in a higher census of persons eligible for specific SSNs that are a part of the social protection model (Mitra, 2005). In addition, while most contemporary models of rehabilitation service delivery already tend to be humanitarian in nature, ecologically oriented models, by definition, have allowed for greater incorporation of mechanisms that encourage empowerment and self-efficacy. The link between ecological and self-determination models is of particular importance to all counselors, including RCs (Lynch & Levers, 2007; O'Sullivan & Strauser, 2009), and the issues of empowerment and self-efficacy have been instrumental in promoting and advancing the rights of PWDs throughout the world.

Defining Disability

The *Convention on the Rights of Persons with Disabilities* (UN, 2007, Article 1—Purpose, para. 2) defines disability as including persons "who have long-term physical, mental, intellectual or sensory impairments which in interaction with various barriers may hinder their full and effective participation in society on an equal basis with others." The ICF also provides an ecological definition of disability, offering a common language and framework for considering health and health-related issues (WHO, 2002), and therefore, is essential as a disability-related tool in an international context. The ICF defines disability as "an umbrella term for impairments, activity limitations and participation restrictions. . . ." further stating that "Functional limitations occur as a result of the interaction between an individual (with a health condition) and that individual's contextual factors (environmental and personal factors)" (WHO, 2001, p. 10). The *ICF* does not focus on the etiology of dysfunction or underlying pathology; rather, these are focal points of its companion classification, the ICD-10 (2007a).

The presence of impairments does not necessarily imply the presence of disorder or disease; rather, according to the WHO (2001, p. 12), they "represent a deviation from certain generally accepted population standards" of functioning. Determinations of impairment are made by "those qualified to judge physical and mental functioning according to these standards" (WHO, p. 12). *Disability*, then, refers to "the outcome or result of a complex relationship between an individual's health condition and personal factors, and of the external factors that represent the circumstances in which the individual lives" (WHO, p. 17). The meaning of *disability*, in this international and ecological context, is intended to imply a focus on the comprehensive individual, societal, and body-related aspects of impairments, along with activity limitations and other participation restrictions in the environment. Its determination, also in this international and ecological context, may be made by various professionals or paraprofessionals, who may or may not look a lot or a little like what are viewed as RCs in a European–American context.

In September 2007, the WHO published the *Children and Youth Version of the International Classification of Functioning, Disability and Health* (ICF-CY). Although a number of ambitious objectives have been associated with the ICF-CY, much like the ICF, the ICF-CY has aimed to shift views regarding disability issues from a more medically oriented model to one that accounts for contextual and environmental factors (Simkiss, 2008).

The ecological model of functioning, as operationally advanced in both the ICF and the ICF-CY, suggests dynamic and reciprocal relationships among various health-related conditions; these relationships occur within the context of multiple personal and environmental influences. Functional level and disability are then conceptualized within dynamic interactions between health conditions and contextual factors, including cultural considerations. The components and interactions that can be used to describe the relationship between disability and functioning are illustrated in Figure 9.1 (borrowed from Pollard et al., 2009, Background, para. 1, which was drawn from WHO, 2001, p. 18).

FIGURE 9.1
Interactions Among the Components of ICF

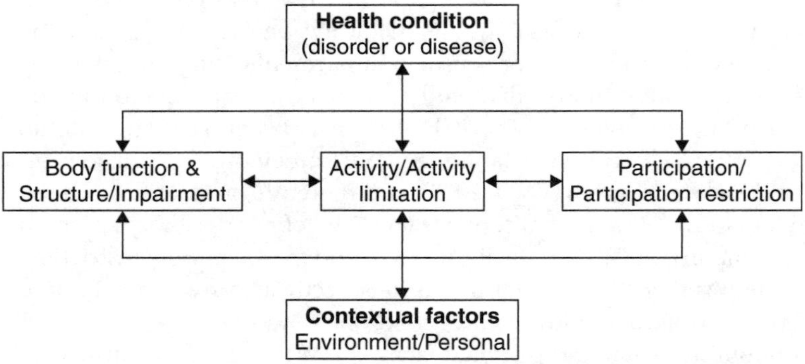

Source: From Pollard et al. (2009) drawn from *The International Classification of Functioning, Disability and Health* (p. 18), by WHO, 2001, Geneva, Switzerland: Author. Reprinted with permission.

Disability, according to the ICF model, is defined by activity and participation limitations due to health conditions, particularly as these are linked to environments in which people live with disabilities. In concert with the underlying theory of the bio-ecological model of human development, social protection policies primarily are intended to mitigate or prevent activity restrictions and participation limitations. For example, poverty is a determinant that can affect environmental context, and disability is associated with poverty in most countries. Although this association suggests a complex situation that is not necessarily determined by a clear cause-and-effect relationship, it ultimately may lead to the socioeconomic exclusion of PWDs, which then influences other dimensions of living. Some performance-based benchmarks even indicate that the extent to which a country provides social protection programs may have a connection with international expenditure norms, thus emphasizing complex interactions between disability and economics (Besley, Burgess, & Rasul, 2003).

Regardless of socioeconomic status, activity restrictions, participation limitations, or environmental barriers, the ICF model recognizes that people can have disabilities and still be healthy (Stein, Stein, Weiss, & Lang, 2009; WHO, 2001). Health or well-being is mediated by cognitive and bodily functions and structures that enable activity and participation. Activity is based on what a person is capable of doing to meet daily living needs, and participation arises from the roles that a person is able to fulfill. Both the environment and the personal factors influence the conditions and pathways for activity and participation by PWDs. For example, people in chronic poverty may have significant health challenges that could be relieved by social protection programs. Due to living in such poverty, PWDs' bodily functions and structures may perform less optimally in enabling a full range of activities and roles that are necessary for successful daily living. Personal factors like self-attitudes can differentiate social outcomes for people who may have the same health conditions; while some may perceive a need to adapt and take control of their situations, others may not. Given the same objective environment and similar health conditions, PWDs may differ in their motivation to acquire the social protection services for which they are eligible. Based on all these assumptions and derived from an ecological perspective of disability, a useful operational definition of disability, suggested by Levers et al. (2008, p. 22) in their evaluation of one African nation's disability system, is: "Any physical, sensory, cognitive, or psychiatric impairment that, when combined with environmental and societal barriers, limits the person's functional ability to perform major life activities."

Role of Rehabilitation Counselors

The Commission on Rehabilitation Counselor Certification web site states that "The CRCC is the world's largest rehabilitation counseling organization . . ." further indicating that "While the vast majority of Certified Rehabilitation Counselors (CRCs) practice in the United States, Certified Rehabilitation Counselors also practice in numerous other countries worldwide and in Canada as Canadian Certified Rehabilitation Counselors (CCRCs)" (CRCC, 2010, About CRC Certification, para. 2). According to the Bureau of Labor Statistics (2010, Nature of the work, para. 8), the scope of practice for RCs is defined in the following way:

> *Rehabilitation counselors* help people deal with the personal, social, and vocational effects of disabilities. They counsel people with both physical and emotional disabilities resulting from birth defects, illness or disease, accidents, or other causes. They evaluate the strengths and limitations of individuals, provide personal and vocational counseling, offer case management support, and arrange for medical care, vocational training, and job placement. Rehabilitation counselors interview both individuals with disabilities and their families, evaluate school and medical reports, and confer with physicians, psychologists, employers, and physical, occupational, and speech therapists to determine the capabilities and skills of the individual. They develop individual rehabilitation programs by conferring with the client. These programs often include training to help individuals develop job skills, become employed, and provide opportunities for community integration. Rehabilitation counselors are trained to recognize and to help lessen environmental and attitudinal barriers. Such help may include providing education and advocacy services to individuals, families, employers, and others in the community. Rehabilitation counselors work toward increasing the person's capacity to live independently by facilitating and coordinating with other service providers.

It may be arguable whether such comprehensive rehabilitation services are available in adequate proportions, even within the industrial societies where the need for such services emerged around industrialization and accelerated after

World War II. For example, the large numbers of military personnel who have returned from Iraq and are returning from Afghanistan, with physical and psychological injuries, may call into question the capacity of U.S. rehabilitation professionals to meet the need (Frain, Bishop, & Bethel, 2010). Further, it is apparent that the onus of activity has tended to be on the RC to perform *for* rather than *with* the client, using a model that is relatively more agentic (for the counselor) than collaborative. Conversely, it is fairly certain that in most low-resource countries such a comprehensive set of rehabilitation services is not available for ordinary citizens, and a scope of practice that favors individualism would not necessarily be as productive in social structures that are more collectivist in nature.

While professionals who work as RCs in the United States typically possess a master's degree or higher, this is not necessarily the case in other parts of the world. First, the field of counseling, regardless of specialty area, is not always viewed as a distinct profession in other countries. Psychology and social work are more universally recognized as organized fields of endeavor, and until very recently, preparing graduate students for careers specifically in professional counseling largely has been a U.S. endeavor. However, there are indications that this approach has been changing, for example, with students being trained in the West and returning to their non-Western homes to provide counseling services (e.g., Cook, Lei, & Chiang, 2010), the international growth of counselor education (e.g., Astramovich & Pehrsson, 2009), promotion of a global counseling identity (e.g., Hoskins & Thompson, 2009), and greater focus on advancing indigenous counseling (e.g., Bhusumane, 2007; Levers, 2006b, 2006c; Msimanga-Ramatebele, 2008). Second, in low-resource countries, human services are not always available, and when they are, it is not probable that they will be provided by a master's-level practitioner. Putting all of this together, it is likely that although the scope of practice for those fulfilling the role of RC is similar throughout the world, it is not as likely that the practitioner will have had the advantage of the same level of training or access to the same level of resources. With this in mind, it is important to identify some of the relevant issues of concern that have global implications for those working in the disability and rehabilitation arena. This summary focuses on international trends that have been identified in the relevant professional literatures and are discussed in the next section.

INTERNATIONAL DISABILITY AND REHABILITATION LITERATURES

The presentation of a thorough and complete examination of global disability and rehabilitation issues is beyond the scope of this chapter. However, several salient trends emerge from the literature as significant and serve to inform the discourse on disability issues and rehabilitation counseling in a global context. Although there is a plethora of transnational literature that relates to disability and rehabilitation issues—for example, comparisons of disability statistics between two or among several specific countries—there is little that integrates and synthesizes relevant international information in a meaningful way. Beyond the documents of global relevance that were identified earlier in this chapter, a review of the international literature reveals two major currents of thought: First, a huge gap exists in terms of any thorough examination of global disability issues, and second, there are a number of identifiable trends or concerns that have emerged and that may have an impact on the delivery of rehabilitation services. These two currents of thoughts are discussed in the following.

Lacunae in the Disability and Rehabilitation Literatures

Lacunae exist in the international literature concerning comprehensive understandings of the epidemiological and evidentiary implications of, as well as the contextual factors associated with, disability and rehabilitation. Although cross-national comparisons can be found in the various relevant literatures, these tend to be limited to a couple or a few countries or to a region, and there is little that sheds light on understanding global disability and rehabilitation from a comprehensive or interdisciplinary perspective. This pattern amplifies the realization that disability is an even more complex and multifaceted issue in the global context.

Epidemiological Implications

Valid health-related statistics are vital across all levels of the health care system; however, the ability to ascertain disease and injury levels and patterns remains lacking in many countries, and derivable knowledge often is fragmentary at best. Although various compilations of data regarding mortality, morbidity, and epidemiological trends exist at national and regional levels, only one publication has attempted to offer "comparable regional and global estimates and projections of disease and injury burden based on a common set of methods and denominated in a common metric" (Murray & Lopez, 1996, p. xxvii). *The Global Burden of Disease: A Comprehensive Assessment of Mortality and Disability from Diseases, Injuries, and Risk Factors in 1990 and Projected to 2020* (Murray & Lopez) is considered a landmark publication for its singularity in this arena. It has offered a mechanism for beginning to gather and analyze international disease- and disability-related data in a comprehensive and aligned fashion, as well as for using historical trends to project the mortality and disease burden forward to 2020.

The Murray and Lopez (1996) study has provided consistent estimates of disease and injury rates, but perhaps more importantly, for the purposes of this chapter, has "attempted to provide a comparative index of the burden of each disease or injury, namely the number of Disability-Adjusted Life Years (DALYs) lost as a result of either premature death or years lived with disability" (Henderson, 1996, p. xiii). The design of this common metric is even more unique in its inclusion of both physical and mental illnesses (Cole et Al., 2000; Lopez, 2005), as psychiatric disability often has been viewed as a low priority in the international disability discourse (WHO, 2010a). Although there is little in the literature that presents a comprehensive picture of globally significant disability and rehabilitation issues, this study offers a foundation for comparative and aggregate transnational research efforts.

Evidentiary Concerns

At the time of preparing this chapter, several sources (e.g., Officer & Groce, 2009; WHO, 2007b) report that WHO and World Bank had been in the process of preparing what promises to be an important text, the *World Report on Disability and Rehabilitation* (Officer et al., 2011). The effort is largely a response to the reality that "There is no global document that compiles and analyses [*sic*] the way countries have developed policies and the responses to address the needs of people with disabilities" (WHO, n.d., I. Background and justification magnitude, para. 3).

The conception for the project was the outcome of the World Health Assembly's Resolution 58.23, of May 2005, regarding the provision *Disability, Including Prevention, Management and Rehabilitation*; the result was a request that the WHO "produce a World report on disability based on the best available scientific evidence" (WHO, n.d., I. Background and justification magnitude, para. 3). For the first time, a report will be available to the public that comprehensively outlines the evidence-based information regarding disability issues from an international perspective.

According to a WHO update (2007b, Box 1: Key messages) about the project, the report has been organized to convey the following key messages: (1) Full and effective participation and inclusion of PWDs in society is essential and within reach; (2) Disability is a human rights issue; (3) Poverty is a cause and effect of disability; (4) Disability affects entire families; (5) Disability is an economic development issue (particularly in low-resource countries); (6) Disability is likely to affect most people at some time in their lives; (7) Disability is a continuum of experience, which varies across the life span; (8) Disability is difficult to define, it is varied, multidimensional, cross-cutting, and complex; (9) Primary prevention needs to be balanced with respect for the integrity of people with disabilities; (10) (Re)habilitation is important; (11) Evidence on what works is presented, it needs to be used, and much remains to be done. Although the report is not yet available to the public at the time that this chapter was written, plans are underway for its official launch (A. Officer, personal communication, August 31, 2010), and the editors anticipate a launch date of June 9, 2011 (WHO, 2010d).

Contextual Factors

Gross inequalities in health care exist among the nations of the world (Marmot, 2005). The reality of so many PWDs throughout the world living in poverty underscores the numerous avoidable health inequities that punctuate the experience of so many PWDs. The notion of *social determinants of health* is an internationally accepted public health concept (Labonté, 2008). WHO's Commission on Social Determinants of Health (CSDH) has identified many contextual factors as social determinants of health and has advanced the following three overarching recommendations and aligned principles of action:

1. Improve the conditions of daily life—the circumstances in which people are born, grow, live, work, and age.

2. Tackle the inequitable distribution of power, money, and resources—the structural drivers of those conditions of daily life—globally, nationally, and locally.
3. Measure the problem, evaluate action, expand the knowledge base, develop a workforce that is trained in the social determinants of health, and raise public awareness about the social determinants of health (CSDH, 2008, p. 2).

The work of the CSDH has informed the discourse on social determinants of health and health inequities, advocating for less focus on individual behavioral change and greater emphasis on nurturing the conditions for health and well-being (Baum, 2008; Baum & Fisher, 2010; Levers, Magweva, & Mpofu, 2007; Springett, Whitelaw, & Dooris, 2010).

Culture.   Nurturing the social conditions that promote health and well-being has everything to do with culture. As noted by Mpofu and Harley (2002), "Conceptions of disability vary widely across societies, and are influenced by the unique sociopolitical and cultural histories of those societies" (p. 26). Yet, the biomedical model of disability and rehabilitation historically has ignored the relevance of local culture in general, and on an international scale, the importance of indigenous knowledge in particular. In terms of cultural understanding, RC education programs have begun to address this by a greater emphasis on including multicultural and diversity issues in the curriculum. In terms of the importance of acknowledging indigenous knowledge, researchers and scholars have begun to examine disability issues within their relevant cultural frameworks (e.g., Berman, 2009; Dalal, n.d.; Durie, 2004; Kakati, Ao, & Doulo, 2006; Levers, 2006a, 2006b, 2006c; Levers & Maki, 1994, 1995; Mpofu & Harley, 2002; Subrick, 2006).

Indigenous knowledge and ethnorehabilitation.   In their inquiry of African traditional healing and indigenous knowledge, Levers and Maki (1994) have proposed consideration for advancing the concept of *ethnorehabilitation* and have advocated for its further examination by suggesting the following:

> Ethnorehabilitation is an eco-systemic, praxeological construct which acknowledges the comprehensive nature of persons with disabilities through functional relationship to their respective cultures and in person/community-appropriate interaction with their environments. It seeks to establish a holistic prescription for a quality of life which entails consideration of biomedical, psychological, personal-social, educational, and vocational dimensions through spiritual dialectics at the individual, familial, community, and cultural levels. This view simultaneously permits a holistic and ecologic perspective which is vertically attentive to the spiritual dimensions of the person and horizontally reflective of the environmental dialectic. It argues for a culturally specific sensitivity to the individual/environmental confluence. It is embedded in the temporal reality of the person's existence and draws meaning from the multiple dimensions of the person/community interface. (Levers & Maki, 1994, p. 86)

Levers and Maki have indicated further that it is only when ethical respect is paid to the person that this perspective can be measured, and the result is a philosophy of empowerment. Mostly, PWDs live in low-resource areas of the world, thereby necessitating reliance on indigenous knowledge systems and traditional healing practices, an issue largely ignored by the Western, biomedically oriented community (Levers, 2006c; Levers, Radomsky, & Shefer, 2009).

Emerging Trends in the International Literature

A number of global trends emerged in the disability and rehabilitation literature. The most salient are highlighted and discussed in the following sections: (1) poverty, (2) trauma, crisis, and disaster, (3) HIV and AIDS, (4) psychosocial issues across the lifespan, and (5) international development.

Poverty

Social protection systems differ greatly in high-resource (developed) versus low-resource (developing) countries. As indicated previously, this has led to numerous avoidable health and other life inequities. The association between poverty and disability is complex (Levers et al., 2007, 2008, 2010), as are the data that are linked to this intricate situation (Braithwaite & Mont, 2009).

Given that approximately 10% of the world's population has some form of disability, Handicap International (2006) reports that an estimated 82% of all PWDs live below the poverty line. According to the World Bank's estimates (as cited in Laurin-Bowie, 2005), PWDs account for as many as one in five of the world's poorest people, suggesting that about 260 million (43%) of the estimated 1.3 billion people globally who are living on less than US$1 per day have a disability.

Social systems often overlook PWDs, and current thinking suggests that it is preferable, more efficient, more cost effective, and less stigmatizing to include PWDs in mainstream programs from the onset (Braithwaite & Mont, 2009; Groce & Trani, 2009). In addition, social and economic exclusion typically does not affect the individual alone; rather, it results in high economic dependency on family members and relatives. People living with disabilities face enormous barriers to obtaining equitable services and opportunities. This phenomenon primarily is due to a combination of stigma, ignorance, discrimination, exclusion, and inaccessible environments. The ways in which poverty and disability interface with and reinforce one another not only negate the rights of PWDs, but also perpetuate vulnerability and advance the vicious cycle of poverty (Handicap International, 2006).

Trauma, Crisis, and Disaster

According to WHO (cited in UNICEF, n.d.), up to 25% of disabilities are the result of injuries and violence. The UNICEF fact sheet states that "Persons with disabilities are more likely to be victims of violence or rape, according to a 2004 British study, and less likely to obtain police intervention, legal protection or preventive care" (UNICEF, Violence, para. 3). In warfare, three children are injured and permanently disabled for every one child killed (UNICEF). Research further indicates that the annual rate of violence against children with disabilities is at least 1.7 times greater than for their peers who are not disabled (UNICEF). Kett and van Ommeren (2009) emphasize the lack of inclusion concerning PWDs and disability issues in trauma-response efforts, particularly situations of armed conflict, disasters, and other emergencies. They also point to the fact that local disabled people's organizations (DPOs) seldom are included in the planning and coordination of crisis responses.

HIV and AIDS

A UN AIDS (2009) web site reported that approximately 33.4 million people worldwide were living with HIV and AIDS in 2008. The pandemic has strained fragile health care systems throughout the world, and although there are resources available to respond to the AIDS crisis, they have been woefully inadequate to meet the needs. Recent data from the United Nations Development Program [UNDP] (2010) indicate that human development has improved in many nations; however, gains have been uneven, and in many developing countries, the effects of HIV and AIDS have shortened actual life expectancy.

Various sources have detailed the disabling effects of HIV and AIDS on the lives of people who contract the virus (e.g., Hanass-Hancock, 2009; Levers, 2006a, 2006b; McReynolds & Garske, 2001), and researchers at Yale University (n.d.), with the World Bank, have conducted a Global Disability Survey to further assess the impact (according to the website, data collection recently concluded). However, perhaps the most salient issue to report here regards the risk of HIV infection for PWDs and the reality that they largely have been ignored by prevention and care services (Levers et al., 2010; World Bank, 2004). Groce (2003) has captured the essence of the problem in the following statement: "Although AIDS researchers have studied the disabling effects of HIV/AIDS on previously healthy people, little attention has been given to the risk of HIV/AIDS for individuals who have a physical, sensory, intellectual, or mental health disability before becoming infected" (p. 1401). It appears that PWDs largely have not been included in outreach efforts due to the stereotype that they are not sexually active, and therefore, not at risk (Groce; World Bank). This fact has obvious and dire implications.

Psychosocial Issues Across the Lifespan

Psychosocial issues, both related and not related to disability, have an impact on PWDs across the lifespan. These are discussed briefly, in global perspective, in the following sections.

Gender. In many developing countries, females report higher incidences of disability than males (UNICEF, n.d.). In addition, females with disabilities typically experience stigma on multiple levels, that is, exclusion due to both gender and disability. Women and girls are particularly vulnerable to maltreatment and abuse. According to the UNICEF fact sheet, a small 2004 survey in India "found that virtually all of the women and girls with disabilities were beaten at home, 25% of women with intellectual disabilities had been raped and 6% of disabled women had been forcibly sterilized" (UNICEF, Overview, para. 9). These findings are consistent with assessments carried out in other developing countries (e.g., Levers, 2006a; Levers & Magweva, 2005; Levers et al., 2008, 2010; Levers, Kamanzi, Mukamana, Pells, & Bhusumane, 2006). Further, gender-related rites of passage across the lifespan—for instance, dating, courtship, marriage, and childbirth—may pose additional challenges for both male and female PWDs.

Children and youth. Although comparative studies of childhood disabilities exist (e.g., Gottlieb, Maenner, Cappa, & Durkin, 2009; Mpofu, 2003), they tend to focus on a cluster of countries or a region, offering little comprehensive information regarding childhood disability issues. Trani (2009) asserts the importance of early screening of children for disabilities.

According to the United Kingdom's Department for International Development, "Mortality for children with disabilities may be as high as 80% in countries where under-5 mortality as a whole has decreased below 20% . . . [and] in some cases it seems as if children are being 'weeded out'" (cited in UNICEF, n.d., Overview, para. 11). Such apprehension begs the question of disability-related infanticide. While a full discussion of this complex issue is beyond the scope of this chapter, in a UNICEF-sponsored report on violence against children with disabilities, Groce and Paeglow (2005) have asserted that infanticide (done immediately or soon after birth) and "mercy killings" (done at a later time after birth, sometimes years later) continue to be global manifestations of violence against children with disabilities. Like information regarding other childhood disability issues, there are little comprehensive data concerning infanticide on an international level.

Education. According to UNESCO, about 98% of children living with disabilities in developing countries do not attend school (cited in ILO, 2009), and approximately 30% of street youths are disabled (UNICEF, n.d.). The UNICEF fact sheet reports that in some developing countries, disability rates are significantly higher among groups with lower educational levels, and that, "On average, 19% of less educated people have disabilities, compared to 11% among the better educated" (UNICEF, Overview, para. 5). Based on a 1998 UNDP study (cited in UNICEF, Education, para. 2), UNICEF reports that "The global literacy rate for adults with disabilities is as low as 3% and 1% for women with disabilities." Assessment (Gottlieb et al., 2009), early intervention (Gottlieb et al., 2009), and access to assistive technology (Borg, Lindström, & Larsson, 2009) are linked with the issue of education and disability.

Work. The International Labour Organization (ILO, 2007, 2009) reports that PWDs face higher unemployment rates and lower earnings than persons without disabilities; they often are excluded and marginalized, being particularly vulnerable during times of economic crisis. Although unemployment rates vary among the types of disabilities, the highest rates tend to exist among those persons having psychiatric disabilities (ILO, 2007). Men with disabilities are nearly twice as likely as women with disabilities to have gainful employment (ILO, 2007).

Clearly, if work conditions are conducive, supportive, and adaptive, PWDs have proven that they can contribute and produce at all levels (ILO, 2007, 2009; Shrey & Hursh, 1999). Yet a prevalent bias is that workers with disabilities cost employers extra money, when in reality, their exclusion from the workplace "deprives societies of an estimated US$1.37–1.94 trillion in annual loss in GDP" (ILO, 2007, Facts on disability in the world of work, para. 1). Assistive technology clearly has implications in this arena (Borg et al., 2009), and greater access is needed. Some of the international donor and nongovernmental organizations (NGOs) have begun to implement income-generation projects among PWDs, but real employment opportunities in the governmental and private sectors have been slow to emerge.

Aging. A number of contemporary issues face aging populations around the world, and this has implications for RCs (Dixon, Richard, & Rollins, 2003). According to the United Nations (n.d.), in higher-resource countries where life expectancies are over age 70, people spend an average of about 8 years, or 11.5% of the lifespan, living with disabilities. Regardless of the geopolitical advantages of living in a high- versus low-resource country, most people surviving to an older age are likely to experience increasing disability in their elder years (Robine & Michel, 2004). Sabat (2009) reports, for example, that dementia is on the rise in developing countries, and Sousa et al. (2009) note the increase of dementia and the contribution of other chronic diseases to disability in elderly people in both low- and middle-income countries.

Economic Development

Officer and Groce (2009, p. 1795) assert that "Disability is a neglected development issue," and PWDs, for the most part, have not benefited from international economic development efforts (Kuipers, 2009). As indicated previously in this chapter, PWDs are disproportionately underrepresented in the development arena, universally, in relationship to their poverty; they also tend to be poorer than people without disabilities (Metts, 2004). MacLachlan and Swartz (2009) advocate for greater inclusion of PWDs in international development efforts.

USEFUL PRACTICES

Trends in the international disability and rehabilitation literatures have raised many important issues, concerns, and challenges; these have been outlined, very briefly, in the preceding. As noted, data are not sufficient and the need for more research related to disability and rehabilitation interventions in an international context is great; therefore, it is difficult to identify *best practices* in the sense that usually is intended in the behavioral and social sciences. However, in terms of the salient issues that have emerged from the relevant international literatures, it is possible to identify several *useful practices* that have real implications for RCs and that hold promise for further examination. These useful practices are discussed briefly in the following sections: (1) rights-based approach, (2) community-based rehabilitation, (3) professional training, (4) web resource access, and (5) research.

Rights-Based Approach

The rights-based approach fortunately has replaced the charity model. The CSDH has emphasized the relevance of Article 25(a) of the United Nations Universal Declaration on Human Rights (UN, 1948, cited in CSDH, 2008, p. 84):

> Everyone has the right to a standard of living adequate for the health and well-being of himself and of his family, including food, clothing, housing and medical care and necessary social services, and the right to security in the event of unemployment, sickness, disability, widowhood, old age or other lack of livelihood in circumstances beyond his control.

The core principles of the UN Convention on the Rights of Persons with Disability (CRPD) include respect for all aspects of human dignity and participation; rights related to equal access to health care are found in separate disability- and rehabilitation-related articles. Additional articles of the CRPD deal with the special needs of women and children with disabilities, as well as with issues of accessibility, mobility, and the responsibilities of the professionals providing care to PWDs, among others. To date, some 143 nation-states have signed, and 71 have ratified the CRPD (Stein et al., 2009).

Clearly, in the international arena disability is viewed as an issue of human rights and social justice. Although this obviously is significant, rights alone do not provide the immediate solution to problems of poverty such as lack of food, shelter, and employment. A tension exists between *human rights* in idealist abstraction, and *human rights* in terms of the pragmatic and concrete reality of everyday needs, and this is articulated by PWDs the world over. Social justice must inform the discourse, and social justice *action* must mediate the results related to fully realizing the rights-based approach. For example, while social justice advocacy for equity is essential, PWDs and DPOs assert that it must be followed by action that leads to ensuring that concrete needs are met, like food and shelter. As noted previously in this chapter, some African consumers of rehabilitation services clearly have echoed this sentiment: "We do not eat rights" (Levers et al., 2010, p. 119).

Community-Based Rehabilitation

First introduced by WHO in the late 1970s, community-based rehabilitation (CBR) has been influenced greatly by PWDs and DPOs as it has developed over the last several decades. According to WHO (2010a, para. 1), CBR "has evolved to become a multisectoral strategy that empowers persons with disabilities to access and benefit from education, employment, health and social services," and its scope has broadened significantly over the last 30 years (WHO, 2010b). Much more than an intervention, CBR is a system of care and service delivery that has involved all relevant stakeholders in the community, including PWDs and their families. Regarded as a general strategy for community development of rehabilitation, CBR has positively affected PWDs' social inclusion as well as equalizing opportunities. Major aims of CBR have included enhancing the quality of life for PWDs and their families and ensuring that basic needs are met in least restrictive environments. As noted by Hartley, Finkenflugel, Kuipers, and Thomas (2009), CBR's goals are to "support access to regular services and opportunities and assist people with disabilities to actively contribute to their own communities as well as encouraging communities to promote and respect their human rights" (p. 1803).

WHO (2010b) recently published guidelines for CBR, including a matrix that covers the five components of health, education, livelihood, social dimension, and empowerment. The information is presented in seven separate booklets, which are available online. The seven booklets include an introduction, examinations of the five components, and a supplementary booklet that focuses on specific issues that have been overlooked, to date, in most CBR programs (i.e., mental health, HIV and AIDS, leprosy, and humanitarian crises). Hartley et al. (2009) report that the WHO guidelines and matrix also reflect critiques of CBR and are aimed at improving the implementation and efficacy of CBR. Although more rigorous research needs to be conducted in this area, CBR shows great promise, especially as it relates to efficacy, and is associated with positive social outcomes.

Professional Training

The preservice training of RCs and other rehabilitation personnel is critical to the enhancement of understanding disability and rehabilitation issues in a global context (Shakespeare, Iezzoni, & Groce, 2009), and a number of examples can be found in the literature. Astramovich and Pehrsson (2009) have promoted the advancement of counselor education, in general, as a means for fostering international perspectives. Stein et al. (2009) have suggested that disability be included with other diversity issues in training programs. Wilson, Henry, Sayles, Senices, and Smith (2003) have suggested that multicultural counseling competencies are imperative to training vocational counselors to meet the demands of globalized understandings of disability. Some academics have espoused the utility of international exchanges of rehabilitation scholars (e.g., Fabian & Madsen, 2007) and cross-cultural field exchanges for rehabilitation students (e.g., Luecking, Cuozzo, McInerney, Cury, & Lorca, 2007) as mechanisms for training RCs about the importance of global context. A special issue of *Rehabilitation Education* (Nemec, Spaniol, & Dell Orto, 2001) was devoted to the necessity of training counselors in psychiatric rehabilitation. Finally, Tingey, Millington, and Graham (2007) have recommended a communities-of-practice approach to training RCs;

"communities of practice" is a term that has been borrowed from social learning theory and here refers to building an evidence-based theory of shared knowledge and practice among RCs. Advancing quality preservice and in-service training for rehabilitation personnel is an essential practice and is important in enhancing service delivery for and with PWDs throughout the world.

Web Resource Access

A UNICEF publication (n.d., Overview, para. 13) notes that in the United Kingdom, "75% of the companies of the FTSE 100 Index on the London Stock Exchange do not meet basic levels of web accessibility, thus missing out on more than $147 million in revenue." Web accessibility for PWDs is a growing concern. The *W3C Web Accessibility Initiative* (W3C WAI, 2010) offers strategies, guidelines, and resources to make the Web accessible to PWDs. Tim Berners-Lee, W3C Director and inventor of the World Wide Web, has stated that "The power of the Web is in its universality. Access by everyone regardless of disability is an essential aspect" (W3C WAI, column 1, text block 3).

Research

The unmet health and rehabilitation needs of PWDs worldwide are open for inquiry. For example, Stein et al. (2009, p. 1797) suggest that more "research is required on how disability affects relative access to health care and medical outcomes"; Salvador-Carulla and Saxena (2009) have identified a research gap between intellectual disability and other neuropsychiatric disorders. While publications such as the *ICF* (WHO, 2001), *The Global Burden of Disease* (Murray & Lopez, 1996), and the *World Report on Disability* (Officer et al., 2011) make the need obvious for robust epidemiological and statistical analyses, Hanley-Maxwell, Al Hano, and Skivington (2007) and Levers (2001) suggest that qualitative and ethnographic understandings of the lived experiences of PWDs and in-depth examinations of disability-related phenomena also are essential in the global context of rehabilitation. Community-based research with indigenous populations with disabilities such as Native American Indians (Marshall et al., 2002), or with indigenous practitioners such as African traditional healers (Levers, 2006c), can yield important information that informs the cross-cultural discourse. Tomlinson et al. (2009) have suggested that, because accurate information about the health patterns of PWDs is inadequate, and in light of the scarcity of resources, disability-related research should be systematically prioritized and involve relevant stakeholders.

CONCLUSION

In this chapter, the reader has been introduced to germane disability and rehabilitation issues, in global context, especially as these have related to defining disability, the scope of rehabilitation counseling in an international context, theoretical perspectives on disability, the role of RCs, the international disability and rehabilitation literatures, and useful practices. A number of available, recently published, and soon-to-be-published resources have been identified concerning disability and rehabilitation in an international context. Additional useful resources are listed in Box 9.1.

A dearth of evidence concerning global disability and rehabilitation issues exists and only begins to link to the lived experiences and needs of people with disabilities. There is a great deal of work yet to be done at the international level that calls for our attention. Several pertinent recommendations can be derived from this discussion; hopefully, these might be taken under consideration for future action by RCs, educators, and researchers in reference to international disability issues.

First, the issue of advocacy merits further consideration. RCs can advocate for improvements for PWDs in terms of infrastructural access, access to services, and, especially in the 21st century, access to Web resources. RCs can advocate for continual reinforcement of the rights-based approach, for poverty mitigation efforts, and for expanded global ways of applying the ecological model. RCs are positioned to advocate for greater professionalization opportunities within the field, especially related to preservice and in-service training, while at the same time understanding that indigenous knowledge systems may offer culturally relevant sources of information as well.

Second, the number of PWDs is growing worldwide, in both low- and high-resource countries. Issues such as poverty, diseases such as HIV and AIDS, illnesses such as psychiatric disabilities, and lifespan conditions such as aging, along

---

BOX 9.1: INTERNET RESOURCES

International Association of Rehabilitation Professionals (IARP)
http://www.rehabpro.org/

Disability World (Disability World Links: International Organizations)
http://www.disabilityworld.org/links/International_Organizations/

International Disability Alliance
http://www.internationaldisabilityalliance.org/

World Institute on Disability
http://www.wid.org/

World Health Organization, External Sources for Health-related Statistical Information
http://apps.who.int/whosis/database/links/external_links.cfm

ICF Browser
http://apps.who.int/classifications/icfbrowser/

Handbook for Parliamentarians on the Convention on the Rights of Persons with Disabilities
http://www.un.org/disabilities/default.asp?id=212

with circumstances involving trauma, crises, and disasters have a global impact on programming aimed at improving the lives of PWDs and at mitigating the negative impact of barriers. RCs have the expertise to construct new ways of building capacity so that relevant rehabilitation services are available to all who need them.

Third, the importance of disability- and rehabilitation-related training beyond the industrialized West cannot be emphasized enough. A number of evaluations have reported the lack of basic training in developing countries, along with a hunger for more education among the people working in such rehabilitation settings (e.g., Levers et al., 2006, 2008, 2010; Levers & Magweva, 2005; Levers & Maki, 1994, 1995). RCs in high-resource countries need to find ways to share instructional resources with and construct training opportunities for colleagues in low-resource countries. RCs can support related endeavors through service learning, volunteerism, and grant writing activities.

Finally, the paucity of research related to international disability and rehabilitation issues illuminates the need for inquiry that is pertinent to the lives of PWDs and the systems that serve them. RCs have a nearly open field for identifying important issues and pursuing research agendas that can contribute to the expansion of thinking and the increased understandings of related global issues.

In summary, although little has been written about international disability issues from a comprehensive perspective, we know that a number of avoidable inequities continue to have deleterious effects on the lives of children and adults living with disabilities. RCs, in all of our international and cultural permutations, have the opportunity and the responsibility to assist PWDs to empower themselves. We also have the opportunity and the responsibility to contribute to the international knowledge base in ways that continue to close the disability-related gaps—gaps in knowledge, practice, service delivery, social justice, and equity—in the global context.

CONTENT REVIEW QUESTIONS

■ How does culture play a role in understanding disability issues on an international scale?

■ How does the *International Classification of Functioning and Health* (ICF) model of rehabilitation differ from the more traditional medical model? Why is this significant?

■ In what ways does the role of the rehabilitation counselor (RC) enhance opportunities for people with disabilities globally, and in what ways can RCs serve in an advocacy capacity for global disability concerns? Why does this matter?

■ What roles do international organizations such as the World Health Organization (WHO) and the United Nations (UN) play in advancing disability issues throughout the world? Why is this important?

- In what ways does a more ecologically oriented model of rehabilitation universally support the rights-based approach and the community-based rehabilitation (CBR) approach? How does this relate to equity and social justice?
- What kinds of training experiences can help prepare RCs for international work?

REFERENCES

Agency for Healthcare Research and Quality. (2009a). *2009 National healthcare disparities report*. AHRQ Publication No. 10-0004. Rockville, MD: U.S. Department of Health and Human Services. Retrieved from http://www.ahrq.gov/qual/nhdr09/nhdr09.pdf

Agency for Healthcare Research and Quality. (2009b). *2009 National healthcare quality report*. AHRQ Publication No. 10-0003. Rockville, MD: U.S. Department of Health and Human Services. Retrieved from http://www.ahrq.gov/qual/nhqr09/nhqr09.pdf

Astramovich, R. L., & Pehrsson, D.-E. (2009). Advancing counselor education: Fostering international perspectives and open access scholarship. *Journal for International Counselor Education, 1*, 1–6. Retrieved from http://digitalcommons.library.unlv.edu/jice

Baum, F. (2008). The Commission on the Social Determinants of Health: Reinventing health promotion for the twenty-first century? *Critical Public Health, 18*, 457–466. doi:10.1080/09581590802443612

Baum, F., & Fisher, M. (2010). Health equity and sustainability: Extending the work of the Commission on the Social Determinants of Health. *Critical Public Health, 20*, 311–322. doi:10.1080/09581596.2010.503266

Berg, K., Finne-Soveri, H., Gray, L., Henrard, J. C., Hirdes, J., Ikegami, N., . . . Teare, G. (2009). Relationship between interRAI HC and the *ICF*: Opportunity for operationalizing the *ICF*. *BMC Health Services Research, 9.* doi:10.1186/1472-6963-9-47. Retrieved from http://www.ncbi.nlm.nih.gov/pmc/articles/PMC2666676/

Berman, N. (2009). Negotiating local knowledge: Networking disability on the community level. *Disability Studies Quarterly, 29(4)*. Retrieved from http://www.dsq-sds.org/article/view/967/1176

Besley, T., Burgess, R., & Rasul, I. (2003). *Benchmarking government provision of social safety nets. Social protection discussion paper series, No. 0315*. Washington, DC: The World Bank.

Borg, J., Lindström, A., & Larsson, S. (2009). Assistive technology in developing countries: National and international responsibilities to implement the Convention on the Rights of Persons with Disabilities. *Lancet, 374*, 1863–1865.

Braithwaite, J., & Mont, D. (2009). Disability and poverty: A survey of World Bank. ALTER. *European Journal of Disability Research, 3*, 219–232. Retrieved from http://siteresources.worldbank.org/DISABILITY/Resources/280658-1239044853210/5995073-1246917324202/braithwaite_and_mont_final_pub_version_ALTER57.pdf

Bruyère, S., VanLooy, S., & Peterson, D. (2005). The International Classification of Functioning, Disability and Health (*ICF*): Contemporary literature overview. *Rehabilitation Psychology, 50(2)*, 113–121.

Bureau of Labor Education. (2001, Summer). *The U.S. health care system: Best in the world, or just the most expensive?* The University of Maine, Orono, Maine. Retrieved from http://dll.umaine.edu/ble/U.S.%20HCweb.pdf

Bureau of Labor Statistics. (2010). Counselors. *Occupational outlook handbook, 2010-11 Edition*. Retrieved from http://www.bls.gov/oco/ocos067.htm

Bhusumane, D.-B. (2007). *Mechanisms of indigenous counseling in Botswana*. Unpublished doctoral dissertation, Duquesne University.

Cole, B., Kane, C., Killeen, M., Mohr, W., Nield-Anderson, L., & Kurlowicz, L. (2000, April). *Responding to the global urden of disease*. International Society of Psychiatric-Mental

Health Nurses White Paper. Retrieved from http://www.ispn-psych.org/docs/4-00Global-Burden.pdf

Commission on Rehabilitation Counselor Certification. (2010). About CRC Certification. Retrieved from http://www.crccertification.com/pages/aboutcertification/46.php

Commission on Social Determinants of Health. (2008). *Closing the gap in a generation: Health equity through action on the social determinants of health.* Final Report of the Commission on Social Determinants of Health. Geneva, Switzerland: World Health Organization.

Cook, A. L., Lei, A., & Chiang, D. (2010). Counseling in China: Implications for counselor education preparation and distance learning instruction. *Journal for International Counselor Education, 2,* 60–73. Retrieved from http://digitalcommons.library.unlv.edu/jice

Dalal, A. K. (n.d.). *Disability rehabilitation in a traditional Indian society.* Retrieved from www.aifo.it/english/resources/online/apdrj/selread102/dalal.doc

DePoy, E. G., & Gilson, S. F. (2011). *Studying disability: Multiple theories and responses.* Thousand Oaks, CA: Sage.

Dixon, C. G., Richard, M., & Rollins, C. W. (2003). Contemporary issues facing aging Americans: Implications for rehabilitation and mental health counseling. *Journal of Rehabilitation, 69*(2), 5–12.

Durie, M. (2004). Understanding health and illness: Research at the interface between science and indigenous knowledge. *International Journal of Epidemiology, 33,* 1138–1143. doi:10.1093/ije/dyh250

Editorial: Disability: beyond the medical model. [Editorial]. (2009). *Lancet, 374,* 1793.

Fabian, E. S., & Madsen, M. K. (2007). International exchange in disability and social inclusion: American educators' perspectives. *Journal of Rehabilitation Counseling, 38*(3), 12–17.

Frain, M. P., Bishop, M., & Bethel, M. (2010). A roadmap for rehabilitation counseling to serve military veterans with disabilities. *Journal of Rehabilitation, 76*(1), 13–21.

Gottlieb, C. A., Maenner, M. J., Cappa, C., & Durkin, M. S. (2009). Child disability screening, nutrition, and early learning in 18 countries with low and middle incomes: Data from the third round of UNICEF's Multiple Indicator Cluster Survey (2005–06). *Lancet, 374,* 1821–1830.

Groce, N. E. (2003). HIV/AIDS and people with disability. Lancet, *26,* 1401–1402.

Groce, N. E., & Paeglow, C. (2005, July). *Summary report: Violence against disabled children.* UN Secretary General's Report on Violence against Children, Thematic Group on Violence against Disabled Children, Findings and Recommendations, Convened by UNICEF at the United Nations, New York, NY. Retrieved from http://www.unicef.org/videoaudio/PDFs/UNICEF_Violence_Against_Disabled_Children_Report_Distributed_Version.pdf

Groce, N. E., & Trani, J.-F. (2009). Millennium Development Goals and people with disabilities. *Lancet, 374,* 1800–1801.

Hanass-Hancock, J. (2009). Disability and HIV/AIDS–a systematic review of literature on Africa. *Journal of the International AIDS Society, 12*(34). doi:10.1186/1758-2652-12-34

Handicap International. (2006). *Annual report 2006 Handicap International.* Retrieved from http://en.handicapinternational.be/download/Annual_report_HI_2006_Eng.pdf

Hanley-Maxwell, C., Al Hano, I., & Skivington, M. (2007). Qualitative research in rehabilitation counseling. *Rehabilitation Counseling Bulletin, 50*(2), 99–110.

Hartley, S., Finkenflugel, H., Kuipers, P., & Thomas, M. (2009). Community-based rehabilitation: Opportunity and challenge. *Lancet, 374,* 1803–1804.

Henderson, R. H. (1996). Foreward to the global burden of disease and injury series. In C. J. L. Murray & A. D. Lopez (Eds.), *The global burden of disease: A comprehensive assessment of mortality and disability from diseases, injuries, and risk factors in 1990 and projected to 2020.* (pp. xiii–xiv). Cambridge, MA: The Harvard School of Public Health on behalf of the World Health Organization and the World Bank, distributed by Harvard University Press.

Hoskins, W. J., & Thompson, H. C. (2009). *Promoting international counseling identity: The role of collaboration, research, and training.* Vistas 2009. Retrieved from http://counselingoutfitters.com/vistas/vistas_2009_Title.htm

International Labour Organization. (2007, November). *Facts on disability in the world of work*. Retrieved from http://www.ilo.org/wcmsp5/groups/public/---dgreports/---dcomm/documents/publication/wcms_087707.pdf

International Labour Organization. (2009, November). *Facts on disability and decent work*. Retrieved from http://www.ilo.org/wcmsp5/groups/public/---ed_emp/---ifp_skills/documents/publication/wcms_117143.pdf

Kaiser Family Foundation. (2010). *US health care costs*. Retrieved from http://www.kaiseredu.org/Issue-Modules/US-Health-Care-Costs/Background-Brief.aspx

Kakati, L. N., Ao, B., & Doulo, V. (2006). Indigenous knowledge of zootherapeutic use of vertebrate origin by the Ao Tribe of Nagaland. *Journal of Human Ecology, 19*(3), 163–167.

Kett, M., & van Ommeren, M. (2009). Disability, conflict, and emergencies. *Lancet, 374*, 1801–1803.

Kuipers, P. (2009). Disability and international development: Towards inclusive global health. *Lancet, 374*, 1813.

Labonté, R. (2008). Global health in public policy: Finding the right frame? *Critical Public Health, 18*, 467–482.

Laurin-Bowie, C. (2005). Poverty, disability and social exclusion: New strategies for achieving inclusive development. *Journal for Disability and International Development, 2*, 51–56.

Levers, L. L. (2001). Representations of psychiatric disability in fifty years of Hollywood film: An ethnographic content analysis. *Theory and Science, 2*(2). Retrieved from http://theoryandscience.icaap.org/content/vol002.002/lopezlevers.html

Levers, L. L. (2006a, April). *Report on the need for trauma counseling in post-genocide Rwanda*. A report prepared for the Kigali Health Institute (KHI), Republic of Rwanda.

Levers, L. L. (2006b). Samples of indigenous healing: The path of good medicine. *International Journal of Disability, Development and Education, 54*, 479–488.

Levers, L. L. (2006c). Traditional healing as indigenous knowledge: Its relevance to HIV/AIDS in southern Africa and the implications for counselors. *Journal of Psychology in Africa, 16*, 87–100.

Levers, L. L., Kamanzi, D., Mukamana, D., Pells, K., & Bhusumane, D.-B. (2006). Addressing urgent community mental health needs in Rwanda: Culturally sensitive training interventions. *Journal of Psychology in Africa, 16*, 261–272.

Levers, L. L., & Magweva, F. I. (2005, March). *Report on a national rehabilitation plan and training programme*. Windhoek, Namibia: Ministry of Lands, Resettlement, and Rehabilitation (Government of the Republic of Namibia).

Levers, L. L., Magweva, F. I., Maundeni, T., & Mpofu, E. (2008). *A report on a comprehensive study of social safety nets for people with disabilities in Botswana*. A study sponsored by the Botswana Ministry of Health, at the request of the Botswana Office of the President. Gaborone, Botswana: Ministry of Health.

Levers, L. L., Magweva, F. I., & Mpofu, E. (2007). Discussion paper 40: A review of district health systems in east and southern Africa: Facilitators and barriers to participation in health. Published online by *Regional Network for Equity in Health in East and Southern Africa* (EQUINET) as an EQUINET Discussion Paper. Retrieved from http://www.equinetafrica.org/bibl/docs/DIS40ehsLOPEZ.pdf

Levers, L. L., Magweva, F. I., & Mufema, E. (2010, March). *Poverty levels among people with disabilities: An evaluation of the need for developing a disability social protection scheme in Zimbabwe*. Final Report to the Terms of Reference Committee Regarding the Consultancy for the National Association of Societies for the Care of the Handicapped (NASCOH), the National Association of Non-Governmental organizations (NANGO), and the Republic of Zimbabwe Ministry of Labour and Social Services (MoLSS). Harare, Zimbabwe: NASCOH.

Levers, L. L., & Maki, D. R. (1994). *An ethnographic analysis of traditional healing and rehabilitation services in southern Africa: Cross cultural implications*. An International Exchange of Experts and Information in Rehabilitation (IEEIR) Research Fellowship Monograph prepared for the World Rehabilitation Fund, National Institute on Disability and Rehabilitation Research, U.S. Dept. of Education, 103 pages. Oklahoma State University, Stillwater, OK: National Clearing House of Rehabilitation Training Materials.

Levers, L. L., & Maki, D. R. (1995). African indigenous healing, cosmology, and existential implications: Toward a philosophy of ethnorehabilitation. *Rehabilitation Education, 9,* 127–145.

Levers, L. L., Radomsky, L., & Shefer, T. (2009). Voices of African traditional healers: Cultural context and implications for the practice of counselling in sub-Saharan Africa. *Journal of Psychology in Africa, 19,* 501–506.

Lopez, A. D. (2005). The evolution of the Global Burden of Disease framework for disease, injury and risk factor quantification: Developing the evidence base for national, regional and global public health action. *Globalization and Health, 1*(5). doi:10.1186/1744-8603-1-5. Retrieved from http://www.globalizationandhealth.com/content/1/1/5

Luecking, R. G., Cuozzo, L., McInerney, C., Cury, S. H. M., & Lorca, M. C. B. C. (2007). Cross cultural field exchange as a rehabilitation professional development experience. *Journal of Rehabilitation Counseling, 38*(3), 18–24.

Lynch, M. F., & Levers, L. L. (2007). Ecological-transactional and motivational perspectives in counseling. In J. Gregoire & C. Jungers (Eds.), *Counselor's companion: Handbook for professional helpers* (pp. 586–605). New York, NY: Earlbaum.

MacLachlan, M., & Swartz, L. (Eds.). (2009). *Disability and international development: Towards inclusive global health.* New York, NY: Springer.

Marmot, M. (2005). Social determinants of health inequalities. *Public Health, 365,* 1099–1104.

Marshall, C. A., Johnson, S. R., Kendall, E., Busby, H., Schacht, R., & Hill, C. (2002, April). Community-based research and American Indians with disabilities: Learning together methods that work. In Work Group on American Indian Research and Program Evaluation Methodology (AIRPEM), *Symposium on research and evaluation methodology: Lifespan issues related to American Indians/Alaska Natives with Disabilities.* Symposium conducted at the meeting of AIRPEM, Washington, DC. Retrieved from http://www.fnbha.org/pdf/AIRPEMMonograph.pdf

Martz, E., Strohmer, D., Fitzgerald, D., Daniel, S., & Arm, J. (2006). Disability prototypes in the United States and the Russian Federation: An international comparison. *Rehabilitation Counseling Bulletin, 53*(1), 16–26.

McReynolds, C. J., & Garske, G. G. (2001). Current issues in HIV disease and AIDS: Implications for health and rehabilitation professionals. *Work: A Journal of Prevention, Assessment and Rehabilitation, 17*(2), 117–124.

Metts, R. (2004). *Disability and development: Background paper prepared for the disability and development research agenda meeting, November 16, 2004.* World Bank Headquarters, Washington, DC. Retrieved from http://siteresources.worldbank.org/DISABILITY/Resources/280658-1172606907476/mettsBGpaper.pdf

Mitra, S. (2004). Viewpoint: Disability—the hidden side of African poverty. *Disability World.* Retrieved November 24, 2009, from http://www.disabilityworld.org/01-03_04/news/africa.shtml

Mitra, S. (2005). Disability and social safety nets in developing countries. Social Protection Discussion Paper Series No. 0509. Social Protection Unit, Human Development Network, World Bank. Retrieved November 26, 2009, from http://www.worldbank.org/sp

Mpofu, E. (2003). Conduct disorder in children: Presentation, treatment options and cultural efficacy in an African setting. *International Journal of Disability, Community & Rehabilitation.* Retrieved from http://www.ijdcr.ca/VOL02_01_CAN/articles/mpofu.shtml

Mpofu, E., & Harley, D. (2002). Rehabilitation in Zimbabwe: Lessons and implications for rehabilitation practice in the United States. *Journal of Rehabilitation, 68*(4), 26–33.

Msimanga-Ramatebele, S. H. (2008). *Lived experiences of widows in Botswana: An ethnographic examination of cultural rituals of death, loss, grief, and bereavement—implications for professional counseling.* Unpublished doctoral dissertation. Duquesne University, Pittsburgh, PA.

Murray, C. J. L., & Lopez, A. D. (Eds.). (1996). *The global burden of disease: A comprehensive assessment of mortality and disability from diseases, injuries, and risk factors in 1990 and projected to 2020.* Cambridge, MA: The Harvard School of Public Health on behalf of the World Health Organization and the World Bank, distributed by Harvard University Press.

Nemec, P. B., Spaniol, L., & Dell Orto, A. E. (2001). Psychiatric rehabilitation education. *Rehabilitation Education, 15*(2), 115–118.

Officer, A. et al. (Eds.). (2011). *World report on disability.* Geneva, Switzerland: World Health Organization.

Officer, A., & Groce, N. E. (2009). Key concepts in disability. *Lancet, 374,* 1795–1796.

Oltman, R., Neises, G., Scheible, D., Mehrtens, G., & Grüneberg, C. (2008). *ICF* components of corresponding outcome measures in flexor tendon rehabilitation—a systematic review. *BMC Musculoskeletal Disorders, 9.* doi:10.1186/1471-2474-9-139. Retrieved from http://www.biomedcentral.com/1471-2474/9/139

O'Sullivan, D., & Strauser, D. R. (2009). Operationalizing self-efficacy, related social cognitive variables, and moderating effects: Implications for rehabilitation research and practice. *Rehabilitation Counseling Bulletin, 52,* 251–258. doi:10.1177/0034355208329356

Pollard, B., Dixon, D., Dieppe, P., & Johnston, M. (2009). Measuring the *ICF* components of impairment, activity limitation and participation restriction: An item analysis using classical test theory and item response theory. *Health and Quality of Life Outcomes, 7.* doi:10.1186/1477-7525-7-41. Retrieved from http://www.hqlo.com/content/7/1/41

Robine, J. M., & Michel, J. P. (2004). Looking forward to a general theory on population aging. *Journal of Gerontology: Medical Sciences, 59A,* 590–597.

Sabat, S. R. (2009). Dementia in developing countries: A tidal wave on the horizon. *Lancet, 374,* 1805–1806.

Salvador-Carulla, L., & Saxena, S. (2009). Intellectual disability: Between disability and clinical nosology. *Lancet, 374,* 1798–1799.

Shakespeare, T., Iezzoni, L., & Groce, N. E. (2009). The art of medicine: Disability and the training of health professionals. *Lancet, 374,* 1815–1816.

Shrey, D. E., & Hursh, N. C. (1999). Workplace disability management: International trends and perspectives. *Journal of Occupational Rehabilitation, 9*(1), 45–59.

Simkiss, D. (2008). The international classification of functioning, disability and health. *Journal of Tropical Pediatrics, 54*(3), 149–150. doi:10.1093/tropej/fmn047

Sousa, R. M., Ferri, C. P., Acosta, D., Albanese, E., Guerra, M., Huang, Y., . . . Prince, M. (2009). Contribution of chronic diseases to disability in elderly people in countries with low and middle incomes: A 10/66 Dementia Research Group population-based survey. *Lancet, 374,* 1821–1830.

Springett, J., Whitelaw, S., & Dooris, M. (2010). Sustainable development, equity and health—time to get radical. *Critical Public Health, 20,* 275–280. doi:10.1080/09581596.2010.502932

Stein, M. A., Stein, P. J. S., Weiss, D., & Lang, R. (2009). Health care and the UN Disability Rights Convention. *Lancet, 374,* 1796–1798.

Steiner, W. A., Ryser, L., Huber, E., Uebelhart, D., Aeschlimann, A., & Stucki, G. (2002). Use of the *ICF* model as a clinical problem-solving tool in physical therapy and rehabilitation medicine. *Physical Therapy, 82,* 1098–1107.

Subrick, R. (2006). AIDS and traditional belief: How an inappropriate AIDS prevention strategy undermined Botswana's health. *International policy network paper.* Retrieved from http://www.policynetwork.net/health/publication/aids-and-traditional-belief

Tingey, K. B., Millington, M. J., & Graham, M. (2007, October). *A communities of practice approach to training and education: Building sociocognitive networks in rehabilitation counseling.* White paper. Logan, UT: National Clearinghouse of Rehabilitation Training Materials.

Tomlinson, M., Swartz, L., Officer, A., Chan, K. Y., Rudan, I., & Saxena, S. (2009). Research priorities for health of people with disabilities: An expert opinion exercise. *Lancet, 374,* 1857–1862.

Trani, J.-F. (2009). Screening children for disability. *Lancet, 374,* 1806–1807.

United Nations. (2000, September 18). *United Nations Millennium Declaration.* Retrieved July 5, 2010, from http://www.un.org/millenniumgoals/bkgd.shtml

United Nations. (2006). *United Nations convention on the rights of persons with disabilities.* Retrieved from http://www.un.org/disabilities/convention/conventionfull.shtml

United Nations. (2007). *Some facts about persons with disabilities,* on the UN Web site, enable! International Convention on the rights of persons with disabilities. Retrieved from http://www.un.org/disabilities/convention/pdfs/factsheet.pdf

United Nations Development Program. (2010, November). *Human development report 2010, The real wealth of nations: Pathways to human development.* 20th Anniversary edition. Retrieved from http://hdr.undp.org/en/media/HDR_2010_EN_Complete.pdf

United Nations International Children's Education Fund (UNICEF). (n.d.). *Voices of youth: Be in the know: Fact sheet.* Retrieved from http://www.unicef.org/explore_3893.html

United Nations Programme on HIV/AIDS. (2009). *Global facts and figures.* Retrieved from http://data.unaids.org/pub/FactSheet/2009/20091124_fs_global_en.pdf

W3C Web Accessibility Initiative. (2010). *W3C: Web accessibility initiative.* http://www.w3.org/WAI/

Weigl, M., Cieza, A., Kostanjsek, N., Kirschneck, M., & Stucki, G. (2006). The *ICF* comprehensively covers the spectrum of health problems encountered by health professionals in patients with musculoskeletal conditions. *Rheumatology, 45,* 1247–1254.

Wilson, K. B., Henry, M. L., Sayles, C. D., Senices, J., & Smith, D. R. (2003). Multicultural counseling competencies in the 21st century: Are vocational rehabilitation counselors primed for the next millennium? *The Journal of the Pennsylvania Counseling Association, 5*(1), 5–18.

World Bank. (2004, November). *At a glance: Disability and HIV/AIDS.* Retrieved from http://globalsurvey.med.yale.edu/Fact%20sheet.pdf

World Health Organization. (1980). *International classification of impairments, disabilities and handicaps* [ICIDH]. Geneva, Switzerland: Author.

World Health Organization. (2001). *International classification of functioning, disability and health* [ICF]. Geneva, Switzerland: Author.

World Health Organization. (2002). *Towards a common language for functioning, disability and health: ICF.* Geneva, Switzerland: Author. Retrieved from http://www.who.int/classifications/icf/training/icfbeginnersguide.pdf

World Health Organization. (2007a). *International classification of disease* (10th ed., ICD-10). Geneva, Switzerland: Author.

World Health Organization. (2007b, April). *WHO world report on disability and rehabilitation update.* UPDATE No. 1. Retrieved from http://siteresources.worldbank.org/DISABILITY/Resources/News---Events/BBLs/20070411WHOissue1.pdf

World Health Organization. (2010a). *Community-based rehabilitation (CBR).* Retrieved from http://www.who.int/disabilities/cbr/en/index.html

World Health Organization. (2010b, October). *Community-based rehabilitation (CBR) guidelines.* Retrieved from http://www.who.int/disabilities/cbr/guidelines/en/index.html

World Health Organization. (2010c). *Concept note: World report on disability and rehabilitation.* Retrieved from http://www.who.int/disabilities/world_report/concept_note_2010.pdf

World Health Organization. (2010d). *Violence and injury prevention and disability: World report on disability.* Retrieved from http://www.who.int/disabilities/world_report/en/index.html

World Health Organization. (n.d.). *Concept note: World report on disability and rehabilitation.* Retrieved from http://www.who.int/disabilities/publications/dar_world_report_concept_note.pdf

Yale University. (n.d.). *HIV/AIDS and global disability survey.* http://globalsurvey.med.yale.edu/

IV
Professional Functions

10

Qualified Providers of Rehabilitation Counseling Services

Michael J. Leahy

LEARNING OBJECTIVES

After reading this chapter, you should be able to:

- Understand how the discipline evolved over time and the specific elements of the discipline that have contributed to the professionalization of practice in rehabilitation counseling.
- Understand the scope of practice for the discipline and how research has provided an evidence-based foundation of the four disciplines in relation to role and function and knowledge requirements.
- Understand how the regulatory mechanisms within the discipline work and how they protect the discipline and the clients served in the rehabilitation process.

Among the various professionals (e.g., physiatrists, psychologists, social workers, and medical case managers) who may provide services to individuals with disabilities during their individual rehabilitation process, the rehabilitation counselor represents a unique professional, who plays a central role in the extra-medical phase of the rehabilitation process, for individuals with both acquired and congenital disabilities (Wright, 1980). Rehabilitation counseling emerged as a full-time occupation over 90 years ago. Unlike the beginnings of other counseling specialties and health-related occupations, rehabilitation counseling was mandated as a specific work role through federal legislation (Smith-Fess Act in 1920), which established the public or state-federal rehabilitation program in the United States. In the years following this landmark legislation, rehabilitation counseling practice in the public and private sectors evolved and expanded to provide a comprehensive array of vocational and independent living services to an ever increasing adult population of persons with a wide range of physical and mental disabilities (Leahy & Szymanski, 1995).

Although the occupational status of rehabilitation counseling was established in the 1920s, it was not until the mid-1950s, with the passage of the 1954 Vocational Rehabilitation Act Amendments, that the discipline embarked on a series of significant ongoing developments (e.g., preservice education, professional associations, code of ethics, and regulation of practice) that have led, over time, to the professionalization of practice in the United States, and to some extent internationally. Although initially a very heterogeneous group of practitioners in terms of educational background and professional competencies, rehabilitation counselors today, as a result of the professionalization process over the past 55 years, represent a group of professionals with a much higher degree of commonalty in relation to preservice preparation, practice, and professional identity than at any previous time in our professional history.

The purpose of this chapter is to review those elements of the discipline that serve to both uniquely identify and provide the foundation for rehabilitation counseling practice in today's health and human services environment. Particular attention will be devoted to discussion of the scope and research-based foundation of practice, the definition of qualified providers, preservice and continuing education, regulation of professional practice (certification and licensure), and professional associations.

SCOPE OF PRACTICE

Rehabilitation counseling has been described as a process in which the counselor works collaboratively with the client to understand existing problems, barriers, and potentials in order to facilitate the effective use of personal and environmental resources for career, personal, social, and community adjustment following disability (Jaques, 1970). In carrying out this multifaceted process, rehabilitation counselors must be prepared to assist individuals with disabilities in adapting to the environment, assist environments in accommodating the needs of the individual, and work toward the full participation of individuals in all aspects of society, with a particular focus on career aspirations (Szymanski, 1985). More recently, the Rehabilitation Counseling Consortium (2005), a relatively new group comprised of the eight major rehabilitation counseling organizations and regulatory bodies, developed the following definition that has been endorsed by all of its member organizations: "A rehabilitation counselor is a counselor who possesses the specialized knowledge, skills and attitudes needed to collaborate in a professional relationship with people who have disabilities to achieve their personal, social, psychological and vocational goals."

Over the years the fundamental role of the rehabilitation counselor has evolved (Jaques, 1970; Rubin & Roessler, 1995; Wright, 1980), with the subsequent functions and required knowledge and skill competencies of the rehabilitation counselor expanding as well. Regardless of variations in their practice setting and client population, most rehabilitation counselors: (1) assess needs, (2) establish a working alliance with the individual to develop goals and individualized plans to meet identified needs, and (3) provide or arrange for the therapeutic services and interventions (e.g., psychological, medical, social, and behavioral), including job placement and follow-up services. Throughout this individualized process, counseling skills are considered essential components of all activities.It is the specialized knowledge of disabilities and of environmental factors that interact with disabilities, as well as the range of knowledge and skills required in addition to counseling that serves to differentiate the rehabilitation counselor from social workers, other types of counselors (e.g., mental health counselors, school counselors, and career counselors), and other rehabilitation practitioners (e.g., vocational evaluators and job placement specialists) in today's service delivery environments (Jenkins, Patterson, & Szymanski, 1992; Leahy & Szymanski, 1995).

In 1994, utilizing the long-standing tradition in rehabilitation counseling research of studying the role and functions of qualified practitioners, an official scope-of-practice statement was developed and adopted by the major professional and regulatory organizations in rehabilitation counseling. This statement, which is consistent with available empirical research, was required to more explicitly identify the scope of practice for the public, clients of services, related professional groups, and regulatory bodies. The official scope-of-practice statement for rehabilitation counseling reads as follows:

> Rehabilitation counseling is a systematic process which assists persons with physical, mental, developmental, cognitive, and emotional disabilities to achieve their personal, career, and independent living goals in the most integrated setting possible through the application of the counseling process. The counseling process involves communication, goal setting, and beneficial growth or change through self-advocacy, psychological, vocational, social, and behavioral interventions. The specific techniques and modalities utilized within this rehabilitation counseling process may include, but are not limited to:
>
> - assessment and appraisal;
> - diagnosis and treatment planning;
> - career (vocational) counseling;
> - individual and group counseling treatment interventions focused on facilitating adjustments to the medical and psychosocial impact of disability;
> - case management, referral, and service coordination;
> - program evaluation and research;
> - interventions to remove environmental, employment, and attitudinal barriers;
> - consultation services among multiple parties and regulatory systems;
> - job analysis, job development, and placement services, including assistance with employment and job accommodations; and
> - the provision of consultation about, and access to, rehabilitationtechnology. (Commission on Rehabilitation Counselor Certification [CRCC], 1994, pp. 1–2)

RESEARCH–BASED FOUNDATION OF PRACTICE

Underlying the practice of any discipline or professional specialty area is the delineation of specific knowledge and skill competencies required for effective service delivery. Job analysis, role and function, professional competency, critical incident, and knowledge-validation research are all terms that describe a process, whereby the professional practice of rehabilitation counseling has been systematically studied to identify and describe important functions and tasks or knowledge and skills associated with the effective delivery of services to individuals with disabilities.

Over the past 50 years, through these various research methods an extensive body of knowledge has been acquired that has empirically identified the specific competencies and job functions important to the practice of rehabilitation counseling. This long-standing emphasis on the development and ongoing refinement of a research-based foundation has served to distinguish rehabilitation counseling from other counseling specialties that are also seeking to define and validate their scope of professional practice. These research efforts have also provided the discipline with evidence of construct validity of rehabilitation counseling knowledge and skill areas (Szymanski, Leahy, & Linkowski, 1993).

Although role and function approaches generally provide an empirically derived description of the functions and tasks associated with the role, the knowledge required to perform these functions is typically more indirectly assessed and inferred on the basis of the described functions and tasks. Roessler and Rubin (1992) in their review of major studies (Emener & Rubin, 1980; Leahy, Shapson, & Wright, 1987; Rubin et al., 1984) concluded that rehabilitation counselors have a diverse role requiring many skills if they are to effectively assist individuals with disabilities improve the quality of their lives. They also concluded that the role of the rehabilitation counselor can be fundamentally described as encompassing the following functions or job task areas: (1) assessment, (2) affective counseling, (3) vocational (career) counseling, (4) case management, and (5) job placement.

Conversely, knowledge validation and professional-competency approaches provide an empirically derived description of the knowledge and skills associated with a particular role, but the actual functions and tasks are more indirectly assessed and inferred on the basis of the knowledge and skills needed by an individual to practice. Recent research by Leahy, Muenzen, Saunders, and Strauser (2009) provided empirical support that the following 12 knowledge domains represent the core knowledge and skill requirements of rehabilitation counselors: (1) individual counseling, (2) group and family counseling, (3) mental health counseling, (4) psychosocial and cultural issues in counseling, (5) career counseling and assessment, (6) job development and placement services, (7) vocational consultation and services for employers, (8) case and caseload management, (9) medical, functional, and environmental aspects of disabilities, (10) foundations, ethics, and professional issues, (11) rehabilitation services and resources, and (12) health care and disability systems. A complete listing of the knowledge domains and subdomains from this study are provided in Table 10.1.

TABLE 10.1
Rehabilitation Counseling Knowledge Domains and Subdomains

Individual Counseling
Individual counseling theories
Individual counseling practices and interventions
Behavior and personality theory
Human growth and development
Multicultural counseling issues related to individual counseling

Group and Family Counseling
Family counseling theories
Family counseling practices and interventions
Group counseling theories
Group counseling practices and interventions
Multicultural counseling issues related to group and family counseling

Mental Health Counseling
Diagnostic and Statistical Manual IV-TR
Rehabilitation techniques for individuals with psychiatric disabilities
Multicultural counseling issues related to mental health counseling
Implications of medications as they apply to individuals with psychiatric disabilities
Dual diagnosis
Substance abuse
Treatment planning
Wellness and illness prevention concepts and strategies

Psychosocial and Cultural Issues in Counseling
Individual and family adjustment to disability
Psychosocial and cultural impact of disability on the individual
Psychosocial and cultural impact of disability on the family
Attitudinal barriers for individuals with disabilities
Societal issues, trends, and developments as they relate to rehabilitation
Working with individuals from various socioeconomic backgrounds
Working with individuals with English as a second language
Gender issues
Human sexuality and disability issues

Career Counseling and Assessment
Theories of career development and work adjustment
Tests and evaluation techniques for assessing clients

(continued)

TABLE 10.1 (*continued*)

Psychometric concepts related to measurement (e.g., reliability, validity, and standard error of measurement)

Interpretation of assessment results for rehabilitation planning purposes

Computer- and Internet-based career resources (e.g., OASYS, O*NET, and Job Accommodation Network [JAN])

Transferable skills analysis

Assistive technology

Job Development and Placement Services

Vocational implications of functional limitations

Job readiness, including seeking and retention skills

Techniques used to conduct labor market surveys

Occupational and labor market information (including but not limited to local/state/national, rural/urban)

Job matching strategies

Employer development for job placement

Employment support services (including but not limited to supported employment, work adjustment, job coaching, on-the-job training, follow up/follow along/job maintenance, and post-employment)

Employment settings (including but not limited to competitive, supported)

Vocational Consultation and Services for Employers

Employer practices that affect the employment or return to work of individuals with disabilities

Marketing rehabilitation services and benefits for employers (including but not limited to financial incentives, federal and state tax credits, and welfare to work credits)

Educating employers on disability-related issues (including but not limited to enhancing workplace culture and environment, Americans with Disabilities Act [ADA] compliance/disability law)

Disability prevention and management strategies

Job analysis and/or job description development

Job modification, accommodation, and restructuring, including ergonomic assessment

Work conditioning or work hardening resources and strategies

Case and Caseload Management

Case management process, including rehabilitation planning, service coordination, and referral to and collaboration with other disciplines

Principles of caseload management, including case recording and documentation

Professional roles, responsibilities, functions, and relationships with clients and other human service providers

Negotiation, mediation, and conflict resolution strategies

Techniques for working effectively in teams and across disciplines

Medical, Functional, and Environmental Aspects of Disabilities

Medical aspects and implications of various disabilities

Medical terminology

Implications of medications as they relate to vocational goals and outcomes

Functional capacities of individuals with physical, psychiatric, and/or cognitive disabilities

Environmental barriers for individuals with disabilities

Rehabilitation terminology and concepts

Foundations, Ethics, and Professional Issues

Philosophical foundations of rehabilitation

Legislation or laws affecting individuals with disabilities

Ethical decision-making models and processes

Ethical standards for rehabilitation counselors

Advocacy for individuals with disabilities

Theories and techniques for providing clinical supervision

Interpretation and application of research findings

Evaluation procedures for assessing the effectiveness of rehabilitation services, programs, and outcomes

Rehabilitation Services and Resources

Financial support/funding resources for rehabilitation services and programs (including but not limited to supported employment, school-to-work, and assistive technology)

Organizations/programs providing rehabilitation services (including but not limited to federal/state/provincial vocational rehabilitation, community-based and private agencies)

Community referral resources and services for rehabilitation planning (including but not limited to support groups, education programs, emergency services, and transportation)

Services available from one-stop career centers

Services available from rehabilitation engineers

Services available through client advocacy programs (including but not limited to Client Assistance Program [CAP] and legal aid)

Programs for specialty populations (including but not limited to school-to-work transition, spinal cord injury, traumatic brain injury, mental health, developmental disability, substance abuse, and correctional)

Forensic rehabilitation services (including but not limited to expert testimony, evaluating earnings capacity and loss, and life-care planning)

(*continued*)

TABLE 10.1 (*continued*)

Health Care and Disability Systems

Managed care concepts (including but not limited to PPO, HMO, POS, provincial/territorial health insurance programs)

Insurance programs (including but not limited to Medicare, Medicaid, group and individual, short- and long-term disability, and personal injury/no-fault liability)

Health care benefits (including but not limited to prescription plans, extended health benefits)

Workers' compensation laws and practices

Social Security programs, benefits, work incentives, and disincentives

Evidence-Based Foundation of Practice

The results of this study (Leahy et al., 2009) provide empirical support for the description of the knowledge base underlying the practice of rehabilitation counseling, and contributes further empirical evidence in relation to the content and construct validity of the knowledge domains identified in this replication and extension of the most recent study completed in 2003 (Leahy, Chan, & Saunders, 2003). Over the past 15 years there have been three, large-scale national research initiatives (Leahy, Szymanski, & Linkowski, 1993; Leahy et al., 2003, 2009) that have identified and defined the specific competencies and job functions important to the practice of rehabilitation counseling and the achievement of positive outcomes with the clients they serve. These last three studies have sampled the same population of interest, and used parallel definitions of variables, research questions, and research instruments. Each successive replication and extension of this line of inquiry has added to the evidence-based foundation of practice (DePalma, 2002) in terms of underlying knowledge dimensions essential for effective rehabilitation counseling. These studies and prior research efforts (e.g., Berven, 1979; Emener & Rubin, 1980; Harrison & Lee, 1979; Jaques, 1959; Leahy et al., 1987; Muthard & Salamone, 1969; Rubin et al., 1984; Wright & Fraser, 1975) have provided the discipline with consistent empirically based evidence of an established and mature discipline that is able to respond appropriately to the evolutionary demands and pressures of a dynamic human service field (Leahy et al., 2009).

Knowledge Translation

In terms of research utilization and knowledge translation, these empirically derived descriptions of the rehabilitation counselor's role, function, and required knowledge and skill competencies have assisted the discipline in a number of important ways. First, they have helped in defining the professional identity of the rehabilitation counselor by empirically defining the uniqueness of the discipline and by providing evidence in support of the construct validity of its knowledge base. Second, the descriptions have been extensively used in the development of preservice educational curricula in order to provide graduate training in areas of knowledge and skill critical to the practice of rehabilitation counseling across major employment settings. Third, the long-standing emphasis on a research-based foundation to practice has greatly contributed to the rehabilitation counseling profession's leadership role in the establishment and ongoing refinement of graduate educational program accreditation through the Council on Rehabilitation Education (CORE), and individual practitioner certification through the Commission on Rehabilitation Counselor Certification (CRCC). Finally, this body of knowledge has also been useful in identifying both the common professional ground (shared competency areas) and the uniqueness of rehabilitation counseling among related rehabilitation disciplines (e.g., vocational evaluators, job placement specialists) and other counseling specialties (e.g., career counselors, school counselors, mental health counselors). This process of further definition in the area of occupational competence is a normal sequence in the professionalization process for any occupation seeking public recognition.

QUALIFIED PROVIDERS

According to the professional associations, qualified providers of rehabilitation counseling services are those professionals who have completed graduate degree training in rehabilitation counseling or a closely related degree program (e.g., counseling) at the master's level, have attained national certification as a Certified Rehabilitation Counselor (CRC), and have acquired the appropriate state licensure (e.g., Licensed Professional Counselor [LPC]) in those states that require this level of credential for counseling practice. As an integral aspect of this professional identity, qualified providers, under this definition, are required to practice rehabilitation counseling within the guidelines and standards of the Code of Professional Ethics for Rehabilitation Counselors (2010) and maintain ongoing professional development through relevant continuing education to maintain and upgrade their knowledge and skills related to practice. In addition to these professional requirements and responsibilities, qualified providers are expected to be a member of a professional association and contribute through professional advocacy to the advancement of the discipline.

There has been a series of studies conducted to investigate the relationship between rehabilitation counselor education and service delivery outcomes that has provided consistent support for the position that rehabilitation counselors, as qualified providers, need to obtain preservice training at the graduate level in rehabilitation counseling or a closely related field prior to practice. Studies of the New York (Szymanski & Parker, 1989), Wisconsin (Szymanski, 1991), Maryland (Szymanski & Danek, 1992), and Arkansas (Cook & Bolton, 1992) state vocational rehabilitation agencies demonstrated that counselors with master's degrees in rehabilitation counseling achieved better outcomes with clients with severe disabilities than did rehabilitation counselors with unrelated master's or bachelor's degrees. In another group of studies involving rehabilitation counselors from a variety of employment settings, preservice education was linked to the rehabilitation counselors' perceived (self-assessed) level of competency. Shapson, Wright, and Leahy (1987) and Szymanski et al. (1993) demonstrated that counselors with master's degrees in rehabilitation counseling perceived themselves to be more competent or better prepared in critical knowledge and skill areas of rehabilitation counseling than did counselors with unrelated preservice preparation (Leahy & Szymanski, 1995).

During the past 35 years, there has been a growing expectation among members of the discipline, employers, and regulatory bodies that rehabilitation counselors who provide services to people with disabilities have the appropriate preservice education and credentials (certification and licensure). Even today, however, there are individuals practicing as rehabilitation counselors in both the public and private rehabilitation sectors in the United States who do not have this type of preservice preparation or appropriate credentials. Although this heterogeneity in professional background was once thought of as a natural consequence of a quickly expanding field, in more recent years the practice of hiring individuals without appropriate professional training and credentials has been heavily criticized by professional, educational, and regulatory bodies in rehabilitation counseling.

One of the key characteristics of any profession is regulation of practice (Rothman, 1987). Individuals who practice rehabilitation counseling outside the discipline are not accountable to or included in such regulation of practice, and are therefore not required to adhere to the discipline's code of ethics or accepted standards of practice. Although this situation has improved over the years, it is still unacceptable. It is clear, however, that in the years to come the trend toward professionalization and particularly the movement toward state licensure and certification in the United States will make it less likely that an individual will be able to practice as a rehabilitation counselor without appropriate training and credentials.

SPECIALIZATION AND RELATED PROVIDERS

Today, a majority of rehabilitation counselors practice in the public, private, and nonprofit rehabilitation sectors. More recently, however, rehabilitation counselors have begun to practice in independent living centers, employee assistance programs, hospitals, clinics, mental health organizations, public school transition programs, and employer-based disability prevention and management programs. Although setting-based factors may affect the relative emphasis or importance of various rehabilitation counselor functions or may introduce new specialized knowledge requirements for the rehabilitation counselor, there remains a great deal of communality in the role and function among rehabilitation counselors regardless of practice setting (Leahy et al., 1987, 1993, 2003, 2009). One aspect that is often affected by these various settings is the specific job title used by the rehabilitation counselor. While the rehabilitation counselor job title is used in the majority of settings, one can also find the use of the title rehabilitation consultant or case manager among today's rehabilitation counselors in practice. In addition, as one advances up the career ladder within these various settings, rehabilitation counselors can assume supervisory, management, and administrative roles within these various organizations.

Although the majority of rehabilitation counselors are viewed as generalists, another aspect of variation among practicing rehabilitation counselors is the degree to which they specialize their practice. One particularly useful model for viewing this issue was developed by DiMichael (1967) who suggested a two-way classification of horizontal and vertical specialization. In DiMichael's model, horizontal specialization refers to rehabilitation counselors who restrict or specialize their practice with a particular disability group (e.g., deaf, blind, head injury, and substance abuse) that requires a significant amount of specialized knowledge or skill specific to the type of disability. Vertical specialization, on the other hand, occurs when rehabilitation counselors attend to only one function in the rehabilitation process (e.g., assessment or job placement) in their work with clients. Vocational evaluators and job placement specialists are examples of vertical specialist in this model.

The previous section on qualified providers does not imply that only rehabilitation counselors should provide rehabilitation services for persons with disabilities. In fact, there are numerous other related work roles that contribute to the rehabilitation process and complement the role and services provided by the rehabilitation counselor. In addition to vocational evaluators and job placement specialists who can assist the rehabilitation counselor and client at critical stages in the rehabilitation process (assessment and job placement), other supportive resources could include physicians and physiatrists, physical and occupational therapists, psychologists, work adjustment trainers, job coaches, and various vocational training personnel. Often, a very critical aspect of the rehabilitation counselors role is the coordination of services provided by these various professionals within the context of a multidisciplinary team approach to effectively address the multifaceted needs of the client in the rehabilitation process.

PRESERVICE EDUCATION AND PROFESSIONAL DEVELOPMENT

Throughout this chapter the importance of appropriate preservice education in rehabilitation counseling has been emphasized. By the 1940s, three universities (New York, Ohio State, and Wayne State) had developed graduate training programs in rehabilitation counseling (Jenkins et al., 1992). In 1954, with the passage of the Vocational Rehabilitation Amendments, federal grant support was provided for the first time to universities and colleges to develop graduate preservice training programs to prepare rehabilitation counselors for employment in the public and private nonprofit rehabilitation sectors. This federal training support, which continues to this day, accelerated the design and development of graduate training in rehabilitation counseling, and can be viewed as the beginning of the professionalization process for the formal discipline of rehabilitation counseling (Leahy & Szymanski, 1995).

During this initial period of program development, a conference report by Hall and Warren (1956), which documented the findings of a comprehensive workshop sponsored by the National Rehabilitation Association (NRA) and the National Vocational Guidance Association (now the American Counseling Association [ACA]), provided the initial guidelines for curriculum planning by the new, federally funded rehabilitation counselor education programs (Wright, 1980). In the years that followed, empirical research in the form of role and function and professional competency studies (covered earlier in this chapter) helped guide curriculum redesign efforts to ensure that critical knowledge and skill areas needed in the field were reflected in the preservice training content.

As rehabilitation counselor education programs expanded in colleges and universities, there was a need to devise a mechanism to standardize and accredit these training programs. In 1972, the CORE was established as the national accreditation body for rehabilitation counselor education programs "to promote the effective delivery of rehabilitation services to individuals with disabilities by promoting and fostering continuing review and improvement of master's degree level programs" (CORE, 1991, p. 2). Research conducted at the University of Wisconsin laid the foundation for a multistakeholder program evaluation process that was recognized in 1975 by the National Commission on Accrediting, a predecessor of the Council on Postsecondary Accreditation (COPA) (Linkowski & Szymanski, 1993). The Council for Higher Education Accreditation (CHEA) was established in 1996 when it replaced COPA and currently recognizes CORE. Currently, there are over 95 accredited master's degree educational programs in rehabilitation counseling. As the oldest and most established accreditation body among the counseling professions, the CORE process remains firmly grounded in research and regularly conducts a systematic review of the adequacy and relevancy of its standards.

Following graduate-level preservice education, practicing rehabilitation counselors need to continue their professional development to maintain and upgrade knowledge and skills associated with the delivery of rehabilitation counseling services to persons with disabilities. For example, CRCs are required to obtain a minimum of 100 hours of relevant continuing education during their 5-year certification period. With the rapid pace of change in the field and the continual dissemination of new knowledge and expanded skills associated with practice, rehabilitation counselors need to be aware of continuing educational opportunities available to them. Although there are numerous organizations and groups that provide this type of training (both face-to-face and distance education opportunities), the primary sources and sponsors of continuing education for the rehabilitation counselor are professional organizations (e.g., ARCA, NRCA, NRA, ACA), research and training centers, and university-based outreach educational programs.

REGULATION OF PRACTICE AND CREDENTIALING

Regulation of practice through professional certification and licensure are important characteristics of professions (Rothman, 1987). Rehabilitation counseling has been widely recognized as the leading counseling specialty in the development and pioneering of credentialing mechanisms through national certification and educational program accreditation, which serve as the cornerstones of the general counseling professionalization system (Tarvydas & Leahy, 1993). However, it has also been widely observed that the order of credentialing development in rehabilitation counseling is atypical of the expected order of progression seen in other, more established professions such as medicine and law. The more classic evolution of credentials, according to Matkin (1983), has been for the discipline to initially achieve state licensure, and then move to develop national specialty certifications or endorsements regulated by the professional organizations. In rehabilitation counseling, national certification was established first, followed by a long period of legislative advocacy in which other counseling specialty groups took the lead role along with rehabilitation counselors to establish state counselor licensure laws in individual states (Tarvydas & Leahy, 1993; Tarvydas, Leahy, & Zanskas, 2009).

In our field, the CRC credentialing process is the oldest and most established certification process in the counseling and rehabilitation disciplines. The purpose of certification is to ensure that the professionals engaged in rehabilitation counseling are of good moral character and possess at least an acceptable minimum level of knowledge, as determined by the Commission, with regard to the practice of their discipline. The existence of such standards is considered to be in the best interests of clients of rehabilitation counseling services and the general public. From a historical perspective, the CRC credentialing program was an outgrowth of the professional concerns of the American Rehabilitation Counseling Association (ARCA) and the National Rehabilitation Counseling Association (NRCA).

Since the inception of the credential and the subsequent development of the CRCC in 1973, over 35,000 professionals have participated in the certification process. Today, there are over 16,000 CRCs practicing in the United States and several foreign countries (Saunders, Barros-Bailey, Chapman, & Nunez, 2009). Certification standards and examination content for the CRC have been empirically validated through ongoing research efforts throughout the 35-year history of the Commission. These standards represent the level of education, experience, and knowledge competencies (see Table 10.1) required of rehabilitation counselors to provide services to individuals with disabilities.

In terms of regulation of practice, the most powerful credential is licensure. As differentiated from voluntary national certification, licensure regulates the practice of a profession through specific state legislation. Beginning in 1976, with the passage of the first counselor licensure bill in Virginia, there has been a long struggle by advocates of the counselor licensure movement to enact legislation on a state-by-state basis to protect the title and regulate the practice of counseling. During the past 34 years, all 50 states have enacted counselor licensure legislation. The trend has been toward the passage of general practice legislation (which covers various counseling specialty groups), which is consistent with the recommendations of the ACA's Licensure Committee in its 1990 model legislation for LPCs (Bloom et al., 1990). Reflecting this trend, the most commonly used title in counselor licensure bills has been that of the LPC.

Counselor licensure legislation has been intended both to regulate the use of the terms by which the statute officially refers to professional counselors and to protect the practice of professional counseling as set forth in its definition and scope of practice provisions. This combination of title and practice bill is the most stringent form of credentialing and would prohibit anyone from practicing counseling unless fully qualified regardless of formal title. Title-only legislation on the other hand prohibits persons from using the specific titles restricted in the bill to those who have met the specified qualifications established by the bill and have achieved licensure. It does not, however, restrict persons from providing counseling services if their job titles avoid restricted language. Most title-only legislation was passed to avoid powerful lobbying efforts that would have been mounted to defeat the more restrictive title and practice bills. Clearly, this type of legislation was seen as a first stage by counselor licensure advocates in the overall drive toward eventual regulation of practice through future revisions of the initial legislation (Tarvydas & Leahy, 1993; Tarvydas et al., 2009).

Although there are presently three states that have passed licensure laws specifically covering rehabilitation counselors (Texas, Louisiana, and Massachusetts), the majority of states have enacted general practice legislation covering all counselors. The professional associations in rehabilitation counseling (ARCA and NRCA) and CRCC have taken the position to strongly advocate for the inclusion of rehabilitation counselors within the general counselor state licensure, whenever possible. With this in mind, the LPC designation, combined with certification as a CRC, would represent the appropriate credentials for rehabilitation counselors working with individuals with disabilities, in states with general practice legislation.

PROFESSIONAL ASSOCIATIONS

Professional associations provide a forum for the exchange of information and ideas among professionals, reflect the philosophical bases of a profession, and, as political entities, are concerned with the organization of the discipline and, relations with external groups (Rothman, 1987). In rehabilitation counseling, professional associations also provide an organizational home for individuals with similar professional identities, interests, and backgrounds who are committed to the further development and refinement of the discipline.

The history of counseling is a fascinating evolutionary process, particularly in relation to how the discipline developed, and how quickly it has evolved through the professionalization process during the past half century. Counseling principally evolved as a profession from the development and maturation of specialty areas of counseling practice (e.g., rehabilitation counseling, mental health counseling, and school counseling) that shared a common core of professional competencies and foundational concepts (Hosie, 1995; Meyers, 1995; Sweeney, 1995). Historical, philosophical, societal trends, and public policy have all contributed to the development of the various counseling specialties. Rather than the profession of counseling evolving first, followed by a logical sequence of specialization of practice (as evident in the medical and legal professions), the specialty areas actually emerged first in response to a variety of human needs and were only later conceptualized as belonging to the common professional home of counseling. This unusual sequence of professional emergence has had a direct impact on the institutions, regulatory bodies, and professional associations that represent the profession and the specialty areas of practice. Meyers (1995) indicated that specializations in the counseling profession have been based upon unique practice settings, clients served, techniques employed, or a blend of required knowledge and client populations (Leahy et al., 2009).

Throughout the modern history of rehabilitation counseling, there have been two divergent models of the discipline that have served to define the professional associations of the rehabilitation counselor. One model postulates that rehabilitation counseling should be viewed as a separate and autonomous profession, organizationally aligned with other related rehabilitation disciplines. The other model views the rehabilitation counseling discipline as a specialty area of general counseling, organizationally aligned with related counseling groups. These early beliefs are presently reflected in the discipline's major professional associations that also represent rehabilitation counseling's dual emphasis in counseling and rehabilitation.

The ARCA was founded in 1958 as a professional division of the American Personnel and Guidance Association (now the American Counseling Association). The NRCA was also founded in 1958 as a professional division of the NRA. The presence of these two organizations, with similar missions and constituencies, has been the topic of much discussion and debate over the years (Leahy & Tarvydas, 2001).

Throughout the years, there have been serious discussions of organizational merger and unification (Leahy & Tarvydas, 2001; Rasch, 1979; Reagles, 1981) and systems of collaboration (Leahy & Tarvydas, 2001; Wright, 1982) to repair the fragmentation and professional and public confusion created by the existence of two such organizations representing rehabilitation counseling (Leahy & Szymanski, 1995). To address these concerns, the ARCA and NRCA boards created the Alliance for Rehabilitation Counseling (ARC) in 1993 as a formal collaborative structure to marshal the strengths of both organizations into a unified professional policy and strategic planning voice for rehabilitation counseling, while at the same time respecting the autonomy, heritage, and value of each of the individual organizations.

Unfortunately, even though the ARC flourished for a number of years in the 1990s, it was disbanded after a failed unification attempt between ARCA and NRCA in 2002. Following these developments, NRCA withdrew from the NRA to become an independent body, and NRA replaced NRCA with the Rehabilitation Counselor and Educators Association (RCEA) soon after. Collectively, these actions, which began as an effort to unify the professional associations in rehabilitation counseling, resulted in further fragmentation at the national level. Of even greater concern is the fact that although we now have more practicing rehabilitation counselors than ever before, we have the lowest level of member participation in professional associations in our contemporary history as a professional discipline. Even though these trends are similar to what other related professional groups have experienced (Bauman, 2008), it remains an alarming limitation for rehabilitation counseling, particularly with the aging out of a large cohort of leaders and members expected to begin in the next few years (Leahy, 2009). Hopefully, the discipline in the coming years will take action on the need to create one national professional organization to represent rehabilitation counselors in the United States, to marshal our strengths, clarify our identity to outside stakeholders and members of the public, and effectively utilize all our resources to continue our leadership role in the counseling and disability fields.

SUMMARY

Rehabilitation counseling, as a professional discipline and specialty area of counseling, has had a rich history of professionalization over the past 55 years. While the occupation has been in existence for over 90 years, we have all witnessed significant growth and development of this specialty area of practice over the past few decades. Today, there are more rehabilitation counselors practicing in a variety of employment settings than at any time in our history, and the future market for these types of trained professionals looks excellent. As indicated previously, while the discipline remains very strong in relation to most of the elements of professionalization (e.g., preservice education, code of ethics, academic program accreditation, and practitioner certification), the fragmented and redundant nature of our professional associations representing rehabilitation counseling is a glaring weakness that will need to be addressed for the discipline to continue to flourish in the future.

CONTENT REVIEW QUESTIONS

- What is the scope of practice and definition of rehabilitation counseling, as a specialty area of counseling practice?
- What are the basic roles and functions of the rehabilitation counselor in practice and what types of knowledge areas are required to practice effectively within the discipline?

- In relation to professionalization, what elements are considered strengths and which are considered weaknesses as the discipline moves forward?
- When we think of regulation of practice as a key element in professionalization, how does rehabilitation counseling regulate practice within the discipline?

REFERENCES

Berven, N. L. (1979). The role and function of the rehabilitation counselor revisited. *Rehabilitation Counseling Bulletin, 22,* 84–88.

Bloom, J., Gerstein, L., Tarvydas, V., Conaster, J., Davis, E., Kater, D., . . . Esposito, R. (1990). Model legislation for licensed professional counselors. *Journal of Counseling and Development, 68,* 511–523.

Commission on Rehabilitation Counselor Certification. (1994). *CRCC Certification Guide.* Rolling Meadows, IL: Author.

Commission on Rehabilitation Counselor Certification. (2010). *Code of professional ethics for rehabilitation counselors.* Schaumburg, IL: Author.

Cook, D., & Bolton, B. (1992). Rehabilitation counselor education and case performance: An independent replication. *Rehabilitation Counseling Bulletin, 36,* 37–43.

Council on Rehabilitation Education. (1991). *CORE policy and procedures manual.* Champaign-Urbana, IL: Author.

DePalma, J. A. (2002). Proposing an evidence-based policy process. *Nursing Administration Quarterly, 26*(4), 55–61.

DiMichael, S. G. (1967). New directions and expectations in rehabilitation counseling. *Journal of Rehabilitation, 33,* 38–39.

Emener, W. G., & Rubin, S. E. (1980). Rehabilitation counselor roles and functions and sources of role strain. *Journal of Applied Rehabilitation Counseling, 11,* 57–69.

Hall, J. H., & Warren, S. L. (Eds.) (1956). *Rehabilitation counselor preparation.* Washington, DC: National Rehabilitation Association and the National Vocational Guidance Association.

Harrison, D. K., & Lee, C. C. (1979). Rehabilitation counselor competencies. *Journal of Applied Rehabilitation Counseling, 10,* 135–141.

Hosie, T. (1995). Counseling specialties: A case of basic preparation rather than advanced specialization. *Journal of Counseling and Development, 74*(2), 177–180.

Jaques, M. E. (1959). *Critical counseling behavior in rehabilitation settings.* Iowa City, IA: State University of Iowa, College of Education.

Jaques, M. E. (1970). *Rehabilitation counseling: Scope and services.* Boston, MA: Houghton Mifflin.

Jenkins, W., Patterson, J. B., & Szymanski, E. M. (1992). Philosophical, historic, and legislative aspects of the rehabilitation counseling profession. In R. M. Parker & E. M. Szymanski (Eds.), *Rehabilitation counseling: Basics and beyond* (2nd ed., pp. 1–41). Austin: PRO-ED.

Leahy, M. J. (2009). Prologue: Rehabilitation counseling credentialing: Research practice and the future of the profession. *Rehabilitation Counseling Bulletin, 52*(2), 67–68.

Leahy, M. J., Chan, F., & Saunders, J. (2003). Job functions and knowledge requirements of certified rehabilitation counselors in the 21st century. *Rehabilitation Counseling Bulletin, 46*(2), 66–81.

Leahy, M. J., Muenzen, P., Saunders, J. L., & Strauser, D. (2009). Essential knowledge domains underlying effective rehabilitation counseling practice. *Rehabilitation Counseling Bulletin, 52*(2), 95–106.

Leahy, M. J., Rak, E., & Zanskas, S. A. (2009). A brief history of counseling and specialty areas of practice. In M. Stebnicki & I. Marini (Eds.), *Professional counselor's desk reference (PCDR)*. New York, NY: Springer Publishing.

Leahy, M. J., Shapson, P. R., & Wright, G. N. (1987). Rehabilitation practitioner competencies by role and setting. *Rehabilitation Counseling Bulletin, 31*, 119–131.

Leahy, M. J., & Szymanski, E. M. (1995). Rehabilitation counseling: Evolution and current status. *Journal of Counseling and Development, 74*, 163–166.

Leahy, M. J., Szymanski, E. M., & Linkowski, D. C. (1993). Knowledge importance in rehabilitation counseling. *Rehabilitation Counseling Bulletin, 37*, 130–145.

Leahy, M. J., & Tarvydas, V. T. (2001). Transforming our professional organizations: A first step toward unification of the rehabilitation counseling profession. *Journal of Applied Rehabilitation Counseling, 32*, 3–8.

Linkowski, D. L., & Szymanski, E. M. (1993). Accreditation in rehabilitation counseling: Historical and current content and process. *Rehabilitation Counseling Bulletin, 37*, 81–91.

Matkin, R. E. (1983). Credentialing and the rehabilitation profession. *Journal of Rehabilitation, 49*, 25–28, 67.

Muthard, J. E., & Salomone, P. (1969). The roles and functions of the rehabilitation counselor. *Rehabilitation Counseling Bulletin, 13*, 81–168.

Meyers, J. (1995). Specialties in counseling: Rich heritage or force for fragmentation? *Journal of Counseling and Development, 74*(2), 115–116.

Puckett, F. D. (1984). Roles and functions of certified rehabilitation counselors. *Rehabilitation Counseling Bulletin, 27*, 199–224.

Rasch, J. D. (1979). The case for an independent association of rehabilitation counselors. *Journal of Applied Rehabilitation Counseling, 10*, 171–176.

Reagles, K. W. (1981). Perspectives on the proposed merger of rehabilitation organizations. *Journal of Applied Rehabilitation Counseling, 12*, 75–79.

Rehabilitation Counseling Consortium. (2005). *Rehabilitation counselor and rehabilitation counseling definitions*. Schaumburg, IL: Commission On Rehabilitation Counselor Certification.

Roessler, R. T., & Rubin, S. E. (1992). *Case management and rehabilitation counseling: Procedures and techniques* (2nd ed.). Austin, TX: PRO-ED.

Rothman, R. A. (1987). *Working: Sociological perspectives*. Englewood Cliffs, NJ: Prentice Hall.

Rubin, S. E., Matkin, R. E., Ashley, J., Beardsley, M. M., May, V. R., Onstott, K., . . . Puckett, F. D. (1984). Roles and functions of certified rehabilitation counselors. *Rehabilitation Counseling Bulletin, 27*, 199–224.

Rubin, S. E., & Roessler, R. T. (1995). *Foundations of the vocational rehabilitation process* (4th ed.). Austin, TX: PRO-ED.

Saunders, J. L., Barros-Bailey, M., Chapman, C., Nunez, P. (2009). Rehabilitation Counselor certification: Moving forward. *Rehabilitation Counseling Bulletin, 52*(2), 77–84.

Shapson, P. R., Wright, G. N., & Leahy, M. J. (1987). Education and the attainment of rehabilitation competencies. *Rehabilitation Counseling Bulletin, 31*, 131–145.

Sweeney, T. (1995). Accreditation, credentialing, professionalization: The role of specialties. *Journal of Counseling and Development, 74*(2), 117–125.

Szymanski, E. M. (1985). Rehabilitation counseling: A profession with a vision, identity, and a future. *Rehabilitation Counseling Bulletin, 29*, 2–5.

Szymanski, E. M. (1991). The relationship of the level of rehabilitation counselor education to rehabilitation client outcome in the Wisconsin Division of Vocational Rehabilitation. *Rehabilitation Counseling Bulletin, 35*, 23–37.

Szymanski, E. M., & Danek, M. M. (1992). The relationship of rehabilitation counselor education to rehabilitation client outcome: A replication and extension. *Journal of Rehabilitation, 58*, 49–56.

Szymanski, E. M., Leahy, M. J., & Linkowski, D. C. (1993). Reported preparedness of certified counselors in rehabilitation counseling knowledge areas. *Rehabilitation Counseling Bulletin, 37,* 146–162.

Szymanski, E. M., & Parker, R. M. (1989). Relationship of rehabilitation client outcome to level of rehabilitation counselor education. *Journal of Rehabilitation, 55,* 32–36.

Tarvydas, V., & Leahy, M. J. (1993). Licensure in rehabilitation counseling: A critical incident in professionalization. *Rehabilitation Counseling Bulletin, 37,* 92–108.

Tarvydas, V. T., Leahy, M. J., & Zanskas, S. A. (2009). Judgement deferred: Reappraisal of the counseling movement toward licensure parity. *Rehabilitation Counseling Bulletin 52*(2), 85–94.

Wright, G. N. (1980). *Total rehabilitation.* Boston, MA: Little and Brown.

Wright, G. N. (1982). Contemporary rehabilitation counselor education. *Rehabilitation Counselor Bulletin, 25,* 254–256.

Wright, G. N., & Fraser, R. T. (1975). *Task analysis for the evaluation, preparation, classification, and utilization of rehabilitation counselor track personnel.* (Wisconsin Studies in Vocational Rehabilitation Monograph No. 22, Series 3) Madison, WI: University of Wisconsin.

11

Assessment

Norman L. Berven and Mary O'Connor Drout

LEARNING OBJECTIVES

After reading this chapter, you should be able to:

- Understand the assessment process in rehabilitation counseling and appreciate the breadth and scope of contemporary assessment practice.
- Understand key concepts in assessment including reliability, validity, and standardization, along with distinctions between "maximum" and "typical" performance.
- Understand the wide variety of categories of assessment instruments and procedures that are typically used in the rehabilitation process.
- Understand interpretation and synthesis of assessment information in developing a "working model" of an individual as a basis for service or clinical decisions, along with some potential sources of bias.
- Understand the use of assessment in clinical and service decisions and in disability determinations.
- Understand some future trends and issues in assessment, including the ever increasing variety of resources and the impact of computer technology.

Assessment is perhaps the most basic of all functions to the practice of rehabilitation counseling, as it "provides the strategic foundation for the provision of rehabilitation services to persons with disabilities" (Bolton & Parker, 2008, p. xv). The *Standards for Educational and Psychological Testing,* published by the American Educational Research Association, American Psychological Association, and National Council on Measurement in Education (AERA, APA, & NCME, 1999), define assessment as "systematic procedures to obtain information from a variety of sources to draw inferences about people" (p. 172). The *systematic procedures* include not only the traditional standardized tests that are usually associated with assessment, but also other procedures, such as interviews, observations, medical examinations, and job tryouts. The *sources* may include consumers or clients themselves, other professionals, and other people who know the individual, including family, friends, and previous employers, as well as the observations made by practitioners themselves. Finally, *inferences* may be drawn about abilities, interests, personality characteristics, likely behavior, and satisfaction in different work and living environments, as well as likely responsiveness to intervention strategies that might be selected for use.

According to the Commission on Rehabilitation Counselor Certification (CRCC, n.d.) Scope of Practice statement, "Rehabilitation counseling is a systematic process which assists persons with physical, mental, developmental, cognitive, and emotional disabilities to achieve their personal, career, and independent living goals in the most integrated setting possible." The CRCC statement goes on to define techniques and modalities used in rehabilitation counseling, including *appraisal* (defined as the use of assessment instruments, in addition to "methods and techniques of understanding human behavior in relation to coping with, adapting to, or changing life situations") and *diagnosis and treatment planning* (defined as the provision of "diagnostic descriptions," exploration of "possible solutions," and "developing and implementing a treatment plan").

Using similar concepts, Berven (2008b) describes the rehabilitation counseling process as

> collaborative with rehabilitation counselors and individuals with disabilities jointly assessing and identifying needs; establishing personal, career, and independent living goals; identifying barriers to accomplishing those goals; identifying needed services and interventions to overcome the barriers and accomplish the goals; organizing those services and interventions into a service plan; and implementing and evaluating progress and success of the plan. (p. 830)

In this conceptualization of rehabilitation counseling as a problem-solving process, all the components listed, except for the implementation of plans, are components of assessment. Thus, the scope of assessment is broad, pervading much of the rehabilitation counseling process.

Further, assessment focuses not only on the person, but also on situational or environmental contexts in which an individual functions, and assessment occurs at many different levels in the rehabilitation counseling process. At a macro level, assessment forms the basis for overall service plans, guiding the rehabilitation counseling process with a particular individual. At a micro level, assessment forms the basis for the identification of appropriate strategies to follow in response to an unexpected crisis; and at an even more specific level, assessment at a particular moment in time forms the basis for determining a verbal response or action to take at that moment that is perceived as consistent with the individual's needs and likely to produce a desired response in a counseling session.

The purpose of this chapter is to discuss the assessment process and contemporary assessment practices in rehabilitation counseling, including assessment methods used, the synthesis and interpretation of assessment information, and the types of decisions and determinations for which assessment is commonly used. In addition, current trends and future developments in assessment are briefly discussed.

REHABILITATION COUNSELOR AND CONSUMER ROLES IN THE REHABILITATION PROCESS

The roles of rehabilitation counselors in relation to clients or consumers served may be conceptualized along a continuum of control over decision making. At one extreme, the more traditional service-delivery model, the rehabilitation counselor maintains control of the process and serves as the primary decision maker in service delivery. Midway along the continuum, the rehabilitation counselor and consumer function as a team, assuming joint control and collaborating in the decisions to be made through an effective working alliance (Chan, Shaw, McMahon, Koch, & Strauser, 1997). At the other extreme the consumer assumes control as the primary decision maker, and the rehabilitation counselor serves as a consultant, providing information and opinions to the consumer to facilitate his or her independent decision making.

A move along the continuum toward greater consumer control of the rehabilitation process is consistent with contemporary views of the practice of rehabilitation counseling, moving away from a medical model of service delivery toward an approach that is more empowering, facilitating control on the part of people with disabilities over their own lives and authority over the decisions that affect them (e.g., Holmes, 1993; National Institute on Consumer-Directed Long-Term Services, 1996; Nosek, 1998; Parker, Hansmann, & Schaller, 2010). As discussed by Berven (2008b), the empowering of people with disabilities to exercise control is consistent with the basic guiding philosophy of rehabilitation counseling regarding the dignity of people with disabilities. Further, informed choice conceptualizes people with disabilities as the ultimate decision makers, with practitioners helping them to obtain the information and understanding required to make good decisions. Kosciulek (2004) has developed a theory of informed consumer choice, along with a consumer-directed theory of empowerment (Kosciulek, 1999), and he has gone on to document the hypothesized relationships among consumer direction, community integration, empowerment, and quality of life (Kosciulek, 2005; Kosciulek & Merz, 2001).

Whatever the procedures followed in making service delivery and treatment decisions in the rehabilitation counseling process, assessment provides the information base for decision making, and the rehabilitation counselor has special expertise in facilitating the development of that information base, typically in collaboration with individuals receiving assistance. To the extent that consumers assume greater control over decision making, they need to be involved as active participants in assessment planning, and the information that is accumulated needs to be communicated to consumers in a form that can be effectively used by them to facilitate their own decision making.

ASSESSMENT PROCESS

Assessment begins when the first information is received by a rehabilitation counselor about an individual to be served, perhaps through a phone call from the individual, a written referral, or a phone call from another professional, sometimes accompanied by previous treatment or service records. From the time that this initial information is obtained, the rehabilitation counselor begins to form impressions about the individual and his or her needs, as well as goals that might be appropriate and services or intervention strategies that might be indicated. As additional information is accumulated, it is interpreted and synthesized with the information previously obtained to develop an increasingly sophisticated and complex understanding of the individual and his or her needs, which can be used to predict how the individual might behave in different situations or how he or she might respond to different intervention strategies. These predictions, in turn, facilitate the decisions to be made in service delivery and treatment. The assessment information is shared with the client or consumer, facilitating self-understanding, predictions about the future, and collaboration in treatment and service decisions, with the full participation of the client or consumer in the overall rehabilitation counseling process.

BASIC CONCEPTS

A distinction, first articulated by Cronbach (1949), between indicators of *maximum performance* and indicators of *typical performance* can be useful in understanding the purposes of various assessment methods in rehabilitation counseling (Berven, 1980; Maki, McCracken, Pape, & Scofield, 1979). Indicators of maximum performance are used to predict the behavior of an individual when performing at his or her best, for example, in training or employment, and may be further categorized into indicators of ability or aptitude, and indicators of current skills or achievement. It is widely accepted that both aptitude and achievement indicators measure developed abilities and are influenced by learning histories (Anastasi, 1992). However, they may be conceptualized as having somewhat different purposes in assessment. Indicators of aptitude assist in determining *potential* to develop skills, if given appropriate opportunities through training or other experiences; in contrast, indicators of skills or achievement can assist in determining *current mastery* of skills. For example, a measure of mathematical aptitude might be used to determine one's potential to learn math skills, whereas a measure of mathematical achievement might be used to determine whether an individual already possesses the math skills required for a particular type of employment or training (e.g., carpentry) or whether some further training in math might be required to improve skills. Indicators of typical performance are used to determine how an individual might typically behave in various situations and may be further divided into indicators of interests, facilitating predictions about likely satisfaction in different work and life situations, and indicators of personality characteristics.

With all assessment methods it is important to consider reliability and validity of the scores or other information provided. According to the AERA et al. standards (1999), *reliability* refers to "the degree to which test scores are . . . dependable and repeatable for an individual test taker; the degree to which scores are free from errors of measurement" (p. 180), and *validity* refers to "the degree to which accumulated evidence and theory support specific interpretations of test scores entailed by proposed uses of a test" (p. 184). As an example, the reliability and validity of the "weight score," provided by a bathroom scale, might be assessed by having an individual step onto and off the scale, each time recording the weight indicated. Reliability of the scale as an assessment device would be reflected by the extent to which the scale consistently indicated the exact same weight on each occasion; if the weights indicated were highly inconsistent, the scale would have little value in measuring weight. In contrast, validity would be reflected in the extent to which the weight indicated provided an accurate measure of the individual's true weight and, if the weight indicated was considerably different from the true weight, the scale would have little value, even if the weight indicated was highly consistent. With any assessment procedure, the reliability and validity of scores or other information produced are largely responsible for determining its value.

Standardization is another concept that is important in understanding the variety of *standardized* or *norm-referenced* assessment devices that are commonly used in rehabilitation counseling practice. A standardized assessment procedure is a test, instrument, or procedure that has been administered to one or more large groups of individuals, referred to as the standardization or normative sample, according to carefully specified procedures. When the device is then used in assessment applications, it is administered according to the same standardized procedures, and the performance of the individual can then be compared to the standardization or normative samples in interpreting scores. However, the comparison of performance to the normative samples can be made *only if* the standardized procedures have been strictly followed. The presence of limitations associated with disability may render standardized administration procedures impossible, and the accommodations required will serve to complicate the interpretation of scores and other performance measures (e.g., see Berven, 1980; Ekstrom & Smith, 2002; Holzbauer & Berven, 1999; Nester, 1993; Sherman & Robinson, 1982; Willingham et al., 1988). In addition, the presence of functional limitations can influence the meaning or inferences to be drawn from test scores in other important ways (e.g., see Berven, 1980; Holzbauer & Berven, 1999).

ASSESSMENT METHODS AND PRACTICES

A wide variety of assessment information typically is used in the rehabilitation process, including scores and other quantitative data from standardized tests and related instruments and procedures, as well as qualitative data obtained through interviews, direct observations, and verbal and written reports from others.

Sources of assessment information include the individuals themselves, other people who have known or have worked with them, and physicians and other professionals who may be called upon to conduct examinations or evaluations of current functioning or potential, as well as the direct observations of the practitioner. Although assessment is heavily concentrated in the initial stages of the rehabilitation process, it continues throughout the entire process. Some of the methods utilized are the same as those used in other counseling and human service specialties and settings, whereas others have been specifically developed to meet the needs of people with disabilities in rehabilitation settings.

Interviews

Berven (2008a, 2010) has discussed the use of interviews for assessment in rehabilitation settings and, as in virtually all counseling and human service disciplines, the interview is probably the most widely used of all assessment methods. It is often the first point of contact between a rehabilitation counselor and an individual seeking assistance and serves to initiate assessment. The interview provides a rich source of self-reported information, as well as an opportunity to observe the individual. Observations may include interpersonal skills, thought processes, affect, memory, and follow-through on plans and commitments made. Unlike standardized tests, the interview is not restricted to prespecified questions and directions of inquiry; rather, the counselor is able to move the information-gathering process in whatever directions seem to be most productive as the interview unfolds.

Types of Assessment Interviews

Rehabilitation counselors, along with other human service professionals, typically begin their work with an *initial* or *intake interview*. In addition to providing information to individuals about the rehabilitation counseling process, services available, and respective roles and responsibilities, the initial interview serves to initiate both the counseling relationship and the assessment process (Farley & Rubin, 2006; Parker & Bolton, 2005; Power, 2006). According to the *APA Dictionary of Psychology* (VandenBos, 2007), initial interviews focus on "relationship building, attending to client behaviors, and developing a beginning picture of the client's cultural context, circumstances, values, needs, aspirations, and goals" (p. 315). The assessment information obtained through initial interviews is limited only by the ability and willingness of individuals to provide information, facts, perceptions, thoughts, and feelings, along with the skills of practitioners in eliciting information and observing behavior.

Due to differences among agencies or programs in services provided, resources available, and eligibility criteria, initial and intake interviews vary considerably across specific rehabilitation service programs. Many programs develop their own interview guides for the initial or intake interview to help ensure that the required information will be obtained. In addition, a number of textbooks on assessment and interviewing provide general interview guides, with topics identified that may be important to explore in initial interviews (e.g., Drummond & Jones, 2006; Farley & Rubin, 2006; Groth-Marnat, 2009; Power, 2006; Sommers-Flanagan & Sommers-Flanagan, 2003). Such guides can help ensure that important points are not missed in the interview (Hood & Johnson, 2007). Standardized intake questionnaires also have been developed, as exemplified by the Quick View Social History, comprised of 130 questions, with responses analyzed by computer to produce a narrative report (Gianetti, 1992).

Diagnostic and *screening interviews* are also conducted in many rehabilitation settings. As the name implies, diagnostic interviews focus specifically on formulating a diagnosis and prognosis. Diagnostic interviews often follow a structured, standardized interview protocol, and most diagnostic interviews are intended to achieve diagnoses per the *Diagnostic and Statistical Manual (DSM)*. (Craig, 2003, 2005). An example is the *Structured Clinical Interview for DSM-IV Axis I Disorders (SCID-I)-Clinician Version* (First, Spitzer, Gibbon, & Williams, 1997), which provides a series of interview questions that lead the interviewer through a decision tree, culminating in a *DSM* diagnosis. Other diagnostic interview protocols focus on specific disorders, including anxiety disorders, mood disorders, schizophrenia, personality disorders, alcohol problems, drug abuse, sexual dysfunctions and deviations, eating disorders, psychophysiological disorders, and both combat and noncombat posttraumatic stress disorders (Hersen & Turner, 2003).

Mental status examinations are another common type of diagnostic interview. Daniel and Crider (2003) point out that comprehensive mental status examinations are similar to physical examinations in medicine, focusing on physical (appearance, behavior, and motor activity), emotional (attitude, mood and affect, thought and perception, and insight and judgment), and cognitive (orientation, attention and concentration, speech and language, memory, and intelligence and abstraction) domains. As with other types of diagnostic interviews, mental status examinations use standardized interview questions to generate responses, along with observations of behavior during the interview. A number of structured interview protocols are available, such as the *Mini Mental State Exam*, comprised of 11 items that focus on orientation, registration, attention, calculation, and language (Folstein, Folstein, & McHugh, 1975).

Finally, protocols and procedures are available for screening interviews directed at specific problems, such as suicide risk and alcohol and other drug use and abuse. Examples of suicide risk assessment protocols include the SAD PERSONS Scale that provides a quick screening on 10 factors indicative of risk (Patterson, Dohn, Bird, & Patterson, 1983); the Suicide Assessment Checklist that includes 12 self-report items for clients and nine items for the counselor that are used to assess risk (Rogers, Alexander, & Subich, 1994); and a decision tree approach to screening, based on the three risk factors of previous suicide attempts, suicide plans and preparation, and desire and suicidal ideation (Joiner, Walker,

Rudd, & Jobes, 1999). An example of a screening interview for alcohol and other drug problems is the CAGE, a brief interview protocol that utilizes four questions associated with alcohol use, with the four letters in the name of the instrument representing key words in each of the four questions (Ewing, 1984; Kitchens, 1994). Hood and Johnson (2007), among other sources, provide reviews of interview protocols that are available for diagnostic and screening purposes.

General Considerations

There are many potential sources of error in information obtained through interviews (see Berven, 2008a, 2010; Kaplan & Saccuzzo, 2009), including subjectivity on the part of the counselor in interpreting statements and observations during the interview; intentional or unintentional distortions in information reported by the individual; the manner in which questions are asked by the counselor that can influence the responses obtained (e.g., leading questions and closed-ended questions); and the relationship established between the counselor and the individual that can influence openness in responding. In addition, observations made during interviews may be situation specific and may not generalize to other situations in which predictions regarding the behavior of the individual need to be made. Critics of traditional testing and assessment procedures may advocate interviews and observational procedures as viable alternatives. However, based on reviews of research (e.g., Garb, 1998; Groth-Marnat, 2009), Berven (2008a) concludes that

> reliability and validity of interview assessments tend to be poor relative to standardized tests and related assessment tools. Further, reliability and validity are highly dependent on the skills of individual practitioners in interviewing and clinical judgment, and those skills tend to vary substantially among practitioners. (p. 259)

Thus, information obtained through interviews may be highly inconsistent from one time to another and may vary substantially depending on the unique biases of the individual practitioner, and the information and observations obtained may not be particularly useful in making accurate inferences and predictions about future behavior.

There are a number of ways to enhance the usefulness of interviews in assessment (Berven, 2008a, 2010). Training in interviewing and other methods to facilitate awareness and sensitivity to potential sources of error in information obtained through interviews can encourage greater vigilance in identifying and attempting to counter sources of error. In addition, reliability and validity of information obtained can be enhanced through the use of more highly standardized, structured interview procedures. Such standardization, if carried too far, however, can reduce some of the advantages of interviews, particularly their flexibility and individualization. Some standardized interview protocols have been developed specifically for use in rehabilitation settings, including the Preliminary Diagnostic Questionnaire (Moriarty, Walls, & McLaughlin, 1987) and the Vocational Decision-Making Interview (Czerlinsky, Jensen, & Pell, 1987). In addition, attempts have been made to comprehensively identify important questions and lines of inquiry, which can facilitate direction and comprehensiveness of initial interviews in rehabilitation settings (e.g., Farley & Rubin, 2006; Power, 2006).

Standardized Tests and Inventories

Standardized psychological and vocational tests and inventories include a wide variety of paper-and-pencil, apparatus, and computer-administered instruments that are widely used in rehabilitation settings. Tests of maximum performance include achievement tests and batteries, particularly those focusing on academic skills such as reading and mathematics. Also included are aptitude tests and batteries focusing on intelligence and other cognitive and neuropsychological abilities, along with a wide variety of vocationally relevant aptitudes, including manual dexterity and clerical and mechanical aptitudes. Tests of typical performance include vocational inventories that focus on vocational interests, attitudes, and values, which may be used to predict likely satisfaction in different occupations and vocational situations and, consequently, the likelihood of persisting in those occupations. Also included are personality inventories and related instruments designed to measure a wide variety of emotions, motives, values, beliefs, attitudes, and related characteristics that are used to facilitate predictions about the ways in which individuals are likely to behave in situations of interest.

Literally, thousands of tests and inventories have been developed, many available through commercial publishers and distributors, and textbooks on testing and assessment typically focus primarily on these types of instruments. Reviews of available instruments are provided through a number of sources, including the *Mental Measurements Yearbook*, originally published in 1938 and currently in its 18th edition (Spies, Carlson, & Geisinger, 2010), which reviews widely used instruments and is also available online at the Buros Institute of Mental Measurements web site (http://buros.unl.edu/buros/jsp/search.jsp) and through academic libraries. In addition, the Buros Institute publishes *Tests in Print*, which is now in its seventh edition (Murphy, Spies, & Plake, 2006) and provides a comprehensive bibliography of tests in print in the English language. Other sources of information on noncommercial tests and related assessment devices include the multivolume *Directory of Unpublished Experimental Mental Measures*, initially published in 1995 and continuing through the most recent Volume 9 (Goldman & Mitchell, 2007), and *A Counselor's Guide to Career Assessment Instruments* (Whitfield, Feller, & Wood, 2009).

Of all assessment methods, reliability and validity tend to be most extensively documented for standardized tests and inventories; however, the reliability and validity of even the best available instruments tend to be more limited than commonly believed, and a great deal of caution should be used in

interpretation of scores and other performance measures. Reliability and validity of tests of maximum performance tend to be more positive than for tests of
typical performance; for example, reliability estimates for tests of maximum performance "tend to cluster in the high .80s and low .90s," while reliabilities of test
of typical performance "tend to fall in the high .70s and low .80s" (Parker, 2008,
p. 141). In a review of research on the validity of psychological tests, Meyer et al.
(2001) concluded that the validities generally are comparable to those of medical
tests, but this conclusion was challenged by others (e.g., Garb, Klein, & Grove,
2002; Hunsley, 2002; Smith, 2002).

Simulations of Work and Living Tasks

Simulations of tasks actually performed in specific occupations or clusters of
occupations, known as work samples, have been widely used in rehabilitation counseling practice. In a similar manner, physical functioning and daily-
living tasks are also often simulated to assess physical capacities, self-care, and
independent-living skills, and these assessments are often conducted by occupational therapists and other allied health professionals. Traditionally, the term
work sample has been used to refer to a simulation of the tasks in a particular
job or cluster of jobs, thus having a direct, one-to-one correspondence with
that job or cluster (Dowd, 1993). For example, a work sample could be developed to simulate an entry-level occupation that individuals who successfully
complete a particular training program may often pursue, and performance
on the work sample may then indicate potential to pursue the training and,
ultimately, employment in the occupation. Alternatively, work samples often
are conceptualized and used as performance aptitude tests, assessing a combination of aptitudes that are important to performance in many different occupations (e.g., the combination of clerical perception and manual dexterity);
inferences may then be drawn from scores and other performance indicators
regarding potential for a variety of occupations requiring that combination of
aptitudes.

Work samples, like tests, are typically standardized and are administered
to individuals being assessed under those same standardized conditions, with
scores compared to norm groups or to industrial standards established through
engineering time studies. In addition to assessment of potential, the completion
of a variety of work samples can provide opportunities for career exploration,
allowing individuals to try a variety of occupational tasks in a short period of
time in order to explore and identify potential interests. A number of commer-
cially distributed work sample and related vocational assessment systems are
available, and Patterson (2008) and Power (2006) have provided summaries of
selected systems. In general, the empirical support for reliability and validity of
information produced through the use of work sample and evaluation systems
varies substantially and tends to not be as well developed as for standardized
tests and inventories.

Simulated and Real Environments

In contrast to work samples, which involve the simulation of tasks in a particular occupation or cluster of occupations, entire work environments may also be simulated. Similarly, living environments, such as a kitchen or entire apartment, may be simulated in a hospital rehabilitation unit to assess independent-living skills, behaviors, and potential. Historically, work environments have been simulated in sheltered employment settings in order to assess work behaviors and potential for employment and to identify behaviors to target for intervention in order to facilitate employability. Although such applications of *situational assessment* are still practiced, contemporary thought has questioned the validity of such assessments because of the contrived nature of the simulated environments, differing in many important ways from real work environments, and the dramatic influence that these differences can have on the behaviors observed.

Observations of individuals functioning in real work or living environments, such as *job tryouts*, can be viewed as the most definitive of all assessment approaches in determining potential, skills, and behavior related to functioning in that specific environment or other similar environments. For example, individuals may be placed in the same environment in which they previously worked prior to the onset of a disability, or in a new occupation and work environment being considered for the future; accommodations can be implemented, training can be provided in vivo, and observations can be made to assess both maximum performance (i.e., aptitudes, skills, and behaviors in relation to the demands of that work environment) and typical performance in that specific environment. Tryouts also are used commonly in assessing potential to succeed in education and training. For example, an individual considering entering a 4-year college or technical college program might take one or two courses to test out potential for success. Similarly, an individual recovering in an inpatient rehabilitation unit from the recent onset of a physical disability can be observed during short stays in the home environment to assess independent living skills and to determine needs for further training in activities of daily living, as well as aids and appliances that might improve independent-living skills, along with the accommodations that might be required in the home environment.

Behavioral observations of individuals in simulated and real environments, as well as in other assessment situations (e.g., work samples and interviews), can be facilitated through the use of systematic behavioral assessment methods and a variety of rating scales (see Galassi & Perot, 1992; Silva, 1993). Many rating scales commonly used in rehabilitation settings are homemade scales that are constructed loosely with little or no reliability or validity data available to support their use. Several scales are available through commercial publishers, however, and reviews of available rating scales have been provided (e.g., Esser, 1975; Harrison, Garnett, & Watson, 1981; Power, 2006).

Ecological assessment emphasizes the use of real environments and has been advocated as a preferred method of assessment for individuals with disabilities, particularly more severe disabilities (Browder, 1991; Parker et al., 2010; Parker, Szymanski, & Hanley-Maxwell, 1989). Ecological assessment minimizes the use of traditional standardized tests and simulations of tasks and work environments in favor of interviews and observations with clients or consumers and others who have had opportunities to observe them in various situations, along with careful analysis of potential work and living environments in relation to individual characteristics identified. A key component of ecological assessment is observation of individuals in real environments of interest, where congruence between the individual and the environment can be assessed in order to identify methods of accommodation and otherwise resolve discrepancies between environmental demands and the capacities, skills, and other characteristics of the individual.

Functional Assessment

Functional assessment may be defined as any systematic approach to describing an individual's functioning in terms of skill (what the individual "can do"), current behavior (what the individual "does do"), or both (Brown, Gordon, & Diller, 1983). Functional assessment typically is conducted with the aid of scales, with the items representing comprehensive listings of areas of functioning, so that each can be rated, evaluated, or described comprehensively. Some scales produce summary scores and score profiles, whereas others rely on checklists and narrative descriptions of an individual's functioning in each area included in the scale. In most cases, multiple sources of information are integrated in the completion of functional assessment measures (e.g., interviews, client self-report, direct observation, and examinations, evaluations, and reports completed by other professionals); in fact, any of the assessment methods described above may contribute information relevant to functional assessment. A number of functional assessment measures are available for use in rehabilitation settings, and reviews and discussions of instruments have been provided (Crewe & Dijkers, 1995; Granger, Gilewski, & Carlin, 2010; Halpern & Fuhrer, 1984; Harley, Smith, & Alston, 2010; Tenth Institute on Rehabilitation Issues, 1983). Crewe and Groomes (2008) provide a review of measures of functioning, organized according to body systems, body structures, activities and participation, and environmental factors, which are categories conceptualized in the World Health Organization (WHO, 2001) *International Classification of Functioning, Disability, and Health* (ICF), which is discussed further in the section "Future Perspectives."

INTERPRETATION AND SYNTHESIS OF ASSESSMENT INFORMATION

As information is gathered regarding a client or consumer, the meaning of the various bits of information must be determined, any inconsistencies with other available information must be resolved, and information gathered must be organized and synthesized into an overall picture of the individual. This process of making sense of diverse bits of information in order to understand individuals and their needs is much like the process of research, which involves the discovery of the order underlying the phenomena under study (Sundberg & Tyler, 1962).

Interpretation of Assessment Information

Several authors have described the process of interpreting assessment information in which they identify different levels of interpretation, each characterized by different degrees of inference (Sundberg, 1977; Sundberg & Tyler, 1962). At the lowest level of inference, items of assessment information can be viewed as samples of behavior in their own right, with full consideration given to the situational context in which the behaviors occurred. At the next higher level of inference, items of information are interrelated in search of consistencies and generalizations. At the next higher level of inference, a hypothetical construct (e.g., depression, motivation, and self-esteem) may be used to describe the essence of the consistencies or generalizations identified. When making such interpretations, it is important to remember that inferences often are far removed from the observations on which they are based and, consequently, interpretations must be made with caution, remaining tentative and open to revision as new information emerges.

Organization of Information According to Assets, Limitations, and Preferences

In order to make sense of the myriad of information typically available in working with clients or consumers in rehabilitation settings, it is important to organize the information in ways that will facilitate the assessment process. The information accumulated includes not only the information about the individual, but also the information about the environmental context surrounding the individual, including barriers to improving quality of life and the resources that may be available to the individual. Relevant information may include such diverse elements as personal characteristics described in terms of hypothetical constructs (e.g., flat affect, positive self-esteem, and perseverance in the face of obstacles to progress); credentials held by an individual (e.g., a driver's license or a high school diploma); and resources available (e.g., social support, financial resources, and stable living arrangements). All such information may have a great deal of relevance to the rehabilitation process in assisting individuals in finding their place in society and improving the quality of their lives.

One approach to making sense of the myriad of information typically available is to organize the information in a continuing process, as it is accumulated, according to assets, limitations, and preferences. *Assets* include the strengths of the individual and his or her surrounding situation that may facilitate the accomplishment of rehabilitation goals and thus may be relevant to rehabilitation planning, whereas *limitations* represent those characteristics that may serve as barriers. *Preferences* represent the individual's likes and dislikes, interests, and needs, which are significant in developing rehabilitation plans that will result in outcomes that will be satisfying to the individual. As assessment information is accumulated, interpreted, and organized, increasingly sophisticated statements can be formulated regarding assets, limitations, and preferences, which can facilitate rehabilitation planning.

Synthesis of Information Into a Comprehensive Working Model of the Individual

A number of authors have described the process by which counselors and other professionals process information and conceptualize individuals with whom they work and their problems and needs (e.g., Goldman, 1971; McArthur, 1954; Pepinsky & Pepinsky, 1954; Strohmer & Leierer, 2000; Strohmer, Shivy, & Chiodo, 1990). In the words of Falvey (2001), "From intake to termination, clinicians must gather and analyze case information, formulate hypotheses, and implement treatment decisions. Given the quantity and ambiguity of information presented, this is a daunting task" (p. 293).

In general, effective clinicians systematically construct a "working model" or conceptualization of an individual and then use that working model as a basis for clinical or service decisions. The process of building the working model begins with *inductive* reasoning in which inferences are drawn about individual bits of information and apparent consistencies between them. To the extent that inconsistencies appear, inferences are revised in an attempt to resolve the inconsistencies, seeking broader inferences to incorporate more and more of the information available and building an increasingly sophisticated working model of the person. *Deductive* reasoning then is used to formulate and test hypotheses regarding the usefulness of the working model in accounting for already available information and for making future predictions. To the extent that hypotheses tested do not account for the information or do not result in accurate predictions, the model of the person is revised so as to account for the new information. In this manner a comprehensive working model or conceptualization of the individual is derived that can then be used to make predictions about the behavior and outcomes likely to be achieved by the individual in a wide variety of situations.

Potential Sources of Bias in Interpretation and Synthesis of Information

Tversky and Kahneman (1974) and Kahneman, Slovic, and Tversky (1982) have described judgmental heuristics or cognitive processing strategies that are used in processing information and making judgments that lead to biased inferences. Nezu and Nezu (1993), among others, have applied these heuristics to understanding sources of bias in clinical inferences. The *availability heuristic* is invoked when a previous experience that is called to mind readily exerts an undue influence on the inferences of a counselor; for example, a counselor may have attended a training program recently on alcohol and other drug abuse that may lead to a quick judgment or inference that an individual is abusing alcohol or other drugs, and the counselor may fail to consider other possible explanations for the behaviors observed. The *representativeness heuristic* is invoked when individuals who share one characteristic also are believed more likely to share another characteristic; for example, stereotypes about women, African Americans, or people with a particular type of disability may lead to inferences from behaviors observed that an individual is "depressed" or "unmotivated," again failing to give adequate consideration to other possible explanations or inferences. The *anchoring heuristic* is invoked when quick determinations are made about an individual on the basis of initial impressions, and these determinations are resistant to change, because any subsequent information that is inconsistent with those impressions will be ignored or discounted, whereas information that is consistent will be given more weight, resulting in a confirmatory bias. A number of authors have empirically examined and discussed these sources of bias in counseling and the importance of recognizing and avoiding them in making inferences in assessment (e.g., Falvey, Bray, & Hebert, 2005; Morrow & Deidan, 1992; Turk & Salovey, 1985).

In addition to heuristics, Garb (1998) identified related cognitive processes that can influence the validity of clinical judgments, including cognitive biases and knowledge structures. One of the most common cognitive biases is confirmatory bias. As an example, counselors may tend to formulate hypotheses very early in their work with a client or consumer and, because of confirmatory bias, they may seek and attend only to that information that supports those hypotheses while ignoring information that is inconsistent (Haverkamp, 1993; Strohmer et al., 1990). Knowledge structures include knowledge and theory about problems and behavior held by counselors, as well as stereotypes, prototypes, and scripts. For example, stereotypes related to race may lead counselors to misdiagnose pathology and other problems (Lopez, 1989) or to underestimate the educational and vocational potential of clients (Rosenthal & Berven, 1999).

MAKING CLINICAL AND SERVICE DECISIONS AND DETERMINATIONS

The use of assessment information involves the translation of that information into any of a number of different clinical decisions and determinations that vary depending on the purposes of the assessment. The most common decisions in rehabilitation counseling practice include selection for service, establishment of vocational objectives, identification of needed interventions and formulation of case service plans, and disability determinations. In making all these decisions and determinations, the "working model" of the individual that has been developed through synthesis and reasoning is used to make predictions corresponding to the decisions and determinations to be made.

Selection for Service

Virtually, all rehabilitation agencies and human-service programs have criteria established for determining who will be served. Some criteria may be relatively objective and easily established, such as the presence of a particular diagnosis or type of disability or the presence of a specified level of financial need. Others rely on more subjective determinations. Perhaps the most universally used criterion concerns the perceived benefits that are likely to occur if treatment or services are provided and whether these likely benefits are sufficient to justify whatever time, effort, and expense would be required to achieve them. In making such determinations, the working model of the individual is projected into the future to predict the likely outcomes of the rehabilitation process if services were to be provided, the extent to which those outcomes would be considered "successful," and the costs that would be associated with the services required to achieve those outcomes. These determinations are highly subjective and are based in part on the experience of the counselor with other individuals judged to be similar to the individual being assessed, along with the outcomes achieved with those individuals. A decision regarding selection of service requires that a value judgment be added, determining whether it is "worthwhile" to proceed with the provision of treatment or service.

In the public sector, or state/federal rehabilitation system, selection for service may also require assessment of severity of disability. In the state/federal system, federal legislation has mandated priority service to consumers with the most significant disabilities, which may necessitate an "order of selection" for services as a result of limited financial resources to serve everyone. Selection of service establishes priority for consumers with multiple impairments, whose mental or physical impairments most significantly limit functional capacities in terms of employment outcomes, and who are likely to require services over an extended period of time (Rubin & Roessler, 2008).

Establishing Career or Vocational Objectives

Career or vocational objectives are common goals established in rehabilitation counseling practice, and interventions and services are then planned and implemented to achieve those objectives. To establish career or vocational objectives, the working model of the individual is projected into work environments associated with different occupations in order to predict likely functioning and, consequently, likely satisfactoriness and satisfaction (Lofquist & Dawis, 1969). To the extent that assets, limitations, and preferences of the individual have been comprehensively identified in developing the working model of the individual, the process will be facilitated, as a suitable vocational objective will capitalize on the assets of the individual, will minimize the impact of limitations, and will be consistent with preferences. Assets and limitations must be considered in terms of any changes that are expected to occur as a result of intervention and service, along with potential accommodations that may be provided. In addition, as the working model of an individual is projected into a potential work environment and likely functioning is predicted, other assets or limitations may be identified that are specific to that particular environment. Information about the ability requirements and sources of satisfaction provided can be found in printed sources of occupational information, such as the O*NET occupational information system (OIS) (Hansen, Matheson, & Borman, 2008; O*Net Resource Center, 2011), as well as through job analyses and other direct observations of work environments. Finally, similar procedures can be used in establishing other types of life objectives and plans to be pursued, such as living arrangements that are consistent with an individual's assets, limitations, and preferences.

Treatment and Case Service Plans

The comprehensive listing of assets, limitations, and preferences of an individual provides the basis for developing treatment and case service plans, as problems or barriers that need to be targeted for intervention will be found among the limitations identified. In those instances in which a career or vocational objective is being pursued through the rehabilitation process, the working model of the individual is projected into work environments consistent with that objective, and the impact of the individual's limitations on functioning in those environments can then be predicted (employability determinations). Similarly, the impact of limitations identified can be determined on *obtaining* employment in that occupation (placeability determinations) and in functioning in whatever environments might be required in preparing for that occupation. Those limitations that are predicted to pose barriers to accomplishment of the objective are then targeted for intervention. Limitations targeted might include skill deficits (e.g., specific vocational skills, academic skills, social skills, independent travel skills, test-taking skills, and job-seeking skills), inconsistencies between typical behavior and environmental expectations (e.g., punctuality, mannerisms, speed, and lack of credentials such as degrees, diplomas, and licenses), or a wide variety of other limitations that may pose barriers (e.g., limitations in self-confidence, social support networks, finances, and transportation).

For each limitation that is targeted for intervention, one or more intervention strategies or services must be identified. Possible interventions would include counseling strategies and other services provided directly by the rehabilitation counselor, whereas other agencies or professionals would be called on to provide other interventions or services. The technique of "brainstorming," which involves the identification of as many alternative intervention strategies as possible while temporarily suspending judgment about their appropriateness, can serve to stimulate creativity in identifying a comprehensive array of alternatives. Decisions regarding the interventions of choice can then be achieved by projecting the working model of the individual into the future to predict the likely outcomes of each alternative intervention, while also considering the practical costs associated with each, including monetary costs, time, and effort. Intervention strategies selected are then organized into a comprehensive, integrated treatment, or service plan that is then implemented.

Disability Determinations

Rehabilitation counselors may be called upon to provide expert opinion regarding the vocational implications of disability in Social Security, workers' compensation, long-term disability, personal injury, and other related proceedings, and some rehabilitation counselors make such forensic assessments as a major part of their professional practice (Cox & Goldberg, 2010; Crystal & Erickson, 2010). Vocational expert opinion has been conceptualized as including both employability and placeability opinions (Lynch, 1983; Sleister, 2000). *Employability opinions* require the identification of occupations that are compatible with an individual's residual capacities. Formulation of those opinions would involve procedures similar to those described in establishing vocational objectives, in which the working model of the individual is projected into work environments associated with different occupations to predict likely functioning. *Placeability opinions* concern the likelihood of actually obtaining employment in particular occupations, and are influenced by the opinions of individuals empowered with hiring decisions regarding the suitability of candidates for employment. To formulate placeability opinions, the working model of the individual is projected into the hiring process to predict the likelihood of a favorable hiring decision. In addition, the availability and competition for jobs in a geographically defined labor market must be determined.

When rehabilitation counselors engage in the formulation of disability determinations, the terms "rehabilitation counselor" and "client" are often replaced by "vocational expert" and "evaluee"; the purpose of assessment is to address the impact of disability on vocational capabilities and to identify options for the resolution of legal disputes (Crystal & Erickson, 2010). The CRCC (2009) has described the informed consent and disclosures needed in situations of disability determination, including written disclosure explaining the purpose of the assessment, the rehabilitation counselor's role including report preparation and the potential of testimony, and limits on confidentiality. Furthermore, the code of ethics for rehabilitation counselors describes the need for objectivity and lack of bias when providing vocational expert opinion.

The determinations required of vocational experts will vary depending on the type of proceeding (Crystal & Erickson, 2010; Field & Sink, 1981; Rothstein, 1991). For example, in Social Security proceedings determinations must be made as to whether an individual is prevented by disability from engaging in substantial and gainful activity in jobs that are available in significant numbers in the national economy, without regard to reasonable accommodation. Vocational experts serve the Office of Disability Adjudication and Review in the Social Security disability process. Experts appear at hearings and provide vocational and employment information to administrative law judges; however, they do not interview applicants (Cox & Goldberg, 2010; Crystal & Erickson, 2010).

An interview commonly provides the foundation for disability determinations. The interview assists in further developing a working model of an individual through the ability to obtain firsthand information; to understand the individual's own perceptions of his or her assets, limitations, and preferences; and to identify concerns about current and future employment status (Berven, 2010; Crystal & Erickson, 2010). Prior to an interview, a vocational expert will review medical reports, functional capacity information, employment records, job descriptions, and other information provided with the referral. The interview allows the practitioner to address inconsistencies in reports and clarify gaps in work history.

In workers' compensation, as well as personal injury proceedings, determinations are often made regarding the loss of earning capacity resulting from a disability, which requires a comparison of earnings in jobs within the capabilities of and available to the individual in the local labor market prior to the onset of the disability, with earnings from jobs within the individual's capabilities and available following onset. However, workers' compensation statutes vary from state to state and may require that statutory-specific factors be considered in the disability determination process. For example, in addition to frequently examined factors such as age, education, training and previous work experience of an injured worker, determinations for loss of earning capacity in the state of Wisconsin should also address an applicant's "willingness to make reasonable change in a residence to secure suitable employment" and "success of and willingness to participate in reasonable physical and vocational rehabilitation program" (Wisconsin Administrative Code 80.34, 2009). In workers' compensation disability determinations in some states, as well as in personal injury, the effects of job accommodations on employability can be considered (Crystal & Erickson, 2010). Furthermore, in personal injury, calculation of actual wage loss in consideration of an individual's remaining work life may be part of the requested determination of impact of disability.

In long-term disability insurance coverage, individuals receive a percentage of wage replacement when they are unable to perform occupational duties as set forth in the long-term disability contract. It is common for individuals to receive wage replacement for a certain period of time when they are unable to perform their "own occupation." Once this phase has ended, many policies including a "change in definition" provision specifies that individuals can continue to receive wage replacement benefits only when they are unable to perform "any occupation" for which they are qualified by virtue of age, education, and transferable skills. Therefore, a disability determination includes identification of occupations that an individual still could perform, in light of current capacities (physical and or mental), and transferable skills which may have been acquired from past employment. Depending on the specifics of the long-term disability contract, a rehabilitation counselor may also be asked to provide labor market survey data.

A *transferable skills analysis* is often a key component of disability determinations. Transferable skills assessments (TSAs) are predicated on trait factor theory, and consider an individual's work history to identify factors such as occupational preferences, aptitudes, interests, and demonstrated skill levels. Many systems are computer based and automate the TSA process; these systems allow for adjustment of a worker profile based on the consequence of disability. In addition, many systems allow modification of the worker profile based on results of achievement, aptitude, and interest testing. The "job matching" approach of these systems is based on occupational information from the fourth and final edition of the *Dictionary of Occupational Titles (DOT)*, the *Classification of Jobs*, and a *Guide to Occupational Exploration*. Patterson (2008) provides a review of job-matching systems such as the Job Browser Pro and SkilTran Online Services.

An issue for disability determination by rehabilitation counselors is that the *DOT*, upon which many TSA systems are based, was last updated in 1991. The Department of Labor, which had maintained the *DOT*, is now supporting the ongoing development of O*NET. The *DOT* provided information on over 12,000 positions; in contrast, O*Net offers detailed, high quality, and current occupational information for only 965 occupations (O*Net Resource Center, 2011). Efforts to provide updated transferable skills information, which will provide valuable resource information for rehabilitation counselors in disability determination, are now under way; for example, the Social Security Administration is developing plans for an occupational classification system for use in the OIS to replace the *DOT* (Social Security Administration, 2009). However, regardless of the system that is devised, the exponential rate of occupational change will no doubt require some type of online access in order to maximize access to updated and current information.

It is important that rehabilitation counseling professionals be able to defend their choice of methods and tools used in disability determinations. Supreme Court decisions in *Daubert* v. *Merrell Dow Pharmaceuticals, Inc.* (1993), and *Kumbo Tire Co.* v. *Carmichael* (1999) have great impact on vocational expert testimony in courtroom situations, as they have established a trial judge's ability to determine whether testimony is relevant and reliable, whether the evidence offered is based on scientific standards, and whether the person offering testimony has sufficient expertise to be considered an "expert" (Crystal & Erickson, 2010; Sleister, 2000; Williams, Dunn, Bast, & Giesen, 2006). The *Daubert* decision provides that expert testimony must be relevant and "assist the trier of fact"; admissibility of testimony depends upon whether the theories and techniques used by an expert have been tested, subjected to peer review and publication, have a known error rate, are subjected to standards governing their application, and enjoy widespread acceptance (Nordberg, 2006).

FUTURE PERSPECTIVES

Assessment devices and resources have grown substantially in numbers and types in past years, and this growth seems likely to continue in the years ahead. The number of assessment devices available is so large that it is virtually impossible for any practitioner to be knowledgeable about all available alternatives for a particular assessment purpose. For example, over 4,000 standardized tests and inventories that are available in print in the English language are indexed in *Tests in Print VII* (Murphy et al., 2006), and more than 5,000 are indexed in the nine-volume *Directory of Unpublished Experimental Mental Measures* series (Goldman & Mitchell, 2007). From these examples, it seems clear that rehabilitation counselors have a wide range of assessment devices from which to choose, and identifying the available alternatives will continue to be increasingly difficult. In addition, the interpretation of assessment reports completed by psychologists, vocational evaluators, and other professionals frequently will include scores and other performance measures on tests and systems that are unfamiliar to rehabilitation counselors. If counselors are to be effective consumers of such assessment information and avoid deferring completely to the judgment of professionals conducting the outside assessments, they will need to maintain access to sources of information on new tests and systems and be diligent in consulting those sources of information when needed.

A relatively recent development facilitating the understanding disability that will have a growing impact on assessment in rehabilitation counseling is the previously mentioned ICF (WHO, 2001), which provides a framework for comprehensively describing the domains of disability and functioning. The ICF is a biopsychosocial approach to conceptualizing the impact of disability in terms of the interplay of factors such as body function and structure and environmental barriers and facilitators on capacity and performance (Bruyère, Van Looy, & Peterson, 2005). As an example of the growing impact of the ICF on assessment, a recently published textbook on assessment, *Rehabilitation and Health Assessment: Applying ICF Guidelines* (Mpofu & Oakland, 2010), has been organized around the ICF model. In addition, Peterson's (2011) *Psychological Aspects of Functioning, Disability, and Health* applies the ICF model to assessment of psychological functioning. As discussed by Peterson, Mpofu, and Oakland (2010), the ICF increasingly will be used as a framework for classifying assessment instruments and procedures in terms of the domains measured, as well as a basis for the development of new measures. This change should contribute to more comprehensive and useful assessments in rehabilitation counseling practice.

The application of computer technology in assessment is another trend that will certainly continue in future years, including greater use of web-based assessment methods. Computers have long been used in testing and assessment for scoring responses to psychological, educational, and vocational tests, in addition to administering and scoring tests and other assessment procedures, including diagnostic, intake, and other assessment interviews (e.g., see Burkhead & Sampson, 1985; Drasgow & Olson-Buchanan, 1999).

Computerized adaptive testing is an application of computer technology that is becoming more widely used in assessment, as exemplified by academic admissions tests such as the *Scholastic Aptitude Test (SAT)* and the *Graduate Record Examination (GRE)*, and computer-adaptive testing, holds much promise for the future (Osterland, Mpofu, & Oakland, 2010; Wainer, 2000; Weiss, 2004; Weiss & Vale, 1987). Computerized adaptive testing involves the construction via computer of an individually tailored test for each person taking the test by oversampling test items near the individual's level of the characteristic being tested (e.g., ability level), while excluding items that are either well above or well below that level (e.g., items that are too easy or too difficult). Computer-adaptive testing should be used more commonly in assessment in rehabilitation settings in the years ahead, and Reid, Kolakowsky-Hayner, Lewis, and Armstrong (2007) have discussed the applications of item response theory (IRT) to improve assessment instruments used with people with disabilities and demonstrate the application of IRT to a subtest of the general aptitude test battery (GATB).

Virtual reality is another application of computer technology that is likely to increase in rehabilitation settings in future years (Uswatte & Schultheis, 2010). Computer games represent one application of virtual reality, providing computer-generated, highly realistic, yet artificial, environments for real-time interaction. A number of applications of virtual reality have been reported for use in assessment in rehabilitation, including driving simulations for people with disabilities (Schultheis, Rebimbas, Mourant, & Mills, 2005). In another application, a shopping experience was simulated to assess cognitive impairment following a stroke (Kang et al., 2008). Virtual reality has been advocated for use in assessment, ranging from measurement of prospective memory abilities (Knight & Titov, 2009) to assessment of abilities for individuals with intellectual disabilities (Standen & Brown, 2005). By providing a close approximation of real-life situations, virtual reality would appear to have great promise in enhancing the ecological validity of assessment in rehabilitation settings.

Finally, evidence-based practice has become increasingly emphasized in psychology and the human services, including rehabilitation services (e.g., Chan, Tarvydas, Blalock, Strauser, & Atkins, 2008). Although treatment is often the primary focus of evidence-based practice, evidence-based assessment practices should also be emphasized (Hunsley & Marsh, 2007). It is important to consider available empirical support for the reliability and validity of procedures used for different assessment purposes and to select those procedures that have the greatest empirical documentation for a particular purpose. It would seem likely that rehabilitation counselors may not be aware of the empirical support available for many different assessment procedures and thus do not consider that information in selecting procedures for use or in interpreting assessment results. In addition, the empirical documentation may often be lacking for many widely used assessment procedures, and research is needed to develop empirical support. Given the importance of assessment to all aspects of rehabilitation counseling, the improvement of assessment methods and practices should be given a high priority if rehabilitation counselors are to assist individuals with disabilities effectively in making life decisions, overcoming barriers to accomplishing their goals, and maximizing quality of life.

CONTENT REVIEW QUESTIONS

■ How is assessment defined and what is its scope? What are the roles of rehabilitation counselors relative to consumers or clients in assessment and the overall rehabilitation process?
■ What is the general assessment process and how does it typically unfold in the overall rehabilitation process?
■ How are the concepts of reliability, validity, and standardization defined, and how do these concepts impact assessment?
■ What roles do initial and diagnostic interviews play in assessment, and what are some of the issues in conducting assessment interviews?
■ What is a "working model" of a client or consumer, how is it constructed, and what roles does it play in the assessment process?
■ What are heuristics and how might they bias clinical judgment?
■ How is assessment information translated into career or vocational objectives and treatment or service plans?
■ How is assessment information translated into different types of disability determinations?
■ How is computer technology influencing assessment practices, including computer-adaptive testing and virtual reality?

REFERENCES

American Educational Research Association, American Psychological Association, & National Council on Measurement in Education. (1999). *Standards for educational and psychological testing*. Washington, DC: American Educational Research Association.

Anastasi, A. (1992). Tests and assessment: What counselors should know about the use and interpretation of psychological tests. *Journal of Counseling and Development, 70,* 610–615.

Berven, N. L. (1980). Psychometric assessment in rehabilitation. In B. Bolton & D. W. Cook (Eds.), *Rehabilitation client assessment* (pp. 46–64). Baltimore, MD: University Park Press.

Berven, N. L. (2008a). Assessment interviewing. In B. F. Bolton & R. M. Parker (Eds.), *Handbook of measurement and evaluation in rehabilitation* (4th ed., pp. 241–261). Austin, TX: Pro-Ed.

Berven, N. L. (2008b). Rehabilitation counseling. In F. T. Leong (Lead Ed.), H. E. A. Tinsley & S. H. Lease (Vol. Eds.), *Encyclopedia of counseling: Vol. 2. Personal counseling and mental health problems* (pp. 827–832). Los Angeles, CA: Sage.

Berven, N. L. (2010). Clinical interviews. In E. Mpofu & T. Oakland (Eds.), *Assessment in rehabilitation and health* (pp. 158–171). Upper Saddle River, NJ: Merrill.

Bolton, B. F., & Parker, R. M. (2008). Preface. In B. F. Bolton & R. M. Parker (Eds.), *Handbook of measurement and evaluation in rehabilitation* (4th ed., pp. xv–xvi). Austin, TX: Pro-Ed.

Browder, D. (1991). *Assessment of individuals with severe disabilities: An applied behavior approach to life skills assessment* (2nd ed.). Baltimore, MD: Brookes.

Brown, M., Gordon, W. A., & Diller, L. (1983). Functional assessment and outcome measurement: An integrative review. In E. L. Pan, T. E. Backer, & C. L. Vash (Eds.), *Annual review of rehabilitation* (Vol. 3, pp. 93–120). New York, NY: Springer.

Bruyère, S. M., Van Looy, S. A., & Peterson, D. B. (2005). The International Classification of Functioning, Disability and Health: Contemporary literature overview. *Rehabilitation Psychology, 50,* 113–121.

Burkhead, E. J., & Sampson, J. P., Jr. (1985). Computer-assisted assessment in support of the rehabilitation process. *Rehabilitation Counseling Bulletin, 28,* 262–274.

Chan, F., Shaw, L. R., McMahon, B. T., Koch, L., & Strauser, D. (1997). A model for enhancing rehabilitation counselor-consumer working relationships. *Rehabilitation Counseling Bulletin, 41,* 122–137.

Chan, F., Tarvydas, V., Blalock, K., Strauser, D., & Atkins, B. J. (2008). Unifying and elevating rehabilitation counseling through model-driven, diversity-sensitive evidence-based practice. *Journal of Applied Rehabilitation Counseling, 39*(4), 46–50.

Commission on Rehabilitation Counselor Certification. (n.d.). *CRC/CCRC scope of practice.* Schaumburg, IL: Author.

Commission on Rehabilitation Counselor Certification. (2009). *Code of professional ethics for rehabilitation counselors.* Schaumburg, IL: Author.

Cox, D. R., & Goldberg, A. L. (2010). Assessment of disability. Social Security Disability evaluation. In E. Mpofu & T. Oakland (Eds.), *Assessment in rehabilitation and health* (pp. 192–204). Upper Saddle River, NJ: Merrill.

Craig, R. J. (2003). Assessing personality and psychopathology by interviews. In I. B. Weiner (Chief Ed.), J. R. Graham, & J. A. Naglieri (Vol. Eds.), *Handbook of psychology: Vol. 10. Assessment psychology* (pp. 487–508). Hoboken, NJ: Wiley.

Craig, R. J. (2005). The clinical process of interviewing. In R. J. Craig (Ed.), *Clinical and diagnostic interviewing* (2nd ed., pp. 21–41). Lanham, MD: Jason Aronson.

Crewe, N. M., & Dijkers, M. (1995). Functional assessment. In L. A. Cushman & M. J. Scherer (Eds.), *Psychological assessment in medical rehabilitation* (pp. 101–144). Washington, DC: American Psychological Association.

Crewe, N. M., & Groomes, D. A. (2008). Assessment of independence. In B. F. Bolton & R. M. Parker (Eds.), *Handbook of measurement and evaluation in rehabilitation* (4th ed., pp. 263–281). Austin, TX: Pro-Ed.

Cronbach, L. J. (1949). *Essentials of psychological testing.* New York, NY: Harper.

Crystal, R. M., & Erickson, A. S. (2010). Forensic assessment. In E. Mpofu & T. Oakland (Eds.), *Assessment in rehabilitation and health* (pp. 172–191). Upper Saddle River, NJ: Merrill.

Czerlinsky, T., Jensen, R., & Pell, K. L. (1987). Construct validity of the Vocational Decision-Making Interview (VDMI). *Rehabilitation Counseling Bulletin, 31,* 28–33.

Daniel, M. S., & Crider, C. J. (2003). Mental status examination. In M. Hersen & S. M. Turner (Eds.), *Diagnostic interviewing* (3rd ed., pp. 21–46). New York, NY: Kluwer Academic/ Plenum.

Daubert v. Merrell Dow Pharmaceuticals (92-102), 509 U.S. 579 (1993).

Dowd, L. R. (1993). *Glossary of terminology for vocational assessment, evaluation, and work adjustment.* Menomonie, WI: University of Wisconsin-Stout, Stout Vocational Rehabilitation Institute.

Drasgow, F., & Olson-Buchanan, J. B. (Eds.). (1999). *Innovations in computerized assessment.* Mahwah, NJ: Erlbaum.

Drummond, R. J., & Jones, K. D. (2006). *Assessment procedures for counselors and helping professionals* (6th ed.). Upper Saddle River, NJ: Pearson.

Ekstrom, R. B., & Smith, D. K. (2002). *Assessing individuals with disabilities in educational, employment, and counseling settings.* Washington, DC: American Psychological Association.

Esser, T. J. (1975). *Client rating instruments for use in vocational rehabilitation agencies.* Menomonie, WI: University of Wisconsin-Stout, Stout Vocational Rehabilitation Institute.

Ewing, J. A. (1984). Detecting alcoholism: The CAGE Questionnaire. *Journal of the American Medical Association, 252,* 1905–1907.

Falvey, J. E. (2001). Clinical judgment in case conceptualization and treatment planning across mental health disciplines. *Journal of Counseling and Development, 79,* 292–303.

Falvey, J. E., Bray, T. E., & Hebert, D. J. (2005). Case conceptualization and treatment planning: Investigation of problem-solving and clinical judgment. *Journal of Mental Health Counseling, 27,* 348–372.

Farley, R. C., & Rubin, S. E. (2006). The intake interview. In R. Roessler & S. E. Rubin (Eds.), *Case management and rehabilitation counseling: Procedures and techniques* (4th ed., pp. 51–74). Austin, TX: Pro-Ed.

Field, T. F., & Sink, J. M. (1981). *The vocational expert.* Athens, GA: VSB.

First, M. B., Spitzer, R. L., Gibbon, M., & Williams, J. B. W. (1997). *Structured clinical interview for DSM-IV axis I disorders (SCID-I)-clinician version.* Washington, DC: American Psychiatric Press.

Folstein, M. F., Folstein, S. E., & McHugh, P. R. (1975). "Mini-Mental State": A practical method for grading the cognitive state of patients for the clinician. *Journal of Psychiatric Research, 12,* 189–198.

Galassi, J. P., & Perot, A. R. (1992). What you should know about behavioral assessment. *Journal of Counseling and Development, 70,* 624–631.

Garb, H. N. (1998). *Studying the clinician: Judgment research and psychological assessment.* Washington, DC: American Psychological Association.

Garb, H. N., Klein, D. F., & Grove, W. M. (2002). Comparison of medical and psychological tests. *American Psychologist, 57,* 137–138.

Giannetti, R. A. (1992). *User's guide for Quickview Social History—Clinical Version.* Minneapolis, MN: National Computer Systems.

Goldman, B. A., & Mitchell, D. F. (2007). *Directory of unpublished experimental mental measures* (Vol. 9). Washington, DC: American Psychological Association.

Goldman, L. (1971). *Using tests in counseling* (2nd ed.). Pacific Palisades, CA: Goodyear.

Granger, C. V., Gilewski, M., & Carlin, M. (2010). Measures of functional performance. In E. Mpofu & T. Oakland (Eds.), *Rehabilitation and health assessment: Applying ICF guidelines* (pp. 547–568). New York, NY: Springer.

Groth-Marnat, G. (2009). *Handbook of psychological assessment* (5th ed.). Hoboken, NJ: Wiley.

Halpern, A. S., & Fuhrer, M. J. (Eds.). (1984). *Functional assessment in rehabilitation.* Baltimore, MD: Paul H. Brookes.

Hanson, M. A., Matheson, L. N., & Borman, W. C. (2008). The O*NET occupational information system. In B. F. Bolton & R. M. Parker (Eds.), *Handbook of measurement and evaluation in rehabilitation* (pp. 337–371). Austin, TX: Pro-Ed.

Harley, D. A., Smith, D. L., & Alston, R. J. (2010). Measures of independent living. In E. Mpofu & T. Oakland (Eds.), *Assessment in rehabilitation and health* (pp. 399–416). Upper Saddle River, NJ: Merrill.

Harrison, D. K., Garnett, J. M., & Watson, A. L. (1981). *Client assessment measures in rehabilitation* (Michigan Studies in Rehabilitation Utilization Series: 5). Ann Arbor, MI: University of Michigan Rehabilitation Research Institute.

Haverkamp, B. E. (1993). Confirmatory bias in hypothesis testing for client-identified and counselor self-generated hypotheses. *Journal of Counseling Psychology, 40,* 303–315.

Hersen, M., & Turner, S. M. (Eds.). (2003). *Diagnostic interviewing* (3rd ed.). New York, NY: Kluwer Academic/Plenum.

Holmes, G. E. (1993). The historical roots of the empowerment dilemma in vocational rehabilitation. *Journal of Disability Policy Studies, 4,* 1–20.

Holzbauer, J. J., & Berven, N. L. (1999). Issues in vocational evaluation and testing related to the Americans with disabilities Act. *Vocational Evaluation and Work Adjustment Bulletin, 32,* 83–96.

Hood, A. B., & Johnson, R. W. (2007). *Assessment in counseling: A guide to the use of psychological assessment procedures* (4th ed.). Alexandria, VA: American Counseling Association.

Hunsley, J. (2002). Psychological testing and psychological assessment: A closer examination. *American Psychologist, 57,* 139–140.

Hunsley, J., & Marsh, E. J. (2007). Evidence-based assessment. *Annual Review of Clinical Psychology, 3,* 29–51.

Joiner, T. E., Walker, R. L., Rudd, M. D., & Jobes, D. A. (1999). Scientizing and routinizing the assessment of suicidality in outpatient practice. *Professional Psychology: Research and Practice, 30,* 447–453.

Kahneman, D., Slovic, P., & Tversky, A. (1982). *Judgment under uncertainty: Heuristics and biases.* New York, NY: Cambridge University Press.

Kang, Y., Ku, J., Han, K., Kim, S. I., Yu, T., Lee, J., & Park, C. (2008). Development and clinical trial of virtual reality-based cognitive assessment in people with stroke: Preliminary study. *CyberPsychology & Behavior, 11,* 329–339.

Kaplan, R. M., & Saccuzzo, D. P. (2009). *Psychological testing. Principles, applications, and issues* (7th ed.). Belmont, CA: Thompson Wadsworth.

Kitchens, J. M. (1994). Does this patient have an alcohol problem? *Journal of the American Medical Association, 272,* 1782–1787.

Knight, R. G., & Titov, N. (2009). Use of virtual reality tasks to assess prospective memory: Applicability and evidence. *Brain Impairment, 10,* 3–13.

Kosciulek, J. F. (1999). The consumer-directed theory of empowerment. *Rehabilitation Counseling Bulletin, 42,* 196–213.

Kosciulek, J. F. (2004). Theory of informed consumer choice in vocational rehabilitation. *Rehabilitation Education, 18,* 3–11.

Kosciulek, J. F. (2005). Structural equation model of the consumer-directed theory of empowerment in a vocational rehabilitation context. *Rehabilitation Counseling Bulletin, 49,* 40–49.

Kosciulek, J. F., & Merz, M. A. (2001). Structural analysis of the consumer-directed theory of empowerment. *Rehabilitation Counseling Bulletin, 44,* 209–216.

Kumho Tire Co. v. Carmichael (97-1709), 526 U.S. 137 (1999).

Lofquist, L. H., & Dawis, R. V. (1969). *Adjustment to work: A psychological view of man's problems in a work-oriented society.* New York, NY: Appleton-Century-Crofts.

Lopez, S. R. (1989). Patient variable biases in clinical judgment: Conceptual overview and methodological implications. *Psychological Bulletin, 106,* 184–203.

Lynch, R. K. (1983). The vocational expert. *Rehabilitation Counseling Bulletin, 27,* 18–25.

Maki, D. R., McCracken, N., Pape, D. A., & Scofield, M. E. (1979). A systems approach to vocational assessment. *Journal of Rehabilitation, 45*(1), 48–51.

McArthur, C. (1954). Analyzing the clinical process. *Journal of Counseling Psychology, 1,* 203–208.

Meyer, G. J., Finn, S. E., Eyde, L. D., Kay, G. G., Moreland, K. L., Dies, R. R., . . . Reed, G. M. (2001). Psychological testing and psychological assessment. A review of evidence. *American Psychologist, 56,* 128–165.

Moriarty, J. B., Walls, R. T., & McLaughlin, D. E. (1987). The Preliminary Diagnostic Questionnaire (PDQ): Functional assessment of employability. *Rehabilitation Psychology, 32,* 5–15.

Morrow, K. A., & Deidan, C. T. (1992). Bias in the counseling process: How to recognize it and avoid it. *Journal of Counseling and Development, 70,* 571–577.

Mpofu, E., & Oakland, T. (Eds.). (2010). *Rehabilitation and health assessment: Applying ICF guidelines.* New York, NY: Springer.

Murphy, L. L., Spies, R. A., & Plake, B. S. (Eds.). (2006). *Tests in print VII. An index to tests, test reviews, and the literature on specific tests.* Lincoln, NE: Buros Institute on Mental Measurements, University of Nebraska Press, University of Nebraska-Lincoln.

National Institute on Consumer-Directed Long-Term Services. (1996). *Principles of consumer-directed home and community-based services.* Washington, DC: Author.

Nester, M. A. (1993). Psychometric testing and reasonable accommodation for persons with disabilities. *Rehabilitation Psychology, 38,* 75–83.

Nezu, A. M., & Nezu, C. M. (1993). Identifying and selecting target problems for clinical interventions: A problem-solving model. *Psychological Assessment, 5,* 254–263.

Nordberg, P. (2006). Daubert in a nutshell. In *The Daubert worldview* (Chap. 2). Retrieved January 22, 2011, from http://www.daubertontheweb.com

Nosek, M. A. (1998). Independent living. In R. M. Parker & E. M. Szymanski (Eds.), *Rehabilitation counseling: Basics and beyond* (3rd ed., pp. 107–141). Austin, TX: Pro-Ed.

O*Net Resource Center. (2011). *About O*Net.* Retrieved February 11, 2011, from http://www.onetcenter.org/overview.html

Osterlind, S. J., Mpofu, E., & Oakland, T. (2010). Item response theory and computer adaptive testing. In E. Mpofu & T. Oakland (Eds.), *Rehabilitation and health assessment. Applying* ICF *guidelines* (pp. 95–119). New York, NY: Springer.

Parker, R. M. (2008). Aptitude testing. In B. F. Bolton & R. M. Parker (Eds.), *Handbook of measurement and evaluation in rehabilitation* (4th ed., pp. 121–150). Austin, TX: Pro-Ed.

Parker, R. M., & Bolton, B. (2005). Psychological assessment in rehabilitation. In R. M. Parker, E. M. Szymanski, & J. B. Patterson (Eds.), *Rehabilitation counseling: Basics and beyond* (4th ed., pp. 307–334). Austin, TX: Pro-Ed.

Parker, R. M., Hansmann, S., & Schaller, J. L. (2010). Vocational assessment and disability. In E. M. Szymanski & R. M. Parker (Eds.), *Work and disability: Contexts, issues, and strategies for enhancing employment outcomes for people with disabilities* (3rd ed., pp. 203–244). Austin, TX: Pro-Ed.

Parker, R. M., Szymanski, E. M., & Hanley-Maxwell, C. (1989). Ecological assessment in supported employment. *Journal of Applied Rehabilitation Counseling, 20*(3), 26–33.

Patterson, J. B. (2008) Assessment of work behavior. In B. F. Bolton & R. M. Parker (Eds.), *Handbook of measurement and evaluation in rehabilitation* (4th ed., pp. 309–336). Austin, TX: Pro-Ed.

Patterson, W. M., Dohn, H. H., Bird, J., & Patterson, G. A. (1983). Evaluation of suicidal patients: The SAD PERSONS Scale. *Psychosomatics, 24,* 343–349.

Pepinsky, H. B., & Pepinsky, N. (1954). *Counseling theory and practice.* New York, NY: Ronald Press.

Peterson, D. B. (2011). *Psychological aspects of functioning, disability, and health.* New York, NY: Springer.

Peterson, D. B., Mpofu, E., & Oakland, T. (2010). Concepts and models in disability, functioning, and health. In E. Mpofu & T. Oakland (Eds.), *Rehabilitation and health assessment: Applying* ICF *guidelines* (pp. 3–26). New York, NY: Springer.

Power, P. W. (2006). *A guide to vocational assessment* (4th ed.). Austin, TX: Pro-Ed.

Reid, C. A., Kolakowsky-Hayner, S. A., Lewis, A. N., & Armstrong, A. J. (2007). Modern psychometric methodology: Applications of item response theory. *Rehabilitation Counseling Bulletin, 50,* 177–188.

Rogers, J. R., Alexander, R. A., & Subich, L. M. (1994). Development and psychometric analysis of the Suicide Assessment Checklist. *Journal of Mental Health Counseling, 16,* 352–368.

Rosenthal, D. A., & Berven, N. L. (1999). Effects of client race on clinical judgment. *Rehabilitation Counseling Bulletin, 42,* 243–264.

Rothstein, M. A. (1991). The law-medicine interface in assessing vocational capacity. In S. J. Sdheer (Ed.), *Medical perspectives in vocational assessment of impaired workers* (pp. 407–422). Gaithersburg, MD: Aspen.

Rubin, S. E., & Roessler, R. T. (2008). *Foundations of the vocational rehabilitation process* (6th ed.). Austin, TX: Pro-Ed.

Schultheis, M. T., Rebimbas, J., Mourant, R., & Mills, S. R. (2005). Examining the usability of a virtual reality driving simulator. *Archives of Physical Medicine and Rehabilitation, 86,* e12.

Sherman, S., & Robinson, N. (Eds.). (1982). *Ability testing of handicapped people: Dilemma for government, science, and the public.* Washington, DC: National Academy Press.

Silva, F. (1993). *Psychometric foundations and behavioral assessment.* Newbury Park, CA: Sage.

Sleister, S. (2000). Separating the wheat from the chaff: The role of the vocational expert in forensic vocational rehabilitation. *Journal of Vocational Rehabilitation, 14,* 119–129.

Smith, D. A. (2002). Validity and values: Monetary and otherwise. *American Psychologist, 57,* 136–137.

Social Security Administration. (2009). *Working paper: Developing an initial classification system.* Retrieved February 12, 2011, from http://www.ssa.gov/oidap/Documents/WEBFORMATTED--071509%20Developing%20an%20Initial%20Classification%20System.pdf

Sommers-Flanagan, J., & Sommers-Flanagan, R. (2003). *Clinical interviewing* (3rd ed.). Hoboken, NJ: Wiley.

Spies, R. A., Carlson, J. F., & Geisinger, K. F. (2010). *The eighteenth mental measurements yearbook.* Lincoln, NE: Buros Institute on Mental Measurements, University of Nebraska Press, University of Nebraska-Lincoln.

Standen, P. J., & Brown, D. J. (2005). Virtual reality in the rehabilitation of people with intellectual disabilities: Review. *CyberPsychology & Behavior, 8,* 272–282.

Strohmer, D. C., & Leierer, S. J. (2000). Modeling rehabilitation counselor judgment. *Rehabilitation Counseling Bulletin, 44,* 3–9, 38.

Strohmer, D. C., Shivy, V. A., & Chiodo, A. L. (1990). Information processing strategies in counselor hypothesis testing: The role of selective memory and expectancy. *Journal of Counseling Psychology, 37,* 465–472.

Sundberg, N. D. (1977). *Assessment of persons.* Englewood Cliffs, NJ: Prentice Hall.

Sundberg, N. D., & Tyler, L. E. (1962). *Clinical psychology.* New York, NY: Appleton-Century-Crofts.

Tenth Institute on Rehabilitation Issues. (1983). *Functional assessment.* Dunbar: West Virginia University, West Virginia Research and Training Center.

Turk, D. C., & Salovey, P. (1985). Cognitive structures, cognitive processes, and cognitive-behavior modification: II. Judgments and inferences of the clinician. *Cognitive Therapy and Research, 9,* 19–33.

Tversky, A., & Kahneman, D. (1974). Judgment under uncertainty: Heuristics and biases. *Science, 185,* 1124–1131.

Uswatte, G., & Schultheis, M. T. (2010). Real and virtual tools for objectively measuring function during everyday activities. In E. Mpofu & T. Oakland (Eds.), *Rehabilitation and health assessment: Applying* ICF *guidelines* (pp. 121–139). New York, NY: Springer.

VandenBos, G. R. (Ed. in Chief). (2007). *APA dictionary of psychology.* Washington, DC: American Psychological Association.

Wainer, H. (2000). *Computerized adaptive testing: A primer* (2nd ed.). Mahwah, NJ: Erlbaum.

Weiss, D. J. (2004). Computerized adaptive testing for effective and efficient measurement in counseling and education. *Measurement and Evaluation in Counseling and Development, 37,* 70–84.

Weiss, D. J., & Vale, C. D. (1987). Adaptive testing. *Applied Psychology: An International Review, 36,* 249–262.

Whitfield, E. A., Feller, R. W., & Wood, C. (Eds.). (2009). *A counselor's guide to career assessment instruments* (5th ed.). Broken Arrow, OK: National Career Development Association.

Williams, J., Dunn, P., Bast, S., & Giesen, J. (2006). Factors considered by vocational rehabilitation professionals in employability and earning capacity assessment. *Rehabilitation Counseling Bulletin, 50,* 24–34.

Willingham, W. W., Ragosta, M., Bennett, R. E., Braun, H., Rock, D. A., & Powers, D. E. (1988). *Testing handicapped people.* Boston, MA: Allyn & Bacon.

Wisconsin Administrative Code § Department of Workforce Development 80.34 (2009).

World Health Organization. (2001). *International classification of functioning, disability and health* (ICF). Geneva, Switzerland: Author.

12
Counseling

Mark A. Stebnicki

LEARNING OBJECTIVES

After reading this chapter, you should be able to:

■ Understand the current scope of practice in rehabilitation counseling and the impact that counselor licensure legislation has on the field concerning eligibility for counselor licensure and becoming an independent rehabilitation practitioner.
■ Define the foundational skills and scope of practice required for effective, competent, and ethical rehabilitation counseling practice.
■ Explain a psychosocial model for rehabilitation counselors who want to structure therapeutic interactions with clients who have chronic illnesses and disabilities.
■ Explore a career path of professional rehabilitation counselor that brings meaning and purpose to a livelihood much better than average occupational outlook of most other counseling professions.

Rehabilitation counseling is a challenging profession that has a prolific history of facilitating counseling strategies, approaches, and services for people with chronic illnesses and disabilities. Rehabilitation counseling as a specialization within the profession of counseling assists individuals in achieving optimal levels of response to their psychological, emotional, sociocultural, medical, physical, career, vocational, environmental, and independent functioning. The scope of practice as affirmed by the Commission on Rehabilitation Counselor Certification (CRCC, 2010) and the Council on Rehabilitation Education (CORE, 2010) suggests that rehabilitation counselors: (1) are ethically obligated to act in beneficent ways to empower persons with disabilities with resources that lead to the best possible outcomes in the least restrictive environments, (2) facilitate the rehabilitation process using a unique set of holistic skills assisting persons to reach their highest level of psychosocial adjustment, and (3) should embrace a philosophy that ultimately results in clients/clients achieving personally fulfilling, socially meaningful, emotionally healthy, independent, and productive lives.

Because rehabilitation counselor education programs are a specialty area of counseling that is comprehensive in nature, most programs prepare graduate students for multiple career options and employment settings. Indeed, rehabilitation counselors possess a unique set of knowledge, awareness, and facilitative skills to understand the challenges people with disabilities face on a day-to-day basis. These challenges go beyond the individual's medical, physical, cognitive, and mental health issues. Accordingly, it is essential that professional rehabilitation counselors know the residual capacities and functional limitations of individuals with disabilities within the context of society's attitudinal and physical barriers to independence, and how this interacts with their career and educational opportunities, and physical, cognitive, and mental health.

DEFINING THE PROFESSION OF COUNSELING AND THE COUNSELING PROCESS

Defining the construct of counseling is an enormous task. It is often misunderstood by clients of services and the general public because of the multiple specialty areas that engage in the practice of professional counseling. State counselor licensure, national certification, and counselor credentialing boards often disagree about the definition and scope of practice for professional counselors. Despite this history, the American Association of State Counselor Licensure Boards (AASCB) in partnership with the American Counseling Association (ACA), the largest professional counseling association with the most membership residing in North American and beyond, defined *counseling* during a meeting of ACA's annual conference that took place on March 31, 2010 (ACA, 2010b). This joint Oversight Committee representing over 29 professional counseling organizations and associations (including the rehabilitation counseling profession) was charged with utilizing a systematic research approach involving work groups, as well as focus/study groups for developing a clear, brief, concise definition for the field of counseling. This committee approved by consensus the following definition:

> *Counseling is a professional relationship that empowers diverse individuals, families, and groups to accomplish mental health, wellness, education, and career goals.*

It is important to note that the delegates to the ACA and AASCB's Oversight Committee anticipate an expanded definition of counseling in the coming years, because we are in an evolving field of professionals that offer therapeutic services to individuals, families, and groups in a variety of settings (e.g., Internet, face-to-face, and health care settings).

To further define the general concept of counseling, Corey and Corey (2011) provide a comprehensive overview that highlights the definition of each counseling specialty (e.g., addiction, career, school, mental health, and rehabilitation counseling) along with scope of practice. These authors suggest that many practitioners and professional counseling associations would concur that the professional counselor's specialty practice is defined by both the population and the setting in which services are provided. Based on these areas of specialty, individuals, groups, and families are offered a distinctive set of programs and services that are unique to a particular environment. For instance, school counselors work primarily in school settings; substance abuse counselors work primarily in residential, inpatient, and/or outpatient rehabilitation treatment programs; career counselors work in vocational and career counseling centers; and pastoral counselors work primarily in faith-based and hospital settings.

Hackney and Cormier (2009) note that the various professional counseling specialties have emerged as a result of the individual's interpersonal and intrapersonal needs. These needs are related to the individual's personality traits, behaviors, cognitive abilities, emotional and psychological wellness, unique cultural aspects, and developmental phase of life. If viewed through this counseling lens, then each professional counselor selects specific therapeutic interventions based on their academic and clinical education. Therapeutic effectiveness is enhanced by knowing each client's coping resources, external supports, and resiliency traits.

Ivey, Ivey, & Zalaquett (2010) suggest that the terms "counseling," "interviewing," and "therapy" have considerable overlap within the counseling literature. Because they are often used interchangeably, there may be some confusion concerning the counseling process. The term "interviewing" typically refers to the basic process of gathering information, problem solving, and dealing with the psychosocial aspects of individuals by facilitating brief short-term counseling strategies. However, the process of counseling and therapy is more long term, intensive, and has the possibilities for forming a more intense personal therapeutic relationship with the individual. Counselors often use the terms "counseling" and "therapy" interchangeably without a standard agreed upon definition. There is continuing interest and attention given to these two terms as professionalization initiatives move forward particularly with regard to regulatory groups and managed care. The term "counseling" will be used throughout this chapter.

COUNSELING AS A RECURSIVE DYNAMIC PROCESS

Early in the process of preparation, the rehabilitation counselor must master the basic theoretical approaches and technical skills of communication. An important component of this preparation is a keen awareness and mastery of relationship values that are fundamental to the counseling process.

The counseling relationship is built on the foundation of a set of values such as respect, warmth, understanding, genuineness, congruency, authenticity, and positive regard. The success of this relationship comes when a partnership can be created with the client. This alliance is developed based on trust and mutual agreement on the client's concern. Based on these building blocks, the client and the counselor engage in a recurrent interaction to develop meaning making of the client's situation and to empower them. This results in a dynamic process that structures the counseling process and helps the client sequentially progress from the problem to the desired change. This recurrent interaction primarily relies on self-reflection as the client works on making meaning and the development of self-awareness and as the counselor uses selected counseling strategies. Clients naturally try to understand the meaning of events and experiences occurring in their lives. The counselor uses this natural tendency to help clients refer to their personal history, knowledge, awareness, and life experiences to derive meaning. The resulting self-discovery and awareness generates energy and focus from the client that is geared toward the desired action. Also, the counselor and the client, through selected counseling strategies and approaches, repeatedly look at the context of the client through insight and self-reflection. Central to this process is the readiness of the client to take action. Once this readiness sets in, positive change can occur at multiple cognitive, emotional, behavioral, and spiritual levels. Typically, this change results in an increased ability for clients to deal with significant concerns or the issues that brought them initially into the counseling process (Lopez Levers, 1997).

Ivey, Ivey, & Zalaquett (2010, p. 15) assert that there are core skills that counselors and psychotherapist use in the helping process, which are required to build a therapeutic relationship and help clients work through their specific issues. These authors propose a hierarchy or pyramid of microskills where the foundation is built upon intentional interviewing skills that integrate the counselors' ethical behavior, cultural competence, and facilitation of client wellness. The foundation for building and sustaining a working alliance is an ongoing task in the counseling process. However, the essential core skills that must be acquired by the professional counselor or psychotherapist include the following skills that can be taught through education, awareness, modeling, and experience:

- Attending and listening
- Open and closed questions
- Client observation skills
- Encouraging, paraphrasing, and summarizing
- Reflection of feeling
- The five-stage interview structure
- Confrontation
- Focusing

- Reflection of meaning and interpretation/reframing
- Influencing skills and counseling strategies
- Skill integration
- Determining personal style and theory

Ivey, Ivey, & Zalaquett (2010) suggest that as the counselor or psychotherapist gains a sense of mastery they will then learn that each client has unique needs that are communicated with an array of verbal and nonverbal response. Thus, it is incumbent upon the professional to identify their client's unique style of expression and communication.

In Egan's (2002, p. 32) perspective, the skilled helper engages in the counseling process within a three-stage Skilled Helper Model as follows:

- Stage I: What is going on? (Counselors help clients clarify key issues for change.)
- Stage II: What solutions make sense? (Counselors help their clients determine outcome.)
- Stage III: What do I have to do to get what I need or want? (Counselors develop strategies for helping clients accomplishing their goals.)

In Egan's (2002) three-stage model the counseling process involves two basic goals. The first is recognizing how clients manage specific problems in their day-to-day life. This goal relates to the way in which professional counselors can assist their clients by facilitating opportunities and resources so that clients can live more optimally. The second goal relates to clients' general ability to manage their problems, develop better coping skills, and recognize opportunities for everyday living. Accordingly, counseling is about increasing the client's levels of emotional and psychological functioning. Egan views a flexible model of skilled helping. However, therapeutic interactions must be structured so as to not let "clients wander around in the morass of problem situations under the guise of flexibility that leads nowhere" (p. 35). Thus, counseling is about helping individuals achieve results, view the outcomes, and have a sense of accomplishment that they have achieved by their difficult work in counseling.

Perhaps universal within the counseling process is an understanding of how to establish client rapport and achieve a meaningful working alliance within a multicultural context. Integrating the knowledge, awareness, and skills to work with the individual's gender, race, ethnicity, gender orientation, socioeconomic status, spiritual and religious beliefs, and disability is of paramount importance. The RESPECTFUL Model provides a comprehensive and functional approach cultural competence within the counseling process (D'Andrea, M., & Daniels, J. 2001). Accordingly, counseling theory and approach should not replace the professional counselor's ability to achieve meaningful rapport with clients in a multicultural context. Without client rapport, a meaningful working alliance will be difficult to achieve and clients will likely terminate services prematurely.

THE EVOLVING DEFINITION AND SCOPE OF
REHABILITATION COUNSELING PRACTICE

The foundational skills of person-centered interactions within a human-istic model of counseling have always been at the foundation of the reha-bilitation counselor's scope of practice (Stebnicki, 2008a, p. 46). Perhaps it is time to revisit our professional identity by reviewing the collective wis-dom of early rehabilitation counselor educators, researchers, and practi-tioners. Mapping a healthy future for rehabilitation counseling begins by honoring past lineage and cultivating our perception and career identity toward new career opportunities, of paramount importance for rehabilitation counselors.

A Brief Historical Perspective of Counseling

The field of counseling evolved primarily as a group of specialty areas (e.g., vocational, school, mental health, and rehabilitation) that practiced a com-mon core of competencies and foundational skills (Leahy, Rak, & Zanskas, 2009, p. 3). Professional counselors were differentiated primarily by their em-ployment setting, the types of clients served, and the counseling approaches facilitated (Meyers, 1995). As Wright (1980) asserted, "no matter what other functions and responsibilities are engaged in by the rehabilitation counselor, counseling is the central function that is provided continuously throughout the rehabilitation process" (p. 54). Rubin and Roessler (1978) comprehensively described the role and function of rehabilitation counselors as they pointed to several defining periods in history when professional rehabilitation asso-ciations and organizations decided that the field was closely aligned with the counseling profession. These authors also contended that rehabilitation coun-selors functioned as case managers and coordinators of services for people with disabilities.

Patterson (1957) was one of the first who sought to resolve the reha-bilitation counselor identity by stressing the "two separate hats theory," suggesting that rehabilitation professionals function as both psychological counselors and as case managers/coordinators. Later, Patterson (1966) advo-cated that vocational rehabilitation state agencies should employ both reha-bilitation case coordinators and rehabilitation counselors to provide services to persons with disabilities. Whitehouse (1975) advocated the "big hat the-ory," in which the rehabilitationist is a counselor, clinician, and professional who works with the holistic needs of the individual. There are multiple roles that all counseling professionals serve in their daily practice. However, it is vital we understand that one of the most essential job functions of rehabilita-tion practitioners encompasses the role as a professional counselor serving diverse individuals, groups, and families that have a variety of disabilities throughout the life span.

Oftentimes, family members will ask individuals preparing for the profession. What is rehabilitation counseling? The short response can be summed up in one sentence: *Rehabilitation counseling is a holistic counseling profession that works with the medical, vocational, and psychosocial aspects of people with chronic illnesses and disabilities.*

CURRENT PRACTICE IN REHABILITATION COUNSELING

Rehabilitation counseling appears much different than it did in the 1990s primarily because there are more occupational titles (i.e., career counselor, licensed professional counselor [LPC], and substance abuse counselor) and job settings (e.g., psychiatric substance abuse hospitals, neuro-rehabilitation units, and career development centers) that exist for rehabilitation counseling professionals. In addition, more state counselor licensure boards have allowed rehabilitation counselors to engage in independent practice by becoming eligible for counselor licensure, diagnosing and treating substance abuse and other mental health conditions, billing third-party payers, and other rights and privileges afforded to psychologists and social workers.

There is only one occupational title in the *Dictionary of Occupational Titles* (DOT, 1991) that represents the specialty area of counseling within the field of rehabilitation. This title makes reference to "Vocational Rehabilitation Counseling," which is a job title that is associated primarily with the state/federal program of vocational rehabilitation. All other occupational titles seen in online career sites, want ads in newspapers, professional and organizational job banks, and other job resources will typically use the titles of "mental health counselor," "substance abuse counselor," "counselor-case manager," as well as other related counseling titles. It should come as no surprise that the general public and clients truly believe that all rehabilitation counselors work for the department of vocational rehabilitation, either at the state or at the federal level.

Today it is a much improved job market for rehabilitation counselors because of the diversity of job settings and titles into which recent graduates of CORE-accredited programs have been hired. In a survey of all CORE-accredited programs, Goodwin (2006) reported that 60% of all RCE programs offer a specialty concentration. The most frequently identified specialties were that of substance abuse counseling, clinical mental health counseling, and deafness and hearing impairment counselling. In regard to RCE programs that offer a specialization in psychiatric rehabilitation, Goodwin identified 11 programs with a psychiatric rehabilitation specialization. Bernacchio, Burker, Falvo, Porter, and Carone (2008) identified four other programs nationally with this particular specialization and two additional that have long-term education grants through the Rehabilitation Service Administration (RSA).

Many state legislators, clients of counseling services, and the general public understand the role and function of psychologists and social workers. However, as evidenced by the diverse specialties or program concentrations offered in rehabilitation counselor education programs, few outside the field know or understand the professional identity of rehabilitation counselors as specialization of the general counseling profession. Thus, state legislators and clients are challenged with trying to understand the identity of rehabilitation counselors because of the many credentials in the general counseling field (e.g., addiction specialists, licensed mental health counselors, LPCs, marriage and family therapists, and certified case managers). It should come as no surprise that the historical question is once again posed by counselor certification, accreditation, and licensing boards outside rehabilitation: Are rehabilitation counselors case managers/coordinators or are they part of the counseling profession?

The Pivotal Shift Within Rehabilitation Counseling

There are multiple indicators that suggest that there is a shift in the foundational principles and practices in rehabilitation counseling. We are in a state of transition concerning our professional identity. Indeed, rehabilitation counseling looks and feels much different now than when it was first conceived by our lineage of creative practitioners, client advocates, highly productive rehabilitation counselor educators, and visionaries from the 1950s to1970s. This is evidenced by state counselor licensure laws that have slowly recognized rehabilitation counseling professionals as eligible for counselor licensure within their state, as well as issues concerning granting graduates of CORE-accredited programs status as a qualified service provider (Stebnicki, 2008a).

Despite that all 50 states have legislation that regulates the counseling profession, some state counselor licensure laws restrict rehabilitation counselors from becoming licensed as professional counselors. This is due partially to the fact that the majority of state counselor licensure laws now require a 60-semester-hours master's program in addition to 3,000 hours of supervised clinical experience (ACA, 2010a). Most CORE-accredited programs are 48–54 semester hours (National Council on Rehabilitation Education [NCRE], 2009) and do not require the intense clinical supervised experiences or client contact as required by other counselor-related education programs.

Tarvydas and Hartley (2009) suggest that one of the most critical components in counselor licensure legislation is the professional scope of practice statement (p. 30). If rehabilitation counselors have limited clinical experiences and insufficient appropriate clinical counseling versus case management interactions, then they may not be perceived by others in the larger counseling profession as being a qualified practitioner. Generally, CORE-accredited programs provide graduate trainees with the foundational knowledge, awareness, and clinical experiences to prepare them for career opportunities as independent practitioners. However, it is important for the professional who wants to become professionally licensed to contact their state counselor licensure board for an evaluation of any deficits there may be in their academic program or supervised clinical experiences. Issues regarding licensing eligibility should become a career decision, and should be made at the beginning, not at the completion, of the counselor education program. The ACA's web site has a listing of contact information for counselor licensure boards across all 50 states.

Indeed, there are critical issues affecting rehabilitation counselors that relate to third-party reimbursement, mental health and disability legislation, the ability to diagnose and treat mental health and substance abuse conditions, and the expanding specialty areas in counseling that require certification and/or a license to practice (e.g., mental health and substance abuse counseling). Issues such as these did not impact rehabilitation counselors a decade ago because many states did not allow graduates of CORE-accredited programs to become licensed counselors. Currently, new and exciting job opportunities exist for rehabilitation counselors. It is imperative that all rehabilitation professionals become advocates for their profession so that they can become eligible providers of counseling services.

The number of private insurance companies and state counselor licensure boards that accept rehabilitation counselors as independent practitioners varies from state to state. We must be vigilant about keeping a watch on our profession. One area in which professional rehabilitation counselors can increase their knowledge is an understanding of the concepts and language of managed health care. This can be quite confusing for rehabilitation counselors who choose to be licensed as independent practitioners such as an LPC. Graduate programs in rehabilitation counseling are designed to teach the necessary skills to become competent and ethical practitioners, rather than developing business skills to promote one's private practice.

Walsh and Dasenbrook (2009) have developed a comprehensive guide for private practitioners that describes the credentialing aspects, becoming a provider and getting on managed care plans, marketing, and promotion of one's private counseling practice. This pivotal shift allows rehabilitation counselors to become entrepreneurs and work with individuals, families, and groups within the system of managed care, as opposed to working only in state and federal programs of rehabilitation. CORE-accredited programs provide new graduates with the foundational knowledge, awareness, and clinical experiences to prepare for new and exciting career opportunities in rehabilitation counseling.

INTEGRATING BEST PRACTICES INTO THE REHABILITATION COUNSELING PROCESS

It is essential that we develop a clear understanding of how to integrate best practices in the rehabilitation counseling process so that we can cultivate therapeutic interactions that go beyond the person-centered approaches of attending, listening, and empathic responding. We must be accountable to those individuals, families, and groups that we serve in terms of providing competent and ethical services. The counseling field itself has taken on a much more outcome-based, solution-focused approach, which has been driven by counselor accreditation standards, managed care, and private practice insurance panels (Stout & Hayes, 2005; Walsh & Dasenbrook, 2009). The implied meaning suggests that "best practices" must be evaluated in more terms of client treatment and termination of services. Rather, the counseling process must be evaluated throughout various phases of the client's individual rehabilitation treatment plan that include, but are not limited to, how the rehabilitation counselor, agency, or organization performs the following:

- Establishes the first contact and makes connections with clients
- Establishes and builds a therapeutic rapport with the clients
- Assesses, evaluates, and defines the clients' presenting problem issues in a culturally sensitive manner
- Identifies salient goals and objectives that include client participation in the rehabilitation treatment plan
- Chooses specific interventions and approaches that are culturally appropriate
- Engages clients in termination of services with appropriate follow-up referral sources and natural support systems

In order for rehabilitation counselors to be perceived by clients, licensing and certification organizations, private and public insurers, state legislators, and other stakeholders, we must uphold best practices standards and strive for competent, ethical, and innovative practices that are accountable and evidence based.The evaluation of outcome must take place on various levels. In other words, the evaluation of "client improvement" or "degree of satisfaction" must be measurable and consistent with rehabilitation accreditation standards, client feedback, and other health and human service practice standards.

Integrating best practices within the rehabilitation counseling process can be communicated and advanced on multiple levels within rehabilitation counseling. This includes, but is not limited to, services provided by a solo practitioner (e.g., where the rehabilitation counselors act in an advocacy role), agency, or organization (e.g., lobbying for a specific program or service for people with disabilities), university-based grant funded programs (e.g., a demonstration program where empirical data are published about the effectiveness of a specific program or approach), or a professional rehabilitation counseling association (e.g., a national voice that promotes services to people with disabilities by the most qualified practitioners—the rehabilitation professionals).

Advancing best practices of rehabilitation counseling on a national level can be communicated at professional rehabilitation conferences. The National Council on Rehabilitation Education (NCRE, 2010) is one example of a professional association concerned with education competent and ethical rehabilitation practitioners for the primary purpose of improving rehabilitation services for persons with disabilities. Both the Eighth Annual National Rehabilitation Educators Conference, held in February of 2008, and Ninth Annual Conference, held in February of 2009, provided an in-depth educational forum suggesting that we are a counseling specialization that has maintained its unique professional identity (Dutta, 2009; Schultz, Holloway, & Wagner Williams, 2008). These particular conferences, as well as other rehabilitation counseling professional associations (e.g., National Rehabilitation Counseling Association [NRCA] and American Rehabilitation Counseling Association [ARCA]), showcase a discipline on the rise. It reflects a model of rehabilitation teaching, research, service, and practice that portrays the ideal standards for best practices. Ultimately, opportunities such as these enrich personal and professional growth that brings meaning and purpose to one's practice.

Personal and Professional Growth as a Standard of Best Practices

Corey (2010) suggests that "counseling professionals tend to be compassionate people who are good at taking care of others, but often we do not treat ourselves with the same level of care" (p. 185). This statement suggests that integrating best practices may begin with the professional who can maintain their own self-care throughout different career experiences that include the ebb and flow of personal and professional growth. Accordingly, some of the most effective rehabilitation counselors are those who are seen by self and others as empathetic, competent, and ethical practitioners. The portrait of the ideal rehabilitation counselor is an empathetic professional who has the awareness, knowledge, and skills to work effectively with the interpersonal challenges posed by their clients. Some of these challenges include working with those who experienced significant loss, grief, trauma, addictions, chronic illness, and disability.

If the professional counselor has a decreased capacity for empathy, they may be at risk for empathy fatigue or other counselor impairments (Stebnicki, 2008b). A word and construct coined by Stebnicki, empathy fatigue results from "a state of mental, emotional, social, physical, spiritual, and occupational exhaustion that occurs as the counselor's own wounds are continually revisited by his or her clients' life stories of chronic illness, disability, trauma grief, loss, and extraordinary stressful events" (p. 16). A functional self-assessment of empathy fatigue suggests that there are multiple variables that coexist on a continuum of low, moderate, to high that measures the professional's qualitative experience (Stebnicki, 2009). These variables include counselors': (1) cognitions and perceptions about therapeutic interactions with their clients, (2) behaviors in session that might detract from exhibiting warmth, genuineness, and empathy, (3) spiritual beliefs that may be imposed on self or others about the clients' mental or physical condition, (4) counseling approach and style that may be culturally insensitive, (5) emotional involvement within a session where there may be diminished mood or negativity toward self and others in session, (6) physical capacity to maintain attention in difficult session, and (7) occupational characteristics of the professional that may include poor job match between professionals and their work environment or the population they serve. The interested reader may want to consult the reference list for greater details on assessing the empathy fatigue experience.

Ideal helpers are also committed to an honest assessment of their own strengths and limitations, have a basic curiosity and openness to learning new approaches, genuinely care about people, are willing to draw upon multiple resources for maintaining self-care practices, have the ability to respect others who are culturally different, have the capacity to establish meaningful relationships, and have a healthy sense of self (Corey & Corey, 2011, p. 13). Other characteristics of effective counselors are professionals who have an increased self-awareness and understanding, good psychological health, sensitivity to cultural differences, open-mindedness, objectivity, are trustworthy, and have interpersonal skills that are genuine and empathic (Hackney & Cormier, 2009, p. 13).

Competent and Ethical Treatment Strategies as Best Practices

There has been a change in recent years toward client or patient rights as evidenced by specific counseling-related state and federal client protection legislation. With the passage of the 1996 Health Insurance Portability and Accountability Act (HIPAA, 2010) there are multiple areas for rehabilitation counselors to be mindful of when providing services. It is beyond the scope of this chapter to fully discuss specific laws relating to health care, mental health, and rehabilitation. However, best practices of rehabilitation counselors include an understanding of client protection laws related to client confidentiality, the provision of treatment, documentation of psychocounseling services, standards governing how information must be kept in electronic files, as well as many other areas.

Tarvydas and Johnston (2009) note that "it is important for counselors to practice good ethics hygiene to minimize the chances of being involved in an ethical or legal complaint" (p. 109). Possessing a good working knowledge of an ethical decision-making model can also assist counselors in providing competent and ethical services to their clients (Cottone & Tarvydas, 2007) and can enhance best practice standards for client protection.

One particular area of client protection salient for rehabilitation counselors to understand is the way in which clients are to be provided with accurate information about the nature and intent of the counseling relationship. Professional disclosure statements are one tool used by professional counselors indicating that clients have been fully informed about the nature and intent of services being offered (Goodwin, 2009). Disclosure statements become a legal contract between the client and the counselor and should include issues that relate to the professional's statement regarding the following:

- Credentials (i.e., certifications and licenses)
- Counseling approaches, strategies, and theoretical orientation
- Populations served, both past and current
- Potential benefits and risks of counseling
- Client confidentiality
- Dual relationships if any
- Length and frequency of sessions or services

- Expectations regarding treatment outcome
- Fees and method of payment
- Billing and insurance reimbursement policies
- Clients' rights to view their files
- Termination of services
- Emergency contact information
- Vacation, retirement, death, or impairment
- Alternatives to counseling
- Complaint procedures

Research supports the notion that many ethical dilemmas can be avoided if the client is provided with the appropriate amount of information that clarifies the nature and intent of treatment and services to be provided (Corey, Corey, & Callahan, 2011; Cottone & Tarvydas, 2007; Remley & Herlihy, 2005). Although the professional disclosure statement is essential for obtaining consent and informing clients of the nature and intent of the counseling relationship, the client's individualized treatment plan is the primary tool used to communicate and define the counseling process for identifying outcomes for client change (Hackney & Cormier, 2009). As part of a best practices approach, rehabilitation counselors need to work with clients and their family members in an active solution-focused manner when it comes to the rehabilitation treatment process. Cormier and Nurius (2003, p. 331) provide the following guidelines for assessing client progress throughout the treatment process:

- A description of all relevant and potentially useful treatment approaches
- A rationale for each procedure that will be used
- A description of the counselor's role in each intervention
- A description of the client's role in each intervention
- Possible discomforts or risks that may occur as a result of the intervention
- Expected benefits that will occur as a result of the intervention
- The estimated time and cost of each intervention

The assumption stated in the above guidelines implies that flexibility is required in any rehabilitation treatment plan and there is not just one "best practice" plan. Rather, there are multiple paths to get to the desired outcome because there are many therapeutic approaches and client variables involved. For instance, the counselor, agency or organization may use affective, cognitive, behavioral, interactional (systemic), or any combination of these interventions. Because client problem issues are multidimensional, each goal may require different needs and resources at different times throughout the counseling process.

BECOMING A SKILLED, COMPETENT, AND ETHICAL REHABILITATION COUNSELOR PRACTITIONER

There are many reasons that students choose to become rehabilitation counselors. They may be drawn to the occupation because either they or a family member may have experienced a significant life event related to addiction, mental health, chronic medical condition, or acquired mental or physical disability. Whatever the motivation and inspiration used to make the career choice, it is essential to understand why they have chosen a career in rehabilitation counseling. Professionals can examine personal motives for choosing rehabilitation counseling by exploring: (1) their personal stress levels and how it relates to working with people that, at times, may have intense psychological, emotional, physical, medical, or occupational needs, (2) their attitudes, values, and beliefs about working with different populations of people (i.e., physical vs. psychiatric disability) they may encounter or different occupational settings, (3) their career goals related to personal and professional growth in a humanistic-oriented work environment, and (4) other areas where the professional has recognized certain reactions that may trigger a sympathy, fatigued, or burnout response. Figure 12.1 provides a guide to processing a career choice.

COUNSELING PEOPLE WITH DISABILITIES

It is beyond the scope of this chapter to provide an overview of the process or helping skills used during therapeutic interactions. There are excellent counseling texts related to counseling theories and strategies that assist professionals in developing the foundational skills to use during therapeutic interactions. These texts basically prepare professional counselors in establishing client rapport (e.g., use of attending, listening, empathic responses, open-ended questioning, clarifying, paraphrasing, and summaries) and in how to gain therapeutic alliance (e.g., use of challenging skills, goal-setting, and cultivating optimal wellness strategies) so that professional counselors can achieve meaningful and working alliances with their clients. Most counseling texts offer strategies and techniques to work with the general mental health needs of individuals requiring counseling services. However, there are unique issues that relate to counseling people with disabilities. Besides considering the reduction in a client's physical capacity, there are psychological, mental, and emotional health concerns to consider. In addition, there are other contextual issues related to the psychosocial reaction to chronic illness or disability that can hinder full participation and achieving optimal wellness across multiple life areas.

There are both universal and specific counseling techniques to use in therapeutic interactions for people with disabilities. However, little is known about best practices in working with individuals who have coexisting mental health issues and physical disability. Most of the research related to the psychosocial reactions of people with disabilities is qualitative in nature. For example, actor Christopher Reeve, now deceased, acquired a C-1 level spinal cord injury and became quadriplegic and ventilator dependent after an equestrian competition in Virginia in May of 1995. As Frey and Hutchins Pirnot (2008, p. 160) account, Reeve's life, he always believed that he would someday walk again. After years of intensive physical and occupational therapy, Reeve was able to move his index finger and later gain some sensation in his left leg and arm. As

FIGURE 12.1
Processing Your Career Choice

Approaching issues of career choice early-on can be processed with thera-pists, peer support groups, faculty mentors and/or clinical supervisors. Ulti-mately, your worldview such as your attitudes, beliefs, feelings, cognitions, and philosophy impacts your theoretical approach, expectations you have for your clients, and the overall nature and intention of the therapeutic rela-tionship with your clients. To begin processing your career choice with self and/or others, you are invited to process the following questions:

- Some reasons why people go to individual and/or group counseling are . . .
- People who are in counseling tend to change when . . .
- Highly effective counselors are professionals that . . .
- Ineffective counseling happens when . . .
- Some reasons why clients do not benefit from counseling are . . .
- For clients that are culturally different than I am, I would especially be mindful of . . .
- If an ethical dilemma or conflict arose in session I would . . .
- Some issues that would be most challenging to me in my new profes-sion are . . .
- One of the most important things that counselors can do for their own personal and/or professional growth is . . .
- Counselors can be more effective at managing their own lives by doing . . .

It is difficult to escape your past because as Kabit-Zinn (1994) states "Wherever you go, there you are". In other words, you cannot ignore your moral beliefs, personality traits and states, religious/spiritual and political ideology, or philoso-phy toward your life and how you believe others should conduct their lives. You should anticipate that by virtue of working in a human service occupation, there will be issues affecting your interpersonal, emotional, social, physical, relational, and occupational functioning. Understanding your career needs early-on will assist you in building resiliency and lessen the possibility of future professional impairments such as empathy/compassion fatigue or burnout. In the Personal and Professional Resources Reference section at the end of this chapter, some personal and professional growth reading is listed that may ben-efit those that are new to rehabilitation counseling progression.

an outside observer, it is unclear whether this rigorous physical regimen or his ability to pay for multiple specialists contributed to the return of sensation and physical capacity or whether the sensation would have returned on its own.

The point being made is that there are multiple physical disabilities and chronic health conditions to consider (e.g., spinal cord injury, diabetes, HIV/AIDS, cancer, chronic pain, and muscular skeletal disorders) when providing psychosocial support and services. This results in a complex interplay between a client's physical, psychological, emotional, social, and independent functioning. Thus, counseling strategies and techniques facilitated by rehabilitation professionals must be culturally centered as it relates to understanding how clients identify themselves in terms of their functioning and health. To assist in understanding these concepts, this section will offer essential guidelines to facilitate therapeutic interactions for counseling people who have a variety of chronic illnesses and disabilities. Common issues related to specific disabilities will be discussed using case study scenarios and discussion questions (Figures 12.2–12.5).

The Culture of Disability

There tends to be the myth that people with disabilities comprise one single group of individuals. However, there are a growing number of chronic illnesses and disabling conditions (i.e., HIV/AIDS, Asperger's syndrome, type I diabetes, and obesity) that affect the individual's mental, physical, cognitive, social, and vocational functioning and each condition has its own unique physiological, psychological, and cultural attributes. Fujiura and Yamaki (2000) suggest that as cultural diversity increases in the United States, the number of individuals with disabilities who come from diverse cultural backgrounds also increases. Counselors across a variety of work settings and theoretical orientations must be proficient, competent, and ethical in working with a range of people with disabilities who may be culturally different.

FIGURE 12.2 CASE STUDY: MARCUS

Marcus is a 21-year-old person who sustained a C-4 level spinal cord injury while driving intoxicated. His accident occurred about 6 months ago and it was reported that he had a blood-alcohol content of 0.20. He also tested positive for barbiturates. You are Marcus's substance abuse and mental health counselor. He has been court-mandated for alcohol/drug treatment and this is your third session with him. Marcus reminds you of one of your family members who is an alcoholic. You are aware of this issue and even after the third session you appear to have difficulty establishing a good rapport and working alliance with Marcus.

- Given this counselor's family history of alcoholism, what are some verbal and nonverbal communication skills that require immediate attention in order for this counselor to build a stronger rapport and try to achieve a good working alliance with Marcus?
- Assume that this particular counselor (inwardly) is feeling sympathy towards Marcus. What are some skills of empathy that could be facilitated by this counselor to overcome sympathy for Marcus's disability?

FIGURE 12.3 CASE STUDY: ALDO

Aldo is a 28-year old construction worker who sustained a traumatic brain injury on the job while he was laying drainage pipe. He is 3 months post-injury, living in a residential facility for persons with brain injury. Aldo has been referred to you for rehabilitation services and he has been very quiet during his intake interview.

- Silence can have many different meanings within a session. Some clients may be intentionally or unintentionally reluctant, resistive, or defensive toward services. Given the nature and characteristics of brain injury and your first contact with Aldo, how would you interpret the meaning of his silence?
- Reluctance is a normal response to something the person has never had to deal with before in his or her life. Discussing the disability experience with someone new may also hinder client disclosure. What are some therapeutic approaches that could be utilized with Aldo to help him open up and trust you?

FIGURE 12.4 CASE STUDY: CHLOE

Chloe is a 24-year old individual who is developmentally disabled. She is a legally competent adult and lives in a small residential facility that has four female and six male residents, all of whom function in the mild-moderate range of mental retardation. She grabs the Team Manager for this residential facility by the elbow and demands: "Hey, why can't I spend some time alone with my boyfriend in my bedroom? You guys treat us like we're in prison here!" Chloe's behavior appears demanding and immature in manner, as she throws a small object and slams the door to her bedroom.

- The Team Manager has set some very rigid standards of interpersonal and intimate contact in the residential facility. As Chloe's rehabilitation counselor, how would you approach this issue with the Team Manager? What exactly would you want to communicate about Chloe's rights as a mentally competent adult with a disability?
- Assume that Chloe has specifically stated to her rehabilitation counselor that she wants to start a sexual relationship with another resident in her house. How would you advocate (or not advocate) for Chloe and what type of guidelines would you offer to either Chloe or the Team Manager?

In a content analysis of multicultural counseling syllabi from CORE-accredited programs, Stebnicki and Cubero (2008) found that multicultural awareness and knowledge areas were addressed in course syllabi in terms of the course content and objectives. However, little attention was given to assisting

FIGURE 12.5 CASE STUDY: JERRY

Jerry is a 26-year old person with a personality disorder who has lived in and out of long-term psychiatric facilities for most of his adult life. You are Jerry's community-based case manager who coordinates most of his psychiatric and vocational rehabilitation services. Jerry is living in a locked psychiatric facility and wants you to help him get discharged to an independent living setting. He perceives that you are avoiding contact with him this week and he gets-up in your face and exhibits very aggressive body language and demands: "Why the hell can't you find me a place to live . . . I thought you were suppose to get me a job also . . . I'm tired of all these people on this psych ward. You better get something done this week, or I may have to hurt myself or someone else."

- Discuss how you would try and understand Jerry's perspective in his current environment and how would you respond to his request to live and work in the community. Assume that transitional living is a possibility if Jerry's psychiatric condition is stable.
- If Jerry had a stable and willing family to take care of him upon discharge (but only on a short-term basis), what types of services could you offer him and his family?

professional rehabilitation counselors in developing the necessary and sufficient skills to work with people from diverse backgrounds in terms of counseling strategies and techniques. Indeed, there are universal and specific ways to engage in therapeutic interactions with persons from a variety of cultural backgrounds. Yet, there is a unique overlay in terms of the level of awareness, knowledge, and skills required to work effectively with individuals who identify themselves as having a chronic illness or disability.

In a comprehensive work relating to the impact that race and culture has on people with disabilities, Balcazar, Suarez-Balcazar, Taylor-Ritzler, and Keys (2010) suggest that guidelines for best practices are rarely discussed in research and practice. As a consequence, the cultural implication of disability and the best counseling practices to facilitate with this group are not clear. This is because there is little empirical evidence to guide rehabilitation counselors in facilitating specific therapeutic strategies, techniques, and services that would potentially work with the diversity of disabilities that exist. In research and practice, the language and constructs related to counseling people with disabilities tends to be described within the context of multicultural counseling skills. Although such models of multicultural counseling can be very applicable in practice, there are unique cultural attributes, differences, and similarities that relate to individuals who have a variety of medical, physical, cognitive, and mental health conditions that should be addressed by counselors.

Particular attention must be given to the counselor's perception of viewing the individual from purely a biological, medical, or psychopathology model of treatment. This is one of the primary differences between rehabilitation counseling and other specialty practice areas (e.g., mental health counseling, community counseling, marriage and family counseling). Because rehabilitation counseling is a profession that works with the medical, psychosocial, and vocational impact of people with disabilities, there is a complex overlay of the disability itself and its own unique cultural attributes that affect the individual's life functioning.

Rehabilitation counselors are not only obligated to work with the mental health aspects of the individual, but also consider the complex psychosocial reactions that one might have with an acquired disability. Thus, it is imperative that professional counselors do not treat people with disabilities from purely a mental health or diagnostic category using traditional treatment protocols and counseling theories that are not culturally sensitive. For some individuals, the disability and the accompanying functional limitations may or may not pose a hindrance, obstacle, or challenge. Rather, it may be societal attitudes or architectural barriers that are the most difficult hurdle for the individual.

As Smart (2009) notes, there is not one single type of individuals that comprises the total population we refer to as "people with disabilities" because there are multiple identities, roles, functional capacities, environments, and assets that encompasses this group of individuals. In fact, people with disabilities consist of many other groups including, but not limited to, people who are older adults, gays or lesbians, African Americans, and Hispanics, as well as people representing a variety of professions (i.e., plumbers, politicians, teachers, lawyers, and physicians). Crabtree, Royeen, and Benton (2006, p. 4) note that being culturally proficient in rehabilitation practice is to truly understand the personal wishes, beliefs, preferences, choices, expectations, and values of people with disabilities. Likewise, Riggar and Maki (2004, p. 4) suggest that individuals with disabilities should be conceptualized as interacting within multiple contexts of life by viewing the person in a holistic and ecological perspective with the counselor facilitating strategies that focus on achieving a meaningful quality of life.

In an ideal world, all counselor education programs would have course work relating to working with the cultural aspects of counseling people with disabilities. This would include the foundational concepts in rehabilitation and content areas related to the medical, psychosocial, and vocational aspects of various chronic illnesses and disabilities. Integral to providing services to people with disabilities in a competent and ethical manner is having the ability to generalize this awareness and knowledge into actual counseling strategies and techniques. Competencies in the rehabilitation counseling scope of practice begin by understanding that there is a continuum of abilities everyone possesses. Any differences that depart from "normal" biological, psychological, physical, cognitive, and developmental functioning should not be viewed as psychopathological or abnormal functioning. Rather, it is an expression of the unique cultural attributes that may have been acquired by birth or somewhere along the continuum of abilities within the personal growth and development of the individual.

Paradigm Shift

There has been a paradigm shift in the last 20 years from working with the individual who has a disability as "the patient" to "the client" (Smart & Smart, 2006; Vash, 1994). Working from the biomedical or "patient" model of disability does little to empower the individual with achieving optimal levels of wellness and independence. Hence, the biomedical model suggests that the "problem of disability" resides within the individual regardless of one's personal assets, attributes, and other abilities. As a consequence of this perceptual pattern, people with physiological deficits and psychopathology are viewed as deviating from the norm.

The use of various classification and diagnostic systems such as the *Diagnostic and Statistical Manual of Mental Disorders* (4th ed., text revision) (*DSM-IV-TR*; American Psychological Association [APA], 2000) further depreciates the individual's worth. As a consequence, the diagnostic category attributed to the person (e.g., borderline personality disorder, depression, and polysubstance abuse disorder) reinforces society's negative attitudes about the individual. This can result in the perception that any mental, physical, or biological difference that deviates from the norm should be considered aberrant, flawed, or abnormal. As a consequence of not being perceived as "normal" in society, it is often concluded that the "problem" of the person's mental or physical condition resides within the individual. When people with disabilities are not provided opportunities or are intentionally marginalized in the workplace, recreational areas, social institutions, educational settings, and other public places, then this creates a majority–minority conflict. The emotional and psychological cost to the individual with the disability can be significant if they integrate such stereotypes and intentional acts of discrimination into their psychological and emotional well-being. As a consequence, Taylor and Epstein (1999) suggest that individuals with disabilities, particularly those with hidden disabilities, have significant mental health challenges of transforming feelings such as anger, depression, doubt, and shame into more healthy coping and resiliency functioning.

It is essential that counseling professionals recognize the paradigm when it comes to diagnosing and treating people with psychological conditions as delineated in the *DSM-IV-TR* (2000). Because there is a wide range of professionals involved with programs and services for persons with psychological problems, it is critical that these professionals understand the fundamental concepts in dealing with people with disabilities during therapeutic interactions. Persons with occupational titles such as psychiatrists, psychologists, licensed clinical social workers, LPCs, rehabilitation counselors, mental health counselors, psychiatric nurses, psychiatric technicians, and mental health workers all have the responsibility and ethical obligation to work in a culturally sensitive manner with this unique population of individuals. Accordingly, any system that classifies the individual in relation to a "disorder" must be taken within context of the person's mental and physical capacity, holistic health functioning, and other contextual factors that may hinder full environmental participation and expression of the person's own unique cultural attributes.

The *International Classification of Functioning, Disability, and Health*; Beta-2 draft (ICFDH-2; World Health Organization [WHO], 2001)—referred to as the ICF—is an example of a classification system that is not based on a "disorder" of abnormal functioning. Peterson's (2011) research contributions with the revised ICF challenge professionals who serve individuals with psychological or psychiatric disabilities to view the person from a biopsychosocial model of diagnosis and treatment. Peterson's work delineates how psychopathology can be integrated into the ICF to assist mental health professionals in viewing their client's mental health functioning from: (1) a body function and structure perspective, (2) the types of activities from which individuals are limited and restricted from participating, and (3) contextual factors such as environmental conditions and other sociocultural and personal factors.

Diagnosis and treatment of mental and physical disabilities require professionals to understand functioning from a holistic or biopsychosocial perspective. This is because disabling conditions can affect multiple life areas such as the individual's mental, physical, cognitive, behavioral, social, vocational, and spiritual health and functioning. Because the *DSM-IV-TR* (2000) differs from the ICF classification system, Peterson (2011) suggests that the stakeholders of the *DSM-IV-TR* (2000) "do not endorse the mind/body duality that separates the physical from mental aspects of disorders and health" (p. 165). Accordingly, rehabilitation professionals must provide services with concern for the individual's level of functioning, disability, and holistic health.

GUIDELINES FOR THE COUNSELING PROFESSIONS

Counseling people with disabilities have primarily focused on the psychosocial aspects of the individual. Historically, the terms used to describe counseling issues have been directed toward psychosocial *adjustment, adaptation,* or *acceptance* of the individual with a disability. Traditionally, these terms have been used to describe individual's coping skills and how successfully they integrate their mental and physical functioning, and overall health into their disability identity. Disability scholars have delineated how psychosocial adjustment and adaptation is expressed through a series of phases or stages that individuals work their way through, finally ending in the theoretical stage of *acceptance* of their disability.

Smart (2001, p. 229) suggests that the more appropriate term *individual's response to disability* communicates more fully that: (1) the disability itself does not define the individual; rather, it is the meaning ascribed by the disability and how the individual views his or her residual functional capacity, (2) *adjustment* does not represent a total life experience or final endpoint of the individual; rather, it reflects a range of experiences that include, but are not limited to, physical, psychological, emotional, cognitive, social, occupational, and spiritual response to a disability, and (3) *adjustment, adaptation,* and *acceptance* tend to pathologize the experience of disability and make the assumption that only those individuals who have a disability go through a phase or stage of *adjustment*, but in reality, all individuals have critical life issues to deal with that cannot be described as having a beginning and end point.

Indeed, all individuals have many critical life events (e.g., divorce, death of a parent, child, or spouse, loss of job and financial security, physical loss of a body part, and acquired disease or chronic illness) that do not fit neatly into a model of *adjustment, adaptation,* or *acceptance*. Besides, what is considered by society to be *acceptance* of a disability does not typically occur as a one-time event. Accordingly, there are unique cultural differences that define the identity of the individual. This accentuates the point that one of the primary differences between the specialty areas of rehabilitation counseling and other counseling disciplines (e.g., school counseling, counseling psychology, clinical social work) is that the society's attitude toward people with disabilities may actually be more disabling than the disability itself. This philosophy is espoused by many authors in the field (Arokiasamy, 1993; Smart, 2009; Smart & Smart, 2006; Vanier, 2007; Vash, 1994; Vash & Crewe, 2004), who further advocate that people with mental and physical disabilities desire the same genuineness, respect, empathy, support, and opportunities as all other clients. Accordingly, the person's psychosocial reaction to disability is a complex interplay of variables that include, but are not limited to, the following issues:

1. *Time of onset*. There are a range of congenital and acquired disabilities that vary across the life span from birth to near death each having have their own unique psychosocial issues. The onset affects the individual emotionally, psychologically, physically, socially, spiritually, cognitively, academically, vocationally, and affects the level of independent functioning throughout the life span.
2. *Type of disability*. Counselors must consider the range of mental, physical, psychological, cognitive, developmental, acquired health, chronic health, life-threatening, and other conditions affecting various functional capacities, body systems, and life areas. It is also important to have a good working knowledge of the course, pattern, prognosis, exacerbation, and remission of the individual's specific type of disability.
3. *Individual's perception toward their disability*. Counselors must consider the individual's perception toward his or her particular disabling condition and view this in terms of the types of losses the individual may be reporting. Depending upon the individual's disability, losses occur in many contexts that include a combination of economic loss, loss of independence, loss of cognitive abilities, loss of physical capacity, loss of immune functioning, loss of emotional or psychological functioning, loss of vocational, educational, occupational, or career opportunities, loss of faith in God or a higher power,

loss of belief in fairness or justice, and the loss of existential meaning of life itself. There is a complex interplay with what the individual experiences with varying degrees of intensity and duration.

4. *Cultural attributes and context of the disability.* Counselors must understand the individual and family within the context of their particular unique cultural attributes, level of acculturation, within-group differences, and overall cultural identity. Culturally competent counselors also try and gain an understanding of the individual's experience with outside influences that may spark negative attitudes, discrimination, stereotyping, or being marginalized by other individuals or groups in society. These outside influences may affect a range of issues related to the individual's self-esteem, confidence, mood, self-depreciation, and other issues related to psychological and emotional well-being.

5. *Continuum of disability.* Counselors must be mindful that disability occurs on a continuum of abilities. There are few, if any, individuals who have absolutely no abilities, and few, if any, who have superior mental, physical, cognitive, or intellectual attributes. Thus, we all exist on a continuum of abilities rather than disabilities.

6. *Psychosocial reaction or response of disability.* Psychosocial reaction or response is a highly individualized experience that is a complex interplay between the person's developmental phase of life, which has varying degrees of intensity, adjustment, and adaptation to the disability. There are physical, psychological, emotional, social, cognitive, vocational, and spiritual reactions to disability that cannot be represented by a theoretical model that has a beginning and end point. It is of paramount importance to also understand that psychosocial reaction or response to disability is a parallel process that affects family, friends, and significant others.

7. *Counseling from a coping skills and resiliency focus.* Competent counselors understand how to work with the individual and family members from a coping skills perspective and know how to assess the individual's resiliency traits. Cultivating resiliency skills are essential so that the individual can generalize past positive coping and resiliency resources to handle future critical life tasks and goals.

8. *Understanding the disability experience.* It is critical for counselors to understand that disability is a unique experience of a particular individual. Professionals and nonprofessionals alike, even if suffering from the same chronic illness or disability (i.e., cancer, diabetes, alcoholism, and spinal cord injury), should not assume that they know what the other person is experiencing. Competent counselors also understand that they should not enable, protect, or sympathize with their clients. Some individuals with disabilities may be difficult to work with, behaviorally and emotionally, because they may have multiple intense issues. Thus, professional counselors must empower their clients with numerous resources, remain objective, facilitate high levels of empathy (not sympathy), and facilitate optimal levels

of functioning to increase the individual's quality of life. If the rehabilitation professional feels that he or she cannot serve the individual client because of his or her own personal issues (i.e., countertransference), has difficulty with being objective, and/or a lack of the appropriate skills or competence to work with a particular individual, then, ethically, the professional needs to consult the CRC Code of Ethics, consult with a supervisor, and perhaps refer this particular client to a different qualified professional.

9. *Recognize the individual as a survivor.* Viewing people with disabilities as *victims* of a traumatic event (e.g., traumatic brain injury and spinal cord injury) or those who have acquired a life-threatening disability (e.g., ALS, cancer, and HIV/AIDS) diminishes the individual's survival, coping, and resiliency skills. The use of *victim* language negatively reinforces the stereotypes of the individual as being helpless and dependent and that their total identity is related to the multiple limitations confronting the individual's functionality and overall well-being. Viewing a person with disabilities as a survivor places the emphasis on the individual's ability to transcend some of life's most difficult challenges. When the individual is empowered with resources that cultivate increased resiliency, independence, and functional capacity, then the individual is a survivor, which is a starting point to live life optimally.

In summary, it is of paramount importance for counselors to recognize and understand that people with disabilities are not a member of one cultural group. Rather, these individuals comprise multiple roles, identities, attributes, and capabilities. There are many other guidelines that could be offered that relate to the individual's reaction to a disability as the individual changes and evolves throughout the life span. However, the above-stated foundational guidelines are, in part, the basis for providing competent and ethical services to people with disabilities. If counselors cannot establish a rapport with their clients, they may have difficulty in forming a therapeutic alliance. Despite the paucity of quantitative data related to best practices, counselors who exhibit honest, direct, and empathic therapeutic relationships in a cultural-centered manner can offer clients a very good beginning point for counseling.

SUMMARY

Building a rapport with a client in a person-centered and culturally sensitive manner requires that the counselor's own attitude toward people with disabilities be open, flexible, and genuine. Corey and Corey (2011) suggest that person-centered approaches emphasize that counselors' attitudes toward their clients will affect the quality of the client–counselor relationship. This is communicated both verbally and nonverbally by genuineness, warmth, accurate empathy, unconditional acceptance, respect, and interpersonal communication skills that model culturally competent strategies and approaches.

Professionals who provide counseling services to people with disabilities must be competent not only in the foundational process skills of counseling, but must also pay particular attention to the cultural differences of disability and how their counseling approaches are communicated both verbally and nonverbally to their clients. Building client rapport and maintaining a strong working alliance can be a prime determinant of a positive outcome during therapeutic interactions.

Case scenarios and discussion questions found in Figures 12.2–12.5 may be helpful in understanding the concepts in counseling people with disabilities.

REFERENCES

American Counseling Association. (2010a). *Licensure and certification*. Retrieved July 8, 2010, from www.counseling.org

American Counseling Association. (2010b). *20/20: A vision for the future of counseling*. Retrieved July 28, 2010, from http://www.counseling.org/20-20/index.aspx

American Psychological Association. (2000). *Diagnostic and statistical manual of mental health disorder* (4th ed., text revision). Washington, DC: Author.

Arokiasamy, C. V. (1993). A theory for rehabilitation? *Rehabilitation Education, 7*, 77–98.

Balcazar, F. E., Suarez-Balcazar, Y., Taylor-Ritzler, T., & Keys, C. B. (2010). *Race, culture, and disability: Rehabilitation science and practice*. Sudbury, MA: Jones and Bartlett Publishers.

Bernacchio, C., Burker, E. J., Falvo, D., Porter, P., & Carone, S. (2008). Specializations in rehabilitation counseling: One Program's vision. *Rehabilitation Education, 22*(3/4), 185–192.

Comier, S., & Nurisu, P. S. (2003). *Interviewing and change strategies for helpers* (5th ed.). Pacific Grove, CA: Brooks/Cole.

Commission on Rehabilitation Counselor Certification. (2010). *The foundation for effective rehabilitation counseling: Scope of practice for rehabilitation counseling*. Retrieved June 10, 2010, from http://www.crccertification.com/mightysite/filebin/pdf/CRCC_CORE_Foundation

Corey, G., Corey, M. S., & Callahan, P. (2011). *Issues and ethics in the helping professions* (8th ed.). Belmont, CA: Brooks/Cole, Cengage Learning.

Corey, M. S. (2010). *Creating your professional path: Lesson from my journey*. Alexandria, VA: American Counseling Association.

Corey, M. S., & Corey, G. (2011). *Becoming a helper* (6th ed.). Belmont, CA: Brooks/Cole Cengage. *Issues and ethics in the helping professions* (7th ed.). Pacific Grove, CA: Brooks/Cole.

Cottone, R. R., & Tarvydas, V. M. (2007). *Counseling ethics and decision making* (3rd ed.). Upper Saddle River, NJ: Merrill/Prentice-Hall.

Council on Rehabilitation Education. (2010). *Rehabilitation counselors and accreditation*. Retrieved June 10, 2010, from http://www.core-rehab.org/accred.html

Crabtree, J. L., Royeen, M., & Benton, J. (2006). Cultural proficiency in rehabilitation: An introduction. In M. Royeen & J. L. Crabtree (Eds.), *Culture in rehabilitation: From competency to proficiency*. Upper Saddle River, NJ: Pearson Prentice Hall. D'Andrea, M., & Daniels, J. (2001). RESPECTFUL counseling: An integrative model for counselors. In D. Pope-Davis & H. Coleman (Eds.). *The interface of class, culture, and gender in counseling* (pp. 417–466). Thousand Oaks, CA: SAGE.

Dictionary of Occupational Titles (4th ed.). (1991). Indianapolis, IN: JIST. Dutta, A. (2009). Rehabilitation practices and practitioner: Innovations and evolution (Advancing the Profession's Identity). *Rehabilitation Education, 23*(1), 5–32.

Egan, G. (2002). *The skilled helper: A problem-management and opportunity-development approach to helping*. Pacific Grove, CA: Brooks/Cole.

Frey, G. L., & Hutchins Pirnot, K. (2008). *As I am: A true story of adaptation to physical disability*. Sarasota, FL: The Peppertree Press.

Fujiura, G. T., & Yamaki, K. (2000). Trends in demography of childhood poverty and disability. *Exceptional Children, 66*(2), 187–199.

Goodwin, L.R. (2006). Rehabilitation counselor specialty areas offered by rehabilitation counselor education programs. *Rehabilitation Education, 20*(2), 133–134.

Goodwin, L. R. (2009). Professional disclosure in counseling. In I. Marini & M. A. Stebnicki (Eds.), *The professional counselor's desk reference* (pp. 114–123). New York, NY: Springer Publishing Company.

Hackney, H. L., & Cormier, S. (2009). *The professional counselor: A process guide to helping*. Upper Saddle River, NJ: Pearson.

Health Insurance Portability and Accountability Act. (2010). *Understanding HIPPA privacy*. Retrieved August 2, 2010, from http://www.hhs.gov/ocr/privacy/hipaa/understanding/index.html

Ivey, A. E., Bradford Ivey, M., & Zalaquett, C. P. (2010). *Intentional interviewing & counseling: Facilitating client development in a multicultural society*. Belmont, CA: Brooks/Cole Cengage.

Kabat-Zinn, J. (1994). *Wherever you go, there you are: Mindfulness meditation in everyday life*. New York, NY: Hyperion.

Leahy, M. J., Rak, E., & Zanskus, S. A. (2009). A brief history of counseling and specialty areas of practice. In I. Marini & M. A. Stebnicki (Eds.), *The professional counselor's desk reference* (pp. 3–13). New York, NY: Springer Publishing Company.

Lopez Levers, L, (1997). In Maki, D. R., & Riggar, T. F. (Eds.), *Rehabilitation counseling profession and practice*. New York, NY: Springer Publishing Company.

Meyers, J. (1995). Specialties in counseling: Rich heritage or force for fragmentation? *Journal of Counseling and Development, 74*(2), 115–116.

National Council on Rehabilitation Education. (2009). *NCRE Directory 2009–2010*. Schaumburg, IL: Council on Rehabilitation Education.

National Council on Rehabilitation Education. (2010). Retrieved August 1, 2010, from http://www.rehabeducators.org/

Patterson, C. H. (1957). Counselor or coordinator. *Journal of Rehabilitation, 23*(3), 13–15.

Patterson, C. H. (1966). The rehabilitation counselor: A projection. *Journal of Rehabilitation, 32*(1), 31, 49.

Peterson, D. B. (2011). *Psychological aspects of functioning, disability, and health*. New York, NY: Springer Publishing Company.

Remley, T. P., & Herlihy, B. (2005). *Ethical, legal, and professional issues in counseling* (2nd ed.). Upper Saddle River, NJ: Person-Merrill/Prentice-Hall.

Riggar, T. F., & Maki, D. R. (2004). *Handbook of rehabilitation counseling*. New York, NY: Springer Publishing.

Rubin, S. E., & Roessler, R. T. (1978). *Foundations of the vocational rehabilitation process*. Baltimore, MD: University Park Press.

Schultz, J. C., Holloway, L., & Wagner Williams, C. (2008). Advancing the profession's identity: Turning vision into reality. *Rehabilitation Education, 22*(1), 5–30.

Smart, J. F. (2001). *Disability, society, and the individual*. Gaithersburg, MD: Aspen Publishers.

Smart, J. F. (2009). Counseling individuals with disabilities. In I. Marini & M. A. Stebnicki (Eds.), *The professional counselor's desk reference* (pp. 640–646). New York, NY: Springer Publishing Company.

Smart, J. F., & Smart, D. W. (2006). Models of disability: Implications for the counseling profession. *Journal of Counseling and Development, 84*, 29–40.

Stebnicki, M. A. (2008a). A call for integral approaches in the professional identity ofrehabilitation counseling: Three specialty areas, one profession. A joint special issue in *Rehabilitation Counseling Bulletin and Journal of Applied Rehabilitation Counseling. Journal of Applied Rehabilitation Counseling, 39*(4), 64–68.

Stebnicki, M. A. (2008b). *Empathy fatigue: Healing the mind, body, and spirit of professional counselors*. New York, NY: Springer Publishing.
Stebnicki, M. A. (2009). Empathy fatigue: Assessing risk factors and cultivating self-care. In I. Marini & M. A. Stebnicki (Eds.), *The professional counselor's desk reference* (pp. 813–829). New York, NY: Springer Publishing Company.
Stebnicki, M. A., & Cubero, C. (2008). A content analysis of multicultural counseling syllabi from rehabilitation counseling programs. *Rehabilitation Education, 22*(2), 89–100.
Stout, C. E., & Hayes, R. A. (2005). *Evidence-based practice: Methods, models, and tools for mental health professionals*. Hoboken, NJ: Wiley.
Tarvydas, V. M., & Hartley, M. T. (2009). What practitioners need to know about professional credentialing. In I. Marini & M. A. Stebnicki (Eds.), *The Professional counselor's desk reference* (pp. 27–37). New York, NY: Springer Publishing Company.
Tarvydas, V. M., & Johnston, S. P. (2009). Managing risk in ethical and legal situations. In I. Marini & M. A. Stebnicki (Eds.), *The professional counselor's desk reference* (pp. 100–111). New York, NY: Springer Publishing Company.
Vanier, J. (2007). The contributions of the physically and mentally handicapped to development. In A. E. Dell Orto & P. W. Power (Eds.),*The psychological and social impact of illness and disability* (5th ed., pp. 101–107). New York, NY: Springer Publishing Company.
Vash, C. L. (1994). *Personality and adversity: Psychospiritual aspects of rehabilitation*. New York, NY: Springer Publishing.
Vash, C. L., & Crewe, N. M. (2004). *Psychology of disability* (2nd ed.). New York, NY: Springer Publishing.
Walsh, R. J., & Dasenbrook, N. C. (2009). Contracting strategies with managed care and other agencies. In I. Marini and M. A. Stebnicki (Eds.), *The professional counselor's desk reference* (pp. 79–87). New York, NY: Springer Publishing Company.
Whitehouse, F. A. (1975). Rehabilitation clinician. *Journal of Rehabilitation, 41*(3), 24–26.
World Health Organization. (2001). *International classification of functioning, disability and health: ICF*. Geneva, Switzerland: Author.
Wright, G. N. (1980). *Total rehabilitation*. Boston, MA: Little, Brown and Company.

PERSONAL AND PROFESSIONAL GROWTH RESOURCES

American Counseling Association. (2010). Aca's taskforce on counselor wellness and impairment. Retrieved August, 9, 2010, from, http://www.counseling.org/wellness_taskforce/index.htm
Corey, M. S. (2010). *Creating your professional path: Lesson from my journey*. Alexandria, VA: American Counseling Association.
Figley, C. R. (2002). *Treating compassion fatigue*. New York, NY: Brummer-Routledge.
Kabat-Zinn, J. (1994). *Wherever you go, there you are: Mindfulness meditation in everyday life*. New York, NY: Hyperion.
Mandala Schilitz, M., Vieten, C., & Amorok, T. (2007). *Living deeply: The art & science of transformation in everyday life*. Oakland, CA: New Harbinger Publications.
Maslach, C. (2003). *Burnout: The cost of caring*. Cambridge, MA: Malor Books.
Seaward, B. L. (1997). *Stand like mountain flow like water: Reflections on stress and human spirituality*. Deerfield Beach, FL: Health Communications.
Stebnicki, M. A. (2008b). *Empathy fatigue: Healing the mind, body, and spirit of professional counselors*. New York, NY: Springer Publishing.
Stebnicki, M. A. (2009). Empathy fatigue: Assessing risk factors and cultivating self-care. In I. Marini & M. A. Stebnicki (Eds.), *The professional counselor's desk reference* (pp. 813–829). New York, NY: Springer Publishing Company.
Taylor, S., & Epstein, R. (1999). *Living well with a hidden disability: Transcending doubt and shame and reclaiming your life*. Oakland, CA: New Harbinger.

13

Case Management

David P. Moxley

LEARNING OBJECTIVES

After reading this chapter, you should be able to:

- Identify the importance of paradigms to the integration of counseling and case management.
- Describe the three paradigms influencing case management practice in counseling: involving the systems-driven, client-centered, and consumer-driven.
- Consider the importance of vulnerability and resilience as advanced organizers of case management.
- Consider the interplay of paradigm and culture in shaping case management practice in counseling.
- Underscore disciplinary focus as influential in shaping case management practice.
- Present implications for career options open to counselors as they increasingly transition to community-based service.

Diversity of case management is a hallmark of this human service function. Whether this variation is found in various sectors of human services, organizational auspices, applications, or strategies, it likely exists because service systems are seeking solutions to the issues that people present to human service personnel. Within human services over the past several decades, there has been considerable diversification of case management across sectors and domains testifying to the perceived usefulness of this form of practice to meet a variety of human needs. Physicians, social workers, counselors, nurses, and lawyers all claim distinctive contributions to case management practice and incorporate it into their roles in health and human service systems.

Elsewhere case management is characterized as useful in helping individuals who face complex situations resolve the issues they face, particularly in the areas of basic social needs, so that they can improve their situations and advance life satisfaction in ways consistent with their preferences (Moxley, 2009). In many service systems, case management is a principal or central strategy for advancing the well-being of individuals who face complex situations in the life domains of health, mental health, employment, and/or housing.

When case management is referred to within this chapter, it is as a broad set of strategies designed to enable a collaborative working arrangement between counselor and client so that together they can bring about tangible, meaningful, and measurable outcomes in prioritized areas of human need (Moxley, 1997). Often, case management involves the assistance clients receive from counselors to access, organize, and use services, opportunities, and/or benefits. Case management may take its priorities from its host system or from individual clients imbuing it with yet more variation in how organizations focus and articulate this form of human service intervention (Moxley, 2003). But what is consistent across this variation is that the relationship formed between client and professional is central to helping (Hasenfeld, 2010).

The extensive variation in case management may result from the efforts human service professionals invest in making case management responsive to specific human needs that emanate from a person's qualities (such as diagnostic or behavioral needs), immediate situation, or social status. By matching response to need, many entities may innovate incrementally in the provision or form of case management and, as a consequence, formulate specific processes and outcome sets as a result (Moxley & Manela, 2001). Diversity in a case management approach may be a product of the effort that systems invest in matching case management to the needs of clients in ways consistent with a particular paradigm or culture. Through this matching the sponsoring organization affirms case management as a principal social and behavioral technology for meeting human needs (Sandfort, 2010). Variation in this technology reveals differences across organizations in their ideologies about the nature of human needs (Sandfort, 2010).

VULNERABILITY AND RESILIENCE AS ADVANCED ORGANIZERS

Within this chapter we move between the discussion of client needs and issues, two very different constructs but both prevalent in contemporary human service work. Depending upon the paradigm of case management and intervention culture, both constructs are visible in theoretical and practice-oriented discussions of case management. For those models that fall into the system-driven paradigm (discussed in the following section), need is a convenient way of thinking about what case management personnel seek to fulfill on behalf of a client. For case management personnel, need may involve a life necessity or a gap between the current situation the client faces and what he or she requires to live (Moxley, 1989).

For example, the discrepancy between homelessness and housed speaks to the client's need for shelter at some normative or base level. A counselor-case manager may take a client through an assessment of multiple domains identifying need at some level and justifying the fulfillment of the need based on community values of adequacy or appropriateness. The actual service plan may incorporate information about the client's status in multiple domains, identifying specific needs as concerns and offering goals as measures of their fulfillment at a given threshold level.

Need implicates a normative conception of human functioning or status. Within American society there is a weak consensus about both what needs are legitimate and at what threshold a community should fulfill a certain need. Previously, poor survivors of Katrina may only be worthy of a tattered mobile home, and may only enjoy some base level of continued support while they wait for permanent housing and employment. What does such a person deserve, and to what extent will a community raise its criteria for guiding the quality of life of people who are marginalized because of event, status, or deprivation?

An alternative to need as an advanced organizer of case management practice has emerged within the consumer movement in the area of social welfare and human services. Adherents to this paradigm recognize that need is intimately linked to diminished status—people with disabilities who are poor, different from the mainstream, deviant from a valued norm experience, or with considerable negative social reaction resulting in numerous forms of deprivation and insult, either explicit or implicit.

Such deprivation stretches across the multiple domains of quality of life, which implicates nutrition, health care, social support, employment, education and literacy, and access to life-enhancing opportunities. Deprivation is also geographic, exposing people who are so deprived to environmental decay and degradation. What Cobb and Sennett (1993) refer to as the hidden injuries of class are far too familiar for people who experience what can amount to institutionalized deprivation. They are not welcome in certain parts of town, they should not make demands on officials, they should not confront, and they should reduce their aspirations if they cannot bring them about through their own means.

From this perspective, people can experience mounting issues that remind them individually or collectively of their diminished status. The issues themselves as seen through the lens of vulnerability are serious (Washington & Moxley, 2009a,b). Listening to people's stories can be stressful for both clients and counselors as themes of deprivation; plight, unfulfilled potential, and illness dominate the story lines of individual narratives. The story of deprivation can reveal a diminished status—because of their position in the social structure, some persons do not enjoy the benefits of the greater society. They go without, and such deprivation is structural in that it is an inherent feature of these persons' position within society.

EXAMPLE OF VULNERABILITY

Marsha Williams meets with the counselor-case manager to discuss her current situation. She has been homeless now for about 8 months and is now in a shelter after living in make-shift circumstances on the streets for several months. Marsha describes her situation to an attentive counselor who is drawing conclusions about her vulnerability. The client describes numerous health problems, that reduce the energy she has available for self-care and disease management. In particular, her diabetes is uncontrolled and she has no safe place to maintain her medication. Symptoms of a serious depression indicate to the counselor that Marsha's medical and psychosocial situation interact to make it seem like the client is slow cognitively. As Marsha describes the issues she faces, including bad debt, damaged credit, and a former landlord who is holding her furnishings because of unpaid rent, the counselor reflects to herself about the high level of vulnerability with which this woman must cope.

SOURCES OF RESILIENCE

As the counselor continues to listen to Marsha's story, she hears different themes of this woman's narrative. Marsha speaks of her great faith and spirituality and how her affiliation with a local church has helped her rekindle her interest in food preparation. She wants to reconnect with a physician who has helped her manage her diabetes and indicates that "Dr. Joe will help me out with my disease." Marsha discusses the support group she attends, and as she describes the members, the woman's affect is positive and strong. The counselor starts inventorying the sources of resilience Marsha presents, and the image of a scale comes into her mind in which factors of strength start to outweigh the factors of plight the client identifies. In her mind's eye, the counselor can now envision a path leading Marsha out of homelessness. Perhaps the church is a viable helping resource.

The narrative of plight likely stands side by side with another narrative, one which involves efficacy. The astute counselor listens deeply for the person's expression of strength, fortitude, and resilience in the face of stress that is a product of overwhelming unresolved issues. Supplementing stories of deprivation, people can articulate what makes them strong as individuals, such as how cultural experiences equip them with tools for resisting the consequences of deprivation, how spirituality fortifies hope, and how friendships formed in adversity help a particular person to garner social support.

Paradigms within case management are conceptual so that advanced organizers handle these factors of plight and efficacy in different ways. As suggested in the following, for one paradigm, which favors the integrity of service systems, case management may view vulnerability as involving a person's constitutional inadequacies while the consumer-driven variant may highlight how the person's exposure to unrelenting oppression (in the form of deprivation) weakens the person in all domains essential to good health—physical, psychological, emotional, cognitive, interpersonal, and cultural.

The reader should remain mindful of the differential use of vulnerability and resilience within the various paradigms offered in the subsequent discussion. (Lopez, Synder, & Rasmussen, 2002). They stand as important constructs, but a counselor's understanding of their dynamics reveals how they come to enact the purpose of case management, advocacy, and assistance, particularly to people who occupy diminished statuses within a community. Counselors will likely serve people with such statuses through community agencies and they should be aware of the differential design and use of case management within any framework of counseling. It is a challenge for a counselor to remain mindful of the causes and consequences of deprivation and, as a result of such insight, craft a meaningful case management response.

IMPORTANCE OF PARADIGM

Borrowing from contingency theory in organizational science, there is no one way of focusing and articulating case management: Rather, it depends on what a service system seeks to achieve in partnership with, or on behalf of, a person in need (Garrow & Hasenfeld, 2010). Central variation in case management can be best explained by the aims a given organization possesses in responding to the needs of individuals who seek assistance, whether this assistance is construed narrowly or broadly, or in simple or complex ways. How an organization comes to construe and fulfill the needs of clients can be pivotal in influencing the development of case management as a central element of a system of helping.

The importance of paradigm is paramount. What a system sees as an acceptable pattern of service provision influences and shapes the form of case management an organization offers to: (1) meet the needs of clients the system defines as desirable to address and (2) determine how it should fulfill what it considers legitimate requests or demands clients make of a given organization. The concept of paradigm highlights how a given system of service sees both the role of the human service professional, which in this case is the counselor, and the role of recipient, client, or consumer. Paradigm, which involves a prevailing general pattern of helping that is accepted widely (or by some important group) to affirm what is correct in framing and taking action in a given area of human service practice, influences the form of case management and its configuration, particularly how it addresses vulnerability and resilience of clients. These two concepts interact and shape how case managers engage in the kind of practices a given service system culture defines as correct and/or legitimate.

THREE PARADIGMS OF CASE MANAGEMENT

Systems-Driven Paradigm

A preferred paradigm positions case management as part of a greater system of human services in which a person's situation is seen by professionals as highly complex. This paradigm is consistent with the founding of case management as a human service methodology in the 1970s. Within this paradigm, complexity of human need requires the coordination and/or integration of multiple forms of human services, multiple organizational venues and/or benefit systems, and/or multiple providers (typically in the form of specialized help). Such a paradigm remains dominant today in human services and expresses itself in forms of case management that incorporate coordination, service integration, and brokering strategies and tactics. Unfortunately, too often a given community may lack the resources a person needs vitiating any possibility of effective or meaningful coordination (Hyduk & Moxley, 2000). The paradigm itself likely favors the aims of organizational management and can amplify the importance of utilization management and the fulfillment of organizational standards of quality, both of which are ascendant in this paradigm (Moxley, 1997).

This paradigm favors the integrity of the larger system and requires case management personnel to preserve this integrity. Indeed, one could argue that case management really serves organizational purposes. What is "managed" within this situation is the case involving a specific person who is seen as a consumer of resources. Perhaps an appropriate label for such a paradigm is "systems focused" or "systems driven." This label is not used in a derogatory manner, but simply to highlight the central focus and purpose of this paradigm, and the forms of case management it favors.

There are other paradigms identified in this chapter as either client-centered or consumer-driven. Both these paradigms reflect other movements in human services that have taken root over the past four decades and serve as alternatives to the systems-integration identified above.

Client-Centered Paradigm

The client-centered paradigm is rooted in the client-centered counseling movement, as well as in the mental hygiene, psychiatric rehabilitation, and community support movements (Moxley, 2002). While it affirms the complexity and multiplicity of human needs emanating out of serious social, physical, and mental health concerns, the paradigm emphasizes the unique qualities of each human being and the formulation of case management direction from the perspective of the client, that is, the client is paramount. For the client-centered case manager advancing quality of life is a function of addressing and fulfilling the multiplicity of needs a person experiences across his or her many life domains.

Individualization of the client's situation based on insight the counselor gains through engagement, relationship formation, and assessment imbues this paradigm with client-centered features (Washington & Moxley, 2009a,b). However,

SYSTEMS-DRIVEN PARADIGM

As a counselor Lindsey is well trained to address in a comprehensive manner the many needs of the people she serves but is unable to do so in her current practice setting. She is amazed at how focused the organization in which she works is on employment and on achieving specific vocational outcomes. The organization, Montgomery Venture Enterprises, focuses the entire helping process on enabling people to get jobs, and their counselors specialize in case management of the employment process. The agency receives substantial funding from the state vocational rehabilitation authority as a result of its focus on employment.

Lindsey is concerned about those clients who are not interested in employment but who nonetheless find their way into the enterprise, typically by referral. The agency stipulates a quick assessment early in the helping process and refers out those individuals who either are not interested in employment or the counselor-case manager determines to be unready for a job search.

Lindsey suggests to the agency leadership that they offer an alternative pathway for those people who normally fall to the wayside because they are not ready for employment. But the leadership is adamant about the agency's exclusive focus on employment. "This is what we do, this is what we are all about," says the executive director. "Everything we do serves employment since this is what our principal funder wants from us." Lindsey appreciates this perspective, but it makes her wonder about what happens to those individuals whose needs the agency does not prioritize.

this approach can only occur when the case manager-counselor is able to engage the person proactively and formulate a strong working alliance as a result of such positive engagement. For the client-centered case manager, the nature of the relationship (engaging one another as authentic human beings) and alliance (creating a partnership in meeting the human needs of the client and in advancing his or her quality of life) forms the essence of case management (Moxley, 2009).

Certainly, the traditions of client-centered counseling are salient and imbue this paradigm with practices consistent with the counselor's authentic presentation of self. Practices include listening and discernment of need as the person articulates his or her concerns from the standpoint of the person's situation or societal location. Within this paradigm, "case" means the individualization and fulfillment of those needs a client finds pressing (Moxley, 1997). An essential quality of client-centered case management is found in a strong alliance in which counselor and client work closely to fulfill those pressing needs the client prioritizes. The system does not dictate what constitutes legitimate need or the priority the client assigns to those needs. The prioritization process is part of the client's own hierarchy of value and is something the counselor-case manager helps the client elicit, elaborate, and understand.

CLIENT-CENTERED PARADIGM

Chuck loves his work as a counselor employed at the Pathways organization. It is here he can actualize what he feels are the best practices of counseling he learned so much about as a graduate student. The agency supports people who are coping with HIV and who are in the process of recovery. Many of the people Chuck serves deal with multiple problems, including substance use, conflict-laden relationships, unemployment, poor housing options, and a range of risk behaviors.

Chuck enjoys working with each of his many clients to help them clarify the direction they wish to take based on their values and preferences. He invests considerably in assessment, working with each client to determine the most promising direction counseling can take, and to determine the client's principal goals.

While some of his clients focus on improving their housing and income, others prioritize wellness, health promotion, and stress management. Chuck assists all his clients, in maintaining their general health so that he helps them become more aware of their CD4 count and viral load, but works with these indicators within the context of the direction and goals his clients set. He feels that case management is a comprehensive process, which takes its focus from what the client seeks to achieve within the comprehensive domains that form quality of life, something HIV can easily threaten.

Most clients move through the helping process at different rates—some will take longer to set goals and develop a plan than others, and still some will require short-term plans because of crisis situations. Chuck may at times prescribe certain plans of action when he recommends harm reduction in situations in which clients' behaviors put them in harm's way or otherwise jeopardize the health of other people. Some of Chuck's colleagues feel that he is being too prescriptive in this regard, but for Chuck the focus on harm reduction is part of responsible counseling work. However, Chuck feels that he must depart from the principles of client-centered practice when he must give specific direction to a client whose behavior creates risky situations.

Consumer-Driven Paradigm

The consumer-driven paradigm has emerged from the consumer movement across a range of domains including service for those persons with infectious disease (e.g., HIV), serious mental illness (e.g., the psychiatric survivors' movement), physical disabilities (e.g., ADAPT), the developmental disabilities movement (e.g., People First), and those who have experienced trauma or violence (e.g., domestic violence). Those movements are consistent in their efforts to focus on the kind of oppression, discrimination, and/or stigma people with such backgrounds or qualities experience in their communities. Such movements also have been at the forefront of fostering rights consistent with ideas of positive segregation, claims on human services, enhanced benefits, and access to advocacy (Freddolino, Moxley, & Hyduk, 2004). Those organizations operating with strong consumerist identities will likely experience considerable conflict within institutional systems (Minkoff, 2010).

The paradigm assumes that clients (who are now consumers or survivors of the very system that has sought to help and, as well, of a greater social reaction) possess strong perspectives on what they want for themselves (Moxley & Freddolino, 1994). The perception that their experiences in traditional service systems have not been productive is likely accurate, and emotionally these experiences may create considerable strain and stress for them. Cognitively, it means that they may experience considerable doubt, skepticism, and uncertainty in obtaining what they want from human services and professionals. Survivors or consumers may bring distrust into the counseling-case management situations and counselors could view such persons as resistant or oppositional (Moxley & Freddolino, 1990).

Rather than being passive consumers, such as those which the systems-driven paradigm likely favors, these consumers are assertive and approach case management mindful that counselors are intended to help them resolve the issues they face. Within this paradigm issues replace needs as advanced organizers. The term "issue" is a construct that highlights the political nature of helping and support. Individuals who experience conflict in their everyday lives often experience injustice within community services from representatives of major societal institutions. Counselors may need to earn legitimacy from clients who may simply discount what they can offer.

The service system itself may generate issues that clients seek to resolve in a manner that brings them satisfaction or reduces the stress they experience. This illustrates how different this particular paradigm is from the other two. In this sense the consumer "drives" the paradigm rather than a system. The paradigm emanates from traditions different from those supporting the other paradigms and is consistent with mutual assistance, self-help, advocacy, social activism, and conflict resolution.

CULTURES OF CASE MANAGEMENT

Consonance as an Integrative Strategy in Case Management

Which paradigm is most relevant to those counselors who engage in case management? This is an interesting question and one worth some contemplation. The choice is likely not one that is under the exclusive control of the individual counselor-case manager. The most relevant one is that which is endorsed and/or favored by the culture of the organization or system within which the case manager works. Consonance—as well as the case manager's preferred approach, the value

CLIENT-DRIVEN PARADIGM

The members of OASIS simply hate the idea of case management. For people like them who have joined together to create an innovative support system, case management is indicative of social control, which means the community's control over choices, direction, activities, time, and expectations. OASIS is a product of a local social movement among people coping with serious mental illness or who too often feel the sting of pervasive negative social reaction in their daily lives.

OASIS members govern their organization as peers who create mutual support to advance collectively their quality of life. Some choose to be part of the local mental health center as clients, while others eschew such an option. After 5 years of hard work, and armed with a small grant from the local community foundation, OASIS secured a building and one case management position. The members were quick to reframe the position—they first named it the ENP on "enhanced navigation person," who helps interested members find and use resources that will contribute something meaningful to their quality of life.

Nancy Adams, a recent counseling graduate of the local state university quickly applied for the position and was told by the search committee, involving some 10 OASIS members, that she was "the best and strongest person for the job," primarily because of her ideology and lived experience with mental health concerns.

Nancy set right to work. She surveyed members and talked with groups and individuals about the best direction ENP could take. Emerging from such dialogue was a common theme that inspired Nancy to engage in the process of mutual support: Just ask members seeking help about what they would like to achieve for themselves given the issues they face in their daily lives.

Nancy found this question to be a real eye-opener. She started tapping into the worries of the members, their concerns for their own well-being, and how best they sought to balance the challenges they faced with the positive directions they sought for themselves. So, when a person came to see Nancy, she asked the question and invariably she quickly sensed themes of injustice, discrimination, and rejection operating in the issues the members shared with her. Soon she found the idea of navigation fading into the background as advocacy became a more prominent form of helping for the OASIS members as they became empowered through a better understanding of the issues they faced and how best to resolve them. By embracing members' lived experiences with negative social reaction, the organization's client-driven qualities resulted in an expansion of the advocacy OASIS could offer its members. Nancy was now the counselor-advocate, a title she cherished. The ENP designation faded quickly as a result.

set and experiences of clients, and the culture of the sponsoring organization—is important here. Counselors who operate with a strong commitment to advancing the effectiveness of a given system may be mindful of the importance of using their energy to improve system performance and protect the integrity of the system while they assist the client to fulfill those needs the system is most willing to address (Moxley, 1997). Integrity is a function of integration, particularly in achieving a good fit between the counselor-case manager and the client.

Implications of the Absence of Good Fit

Assertive clients may be seen by providers as problematic because they make demands of the system that neither counselors nor system leaders may see as reasonable. The culture itself identifies the importance of preserving the system's aims and may find itself working more effectively or responsively with those clients who may be passive in their orientation to authority, highly motivated to please, or perhaps willing to subjugate their own self-perceived priorities to those of the system (Moxley, 2003). Also, the system may place limits on its own responsiveness and the scope of the opportunities or services it is willing to offer consumers. Those human service systems that incorporate managed care practices may prioritize medical necessity as the criterion for determining the nature and amount of services they are willing to offer. While the system may justify these practices—because of cost and resource considerations—clients themselves may see such practices as inequitable given the nature and magnitude of the issues they face in daily life.

Alternatively, a culture that is client-centered likely favors those clients who are willing to engage in service, form strong relationships, build suitable alliances, and participate readily in planning and implementation activities. Here the culture may prioritize a process in which deviations from the norm may find little tolerance within a given program. The counselors themselves may prize the integrity of their own counseling or case management process and seek to achieve the right kind of client who can benefit from the model they offer. Those clients who respect the process and who are cooperative, who learn the appropriate client-centered behaviors, and who are willing to enact them in practice may be seen within such a culture as the most appropriate candidates.

Responding to a Dissonant Fit

The assertive client, or consumer, may experience strong dissonance within such cultures. Indeed, the cultures themselves may amplify the limitations of the person (framed as deficits in character of behavior), or explain them using diagnostic perspectives. Such cultures may easily overlook what people require in effective case management; that is, a good match between their own lived experience, values and preferences, and the human development context. A given culture and paradigm can interact to form this context of human development in which some clients (rather than others) find a good situation conducive to addressing their needs. The absence of such a fit is manifest in the dissatisfaction of the client with the case management experience, and can alert a counselor to the necessity of helping individuals who are not satisfied in finding the best home for themselves.

To clarify whether a good fit exists between paradigm and client expectations, the counselor may position an explicit screening effort at the beginning of the case management process as part of an engagement process in which the client can articulate what he or she values in terms of both process and outcome. Assessing the kind of fit a person requires may be an important aim of case management early in the process of counseling, or later when the counselor and client must troubleshoot what is not working. For those clients who are not clear about their preferences or expectations, the counselor can arrange for a brief provision of case management service followed by a mutual appraisal of the fit between the client and the service or helping culture. Advocacy is all too often limited to fostering access to services (inherent within brokering or coordinative forms of case management). It may result in the counselor fostering changes in organizational culture, or in helping a client to navigate another, more appropriate culture-paradigm of assistance (Hyduk & Moxley, 1997).

Without such provisional arrangements, the counselor risks the attribution of failure to those clients who may not find relevance in what the counselor offers or what is available through the immediate service situation. Blaming the victim can ensue and the culture itself may resolve the poor fit through a client's expulsion. Ultimately, culture mediates fit and enables groups to manage deviance. Therefore, counselors want to remain mindful of how the helping culture in which they practice influences the satisfaction of those people who hold the status of client. The idea of status amplifies whether—within a given paradigm—a client holds a diminished or empowered status. Valorization of the client's status may itself serve as an important intervention within human services (Wolfensberger, 1983).

Those clients who disengage from the system either voluntarily or involuntarily may say something important about the culture of the system and its prevailing paradigm. Such disengagement changes the membership qualities of the system and can limit the range of qualities (whether demographic, physical, cognitive, emotional, motivational, interpersonal, or behavioral) that participants bring to the culture. Those systems with attributes that make them a "no wrong door" system and that operate on "zero reject" philosophies with wrap-around practices may possess the most flexible cultures accommodating a wide range of diverse qualities that clients may introduce into a service setting. Such diverse clients not only reflect different needs, but also introduce different perspectives on what is useful within a given configuration of counseling, case management, and assistance. It is important for counselors to recognize the possibility that the alliance emulates the prevailing culture within a given system—at least this is an important hypothesis for readers to consider.

Reframing Case Management in Counseling Practice

With this content in mind, case management will be reframed when it is brought into a framework of counseling. Assisting individuals to determine what for them constitutes a good situation, particularly those who have experienced disability or trauma and/or those who face considerable discrimination resulting in marginalization, is a powerful approach to practice within case management. That is, for them a good situation is one in which they can thrive and achieve what matters most to them. Such an approach demands much of counselor-case managers because they must identify honestly for clients the strengths and limitations of a given system, organizational form, and cultural configuration. These counselors may need to inform clients about the potential of the system/paradigm to help them fulfill their needs or resolve the issues they face.

This form of case management may diverge greatly from those practices indicative of a more diagnostic clinical form, or those that embrace brokering and coordination methods. Within such a form of case management, consumer-centered or consumer-controlled values dominate the working agenda. The client and counselor establish methods to operationalize the direction of case management. The client and counselor will come to see vulnerability as situational or as influenced by social situation, the compounding and intractability of issues, and the client's experience of discrimination resulting in marginalization. They recognize clients' sources of resilience including those involving personal virtues, strengths, and character-forming experiences (Rapp & Gocha, 2006). What can emerge here is a kind of hybrid paradigm, one that integrates best practices from client-centered and consumer-driven paradigms. The following schema for this paradigm is adopted from previous work (Moxley, 2009):

Value Assigned to the Client's Perspective → Narrative as a Tool to Highlight Desire and Direction → Narrative to Identify Strengths, Assets, Issues, and Barriers → Formulation of Person-Centered Plan → Collaborative Action to Achieve Person-Centered Outcomes → Realization of Outcomes the Client Values

DISCIPLINARY CONFIGURATION OF CASE MANAGEMENT

The disciplinary configuration of case management also may be an expression of the culture of a given service system with variation found in multidisciplinary, interdisciplinary, or transdisciplinary forms. The term "discipline" refers to how knowledge, methods, and tools adhere to a given professional role in human services (Moxley, 2008). For counselors, case management can be a natural expression of their training and knowledge base. They muster their distinctive methods and tools within a framework of action that affirms what counselors "do" within a given service system.

Service systems may differ in how much and to what extent they legitimize specific human service or health disciplines. For example, one system may differentiate counselors and social workers in terms of roles and activities, while still another system may discount such differences and focus more on unifying the knowledge or practice base across disciplines. Whether discipline does or does not matter influences the kind of helping culture a particular system forms.

Multidisciplinary Configuration

The service system itself may offer specialized roles for specific disciplines within discrete or discipline-based organizational structures. Counselors, as opposed to psychiatrists, may handle the bulk of patient education, guidance, and personal change technologies that involve psychosocial processes. Such discipline-specific organizations face a challenge of integrating service structures and may resort to various integrative strategies cutting across departments or units. Counselors within such organizations may specialize in case management or, more likely, in specific case management functions like outreach and engagement, navigation through complex services, and discharge planning and community reentry. In such instances, counselors will integrate their counseling knowledge and skills base into the case management functions for which they are accountable.

Interdisciplinary Configuration

Over the years, discipline-specific organizations have evolved into more interdisciplinary ones in which professionals of diverse backgrounds meld naturally into team structures, often creating integrative tools and routines for directing action within their own working groups. Although discipline identity (e.g., social worker or counselor) may remain salient in day-to-day practice, it is the knowledge of how multiple professionals work to bring about desired outcomes and the sociotechnical knowledge of the group that ultimately foster interdisciplinary practice. Sociotechnical practice is inherently integrative, an aim of interdisciplinary practice. It integrates the personal qualities of the practitioners with the various disciplines within a specific work structure, which most likely is a team. Note that where practice is undertaken in discrete departments, as in multidisciplinary interaction, action within interdisciplinary practice is centered in team structures that likely exercise considerable independence within a broader framework of organizational policies, managerial procedures, ethics, and practices (Moxley, 2008).

A given team may manage a large caseload by allocating roles across team members in a way that makes the most sense for those clients whose needs the team addresses. A given team may engage in considerable role innovation bringing on board specialists who offer expertise in disability management, vocational development, and employment and housing. Role innovation may involve the recruitment and inclusion of peers, those individuals who share common characteristics and experiences with members of the service population (Moxley & Mowbray, 1997). Peer support specialists may bring a distinctive world view and paradigmatic orientation to a team making its practices more sensitive and responsive to clients.

Case management within interdisciplinary team-based practice likely will become the responsibility of the team as a whole. Such practice innovates in protocol development, process management, and outcome management to make such functions and their associated activities regular attributes of team work. Counselors who hold tight to disciplinary identities may find considerable challenge here as counseling knowledge, skills, and competencies blend with the distinctive knowledge, skills, and competencies of other disciplines. Through interdisciplinary practice, the counselor may come to know a lot about and appreciate better other professions such as physical therapy, occupational therapy, social work, or nursing.

Mutuality of respect becomes a signature of effective interdisciplinary practice within team contexts. Following this line of reasoning, the integration of disciplines means that the counselor will relinquish the idea that they do case management alone, and embrace the unity of case management activity within the team as a whole. For the counselor within interdisciplinary practice, the idea of case management does not involve the question of "How do I engage in case management as a counselor?," but rather "How does the team as a whole engage in case management given all of its diversity?" and "What is the distinctive contribution counselors make to case management undertaken by a team?"

Transdisciplinary Configuration

For case management within either multidisciplinary or interdisciplinary configurations, the discipline identity of practitioners remains both salient and important. But this statement is not necessarily true within those configurations that are transdisciplinary in nature. Team structures remain important, but a common base of theory, a common conception of purpose, and roles differentiated by the functional requirements of outcome influence practice within such teams. Transdisciplinary models seek unity and integration to bring about a valued outcome within a team context. Unlike interdisciplinary practice models, in which disciplines meld their knowledge and practices while preserving discipline identity, within the transdisciplinary approach other factors are important to personnel including their functional contributions, personal suitability, and mastery of core knowledge and best practices that all team members hold in common.

Counselors, social workers, and occupational therapists, for example, may all fulfill roles as employment specialists and bring to such roles insight into relevant core helping processes, a deep commitment to service, and specialized skills in vocational development and rehabilitation earned through considerable experience. Case management within this context may be a product of the entire team's efforts at service integration, and process and outcome management is undertaken by team members in a manner that fosters performance. To formulate its case management best practice base, a team forms a common skill base from which they pull process and outcome theories of rehabilitation (e.g., psychiatric rehabilitation). The team membership may pursue a common agenda of service integration differentiated theoretically by the practice model it adopts.

Imagine a team of six professionals integrating practice theories involving stress reduction, solution-focused work, and family systems work from which they derive pragmatic guidelines for implementing case management. Any team member should be prepared to engage in such practices at a level of quality the team as a whole stipulates. Clients enter the team and form a relationship with its members and can come to expect that each team member with whom they interact responds in a fairly consistent manner. This approach means that any team member can step in for another whose other responsibilities may take them away from direct practice for a time. The team as a whole shares a strong culture in which practices and their implementation are well defined and outcomes are clearly identified. Teams internally may differentiate members by their specializations and designate a member who focuses on housing, employment, socialization, education, or disability management. However, the factor that unifies them is a common intervention theory and practice base. The strong and enduring relationships they form with one another are yet another integrative device.

Through such a configuration counselors may find that they have opportunities to integrate case management into their work as specialists who also carry generalist responsibilities for rehabilitation within the team. Unlike the interdisciplinary configuration in which the counselors seek to preserve their discipline identity, the counselors in transdisciplinary practice may reduce their professional identity as a functional perspective ascends within the counselor's job duties. Within the transdisciplinary configuration, personnel likely ask: "How do we implement our specialist functions while engaging in broad-based case management, employing a common theory and practice base across team members?" In transdisciplinary practice, service providers may identify more with their specialization, team, and function than they do with their discipline.

The maturation of transdisciplinary models within human services is a salient innovation of the past two decades (Moxley, 2008). There has been a convergence of knowledge and practice in principal domains of human services, such as rehabilitation, and their development is one very important driver of transdisciplinarity. Such models challenge professional education and professional identities, but they focus attention and energy on what matters most to clients: "How do I advance my quality of life with a level of support I find useful and acceptable?"

Within transdisciplinary practice the criteria of usefulness and accept-ability stand as important values of client support. Usefulness implies the practical outcome of unified and integrated effort. Here quality of environment, quality of day, and quality of life take on important meaning, as people who are vulnerable or at risk of poor life outcomes seriously consider with considerate, knowledgeable, and well-motivated professionals how they wish to lead their lives.

Specialization among team members can be introduced, for example, through various role assignments, such as that of housing specialist. This addition implies the importance of helping people make headway in specific areas of their daily living. The integration of functional specialization into good team work reflects capacity building. A team's capacity for case management is a function of the extent to which it can address proactively the scope of clients' needs. Such requisite variety is an indicator of the quality of case management within transdisciplinary practice. In other words, a team's scope mirrors the scope of need experienced by people who are clients of case management.

Whether clients find certain actions desirable and relevant can factor into case management in important ways. Transdisciplinary practitioners are not preoccupied with disciplinary or professional status, but come to recognize the importance of respecting the choices of the people they serve. They understand that helping people will bring their preferences into a plan and action, and the team and client will solidify a stronger partnership and alliance. The strength of alliance, the concordance among team members and clients, and a practical outcome that clients find satisfying may be the strongest factors influencing the potency of case management.

PARADIGMATIC FACTORS INFLUENCING COUNSELING AND CASE MANAGEMENT

The Importance of Organizational Auspices

A sound argument for the differentiation of case management into three principal paradigms has been made—the systems-driven, client-centered, and consumer-driven forms in which each form emerges from an alternative tradition within the human and helping services. The aim of this chapter is descriptive rather than prescriptive; it should be emphasized that both client-centered and consumer-driven forms are likely more prevalent within community-based services as counselors and other helping professionals work with people entering street-level structures searching for assistance.

Such structures likely exist outside the bureaucratic matrix of state and local government, although they may garner a portion of their funds from these entities given the propensity of government to transfer responsibility for service to community organizations. Such organizations are likely nonprofit or hybrid public-private entities—such as those found in community mental health systems—that reflect the emergence over the past 30 years of community-based systems located outside the public sphere. Helping organizations may be well integrated into larger systems or may stand alone but be networked with other organizational entities within local communities. Still others may exist as more marginalized collectives of people who commonly share certain social issues, such as consumer-run organizations. The standing of consumer-run organizations within service systems may be diminished because more powerful entities see them as deprofessionalized or limited in their capacities. Such entities still may present powerful strategies for meeting the needs of people who do not find relevance or value in more mainstream settings.

Alternatively for state bureaucracies, outcomes and processes likely are well defined and case management is seen as a process for moving people in need through highly structured benefit systems in which access, eligibility, service provision or amount, and outcome are specified by law, regulation, and procedure. Such systems like state vocational rehabilitation organizations possess very clear criteria for eligibility. Counselors may work in highly structured service settings with little discretion or control over the specification of outcome. They may engage in navigation activities moving people through the system from intake to discharge.

As counseling radiates into community settings, such narrow role specification may literally dissolve as counselors increasingly gain discretion over their practices. The counselor, particularly within client-centered paradigms, can exercise considerable control over his or her decisions. The counselor may determine who receives service, particularly in partnership with clients who participate considerably in determining the direction service will take, the amount of service an organization offers, and the focus and nature of outcome. How counselor-case managers help clients articulate their needs and find relevant directions they value will influence case management, particularly in an agency in which a client-centered form is dominant.

In a client-centered form, outcome cannot be readily defined (unlike systems-driven forms that may specify a limited set of outcomes) until people who receive services articulate what they need and the counselor-case manager interprets such need within the framework of the host organization's purpose and aims. Depending upon the needs a counselor-case manager addresses (and based on the acuity level of the client), either a directive or nondirective approach may be salient. The integration of model of practice (such as solution-focused counseling) into this matrix may be under the discretionary control of the counselor.

Case Management in Community Counseling

Broad-based assessment processes will figure into such case management in important ways as the client-centered counselor-case manager seeks to understand fully what is occurring in the life of the person, what brings the person into the community agency for assistance, and how the person's strengths influence his capacity for self-care and self-directed action. Counselor-case managers practicing from the perspective of a client-centered paradigm will likely frame their approach using a broad framework like quality of life (Washington & Moxley, 2009a,b). Such a framework will incorporate multiple domains of daily life and offer the counselor-case manager and client a starting point for considering need, identifying requirements of daily living, and formulating any initial and/or subsequent direction the helping process can take.

For the client-centered counselor-case manager, important initial questions emerge when the professional considers the quality of life of the person he or she will assist: How satisfying is your quality of life? What gaps exist for you or what deficiencies do you experience? What ways do you want to improve your quality of life? What aims emerge for you that you would invest in with some urgency (particularly in crisis situations) or priority (particularly in situations in which the counselor and client take a long-term perspective)?

Understanding that it is the quality of people's environment that influences their quality of life in fundamental ways, counselors cannot distance themselves from more basic aspects of helping that are linked directly to environment, such as safety, housing, and nutrition. The life-enhancing aspects of the environment can reveal themselves as strengths during an assessment process, while the negative consequences the environment produces for particular individuals may become readily visible through a well-articulated assessment (Washington & Moxley, 2009a,b; Wright & Lopez, 2002). People who face considerable discrimination, stigma, and ultimately diminished status will likely struggle with poor environments, ones that fail to meet their needs, and foster their development, and, such as in the case of pollution, can literally expose people to toxins.

In some cases, people will present symptoms indicative of a failure to thrive in which unmet needs for medical care, nutritional adequacy, and suitable housing are salient. Counselors, particularly those working in impoverished communities, cannot overlook such immediate needs. Melding immediate assistance to fulfill a person's needs with other forms of action, such as advocacy, supplemented with supportive activities sometimes achieved, for example, through group work, means a counselor in those situations integrates case management within the overall structure of counseling, helping, and practical assistance (Washington & Moxley, 2001). The integration of group work and case management may form a powerful synergy for helping people who face numerous issues, particularly ones that can dampen their motivation for self-care (Washington & Moxley, 2001; Washington & Moxley, 2003a–c).

By incorporating structured activities, spirituality, and narrative forms of knowledge into group work, counselors can encourage the formation and perpetuation of mutual support (Washington, Moxley, & Garriott, 2009; Washington, Moxley, Garriott, & Crystal-Weinberger, 2009). Additional structured activities can support further development of self-efficacy among group members (Moxley, Washington, Garriott, & Feen-Calligan, 2010; Washington, Moxley, & Taylor, 2009). Supportive group work can enhance clients' motivation and equip them with ideas and skills to resolve the issues they face (Toseland & Rivas, 2005). Groups also can serve a calming function helping people under stress to focus attention and energy on the issues they face within the context of a supportive environment (Feen-Calligan, Washington, & Moxley, 2008; Moxley & Washington, 2001).

Such integration is highly indicative of community counseling models in which the counselor links specific strategies of assistance through support, case management, group work, and advocacy (Washington, Moxley, Garriott, & Crystal, 2009). More systems-driven counselors may not engage in such high levels of role integration, favoring a more well-focused, outcome-set of limited scope, process limited, and well-bounded form of practice. Bureaucratic auspices in which counselors operate can set limits on helping in which rationing, cost containment, and medical orientation may constrain the clients' specification of their own aims.

Importance of an Environmental Focus

An environmental focus within counseling-case management may prove to be a central feature of either a client-centered or consumer-driven approach. Counselors operating within community counseling organizations may witness firsthand how poor or unsupportive environments can attenuate the functioning of the people they serve and create negative emotional experiences for people who are coping with the consequences of environmental deprivation and/or degradation.

In particular, for people with disabilities, the environment is a critical factor in influencing opportunity, community involvement, and a sense of social support. Environments that are highly accessible and that foster inclusion may result in a very different expression of disability for persons who find physical, social, and instrumental supports readily available within their communities. Those environments that establish serious barriers to human development and expression of diversity may amplify a person's limitations, thereby reducing functioning and obviating success. Environment can become a focal point of counseling-case management. Particularly, assessment within the client-centered form can begin with an appraisal of the multiple features of environment and address how people's adaptation to "what is" creates negative consequences in the physical, cognitive, emotional, and social domains (Boeck, Wachter, & Moxley, 2010). Fully understanding adaptation is a key tactic within a client-centered approach that can reveal strengths of the person receiving assistance and amplify the nature of those issues that serve as barriers to the person's realization of a life style he or she prefers (Moxley, Washington, & Feen-Calligan, 2010).

Counselors serving as case managers within community settings will interact with people who bring a range of life experiences and situations that demand a rich understanding of environment. People living with HIV or serious mental illness face numerous adaptive challenges within environments that may be unprepared to support their functioning and well-being. People leaving incarceration and reentering community life likely face similar environments. People experiencing serious economic disruption likely face unresponsive environments. The counselor-case manager seeks to integrate different forms of practice (e.g., case management and advocacy), and will see the negative consequences of unresponsive environments. This awareness raises the question of "How best to help?" Responding effectively to such a question demands the best of a counselor's ingenuity. Being ready to meet such challenges with a plethora of tools geared to the needs of an individual who requires considerable assistance reveals one of the distinct properties of the client-centered paradigm. A key strategy involves helping individuals strengthen social networks and enhance social support (Tracy, 2009).

Criteria Guiding Adoption of Consumer-Driven Case Management

When does a counselor-case manager embrace a consumer-driven form? Briefly reflecting on the organization of human services within most local communities will help guide the determination. The differences between bureaucratic and community-based organizations have been described previously. There is another option, known as alternative service organizations, which is too often formed out of frustration and anger among people who bear the negative effects of unresponsive service systems, social institutions, environments, and communities. These are founded by people who seek a different, more informed, or more enlightened way of offering support.

Typically built on tenets of self-help, mutual support, and social action, such alternative organizations may remain small and informal in their governance and operations. They often serve as a refuge for those individuals who experience considerable stigma, discrimination, neglect, and abuse within the general community. The grand narrative of an alternative service organization typically articulates the harsh treatment people with certain qualities or characteristics have faced, thereby justifying the formation of an alternative to what exists.

It is not surprising that within American society alternative service organizations first emerged to support people who were devalued—people with serious mental illness, people with mental retardation, people facing domestic violence, and people with physical disabilities. All these groups have one thing in common—they likely experience considerable stigma and face negative social reaction (Washington & Moxley, 2009a, 2009b). To find an organization with a culture that supports people who otherwise face social rejection is a principal step toward empowerment. Successfully advancing such an organization strengthens the standing and voice of the individuals who form its membership.

Working with alternative service organizations may serve as a viable way the counselor-case manager can partner with people to build and expand support systems when more institutionalized systems fail to resolve the issues they face. The members of such organizations may not be receptive to a strong professional identity on part of the counselor and may see case management as a form of social control. Alternatively, they may relate directly to the personal qualities of the counselor and to his or her own experience with the forces of marginalization. Pragmatism in helping may ascend as an important value steering assistance a counselor offers in the direction of practical outcome.

For counselors this distinction may be difficult to manage personally, particularly since years of educational preparation and development equips them with strong professional identities. To relinquish this identity within the context of an alternative service organization may create a crisis for counselors who come to understand that by identifying marginalization and the plight it creates for people (inherent in a consumer-run organization) they relinquish their professionalism. Reframing identity may occur here when the counselor shifts from doing case management to serving as an issue-oriented advocate.

As an advocate the counselor understands the grand narrative of marginalization guiding the development of the alternative service organization and works to empower the members of such a support system. Two forms of expertise may emerge within such an organization. First, the alternative service organization is adept at supporting its members in the face of social reaction and at buffering negative consequences members experience. Second, the alternative service organization builds a capacity to help members bring about satisfying resolutions to the issues they face. The practice of a counselor may come to reflect personally (and professionally) such strengths.

Ultimately, consumer-driven practice means that the counselor identifies directly the plight of clients. Counselors are willing to represent the issues of those who experience this plight directly as if they were their own, a form of advocacy found in public interest legal practice (Freddolino et al., 2004). Alternatively, counselors may see the advancement of the status of the people they work with as a principal focus of assistance offering a more sociological perspective on advocacy. What matters most, however, is that consumer-driven practice is different compared to either systems-driven or client-centered forms. Within the consumer-driven form, the counselor engages in social action designed to advance the well-being of people whose status is diminished within society and/or to promote the formation of alternative support systems, ones involving self-help or mutual assistance (Washington & Moxley, 2008). The counselor likely undertakes this social action in partnership with those who have firsthand experience of a serious issue.

Variation in Advocacy

Certainly, advocacy is part of the role constellation of counseling and case management within each paradigm (Freddolino et al., 2004). Within the systems-driven or client-driven forms, advocacy may be more limited than within the consumer-driven variant. Advocacy influenced by systems-driven paradigm may simply involve navigating people through complex bureaucracies. Helping them pass through rigid systems of eligibility, access, and service provision within bureaucracies or rendering assistance so that people gain access to community-based services is a common form of advocacy within human services work (Moxley & Hyduk, 2003). Advocacy within the consumer-driven form is more potent—it addresses both the social status of the person who experiences marginalization and the conflict that ensues from diminished status (Moxley & Washington, 2009a,b). Thus, helping a person improve his or her status is a hallmark of advocacy within the consumer-driven paradigm (Moxley & Paul, 2005).

CAREER PATHS FOR THE COUNSELOR-CASE MANAGER

Differential Foci for the Integration of Counseling and Case Management

Counseling and case management can come to involve different foci within the three paradigms. For the counselor it raises choices about the nature of counseling strategy and career development. What paradigm best suits a given individual and how do they come to enact such a paradigm from a career development perspective? Imagine a person in recovery from serious mental illness who at midlife embarks on a career in counseling, but does so within an alternative service organization, the mission of which is to support people who do not find value in prevailing client-centered or system-driven services. Our hypothetical counselor subscribes to self-help and mutual support and develops as an advocate of people who seeks to create and sustain an alternative service organization for people who are recovering from societal neglect and social reaction. The counselor's identity melds both his or her first-person lived experience and professional development.

Another person embarks on what comes to be a systems-driven career. This person takes an entry-level position as a counselor-case manager in a specialized rehabilitation environment and focuses on helping people navigate the process of community reentry after stabilization from a serious physical disability. This counselor is well focused on a specific step of the rehabilitation process, reentry, and facilitates this process addressing a person's fears and anxieties about independent living, issues an unresponsive environment may play in the daily life of the person, and links for the person to community-based services.

In this situation, the counselor serves as a clinical case manager working on the person's adjustment, at the same time addresses the adequacy and responsiveness of the receiving environment to the person's needs. Within this role as a clinical case manager, the counselor integrates linkage, brokering, and coordinating activities, ones indicative of traditional case management with those supportive features of a clinical approach. For this counselor, professional development may involve the acquisition of social capital within a community that would be useful in facilitating the person's successful reentry and stabilization within independent living.

For the client-centered counselor, a career likely means interdisciplinary engagement of other professionals to best meet the quality of life needs of those individuals who seek services and support from a community agency. This focus may be an emergent one in which counselors, particularly those focusing on rehabilitation, move from bureaucratic settings to community-based ones. Here frameworks such as biopsychosocial and holistic ones take on immediate importance as counselors use such perspectives to foster individualization or personalization in processes of engagement, relationship enhancement, assessment, service planning, service enactment, and evaluation orchestrated by the counselor in a seamless manner and in such a way that helps those served achieve substantive improvements to their quality of life.

Career development for the client-centered counselor may take either a generalist or specialist path. For the generalist, client-centered practice will involve a diverse case load of people who present different situations but whose needs may be addressed in similar ways through a systematic process of counseling and case management. For the specialist, the client-centered practitioner will focus on specific populations, such as people with serious mental illness.

The Aim of Integration Within a Matrix of Choice

For sure, in all three scenarios, how counselors working within a given paradigm, culture, and organization come to see vulnerability and resilience of those people with whom they work is an important way of framing action. Integration here assumes multiple parts creating a complex helping situation. Harmonizing these parts into a whole, ensuring that the distinct elements of counseling and case management join together into a powerful synergy, and imbuing practice with a particular kind of style that emanates from the best practices of a particular paradigm demands much of a counselor who is in search of integrity. In the words of O'Donohue (2004), the achievement of integrity occurs when there is "complete realization of whatever a thing is supposed to be." For the counselor, this realization is an important part of working closely with people who experience considerable vulnerability. For people whose needs go unmet (and, as a result, serious negative consequences ensue) or who experience mounting unresolved issues, "realization" may be elusive until they engage a helpful, caring, and committed counselor.

Diverse practice settings and pluralistic roles suggest a broad matrix of choice for counselors who seek to advance the lives of individuals and communities in ways they find creative, innovative, and meaningful. For the counselor-case manager, the "how" of case management follows from its "why," making paradigm and culture powerful forces in shaping practice.

SUMMARY

In conclusion, the three variants offer a differential way of thinking about the influence of paradigms, organizational cultures, and systems. The alternative career paths they offer counselors who integrate in some fashion or to some degrees can challenge professional self-concept and make counselors more mindful of the structural aspects of their work. Diversity in the auspices of counseling opens up numerous paths in which there is no longer one set of techniques, one model, or one setting. The counselor can choose and the results of such choice define professional character.

CONTENT REVIEW QUESTIONS

- What constitutes case management in counseling practice for a practitioner?
- What is the role of case management within practice? Within counseling in general?
- To what extent is each of the three paradigms operating in the world of counseling practice?
- Compare the systems-driven paradigm, client-centered paradigm, and consumer-driven paradigm. Discuss aspects of these paradigms that are influential in shaping case management practice for counselors.
- What are the implications of each paradigm for a counselor? How does each paradigm influence the development of a counselor?
- How do you see vulnerability as an advanced organizer of counseling? What are its implications for a counselor?
- How does the idea of intervention or service culture influence thinking about how counselors can undertake case management?
- How can counselors form "hybrid" models of case management through the interplay of paradigms? How does this formation influence innovation in counseling practice?
- Distinguish a multidisciplinary, interdisciplinary, and transdisciplinary form of case management and describe the relative strengths and limitations of each practice.
- Given the principal themes of this chapter, how do you view case management practice within counseling? What are the implications, if any, for a career in counseling?

REFERENCES

Boeck, D., Wachter, H., & Moxley, D. (2010). Designing Health: Aging Needs Assessment and The Environment for Positive Aging in Norman, OK. *Action Research for Expanding Positive Aging Resources in Town Development*. Proceedings of the 2010 Design Research Conference, Riverpoint Campus, Spokane, WA.
Cobb, J., & Sennett, R. (1993). *Hidden injuries of class*. New York, NY: Norton.
Feen-Calligan, H., Washington, O., & Moxley, D. (2008). Use of artwork as a visual processing modality in group treatment of chemically dependent minority women. *The Arts in Psychotherapy Journal, 35*(4), 287–295.

Freddolino, P., Moxley, D., & Hyduk, C. (2004). A differential model of advocacy in social work practice. *Families in Society, 85*(1), 119–128.

Garrow, E., & Hasenfeld, Y. (2010). Theoretical approaches to human service organizations. In Y. Hasenfeld (Ed.), *Human services as complex organizations* (2nd ed., pp. 33–57). Thousand Oaks, CA: Sage.

Hasenfeld, Y. (2010). The attributes of human service organizations. In Y. Hasenfeld (Ed.), *Human services as complex organizations* (2nd ed., pp. 9–32). Thousand Oaks, CA: Sage.

Hyduk, C., & Moxley, D. (1997, April). A personal advocacy model for serving older adults. *Journal of Gerontological Social Work, 28*(4), 75–90.

Hyduk, C., & Moxley, D. (2000). Challenges to the implementation of a personal advocacy program for older adults. *Families in Society, 81*(5). 455–466.

Lopez, S., Snyder, C., & Rasmussen, H. (2002). Striking a vital balance: Developing a complementary focus on human weakness and strength through positive psychological assessment. In C. R. Snyder & S. J. Lopez (Eds.), *Handbook of Positive Psychology* (pp. 3–20). New York, NY: Oxford University Press.

Minkoff, D. C. (2010). The emergence of hybrid organizational forms: Combining identity-based service provision and political action. In Y. Hasenfeld (Ed.), *Human services as complex organizations* (2nd ed., pp. 117–138). Thousand Oaks, CA: Sage.

Moxley, D. (1989). *The practice of case management.* Thousand Oaks, CA: Sage.

Moxley, D. (1997). *Case management by design: Reflections on principles and practices.* Chicago, IL: Nelson-Hall.

Moxley, D. (2002). The emergence and attributes of second-generation community support services for persons with serious mental illness: Implications for case management. *Journal of Social Work in Disability and Rehabilitation, 1*(2), 25–52.

Moxley, D. (2003). Outcomes and alternative cultures of case management. *Australian Journal of Case Management, 5*(1), 3–11.

Moxley, D. (2008). Interdisciplinarity. In T. Mizrahi & L. Davis (Eds.), *Encyclopedia of social work* (20th ed.). New York, NY: Oxford University Press.

Moxley, D., & Freddolino, P. (1990). A model of advocacy for promoting client self-determination in psychosocial rehabilitation. *Psychosocial Rehabilitation Journal, 14*(2), 69–82.

Moxley, D., & Freddolino, P. (1994). Client-driven advocacy and psychiatric disability: A model for social work practice. *Journal of Sociology and Social Welfare, 21*(2), 98–108.

Moxley, D., & Hyduk, C. (2003). The logic of personal advocacy with older adults and its implications for program management in community gerontology. *Administration in Social Work, 27*(4), 5–23.

Moxley, D., & Manela, R. (2001). Expanding the conceptual basis of outcomes and their use in the human services. *Families in Society, 82*(6), 569–577.

Moxley, D., & Paul, M. Advocacy and guardianship. (2005). In W. Crimando & T. F. Riggar (Eds.), *Community resources: A practical guide for human service professionals* (pp. 200–217). Prospect, Ill: Waveland Press.

Moxley, D., & Washington, O. (2001). Strengths-based recovery practice in chemical dependency: A transpersonal perspective. *Families in Society, 82*(3), 251–262.

Moxley, D., & Washington, O. (2009). The role of advocacy assessment and action in resolving health compromising stress in the lives of older African American homeless women. In L. Napier & Paul Waters (Eds.), *Social work and global health inequalities: policy and practice developments.* London, UK: Policy Press.

Moxley, D., Washington, O., & Feen Calligan, H. (2010). *Narrative insight into risk, vulnerability and resilience among older homeless African American women.* Paper submitted for publication.

Moxley, D., Washington, O., Garriott, L., & Feen Calligan, H. (2010). *Quilting as self-efficacy group work with older African American women transitioning out of homelessness.* Paper submitted for publication.

Moxley, D. P. (2009). Case management in psychosocial rehabilitation. In A. R. Roberts (Ed.), Social workers' desk reference (2nd ed., pp. 770–778). New York, NY: Oxford University Press.

Moxley, D. P., & Mowbray C. T. (1997). Consumers as providers: Social forces and factors legitimizing role innovation in psychiatric rehabilitation. In C. T. Mowbray, D. Moxley, C. Jasper, & L. Davis (Eds.), Consumers as providers in psychiatric rehabilitation. International Association of Psychosocial Rehabilitation Services.

O'Donohue, J. (2004). Beauty: The invisible embrace. New York, NY: Harper Perennial.

Rapp, C. A., & Gocha, R. J. (2006). The strengths model: Case management with people with psychiatric disabilities. New York, NY: Oxford University Press.

Sandfort, J. (2010). Human service organizational technology: Improving understanding and advancing research. In Y. Hasenfeld (Ed.), Human services as complex organizations (2nd ed., pp. 269–290). Thousand Oaks, CA: Sage.

Toseland, R. W., & Rivas, R. F. (2005). An introduction to group work (5th ed.). Boston, MA: Allyn & Bacon.

Tracy, E. M. (2009). Working with and strengthening social networks. In A. R. Roberts (Ed.), Social workers' desk reference (2nd ed., pp. 710–714). New York, NY: Oxford University Press.

Washington, O. G. M., & Moxley, D. P. (2001). The use of prayer in group work with African American women recovering from chemical dependency. Families in Society, 82, 49–59.

Washington, O., & Moxley, D. (2001). A model of group treatment to facilitate recovery from chemical dependence. Journal of Psychosocial Nursing and Mental Health Services, 39(7), 30–41.

Washington, O., & Moxley, D. (2003a). Developing psychological readiness for employment rehabilitation among chemically dependent women. Journal of Social Work Research and Evaluation: An International Publication, 4(1), 67–81.

Washington, O., & Moxley, D. (2003b). Group interventions with low-income African American women recovering from chemical dependency. Health and Social Work, 28(2), 146–156.

Washington, O., & Moxley, D. (2003c). Promising group practices to empower low income women coping with chemical dependency. American Journal of Orthopsychiatry, 73(1), 109–116.

Washington, O., & Moxley, D. (2008). Telling my story: From narrative to exhibit in illuminating the lived experience of homelessness among older African American women. Journal of Health Psychology, 13(2), 154–165.

Washington, O., & Moxley, D. (2009a). Development of a multimodal assessment framework for helping older African American women transition out of homelessness. Smith College Studies in Social Work, 79(2), 103–124.

Washington, O., & Moxley, D. (2009b). "I Have Three Strikes against Me": Narratives of Plight and Efficacy among Older African American Homeless Women and Their Implications for Engaged Inquiry. In S. Evans (Ed.), African Americans and Community Engagement in Higher Education. New York, NY: State University of New York Press.

Washington, O., Moxley, D., & Garriott, L. (2009). The Telling My Story Quilting Workshop: Innovative Group Work with Older African American Women Transitioning Out of Homelessness. Journal of Psychosocial Nursing and Mental Health Services, 47(11), 1–11.

Washington, O., Moxley, D., Garriott, L., & Crystal, J. (2009). Building a responsive network of support and advocacy for older African American homeless women through developmental action research. Contemporary Nurse, 33(2), 140–161.

Washington, O., Moxley, D., Garriott, L., & Crystal-Weinberger, J. (2009). Five dimensions of faith and spirituality of older African American women transitioning out of homelessness. Journal of Religion and Health, 48(4), 431–444.

Washington, O., Moxley, D., & Taylor, J. (2009). Enabling older homeless minority women to overcome homelessness by using a life management enhancement group intervention. *Issues in Mental Health Nursing, 30*(2), 86–972.

Wolfensberger, W. (1983). Social role valorization: A new term for the principle of normalization. *Mental Retardation, 21*(6), 234–239.

Wright, B., & Lopez, S. (2002). Widening the diagnostic focus: As case for including human strengths and environmental resources. In C. R. Snyder & S. J. Lopez (Eds.), Handbook of Positive Psychology (pp. 26–44). New York, NY: Oxford University Press.

14

Advocacy

William Ming Liu and Rebecca L. Toporek

LEARNING OBJECTIVES

After reading this chapter, you should be able to:

■ Understand the relationship of advocacy, empowerment, and social justice
■ Understand advocacy in connection to multicultural competencies and rehabilitation
■ Understand the advocacy competencies

Advocacy in rehabilitation counseling is not new. In fact, "Advocacy is embedded in the very nature of the rehabilitation counseling field" (Middleton, Robinson, & Mu'min, 2010, p. 175). Rehabilitation counselors, in many professional practices, often find themselves at the forefront of helping clients in multiple ways to create optimal environments for their growth and development (Maki & Riggar, 1997; Toporek, Blando, et al., 2009). Yet finding empirical and theoretical literature regarding the practice of advocacy in rehabilitation counseling is difficult. Moreover, misconceptions about effective advocacy have led some to confusion and, in some cases conflict, regarding the place of advocacy in this counseling specialty. Advocacy in rehabilitation counseling has tended to focus on facilitating access to services; yet the field has been somewhat slower to address advocacy with individuals who are marginalized within the rehabilitation system (Middleton et al., 2010). Thus, to advance the practice of advocacy within rehabilitation counseling, one possible area to gain some understanding may be from multicultural counseling.

The multicultural counseling literature has critiqued traditional counseling practices, research, and education for cultural bias toward individualism, middle-classness, and certainly ability (Olkin, 1999, 2002; Prilleltensky, 1997). Parallel to this tendency within the rehabilitation field has been the use of the medical model. Operating from this model, rehabilitation practice focuses on the disability and the characteristics of the individual with the intent of mini-mizing pathology and treating symptoms rather than addressing problems in the environment (Middleton et al., 2010). Within the framework of the medical model, it is the individual that is the problem. Typically, the denial of power systems that perpetuate the marginalization of "minority" peoples has been a problematic theme in many theoretical orientations (Caldwell & Vera, 2010; Liu & Hernandez, 2010; Pieterse, Evans, Risner-Butner, Collins, & Mason, 2009; Singh et al., 2010; Toporek & Liu, 2001; Toporek & Vaughn, 2010). Consequently, the failure to be "self-actualized" and productive is often considered to be the fault of the client rather than context, history, or access to resources. To correct these issues and more fully integrate context into professional practice, many in our counseling professions have taken upon themselves the responsibility to work beyond the confines of the counseling space and to engage directly into social action and advocacy.

The focus of this chapter is to describe advocacy in rehabilitation counsel-ing by attending to the contribution of multicultural counseling perspectives. To meet this goal, we will first discuss the relevance of incorporating multicultural competency into the definition of advocacy in rehabilitation counseling. Second, we will discuss the role of advocacy in professional practice and describe vari-ous models and definitions of advocacy. Finally, we will discuss education and practice implications, with particular attention to the professional responsibili-ties of rehabilitation counselors and the challenges they face as they attempt to advocate for their clientele.

MULTICULTURAL COUNSELING COMPETENCIES

By now, many counselors understand the necessity of multicultural competen-cies. The best-known framework for multicultural competencies—as articulated by Sue, Arredondo, and McDavis (1992)—stated that counselors need to have knowledge, awareness, and skills in three areas of understanding: their biases, their client's worldviews, and culturally congruent interventions. The argument for the integration of multiculturalism into counseling has rested on the chang-ing racial and ethnic demographics of the United States (Ridley & Kleiner, 2003). Problematically, however, this argument often overlooks other existing aspects of diversity (e.g., sexual orientation, women, and ability) and situates multicultur-alism with race and ethnicity. On the contrary, it is important that multicultural-ism be defined in general and overarching cultural dimensions—to be expansive and inclusive (Stone, 1997). There are several works that may contribute to the relevance of multicultural competencies to rehabilitation counseling. First, Arredondo et al. (1996) discussed an inclusive perspective of multiculturalism and elaborated the competencies within the framework of personal dimensions of identity. They suggested that counselors must consider the multiple ways that individuals define themselves and the multiple communities of importance to clients, and strive for competence in these different realms. In keeping the expansive definition of multiculturalism, it is easy to understand how advocacy, multiculturalism, and rehabilitation counseling may form a strong partnership.

The multicultural rehabilitation competencies articulated the importance of cultural competence including awareness, knowledge, and skills (Middleton et al., 2000). Middleton and her colleagues endorsed and provided practical guidance regarding the implementation of these competencies. This move reinforced the connection between rehabilitation counseling and multicultural competence. Later, Middleton et al. (2010) noted that, although the multicultural rehabilitation competencies had been developed, the field was still slow to advocate for underrepresented groups.

Toporek and Reza (2000) used the base of multicultural counseling competencies provided by Sue et al. (1992) to assert that multicultural competencies should include attention to institutional dimensions as well as professional and personal realms. They described institutional cultural competence as actions that counselors may need to take in addressing institutional issues that impact the well-being of clients. Counselors may do this through administrative roles, coordinator roles, as members of an organization, or in a variety of other functions. This attention to institutional competence directly suggests that advocacy may be critical in working in culturally competent ways—beyond one-on-one work with clients.

Focusing on rehabilitation counseling specifically, we see that this counseling specialty is very appropriate for an integration of advocacy and multiculturalism. Middleton et al. (2010) asserted that advocacy is inherent in the multicultural counseling competencies (Sue et al., 1992) and the multicultural counseling rehabilitation competencies. Acknowledging the importance of self-advocacy within rehabilitation, Middleton and her colleagues also noted that access to institutional power varies based on a number of identity variables such as race, gender, sexual orientation, and disability status. Consequently, advocacy may be needed from others who have greater access to institutional power, namely counselors. Middleton and her colleagues charged that there are two major gaps in the rehabilitation counseling profession: the lack of endorsement of multicultural competencies and the absence of common language, definitions, and competencies for advocacy.

Hershenson's (1990) "C-C-C" model of rehabilitation counseling may be used as a framework for considering how advocacy may be an integral part of the role. In this model, the rehabilitation counselor's role includes three primary functions: coordinating, counseling, and consulting. Within each aspect of this role, the counselor may find that some form of advocacy is an appropriate intervention. Multiculturalism, in general, encourages institutions and individuals to seek out transformation of systems rather than to settle for additive changes or superficial reorganizing (Liu & Pope-Davis, 2003). As such, advocacy becomes an implicit activity of those who identify themselves as multiculturally competent counselors. In a similar manner, rehabilitation counselors may find themselves in situations where they must facilitate client self-advocacy or advocate for client welfare—with or on-behalf of the client—to make environmental accommodations and facilitate change with and for the client. This advocacy activity is congruent with the aims of multiculturalism because environments that are not adaptive or accommodating may be construed as marginalizing and oppressive milieus for some clients. As a function of their role, rehabilitation counselors acting as advocates in promoting changes in a client's environment are engaging in multiculturally competent work for the betterment of their clients.

Although it may appear that there is a dichotomy between counseling and advocacy, Lerner (1972) believed that this perception results in a false dichotomy between social action and counseling. For some counselors, the idea of advocacy is perceived as a confluence between the personal and the private world of counseling versus the public and the political world of social action (Pope-Davis, Liu, Toporek, & Brittan, 2001). Consequently, reluctance toward advocacy may be construed as a fear of politicizing counseling (Pope-Davis et al., 2001). This fear, of course, assumes that counseling is a nonpolitical activity (Liu & Pope-Davis, 2003). But if counselors understood "political and politics" as a venue or situation in which a person's values, beliefs, and worldviews are used to facilitate another person's movement toward some intrapersonal and interpersonal change, then counselors would see that politics is inflected in every personal and professional activity.

Advocacy in counseling, especially rehabilitation counseling, challenges many of the values inherent in traditional counseling and psychotherapy (Toporek & Liu, 2001). Among these conflicts are the value of individualism, insight as a cure, and ableism (Olkin, 2002). It also challenges the notion of time-limited or brief therapy, psychological distance between the client and the counselor, and dual relationships. Advocacy and being an advocate confronts the notion that clients are, by themselves, responsible for their situation (i.e., it is their distorted perceptions that are creating the problem) and that only they can change their environment. Often, many of these values are implicit in the way clients are treated (i.e., diagnosed) in counseling (Follette & Houts, 1996). Moving away from this dualistic worldview, rehabilitation counseling recognizes that the environment significantly impacts their clients. However, the controversy in rehabilitation counseling is often the extent to which counselors may use their own power and privilege for the benefit of their client (Liu, Pickett, & Ivey, 2007). Consequently, advocacy actions risk and threaten the status quo on which the counselor may depend. That is, rehabilitation counselors may be at risk of losing their job if their advocacy actions challenge the system in which they exist. Although self-advocacy is certainly an important counseling goal, we also believe that the counselor may need to consider situations in which it is appropriate to intervene directly into organizations or systems. Within the model presented by Hershenson (1990), the roles of consultation or coordination may represent such examples.

One of the principles in multicultural counseling is the idea of collaboration with clients. Rather than wallow in the ambiguity between what we do "with" or "for" a client (Lerner, 1972), the focus needs to be always upon what we can do "along" with clients in order to better their environment, situation, or condition (e.g., Freire, 1989). In traditional psychotherapy, clients tend to be disempowered and may feel a lack of agency due to assumptions many counselors may have of clients. These assumptions may be that the counselor knows what is best for the client, does not include clients in decisions, and stigmatizes individuals through deficit-oriented labels (i.e., disabled client versus a client with a disability) (Prilleltensky, 1997). It is particularly important in rehabilitation counseling to work collaboratively with clients to identify the part of the problem that is internal (intrapsychic) and the part that is external (systemic) as well as actions that the client may take to change the systemic issues. In addition, we argue that there are times when it is appropriate for counselors to recognize their responsibility in addressing systemic issues. For example, when the help-giving organization is one that is perpetuating barriers, not only it is important for clients to voice their concerns, but it is a responsibility of the counselor—as a member of the organization—to actively facilitate change within the organization (Hopps & Liu, 2006). If the counselor does not take such action, they are in danger of colluding with the problematic system. In addition, the client may sense the counselor's implicit collusion and may interpret counselor–client discourse in counseling as a double-bind message of "I'll help you only if I don't risk anything on my part." Consequently, the counselor's trustworthiness and credibility and ability to conduct counseling may be jeopardized (Sue & Zane, 1987).

It is important to see counseling as an interactional process—the client and counselor are conceived as collaborators. The counselor is open to change as much as the client, and they both must envision potential changes within their environment. Because it is important to construe the "client" or "consumer" as a participant in his/her own change, we would like to posit that the consumer language often used in rehabilitation counseling be challenged for not fully incorporating the notion of client agency in the environment. Although the consumer label for clientele is popular because it puts the potential "power" within the consumer and not necessarily with the service provider, the marketplace metaphor still resonates with an adversarial theme. If the consumer is unhappy with a particular service, then the service provider is to change and meet the new demands. Yet implicit in this notion of the consumer and the market is also a "bottom-line." Based upon cost-benefits, some agencies may not change at all, and eventually clients may find themselves without adequate services altogether. The notion of collaboration or equality is not inherent in an economic model of service provision (e.g., Eriksen, 1997, 1999). Consequently, we will use the language of collaboration to denote the role of the client and counselor rather than using the common language of the consumer in this chapter.

Before continuing further, it is necessary to understand the role advocacy has in counseling and in the counseling profession. In addition, we will discuss the various models from which advocacy can be operationalized. The following section is a brief overview of these two facets of advocacy in counseling.

ADVOCACY IN COUNSELING

Historical Perspective

For us, the issue of advocacy is partly a professional identity issue and not solely a practical concern. Actions that benefit clients by eliminating or diminishing institutional and cultural barriers may have a secondary effect of empowering clients and encouraging future social action by clients and counselors. Many sentiments toward institutional and cultural change were elements of advocacy and community organizing in the 1970s when changing structural inequities was considered an appropriate professional role (Lewis & Lewis, 1983). Yet, through the 1980s and 1990s, the advocacy perspective seemingly lost its prominence (McClure & Russo, 1996; Toporek & Liu, 2001). McClure and Russo (1996) speculated that a focus by the counseling profession toward credibility and individualism has contributed to the decreasing emphasis on advocacy as a legitimate professional role.

With the increasing emphasis on multiculturalism and multicultural competencies, it appears that the pendulum may be swinging back toward advocacy and social justice. With the advent of multiculturalism and feminist orientations, traditional notions of psychotherapy and counseling are being challenged to become relevant for historically marginalized groups (Toporek & Liu, 2001). Because multiculturalism is concerned with social justice, especially for disenfranchised and marginalized groups, and because advocacy also is typically aligned with combating marginalization (Chesler, Bryant, & Crowfoot, 1976), advocacy is becoming an important professional concern. Recognizing that counseling has differentially been effective and sometimes biased against minority individuals, there have been increasing challenges to the profession to explore the individual, cultural, and institutional barriers that perpetuate oppression (Hopps & Liu, 2006; Middleton et al., 2010; Ridley, 1995; Sutton & Kessler, 1986). Although some oppression can be acted upon in dyadic interactions, some can only be targeted through advocacy (Atkinson, Thompson, & Grant, 1993; Middleton et al., 2010). For instance, a negative sense of self related to internalizing negative stereotypes of his/her racial group (i.e., internalized racialism) (Cokley, 2002) can be a pertinent dyadic issue in individual counseling. But if a client reports that he/she cannot gain access to a building due to wheelchair restrictions to doorways and steps, the "in-session" (individual-focused) counseling is likely to be unsuccessful in ameliorating client distress, anger, and frustration. Only through appropriate advocacy and "out-of-session" actions will clients start to build a sense of efficacy and empowerment (McWhirter, 1994). Gruber and Trickett (1987) posit that advocacy operationalizes the privileges and power of the advocate, which are the intimate knowledge of rules, norms, and systems and are the resources that counselors can use to work with clients in a concerted and effective way for change. In the latter case, the counselor is the most effective agent to start the change process to make the agency more accessible.

Definitions and Models

Although we focus specifically on advocacy in this chapter, one of the confusions that can occur is between definitions of advocacy, empowerment, and social action. Sometimes all three labels can be used synonymously to describe a particular activity, and we would draw some distinctions that may not be apparent. For us, advocacy is "the action a mental health professional, counselor, or psychologist takes in assisting clients and client groups to achieve therapy goals through participating in clients' environments" (Toporek & Liu, 2001, p. 387).

Historically, authors have sought to refine the overall idea of advocacy to include a variety of activities. Lewis and Lewis (1983) differentiate between case advocacy, which is advocacy on behalf of a client, and class advocacy, which is advocacy on a systemic level. They also describe three types of advocacy as "here and now" advocacy or responding to a situation, "preventive" advocacy or actions to create a just environment, and "citizen" advocacy or action encouraging others to challenge social issues. Chan, Brophy, and Fisher (1981) elaborate further on the concept of advocacy and suggest three types of advocacy that may be used. First, "representative advocacy" is when a counselor takes on the issues of his/her client because the client is unable to express or act upon his/her needs. This is similar to the counselor–advocate model of Atkinson, Morten, and Sue (1993) where the counselor "speaks on behalf of the client, often confronting the institutional sources of oppression that are contributing to the client's problem" (p. 301). Second, "group advocacy" is when a "group seeks to intervene in a problem situation in order to achieve a goal consistent with the interest of the members of the group or others" (Chan et al., 1981, p. 195). Finally, there is "self-advocacy" when the individual is taught agentic knowledge, actions, and behaviors. In this last case, Chan et al. (1981) illustrated their "self-advocacy" by presenting cases wherein clients are faced with a problematic situation. Counselors, working in this model, help clients define the problem and develop a list of possible actions from which the client chooses alternatives.

In considering advocacy in counseling, we have found it useful to describe advocacy as a continuum of activity on which empowerment and social action reside (Toporek & Liu, 2001). For us, empowerment is considered to be on one end of the agentic continuum. In this model, empowerment implies that counselor and client work to develop efficacy within the client's and counselor's sociopolitical world (McWhirter, 1994, 1997; Toporek & Liu, 2001). Thus, empowerment encompasses a specific action and behavior with a specific client. As a result of empowerment, clients are able to cope with specific situational problems and concerns, and have a sense of self-efficacy to contend with similar problems in the future. Social action, on the other hand, means that the counselor is constantly working on removing institutional and cultural barriers for a community or population. Social action implies advocacy on a societal level on issues such as legislation or public policy that affect all clients. Thus, social action implies broad-based action and not specific activities focused on the issues of just one individual. Social action also means that counselors are working toward a socially just world; one in which benefits, rights, privileges, and resources are equally distributed as well as social costs and vulnerabilities (i.e., everyone shares equally in the good and bad in society) (Lewis, 2010). Within this model there are a range of behaviors in which counselors may engage to remove barriers and address injustice. We assert that all these activities may be considered under the umbrella of advocacy and that each of these behaviors may be appropriate at various times in work with clients.

In recognition of the fact that many counselors across specializations utilize advocacy in their work, the American Counseling Association (ACA) adopted a set of Advocacy Competencies (Lewis, Arnold, House, & Toporek, 2002). The Advocacy Competencies were designed to facilitate the ethical implementation of advocacy and assist counselors in identifying advocacy actions that would be appropriate at individual, community or school, and public or societal levels (Toporek, Lewis, & Crethar, 2009). Further, the Advocacy Competencies acknowledged that some types of advocacy may be collaborative actions in which the client and the counselor work together and other types where the counselor may take action on behalf of the client. This framework resulted in six domains, including empowerment and client advocacy (individual level), community collaboration and systems advocacy (community or school level), and public information or social/ political action (societal). Middleton et al. (2010) examined the Advocacy Competencies and integrated the Multicultural Rehabilitation Counseling Competencies providing guidelines for appropriate advocacy within rehabilitation counseling. Further, they illustrate concrete examples of advocacy for a number of common situations that rehabilitation counselors may encounter.

A common thread through advocacy, empowerment, and social action is that any action along all these dimensions may be positive for clients and counselors alike. In all of these cases, changing environments for the optimal growth and development of the client is the goal. Although these actions are necessary and important in the professional lives of rehabilitation counselors, it is unclear as to how counselors learn or train to be effective advocates for their clients.

PRACTICE

Advocacy in practice may take many forms as suggested by the continuum model we described earlier. Because the practice of rehabilitation counseling also takes many forms, we will address examples and possible advocacy roles throughout counseling, coordination, and consultation.

The counseling function of rehabilitation counseling lends itself to advocacy in relation to individual issues. Chan et al. (1981) provide some excellent examples of self-advocacy and a model for working with individual clients to facilitate their knowledge and agency in addressing barriers. In addition to self-advocacy, there are other examples of advocacy behaviors in counseling. For example, advocating for clients in their presence can serve as a model of agentic behavior for clients as well as serve as an advocate function. With this type of behavior, it is critical that the counselor and client collaboratively decide on what action the counselor might take including goals and strategy for the action. This type of behavior may be appropriate in a situation in which the power and privilege of the counselor's role lends something that is not attainable by the client. The modeling involved in this action can provide a visible demonstration for situations in which self-advocacy is more important.

The coordinating function of rehabilitation counseling also lends itself to advocacy. Advocacy at this level may address individual or group concerns. Within the coordination function, counselors may be participants in decision- and policy-making bodies such as clinical and administrative management teams, and as such have access at a level different from that available to the client or client groups. Advocacy at the coordination level may also include actions such as identifying client needs that are not being met by the institution and then working to establish funding and institutional support for programs that may meet the needs of a specific population.

The consultation role provides a noteworthy avenue for advocacy. As with coordination, advocacy in this role may serve individuals or groups. One example of advocacy at this level would be to engage legislators as consultees around issues that represent barriers to clients from marginalized groups. Other examples might include consulting with social service agency staff to provide training around multicultural competence, prejudice and discrimination, or consulting with faculty to ensure that new curriculum includes issues-related disabilities and other issues. A final example of this would be lobbying the institution to include a permanent advocate on planning committees for access issues in re-modeling or construction.

Considering the multifaceted role required in the practice of rehabilitation counseling, effective training for advocacy is a complex endeavor.

Training

Advocacy training is one of the most challenging issues in counselor education. Along with course work, counselor education implies the need for face-to-face work with clients as well as "competent" supervision. But how does one go about receiving competent supervision for advocacy work? One possible answer may come from the advocacy literature as well as training strategies described within multicultural competencies.

First, a distinction needs to be made between advocacy self-efficacy and specific competent behaviors (Lewis, 2010). For example, multicultural competency can be perceived as the sense of self-efficacy that counselors may have about working with diverse peoples and groups, and multicultural competencies may be the specific proficiencies counselors have in working with diverse peoples (Pieterse et al., 2009). Although counselors sometimes have a high sense of self-efficacy (competency), they may not have the exact proficiencies that allow them to work effectively with diverse peoples and groups (Ridley & Kleiner, 2003). For instance, it is possible that counselors who perceive themselves as highly multiculturally competent may not be experienced as such by their clients (Pope-Davis et al., 2002). This issue is pertinent to advocacy in rehabilitation counseling because counselors may have a sense of competency in being an advocate for their clients, but may find themselves at a loss when it comes to the real behavior and action of advocacy. Thus, training and supervision become integral aspects of rehabilitation counseling advocacy.

Another training issue for rehabilitation counselors is that the very environment that they are challenging for their client may be the one that employs them. Hence, as rehabilitation counselors seek to engage and transform environments for their clients, they may become acutely aware that their jobs may be threatened. Power differentials in supervision and in the field are considerable forces for trainees (Toporek & Vaughn, 2010). For many trainees, there is a delicate balance between maintaining openness to a new system while also recognizing systemic barriers that may require advocacy. This balance is difficult and trainees often need guidance regarding the timing and appropriateness of challenging the systems in which they are often some of the least powerful players. At the same time, trainees may have a tendency to observe injustice and feel angry with the system without a full understanding of the larger context. Training regarding ways of identifying and resolving these dilemmas would be useful.

One model that may provide a good guide is that of a portfolio approach to advocacy training. Coleman and Hau (2003) provide a model of using portfolio assessment to evaluate and support students' development around multicultural issues. A similar model may be applied for advocacy in rehabilitation counselor education. Using this type of model, students would develop a portfolio of training and practice activities related to advocacy work they have completed throughout the program. The portfolio may include examples of specific cases within practicum, papers they have written, workshops they have attended, and so forth. This would provide the student with the opportunity to do a comprehensive self-review and the program faculty with more data on which to evaluate the students' progress.

Currently, a major challenge in rehabilitation counseling may be that there is not enough training on the issue of being an advocate for clients (Collison et al., 1998; Eriksen, 1997, 1999). Effective training would include skills in identifying problem situations and determining which type of advocacy might be appropriate. The ACA Advocacy Competencies (Lewis et al., 2002) may be helpful with that. In addition, it would be important for counselors to be able to identify the consequences of advocacy actions for both clients and themselves; for example, living with a changed system, or less optimistically, the ramifications of challenging a hostile system. Although advocacy issues are not new for rehabilitation counseling, there is a need for more attention to coursework, curriculum, and supervision necessary to be an effective rehabilitation counseling advocate.

CHALLENGES IN IMPLEMENTING ADVOCACY
IN REHABILITATION COUNSELING

The movement toward advocacy within the counseling professions is not without its detractors. Some argued that counselors cannot be involved in clients' environments and that advocacy is an unrealistic expectation (Weinrach & Thomas, 1998), or that it is a dangerous ideology (Ramm, 1998). This attitude, of course, assumes that the counseling profession is value neutral and that we are not constantly practicing our politics in session (Pope-Davis et al., 2001). In fact, counselors are constantly negotiating their values in session and practicing their worldviews out of session.

Others note the need for intentionality and awareness in advocacy so as to not create unrealistic dependencies (Pinderhughes, 1983) or disempower clients (McWhirter, 1994). It is important to emphasize that dependency building does not represent the type of advocacy we are talking about. Rather, actions that promote dependency building are problematic and represent values and worldviews imposed by the counselor upon the client in a noncollaborative relationship, wherein the counselor retains his or her position as "healer" and the client's position as that of the "sick person." Both are examples of nonadvocacy relationships and are more likely "traditional" counseling relationships masquerading as advocacy.

CONCLUSION

Rehabilitation counseling provides a natural forum for integrating advocacy into practice and education, and there is an increasing body of literature and models to facilitate with implementation. In order for the field to advance, there are some philosophical and ethical issues as well as skills training that must be included in order for counselors and education programs to effectively use this approach with clients. Some of these issues include concerns about creating dependency, balancing client agency with counselors' responsibilities to address systemic barriers, dilemmas regarding conflict of interest between counselors and their home institution, and many others. In addition, research is needed regarding the nuances of process and client outcomes using advocacy in rehabilitation practice. Training will be critical in providing rehabilitation counselors an avenue for developing appropriate skills in resolving these issues and identifying appropriate times and strategies for advocacy. Multicultural counseling competencies can provide useful guidance in terms of training models and the establishment of competency standards that recognize issues faced by clients who are marginalized and impeded by systemic barriers. It is hoped that this chapter provided a useful framework as well as tools that may help rehabilitation counselors and educators in integrating advocacy thoughtfully and effectively.

CONTENT REVIEW QUESTIONS

- How are the definitions of advocacy and empowerment similar and divergent?
- What is the C-C-C model?
- What are the professional and ethical issues related to advocacy?
- What is a double-bind message in advocacy?
- What is the definition of social justice and social action?
- What is the relationship of the Multicultural Counseling Competencies and the Multicultural Rehabilitation Counseling Competencies?

REFERENCES

Arredondo, P., Toporek, R., Brown, S., Jones, J., Locke, D., Sanchez, J., ... Stadler, H. (1996). Operationalization of multicultural counseling competencies. *Journal of Multicultural Counseling and Development, 24*(1), 42–78.

Atkinson, D. R., Morten, G., & Sue, D. W. (1993). *Counseling American minorities: A cross-cultural perspective* (4th ed.). Dubuque, IA: William C. Brown.

Atkinson, D. R., Thompson, C. E., & Grant, S. K. (1993). A three-dimensional model for counseling racial/ethnic minorities. *The Counseling Psychologist, 21,* 257–277.

Caldwell, J. C., & Vera, E. M. (2010). Critical incidents in counseling psychology professionals' and trainees' social justice orientation development. *Training and Education in Professional Psychology, 4,*163–176.

Chan, A., Brophy, M. C., & Fisher, J. C. (1981). Advocate counseling and institutional racism. In *National Institutes of Mental Health, Institutional racism and community competence (ADM 81-907)* (pp. 194–205). Washington, DC: U.S. Department of Health and Human Services.

Chesler, M. A., Bryant, B. I., & Crowfoot, J. E. (1976). Consultation in schools: Inevitable conflict, partisanship, and advocacy. *Professional Psychology, 7*(4), 637–645.

Cokley, K. O. (2002). Testing cross's revised racial identity model: An examination of the relationship between racial identity and internalized racialism. *Journal of Counseling Psychology, 49,* 476–483.

Coleman, H. L. K., & Hau, J. M. (2003). Multicultural counseling competency and portfolios. In D. B. Pope-Davis, H. L. K. Coleman, W. M. Liu, & R. L. Toporek (Eds.), *Handbook of multicultural counseling competencies.* Thousand Oaks, CA: Sage Publications.

Collison, B. B., Osborne, J. L., Gray, L. A., House, R. M., Firth, J., & Lou, M. (1998). Preparing counselors for social action. In C. C. Lee & G. R. Walz (Eds.), *Social action: A mandate for counselors* (pp. 263–278). Alexandria, VA: American Counseling Association.

Eriksen, K. (1997). *Making an impact: A handbook on counseling advocacy.* Washington, DC: Taylor & Francis/Accelerated Development.

Eriksen, K. (1999). Counseling advocacy: A qualitative analysis of leaders' perceptions, organizational activities, and advocacy documents. *Journal of Mental Health Counseling, 21*(1), 33–49.

Follette, W. C., & Houts, A. C. (1996). Models of scientific progress and the role of theory in taxonomy development: A case study of the DSM. *Journal of Consulting and Clinical Psychology, 64,* 1120–1132.

Freire, P. (1989). *Pedagogy of the oppressed.* New York, NY: Continuum.

Gruber, J., & Trickett, E. J. (1987). Can we empower others? The paradox of empowerment in the governing of alternative public schools. *American Journal of Community Psychology, 15*(3), 355–371.

Hershenson, D. (1990). A theoretical model for rehabilitation counseling. *Rehabilitation Counseling Bulletin, 33*, 268–278.

Hopps, J., & Liu, W. M. (2006). Working for social justice from within the health care system: The role of social class in psychology. In R. L. Toporek, L. H. Gerstein, N. A. Fouad, G. Roysircar, & T. Israel (Eds.), *Handbook for social justice in counseling psychology: Leadership, vision, and action* (pp. 318–337). Thousand Oaks, CA: Sage.

Lerner, B. (1972). *Therapy in the ghetto: Political impotence and personal disintegration.* Baltimore, MD: Johns Hopkins University.

Lewis, B. L. (2010). Social justice in practicum training: Competencies and developmental implications. *Training and Education in Professional Psychology, 4*, 145–152.

Lewis, J. A., Arnold, M. S., House, R., & Toporek, R. L. (2002). *ACA advocacy competencies.* Retrieved September 13, 2008, from http://www.counseling.org/Publications/

Lewis, J. A., & Lewis, M. D. (1983). *Community counseling: A human services approach.* New York, NY: John Wiley.

Liu, W. M., & Hernandez, N. (2010). Counseling those in poverty. In M. J. Ratts, J. A. Lewis, & R. L. Toporek (Eds.), *American Counseling Association Advocacy Competencies: An advocacy framework for counselors* (pp. 43–54). Alexandria, VA: ACA.

Liu, W. M., Pickett, T., Jr., & Ivey, A. E. (2007). White middle-class privilege: Social class bias and implications for training and practice. *Journal of Multicultural Counseling and Development, 35*, 194–206.

Liu, W. M., & Pope-Davis, D. B. (2003). Moving from diversity to multiculturalism: Exploring power and the implications for psychology. In D. B. Pope-Davis, H. L. K. Coleman, W. M. Liu, & R. L. Toporek (Eds.), *The handbook of multicultural competencies.* Thousand Oaks, CA: Sage.

Maki, D. R., & Riggar, T. F. (1997). Rehabilitation counseling: Concepts and paradigms. In D. R. Maki & T. F. Riggar (Eds.), *Rehabilitation counseling: Profession and practice* (pp. 3–31). New York, NY: Springer Publishing.

McClure, B. A., & Russo, T. R. (1996). The politics of counseling: Looking back and forward. *Counseling & Values, 40*(3), 162–174.

McWhirter, E. H. (1994). *Counseling for empowerment.* Alexandria, VA: American Counseling Association.

McWhirter, E. H. (1997). Empowerment, social activism, and counseling. *Counseling and Human Development, 29*(8), 1–14.

Middleton, R. A., Robinson, M. C., & Mu'min, A. S. (2010). Rehabilitation counseling: A continued imperative for multiculturalism and advocacy competence. In M. J. Ratts, R. L. Toporek, & J. A. Lewis (Eds.), *ACA Advocacy Competencies: A social justice framework for counselors* (pp.173–183). Alexandria, VA: American Counseling Association.

Middleton, R. A., Rollins, C., Sanderson, P., Leung, P., Harley, D., & Leal-Idrogo, A. (2000). Endorsement of professional multicultural rehabilitation competencies and standards: A call to action. *Rehabilitation Counseling Bulletin, 48*, 233–244.

Olkin, R. (1999). *What psychotherapists should know about disability.* New York, NY: Guildford Press.

Olkin, R. (2002). Could you hold the door for me? Including disability in diversity. *Cultural Diversity and Ethnic Minority Psychology, 8*, 130–137.

Pieterse, A. L., Evans, S. A., Risner-Butner, A., Collins, N. M., & Mason, L. B. (2009). Multicultural competence and social justice training in counseling psychology and counselor education: A review and analysis of sample multicultural course syllabi. *The Counseling Psychologist, 37*, 93–115.

Pinderhughes, E. B. (1983). Empowerment for our clients and ourselves. *Social Casework, 64*(6), 331–338.

Pope-Davis, D. B., Liu, W. M., Toporek, R., & Brittan, C. (2001). How do we identify cultural competence in counseling: Review, introspection, and recommendations for future research. *Cultural Diversity and Ethnic Minority Psychology, 7,* 121–138.

Pope-Davis, D. B., Toporek, R. L., Ortega-Villalobos, L., Ligiero, D. P., Brittan-Powell, C. S., Liu, W. M., … Liang, C. T. H. (2002). A qualitative study of clients' perspectives of multicultural counseling competence. *The Counseling Psychologist, 30,* 355–393.

Prilleltensky, I. (1997). Values, assumptions, and practices: Assessing the moral implications of psychological discourse and action. *American Psychologist, 52,* 517–535.

Ramm, D. R. (1998). Consider the scientific study of morality. *American Psychologist, 53,* 323–324.

Ridley, C. R. (1995). *Overcoming unintentional racism in counseling and therapy.* Thousand Oaks, CA: Sage.

Ridley, C. R., & Kleiner, A. J. (2003). Multicultural counseling competence: History, themes, and issues. In D. B. Pope-Davis, H. L. K. Coleman, W. M. Liu, & R. L. Toporek (Eds.), *The handbook of multicultural competencies.* Thousand Oaks, CA: Sage.

Singh, A. A., Hofsess, C. D., Boyer, E. M., Kwong, A., Lau, A. S. M., McLain, M., … Haggins, K. L. (2010). Social justice and counseling psychology: Listening to the voices of doctoral trainees. *The Counseling Psychologist, 38,* 766–795.

Stone, G. L. (1997). Multiculturalism as a context for supervision: Perspectives, limitations, and implications. In D. B. Pope-Davis & H. L. K. Coleman (Eds.), *Multicultural counseling competencies: Assessment, education and training, and supervision* (pp. 263–289). Thousand Oaks, CA: Sage.

Sue, D. W., Arredondo, P., & McDavis, R. J. (1992). Multicultural counseling competencies and standards: A call to the profession. *Journal of Counseling and Development, 70,* 477–486.

Sue, S., & Zane, N. (1987). The role of culture and cultural techniques in psychotherapy: A critique and reformulation. *American Psychologist, 42,* 37–45.

Sutton, R. G., & Kessler, M. (1986). National study of the effects of socioeconomic status on clinical psychologists' professional judgment. *Journal of Consulting and Clinical Psychology, 54,* 275–276.

Toporek, R. L., Blando, J. A., Chronister, J., Kwan, K.-L. K., Liao, H.-Y., & VanVelsor, P. (2009). Counselor to the core: Serving the whole client through creative blending of counselor roles. *Counseling and Human Development, 41*(5), 1–16.

Toporek, R. L., Lewis, J., & Crethar, H. C. (2009). Promoting systemic change through the advocacy competencies. special section on ACA advocacy competencies. *Journal of Counseling and Development, 87,* 260–268.

Toporek, R. L., & Liu, W. M. (2001). Advocacy in counseling: Addressing race, class, and gender oppression. In. D. B. Pope-Davis & H. L. K. Coleman (Eds.), *The intersection of race, class, and gender in multicultural counseling* (pp. 385–416). Thousand Oaks, CA: Sage Publishers.

Toporek, R. L., & Reza, J. V. (2000). Context as a critical dimension of multicultural counseling: Articulating personal, professional, and institutional competence. *Journal of Multicultural Counseling and Development, 29*(1), 13–30.

Toporek, R. L., & Vaughn, S. R. (2010). Social justice in the training of professional psychologists: Moving forward. *Training and Education in Professional Psychology, 4,* 177–182.

Weinrach, S. G., & Thomas, K. R. (1998). Diversity-sensitive counseling today: A postmodern clash of values. *Journal of Counseling and Development, 76,* 115–122.

15

Career Development, Vocational Behavior, and Work Adjustment

David R. Strauser, Alex W. K. Wong, and Deirdre O'Sullivan

LEARNING OBJECTIVES

After reading this chapter, you should be able to:

■ Understand the relationship between work and human needs and development.
■ Know how to assess basic human needs related to survival and power, social connection, and well-being and self-determination.
■ Understand the basic tenets of five important career development theories, as well as the limitations of each when working with individuals with disabilities.
■ Understand the INCOME model and how rehabilitation counselors can implement this framework when working with persons with disabilities.
■ Understand the strengths of the INCOME model.

Historically, the field of rehabilitation counseling has been concerned with the career development, employment, and vocational behavior of individuals with disabilities (Patterson, Szymanski, & Parker, 2005; Wright, 1980). Underlying the vocational focus of rehabilitation counseling is the philosophy that work is a fundamental and central component of people's lives and is the primary means by which individuals define themselves in society (Blustein, 2008; Gottfredson, 2002; Super, 1969; Szymanski & Hershenson, 2005). Rehabilitation counselors who provide career and vocational services to individuals with disabilities must understand the complex interaction among work, society, and the individual in order to facilitate and maximize individuals with disabilities in career development, employment, and overall work adjustment. This chapter will provide an introduction to the constructs, theories, and strategies that are relevant for practicing rehabilitation counselors to assist individuals with disabilities attain work, maximize productivity, and successfully adjust to the contemporary social, organizational, and personal dynamics in the work environment. Topics covered in this chapter that highlight the vocational focus of rehabilitation counseling are: (1) centrality of work in peoples' lives, (2) how work relates to individuals' basic needs (Blustein, 2008) and how these needs can be used to develop multidimensional outcomes to measure the effectiveness of rehabilitation counseling, (3) relevant theories of career development and work adjustment, and (4) the application of the INCOME framework to guide rehabilitation counseling service delivery.

In addition to the core value that work is central to people's lives, this chapter is based on several assumptions that the authors believe are not only relevant, but also fundamental to the field and practice of rehabilitation counseling. First, the practice of rehabilitation counseling is focused on bringing about positive behavior change. This change in behavior can be big or small, involve the development of new skills, or the enhancement of existing skills; nevertheless, there is focus on positive change. Even when the focus of rehabilitation counseling is on job maintenance, we believe that this is a focus on positive behavior change because the individual would not need rehabilitation counseling services if the individual had the necessary skills to achieve this goal independently. Second, the focus of rehabilitation counseling is to maximize the individual's ability to function independently in the environment of his or her choice. We think that the key words are "independently" and "choice." Individuals with disabilities must have the independent desire to bring about change and be empowered to be change agents in their lives. Third, as discussed in other chapters of this book, we feel that counseling and the relationship between the rehabilitation counselor and the individual with disability are the fundamental tools that rehabilitation counselors have to bring about effective and positive behavioral change.

CENTRALITY OF WORK

Work has been—and will undoubtedly continue to be—central to all human societies. Work provides opportunities to advance, for social support systems, and for self-expression and self-determination—all necessary components of psychological health (Blustein, 2008; Neff, 1985). In a sense, the activity of work itself is healthy and can be therapeutic for all people, but may be particularly beneficial for persons with disabilities due to the common experiences of greater social isolation, stigma, and financial burdens compared to people without disabilities (Blustein, 2008; Strauser, O'Sullivan, & Wong, 2010). Besides the commonly experienced negative financial impact following a chronic illness or disability, people often become isolated and experience a decrease in self-esteem. The work environment can offset this experience by providing opportunities for income, social interaction, and support. According to Neff (1985), most work environments provide social environments that require a person to interact with others, perform rituals and customs that are meaningful, and provide opportunities for growth. These are the activities that sustain mental health (Blustein, 2006, 2008).

The evidence supporting the positive mental health impact of work is not meant to dismiss the potentially hazardous impact of certain working environments on individuals. Specifically, an incongruent person–environment fit can lead to higher levels of depression and stress (Neff, 1985; O'Sullivan & Strauser, 2010). An incongruent fit is one where the individual's personal work style and value system does not fit well with the work environment (Hershenson, 1981; Holland, 1985; Neff, 1985). Service sector positions, common employment sites for individuals with disabilities, and work environments that are noisy, dirty, require long hours, and extreme weather conditions will also likely lead to increased stress levels (Szymanski & Parker, 2010). Other factors that contribute to reduction in mental health include job role ambiguity, lack of control or input, lack of support in high-responsibility jobs, and very low pay (Neff, 1985; Strauser et al., 2010). Work stress has been a topic of considerable concern for both psychology and business and has a significant negative impact on the overall work environment (Baron & Greenberg, 1990; Kahn & Byosiere, 1990; Quick, Quick, Nelsom, & Hurrell, 1997; Szymanski & Parker, 2010). For an individual with disabilities, the relationship between the individual's job and work stress is complex, with the presence of a disability or chronic health condition further complicating the individual's ability to manage stress in the workplace. Managing work stress for individuals with disabilities is an important factor for rehabilitation counselors to consider and much more research is needed in this particular area.

Because of its centrality across the lifespan and its impact on well-being, an understanding of how people must adapt to work after any life-changing event or congenital illness is worthy of exploration and an important and necessary goal of rehabilitation researchers, educators, and counselors. Competitive employment not only improves a person's financial standing, but has also been shown to improve self-esteem and mental health (Blustein, 2008). Competitive employment leads to improvements in physical and psychological health for many reasons. First, employment means income and a social role, both of which lead to improvements in social status (Wolfensberger, 2002). There can also be an improved access to better housing, health care, nutrition, neighborhood, and school districts, as well as crime-free communities and better family relationships (Blustein, 2008; Bond et al., 2001; Larson et al., 2007). From a community perspective, a study of urban Chicago (Wilson, 1996) found loss of employment empirically connected to a lower quality of life, including increased drug use, violence, and crime. According to Wilson (1996), employment status is more important than poverty for predicting family discord, violence in neighborhoods, and low functioning school systems. Wilson (1996) explains that families who function in communities with high employment and who are poor experience fewer problems than families who function in communities with high unemployment and high poverty. From the individual perspective, loss of employment is linked to higher rates of depression, anxiety, and substance abuse (Blustein, 2008), as well as overall reduction in well-being and health status. These states were found not to rebound back to levels prior to loss of employment despite eventual reemployment (Blustein, 2008; Blustein, Kenna, Gill, & DeVoy, 2008). This finding points to the lasting negative physical and psychological impacts experienced by those who lose their employment status, even after regaining it.

Across disability categories, employment rates are much lower for persons with disabilities compared to the national average. Despite the passage of the Americans with Disabilities Act (ADA), a recent report on the employment of individuals with disabilities has indicated that only 35% of working-age people with chronic illness or disability are employed compared to 78% of those without disabilities (National Council on Disability, 2007). Over the last two decades, the employment rate of individuals with disabilities has been hovering around 35%. Importantly, two-thirds of the unemployed persons with chronic illness and disability surveyed indicated that they would like to work but could not find a job (Amir, Strauser, & Chan, 2009). Examination of specific disability groups reveals a similar trend. For persons with severe mental health conditions, only 15% are employed compared to the 77% of the general working-age population (Bond et al., 2001). For persons with mild mental retardation, roughly 2–9% are competitively employed (Moore, Feist-Price, & Alston, 2002). For persons who are visually impaired, only 40–45% of working-age persons are employed (Capella-McDonnall, 2005). For persons with spinal cord injuries, only 54% are employed (Marini, Lee, Chan, Chapin, & Romero, 2008). As a result of the low employment and underemployment rates, individuals with disabilities are at increased risk for experiencing decreased levels of physical and psychological health—further complicating future career development and employment.

WORK AND HUMAN NEEDS

Due to the centrality of work and its positive effect on individuals' physical and psychological health, work has been identified as a foundation for meeting human needs. According to Blustein (2006, 2008) and Blustein et al. (2008), work provides a means in which individuals can fulfill the following three basic human needs: (1) survival and power, (2) social connection, and (3) self-determination and well-being. In providing vocational and career services, it is important for rehabilitation counselors to understand from the perspective of the individual with disability how his or her educational experiences, conceptualization of work, work experience, familial and cultural background, and disability-related factors impact these three basic human needs. Understanding the impact of work on these three fundamental human needs also highlights the complex way in which working functions in the human experience and the need for multidimensional outcomes in measuring the effectiveness of rehabilitation counseling interventions. Specifically, the traditional dichotomous outcome of *employed* versus *unemployed* does not cover the multidimensional impact of work in the lives of individuals with disabilities. Being employed only tells us that the person is working and nothing about the quality of employment, how integrated the individual is in the social environment, and the autonomy with which the individual is functioning as a result of working or not working. Therefore, to gain a true understanding of the effectiveness of rehabilitation counseling, it is critical to employ a multidimensional outcome analysis framework. In the remainder of this section, we will provide a brief overview of the three sets of human needs that can be fulfilled by working (Blustein, 2008) and then provide domains that can be used to guide the evaluation of the impact of rehabilitation services on enhancing the career development and employment of individuals with disabilities.

Basic Need of Survival and Power

Work provides a means for individuals with disabilities to survive and derive power (Blustein, 2006; Blustein et al., 2008). In contemporary labor market terms, survival can be equated with the individual being able to meet his or her basic needs. Ideally, through competitive employment, individuals with disabilities should be able to generate enough income and benefits to meet their most basic needs. However, research continuously has found that individuals with disabilities are employed at a much lower rate than their counterparts without disabilities, are likely employed in positions with no real career path and no benefits, are underemployed, and when employed, occupy low-paying positions (Lustig & Strauser, 2007). A reciprocal relationship between disability and poverty has been established and is exacerbated by high rates of unemployment and underemployment for individuals with disabilities (Edgell, 2006; Lustig & Strauser, 2007). Globalization and the changing labor market have made it more difficult for individuals with disabilities to escape poverty (Szymanski & Parker, 2010). As a result, many individuals with disabilities are unable to meet their most basic human needs independently—often creating a state of dependence with no real promise for achieving higher states of vocational or career functioning.

The human need for the acquisition of psychological, economic, and social power is closely tied to meeting basic needs (Blustein, 2006). What this means for individuals with disabilities is that working should provide material and social resources that increase an individual's agency within society. In essence, work should give an individual purpose and relevance within the broader environment. Individuals who are working assume an increased social role that ultimately increases their ability to derive psychological, social, and economic power (Wolfensberger, 2002). However, there are many structural and cultural barriers that negatively impact individuals' (with disabilities) access to high status employment, ultimately relegating them to disempowered and low-status occupational and social roles (Szymanski & Parker, 2010). Occupying these disempowered and low-status roles perpetuates dependence on others (individuals, institutions, and programs) and does not fulfill the individual's personal needs.

Rehabilitation counselors need to be aware that individuals with whom they work have an inherent need for survival and power, and that work is critical to meeting these individual needs. Vocational and career services should be directed at increasing career and employment opportunities to maximize individuals' abilities to sustain themselves and increase their power by obtaining positions that have increased social value. Table 15.1 provides a list of potential outcomes that could be used to measure individuals' ability to meet their needs for survival and power.

TABLE 15.1
Need, Outcome Construct, and Specific Outcome Domains Related to Rehabilitation Counseling Outcomes

Need	Outcome Constructs	Specific Outcome Domains
Survival and power	Compensation	Salary
		Benefits
		Pay incentives
		Indirect compensation
	Employee development	Internal development
		External development
	Perceived occupational status	Low status positions
		High status positions
Social connection	General integration	Conformity
		Acceptance
		Orientation
	Social support	Close interpersonal relationships
		Diffuse relationships
	Leisure	Leisure activities
		Recreational activities
	Independent living	Individual's living situation
Self-determination and well-being	Well-being	Quality of life
		Satisfaction with life
		Physical health status
		Psychological health status
	Self-determination	Autonomy
		Relatedness
		Capacity
		Values and goals

Basic Need for Social Connection

Individuals are social beings who have strong needs to be connected with broader society and develop strong interpersonal relationships (Blustein, 2006; Bowlby, 1982). Participation in work-related activities provides an opportunity for individuals with disabilities to connect with other individuals and their broader social and cultural environments (Blustein, 2008). Ideally, through work, individuals develop positive relationships that supply the support needed to manage work-related stress and foster identity development (Blustein, 1994; Schein, 1990). In contrast, if individuals experience a negative work environment, where the individual feels isolated, disconnected, and under stress, the individual's job performance and work adjustment will most likely be negatively affected. Finally, working provides a mechanism for individuals with disabilities to develop a sense of connection with their broader social world through contributing to the larger economic structure of society (Blustein, 2006). Earning a paycheck and contributing to society's well-being by paying fair and reasonable taxes is a valued social role.

Rehabilitation counseling should not only be focused on finding employment, but also on how employment can increase individuals' levels of social integration. Many times in rehabilitation counseling, the focus of work and socialization are directed at enhancing the person's socialization on the job and with coworkers. However, Blustein (2008) highlights that the social impact and benefits of work are not limited to the work environment, but also include the broader community. As a result, rehabilitation counselors need to ensure that their efforts regarding socialization not only include the work environment, but also how work can be leveraged to increase individuals' overall level of social integration in roles and communities that they wish to occupy and participate. Potential outcomes for measuring an individual's level of social connection are highlighted in Table 15.1.

Basic Need for Self-Determination and Well-Being

Individuals search for environments that promote self-determination, self-expression, and well-being. Rehabilitation counselors have been instrumental in conceptualizing and facilitating work environments that promote physical and psychological well-being for people with disabilities. This work has included job placement in safe environments, promotion of accommodations such as flexibility, and facilitation of environments and tasks that do not exacerbate symptoms. Although all these met objectives are necessary for well-being, they are not sufficient. Ideally, individuals work in environments that provide them with opportunities to exercise self-determination, self-expression, and promote individual well-being by participating in work that is consistent with their skills and interests. However, very few individuals with disabilities have the opportunity to participate in work-related activities that correspond to their personal skills and interests, and they often pursue employment for extrinsic reasons such as income (Blustein, 2008). Research has suggested that promoting *autonomy, relatedness,* and *competence* in relation to work that is initially pursued for extrinsic reasons can increase the individual's level of self-determination and well-being related to work (Ryan & Deci, 2000). Blustein (2008) also suggested that when an individual's personal values and goals coincide with those of the work organization, and when the work environment provides individuals with resources and supports that foster successful work experiences, the individual's level of well-being increases.

It is important to note that we are not suggesting that the promotion of autonomy, relatedness, and competence can transform a job with low pay, high stress, and an overall poor work environment into a positive and rewarding work experience. What we are suggesting is that for individuals with disabilities who are not employed in jobs that are consistent with their interests and abilities, rehabilitation counselors can address these constructs of *autonomy, relatedness,* and *competence* to promote a better work experience for individuals with disabilities. Specifically, addressing these issues through counseling and careful analysis of how individuals with disabilities derive meaning from their work is important. It can help provide rehabilitation counselors the knowledge to enhance the employment conditions that frame the experience of most people with disabilities who must accept employment options that have low pay, no benefits, and limited opportunities for advancement, so that they can support themselves and their family (Blustein, 2008). Potential outcomes for measuring self-determination and well-being are highlighted in Table 15.1.

THEORIES OF VOCATIONAL BEHAVIOR AND CAREER DEVELOPMENT

Vocational and career development theories provide the foundation for rehabilitation counselors' ability to understand, conceptualize, and explain different aspects of the career development process and explain the vocational behavior of individuals with disabilities (Super, 1969; Szymanski & Hershenson, 2005). Although the theories of career development and vocational behavior have limitations in their application to rehabilitation counseling (Conte, 1983; Curnow, 1989), we believe that it is important for rehabilitation counselors to gain familiarity with the theories so that they can apply specific facets of various theories selectively to the career development of individuals with disabilities. Understanding career and vocational theories is important because many career instruments and software programs are based on specific career theories. Career theories also provide rehabilitation counseling practitioners with a framework to understand career problems and facilitate effective career choices. Most importantly, career and vocational theories are used by skilled rehabilitation counseling practitioners to generate and test hypotheses about individuals and scientifically guide and evaluate their practices (Szymanski & Hershenson, 2005; Tracey, 1991). In this section we provide a brief overview of five career and vocational theories that are relevant to the practice of rehabilitation counseling. As mentioned, no specific theory discussed is without limitations. However, in piecing together different aspects of these theories, we feel that rehabilitation counselors would have adequate tools to develop a conceptual framework to guide their respective practices and to work with individuals with disabilities. In reviewing the following theories we suggest that rehabilitation counselors evaluate how each of the career theories presented address three important aspects related to career and vocational behavior. First, how does the theory account for the individual development of career and vocational behavior? Second, how does the theory account for the interaction between the individual and the environment? Finally, how does the theory account for social cognitive factors that impact career and vocational behavior?

Super's Life-Span and Life-Space Theory of Career Development

Super's theory is a multifaceted view of career development based on constructs from developmental, social, and personality psychology combined with learning and self-concept theory (Super, 1990, 1994). Super's theory is developmental in nature and examines the notion of trait and factor congruence (Szymanski, Enright, Hershenson, & Ettinger, 2010; Szymanski & Hershenson, 2005). Super (1990) posited that each occupation requires a characteristic pattern of ability and personality characteristics (i.e., needs, values, interests, traits, and self-concept). As a result of these characteristics, people are qualified for a number of occupations. The vocational preferences, competencies, and environments in which people live and work change with time and experience. A key component of Super's model is the "life career rainbow" that combines situational and personal determinants with life roles and life stages. Life roles proposed by Super include *child, student, leisurite, citizen, worker,* and *homemaker.* The following life stages and corresponding ages reflect the developmental nature of Super's theory: *growth (birth–14), exploration (15–24), establishment (26–44), maintenance (45–64),* and *decline (65+).* Although age ranges for stage transition are offered, actual transition ages are flexible and "each transition involves a recycling through one or more stages—a mini-cycle" (Super, 1990, p. 215). Super (1994) further suggested that the success in coping with demands of the environment depends on the readiness of the individual to cope with these demands (i.e., career maturity). The nature of an individual's career pattern is determined by the individual's parental socioeconomic level, mental ability, education, skills, personalities, and career maturity, and by the opportunities to which he or she is exposed.

Super's (1990) conceptualization of career development has been applied frequently to the practice of career counseling. For example, his work on the life career rainbow, which combines situational and personal antecedents with life roles and stages and career maturity, has been applied in a number of ways including underpinning instruments such as the *Career Development Inventory* (Thompson & Linderman, 1984) and *Career Maturity Inventory* (Crites, 1978).

Super's theory has been found to be useful in addressing the special career needs of individuals with disabilities, particularly those with congenital problems. The limitations in early experiences—including opportunities for play, work-role fantasies, and career-related role playing—hinder people with congenital disabilities from full participation in career planning and decision making (Szymanski et al., 2010; Szymanski & Hershenson, 2005; Thomas & Parker, 1992; Turner & Szymanski, 1990).

Holland's Theory of Vocational Personalities and Work Environments

Holland's theory, as its name implies, focuses on a person–environment fit that depends upon the congruence between individual personalities and environmental characteristics (Holland, 1997). According to Holland's theory upon individuals exhibit aspects of the following six work personalities: realistic (R), investigational (I), artistic (A), social (S), enterprising (E), and conventional (C). "The more closely a person resembles a particular personality type, the more likely he or she is to exhibit the personal traits or behaviors associated with that type" (Holland, 1997, pp. 1–2). The work environment consists of the same six traits that can be applied to describe the characteristics of various educational and employment opportunities (Holland, 1997). The matching of the individuals and environment leads to the increased prediction of vocational and educational outcomes, including vocational choice and achievement, educational choice and achievement, competence, social behavior, and vulnerability to influence. The RIASEC hexagon is a structural model used to represent the interrelationships among the six types and work environments, and it has been central to Holland's theory and its application in applied settings (Tracey & Rounds, 1995). Over the last 20–30 years, comprehensive meta-analyses (Rounds & Tracey, 1996; Tracey & Rounds, 1993), combined with research using more representative samples (Day, Rounds, & Swaney, 1998; Fouad, Harmon, & Borgen, 1997), and increasingly sophisticated structural methods (Armstrong, Hubert, & Rounds, 2003; Deng, Armstrong, & Rounds, 2007) have provided some empirical support for Holland's structural model. *Personal identity* and *environmental identity* are important constructs related to Holland's theory. *Personal identity* is defined as "the possession of a clear and stable picture of one's goals, interests, and talents," and *environmental identity* is defined as being "present when an environment or organization has clear and integrated goals, tasks, and rewards that are stable over time intervals" (Holland, 1997, p. 5).

Due to its ease of use and strong research support, Holland's model has been applied widely in current counseling settings, although some criticisms have appeared that question the possibility of application to various disability populations (Conte, 1983; Hagner & Salomone, 1989). However, Szymanski et al. (2010) and Szymanski and Hershenson (2005) suggested that this model can be applied with important precautions. For example, the *My Vocational Situation* assessment (Holland, Daiger, & Power, 1980), which addresses vocational identity, is also useful for appraising the readiness of career planning for people with disabilities. The *Self-Directed Search* (Holland, 1985) is another instrument that operationalizes the RIASEC typology, and it has a version for persons with low reading levels. It is useful for engaging people with disabilities in career planning. Rehabilitation counselors should be aware of the potential impact of disability in limiting expressed interests, whereas individuals with disabilities are responding to SDS items because they may believe that they cannot perform the required tasks due to physical and cognitive limitations. Another caution of which rehabilitation counselors should be aware is that limited early life and educational experiences may hinder the vocational development of people with congenital disabilities resulting in a flat interest profile (Conte, 1983; Turner & Szymanski, 1990).

Minnesota Theory of Work Adjustment

The original development of the Minnesota theory of work adjustment was supported by the federally funded rehabilitation program to address how the individuals being evaluated in the vocational rehabilitation program adjusted to work (Lofquist & Dawis, 1969). This theory is based on a series of person–environment theories emphasizing the work personality–work environment correspondence leading to job satisfaction and satisfactoriness (Dawis, 2000, 2005). Theoretically, work adjustment is defined as the process by which the person achieves and maintains correspondence with the work environment (Lofquist & Dawis, 1969). According to this model, the constructs of *skills* and *needs* are used to describe the person's work personality, whereas the two complementary terms, *reinforcers* and *skill requirements*, are used to describe the work environment. The correspondence between the person's skills and the skill requirements of the work environment determines satisfactoriness (i.e., the extent to which the individual is capable to perform the job). The correspondence between the person's needs and the reinforcers of work environment determines the person's satisfaction with the job. Satisfactoriness and satisfaction result in tenure (i.e., the period of time the individual holds the job) which is the principal indicator of work adjustment (Lofquist & Dawis, 1969). Work adjustment is defined as "the continuous and dynamic process by which the individual seeks to achieve and maintain correspondence with the work environment" (Lofquist & Dawis, 1969, p. 46).

Lofquist and Dawis (1969) initially suggested that due to the ease of administration of the instruments associated with the theory, rehabilitation counselors should be able to spend more time and resources on counseling individuals with disabilities. Assessment instruments and supporting materials used to operationalize, test, and apply the Minnesota theory of work adjustment have been developed widely. Readers are referred to the Web site (http://www.psych .umn.edu/psylabs/vpr/default.htm) from Vocational Psychology Research Program of the Department of Psychology, University of Minnesota, to get more information. Readers can also review two textbooks from Szymanski et al. (2010) as well as Szymanski and Hershenson (2005) for a detailed description of the theory and its application.

Social Cognitive Career Theory

The development of the social cognitive career theory is based on Bandura's general social cognitive theory (Bandura, 1986), which emphasizes the complex ways in which individuals' personal attributes, external environmental factors, and overt behaviors operate as interlocking mechanisms that mutually influence one another and the individuals' learning experiences (Lent, 2005; Lent, Brown, & Hackett, 1996, 2002). Following the basic tenets of social cognitive theory, social cognitive career theory highlights the interplay of three variables, namely *self-efficacy* (i.e., judgments of one's own capabilities to attain specific tasks), *outcome expectations* (i.e., beliefs about the anticipated results of performing particular behaviors), and *personal goals* (i.e., intention to carry out a particular activity or to produce a particular outcome) that enables the exercise of personal agency in career development. It acknowledges that people are capable of directing their own vocational behavior (human agency) and even negotiating personal (e.g., predispositions, race-ethnicity, gender, disability, and health status) and contextual variables (e.g., socio-structural barriers, support, and culture) to prevail in career development. Social cognitive career theory intends to provide a potentially unifying framework to explain how people develop vocational interests, make career choices, and achieve varying levels of career success and stability (Lent, 2005; Lent et al., 1996, 2002).

Social cognitive career theory shares certain goals and features with trait-factor (or person-environment fit) and developmental career theories. It has been useful in guiding practice and research on career counseling and vocational intervention for people with disabilities (Strauser, Ketz, & Keim, 2002) and minorities (Lent et al., 2002). In particular, this theory offers a unifying framework to guide rehabilitation counselors to assist clients in examining and overcoming barriers engendered by personal limitations, environmental factors, and/or learning experiences. In addition, this theory also provides the blueprint for guiding rehabilitation counseling research and practice of facilitating career choice making, promoting career aspirations, expanding vocational alternatives, improving self-efficacy, and promoting work satisfaction among people with disabilities.

Hershenson's Theory of Work Adjustment Development

Work adjustment is comprised of two essential elements: the person and the person's environment (Hershenson, 1996b). The person consists of the following three subsystems that develop sequentially: *work personality, work competencies*, and *work goals*. *Work personality* develops during the preschool years and is influenced mostly by the family. It consists of one's self-concept as a worker, work motivation, and work-related needs and values. *Work competencies* develop during the school years and are influenced by successes and failures in school settings. *Work competencies* consist of work habits, physical and mental skills, and work-related interpersonal skills (Strauser et al., 2002; Szymanski & Hershenson, 2005). Appropriate *work goals* develop prior to leaving school and are influenced by one's peer or reference groups (Hershenson, 1996a). *Work goals* should be clear, realistic, and consistent with the person's *work personality* and *work competencies*. Hershenson (1996b) mentioned three components in the person's environment, including *organizational culture and behavioral expectations, job demands and skill requirements*, and the *rewards and opportunities* available to the worker. Szymanski et al. (2010) and Szymanski and Hershenson (2005) suggested that the product of the interaction of the person's subsystems and work environment is work adjustment. Hershenson also discussed the following three domains of work adjustment: work role behavior, task performance, and work satisfaction. Work role behavior refers to displaying appropriate behaviors in the work setting, which is primarily related to work personality in the person and the behavioral expectations of the work setting. Task performance refers to the quality and quantity of one's work output, which is related primarily to work competencies in the person and the skill requirements of the work setting. Work satisfaction refers to one's degree of gratification resulting from work, which is related primarily to the work goals of the person, and the rewards and opportunities in the work setting.

Hershenson's theory was designed particularly to be applicable to people with disabilities. Theoretically, individuals must address two major environmental transitions in facilitating work adjustment: the transition from home to school and the transition from school to work. However, for individuals who experience an impediment in the course of their career track, there may be a third or fourth environmental transition (rehabilitation counseling or a shifting of careers). Success in the current transition will depend upon the individual's experience during previous transitions (Szymanski et al., 2010; Szymanski & Hershenson, 2005). Research has found that individuals with disabilities who had higher levels of work personality have higher levels of job readiness, self-efficacy, and more internalized work locus of control (Strauser et al., 2002).

THE INCOME FRAMEWORK

The five career development and work adjustment theories discussed in the previous section have limitations that preclude their exclusive application to the career and vocational counseling of individuals with disabilities (Conte, 1983; Szymanski & Hershenson, 2005). Research regarding the career development and employment of individuals with disabilities has identified the following three factors related to the lives of individuals with disabilities that limit the application of existing career and vocational theories: (1) limitations in career exploratory experiences, (2) limited opportunities to develop decision-making abilities, and (3) a negative self-concept resulting from negative societal attitudes toward individuals with disabilities (Curnow, 1989). Because of the various limitations, the five theories discussed herein are of questionable use in describing, predicting, planning, and implementing career development and employment interventions designed to facilitate increased career and employment outcomes of individuals with disabilities.

Over the past 15 years several attempts have been made to address the limitations noted and develop a comprehensive model that would address these issues (Hershenson & Szymanski, 1992; Szymanski & Hershenson, 1998; Szymanski, Hershenson, Enright, & Ettinger, 1996). Despite the efforts to develop a comprehensive theory, some have questioned this need given the diversity and heterogeneity of individuals with disabilities (Thomas & Berven, 1990). One alternative to developing a comprehensive theory is employing a framework to guide rehabilitation counselors in their provision of vocational rehabilitation services to individuals with disabilities. The INCOME framework is a comprehensive framework that consists of six statuses through which individuals with disabilities can move: Imaging, iNforming, Choosing, Obtaining, Maintaining, and Exiting (Beveridge, Craddock, Liesener, Stapleton, & Hershenson, 2002). The development of this framework is based upon career development theories applicable to individuals with disabilities (Danley & Anthony, 1987; Dawis & Lofquist, 1984; Hershenson, 1996a, 1996b; Super, 1957, 1990). Other theories that are intended to be applicable to diverse groups such as Maslow's hierarchy of needs (Maslow, 1987), Bandura's social cognitive theory (Bandura, 1986, 1997), and career development theories based on social cognitive theory (Hackett & Betz, 1996; Lent et al., 2002; Mitchell & Krumboltz, 1996) were also utilized in developing the INCOME framework (Beveridge et al., 2002).

In examining the components of the INCOME framework, there are several important factors to consider. First, the INCOME framework consists of statuses—not stages—to address the heterogeneity of the individual with disabilities. The distinction of employing statuses versus stages is important because stages imply a sequential progression, cultural universality, hierarchic integration, and stage resolution sequencing that limit application to the unique needs and development of individuals with disabilities (Beveridge et al., 2002; Kohlberg, 1968). In contrast to stages, statuses are more flexible, allowing individuals to occupy more than one status at a time (e.g., Choosing a different occupation while Maintaining a job in one occupation), statuses are not bound by order or sequential progression, and statuses allow individuals freedom to skip and revisit statuses as needed (Helms, 1995). Second, within each of the six statuses, one must consider the interaction of three dynamic factors: (1) the individual, (2) his or her environment, and (3) the culture and subcultures within which the other two factors reside (Vondracek, Lerner, & Schulenberg, 1986). Finally, application of the INCOME framework recognizes that age of disability onset and the progressive nature of certain disabilities are factors that impact career development and vocational behavior. Therefore, within each status the following three distinct subgroups of individuals with disabilities are recognized as having their own unique needs: pre-career onset, mid-career onset, and episodic disabilities.

Listed below are the six statuses of the INCOME framework.

Imagining. The imagining status is highlighted by the individual developing an awareness of work, jobs, or careers that exist in the broader environment. This may include an individual becoming aware of a new job or career that existed, but of which he or she was personally unaware. This status consists of the following three substatuses: *awareness, fantasy,* and *reality-based imagining.* During early childhood the family has a strong impact, but as individuals develop they acquire information regarding the world of work from the media and school. Social learning provides the mechanism in which children acquire information from their environment resulting in the development of the individual's attitudes about work and occupations. Individuals who occupy this status as children and adults derive meaning and assess their values regarding their conceptualization of work and careers.

iNforming. Obtaining information about one's self, the world of work, opportunities that exist within the environment, and one's cultural context highlight the iNforming status. This status includes: (1) developing individual work competencies, (2) acquiring information about him- or herself and the world of work, (3) developing an awareness of the cultural supports and barriers that exist within the environment, and (4) the moderating effect of the cultural supports and barriers on work competencies and information regarding the world of work. This dynamic interaction provides the foundation for the development of the individual's career-related self-efficacy and outcome expectations.

Choosing. Integrating information from the Imagining and iNforming status, and selecting from the known occupations highlight the Choosing status. When choosing an occupation, the individual analyzes the degree of congruence between the environment and his or her personality type, the fit between job benefits and his or her personal needs and values, the individual's decision-making style, and chance effects. Career self-efficacy and outcome expectations also influence choice by acting as a filter for information that the individual has developed regarding him- or herself and the world of work. During this status, motivation for choosing is impacted by how well the individual's basic needs are met. If basic needs are not met, an individual will not be motivated to seek satisfaction of higher needs and make occupational or vocational choices.

Obtaining. The Obtaining status is defined by the individual implementing a specific career decision and obtaining a job in the occupation of his or her choice. The broader environment and labor market have a significant impact on the individual's choice and outcome of this particular status. The obtaining status is also influenced considerably by the person's family, culture, and society.

Maintaining. The Maintaining status involves the individual with a disability adapting to, performing, and sustaining a position. Maintaining a job involves the dynamic process of work adjustment where the individual needs to adjust continuously to the work demands and the work environment. Work personality, work competencies, job-related physical and mental skills, and interpersonal skills are important in maintaining the necessary balance between the individual, environment, and job maintenance (Strauser et al., 2010).

Exiting. Leaving one's job either voluntarily or involuntarily defines the Exiting status. In voluntarily leaving, the individual chooses to leave for a new position, retires, or chooses to take a break from labor market participation. Involuntary termination involves the individual being fired or separated from the job due to poor performance or potentially because of disability or medical-related issues. Factors that influence exiting are the individual's desire to exit, individual needs, physical and psychological health, satisfaction with the job and work environment, personal goals, and condition of the work environment. These factors are dynamic and change throughout the person's career and are influenced by the environment, psychological, social, and economic forces.

REHABILITATION COUNSELING INTERVENTIONS

In applying the INCOME framework and other various career and vocational counseling theories outlined in this chapter, rehabilitation counselors have a variety of interventions at their disposal. When choosing the type and intensity of career and vocational intervention, rehabilitation counselors should consider whether the intervention (1) is consistent with the applicable code of ethics, (2) ensures that the client learns a process that can be applied to similar career situations that may arise in the future, (3) assists the client in acquiring skills needed to cope with changes in the labor market, (4) assists the individual with future changes in career plans, and (5) is not overly disruptive to the overall work environment (Szymanski et al., 1996). When considering interventions, it is also important to consider whether the intervention enhances the client's sense of control, competence in self, and promotes environmental exploration to increase the range of career and employment options (Blustein, 2006). Finally, all career and vocational interventions should be provided in the context of the counseling relationship that is based on the fundamental principles of the working alliance: (1) developing a strong relationship with the client, (2) identifying reasonable and obtainable goals, and (3) identifying the tasks need to achieve the identified goals (Donnell, Lustig, & Strauser, 2004; Lustig, Strauser, Weems, Donnell, & Smith, 2003; Strauser, Lustig, & Donnell, 2004). In the following section, we provide a brief overview of various career and vocational interventions that rehabilitation counselors can employ in their work with individuals with disabilities.

Individual and Group Career Counseling

Individual career counseling is a largely verbal process in which the counselor and client are engaged in a dynamic interaction where the counselor employs a repertoire of diverse behaviors. These are used to help bring about self-understanding and action in the form of "good" decision making on the part of the individual who has responsibility for his or her own actions (Herr & Cramer, 1996). Recent research regarding the vocational behavior of individuals receiving vocational rehabilitation services has indicated that the core elements of the working alliance are especially powerful facilitators of change when providing individual career counseling services (Strauser et al., 2004). The working alliance is a transtheoretical process that consists of the following three elements: (1) bonds, (2) goals, and (3) tasks (Strauser et al., 2004). Individuals who reported higher levels of working alliance with their vocational rehabilitation counselor reported more satisfaction with their rehabilitation services and increased vocational outcomes (Lustig et al., 2003). Research has also suggested that individuals receiving vocational services reported that they would have liked to receive more vocational counseling and desired a strong working relationship with their rehabilitation counselor (Lustig et al., 2003). Group counseling is beneficial when counseling for career exploration, using visual imagery, developing locally relevant occupational information, teaching career decision making, and teaching job interviewing skills (Pope, 1999).

Vocational Evaluation

Vocational evaluation is a comprehensive and systematic process in which rehabilitation counselors and clients work together to assess and identify the client's vocational interests, abilities, aptitudes, work values, functional limitations, and barriers to employment. The main function of vocational evaluation services provided by rehabilitation counselors is to identify the client's strengths and weaknesses relative to the rehabilitation goal and employment outcome. According to the INCOME framework, the client in the iNforming status may benefit from a vocational evaluation, in which the client acquires information about himself or herself, the world of work, and potential supports and barriers.

Situational Assessment

Situational assessment is a valuable tool for rehabilitation counselors when assisting clients to make choices about the types of jobs and work environments that would be of interest. A situational assessment is an assessment that commonly involves actual employment and community settings, but can also be developed within the private sector for people with disabilities to explore their interests, assess current skill level, and provide training (Fraser & Johnson, 2010). Situational assessment allows for information to be generated quickly concerning employment options that are worth pursuing further, avoid time wasted on inappropriate job searches. In addition, many situational assessments can provide a transition to actual paid employment. Situational assessments can assist rehabilitation counselors and individuals with disabilities in determining potential accommodations that will be necessary for successful competitive employment. The client in the Choosing and Obtaining statuses may benefit from situational assessments. Rehabilitation counselors can assist clients in the Choosing status make career choices by understanding the fit between the individual and the work environment. Rehabilitation counselors working together with the client in the Obtaining status can identify barriers to obtaining employment.

Job Site Accommodation

The ADA of 1990 instituted the policy that employers must make a reasonable accommodation to the known physical and mental limitations of a qualified applicant or employee with a disability. Rehabilitation counselors involved in the accommodation process can work with other rehabilitation professionals to determine what type of workplace accommodation may be needed or beneficial to facilitate competitive employment. According to the INCOME framework, a client in the Maintaining status may benefit from a job site accommodation, so that the client can adjust to the work demands and the work environment in order to maintain the job.

Job Development and Placement

Job development and placement interventions help clients with disabilities connected with the jobs that meet their knowledge, skills, and abilities. Rehabilitation counselors can assist with revising a resume, preparing the individual for a job interview, finding job leads, assisting with the submission of a job application, and setting up and attending interviews, and can provide assistance and support needed to help the individual attain the desired employment outcome. In accordance with the INCOME framework, the client in the Choosing and Obtaining statuses may benefit from job development and placement services.

Supported Employment

According to the Rehabilitation Act Amendments of 1998, supported employment is a program to assist people with the most significant disabilities to become and remain successfully and competitively employed in integrated workplace settings. It is targeted at individuals with the most significant disabilities for whom competitive employment has not traditionally occurred, or for whom competitive employment has been interrupted or has been intermittent because of a disability. Supported employment usually provides assistance such as job coaches, transportation, assistive technology, specialized job training, and individually tailored supervision. Typically, supported employment is a way to move people from dependency on a traditional service delivery system to independence via competitive employment (Wehman, 1996). There are several features of supported employment programs that differ from traditional job placement service approaches. First, supported employment programs seek to identify jobs that provide wages above the minimum wage, fringe benefits, and positions with career trajectories. Second, supported employment programs focus on providing ongoing support required to get and keep a job rather than on getting a person a job ready for future employment. Third, supported employment programs emphasize creating opportunities to work rather than simply providing services to develop job skills for people with disabilities. Fourth, supported employment programs encourage full participation. Thus, all people—regardless of the degree of their disability—have the capacity to undertake supported employment if appropriate support services can be provided. Fifth, supported employment programs promote social integration in which people with disabilities are encouraged to interact with coworkers, supervisors, and others at work during lunchtimes or breaks and during nonwork hours as a result of wages earned. Lastly, supported employment programs promote flexibility in which people with disabilities are provided with various work options consistent with the wide range of job opportunities available in the community.

Benefits Counseling

Obtaining and Maintaining competitive employment may have a significant impact on the benefits that individuals with disabilities receive. The provision of benefits counseling focuses on reviewing with the individual and rehabilitation counselor what can be earned through work without jeopardizing or losing existing benefits if this is a concern for the individual with a disability. The goal of benefits counseling would be to develop a plan for achieving self-sufficiency or a work-related expense plan, so that the individual can maximize workplace participation while retaining important benefits (Fraser & Johnson, 2010).

Assistive Technology

Assistive technology is a class of interventions in which people with disabilities use technology to facilitate the performance of functional tasks (Kirsch & Scherer, 2010). Assistive technology not only includes mobility devices such as walkers and wheelchairs, but also includes computerized devices, software, and peripherals that assist people with disabilities in assessing computers or other information technologies. Various service delivery models regarding the application of assistive technology for people with disabilities have been developed in state rehabilitation agencies. Some of these services are provided by a vendor who is a rehabilitation counselor who has special responsibility to providing assistive technology services, some other pertinent health care providers, such as an occupational therapist, or an assistive technologist. Evidence also showed that assistive technology can also be used to enhance the employment opportunities for people with disabilities (Noll, Owens, Smith, & Schwanke, 2006). Thus, it is important that rehabilitation counselors should be knowledgeable and competent in assistive technology services. Rehabilitation counselors should identify the need for assistive technology services or devices for people with disabilities, provide information regarding assistive technology to people with disabilities, and coordinate assistive technology services.

SUMMARY AND RECOMMENDATIONS

Career development, vocational behavior, and employment of individuals with disabilities is a complex and dynamic process that is developmental in nature; it involves the person interacting with the environment and is moderated by social cognitive factors. In this chapter, we attempted to provide rehabilitation counselors with an overview of information that is important to understanding career and vocational behavior and ultimately enhance the career and employment outcomes of individuals with disabilities. In discussing the centrality of work and discussing how work is critical in meeting human needs, rehabilitation counselors gain an understanding that work plays an important role in the individual's level of mental health and social integration. Theories of career development were reviewed briefly in an effort to provide rehabilitation counselors with a framework to understand the complex nature of vocational behavior. The INCOME framework was introduced as a mechanism that rehabilitation counselors can use in conceptualizing and strategizing the delivery of rehabilitation services. Finally, we briefly described various interventions that can be used by rehabilitation counselors in facilitating vocational behavior change.

Overall, much work is still needed to gain a better understanding of work and disability. There is a very significant need to conduct studies that evaluate the impact of career counseling and vocational interventions for individuals with disabilities. To date, most of the research in this area has focused on supported employment and related interventions. Although these types of interventions appear to be very robust for those with severe disabilities, little, if any, research has been done to examine the development and efficacy of interventions directed at those without severe disabilities. Expanding research beyond those with severe disabilities would seem to be a needed priority over the next 10–15 years.

CONTENT REVIEW QUESTIONS

- What are the assessment methods that rehabilitation counselors can use to evaluate clients' needs? Use Table 15.1 as a guide.
- For each of the five career theories presented, describe how each theory accounts for the following: individual development, career development, vocational behavior, the person–environment interaction, and important social cognitive variables.
- What are the six statuses of the INCOME model?
- Explain how statuses, rather than stages, are more appropriate when working with persons with disabilities.

■ Explain how rehabilitation counselors can implement traditional vocational evaluation and counseling strategies using the INCOME framework?

REFERENCES

Amir, Z., Strauser, D. R., & Chan, F. (2009). Employers' and survivors' perspectives. In M. Feuerstein (Ed.), *Work and cancer survivors* (pp. 73–89). New York, NY: Springer.

Armstrong, P. I., Hubert, L., & Rounds, J. (2003). Circular undimensional scaling: A new look at group differences in interest structure. *Journal of Counseling Psychology, 51,* 299–313.

Bandura, A. (1986). *Social foundations of thought and action: A social-cognitive theory.* Englewood Cliffs, NJ: Prentice Hall.

Bandura, A. (1997). *Self-efficacy: The exercise of control.* New York, NY: W. H. Freeman.

Baron, R. A., & Greenberg, J. (1990). *Behavior in organizations: Understanding and managing the human side of work.* Boston, MA: Allyn & Bacon.

Beveridge, S., Craddock, S. H., Liesener, J., Stapleton, M., & Hershenson, D. B. (2002). INCOME: A framework for conceptualizing the career development of persons with disabilities. *Rehabilitation Counseling Bulletin, 45*(4), 195–206.

Blustein, D. L. (1994). "Who am I?": The question of self and identity in career development. In M. L. Savickas & R. W. Lent (Eds.), *Convergence in career development theories: Implications for science and practice* (pp. 139–154). Palo Alto, CA: Consulting Psychologists Press.

Blustein, D. L. (2006). *The psychology of working: A new perspective for career development, counseling, and public policy.* Mahwah, NJ: Lawrence Erlbaum.

Blustein, D. L. (2008). The role of work in psychological health and well-being. *American Psychologist, 63*(4), 228–240. doi:10.1037/0003-66X.63.4.228

Blustein, D. L., Kenna, A. C., Gill, N., & DeVoy, J. E. (2008). The psychology of working: A new framework for counseling practice and public policy. *The Career Development Quarterly, 56,* 294–308.

Bond, G. R., Resnick, S. G., Drake, R. E., Xie, H., McHugo, G. J., & Bebout, R. R. (2001). Does competitive employment improve nonvocational outcomes for people with severe mental illness? *Journal of Consulting and Clinical Psychology, 69*(3), 489–501.

Bowlby, J. (1982). Attachment and loss: Retrospect and prospect. *American Journal of Orthopsychiatry, 52,* 664–678.

Capella-McDonnall, M. E. (2005). The effects of single and dual sensory loss on symptoms of depression in the elderly. *International Journal of Geriatric Psychiatry, 20*(9), 855–861.

Conte, L. (1983). Vocational development theories and the disabled person: Oversight or deliberate omission. *Rehabilitation Counseling Bulletin, 26,* 316–328.

Crites, J. O. (1978). *Career maturity inventory.* Monterery, CA: McGraw-Hill.

Curnow, T. C. (1989). Vocational development of persons with disability. *Vocational Guidance Quarterly, 37,* 269–278.

Danley, K. S., & Anthony, W. A. (1987). The choose-get-keep model: Serving severely psychiatrically disabled people. *American Rehabilitation, 13*(4), 6–9, 27–29.

Dawis, R. V. (2000). The person-environment tradition in counseling psychology. In W. E. Martin Jr. & J. L. Swartz-Kulstad (Eds.), *Person-environment psychology and mental health* (pp. 91–111). Mahwah, NJ: Erlbaum.

Dawis, R. V. (2005). The Minnesota theory of work adjustment. In S. D. Brown & R. W. Lent (Eds.), *Career development and counseling: Putting theory and research to work* (pp. 3–23). New Jersey: John Wiley & Sons.

Dawis, R. V., & Lofquist, L. H. (1984). *A psychological theory of work adjustment: An individual-differences model and its application*. Minneapolis, MN: University of Minnesota Press.

Day, S. X., Rounds, J., & Swaney, K. (1998). The structure of vocational interests for diverse racial-ethnic groups. *Psychological Science, 9*, 40–44.

Deng, C.-P., Armstrong, P. I., & Rounds, J. (2007). The fit of Holland's RIASEC model to US occupations. *Journal of Vocational Behavior, 71*, 1–22. doi:10.1016/j.jvb.2007.04.002

Donnell, C., Lustig, D. C., & Strauser, D. R. (2004). The working alliance: Rehabilitation outcomes for persons with severe mental illness. *Journal of Rehabilitation, 70*(2), 12–17.

Edgell, P. (2006). *Religion and family in a changing society*. Princeton, NJ: Princeton University Press.

Fouad, N. A., Harmon, L. W., & Borgen, F. H. (1997). Structure of interests in employed male and female members of US racial-ethnic minority and non-minority groups. *Journal of Counseling Psychology, 44*, 339–345.

Fraser, R. T., & Johnson, K. (2010). Vocational rehabilitation. In R. G. Frank, M. Rosenthal, & B. Caplan (Eds.), *Handbook of rehabilitation psychology* (pp. 357–363). Washington, DC: American Psychological Association.

Gottfredson, L. (2002). Gottfredson's theory of circumscription, compromise, and self-creation. In D. Brown & Associates (Eds.), *Career choice and development* (pp. 85–148). San Francisco, CA: Jossey-Bass.

Hackett, G., & Betz, N. E. (1996). A self-efficacy approach to the career development of women. *Journal of Vocational Behavior, 18*, 326–339.

Hagner, D., & Salomone, P. (1989). Issues in career decision making for workers with developmental disabilities. *Career Development Quarterly, 38*, 148–159.

Helms, J. E. (1995). An update of Helm's White and people of color racial identity models. In J. G. Ponterotto, J. M. Casas, L. A. Suzuki, & C. M. Alexander (Eds.), *Handbook of multicultural counseling* (pp. 181–198). Thousand Oaks, CA: Sage.

Herr, E. L., & Cramer, S. H. (1996). *Career guidance and counseling through the lifespan: Systematic approaches*. New York: Harper Collins College.

Hershenson, D. B. (1981). Work adjustment, disability, and the three r's of vocational rehabilitation: A conceptual model. *Rehabilitation Counseling Bulletin, 25*, 91–97.

Hershenson, D. B. (1996a). A systems reformulation of a developmental model of work adjustment. *Rehabilitation Counseling Bulletin, 40*, 2–10.

Hershenson, D. B. (1996b). Work adjustment: A neglected area in career counseling. *Journal of Counseling & Development, 74*, 442–446.

Hershenson, D. B., & Szymanski, E. M. (1992). Career development of people with disabilities. In R. M. Parker & E. M. Szymanski (Eds.), *Rehabilitation counseling: Basics and beyond* (pp. 273–303). Austin, TX: Pro-Ed.

Holland, J. L. (1985). *The self-directed search professional manual*. Odessa, FL: Psychological Assessment Resources.

Holland, J. L. (1997). *Making vocatinal choices: A theory of vocational personalities and work environments*. Odessa, FL: Psychological Assessment Resources.

Holland, J. L., Daiger, D. C., & Power, P. G. (1980). *My vocational situation*. Palo Alto, CA: Consulting Psychologists Press.

Kahn, R. L., & Byosiere, P. (1990). Stress in organizations. In M. Dunnette (Ed.), *Handbook of industrial and organizational psychology* (2nd ed., Vol. 3, pp. 571–650). Chicago, IL: Rand-McNally.

Kirsch, N. L., & Scherer, M. J. (2010). Assistive technology for cognition and behavior. In R. G. Frank, M. Rosenthal, & B. Caplan (Eds.), *Handbook of rehabilitation psychology* (pp. 273–284). Washington, DC: American Psychological Association.

Kohlberg, L. (1968). Early education: A cognitive-developmental approach. *Child Development, 39*, 1013–1062.

Larson, J. E., Barr, L. K., Corrigan, P. W., Kuwabara, S. A., Boyle, M. G., & Glenn, T. L. (2007). Perspectives on benefits and costs of work from individuals with psychiatric disabilities. *Journal of Vocational Rehabilitation, 26*(2), 71–77.

Lent, R. W. (2005). A social cognitive view of career development and counseling. In S. D. Brown & R. W. Lent (Eds.), *Career development and counseling: putting theory and research to work* (pp. 101–127). New Jersey: John Wiley & Sons.

Lent, R. W., Brown, S. D., & Hackett, G. (1996). Career development from a social cognitive perspectives. In D. Brown & L. Brooks (Eds.), *Career choice and development* (pp. 373–421). San Francisco, CA: Jossey-Bass.

Lent, R. W., Brown, S. D., & Hackett, G. (2002). Contextual supports and barreirs to career choice: A social cognitive analysis. *Journal of Counseling Psychology, 47*, 36–49.

Lofquist, L. H., & Dawis, R. V. (1969). *Adjustment to work: A psychological view of man's problems in a work-oriented society*. New York, NY: Appleton-Century-Crofts.

Lustig, D. C., & Strauser, D. R. (2007). Causal relationships between poverty and disability. *Rehabilitation Counseling Bulletin, 50*(4), 194–202.

Lustig, D. C., Strauser, D. R., Weems, G. H., Donnell, C., & Smith, L. D. (2003). Traumatic brain injury and rehabilitation outcomes: Does working alliance make a difference. *Journal of Applied Rehabilitation Counseling, 34*(4), 30–37.

Marini, I., Lee, G. K., Chan, F., Chapin, M. H., & Romero, M. G. (2008). Vocational rehabilitation service patterns related to successful competitive employment outcomes of persons with spinal cord injury. *Journal of Vocational Rehabilitation, 28*(1), 1–13.

Maslow, A. H. (1987). *Motivation and personality*. New York, NY: Harper & Row.

Mitchell, L. K., & Krumboltz, J. D. (1996). Krumboltz's learning theory of career choice and counseling. In D. Brown & L. Brooks (Eds.), *Career choice and development* (pp. 233–280). San Francisco, CA: Jossey-Bass.

Moore, C. L., Feist-Price, S., & Alston, R. J. (2002). VR services for persons with severe/profound mental retardation: Does race matter? *Rehabilitation Counseling Bulletin, 45*(3), 162–167.

National Council on Disability. (2007). Empowerment for Americans with disabilities: Breaking barriers to careers and full employment. Retrieved November 15, 2010, from http://www.ncd.gov/newsroom/publications/2007/NCDEmployment_20071001.htm

Neff, W. S. (1985). *Work and human behavior*. New York, NY: Aldine.

Noll, A., Owens, L., Smith, R. O., & Schwanke, T. (2006). Survey of state vocational rehabilitation counselor roles and competencies in assistive technology. *Work: A Journal of Prevention, Assessment and Rehabilitation, 27*(4), 413–419.

O'Sullivan, D., & Strauser, D. (2010). Validation of the developmental work personality model and scale. *Rehabilitation Counseling Bulletin, 54*(1), 46–56. doi:10.1177/0034355210378045

Patterson, J. B., Szymanski, E. M., & Parker, R. M. (2005). Rehabilitation counseling: The profession. In R. M. Parker, E. M. Szymanski, & J. B. Patterson (Eds.), *Rehabilitation counseling: Basics and beyond* (pp. 1–25). Austin, TX: Pro-Ed.

Pope, M. (1999). Applications of group career counseling techniques in Asian cultures. *Journal of Multicultural Counseling and Development, 27*, 18–31.

Quick, J. C., Quick, J. D., Nelsom, D. L., & Hurrell, J. J., Jr. (1997). *Preventative stress management in organizations*. Washington, DC: American Psychological Association.

Rounds, J., & Tracey, T. J. (1996). Cross-cultural structure equivalence of RIASEC models and measures. *Journal of Counseling Psychology, 43*, 310–329.

Ryan, R. M., & Deci, E. L. (2000). Self-determination theory and the facilitation of intrinsic motivation, social development, and well-being. *American Psychologist, 55*, 68–78.

Schein, E. (1990). Organizational culture. *American Psychologist, 45*, 109–119.

Strauser, D. R., Ketz, K., & Keim, J. (2002). The relationship between self-efficacy, locus of control and work personality. *Journal of Rehabilitation, 68*(1), 20–26.

Strauser, D. R., Lustig, D. C., & Donnell, C. (2004). The impact of the working alliance on therapeutic outcomes for individuals with mental retardation. *Rehabilitation Counseling Bulletin, 47*, 215–223.

Strauser, D. R., O'Sullivan, D., & Wong, A. W. K. (2010). The relationship between contextual work behaviors self-efficacy and work personality: An exploratory analysis. *Disability and Rehabilitation, 32*(24), 1999–2008. doi:10.3109/09638281003797380

Super, D. E. (1957). *The psychology of careers: An introduction to vocational development*. New York, NY: Harper & Brothers.

Super, D. E. (1969). The development of vocational potential. In D. Malikin & H. Rusalem (Eds.), *Vocational rehabilitation of the disabled: An overview* (pp. 75–90). New York, NY: New York University Press.

Super, D. E. (1990). A life-span, life-space approach to career development. In D. Brown & L. Brooks (Eds.), *Career choices and development: Applying contemporary theories to practice* (pp. 197–261). San Francisco, CA: Jossey-Bass.

Super, D. E. (1994). A life span, life space perspectives on convergence. In M. L. Savickas & R. W. Lent (Eds.), *Convergence in career development theories: Implications for science and practice* (pp. 63–74). Palo Alto, CA: Consulting Psychologists Press.

Szymanski, E. M., Enright, M. S., Hershenson, D. B., & Ettinger, J. M. (2010). Career development theories and constructs: Implications for people with disabilities. In E. M. Szymanski & R. M. Parker (Eds.), *Work and disability: Contexts, issues, and strategies for enhancing employment outcomes for people wtih disabilities* (pp. 87–131). Austin, TX: Pro-Ed.

Szymanski, E. M., & Hershenson, D. B. (1998). Career development of people with disabilities: An ecological model. In R. M. Parker & E. M. Szymanski (Eds.), *Rehabilitation counseling: Basics and beyond* (pp. 327–378). Austin, TX: Pro-Ed.

Szymanski, E. M., & Hershenson, D. B. (2005). An ecological approach to vocational behavior and career development of people with disabilities. In R. M. Parker, E. M. Szymanski, & J. B. Patterson (Eds.), *Rehabilitation counseling: Basics and beyond* (pp. 225–280). Austin, TX: Pro-Ed.

Szymanski, E. M., Hershenson, D. B., Enright, M. S., & Ettinger, J. M. (1996). Career development theories, constructs, and research: Implications for people with disabilities. In E. M. Szymanski & R. M. Parker (Eds.), *Work and disability: Issues and strategies in career development and job placement* (pp. 79–126). Austin, TX: Pro-Ed.

Szymanski, E. M., & Parker, R. M. (2010). Work and disability: Basic concepts. In E. M. Szymanski & R. M. Parker (Eds.), *Work and disability: Contexts, issues, and strategies for enhancing employment outcomes for people wtih disabilities* (pp. 1–15). Austin, TX: Pro-Ed.

Thomas, K. T., & Berven, N. (1990). Providing career counseling for individuals with handicapping conditions. In N. Gysbers & Associates (Eds.), *Designing careers* (pp. 403–432). San Francisco, CA: Josssey-Bass.

Thomas, K. T., & Parker, R. M. (1992). Application of theory to rehabilitation counseling practice. In S. E. Robertson & R. I. Brown (Eds.), *Rehabilitation counseling: Approaches in the field of disability* (pp. 34–78). London, UK: Chapman & Hall.

Thompson, A. S., & Linderman, R. H. (1984). *Career development inventory: Technical manual*. Palo Alto, CA: Consulting Psychologists Press.

Tracey, T. J. (1991). Counseling research as an applied science. In C. E. Watkins, Jr. & L. J. Schneider (Eds.), *Research in counseling* (pp. 3–31). Hillsdale, NY: Erlbaum.

Tracey, T. J., & Rounds, J. (1993). Evaluating Holland's and Gati's vocational-interest models: A structural meta-analysis. *Psychological Bulletin, 113*, 229–246.

Tracey, T. J., & Rounds, J. (1995). The arbitrary nature of Holland's RIASEC types: A concentric-circles structure. *Journal of Counseling Psychology, 42*, 431–439.

Turner, K. D., & Szymanski, E. M. (1990). Work adjustment of people with congenital disabilities: A longitudinal perspective from birth to adulthood. *Journal of Rehabilitation, 56*(3), 19–24.

Vondracek, F. W., Lerner, R. M., & Schulenberg, J. E. (1986). *Career development: A life-span developmental approach*. Hillsdale, NJ: Erlbaum.

Wehman, P. (1996). Supported employment: Inclusion for all in the workplace. In W. Stainback & S. Stainback (Eds.), *Controversial issues confronting special education: Divergent perspectives* (pp. 293–304). Boston, MA: Allyn & Bacon.

Wilson, W. J. (1996). *When work disappears. The world of the new urban poor*. New York, NY: Alfred A. Knopf.

Wolfensberger, W. (2002). Social role valorization and, or versus, "empowerment". *Mental Retardation, 40*(3), 252–258.

Wright, G. N. (1980). *Total rehabilitation*. Boston, MA: Little, Brown, and Company.

V

Professional Competencies

16

Ethics and Ethics Decision Making

Vilia M. Tarvydas

LEARNING OBJECTIVES

After reading this chapter, you should be able to:

■ Summarize the major characteristics of the three components of professional standards
■ Discuss the elements and processes of ethics governance
■ Explain the decision-making process as a value-laden, but rational, process
■ Summarize and apply an integrative model of ethical decision making

---

INTRODUCTION

Increased quality of life for clients with disabilities depends upon professional counselors heeding the caution embodied in the words of Samuel Johnson: "Integrity without knowledge is weak and useless, and knowledge without integrity is dangerous and dreadful." The development of a strong professional identity rests on clear professional standards of practice. Clients need solution-focused, respectful, nonexploitative and empowering, and, therefore, ethical relationships with their counselors.

Clearly, clients require the services of professionals who are grounded firmly in the awareness of their value-laden mission and who are willing and able to assist people through appropriate knowledge and competencies (Gatens-Robinson & Rubin, 1995). The unusually strong tradition of explicit philosophical foundations is critical to the profession of rehabilitation and led to an early recognition of the value-based nature of rehabilitation counseling (Wright, 1983). This treasured legacy provides a strong basis for understanding the ethical principles at the heart of the ethical decision-making skills needed within the practice of rehabilitation counseling.

COMPONENTS OF PROFESSIONAL STANDARDS

The practice of counseling is both an art and a science—requiring the practitioner to make both value-laden and rational decisions. Rather than being incompatible stances, both facts and values must be considered in juxtaposition to one another to engage in rational decisions (Gatens-Robinson & Rubin, 1995). Within ethical deliberation, the practitioner blends such elements as personal moral sensitivities and philosophies of practice with clinical behavioral objectivity and the quest for efficient care of clients.

The nature and complexity of standards of practice for all of the professions have changed and grown over the last several decades. The phrase *professional standards* no longer simply mean specifically the ethical standards of the profession. This term is a general term meaning professional criteria indicating acceptable professional performance (Powell & Wekell, 1996) and may encompass ethical and/or clinical care standards. There are three types of standards relevant to describing professional practice: (1) the *internal standards* of the profession; (2) *clinical standards* for the individual practitioners within a profession; and (3) *external, regulatory standards*. Taken together, these professional standards increase the status of the profession and its ability for self-governance, as well as enhancing the external representation and accountability for the profession's competence with clients, the general public, employers, external regulators, and payers (Rinas & Clyne-Jackson, 1988). These types of standards, their major characteristics, and principal components are depicted in Figure 16.1.

Internal Standards

First, the internal standards of the profession form the underpinnings of the appropriate role and functions of the profession. Internal standards are characterized by being focused on advancing the professionalism of the group in question, having the intent of setting a profession-wide standard of practice, and assisting individual practitioners through defining their professional identity and obligations. Prominent examples of mechanisms in this category are the profession's code of ethics and any guidelines for specialty practice relevant to the discipline.

Clinical Standards

The clinical standards for professional practitioners are close to the internal standards described in that both are directly relevant to services delivered to the individual client or patient. Additional characteristics include focusing on single disciplinary or multidisciplinary standards of clinical care. These standards may be specific to a particular setting or client population—they evaluate the

FIGURE 16.1
The Structure of Professional Standards

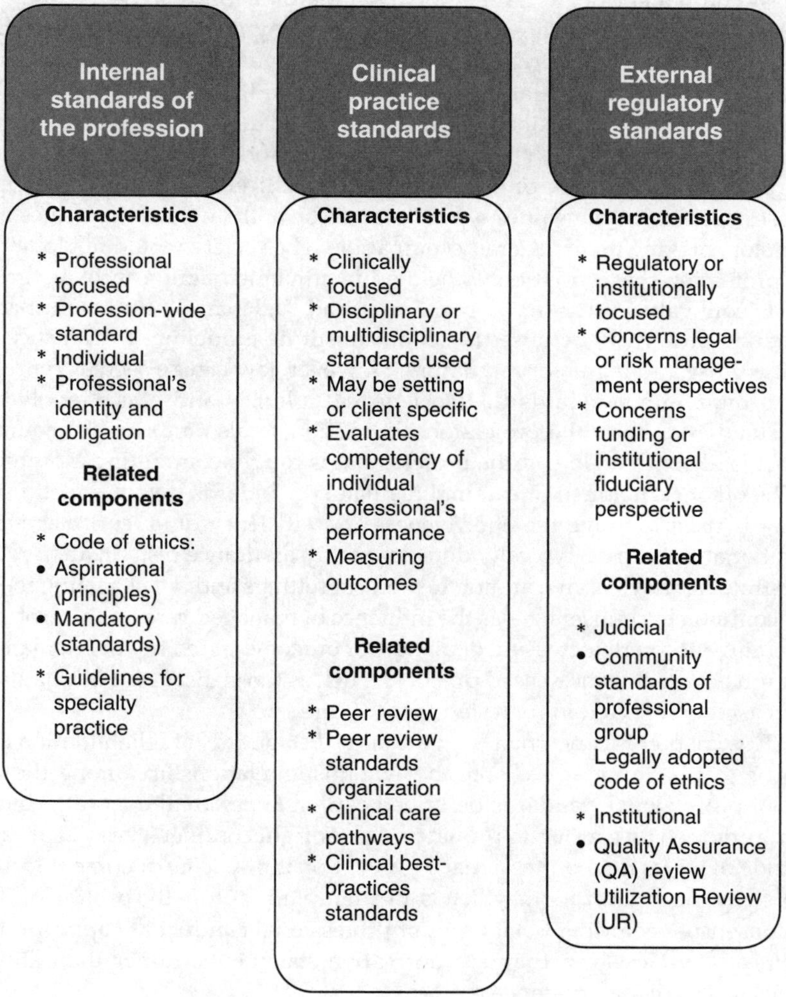

Internal standards of the profession	Clinical practice standards	External regulatory standards
Characteristics	**Characteristics**	**Characteristics**
* Professional focused * Profession-wide standard * Individual * Professional's identity and obligation	* Clinically focused * Disciplinary or multidisciplinary standards used * May be setting or client specific * Evaluates competency of individual professional's performance * Measuring outcomes	* Regulatory or institutionally focused * Concerns legal or risk management perspectives * Concerns funding or institutional fiduciary perspective
Related components		**Related components**
* Code of ethics: • Aspirational (principles) • Mandatory (standards) * Guidelines for specialty practice	**Related components** * Peer review * Peer review standards organization * Clinical care pathways * Clinical best-practices standards	* Judicial • Community standards of professional group Legally adopted code of ethics * Institutional • Quality Assurance (QA) review Utilization Review (UR)

competency of individual professionals based on the specific care rendered, and they have a client- or patient-care outcome measurement focus. Peer review processes and standards, as well as clinical care pathways, are examples of this type of standard.

External Regulatory Bodies

The last component of the professional standards trio involves the standards of external regulatory bodies of diverse sorts. They are focused on regulatory or institutional-level concerns. They usually involve legal or risk-management questions and deal with funding or institutional fiduciary perspectives. There is a judicial type of component in which legal or quasi-legal processes are at play—such as community standards of a professional group being used in a malpractice suit or a code of ethics adopted by a licensure board to discipline licensees. General social values typically underlie both law and the values of the profession, making them generally compatible. The society would not long tolerate a profession that is routinely operated in a manner significantly at variance with its core value structure. Corey, Corey, and Callanan (2010) noted that law and ethics are similar, because they both constitute guidelines for practice and, in some sense, are regulatory in nature. However, law can be seen as representing the minimum standards that society will tolerate, and ethics involves the ideal standards set by the profession itself. The law also informs the counselor of what is likely to happen if the professional is caught committing a prohibited act. The other component of external regulatory standards involves institutional standards used to judge the effectiveness and efficiency of an entire agency or institutional unit—as is typically done in quality assurance or utilization review. Such strategies have been common in medical settings and are becoming increasingly common in counseling—as the influence of managed care on the profession accelerates—through increasing demands for outcome-based treatment planning. An emphasis on evidence-based practices (such as those discussed in Chapter 18) is increasingly reflected in such standards of care.

This chapter is concerned with the ethical standards of rehabilitation counseling, but it is important to note the synergistic relationship among the three types of professional standards described earlier. *Ethics* are the moral principles that are adopted by a group to provide rules for right conduct (Corey et al., 2010). The code of ethics for a professional organization is a specific document formally adopted by the organization, which is an attempt to capture the profession's current consensus regarding what types of professional conduct are appropriate or inappropriate. However, they are normative statements, rather than absolute dictates of situational guidance.

ETHICS GOVERNANCE

Effective processes to govern ethics practice are necessary to give meaning to professional standards of practice and to enhance the societal stature of the profession. These governance processes guide the profession's practitioners through education and socialization into the professional role, and subsequently discipline them if they do not practice within the proscribed standards established.

Ethical components of the standards of practice can be thought of as being either mandatory or aspirational in the level of direction they provide the practitioner (Corey et al., 2010). The most basic level of ethical functioning is guided by mandatory ethics. At this level, individuals focus on compliance with the law and the dictates of the professional codes of ethics that apply to their practice. They are concerned with remaining safe from legal action and professional censure. The more ethically sophisticated level is the aspirational level. At this level, individuals additionally reflect on the effects of the situation on the welfare of their clients, and the effects of their actions on the profession as a whole.

These same concepts of mandatory and aspirational ethics can be applied to the overall structure of governance for a profession's ethical standards of practice as a whole. Codes of ethics are binding only on persons who hold that particular credential (e.g., certification through the Commission on Rehabilitation Counselor Certification [CRCC]), or have membership in that organization (e.g., member of the American Counseling Association [ACA]). Those professionals so governed must take ethical guidance, and sanctions may be applied based upon the specific ethical codes and disciplinary process of this specific professional entity. The disciplinary process of CRCC is an example of such a process applicable to rehabilitation counseling practice. If a credential holder or member of a particular professional entity violates its code of ethics, the entity has the responsibility to provide a disciplinary procedure to enforce its standards. After due process, the entity applies an appropriate sanction to the violator. In the case of a professional organization, the ultimate sanction would typically be removal from membership, with possible referral of the findings to other professional or legal jurisdictions. For a credentialing entity such as CRCC or a counselor licensure board, the violator could face the more serious option of certificate or license revocation, thus possibly removing an individual's ability to practice. Less-serious levels of sanction, such as reprimand or probation, are also available. Often these statuses are coupled with significant educational or rehabilitative conditions, such as taking an ethics course or treatment of an addiction and supervised practice, to assist practitioners in regaining appropriate ethical standards of practice, while protecting their clients. A letter of instruction may be used when there is no ethical violation found, but the disciplinary body determines that information could be provided to the practitioner about the best ethical practices that might improve the future provision of services to clients. The assessment of the level of seriousness of the ethical violation will affect the actual choice of sanction, once the individual is adjudicated as being in violation of the code of ethics. Factors often considered include intentionality, degree of risk or actual harm to the client, motivation or ability of violator to change, and recidivism of the violator (Koocher & Keith-Spiegel, 2007).

Responsible practitioners supplement this basic mandatory level of practitioner ethics with advanced knowledge of the clinical wisdom and scholarly literature on best practices in ethics. In addition, they will gain guidance from other codes of ethics and specialty guidelines for ethical practice that are relevant to their practices. These sources should be sought to supplement the required mandatory ethical standards with the more aspirational principles and ethical concepts to which the more sophisticated practitioner should aspire. In fact, for certain situations, the course of action suggested by the aspirational ethics perspective may contradict that required by the dictates of mandatory ethics. Such a situation leaves the practitioner in the stressful position of needing to responsibly reconcile the two directions.

The contemporary structure of ethics governance for counselors is presented in Figure 16.2. This representation depicts types of professional organizational entities in counseling—organized hierarchically in the shape of a pyramid. The levels of ethical governance are represented by the vertical arrow to the side of the pyramid, depicting the entities as existing roughly on a continuum from a primarily aspirational to a primarily mandatory level of function.

FIGURE 16.2
Model of Ethics Governance for Rehabilitation Counselors

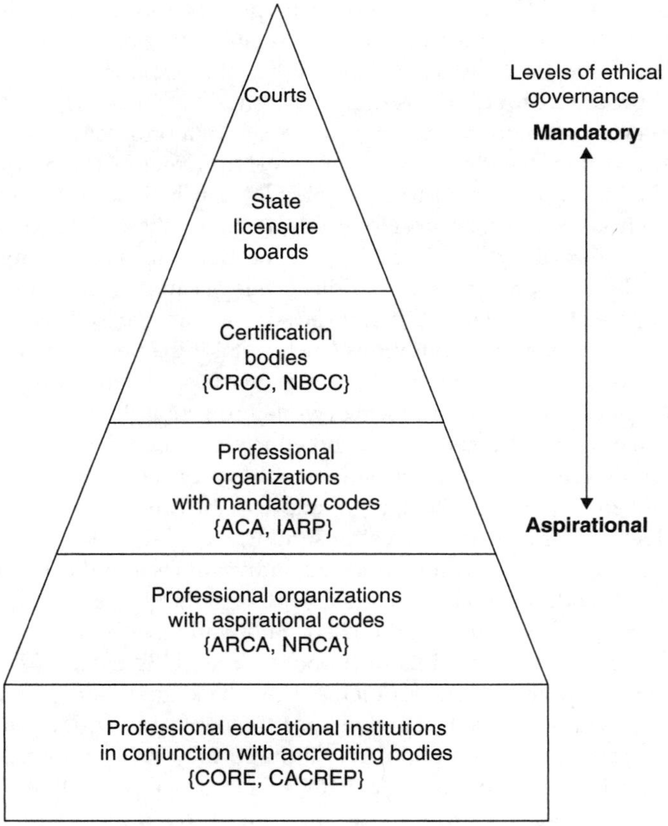

Colleges and universities provide professional education and research services, doing so under the review of credentialing bodies such as the Commission on Rehabilitation Education (CORE) or the Commission on the Accreditation of Counseling and Related Educational Programs (CACREP). As such, they are entities that have the broadest function to provide aspirational education and guidance in ethics, and that represent the foundation of the structure of ethics governance. In additional, they build the theoretical and research base for understanding ethical issues, decision-making processes, and ethics educational methods. These aspects of the aspirational knowledge base are needed to support ethical development of the profession. Colleges and universities also ensure that proper preservice education and professional socialization occur to inculcate future practitioners and educators with a proper ethics base from which to conduct their future practice of counseling. This obligation includes active role-modeling and supporting ethical analysis and ethical behavior in teaching, supervision, and actual clinical practice. Educational institutions also serve as a resource to other professional organizations and regulatory bodies to provide teaching, research, and service, supporting aspirational and mandatory ethical practice in the community.

At the next level sit the professional organizations with aspirational codes of ethics, but with no internal mandatory enforcement mechanisms for them. For example, the Association for Specialists in Group Work and the American Rehabilitation Counseling Association (ARCA), as divisions of ACA, occupy this position. For such organizations, the primary task is to encourage aspirational ethical levels of function in their members. Mandatory enforcement tasks are not undertaken by such professional organizations because of such factors as lack of appropriate consumer access and protection in the disciplinary process; appropriate remedies for serious infractions; and the substantial financial, staff, and professional resources necessary for responsible enforcement. In some cases, the mandatory enforcement function of the organization is referred to a parent organization (e.g., to ACA, in the case of ARCA members who are ACA members), or the complainant is referred to another appropriate jurisdiction to initiate a disciplinary process.

Nonetheless, professional organizations with aspirational codes perform several significant functions within the ethics governance structure. They may provide supplemental, complementary codes of ethics for their members, which extend and explicate other more general codes of ethics. Such a document provides guidelines for ethical practice for special issues frequently encountered or of particular concern to these professionals. For rehabilitation counselors, examples of such issues might include assessment of persons with functional limitations caused by disability, interdisciplinary team practice relationship issues, managed care practice, and the responsibility of advocacy for persons with disabilities. A supplementary code may take the form of specialty guidelines for practice, which address specialty setting or function specific issues. One example of this type of guideline is the *American Psychological Association Revised Guidelines for Child Custody Evaluations in Family Law Proceedings* (2009).

346 V. PROFESSIONAL COMPETENCIES

In addition to maintaining supplementary, specialty ethical standards for practice, some professional organizations, with an aspirational ethical level of function, collect information regarding ethical trends and needs for revision of either the specialty or the generalist ethics codes. Their leadership also should participate in the code revision and writing processes for both types of codes. These organizations should identify and supply qualified professionals to serve on the various mandatory enforcement bodies. They provide educational programs to further knowledge and the quality of ethical practice, performing significant educational and socialization functions. An innovative role—yet one that is potentially most meaningful—is the provision of mechanisms and expertise to offer remediation or rehabilitation programs for impaired professionals who have been found in violation (or are at risk of violation) of ethical standards.

At the third level of ethical governance are professional organizations that maintain and enforce a mandatory code of ethics, such as ACA and the International Association of Rehabilitation Professionals (IARP). These organizations provide an entry-level mandatory code of ethics and enforcement process for their members, and, in the case of ACA, the enforcement for referred complaints of its specialty memberships. This level of organization consults with certification and licensing bodies and the specialty professional organizations to ensure active participation of all parties in the ethics enforcement process, and attempts to incorporate specialty viewpoints into a compatible and continually revise codes of ethics. They provide referral to other jurisdictions for complaints against accused parties, as appropriate. They may provide important educational programs to increase practitioner expertise in ethical practice, and may issue advisory opinions to members who inquire to assist in proactively guiding ethical practice.

At the next two levels of ethics governance are professional regulatory bodies that either certify or license professionals, and that constitute the preeminent enforcers of the mandatory code. National certification bodies, such as CRCC and the National Board for Counselor Certification (NBCC), as well as the state counselor licensure boards operate at this level. They perform a pivotal role in the promulgation and enforcement of ethical standards. However, they draw their specific codes of ethical standards from the professional organizations, because they do not constitute the profession, but rather regulate it, based upon the profession's own internal standards. They may provide information and consultation to professional organizations in revising and maintaining as current the codes of ethics. Beyond the ethical regulatory function, the regulatory bodies encourage ethical proficiency of their licensees and certificants through requiring preservice education and continuing education in the area of ethics.

As a practical matter, many states that license professional counselors adopt the ACA Code of Ethics and Standards of Practice, and a counselor licensed in a state that has adopted the ACA code would be governed by that code or one very closely related to it. In additionally, the 2010 CRCC Code of Professional

Ethics for Rehabilitation Counselors (Appendix C in this book) is very similar to the ACA code of ethics (Tarvydas & Cottone, 2000). In essence, this consistency provides rehabilitation counselors with a unified code of ethics within the profession, which is highly compatible with ethical standards of ACA and most counseling licensure boards.

At the pinnacle of the ethics governance hierarchy are found the civil and criminal courts and other legal jurisdictions that impact the ethical practice of counselors. For example, engaging in sexual intimacy with a client is a criminal offense in many states, and may even result in arrest and incarceration if practitioner is found guilty of this offense (Corey et al., 2010). However, one of the primary mechanisms of legal governance of ethics still is through the use of malpractice suits in civil courts. In malpractice actions, one of the central points is to establish a violation of duty, requiring determination of the standard of what constitutes "good professional practice" as applied to the matter at hand. This issue is difficult to determine because it is often ill-defined and requires many types of considerations. It is not unusual that various expert witnesses would be called to testify regarding such practices. In addition, there might be an attempt to establish that a blatant violation of the general rules of the profession occurred, by reference to the profession's ethical standards (Thompson, 1990).

Another standard of practice that might be applied would be consideration of whether the action or service in question was both within the scope of practice of the profession and within the individual's personal scope of practice (see Appendix B of this book for the CRCC Scope of Practice). The profession of rehabilitation counseling has established its scope of practice, with which its practitioners must be familiar, to appropriately and ethically establish their personal scopes of practice. In addition, state licensed professional counselors are governed by the scope of practice described for counselors within their state's licensure regulatory language, and may be required to declare their personal scopes of practice at the time they are licensed and to revise them as appropriate. Practitioners are ethically bound to limit their own scopes of practice to areas within the profession's scope, in which they are personally competent to practice, by virtue of appropriate types and levels of education, supervision, and professional experience.

Through these six levels, the various professional governance entities interact to provide a network of mandatory and aspirational ethics functions. Concern for the protection of clients is very strong among these professional governance structures, and they have cooperated to share information about the most serious ethical infractions that are adjudicated within their organizations. In their totality, they are an interactive system of research, educational, and enforcement services to shape and regulate the ethical practice of counselors. Taken together, these systems of knowledge, traditions, rules, and laws form the regulatory content, but they do not provide the practitioner with possibly the most crucial tool for ethical practice—knowledge and experience in application of a decision-making process that can be applied to this form and content.

ETHICAL DECISION-MAKING PROCESSES

The intent of an ethics code is to provide rehabilitation counselors with guidance for specific situations they experience in their practices. However, authorities have long recognized that ethics codes must be written in general enough terms that they apply across a wide range of practice settings. They also are reactive in nature; that is, they address situations that have already been part of the profession's experience (Kitchener, 1984; Mabe & Rollin, 1986). As a result, even with the knowledge of the profession's code of ethics, rehabilitation counselors may find that they do not have sufficient guidance to resolve the dilemma in question. They may find that the particular situation with which they are faced is not addressed in their code; that their practice is governed by more than one code, providing conflicting direction in the situation; or that conflicting provisions within any one code appear to apply to the situation. For that reason, the rehabilitation counselor must be prepared to exercise their professional judgment in ethics responsibly. This type of occurrence is not so much a failure of ethical codes, but rather a natural and appropriate juncture recognizing the importance and role of professional judgment. In other words, it is affirmation that one is involved in practice of a profession, rather than doing a job, however skilled. In order to exercise professional judgment, the rehabilitation counselor must be prepared to recognize underlying ethical principles or conflicts between competing interests, and to apply appropriate ethical decision-making skills to resolve the dilemma and act in an ethical manner (Cottone & Tarvydas, 2007; Francouer, 1983; Kitchener, 1984). In fact, expanding upon the expectation stated in the 2005 ACA Code of Ethics for use of an ethical decision-making model, CRCC's Code of Professional Ethics charges counselors with the responsibility to "be familiar with and apply a credible model of decision making that can bear public scrutiny" (CRCC, 2010, p. 104) through inclusion of an ethical standard to apply one as well as to "recognize underlying ethical principles and conflicts among competing interests" (p. 136). This trend is in keeping with the growing recognition that mental health professionals must be prepared to go well beyond the simple knowledge of codes of ethics to know how to reason about complex and sometimes seemingly conflicting types of information through application of a formal ethical decision-making model (Cottone, in press). Fortunately, the professional is assisted in this task by examination and refinement of their ordinary moral sense, as well as by the availability of thoughtful models for the ethical decision-making process. Many components of ethical decision making involve teachable, learnable skills to supplement the professional's developing intuitive professional judgment.

Several types of models exist, which seek to explain and structure the process of ethical decision making (Cottone, in press; Cottone & Claus, 2000). Some prominent examples view the ethics decision-making process as: professional self-exploration (Corey et al., 2010); a moral reasoning discourse (Kitchener, 1984); the result of a moral developmental process (VanHoose & Kottler, 1985);

a multidimensional, integrative psychological process (Rest, 1984); and involving a hierarchy of four contextual levels that affect the process of decision making (Tarvydas & Cottone, 1991). Generally, ethical decision-making models can be thought of as having the characteristics of either principle or virtue ethics (Corey et al., 2010). *Principle* ethics focuses on the objective, rational, cognitive aspects of the process. Practitioners who adhere to this perspective tend to view the application of universal, impartial ethical principles, rules, codes, and laws as being the core elements of ethics. *Virtue* ethics considers the characteristics of the counselors themselves as the critical element for responsible practice. Thus, proponents of virtue ethics approaches would tend to concern themselves more with counselors reflecting upon and clarifying their moral and value positions. In addition, they would examine other personal issues that might impact their ethical practice, such as unresolved emotional needs, which might negatively affect their work with their clients. Preferred approaches to ethical decision making should include both aspects (Corey et al., 2010; Meara, Schmidt, & Day, 1996). Among other positive contributions of such a synergistic approach, Vasquez (1996) has speculated that the addition of virtue ethical perspectives may improve ethical conduct in multicultural and diverse interactions and settings. Cottone (in press) has identified multicultural sensitivity as a major theme in the evolution of ethical decision-making models, and Garcia, Cartwright, Winston, and Borzoukowska (2003) have addressed it through infusing multicultural elements into the Tarvydas integrative decision-making model of ethical behavior discussed in the following.

TARVYDAS' INTEGRATIVE DECISION-MAKING MODEL OF ETHICAL BEHAVIOR

The Tarvydas integrative decision-making model of ethical behavior builds on several well-known decision-making models widely used by professionals in the mental health and counseling communities. It incorporates the most prominent principle and virtue aspects of several decision-making approaches and introduces some contextual considerations into the process. The Tarvydas integrative model emphasizes the constant process of interaction between the principle and the virtue elements, and places a reflective attitude at the heart of the process. The model also focuses on the actual production of ethical behavior within a specified context, rather than prematurely terminating analysis by merely selecting the best ethical course of action. The model is shown in Table 16.1. This approach respects the importance of setting and environmental factors, which are crucial in counseling. Indeed, in reviewing the various approaches to ethical decision making, Garcia et al. (2003) observed that this model uses virtue ethics and behavioral strategies that are consistent with a multicultural approach to counseling and ethical decision making, and have proposed an integrative transcultural ethical decision-making model that is based primarily on the Tarvydas integrative model.

Table 16.1
Tarvydas Integrative Model for Ethical Behavior

Themes or Attitudes in the Integrative Model

Maintain an attitude of *reflection*.

Address *balance* between issues and parties to the ethical dilemma.

Pay close attention to the *context(s)* of the situation.

Utilize a process of *collaboration* with all rightful parties to the situation.

Stage I. Interpreting the Situation

Component 1. Enhance *sensitivity* and *awareness*.

Component 2. Determine the major *stakeholders* and their ethical claims in the situation.

Component 3. Engage in the *fact-finding* process.

Stage II. Formulating an Ethical Decision

Component 1. Review the problem or dilemma.

Component 2. Determine what *ethical codes, laws, ethical principles*, and *institutional policies and procedures* exist that apply to the dilemma.

Component 3. Generate possible and probable courses of action.

Component 4. Consider potential positive and negative *consequences* for each course of action.

Component 5. Consult with supervisors and other knowledgeable professionals.

Component 6. Select the best *ethical course* of action.

Stage III. Selecting an Action by Weighing Competing, Nonmoral Values

Component 1. Engage in reflective recognition and analysis of *competing nonmoral values, personal blind spots*, or *prejudices*.

Component 2. Consider *contextual influences* on values selection at the counselor–client, team, institutional, and societal levels.

Component 3. Select *preferred course* of action.

Stage IV. Planning and Executing the Selected Course of Action

Component 1. Figure out a reasonable *sequence of concrete actions* to be taken.

Component 2. Anticipate and work out *personal and contextual barriers* to effective execution of the plan of action, and effective *countermeasures* for them.

Component 3. Carry out, document, and *evaluate* the course of action as planned.

Themes and Attitudes

In addition to the specific elements or steps of the Tarvydas integrative model, there are four underlying themes or attitudes that are necessary for the professional counselor to enact. These attitudes involve mindfully attending to the tasks of: (1) maintaining a stance of *reflection* concerning one's own conscious awareness of personal issues, values, and decision-making skills, as well as extending an effort to understand those of all others concerned with the situation, and their relationship to the decision maker; (2) addressing the *balance* among various issues, people, and perspectives within the process; (3) maintaining an appropriate level of attention to the *context* of the situation in question, allowing awareness of the counselor–client, treatment team, organizational, and societal implications of the ethical elements; and (4) seeking to use a process of *collaboration* with all rightful parties to the decision, but most especially the client.

By adopting these background attitudes of reflection, balance, context, and collaboration, counselors engage in a more thorough process that will help preserve the integrity and dignity of all parties involved. This will be the case even when outcomes are not considered equally positive for all participants in the process, as is often true in a serious dilemma when such attitudes can be particularly meaningful. Indeed, Betan and Stanton (1999) studied students' responses to ethical dilemmas, analyzing how emotions and concerns influence willingness to implement ethical knowledge. They concluded that "subjectivity and emotional involvement are essential tools for determining ethical action, but they must be integrated with rational analysis" (p. 295).

Reflection is the overriding attitude of importance throughout the enactment of the specific elements of stages and components that constitute the steps of the Tarvydas integrative model. Many complex decision-making processes easily become overwhelming, either in their innate complexity or in the real-life press of the speed or intensity of events. In the current approach, the counselor is urged always to "Stop and think!" at each point in the process. The order of operations is not critical or absolute, or is it more important than being reflective and invested in a calm, dignified, respectful, and thorough analysis of the situation. Not until we recognize that we are involved in the process and appreciate its critical aspects can we call forth other resources to assist the process and persons within it. Such an attitude of reflection will serve the counselor well at all stages of this process.

Elements

The specific elements that constitute the operations within the Tarvydas integrative model have four main stages with several components, including the steps to be taken within each stage. The concepts summarized below are drawn, in the main, from the work of Kitchener (1984), Rest (1984), and Tarvydas and Cottone (1991).

Stage I: Interpreting the Situation Through Awareness and Fact Finding
At this stage, the primary task of counselors is to be sensitive and aware of the needs and welfare of the people around them, and of the ethical implications of these situations. This level of awareness allows counselors to imagine and to investigate the effects of the situation on the parties involved and the possible effects of various actions and conditions. The sense of this state is somewhat like the idea of "situational awareness" as used in military parlance, through which

the agents scan the circumstances for potential threats and resources that are relevant to addressing the conflict at hand. This research and awareness must also include emotional, as well as cognitive and fact-based considerations. Three components constitute the counselors' operations in this stage.

Component 1 involves enhancing one's sensitivity and awareness. In *Component 2*, the counselor takes an inventory of the people who are major stakeholders in the outcome of the situation. It is important to reflect on any parties who will be affected and who play a major role in the client's life, as well as considering what their exact relationship is—ethically and legally—to the person at the center of the issue—the client. Imagine dropping a rock into a pond—the point of impact is where the central figure, the client, is situated; however, the client is surrounded by people at varying levels of closeness to them, such as parents, foster parents, intimate partners, spouse, children, employer, friends, and neighbors, all radiating out from the client in decreasing levels of intimacy and responsibility to the client.

Figure 16.3 depicts how the spheres of influence of these stakeholders in the client's life, as well as the stakeholders at each of the four levels in the professional world of the counselor, may be seen as intersecting. This way of thinking about the relationships among the different stakeholders in the situation allows for a fuller appreciation of the specific people and contexts of the counselor's practice and the client's situation.

A number of people and levels of the professional service hierarchy will (or should) play a part in the ethics decision. These social forces will create both positive and negative influences in the ethical situation, and should be taken into account in the ethical analysis. The ethical claims of these parties on the counselor's level of duty are not uniform. Almost all codes of ethics in counseling make it clear that the client is the person to whom the first duty is owed, but there are others to whom the counselor has lesser, but important levels of duty. It is always important to determine whether any surrogate decision makers for the client exist, such as a foster parent, guardian or person with power of attorney, so that they may be brought into the central circle of duty early in the process. Sensitivity and proactivity are useful in working through situations in which the legal relationships involved do not coincide with the social and emotional bonds between the client and other people involved in the dilemma.

The final element in Stage I is *Component 3*, in which the counselor undertakes an extensive fact-finding investigation, with a scope appropriate to the situation. The nature of the fact-finding process should be carefully considered and is not intended to be a formal investigative or quasi-legal process. The intent is that the counselor should carefully review and understand the information at hand, then seek out new information. Only information that is appropriately available to a counselor should be involved. The scope and depth of information that would be rightfully available to the counselor is surprising, but it is often not fully utilized. For example, information might be gained from such sources as further discussion with the client, contacts with family (with appropriate permission of the client), case records, expert consultation and reports, legal resources, or agency policy and procedures.

FIGURE 16.3
The Intersection of the Client's Personal World With the Counselor's
Professional Hierarchical Contexts

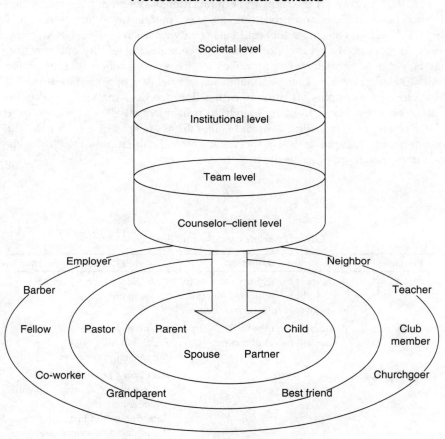

Stage II: Formulating an Ethical Decision
This aspect of the process is most widely known by professionals, and many may erroneously think it is the end of the process. The central task in this stage is to identify which of the possible ethical courses of action appears to come closest to the moral ideal in the situation under consideration (Rest, 1984). Many decision-making models in other areas of counseling can be applied as a template at this stage, but the following components are drawn from the work of Van Hoose and Kottler (1985).

Component 1 suggests that the counselor review the problem or dilemma to be sure that it is clearly understood in light of any new information obtained in Stage I. In *Component 2*, the counselor researches the standards of law and practice applicable to the situation. This component includes Kitchener's (1984) attention to ethical codes, laws, and ethical principles, and Tarvydas and Cottone's (1991) concern for the team and organizational context in the examination of institutional policies and procedures to make mention of other useful areas for consideration. The counselor would also analyze which of the six core ethical principles (autonomy, beneficence, nonmaleficence, justice, fidelity, and veracity) may be either supported or compromised by the types of actions that are being contemplated in the situation (see Table 16.2 for brief description of these ethical principles and examples of common counseling practices that are based upon them). This operation is formally known as principle analysis and is one of the most challenging, yet critical aspects of the ethical analysis of a dilemma. The core, or main, principle analysis concerns the ethical obligations owed to the client, rather than to other parties to the situation.

TABLE 16.2
Ethical Principles and Related Practices

Principle	Brief Definition	Related Counseling Practice
Autonomy	To respect the rights of clients to be self-governing within their social and cultural framework	Obtaining informed consent Keeping confidentiality
Beneficence	To do good to others; to promote the well-being of clients	Hospitalizing a suicidal client Providing high-quality counseling services
Nonmaleficence	To do no harm to others	Avoiding a potentially detrimental dual relationship with a client Referring or not providing counseling services when not fully qualified
Fidelity	To be faithful; to keep promises and honor the trust placed in one	Keeping promises to clients Respecting client's privacy
Justice	To be fair in the treatment of all clients; to provide appropriate services to all	Advocating on behalf of client Ensuring services are fully accessible to all Providing fair access to services to all, even difficult clients
Veracity	To be honest	Providing detailed professional disclosure Describing completely who will have access to client files

Component 3 initiates the process of formally envisioning and generating of possible and probable courses of action. As with all decision-making processes, it is important not to truncate this exploratory process by prematurely censoring the possibilities, or succumbing to a sense of being too overwhelmed, or too limited, in options. *Component 4* is the logical outgrowth of considering courses of action. Positive and negative consequences are identified and assessed in relation to risks, as well as to material and personal resources available. In *Component 5,* the counselor is reminded to consult with supervisors and trusted and knowledgeable colleagues for guidance, if this has not been done before this point. Professional standards of practice emphasize the importance of appropriate collegial consultation to resolve difficult clinical and ethical dilemmas. Research has also demonstrated that such consultations can have a significant influence on those seeking such consultation (Butterfield, Trevino, & Weaver, 2000; Cottone, Tarvydas, & House, 1994). There is value in reviewing the reasoning employed in working through the ethical dilemma to this point, and the solutions and consequences envisioned to be sure that all potentially useful and appropriate considerations have been taken into account. Finally, the best ethical course of action is determined and articulated in *Component 6.* The ethical decision at this stage of the model should be contrasted with the decision about what the counselor actually decided to do, which is the product of Stage III.

Stage III: Selecting an Action by Weighing Competing, Nonmoral Values, Personal Blind Spots, and Prejudices

Many people would think that the ethical decision-making process is concluded at the end of Stage II. This impression is limited in its realization of the many additional forces that may affect the counselor and result in the counselor not actually executing the selected ethical course of action. *Component 1* of Stage III interjects a period of reflection and active processing of what the counselor intends to do, in view of competing, nonmoral values (Rest, 1984). At this point, the counselor considers any personal factors that might intervene to pull them away from choosing the ethical action or cause that action to be substantially modified. Nonmoral values involve anything that the counselor may prize or desire, which is not in and of itself a moral value, such as justice. Such values may include such things as valuing social harmony, spending time with friends or working on one's hobby, desiring control or power, or having personal wealth. In this component, counselors are also called upon to examine themselves to determine if they have some personal blind spots or prejudices that might affect their judgment or resolve to do the ethical thing, such as a fear of HIV infection, or the conviction that gay men are also likely to molest children. This portion of the model provides an excellent opportunity for counselors to carefully evaluate whether they have adequately incorporated multicultural considerations and competencies in their work on this ethical dilemma and to be sure that they are not operating from a culturally encapsulated frame of reference.

Counselors must allow themselves to become aware of the strength and attractiveness of other values they hold, which may influence whether they will discharge their ethical obligations. If they are self-aware, they may more effectively and honestly compensate for their conflicted impulses at this point. Counselors may have strong needs for acceptance by peers or supervisors—for prestige and influence—to avoid controversy or to be financially successful. These value orientations may come into conflict with the course of action necessary to proceed ethically, and must be reconciled with ethical requirements if the client is to be ethically served. On the other hand, counselors may place a high value on being moral or ethical and on being accepted as respected professionals with high ethical standards, or they may value the esteem of colleagues who place a high value on ethical professional behavior. Those forces should enhance the tendency to select ethical behavioral options [the influence of the ethical climate on the ethical behavior of the counselor is more fully explored in Tarvydas, O'Rourke, and Urish (2007)]. Therefore, the importance of selecting and maintaining ethically sensitized and positive professional and personal cultures should be recognized as critical to full professional functioning, as the next component would suggest.

In *Component 2,* counselors systematically inventory the contextual influences on their choices at the counselor–client, team, institutional, and societal levels. This is not a simple process of weighing influences, but it should serve as an inventory of influences, which may be either dysfunctional or constructive, for selecting the ethical course over other types of values present in these other interactions. Counselors may also use this type of information to think strategically about the influences they will need to overcome to provide ethical service in the situation. Beyond the immediate situation, counselors should control their exposure to contexts that consistently reinforce values that run counter to the dictates of good ethical practices. For example, rehabilitation counselors working in private practices where their employers consistently pressure them to favor the attorneys that hire them in their forensic evaluations run the risk of eventually succumbing to these pressures.

Component 3 is the final aspect of Stage III, in which the counselor selects the preferred course of action or the behavior that they plan to undertake.

This decision may be a reaffirmation of the intention to take the ethical course of action, as determined at the conclusion of Stage II, but augmented to deal with some contextual barriers discovered in Stage III. However, it may be some other course of action that may even not be ethical, or a modified version of the ethical course of action selected in Stage II. Whatever the choice, the counselor has selected it after this more extensive reflection on his or her own competing values and personal blind spots, as well as the contextual influences in the situation in question.

Stage IV: Planning and Executing the Selected Course of Action
Rest (1984) described the essential tasks of this stage as planning to implement
and executing what one plans to do. This operation includes *Component 1*, in
which the counselor figures out a reasonable sequence of concrete actions to be
taken. In *Component 2*, the task is to anticipate and work out all personal and
contextual barriers to effectively executing the plan. Preparing countermeasures
for barriers that may arise is useful. Here, the earlier attention to other stakeholders and their concerns may suggest problems or allies to the process. In addition, earlier consideration of the contextual influences in Stage III assists the
counselor in this type of strategic planning. *Component 3* is the final step of this
model, in that it provides for the execution, documentation, and evaluation of
the course of action as planned. Rest noted that the actual behavioral execution
of ethics is often not a simple task, frequently drawing heavily on the personal,
emotional qualities and professional and interpersonal skills of the counselor.
He mentions such qualities as firmness of resolve, ego strength, and social assertiveness. To this list could be added countless skills, such as persistence, tact,
time management, assertiveness skills, team collaboration, and conflict-resolution
skills. Considerations are limited only by the characteristics and requirements
of the counselor and specific situation involved. Clear and thorough documentation of the entire plan and the rationale behind it, and ethical decision-making
steps taken in responding to the ethical dilemma as the process unfolds are critical to protect the interests of both counselor and client. The information gained
in this documentation process will prove critical to assisting in evaluating the
effectiveness of the entire ethical decision-making process.

Practicing the Tarvydas Integrative Model

Just like the basic counseling microskills, the skills of ethical decision making as
described do not come automatically, or even easily, after merely reading about
the concepts in a book. Practice in solving mock ethical dilemmas—working to address actual ethical dilemmas under the supervision of an ethically knowledgeable
instructor, clinical supervisor, master counselor, or mentor—and incorporating ethical analysis into clinical training process are all essential to gradual progression in
gaining practical skills and sensitive, accurate ethical knowledge. A complex ethical scenario, with a full ethical analysis using the Tarvydas integrative model and
all its stages and components, is presented in Table 16.2 to begin an exploration of
how to use this rich approach to ethical decision making.

The following analysis does not represent the one and only correct answer
to this dilemma. Sometimes, information discovered, or concerns raised by other
reasonable people, can lead to important shifts in the elements of a case. Also, because reasonable professionals can judge and weigh even the same ideas or risks
differently, there may be other valid conclusions to the same case. This process is
not so much about getting the hidden, correct answer, but rather is about going
through the process of decision making thoroughly and carefully, and exercising

due care and good, reasonable professional judgment throughout. If this is done, in the end, the counselor is more likely to have arrived at an explicable judgment that minimizes risk to the client, the counselor, and others. The counselor will also benefit from increased confidence and peace of mind, assured that he or she has done the best in the situation, having used a thorough, thoughtful approach to solving a dilemma that may not have a solution that is satisfying to the parties involved.

CASE STUDY 16.1

Case Study Illustration of the Tarvydas Integrative Model for Ethical Behavior

Narrative of Case Example

John is a 43-year-old man who is meeting with a counselor at the Department of Correctional Services (DCS). He has recently been released from prison on parole, and is meeting with a counselor voluntarily to deal with some issues of depression. He is currently on medication for depression, and has made previous suicide attempts. He was married to a woman for 9 years, and they had two children together, now 7 and 5 years old. She also had two children from a previous relationship, now 12 and 8 years old, which John also considers to be his children. He and his wife are recently divorced. At first, she would not allow the children to visit their dad, but just recently John says they have been talking again, and his ex-wife has started to trust him again and let the children visit whenever they wanted. Just recently, his youngest girl confided in him that their mom and her new friends are still using drugs, and are also selling them from the house. She had found a syringe at the home, which her mom had thought was hidden. John is very adamant that he does not want to contact the Department of Human Services (DHS) or any other similar agency about this. He had contacted DHS for a similar situation a few years ago, and had a bad experience. DHS had "done nothing," and his ex-wife had found out that he had made the report. She did not let him see the kids for a long time after the incident. He feels that, at this point, he can do the most good by keeping a close relationship with his children and a civil relationship with his ex-wife. He is living a clean and drug-free life, and feels that he is his ex-wife's best hope right now to straighten out. He says that, if a report is made, the only thing he is sure of is that his ex-wife would not let him see the children, and he does not know if he could live without being part of his children's life. In this case, the client has his reasons for not wanting to contact DHS, and client autonomy needs to be respected. The client also raises the issue that maybe contacting the authorities really is not in the best interest of the children. He also made some statements regarding not being able to live without being a part of his children's lives, which need to be taken seriously, given the client's suicidal history and current state of depression. On the other hand, young children are involved in a dangerous situation. There is no report of physical or sexual abuse occurring, yet drug use in the home and young children coming across needles is dangerous and could be considered abuse. At this point, the counselor feels there may be a potential dilemma that needs to be explored further.

Stage I: Interpreting the Situation Through Awareness and Fact Finding

The primary task of the counselor in Stage I is to be sensitive and aware of the needs and welfare of the people around them, and of the ethical implications of these situations. This level of awareness allows counselors to imagine and to investigate the effects of the situation on the parties involved and the possible effects of various actions and conditions. This research and awareness must also include emotional as well as cognitive and fact-based considerations.

Component 1: Sensitivity and Awareness

At this point, the counselor talks to John and gets his impression of who will be affected by this situation, and how they will be affected. John clearly cares about his children, but firmly believes that the best chance they have is if he continues to be a part of their lives. He has no guarantee what would happen if he did contact DHS, and he does not want to take that risk. Given what happened the last time he called, John is very distrustful of the system. He also expressed some concerns for his ex-wife and, even though they parted on unfriendly terms, he still seems to care about her and wants what is best for her also. He says that they are just starting to talk again, and he feels that he may be the only one who truly understands what she is going through with the drugs and might be able to help her kick the habit. Although he admits that he worries what kind of environment his children are living in, John feels that this is the best chance they have.

The counselor also notes that there are four children in the house of varying ages. An 18-year-old might understand how dangerous finding a needle in the house really is, but a 5-year-old most likely would not. Even aside from needles being in the house, there is also the potential for danger with what kind of people are around the children. If their mother is dealing drugs from the home, many of those she sells to are probably in the house also, and around the children.

The client says he understands all of this, but still feels that he is making progress with his ex-wife, and that he is the best chance for his children. John acknowledges that he is taking on a lot of responsibility, but says that he would do anything for his children and truly believes that he is doing the best for them in the long run.

Component 2: Major Stakeholders and Their Ethical Claims

The counselor identifies the parties who will be affected and what their exact relationship is—ethically and legally—to the person at the center of the issue. There are often others to whom the counselor has lesser, but important, levels of duty, such as parents, intimate partners, spouse, children, employer, friends, neighbors, guardian, or persons with power of attorney. List below all important parties with an ethical or legal claim in the situation.

Parties	Ethical Claim
The client John	He does not want to contact any authorities.
The children	They may be in danger, may not know all of their options or how they could get help.
DCS	They are responsible for their counselors, and could be held liable for mistakes made by their employees.
The counselor	They may be held liable for any harm that befalls the children or the client.
The ex-wife	She could face an abuse investigation and the subsequent consequences.
Grandparents	If DHS did find abuse, they would most likely get custody of the children.

Component 3: Fact-Finding Process

The counselor undertakes an extensive fact-finding investigation, of a scope appropriate to the situation, by reviewing and understanding current information and seeking out new information. This investigation involves gathering information appropriately available to the counselor, either through professional records and channels (with appropriately obtained releases of information) or through part of public domain information. Sources might include further discussion with the client, contacts with family (with client's permission), current and old client records in one's own or another agency, expert consultation and reports, legal resources, or agency policy and procedures. List below all facts or factual questions the counselor should reasonably be able to research or answer.

A call was made anonymously to DHS to find out if the situation in general fell under the guidelines for mandatory reporters, which it did not. DHS stated that it did not fall under mandatory guidelines because it was third-party information.

The counselor talked to the supervisor and found out that they have an unwritten rule or policy at DCS. This policy is to convince the client to call authorities and report the situation.

John stated that, if DHS was contacted, an investigation was conducted, and action was taken to remove the children from their mother—her parents would probably receive custody. The client stated that he has a good relationship with her parents. He thought that they would allow him to see the children if they did get custody of the children.

The counselor was informed by a supervisor that one reason DHS may not have done anything the last time John reported was that there may have been some type of drug investigation going on. If there is a current investigation into drug trafficking or selling, they can postpone going into the house for a child abuse charge, because the house is under supervision as part of a larger investigation.

Stage II: Formulating an Ethical Decision

The counselor's task in this stage is to identify which of the possible ethical courses of action appears to come closest to the ethical ideal in the situation under consideration.

Component 1: Review Problem or Dilemma

Review the problem or dilemma to be sure that it is clearly understood in relation to any new information.

Because this situation does not fall into the category of mandatory reporting, the counselor is not legally bound to break the client's confidence. However, we now know that the unwritten policy of the institution (DCS) is to try to convince or coerce the client to call DHS on his own. Thus, the counselor must decide whether to respect the client's wishes not to call DHS or to try to coerce the client to call, in accordance with the institution's unwritten policy.

Component 2: Determine Ethical Codes, Laws, Principles, and Institutional Policies and Procedures

The counselor must determine and research the standards of law (in any and all applicable local jurisdictions) and professional practices applicable to the situation. The latter material includes ethical codes and related standards of care, laws, ethical principles, and institutional policies and procedures. List these below.

Ethical Codes

List any rules or canons from applicable ethics code(s) and provide a summary of the dictate. For counselors, the ACA Code of Ethics and any applicable specialty standards such as the CRCC Code of Professional Ethics for Rehabilitation Counselors are recommended. If the counselor is licensed or holds national certification, the codes of ethics that apply to that credential also must be consulted.

ACA Code of Ethics

Section A. Introduction. Counselors encourage client growth and development in ways that foster the client's interest and welfare—counselors avoid fostering dependent counseling relationships.
Section A.1.a Primary Responsibility. The primary responsibility of counselors is to respect the dignity and promote the welfare of the clients.

Section B.2.a Danger and Legal Requirements. The general requirement that counselors keep information confidential does not apply when disclosure is required to protect clients or identified others from serious and foreseeable harm or when legal requirements demand that confidential information must be revealed. Counselors consult with other professionals when in doubt as to the validity of an exception.

Section D.1.h Negative Conditions. Counselors alert their employers of inappropriate policies and practices. They attempt to effect changes in such policies or procedures through constructive action within the organization. When such policies are potentially disruptive or damaging to clients or may limit the effectiveness of services provided and change cannot be affected, counselors take appropriate further action.

Section D.1.g Employer Policies. The acceptance of employment in an agency or institution implies that counselors are in agreement with its general policies and principles. Counselors strive to reach agreement with employers as to acceptable standards of conduct that allow for changes in institutional policy conducive to the growth and development of clients.

Laws/Legal Considerations

List any laws or legal considerations that may apply. Research those relevant to your own jurisdiction. The example is provided, based upon Iowa law, circa 2009. This example is not to be considered a legal opinion, only an example. For further information, consult legal counsel and resources in your own area.

Iowa Code

Section 232.69 Mandatory and permissive reporter–straining required. [A counselor is considered to be a mandatory reporter] ". . . who, in the scope of professional practice or in their employment responsibilities, examines, counsels, or treats a child and reasonably believes a child has suffered abuse".

Section 232.68 [Included in the definitions of child abuse] An illegal drug is present in a child's body as a direct and foreseeable consequence of the acts or omissions of the person responsible for the care of the child.

Ethical Principles

List all ethical principles that describe relevant obligations. Describe the courses of action, the principles upheld, the principles compromised, and the obligations. Sometimes this process is referred to as *principle analysis,* a process wherein ethical principles are specified and subjected to balancing considerations.

Each of the two courses of action can be supported by one or more ethical principles. Contacting authorities could fall under the category of beneficence on the part of the children. Keeping John's confidence could fall under the category of autonomy for honoring the right to individual decisions. There is also the possibility that both scenarios could fit into the category of nonmaleficence. Not telling anyone could lead to harm for the children, in some way. Also, by telling, it is possible that John's fears could materialize and the ex-wife could keep the children away from him. In this way, it may be harmful to the client and also for the children if they are not allowed to see their father.

The ethical principles supporting the other course of action will be compromised. If the authorities are told, the counselor is not respecting the client's autonomy. If authorities are not told, the counselor may be compromising the principles of nonmaleficence toward the children and the concept of beneficence, in the same way.

This situation is an ethical dilemma, not just an ethical issue. An ethical issue has a fairly identifiable course of action that is appropriate, even if taking that action is not necessarily easy in practice (i.e., as in the case of involuntarily committing a seriously suicidal individual).

Action A. Pressuring the Client

Principles Upheld	*Principles Compromised*
Beneficence (to children)	Beneficence (to client)
	Nonmaleficence (to client)
	Autonomy (of client)
	Fidelity (to client)
	Veracity (to client)

Resultant Obligations: Work with client?*

Action B. Not Pressuring the Client

Principles Upheld	*Principles Compromised*
Beneficence (to client)	Beneficence (to children)
Nonmaleficence (to client)	Nonmaleficence (to children)
	Autonomy (of client)
	Fidelity (to client)
	Veracity (to client)

Resultant Obligations: Work with client?*

*Note: In principle analysis, the principle obligations owed to the client normally outweigh those to others. Therefore, frequently they are the only ones considered; if obligations to others are considered, those owed to the client generally supersede them, because the counselor incurs these primary obligations by virtue of entering into a professional relationship with the client. The exception to this case would involve obligations to vulnerable others (e.g., small children), and/or those situations in which there a high degree of serious danger or risk. This reasoning is why this case is a particularly troublesome dilemma.

Institutional/Agency Rules or Policies

List any institutional/agency rules or policies that may apply.

In the experience of the counselor, the unwritten policy of DCS is to try to coerce the client into reporting the possible child abuse to DHS.

Component 3: Courses of Action

List all possible and probable courses of action. If you can boil this selection down to two opposing options, this strategy is recommended.

Action A: Attempt to coerce the client into reporting.
Action B: Do not try to coerce the client into reporting.

Component 4: Positive and Negative Consequences

Consider potential positive and negative consequences for each course of action, in light of the risks.

Action A: Pressure the Client

Positive Consequences	*Negative Consequences*
May protect the children from abuse	Does not respect client's autonomy or confidentiality
Follows unwritten DCS policy	
Hurts client's trust of counselor	Ex-wife may cut off child visitation
DCS would not step in to coerce the client	Negative relationship with ex-wife
Less time for other pressing issues of client	May evoke suicidal thoughts
Protects DCS from liability	

Action B: Do Not Pressure Client

Positive Consequences	*Negative Consequences*
Respects client's autonomy and confidentiality	Does not protect children from possible abuse
Time for other client issues	Counselor is defying employer (DCS)
Does not evoke suicidal thoughts	
Child visitation is preserved	DCS might step in and coerce client anyway
Positive relationship with ex-wife	DCS might be liable (if child is harmed)

Component 5: Consult With Others
Consult with supervisors and other knowledgeable professionals. Review the reasoning employed so far in working through the ethical dilemma in consulting with others.

Individual	*Type of Consultation*
1. ACA Ethics Committee	Review situation, obtain suggestions and opinion.
2. Counselors from other corrections	
3. Other colleagues	
4. DHS anonymously again	
5. Attorney	

Component 6: Determine Best Ethical Action
Select the best ethical course of action.

The best ethical course of action would be not to pressure the client to report to DHS, for the following reasons:

1. More ethical principles support this course of action, especially for client.
2. More positive than negative consequences are likely to result.
3. The Iowa Code does not consider this a situation of mandatory child abuse reporting, because the counselor is not working directly with the children, and the only information is "hearsay."

Stage III: Selecting an Action by Weighing Competing, Nonmoral Values, Personal Blind Spots, or Prejudices
The counselor, in this stage, must realize the many additional forces that may affect the counselor and tempt the counselor to not actually execute the selected ethical course of action.

Component 1: Competing Values or Concerns
The counselor engages in a period of reflection and active processing of personal competing values (e.g., need to be liked by coworkers or the supervisor, or a desire to be seen as a team player, so as to be promoted by the supervisor), personal blind spots, or prejudices that may influence whether or not they will discharge their ethical obligations. These value orientations may either come into conflict with the course of action necessary to proceed ethically or enhance the tendency to select ethical professional behavior.

Conflicting Concern	Potential Effects
1. Fear of a negative evaluation by DCS, if unwritten policy is not followed	Loss of job, license, respect Financial consequences
2. Feel the need to protect the children at all costs, no matter what the situation	Loss of reputation and seen as a confidential risk
3. Fear of legal repercussions if abuse situation is not reported to DHS	Children are harmed Loss of license of job
4. Fear of harm to DCS	Personal mental health Financial impact on agency/self
5. Fear of losing respect of colleagues	Personal mental health Future relationships
6. Feeling that client should not be pressured and have autonomy in the decision	Harm to children Increased client confidence
7. Feeling that counseling session should be used to work on the client's problems (e.g., depression), rather than using all of the time trying to convince client to call DHS	DHS not contacted and children are harmed Client benefits from counseling

Component 2: Contextual Influences

The counselor systematically inventories the contextual influences on their choices at the collegial, team, institutional, and societal levels. These influences might be either dysfunctional or constructive for selecting the ethical course over other types of values.

Level 1: Clinical (Counselor–Client)
1. Counselor's professors/supervisors have recommended advocating for clients' autonomy in the past.

Level 2: Team
1. A few coworkers note that DHS said that the counselor is not required to report the situation to DHS, because it is third-party information.

Level 3: Institutional/Agency
1. DCS has an unwritten policy of convincing clients to report abuse on their own.
2. Counselor's supervisor and most colleagues support the institution's policy and feel that all counselors at DCS should adhere to both written and unwritten policies.

Level 4: Social Policy/General Cultural
1. Society values children and children's welfare.
2. Society has little tolerance for drug abuse or the selling of drugs, especially when children are involved.
3. There is a fear of transmitted diseases in society, especially HIV and AIDS, which can be passed through intravenous drug use.
4. Society has a prejudiced attitude toward ex-cons on parole, and makes little distinction between those who are successfully recovering and those who are not.

Component 3: Select Preferred Action
The counselor selects the preferred course of action.

This course of action is to attempt to convince the client to call DHS anonymously. Yet, he still respects the client's autonomy and will not coerce John to report the situation to DHS.

Stage IV: Planning and Executing the Selected Course of Action
The counselor in this stage plans to implement and execute the selected course of action.

Component 1: Possible Sequences of Actions
The counselor figures out a reasonable, practical sequence of concrete actions to be taken. List the action steps to be taken.

1. Talk with client about the consequences of his reporting versus not reporting the situation (anonymously, at least) to DHS.
2. Attempt to convince the client to call DHS anonymously for information about what would happen if the situation were reported.
3. If the client does not call, do not continue to convince him any further.
4. If the client does call and receives the information, give support for what he decides to do next.

Component 2: Contextual Barriers and Countermeasures
The counselor will need to anticipate and work out all personal and contextual barriers to effectively execute the plan. It is useful to prepare countermeasures for any contextual barriers that may arise.

Possible Barriers	*Possible Countermeasures*
1. Client does not wish to call.	Document the attempts to get him to call and not press the issue any further.
2. Supervisor may want the counselor to continue to coerce the client to call.	Counselor could let the supervisor know what he or she is not comfortable doing and apprise someone in authority above the supervisor of the situation.
3. DCS may assign the case to someone else.	No countermeasure, unless client insists upon seeing the current counselor.
4. John's ex-wife may refuse to let him see the children, if he reports the situation to DHS.	Counselor could encourage the client to speak with an attorney about his rights with the children.

Component 3: Carry Out, Document, and Evaluate

This step provides for the execution, documentation, and evaluation of the course of action as planned. Describe here the planned goal(s) and potential types of measurements of plan effectiveness and sources of information.

The counselor would carry out the plan by talking to the client about the consequences of reporting versus not reporting the abusive situation to DHS and attempt to get the client to call for information. If the client decides to call, the counselor would support his next step. The counselor would document the ethical decision-making steps taken. Finally, the counselor would evaluate the effectiveness of the plan of action and the entire ethical decision-making process.

Goal	*Measure*
1. Review consequences of reporting or not reporting and attempt to get the client to call DHS for information.	Weigh benefits and costs of client's decision; assess client's level of comfort with either decision.
2. Support client if he decides to call.	Assess what client needs from counselor.
3. Prevent harm to children and help mother.	Follow up with treatment referrals for mother and on the children's welfare.

This case study was developed by Vilia Tarvydas, PhD, LMHC, CRC, and uses the Tarvydas Integrative Decision-Making Model for Ethical Behavior.

SUMMARY

Rehabilitation counseling continues to grow in stature and visibility, as a specialty practice within the counseling profession. As a result, contemporary rehabilitation counselors should anticipate the need to demonstrate high levels of competency in the ethical aspects of their practices. The professional practice as a whole has provided substantial tools to inform this process, including the revised 2010 ethical standards of practice (Appendix C of this book), mechanisms to educate and govern the practice of these ethical standards, and knowledge and wisdom for individual counselors, embodied within models of ethical decision making and behavior. With responsible utilization of these sizable assets for ethical practice, rehabilitation counseling should continue its leadership in the counseling professionalization movement.

CONTENT REVIEW QUESTIONS

- What are the three components of professional standards? Provide examples of each, and describe how they contribute to the quality of care in the profession.
- What are the major levels of ethics governance and what role does each play in the enforcement of ethical standards? What bodies represent counseling and rehabilitation counseling at each level?
- What is the difference between mandatory and aspirational ethics? Provide an illustration of a set of ethical standards that represents each type of ethical standard and discuss why, as well as how they serve complementary roles.
- What themes or attitudes must one consider when using the Tarvydas Integrative Decision-Making Model? Why do you think these are important in the process?
- What are the major stages of the Tarvydas Integrative Decision-Making Model? What main processes and goals are characteristic of each one?

REFERENCES

American Psychological Association. (2009). *Revised guidelines for child custody evaluations in family law proceedings.* Washington, DC: Author.

Betan, E. J., & Stanton, A. L. (1999). Fostering ethical willingness: Integrating emotional and contextual awareness with rational analysis. *Professional Psychology: Research and Practice, 30,* 295–301.

Butterfield, K., Trevino, L., & Weaver, G. (2000). Moral awareness in business organizations: Influences of issue-related and social context factors. *Human Relations, 53,* 981–1018.

Commission on Rehabilitation Counselor Certification. (2010). *The CRCC desk reference on professional ethics: A guide for rehabilitation counselors.* Athens, GA: Elliott & Fitzpatrick.

Corey, G., Corey, M. S., & Callanan, P. (2010). *Issues and ethics in the helping professions* (8th ed.). Pacific Grove, CA: Brooks/Cole.

Cottone, R.R. (in press). Ethical decision making in mental health contexts: Representative-models and an organizational framework. In S. Knapp (Ed.), *The handbook on ethics in psychology*. Washington, DC: American Psychological Association.

Cottone, R. R., & Claus, R. E. (2000). Ethical decision making models: A review of the literature. *Journal of Counseling and Development, 78,* 275–283.

Cottone, R. R., & Tarvydas, V. M. (2007). *Counseling ethics and decision making* (3rd ed.). Upper Saddle River, NJ: Merrill/Prentice-Hall.

Cottone, R. R., Tarvydas, V., & House, G. (1994). The effect of number and type of consulted relationships on the ethical decision making of graduate students in counseling. *Counseling and Values, 39,* 56–68.

Francouer, R. T. (1983). Teaching decision making in biomedical ethics for the allied health-student. *Journal of Allied Health, 12,* 202–209.

Garcia, J., Cartwright, B., Winston, S. M., & Borzuchowska, B. (2003). A transcultural integrative ethical decision-making model in counseling. *Journal of Counseling and Development, 81,* 268–277.

Gatens-Robinson, E., & Rubin, S. E. (1995). Societal values and ethical commitments that influence rehabilitation service delivery behavior. In S. E. Rubin & R. T. Roessler (Eds.), *Foundations of the vocational rehabilitation process* (pp. 157–174). Austin, TX: Pro-Ed.

Kitchener, K. S. (1984). Intuition, critical evaluation and ethical principles: The foundation for ethical decisions in counseling psychology. *The Counseling Psychologist, 12*(3), 43–55.

Koocher, G. P., & Keith-Spiegel, P. (2007). *Ethics in psychology and the mental health professions: Standards and cases* (2nd ed.). New York, NY: Oxford University Press.

Mabe, A. R., & Rollin, S. A. (1986). The role of a code of ethical standards in counseling. *Journal of Counseling and Development, 64,* 294–297.

Meara, N. M., Schmidt, L. D., & Day, J. D. (1996). Principles and virtue: A foundation for ethical decisions, policies, and character. *The Counseling Psychologist, 24*(1), 4–77.

Powell, S. K., & Wekell, P. M. (1996). *Nursing case management.* Philadelphia, PA: Lippincott.

Rest, J. R. (1984). Research on moral development: Implications for training psychologists. *The Counseling Psychologist, 12*(3), 19–29.

Rinas, J., & Clyne-Jackson, S. (1988). *Professional conduct and legal concerns in mental health practice.* Norwalk, CT: Appleton & Lange.

Tarvydas, V. M., & Cottone, R. R. (1991). Ethical responses to legislative, organizational and economic dynamics: A four level model of ethical practice. *Journal of Applied Rehabilitation Counseling, 22*(4), 11–18.

Tarvydas, V. M., & Cottone, R. R. (2000). The code of ethics for rehabilitation counselors: What we have and what we need. *Rehabilitation Counseling Bulletin, 43,* 188–196.

Tarvydas, V. M., O'Rourke, B. J., & Urish C. (2007). Ethical climate. In R. R. Cottone & V. M. Tarvydas (Eds.), *Counseling ethics and decision making* (3rd ed., pp. 116–137). Upper Saddle River, NJ: Merrill/Prentice-Hall.

Thompson, A. (1990). *Guide to ethical practice in psychotherapy.* New York, NY: John Wiley & Sons.

VanHoose, W. H., & Kottler, J. A. (1985). *Ethical and legal issues in counseling and psychotherapy.* San Francisco, CA: Jossey-Bass.

Vasquez, M. J. T. (1996). Will virtue ethics improve ethical conduct in multicultural settings and interactions? *The Counseling Psychologist, 24*(1), 98–104.

Wright, B. A. (1983). *Physical disability—A psychosocial approach.* New York, NY: Harper & Row.

17

Cultural Competence

Brenda Y. Cartwright, Debra A. Harley, and Jennifer L. Burris

---

LEARNING OBJECTIVES

After reading this chapter, you should be able to:

- Understand how the interaction of multiple factors in the RESPECTFUL counseling model might be manifested among clients with whom they work.
- Recognize the need to continually assess the ways in which these multiple factors may impact rehabilitation practitioners' own development and ways of approaching clients from diverse groups and backgrounds.
- Address individual and group identity development when developing cultural assessments.

Concerns regarding the status of individuals with disabilities from traditionally underserved populations (i.e., African Americans, Asian Americans/Pacific Islanders, Latino/Latina Americans, and Native Americans/Native Alaskans) have provided the impetus and need for cultural competency on several levels in the field of rehabilitation. On one level, federal legislation (i.e., Section 21 of the U.S. Rehabilitation Act Amendments) mandated that rehabilitation counseling professionals in the state-federal system must develop and maintain culturally competent services to individuals with disabilities from these groups. On a second level, professional organization goals have included equity and fairness in the delivery of rehabilitation services for culturally diverse populations. For example, in its mission statement the National Association of Multicultural Rehabilitation Concerns (NAMRC) and its forerunner, the National Association of Non-White Workers (NANRW) advocate for quality and equitable services to individuals with disabilities from culturally diverse populations. On a third level, justice on ethical grounds has also propelled cultural competency (Whaley & Davis, 2007). In fact, the Commission on Rehabilitation Counselor Certification (CRCC) 2010 Code of Professional Ethics for Rehabilitation Counselors articulated specific guidelines outlining ethical responsibilities for recognizing the special needs of diverse client populations. On a final level, the call for cultural competence has been formalized in program accreditation standards. The Council on Rehabilitation Education (CORE) specifies in its proposed accreditation standards that rehabilitation counseling programs must educate faculty and students to guard the individual rights and personal dignity of all clients, including those from protected groups as a result of antidiscrimination laws (e.g., race, color, religion, age, disability status, gender identity).

Although the field has made progress in understanding the need for cultural competence, the gap between theory, research, and application remain. Evidence suggests that beginning with the Atkins and Wright (1980) seminal study, an ongoing struggle continues among rehabilitation counseling professionals to provide quality and equitable services to individuals from traditionally underrepresented groups, including those from nonwhite populations, as well as persons from specific disability groups, such as Deaf, hard of hearing, and individuals with mental illnesses (Boutin & Wilson, 2009; Bowe, 1984; Gao, Gill, Schmidt, & Pratt, 2010; Hasnain & Balcazar, 2009; Houston, Lammers, & Svorny, 2010; Jacobs, Wissusik, Collier, Stackman, & Burkeman, 1992; Moore, 2001; Patterson, Allen, Parnell, Crawford, & Beardall, 2000; Rimmerman, Botuck, & Levy, 1995; Wilson, 2002). Although rehabilitation counseling professionals are beginning to become more aware of some of the ways in which diverse cultural contexts impact their clients' lives, many of these professionals fail to effectively implement this knowledge in ways that result in maximized employment, economic self-sufficiency, independence, inclusion, and integration.

This chapter is designed to increase rehabilitation counselors' awareness and knowledge of a broad range of diversity issues that need to be addressed when serving persons from culturally diverse groups and backgrounds. First, definitions of cultural competence and cultural responsiveness will be discussed. Second, particular attention will be directed to the multidimensional nature of clients' development as described in the RESPECTFUL model of counseling (D'Andrea & Daniels, 1997, 2001, 2010). Third, because research suggests a relationship between identity development and cultural competence, definitions, key concepts and models associated with personal and group identity development will be described. A case scenario is included at the end of this chapter to demonstrate the usefulness of the RESPECTFUL counseling model to assess the clients' and counselors' multidimensionality, as well as assess the level of identity development.

The most widely used definition of cultural competence involves a constellation of three characteristics: (1) an *awareness* of one's own assumptions about human behavior, values, preconceived notions, limitations and biases, (2) *knowledge* or understanding of the worldviews of clients who are culturally different without imposing negative judgments, pathologizing, blaming, or invalidating others' experiences, and (3) *skills*, or the ability to develop and practice appropriate, relevant, and sensitive intervention strategies in working with culturally different clients (Sue, Arredondo, & McDavis, 1992). It is important to note that cultural competence is not a concept at which one arrives, but more a process that is lifelong and ever evolving.

Cultural responsiveness conveys the give and take as well as the adjustments and reactions to cultural aspects of service delivery. Cultural responsiveness also communicates a state of being open to the process of building mutuality with a client and to accepting that the culture-specific knowledge one has about a group may or may not apply to the person being served (Munoz, 2007).

THE RESPECTFUL COUNSELING MODEL

The RESPECTFUL counseling model specifically focuses on a host of diversity and contextual issues that rehabilitation counselors are encouraged to consider as they strive to work more responsively, ethically, and respectfully with persons from diverse client populations (D'Andrea & Daniels, 1997, 2001, 2010). These researchers recognized that as cultural beings, counselors and the individuals they serve may be members of more than one cultural or identity group, and that some group identities may be more salient than others.

This model addresses the multidimensional nature of human development by directing attention to 10 factors that are known to significantly impact the psychological development of both counselors and their clients. The 10 factors that comprise the RESPECTFUL counseling model include religious/spiritual identity, economic class background, sexual identity, psychological maturity, ethnic/racial identity, chronological/developmental challenges, trauma and other threats to one's well-being, family background and history, unique physical characteristics, and location of residence and language differences. Each of these factors will be briefly described below.

Religious/Spiritual Identity

The first component focuses on the way in which individuals personally identify with established religions or hold beliefs about extraordinary experiences that go beyond the boundaries of the strictly objective, empirically perceived world that characterizes Western, modern, psychological thought. Kelly (1995) noted that the terms *religion* and *spirituality* are both grounded in an affirmation of transcendental experiences that are typically manifested in religious forms that extend beyond the boundaries of the ordinary and tangible. As used in the RESPECTFUL counseling framework, *religion* and *spirituality* generally refer to a person's belief in a reality that transcends physical nature and provides individuals with an "extraordinary" meaning of life in general and human existence in particular.

Although the terms *religion* and *spirituality* include the affirmation of a transcendental dimension of reality, they also hold different meanings as well. As D'Andrea and Daniels (1997) explain:

> While the term spirituality is often used to refer to a person's belief and affirmation of a transcendental connectedness with the universe, religion is typically used to denote the specific ways in which the belief is manifested institutionally within the creeds and dogmas of different religious groups and denominations. As used in the RESPECTFUL counseling model, the term religious/spiritual identity refers to a person's beliefs about the afterlife and the interconnectedness of all things in the universe as well as one's views about the meaning of such concepts as "God," "enlightenment," and "grace" to name a few. (p. 30)

Economic Class Background

To help rehabilitation counselors gain a greater understanding about the different economic classes or groups of which many clients are a part, D'Andrea and Daniels (2001) extended the three general classes (i.e., low, middle, upper) that have been traditionally used by social scientists by describing six socioeconomic classes or categories into which most persons in the United States can be classified. This classification system includes: (1) *poor persons* (e.g., unemployed individuals with less than a high school degree who are in need of economic assistance to meet their basic living needs), (2) *working poor persons* (e.g., individuals who have a high school or equivalency degree and/or some college experience employed as unskilled workers, whose annual incomes fall below the federal poverty guidelines), (3) *working class persons* (e.g., individuals who have a high school degree, some college experience, or have received a certificate or license in a particular trade, whose annual incomes fall above the federal poverty guidelines), (4) *middle class nonprofessionals* (e.g., persons with at least a high school degree, but more likely have an advanced degree or specialized training in a given vocational-career whose annual income is above the national average), (5) *middle class professionals* (e.g., individuals with at least a college degree, but more likely have an advanced degree in some professional field such as education, law, medicine, etc., whose annual income is above the national average), and (6) *persons in the upper class* (e.g., individuals whose annual income falls within the upper 10% of the national average).

Sexual Identity

As used in the RESPECTFUL counseling model, the term sexual identity relates to a person's gender identity, gender roles, and sexual orientation. The term *gender identity* refers to an individual's subjective sense of what it means to be either male or female. A person's gender identity is clearly impacted by the different roles men and women are expected to play within a given cultural-ethnic context. Savin-Williams and Cohen (1996) noted that the type of gender identity that one develops is markedly influenced by "those behaviors, attitudes, and personality traits that a society designates as masculine or feminine, that is, more 'appropriate' for or typical of the male or female role" (p. 72).

A person's sexual identity can be manifested in a broad range of ways that extend beyond the narrow notion of masculinity and femininity. Transsexuals, for example, are described as individuals who are convinced that they were born the wrong biological sex. Thus, the term *transsexualism* refers to those persons who experience discordance between their gender identity and their anatomical sex (Bailey, 1997).

Sexual identity is also influenced by one's sexual preference. There are a number of ways to conceptualize this dimension of a person's sexual identity. Generally speaking, it includes such concepts as *bisexuality*, *heterosexuality*, and *homosexuality*. *Bisexuality* refers to individuals who demonstrate a sexual interest in both males and females. *Heterosexuality*, in contrast, refers to individuals whose sexual interest is directed toward persons of the opposite sex. A third way of viewing this dimension of one's sexual identity involves the concept of *homosexuality*—a term that has been used to identify individuals whose sexual preference involves persons of the same sex. In light of the negative stereotypes that have historically been associated with the term *homosexuality*, words like gay males, gays and lesbians are considered more acceptable and respectful terms to use in describing this dimension of a person's sexual identity.

Psychological Maturity

Rehabilitation counselors often work with clients who share common demographic characteristics (e.g., age, gender, socioeconomic, and cultural-racial backgrounds), but appear to be very different in psychological terms. In these situations one might refer to a client as being "more psychologically mature" than another client who is the same age, identifies with the same cultural-racial reference group, and shares a similar sexual identity. Some descriptors that are commonly used by counseling professionals to describe this "immature" client include statements such as "He demonstrates limited impulse control in social interactions" or "She has a low capacity for self-awareness." Statements that are commonly used to describe "more mature" clients include the following: (1) "He is able to discuss his or her problems with much insight," (2)"She is highly self-aware," and (3) "She has developed a much broader range of interpersonal and introspective skills than many of the other clients with whom I am working."

Over the past three decades, there has been a tremendous increase in understanding the developmental stages that individuals pass through as they mature psychologically. Much of this knowledge comes from the work of a variety of structural-developmental psychologists who have presented numerous models that help explain the process of psychological maturity. This includes the work of Piaget (1977) (cognitive development), Perry (1970) (ethical development),

Kohlberg (1981) and Gilligan (1982) (moral development), Selman (1980) (social/ interpersonal development), and Loevinger (1976) (ego development).

Structural-developmental theories view psychological development as a process in which individuals move from simple to more complex ways of thinking about themselves and their life experiences. This movement can be traced along a set of invariant, hierarchical stages that reflect qualitatively different ways of thinking, feeling, and acting in the world (Sprinthall, Peace, & Kennington, 2001). According to Young-Eisendrath (1988), each developmental stage represents a uniquely different frame of reference for meaning making. She goes on to point out that developmental stages "are not entirely dependent on chronological maturation.... Stages evolve with aging up to a point. However, when further development is not supported by environmental factors, a person may stop developing" (p. 71).

Ethnic/Racial Identity

The term "ethnic" is derived from the Greek word "ethnos" meaning "nation." Thus, the concept of "ethnic identity" refers to persons who identify with and are distinguished from others by the unique social–cultural characteristics, values, and traditions that have evolved within the nation-states in which a person lives or has descended. Although individuals are commonly associated with large cultural-racial groups (e.g., African Americans, European Americans, Native Americans), people commonly demonstrate strong personal identification with specific ethnic groups (e.g., Italian-Americans, Irish-Americans) whose values and traditions have substantially impacted their development and view of the world.

The various privileges, discrimination, and types of oppression that have been and continue to be bestowed among persons who are associated with different racial groups have a profound psychological effect on the way individuals construct meaning of the world and themselves. Over the past 15 years, numerous researchers have helped shed light on some of the ways persons from diverse groups develop a personal sense of identity that integrates reactions to one's racial background and experiences. A more extensive discussion on personal and group identity follows the description of the RESPECTFUL model to describe the different stages/periods and unique psychological characteristics that distinguish persons who operate from the various identity developmental levels.

Chronological/Developmental Challenges

Besides the types of developmental changes that were discussed under section "Psychological Maturity," individuals also undergo systematic changes that are chronologically based. These age-related, developmental changes represent what are referred to as *chronological challenges* that individuals face at different points across the lifespan. Rehabilitation counselors are familiar with many of the challenges representing the characteristics that are normally associated with infancy, childhood, adolescence, and adulthood.

Theorists who explain human development from a chronological perspective are commonly referred to as lifespan development (Craig, 1992; Havighurst, 1953; Shaffer, 1993) or maturational theorists (Erikson, 1968). Unlike the structural developmental theorists who tend to look at a particular aspect of a person's psychological maturity (e.g., intellectual, moral, social development), lifespan development theorists examine a person's growth from a more holistic perspective, which includes taking into account the types of physical, cognitive, and psychological changes that predictably occur at different times in an individual's life (D'Andrea & Daniels, 2001).

The specific changes lifespan researchers have noted individuals normally undergo as they develop from infancy through adulthood include physical growth (e.g., bodily changes and the sequencing of motor skills); the emergence of different cognitive competencies (e.g., the development of perceptual, language, learning, memory, and thinking skills); and the manifestation of a variety of psychological skills (e.g., including the ability to manage one's emotions and the demonstration of more effective interpersonal competencies) that occur over time (Shaffer, 1993). The ways in which individuals successfully negotiate the chronological challenges that are commonly associated with infancy, childhood, adolescence, and adulthood largely determine the degree to which they develop a positive sense of self-esteem, lead productive lives, and experience personal satisfaction in life.

Trauma and Other Threats to One's Well-Being

Trauma and threats to one's well-being are included in the RESPECTFUL counseling and development model to emphasize the complex ways in which stressful situations put people at risk of psychological danger and harm. Such harm typically occurs when the stressors individuals experience in their lives exceed their ability to cope with them in constructive and effective ways. An individual's personal resources (e.g., coping skills, self-esteem, social support, and the personal power derived from his or her cultural group) may be overtaxed when one is subjected to ongoing environmental stressors for extended periods of time. When individuals experience similar stressors for extended periods of time, they are commonly referred to as a *vulnerable* or an *at-risk* group (Lewis, Lewis, Daniels, & D'Andrea, 2003).

Rehabilitation counselors are frequently called upon to work with persons in various vulnerable, at-risk groups (e.g., poor, homeless and unemployed people; adults and children in families undergoing divorce; pregnant teenagers; individuals living with HIV or AIDS; persons diagnosed with cancer; and individuals who are victimized by various forms of ageism, racism, sexism, and cultural oppression). Although persons in these vulnerable populations greatly differ from one another, they all routinely experience high levels of environmental stress that tax their personal resources and coping abilities. Heightened, prolonged, and historical stressors often result in more severe and adverse psychological outcomes for many persons from oppressed cultural-ethnic-racial groups in contemporary society. These stressors can and do result in traumatic life experiences that underlie many of the intergenerational problems that are manifested among many persons from diverse and vulnerable groups in this nation (Salzman, 2001).

Family Background and History

The rapid cultural diversification of the United States includes an increasing number of families that are very different from the traditional notion of "family" that many rehabilitation counselors have historically used as a standard for determining "normal family life" and "healthy family functioning." The different types of families (e.g., single-female headed families, blended families, extended families, families headed by gay and lesbian parents) that counselors increasingly encounter in their work challenge them to reassess the traditional concept of the nuclear family that was used as a standard to which all types of other families were compared.

Unique Physical Characteristics

The RESPECTFUL counseling framework emphasizes the importance of being sensitive to the ways in which society's idealized images of physical beauty negatively impact the psychological development of many persons, whose physical nature does not fit the narrow views of beauty that are fostered by modern culture. McWhirter (1994) noted that "one of the most disheartening and frightening phenomena in our society is the relentless and all-consuming desire for physical beauty" (p. 203). This obsession is rooted in an idealistic image of persons who are thin and muscular. In reality, few persons match up to this idealistic image and many experience a sense of reduced self-esteem and increased feelings of personal inadequacy as a result of not living up to this socially constructed view of a *beautiful person* (McWhirter). In other instances, persons who possess certain unique physical characteristics that have traditionally been referred to as "physical, mental, and emotional disabilities" have also suffered from various forms of discrimination and stigmatization whose genesis is rooted in misperceptions and stereotypes about physical beauty and health.

Location of Residence and Language Differences

The location of one's residence refers to the geographical region and setting where one resides. Five areas that many persons commonly refer to when talking about the major regions in the United States include the Northeast, Southeast, Midwest, Southwest, and Northwest. These geographical areas are distinguished by the types of persons who reside in these areas, as well as differences in terms of climate patterns, geological terrain, and to some degree the types of occupations and industries that are available to workers who reside in these areas. These geographical locations are also often characterized by their own unique "subcultures" that reflect the types of values, attitudes, and language/dialects that are commonly manifested by many of the individuals who reside in these areas.

The location of one's residence also includes the type of setting in which a person resides. Rehabilitation counselors are most likely familiar with three major types of residential settings in which clients live. This includes rural, suburban, and urban settings. As defined by the U.S. Bureau of the Census (2000), rural populations consist of people who live in places or towns of less than 2,500 inhabitants and in open country outside the closely settled suburbs of metropolitan cities. In contrast, urban areas consist of cities with 50,000 or more inhabitants (U.S. Bureau of the Census).

PERSONAL AND GROUP IDENTITY

Personal and cultural identity has internal and external qualities. Erickson (1968) described such an identity to involve a coherent sense of the internal self, in development over time, in relationship to others, and a sense that others have a consistent sense of who and what they are. This coherency is a function of individuals' biological capabilities, their interactions with the contexts that facilitate and constrain their development, and their interpretation of their experience. In other words, "identity is the acquisition of cognitive coherence and stability, which includes affective and cognitive components of self in relationship to the context in which one is living" (Coleman, Norton, Miranda, & McCubbin, 2003, p. 41). Coleman et al. suggest that cultural identity involves one's sense of self in relationship to his or her ecological system (i.e., microsystems, mesosystem, exosystem, macrosystem). Moreover, the more complex the macrosystem in which a person develops, the more complex the person's sense of cultural self and the greater challenge the person will have in achieving that sense.

People develop their sense of belonging and their place in the world based on multiple identities. Perhaps the identity with the most overwhelming presence is that of ethnicity and/or race. Ethnic and racial identity development is a complex process consisting of multiple dimensions. Ethnicity refers to an individual's sense of belonging to an ethnic group and the part of a person's thinking, perceptions, feelings, and behavior that is a function of that ethnic group's membership. Ethnic identity can involve such notions as positive attitudes about one's ethnic group and a sense of belonging to it, voluntary and frequent association with other ethnic group members, and ethnic practices (e.g., food, music, language, ethnic festivities) (Johnson, 2004). Ethnic identity is a fundamental aspect of acculturation, which has a reciprocal relationship focusing on the self and includes a sense of connection to an ethnic group (Maldonado, Kushner, Barr, & Korz, 2009; Phinney, 1990, 2003; Shin & Munoz, 2009).

Racial identity describes the stages of identity formation related to racial characteristics and examines the degree to which people affiliate or disassociate with others from their racial heritage (Helms & Cook, 1999). An individual's racial identity is a composite of psychological aspects (i.e., sense of belongingness and commitment), cultural awareness, knowledge, and acceptance of cultural and social traditions, physical aspects (i.e., acceptance of physical features of the racial group), and sociopolitical aspects (i.e., attitudes toward social and economic issues of the racial group) of being a member of one's racial group along with the value and emotional significance associated with that membership (Alston, Bell, & Feist-Price, 1996).

Both ethnic and racial identities are defined by cultural influences. Culture refers to all the knowledge and values shared by a society (e.g., language, familial roles, communication patterns). Cultural influences include the way an individual views self and identity through socialization, enculturation (i.e., deliberate cultural learning), and acculturation, and through characteristics (i.e., sense of "peoplehood," culture, ethnocentrism, territoriality) of an ethnic group (Phinney, 2003). The strength of racial/ethnic identity is influenced by four factors: size, power, discrimination, and appearance.

Another aspect of identity development is that of multiracial identity. It is acknowledged that the United States has experienced an increased number of multiracial individuals and a growing multiracial identity movement (Jones & Smith, 2001). Multiracial individuals may change the way they self-identify racially throughout their lives, or how they verbally identify their race or ethnicity in different situations. Although people who are multiracial in the United States are not new, those who identify themselves as belonging to two or more races is increasing. High profile multiracial individuals such as President Barack Obama, golfer Tiger Woods, actors Keanu Reeves and Vin Diesel, and actress Halle Berry have bought increased attention to multiracial identity. Many individuals in the United States are of mixed heritage; however, the miscegenation laws deemed interracial marriage (most notably between Blacks and Whites) illegal. Until 1989, biracial children with White parents were assigned the racial status of the non-White parent, which barred their entrance into the White race and did not necessarily ensure them welcome acceptance within the other racial/ethnic group (Thompson, 2006). Multiracial identity in America today has raised the question of whether being multiracial is an identity all its own or a balance of "old divides" (NPR, 2007).

The concept of acculturation applies to both immigrants (i.e., those who have chosen to enter a new society) and to nonimmigrant ethnic groups (i.e., those who have been involuntarily subjected to the dominance of a majority group). Acculturation refers to "absorption of the 'host' society's cultural norms, beliefs, attitudes, and behavior patterns by immigrants, or by other groups historically excluded from the larger society" (Johnson, 2004, p. 1280). Acculturation occurs at group, individual, and multigenerational levels. Group-level acculturation refers to changes resulting from interaction between two autonomous and independent cultural groups. On an individual level, acculturation refers to the changes an individual experiences as a result of interacting with other cultures, and as a result of participating in the process of acculturation as a member of ethnic group who is undergoing the process. Multigenerational acculturation refers to the role of culture within a family or subsystem.

Identity development is a series of stages everyone must go through to determine who he or she is as an individual. In addition, identity development affects how individuals perceive themselves and feel emotionally. As for ethnic identity, those who have explored options and made commitments to their ethnic group exhibit fewer symptoms of depression and higher self-esteem (Wilcots, 2000).

Identity Development Models

Numerous models have been integrated into counseling to describe identity development models (e.g., Nigrescence model of Black identity development, Asian American Identity Models, Latino/Hispanic American Identity Development Models). Atkinson, Morten, and Sue (1989) proposed the Racial/Cultural Identity Development Model (R/CID), formerly known as the Minority Identity Development Model (MID). The R/CID Model seeks to identify common features that are found in minority populations and consists of five stages: conformity, dissonance, resistance and immersion, introspection, and integrative awareness. With this model, Atkinson et al. proposed that an understanding of cultural identity development should sensitize counselors to the role that oppression plays in a minority individual's development. This model will assist counselors to: (1) recognize intracultural differences with respect to their cultural identity, (2) serve as an assessment and diagnostic tool for counselors to gain a better understanding of culturally diverse clients, and (3) recognize the changing and developmental nature of cultural identity among clients. The five stages of the R/CID Model are presented below (Atkinson et al., 1989; Lee, Blando, Mizelle, & Orozco, 2007).

Conformity Stage
In the conformity stage, an ethnic/racial minority individual holds the same values as those of persons in the dominant cultural group and tends to devalue self and other ethnic/racial minority people. People at the conformity stage possess the following characteristics: (1) self-depreciating attitudes and beliefs, (2) group-depreciating attitudes and beliefs toward members of the same minority group, (3) discrimination toward members of different minorities, and (4) group-appreciating attitudes and beliefs toward members of the dominant group. Individuals in this stage would probably prefer a counselor who is a member of the dominant cultural group and might be more prone to accept a problem-solving approach to counseling.

Dissonance Stage

The dissonance stage is characterized by: (1) conflict between self-depreciating and self-appreciating attitudes and beliefs, (2) conflict between group-depreciating and group-appreciating attitudes and beliefs toward members of the same minority, (3) conflict between dominant-held views of minority hierarchy and feelings of shared experience, and (4) conflict between group-appreciating and group-depreciating attitudes toward members of the dominant group. Individuals in this stage are in a state of psychological conflict. Individuals are beginning to question their cultural identity and sense of self-esteem as they come to realize the impact of culture in their own lives. Movement into the dissonance stage is a gradual process.

Resistance and Immersion Stage

This stage involves a new sense of self and cultural group appreciation and a rejection of the dominant cultural group. The desire to eliminate oppression of the individual's minority group becomes an important motivation of the individual's behavior. During this stage, trust issues, racism, and feelings of guilt, shame, and anger may be important in counseling a client. Individuals in this stage may experience: (1) self-appreciating attitudes and beliefs, (2) group-appreciating attitudes and beliefs toward members of the same minority group, (3) conflict between feelings of empathy for other minority group experiences and feelings of culturocentrism, and (4) group-depreciating attitudes and beliefs toward members of the dominant group.

Introspection Stage

The introspection stage is characterized by concern about: (1) the basis of self-appreciating attitudes and beliefs, (2) the unequivocal nature of group appreciation toward members of the same minority, (3) ethnocentric bias for judging others, and (4) the basis of group depreciation toward members of the dominant group. Individuals in this stage exhibit a growing concern over the basis of self-appreciation and a questioning of ethnocentrism as a premise for judging others. Individuals begin to discover that the level of intensity of feelings is psychologically draining and does not permit them to devote crucial energies to understanding themselves or to their own racial/cultural group. In addition, the minority individual experiences feelings of discontent and discomfort with resistance and immersion stage group views that may be quite rigid. An individual in this stage may benefit from a counselor with a broad worldview who can assist in a process of self-exploration to help the client differentiate his/her individual views from those of others.

Integrative Awareness Stage

Persons in the integrative awareness stage have: (1) self-appreciating attitudes and beliefs, (2) group-appreciating attitudes and beliefs toward members of the same minority group, (3) group-appreciating attitudes toward members of a different minority, and (4) attitudes and beliefs of selective appreciation toward members of the dominant culture. Minority persons in this stage have developed a capacity to appreciate themselves as well as others. An individual at this stage may have a strong commitment and desire to eliminate all forms of oppression. A counselor with a broad worldview would be most desired.

As previously mentioned, there is a growing proportion of the population that is biracial and multiracial. In general, individuals from multiple heritages experience life and development differently from those from a monoracial heritage (Henriksen & Paladino, 2009). The Multiple Heritage Identity Development (MHID) Model (Henriksen, 2000) involves six periods, which are not distinct and linear stages. These stages identify an individual's movement toward the development of a racial identity. Individuals may not encounter all periods and may reexperience the periods of development. The six periods are neutrality, acceptance, awareness, experimentation, transition, and recognition. Each of these periods is presented below.

Neutrality. During this period, an individual is unaware of racial or ethnic differences, or even accepts that they exist. In addition, an individual could be unaware of how race and ethnicity affect social interactions with individuals of other backgrounds.

Acceptance. Individuals initially recognize and accept themselves as having a racial or ethnic heritage on the basis of statements made by family and peers. There is acceptance that they are different racially and ethnically, but individuals do not necessarily see that difference as a problem or know what it means. During this period, individuals first recognize and acknowledge that they belong to a racial or ethnic reference group, with family having the greatest impact on their identity development.

Awareness. This is the period during which individuals from mixed heritages begin to understand what it means to be racially different from others. This period is often accompanied by a significant interaction that leads to feelings of isolation as a result of the lack of an identified reference group. Acceptance and awareness can occur simultaneously or separately.

Experimentation. During this period, an individual tries to fit into only one part of his or her racial identity to experience a sense of connection with others. Situational influences lead individuals into this period. For example, the kinds of activities an individual may become involved in may attract more people of one racial or ethnic group than of others, which can result in an attempt to identify with the group that maintains similar interests. This period is a time when an individual is moving toward determining his or her own racial or ethnic group identity as well as his or her sexual identity, religious identity, and other aspects of his or her identity.

Transition. Transition is the period during which some individuals move toward a sense of racial self-recognition, fueled by internal turmoil and a search for a racial identity or racial group with which to identify. During this period, some individuals begin to realize that they cannot choose to identify as a member of any one group.

Recognition. This is the period during which many individuals may decide who they are racially, ethnically, religiously, and sexually and accept the family heritage to which they were born. Individuals verbally define themselves as biracial during this period and also identify themselves with terms such as *Black, White, Mexican, Iranian, mulatto, biracial, multiracial, Indian, Native American,* and *mixed.* In addition, they begin to describe themselves in terms of their religious affiliation and sexual orientation.

The R/CID Model, MHID Model and other racial/cultural identity development models are designed to aid in the understanding of the process involved in developing a racial identity. Included in racial and ethnic identity development are language, sexuality, spirituality, gender, national origin, and indigenous heritage (Atkinson et al., 1989; Henriksen & Paladino, 2009). Racial/cultural identity development models assist in reducing the stereotypic manner of counselor responses to culturally diverse clients, as well as increasing their ability to recognize within-group or individual differences. A second strength of racial/cultural identity models lies in their potential diagnostic value (Sue & Sue, 2008). Racial and ethnic minority clients have a higher rate of premature termination of services than White clients (Wilson, 2002). The high failure rate of many clients can be connected to the mental health professional's inability to assess the cultural identity of clients accurately (Sue & Sue, 2008).

THE CASE OF LENA

Padit Lena Paul is a 46-year-old widow who moved from India 8 years ago to live with her eldest daughter after her husband died from a massive heart attack. Lena's transition to America has been very difficult since her husband used to handle all major responsibilities. Lena is accompanied by Sara, her daughter, and her husband, Neville for her initial appointment. Due to a blow to the head by an abusive boyfriend, Lena developed a moderate hearing loss. She wears binaural hearing aids that enable her to communicate in English fairly well. She takes medication for depression. Lena is requesting your assistance to obtain full-time employment to care for herself since Neville's job will soon be relocating to Canada. She wishes to remain in San Francisco to be near her Christian church family and Indian friends. Lena received her MBA in Business Administration while living in India, but has had difficulty finding full-time work in this field.

In addition to addressing the multidimensional nature of clients' development, counselors may use culturagrams to better understand multigenerational acculturation and ethnic/racial identity (Congress, 2004). Culturagrams gather information on the unique family structures and beliefs about power dynamics, rules, and myths, often influenced by culture. Following the case scenario below, we encourage rehabilitation counselors to develop a cultural assessment to work more responsively, ethically, and respectfully with Lena and future clients from culturally diverse backgrounds.

When developing a cultural assessment, a few questions that rehabilitation counselors may wish to explore include:

How has Lena's religious upbringing, spiritual beliefs, and values influenced her life?

How does the socioeconomic class in which Lena was raised influence her current way of thinking?

How does Lena's sexual identity affect her psychological disposition?

What is Lena's level of psychological development?

In what ways is Lena psychologically different?

What are some of the challenges that Lena is encountering from a chronological perspective?

Why are the identified stresses considered problematic for Lena?

How have Lena's family dynamics affected her life?

How have physical challenges influenced Lena's development psychologically?

What are the different types of needs, stresses, and sources of support if Lena remains in San Francisco?

What were other reasons leading to Lena's relocation to San Francisco-economic, political, and religious?

Is it possible for her to return to India?

What is Lena's legal status (undocumented vs. documented)?

What is the length of time in her current community (it may differ for each family member, various levels of acculturation, or assimilation)?

What is the impact on family relationships, development of her children, and grandchildren?

What is her language—skill level, specific languages, and intergenerational languages?

What are her health beliefs—mental health, family obligations, and cultural treatments?

What were crisis events for Lena—developmental, family, and situational crisis?

What holiday and special events are culturally relevant for Lena?

What contact does Lena have with cultural and religiously relevant institutions?

What are Lena's values about work and education—family togetherness versus education, patriarchal breadwinner issues?

What is the family structure and power—myths and rules?

In examining how your own beliefs and attitudes affect how you react to the situation presented, rehabilitation counselors may consider these questions:

How does your own religious/spiritual beliefs and values (or lack of) influence this counseling session?

What biases do you bring from your own economic background?

Are you genuinely comfortable and confident working with persons with a different lifestyle?

Given your own level of psychological maturity, how comfortable are you working with Lena?

How might your own cultural biases/preferences influence your work with Lena?

How might your individual and group identity affect your perception of Lena?

How might the way Lena identifies as an individual and with others in her culture affect your perception and ability to work with her?

What are the strengths and limitations of your age as you work with Lena?

How do the daily stresses you experience impact your work with Lena?

How have your family experiences influenced your comfort level in working with Lena?

What are your biases regarding Lena's "physical-ness" and how do these biases impact your work with her?

How might your residence preference influence your work with Lena?

CONCLUSION

We anticipate that this chapter will offer practical utility to help expand rehabilitation counselors' thinking about the various considerations that underlie a culturally competent approach to rehabilitation counseling practice. We also recognize that this overview does not represent an exhaustive listing of all the factors impacting human development; therefore, we expect that counselors and researchers will work collaboratively in the future and continue adding to a better understanding of the multidimensional nature of human development—personally and professionally.

CONTENT REVIEW QUESTIONS

- Discuss the several levels of rationale for rehabilitation counselors to be culturally competent.
- Define cultural competence and cultural responsiveness.
- What are the 10 factors that comprise the RESPECTFUL counseling model?
- Describe five stages of the Racial/Cultural Identity Development Model (R/CID) and six periods of the MHID Model.

- Discuss how the constructs of ethnic, racial, and cultural identity interact to inform identity development. Discuss the importance of exploring/understanding the significance of each of these constructs with consumers/clients. How can this help to facilitate positive outcome attainment?
- Why is gaining an understanding of one's own cultural identity development integral to the development of cultural competence? How can negating or neglecting counselor development in this area impact the work done with consumers/clients?

QUESTIONS FOR EXPLORATION

- In the process of building mutuality with the consumer/client, what factors can influence consumer/client perceptions of counselor cultural competence? Why is it important for rehabilitation professionals to attend to this process?
- How can rehabilitation professionals utilize the RESPECTFUL counseling model to deepen their own understanding of the contextual influences they bring to the counselor–consumer/client alliance (relationship)?
- What actions can you take as a counselor when you become aware of the need to further engage the process of cultural competence development?

REFERENCES

Alston, R. J., Bell, T., & Feist-Price, S. M. (1996). Racial identity and African Americans with disabilities: Theoretical and practical considerations. *The Journal of Rehabilitation, 62*(2), 11–15.

Atkins, B. J., & Wright, G. N. (1980). Three views: Vocational rehabilitation of blacks. The statement, the response, the comment. *Journal of Rehabilitation, 46*(2), 40–49.

Atkinson, D. R., Morten, G., & Sue, D. W. (1989). *Counseling American minorities: A cross-cultural perspective* (3rd ed.). Dubuque, IA: Wm. C. Brown.

Bailey, J. M. (1997). Gender identity. In R. C. Savin-Williams & K. M. Cohen (Eds.), *The lives of lesbians, gays, and bisexuals: Children to adults* (pp. 71–93). For Worth, TX: Harcourt Brace.

Boutin, D. L., & Wilson, K. B. (2009). Professional jobs and hearing loss: A comparison of deaf and hard of hearing consumers. *Journal of Rehabilitation, 75*(1), 36–40.

Bowe, F. (1984). *U. S. Census and disabled adults.* Hot Springs, AR: University of Arkansas, Arkansas Services, Arkansas Rehabilitation Research and Training Center.

Coleman, H. L. K., Norton, R. A., Miranda, G. E., & McCubbin, L. (2003). An ecological perspective on cultural identity development. In D. B. Pope-Davis, H. L. K. Coleman, W. M. Liu, & R. L. Toporek (Eds.), *Handbook of multicultural competencies in counseling & psychology* (pp. 38–58). Thousand Oak, CA: Sage.

Congress, E. P. (2004). Cultural and ethical issues in working with culturally diverse patients and their families: The use of the culturagram to promote cultural competent practice in health care settings. *Social work visions around the globe: Citizens, methods, and approaches* (pp. 249–264). Philadelphia, PA: Haworth press.

Craig, G. J. (1992). *Human development* (6th ed.). Englewood Cliffs, NJ: Prentice Hall.

D'Andrea, M., & Daniels, J. (1997, December). RESPECTFUL counseling: A new way of thinking about diversity counseling. *Counseling Today, 40*(6), 30, 31, 34.

D'Andrea, M., & Daniels, J. (2001). RESPECTFUL counseling: An integrative model for counselors. In D. Pope-Davis & H. Coleman (Eds.), *The interface of class, culture and gender in counseling* (pp. 417–466). Thousand Oaks, CA: Sage.

D'Andrea, M., & Daniels, J. (2010). *Multicultural counseling: Empowerment strategies for a diverse society.* Pacific Grove, CA: Brooks/Cole.

Erikson, E. (1968). *Identity: Youth and crisis.* New York, NY: Norton.

Gao, N., Gill, K. J., Schmidt, L. T., & Pratt, C. W. (2010). The application of human capital theory in vocational rehabilitation for individuals with mental illness. *Journal of Vocational Rehabilitation, 32*(1), 25–33.

Gilligan, C. (1982). *In a different voice: Psychological theory and women's development.* Cambridge, MA: Harvard University Press.

Hasnain, R., & Balcazar, F. (2009). Predicting community versus facility-based employment for transition-aged young adults with disabilities: The role of race, ethnicity, and support services. *Journal of Vocational Rehabilitation, 31*(3), 175–188.

Havighurst, R. J. (1953). *Human development and education.* New York, NY: Longman.

Helms, J. E., & Cook, D. A. (1999). *Using race and culture in counseling and psychotherapy: Theory and process.* Boston, MA: Allyn and Bacon.

Henriksen, R. C. (2000). Black/White biracial identity development: A grounded theory study (Doctoral dissertation, Texas A&M University-Commerce, 2000). *Dissertation Abstracts International, 61/07*, 2605.

Henriksen, R. C., & Paladino, D. A. (2009). Identity development in a multiple heritage world. In R. C. Henriksen Jr. & D. A. Paladino (Eds.), *Counseling multiple heritage individuals, couples, and families* (pp. 25–43). Alexandria, VA: American Counseling Association.

Houston, K., Lammers, H. B., & Svorny, S. (2010). Perceptions of the effect of public policy on employment opportunities for individuals who are deaf or hard of hearing. *Journal of Disability Policy Studies, 21*(1), 9–21. doi:10.1177/1044207309357428

Jacobs, H. E., Wissusik, D., Collier, R., Stackman, D., & Burkeman, D. (1992). Correlations between psychiatric disabilities and vocational outcome. *Hospital and Community Psychiatry, 43*, 365–369.

Johnson, B. B. (2004). Arguments for testing ethnic identity and acculturation as factors in risk judgments. *Risk Analysis, 24*, 1279–1287.

Jones, N. A., & Smith, A. S. (2001). The two or more races population: 2000. *Census 2000 Brief.* Retrieved from http://www.census.gov/prod/2001pubs/c2kbr01-6.pdf

Kelly, E. W. (1995). *Spirituality and religion in counseling and psychotherapy: Diversity in theory and practice.* Alexandria, VA: American Counseling Association.

Kohlberg, L. (1981). *The philosophy of moral development.* San Francisco, CA: Harper & Row.

Lee, W. M. L., Blando, J. A., Mizelle, N. D., & Orozco, G. L. (2007). *Introduction to multicultural counseling for helping professionals.* New York, NY: Routledge.

Lewis, J., Lewis, M., Daniels, J., & D'Andrea, M. (2003). *Community counseling: Empowerment strategies for a diverse society.* Pacific Grove, CA: Brooks/Cole.

Loevinger, J. (1976). *Ego development.* San Francisco, CA: Jossey-Bass.

Maldonado, J. M., Kushner, J. D., Barr, J., & Korz, K. (2009). Ethnic identity and acculturation of English as second language learners: Implications for school counselors. *Michigan Journal of Counseling, 36*(1), 13–23.

McWhirter, E. H. (1994). *Counseling for empowerment.* Alexandria, VA: American Counseling Association.

Moore, C. L. (2001). Disparities in job placement outcomes among deaf, late-deafened, and hard of hearing consumers. *Rehabilitation Counseling Bulletin, 44*(3), 144, doi:10.1177/003435520104400304

Munoz, J. P. (2007). Culturally responsive caring in occupational therapy. *Occupational Therapy International, 14*(4), 256–280. doi:10.1002/oti.238

NPR Radio. (2007, April 26). *Multiracial identity in America today*. Available at http://www.npr.org/templates/story/story.php?storyId=9849015.

Patterson, J. B., Allen, T. B., Parnell, L., Crawford, R., & Beardall, R. L. (2000). Equitable treatment in the rehabilitation process: Implications for future investigations related to ethnicity. *The Journal of Rehabilitation, 66*(2), 14.

Perry, W. G. (1970). *Forms of intellectual and ethical development in the college years: A scheme.* New York, NY: Holt, Rinehart & Winston.

Phinney, J. (1990). Ethnic identity in adolescents and adults: Review of research. *Psychological Bulletin, 108*, 499–514. doi:10.1037/0033-2909.108.3.499

Phinney, J. (2003). Ethnic identity and acculturation. In K. Chun, P. B. Organista, & G. Marin (Eds.), *Acculturation: Advances in theory, measurement, and applied research* (pp. 63–81). Washington, CD: American Psychological Association.

Piaget, J. (1977). *The development of thought: Equilibrium of cognitive structure.* New York, NY: Viking.

Rimmerman, A., Botuck, S., & Levy, J. M. (1995). Job placement for individuals with psychiatric disabilities and supported employment. *Psychiatric Rehabilitation Journal, 19*, 37–43.

Salzman, M. B. (2001). Cultural trauma and recovery: Perspectives from terror management theory. *Trauma, Violence, & Abuse, 2*, 172–191. doi:10.1177/1524838001002002005.

Savin-Williams, R. C., & Cohen, K. M. (1996). *The lives of lesbians, gays, and bisexuals: Children to adults.* Fort Worth, TX: Harcourt Brace College Publishing.

Selman, R. (1980). *The growth of interpersonal understanding: Developmental and clinical analysis.* New York, NY: Academic Press.

Shaffer, D. R. (1993). *Developmental psychology: Childhood and adolescence* (3rd ed.). Pacific Grove, CA: Brooks/Cole.

Shin, H., & Munoz, O. (2009). Acculturation: Context, dynamics, and conceptualization. In C. C. Lee, D. A. Burnhill, A. L. Butler, C. P. Hipolito-Delgado, M. Humphrey, O. Munoz et al. (Eds.), *Elements of culture in counseling* (pp. 57–76). Upper Saddle River, NJ: Pearson.

Sprinthall, N. A., Peace, S. D., & Kennington, P. A. D. (2001). Cognitive-developmental stage theories for counseling. In D. C. Locke, J. E. Myers, & E. L. Herr (Eds.), *The handbook of counseling* (pp. 109–130). Thousand Oaks, CA: Sage.

Sue, D. W., Arredondo, P., & McDavis, R. (1992). Multicultural counseling competencies and standards: A call to the profession. *Journal of Multicultural Counseling & Development, 20*, 64–88.

Sue, D. W., & Sue, D. (2008). *Counseling the culturally different: Theory and practice* (5th ed.). New York, NY: John Wiley & Sons.

Thompson, B. Y. (2006). *The politics of bisexual/biracial identity: A study of bisexual and mixed race women of Asian/Pacific Islander descent.* Snakegirl Press.

U.S. Bureau of the Census. (2000). *Geographic tools (Fact finder for the nation).* Washington, DC: U.S. Government Printing Office.

Whaley, A., & Davis, K. (2007). Cultural competence and evidence-based practice in mental health services: A complementary perspective. *American Psychologist, 62*, 563–574. doi:10.1037/0003-066X.62.6.563.

Wilcots, K. D. (2000). *The relationship between racial identity, ethnic identity, and African-American acculturation and their contribution to psychological well-being.* Dissertation, University of North Texas, Denton, TX.

Wilson, K. B. (2002). Exploration of VR acceptance and ethnicity: A national investigation, *Rehabilitation Counseling Bulletin, 45* (3), 168–169. doi:10.1177/003435520204500306 .

Young-Eisendrath, P. (1988). Making use of human development theories in counseling. In R. Hayes & R. Aubrey (Eds.), *New directions for counseling and human development* (pp. 66–84). Denver, CO: Love Publishing.

18

Evidence–Based Practice and Research Utilization

*Fong Chan, Connie Sung, Veronica Muller, Chia-Chiang Wang,
Mayu Fujikawa, and Catherine A. Anderson*

LEARNING OBJECTIVES

After reading this chapter, you should be able to:

- Understand how the transformation of the health care system in the United States has impacted service delivery of health care disciplines including rehabilitation counseling in providing the most effective clinical services.
- Understand how research has provided an evidence-based foundation for the discipline in relation to role, function, and knowledge requirements.
- Understand how rehabilitation professionals can become more effective evidence-based practitioners through enhancing their knowledge in evidence-based methodologies, research utilization, and effective vocational rehabilitation (VR) service delivery practices.
- Understand the concepts of systematic reviews, meta-analysis, effect size, and knowledge translation.
- Understand how the mechanisms of theory development, empirical evidence, and clinical application inform practice in VR service delivery, improving evidence-based practice to enhance outcomes and quality of life of people with disabilities.
- Recognize the value of continually assessing the way clinical services are provided to increase effectiveness of intervention strategies.

Because of skyrocketing health insurance costs, the American health care system has undergone significant transformation over the last two decades, with considerable efforts directed toward the integration of both the financing and the delivery of health care within a system that seeks to manage accessibility, cost, and quality of service and outcomes (Chronister, Cardoso, Lee, Chan, & Leahy, 2005). One way to respond to these managed care efforts is through evidence-based practice. Evidence-based medicine espouses that all health care professionals should provide their patients with the most effective clinical services based on sound research evidence (Chan et al., 2010). This philosophy of clinical practice has since pervaded a range of health care and rehabilitation disciplines including the rehabilitation counseling profession (Chan et al., 2010; Chan, Rosenthal, & Pruett, 2008; Chronister, Chan, Cardoso, Lynch, & Rosenthal, 2008; Pruett, Swett, Chan, Rosenthal, & Lee, 2008). For example, the state-federal VR program was placed by the U.S. Government Accountability Office (GAO) on a list of high-risk programs for not keeping up with *scientific advances* and economic and social changes (GAO, 2005). As a result, the Rehabilitation Services Administration has begun to encourage state VR agencies to integrate the best scientific evidence with clinical expertise and client perspectives (Thirty-Third Institute on Rehabilitation Issues, 2008). The National Institute on Disability and Rehabilitation Research (NIDRR) in recent years has underscored the need for its sponsored research studies to meet standards for inclusion in evidence-based systematic reviews (Schlosser, 2006), and emphasized the importance of knowledge translation to facilitate research utilization in rehabilitation practices.

Without a doubt, VR agencies and rehabilitation counselors are under increasing pressure to demonstrate that they are using empirically supported interventions to improve the effectiveness of rehabilitation service delivery practices (Chan, Keegan, et al., 2009; Rubin, Chan, & Thomas, 2003). According to Chan, Tarvydas, Blalock, Strauser, and Atkins (2009), the use of high-quality research evidence to guide clinical practices also has the benefit of helping counselors fulfill their ethical obligations to consumers by protecting consumers from harm (nonmaleficence), improving efficiency in utilization of scarce resources (justice), and empowering consumers to exercise knowledgeable self-determination and truly informed choice (autonomy). Not surprisingly, a recent survey conducted by Bezyak, Kubota, and Rosenthal (2010) found that rehabilitation counselors generally hold positive attitudes toward evidence-based practice. However, they also identified a lack of knowledge and insufficient academic preparation in evidence-based practice and research utilization as major barriers for implementation (Bezyak et al., 2010).

Knowledge of basic concepts of research methods acquired from a traditional master's level rehabilitation counseling research course is insufficient to be an effective evidence-based practitioner. Rehabilitation counseling professionals must become more knowledgeable about evidence-based methodologies, knowledge translation, research utilization, and effective VR service delivery practices. The purpose of this chapter is to provide a review of these key evidence-based practice concepts and to discuss how they can be implemented to improve the professional practice of rehabilitation counseling.

EVIDENCE-BASED PRACTICE

DePalma (2002) described evidence-based practice as a total process beginning with knowing what clinical questions to ask, how to find the best practice, and how to critically appraise the evidence for validity and applicability to the particular care situation. The best evidence then must be applied by a clinician with expertise in considering the patient's unique values and needs. The final aspect of the process is evaluation of the effectiveness of care and the continual improvement of the process.

Formulating an unambiguous clinical question from a client's presenting problem is the important first step in evidence-based practice. The ability to ask appropriate background and foreground questions is important in this crucial step of the clinical decision-making process. Specifically, background questions (or general questions) ask about a setting or context, whereas foreground questions ask about a specific case within that context (Walker, Seay, Solomon, & Spring, 2006). Examples of typical background questions include:

1. What are the most effective treatments for presenting problem Y?
2. Is treatment X an effective treatment for presenting problem Y?
3. Are there any significant risks associated with treatment X?

Regarding foreground questions, they should be asked using the PICO format: patient group (P), intervention (I), comparison group (C), and outcome measures (O). The following is an example of a foreground PICO question: For an African American man with schizophrenia (patient group), is there any evidence that the individual placement and support (IPS) model of supported employment (intervention) is superior to state VR services, assertive community treatment, and the clubhouse approach (comparison group) in improving his employment outcome and the quality of his outcome (outcome)? A set of well-built background and foreground questions provide direction for determining what evidence to look for and where to search for the best evidence.

To search for current best evidence, an evidence-based practitioner in rehabilitation must be knowledgeable about specific methods and resources for locating research evidence and incorporating this clinical information into treatment. The most reliable and scholarly approach to searching for scientific research papers and systematic reviews documents is through academic databases such as Academic Search Elite, CINAHL Plus with Full Text, MEDLINE, PsycINFO, Cochrane Collaboration, and Campbell Collaboration.

After formulating well-defined, answerable questions and seeking the best evidence available to answer the questions, the rehabilitation counselor must critically appraise the evidence. Chambless and Hollon (1998) indicated that best evidence for psychosocial treatments should be evaluated in terms of efficacy (statistical and clinical significance), effectiveness (clinical utility), and efficiency (cost effectiveness). In evidence-based medicine, the gold standard for best evidence is randomized clinical trials or experimental studies. A five-level hierarchical framework emphasizing the importance of experimental studies offers health care and rehabilitation professionals a format for determining the strength of the evidence based on methodological rigor (Holm, 2000; Nathan & Gorman, 1998). This hierarchy of levels of evidence follow:

1. Level 1 evidence is defined as strong evidence from at least one systematic review of multiple, well-designed, randomized controlled trials.
2. Level 2 evidence is defined as strong evidence from at least one properly designed, randomized controlled trials of appropriate size.
3. Level 3 evidence is defined as evidence from well-designed trials without randomization, single group pre-post, cohort, time series, or matched case-controlled studies.
4. Level 4 evidence is defined as evidence from well-designed nonexperimental studies from more than one center or research group.
5. Level 5 evidence is defined as opinions of respected authorities, based on clinical evidence, descriptive studies, or reports of expert committees.

However, professionals should be mindful that randomized clinical trials as the gold standard for scientific evidence work well in medicine, but may be too restrictive for other behavioral and social sciences because they do not always take into account the full complexity of human behavior and clinical condition (Wampold, 1997). The complex nature of VR both in the scope of services provided through an array of disciplines and diverse clinical populations definitely make rehabilitation process and outcome research challenging. Tucker and Reed (2008) suggested that rehabilitation professionals should embrace evidentiary pluralism as a strategy for research and evidence-based practice in rehabilitation. They do not dispute that randomized controlled trials are vital for establishing treatment efficacy, but question whether randomized clinical trials are uniformly the best evidence to inform rehabilitation practice. Tucker and Reed argued that other multivariate approaches used to test mediator effects (e.g., hierarchical regression analysis), person–environment interactions (e.g., multilevel analysis), and complex theoretical models (e.g., structural equation modeling) in the natural environment can provide invaluable information about contextual, psychological, and treatment influences on functioning, disability, and community participation. Chwalisz, Shah, and Hand (2008) also made a compelling argument that rigorous qualitative research methods have much to contribute to theoretical and applied knowledge in rehabilitation. Therefore, different empirical questions are better addressed using different methods and when considered together with experimental studies, nonexperimental quantitative and qualitative studies can expand the scope and impact of rehabilitation and health-related research.

After locating, appraising, and synthesizing the research evidence, the rehabilitation counselor must incorporate the evidence into a client's treatment plan by taking into account the significance of the evidence, his or her own professional expertise and judgment, and the client's characteristics, values, and context. The American Psychological Association (APA) defines best evidence as "evidence based on systematic reviews, reasonable effect sizes, statistical and clinical significance, and a body of supporting evidence" (APA, 2005, p. 1). Professional judgment is used to identify each client's unique disability and health status and to integrate the best evidence with the rehabilitation context. Client characteristics, values, and context are the preferences, values, strengths, weaknesses, personality, sociocultural factors, and expectations that a consumer brings to the rehabilitation process. Indeed, in evidence-based practice, clinical decisions are made in collaboration with the client.

In summary, evidence-based practice is a clinical decision-making process that involves conscientious, explicit, and judicious use of current *best evidence* in making decisions about the care of individual clients (Sackett, Rosenberg, Gray, Haynes, & Richardson, 1996). The use of current best evidence to guide clinical decision making and the provision of interventions using best evidence has the potential to improve the likelihood of positive clinical and vocational intervention outcomes for people with chronic illness and disability.

RESEARCH UTILIZATION

Despite research utilization being a desirable goal, it is also quite elusive. Bezyak et al. (2010) identified a lack of knowledge and insufficient academic preparation in evidence-based practice and research utilization as major barriers for implementation. Other challenges to utilization can be attributed to several negative perceptions about rehabilitation research, including a weak theoretical foundation, lack of practical relevance for professionals and consumers, a dearth of well-designed experimental design studies aimed at validating the efficacy of rehabilitation counseling interventions, and the underutilization of qualitative research methodologies (Berkowitz, Englander, Rubin, & Worrall, 1975, 1976; Chan, Miller, Lee, Pruett, & Chou, 2003; Parker & Hansen, 1981; Rubin & Rice, 1986). To train master's level rehabilitation counseling students and professional counselors to be intelligent consumers of research, it is important, although not sufficient, to teach them the basic concepts of research designs and statistical methods. They need to be knowledgeable about evidence-based methodologies and concepts including research databases, systematic reviews/meta-analysis, and knowledge translation. Finally, they need to be able to see clearly how research evidence can be a practical and integral part of their professional practice.

Research Databases

To critically appraise evidence from a single properly designed randomized control trial requires a relatively strong background in research methods and a working knowledge of concepts related to internal and external validity (Schlosser, 2006). Given the potential for a vast number of research articles with contradictory findings, the most efficient way for master's students and practicing counselors to learn how to find the best evidence may be to use databases and/or specific evidence-based intervention Web sites to search for high-quality systematic reviews. The most useful Web sites for systematic reviews related to evidence-based medical, rehabilitation, and behavioral science intervention information include the Cochrane Collaboration (www.cochrane.org), Campbell Collaboration (http://www.campbellcollaboration.org), Agency for Healthcare Research and Quality (http://www.ahrq.gov), American Congress of Rehabilitation Medicine (http://www.acrm.org/evidence-based-practice.cfm), and the Substance Abuse and Mental Health Services Administration's National Registry of Evidence-based Programs and Practices (http://www.nrepp.samhsa.gov/Search.aspx). Rehabilitation professionals and students can also search for systematic reviews and meta-analytic studies through Academic Search Elite, CINAHL Plus with Full Text, MEDLINE, and PsycINFO databases.

Systematic Reviews

Systematic reviews answer a specific clinical question by using predetermined rules for capturing the evidence, appraising it, and synthesizing it in a manner that is easily accessible to clinicians. Systematic reviews are based on work by scholars with expertise in a substantive area who review and critique the available data in the field (Schlosser, 2006). It typically involves several steps, including: (1) asking an answerable clinical question, (2) identifying one or more databases to search, (3) developing an explicit search strategy, (4) selecting titles, abstracts, and manuscripts based on explicit inclusion and exclusion criteria, and (5) abstracting data in a standardized format. Strong evidence from at least one systematic review of multiple well-designed randomized clinical trials is considered the highest level of best evidence (Level 1) and is frequently labeled a meta-analytic review. Meta-analysis is a particular type of systematic review that uses quantitative methods to combine the results from a number of studies.

Meta-analysis

The goal of any science is the production of cumulative knowledge. However, the small-sample studies commonly reported in behavioral science research and the overreliance on statistical tests can produce seemingly conflicting results (Schmidt & Hunter, 2003). Meta-analytic studies review the results of a collection of empirical studies in a specific research domain through statistical integration and analysis, and synthesize the results to reveal the simpler patterns of relations that underlie the topical research area, thus providing a basis for theory development (Durlak, 1995; Schmidt & Hunter, 2003). Importantly, meta-analysis can correct for the distorting effects of sampling error, measurement error, and other artifacts that produce the false impression of contradictory findings. Similar to an individual experiment, a meta-analysis contains both independent and dependent variables, with the independent variables being such characteristics as participants, interventions, and outcome measures, and with the dependent variable being the effect size or the outcome of the results of each study selected for review, transformed into a common metric across studies.

In evidence-based practice methodology, the focus of meta-analysis is on treatment effectiveness (e.g., is cognitive-behavioral therapy more effective than psychotherapy in treating depression?). The advantages of this statistical technique are its ability to: (1) synthesize the results from many studies succinctly and intuitively to nonscientific communities, (2) illustrate the amount and relative impact of different programs on different criteria for policy decision-making purposes, and (3) identify the most effective programs and highlight gaps or limitations in the literature to suggest directions for future research (Durlak, 1995). A meta-analysis is conducted by following six major steps, which include: (1) formulating research questions, (2) identifying relevant studies through a comprehensive review of the literature (computer searches, manual searches, and examination of the reference lists of each identified study), (3) coding the studies (e.g., participants, research designs, therapist qualifications, control group, treatment type, presenting problem, number of sessions, and method of administration), (4) computing the index of effect, (5) conducting the statistical analysis of effects, and (6) offering conclusions and interpretations (Durlak, 1995).

A common index representing the size of the effect produced by each study is Cohen's d, which is the standardized difference between the sample mean of the treatment group and the sample mean of the control group (Borenstein, Hedges, Higgins, & Rothstein, 2009). It should be noted that the population estimator ⊠ for describing the size of effects for statistical power analysis is also sometimes called d, creating some confusion in the literature. Borenstein et al. (2009) recommend the use of the symbol ⊠ to represent the effect size parameter and d for the sample estimate of the parameter. However, d tends to overestimate the absolute value of δ in small samples. This bias can be corrected using a correction factor J proposed by Hedges (1981) and the resulting unbiased estimate is called Hedges's g. Because of this confusion, currently, both d and g can be found reported in the literature as unbiased effect size indexes. A positive score indicates that the treatment group outperformed the control group, and a negative score has the reverse meaning. A typical way to interpret the size of an effect is to compare the d or g index with the standards set by Cohen (1988), with small, medium, and large effect represented by 0.20, 0.50, and 0.80, respectively. To examine the overlap of the control and treatment distributions, the effect size index (d or g) should be converted to the value of the standard normal cumulative distribution. For example, if $d = 0.85$ then $z = 0.85$ and compared to the normal distribution curve, a z-score of 0.85 covers 80% of the normal curve and would indicate that the average client receiving treatment will be better off than 80% of untreated clients. Other related mean difference effect size indexes include the proportion of variability (PV) and partial eta-squared (η^2). For correlational studies, the effect size is reported as r; for multiple regression analysis, the effect size

TABLE 18.1
Effect Size Measures

Effect Size	PV	r	d/g	η^2	w	f^2
Small effects	0.01	0.10	0.20	0.01	0.10	0.02
Medium effects	0.10	0.30	0.50	0.06	0.30	0.15
Large effects	0.25	0.50	0.80	0.14	0.50	0.35

is f^2; and for a Pearson chi-square test, the effect size is reported as w. A typical way to interpret the size is to use the standards established by Cohen and presented here in Table 18.1.

There are many factors that can influence the effect size of a meta-analytic study including sample size, sensitivity of measurement instruments, design characteristics, and clinical significance. Of particular importance are the issues of homogeneity and power. The power of a statistical test is the probability that it will yield statistically significant results. However, Kosciulek and Szymanski (1993), after analyzing empirical articles from five rehabilitation journals, concluded that because of low statistical power, rehabilitation counselor researchers had little chance of finding small relationships or differences that exist in population of interest.

In regard to homogeneity, it can be argued that studies included in a meta-analysis may have an array of different independent or dependent variables, and may not have a common population parameter. For this reason, researchers have developed a way to empirically test the heterogeneity and homogeneity of the studies. Hedges and Olkin (1985) developed a Q statistic for a large sample test of homogeneity and suggested that if the null hypothesis of homogeneity is rejected (i.e., Q statistic is significant), the studies should be partitioned based on meaningful categories. Specifically, a meta-analysis may include studies that differ in categorically predictable ways; for example, a "better designed" study would produce a larger effect than a "poorer designed" study; therefore, to control for this difference, the independent variable "quality of research design" can be used to partition studies into two groups (good design studies vs. poor design studies). The between group differences can then be tested using QB—a goodness-of-fit statistic—also developed by Hedges and Olkin. If a significant difference between groups (QB) is determined, and no difference within groups (Q), then $d+$ can be computed to estimate the effect size for each group of studies. If there is a significant difference within groups, then the groups should be further partitioned. Because the test of homogeneity typically has low power to detect variations beyond sampling error, Hedges and Olkin recommended that if theory suggests the existence of moderators, a moderator analysis should be conducted even if the homogeneity test is not significant.

Knowledge Translation

Despite the increasing acceptance of evidence-based practice, high-quality evidence is not being used consistently in practice. Straus, Tetroe, and Graham (2009) attributed failures to use evidence from research to make informed decisions to the lack of skills in knowledge management and infrastructure (i.e., the sheer volume of research evidence currently produced, access to research evidence, time to read and the skills to appraise, and understand and apply research evidence). One way to improve research utilization is through better knowledge translation processes. The National Center for the Dissemination of Disability Research (NCDDR, 2006) defined knowledge translation as the collaborative and systematic review, assessment, identification, aggregation, and practical application of high-quality disability and rehabilitation research by key stakeholders (i.e., consumers, researchers, practitioners, and policymakers) for the purpose of improving the lives of individuals with disabilities. In the context of evidence-based practice, knowledge translation is the process of moving what we learned through research to the actual applications of such knowledge in a variety of practice settings and circumstances. Sudsawad (2007) suggested that, essentially, knowledge translation is an interactive process underpinned by effective exchanges among researchers who create new knowledge and clinicians who use the information. Continuing dialogues, interactions, and partnerships within and between different groups of knowledge creators and users in all stages of the research process are integral parts of knowledge translation.

The knowledge-to-action framework for the practice of knowledge translation has received considerable attention in recent years (Graham et al., 2006). It has great potential for improving the knowledge translation process in rehabilitation counseling. The structural relationships among knowledge creation and those associated action steps in the knowledge-to-action model are depicted in Figure 18.1.

In this model, knowledge creation is composed of three phases: (1) knowledge inquiry, (2) synthesis of knowledge, and (3) creation of knowledge tools. Knowledge inquiry involves the completion of the primary research. The synthesis stage required appropriate research findings would be considered in the totality of the evidence (i.e., systematic reviews) to identify common patterns. At the stage of development of tools and products, the best-quality knowledge is further synthesized and distilled into decision-making tools such as practice guidelines—aids for patient decisions or algorithms (Straus et al., 2009). In rehabilitation counseling, toolkits including empirically validated assessment, planning, and interventions can be developed and distributed to practicing counselors.

The action cycle is composed of seven phases based on theories of planned action. These actions can occur sequentially or simultaneously and can be influenced by activities of the knowledge phases at any point in the cycle. Included are the processes needed to use knowledge in health care and rehabilitation

FIGURE 18.1
Knowledge-to-Action Framework of Knowledge Translation

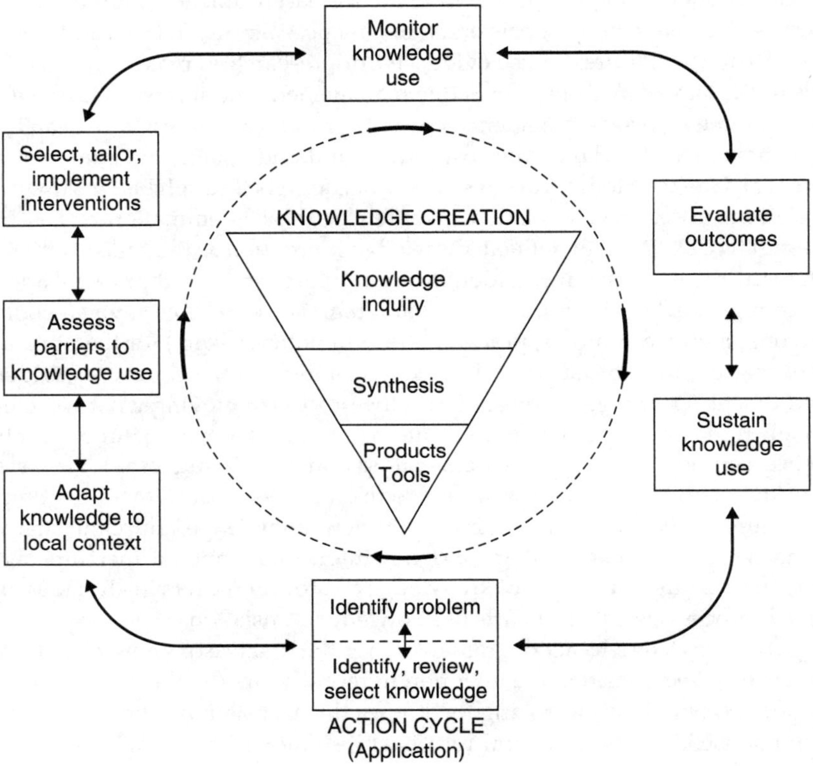

settings. Specifically, these processes are: (1) identifying the problem, (2) identifying, reviewing, and selecting the knowledge to implement, (3) adapting or customizing the knowledge to the local context, (4) assessing the determinants (barriers) of knowledge use, (5) selecting, tailoring, implementing, and monitoring interventions related to knowledge translation, (6) evaluating outcomes or impacts of using the knowledge, and (7) determining strategies for ensuring sustained use of knowledge. Salient to this knowledge translation framework is its emphasis on the need to incorporate input from the various stakeholders (including clients, clinicians, managers, or policy makers) who are the end users of the knowledge that is being implemented. Inclusion of the end users of the knowledge will ensure that the knowledge and its subsequent implementation are relevant to their needs, promoting the applications of research and the process of knowledge translation.

An exemplary application of knowledge translation to improve rehabilitation practice is the series of evidence-based practice toolkits developed by

SAMHSA for mental health practitioners. For example, the Assertive Community Treatment Knowledge Informing Transformation (ACT KIT) includes an array of materials designed to help agencies implement, sustain, and evaluate ACT programs and ensure that people with serious mental illness have access to these effective services. At the core of the newly released ACT KIT are three detailed volumes that cover implementation, training, and evaluation. The first volume—*Building Your Program*—is designed to help mental health authorities, agency administrators, and ACT leaders think through and to develop the structure of ACT programs. The second core volume—*Training Frontline Staff*—is a workbook intended for use as both a training manual for group sessions and a basic desk reference. The 110-page workbook divides training into four modules: basic elements of ACT, recovery and the stress–vulnerability model, core processes of ACT, and the array of services that ACT programs provide, from medication support to health promotion to housing assistance and employment. The third volume—*Evaluating Your Program*—shows quality assurance team members how to assess the effectiveness of the ACT program and includes a readiness assessment, the ACT Fidelity Scale, the General Organizational Index, and outcome measures that are specific to ACT. The ACT KIT also contains materials designed to introduce the practice to a wide variety of stakeholders—mental health authorities, community members, employers, consumers, families and other supporters, and agency staff. Videos, brochures, and handouts in Spanish and English and a PowerPoint presentation are included, along with instructions for making the best use of these resources. Finally, a 32-page booklet—The Evidence—introduces all stakeholders to the research literature. It presents a review of the ACT literature, a selected bibliography for further reading, and references for the citations presented throughout the ACT KIT. The ACT KIT can be downloaded from the Web site of the Center for Mental Health Services (http://store.samhsa.gov/home).

The NIDRR has made knowledge translation a high priority in all of its funded research projects. It has funded the NCDDR (http://www.ncddr.org/) as the national resource for disability and rehabilitation research information. In addition, all NIDRR funded Rehabilitation Research and Training Centers (RRTCs), Disability and Rehabilitation Research Programs (DRRPs), Disability and Business Technical Assistance Centers (DBTACs), Traumatic Brian Injury Model Systems, and Spinal Cord Injury Model Systems are required to conduct research that meets the highest standards for inclusion in evidence-based systematic reviews and knowledge translation must be an integral component of their systematic research program. These centers are excellent resources for best evidence information related to psychosocial and vocational interventions for people with disabilities. Some of the RRTCs and DRRPs that are particularly relevant to evidence-based practice include the RRTC-Individual Characteristics, RRTC-Employer Practice, RRTC-Effective Vocational Rehabilitation Service Delivery Practices, and DRRP-Center on Knowledge Translation for Employment Research. The Johnson & Johnson—Dartmouth Community Mental Health

Program and the Substance Abuse and Mental Health Services Administration's National Registry of Evidence-Based Programs and Practices are excellent resources for evidence-based mental health interventions.

Effective VR Interventions

Current rehabilitation practices have been characterized by some scholars as "experience-based," "eminence-based," or "habit-based" (Law, 2002). The lack of strong theory-driven research and empirical evidence to inform assessment, planning, and intervention in the rehabilitation process is one of the most recurring and frequent criticisms of rehabilitation counseling research (Berkowitz et al., 1975; Chan et al., 2003). However, research evidence from multiple disciplines can be used to inform VR service delivery practices in the rehabilitation process. Within this context, a variety of high-quality evidence exists to suggest that the provision of rehabilitation counseling services can have significant benefits to clients. Some examples of empirically supported interventions frequently used in rehabilitation counseling are described in the following.

Counseling/Psychotherapy

Counseling is a central rehabilitation counseling function that serves to unify the entire rehabilitation service delivery process (Leahy, Chan, & Saunders, 2003). Literally hundreds of experimental studies of the efficacy of counseling have been reported in the research literature during the past 50 years. The initial meta-analysis of these investigations concluded that clients benefit considerably from the various types of psychotherapeutic and counseling interventions (Smith & Glass, 1977; Smith, Glass, & Miller, 1980; Wampold, 2001). In a meta-analysis of 475 controlled outcome studies, Smith et al. (1980) demonstrated an average effect size of 0.85 standard deviation on the outcome measure of the treatment over the control group, indicating that the typical client receiving counseling was better off than 80% of those untreated but in need of counseling. Wampold (2001) reviewed several major meta-analyses conducted between 1993 and 1996 and reported that the effect size related to absolute efficacy of counseling/psychotherapy falls within the range of 0.75–0.85. He concluded that a reasonable and defensible point estimate for the efficacy of counseling/psychotherapy should be 0.80, a large effect size in the behavioral and social sciences.

Working Alliance

Working alliance can be defined as: (1) the client's affective relationship with the therapist, (2) the client's motivation and ability to accomplish work collaboratively with the therapist, (3) the therapist's empathic responding to and involvement with the client, and (4) client and therapist agreement about the goals and tasks of therapy (Horvath & Symonds, 1991). In a meta-analysis involving thousands of studies designed to investigate the efficacy of counseling interventions on client outcomes, Wampold (2001) determined that it was common factors such as working alliance, empathic listening, and goal setting that underlie all psychotherapeutic approaches that affect outcomes, not techniques associated with specific theoretical orientations. He found that at least 70% of psychotherapeutic effects are due to common factors, 8% are due to specific factors (i.e., different theoretical orientations and techniques), and the remaining 22% was partially attributed to individual client differences. In a meta-analysis that used 24 studies related specifically to the efficacy of working alliance, Horvath, Del Re, Flückiger, and Symonds (2011) found a "relatively robust" relationship between working alliance and positive counseling outcomes ($r = 0.275$). Working alliance is especially conducive to active participation between clients and counselors in the rehabilitation process (Chan, Shaw, McMahon, Koch, & Strauser, 1997). Lustig, Strauser, Rice, and Rucker (2002) examined survey data of 2,732 VR clients during fiscal year 2000 and found that: (1) employed clients had a stronger working alliance than unemployed clients ($d = 0.73$; large effect), (2) a stronger working alliance was related to a more positive client perception of future employment prospects ($r = 0.51$; large effect), and (3) a stronger working alliance was related to employed rehabilitation clients' satisfaction with their current jobs ($r = 0.15$; small effect).

Self-efficacy

Promoting self-efficacy is another important aspect of VR. Although skills training is used frequently to promote the self-efficacy of individuals with severe and persistent mental illness and alcohol and other drug abuse problems, the concept of skills training in the areas of social skills, coping skills, general life skills, and specific job skills also is applicable to individuals with other disabilities. Huffcutt, Conway, Roth, and Stone (2001) in a meta-analysis of predictors of job performance found that interpersonal skills are highly related to job performance (with a large average effect size of $r = 0.39$). Bolton and Akridge (1995) conducted a meta-analysis of skills training interventions for people with disabilities in VR and found that outcome measures resulted in an aggregate effect size of $d+ = 0.82$, 95% confidence interval (CI) 0.55–1.31, and a disattenuated effect size of $d+ = 0.93$, suggesting substantial benefit to the typical participant. Dilk and Bond (1996) conducted a meta-analysis of 68 studies, 59 between-group studies and 9 within-group studies (i.e., one-group, pretest-posttest), to determine the effectiveness of skills training for individuals with mental illness and the influence of such factors as methodological rigor, choice of outcome measures, and service settings. For between-group studies, the overall effect size was medium at posttest ($d = 0.40$) and at follow-up ($d = 0.56$). For the within-group studies, the overall effect size was also medium at posttest ($d = 0.48$), but small at follow-up ($d = 0.30$). Dilk and Bond concluded that behavioral skills training for persons with mental illness can be effective for teaching inpatients interpersonal and assertiveness skills, as indicated by measures of skill acquisition and symptom reduction.

Motivational Interviewing

Motivational interviewing is an empirically supported, client-centered, directive counseling approach designed to promote client motivation and reduce motivational conflicts and barriers to change. Wagner and McMahon (2004) have identified an array of motivational interviewing applications that can be used to address motivational issues in rehabilitation counseling practice such as managing medical issues and adjusting to physical disability, adjusting to cognitive impairment, improving psychosocial functioning, and returning to work. Hettema, Steele, and Miller (2005) conducted a meta-analysis of 72 studies to examine the efficacy of motivational interviewing. The majority of the studies (71%) have a focus on alcohol, smoking, and drug use. Generally, motivational interviewing was found to have a large effect size of 0.77 (95% CI 0.35, 1.19) immediately after treatment, a medium effect size of 0.30 (95% CI 0.16, 0.43) at more than 3–6 months, and dropped to a small effect size of 0.11 (95% CI 0.06, 0.17) at follow-ups longer than 12 months. The effect of motivational interviewing on alcohol and other drug abuse treatment outcome is more consistent than other studies, with a mean of 0.26 across all follow-up points. Recently, Lundahl, Kunz, Brownell, Tollefson, and Burke (2010) conducted a meta-analysis of 25 years of motivational interviewing empirical studies with substance use (tobacco, alcohol, drugs, and marijuana), health-related behaviors (diet, exercise, and safe sex), engagement in treatment, and gambling variables as targeted outcomes. They found a smaller overall effect size of $g = 0.22$ (95% CI 0.17, 0.27). Although motivational interviewing did not perform any better than other strong substance abuse treatments such as cognitive behavior therapy and 12-step, motivation interviewing interventions on average require significantly less time (over 100 fewer minutes) to produce equal effects. Motivational interviewing is effective for increasing clients' engagement in treatment and their intention to change. It works relatively well for individuals with all range of distress levels. The effect of motivational interviewing also was found to be durable at the 2-year mark and beyond.

Vocational Rehabilitation (VR) Services

Although it is not possible to conduct experimental studies for state VR services as an independent variable, the Rehabilitation Act requires the state-federal VR program to conduct ongoing research to demonstrate the effectiveness of rehabilitation interventions on employment rates and quality of employment outcomes of people with disabilities. There is research evidence from nonexperimental studies to support the association between VR services and successful employment outcomes. In a recent study, Dutta, Gervey, Chan, Chou, and Ditchman (2008) analyzed the Rehabilitation Services Administration case services report (RSA-911) data for fiscal year 2005 using logistic regression analysis and found job placement, on-the-job support, maintenance, and other services (e.g., medical care for acute conditions) as significant predictors of employment success across all impairment groups. They found that job placement and support services could improve the odds for obtaining competitive employment: job search assistance (odds ratio [OR] = 1.24; 95% CI [1.08, 1.43]), job placement assistance (OR = 1.89; 95% CI [1.66, 2.16]), and on-the-job support (OR = 2.20; 95% CI [1.90, 2.55]). In addition, diagnostic and treatment (D&T) services (OR = 1.57; 95% CI [1.35, 1.82]) and rehabilitation technology services (OR = 1.97, 95% CI [1.67, 2.33]) were found to contribute uniquely to employment outcomes for the sensory impairments group as well as the physical impairments group (D&T services: OR = 1.31, 95% CI [1.15, 1.48]; RT services: OR = 1.41, 95% CI [1.13, 1.75]), but not the mental impairments group. Substantial counseling was associated with employment outcomes for the physical (OR = 1.16, 95% CI [1.02, 1.32]) and mental impairments groups (OR = 1.18, 95% CI [1.03, 1.35]). Miscellaneous training (OR = 1.31; 95% CI [1.09, 1.49]) was specifically associated with employment outcomes of the mental impairments group.

Psychiatric Rehabilitation

Drake, Merrens, and Lynde (2005) identified supported employment as a high-quality evidence-based intervention in mental health practice. There is strong evidence including randomized clinical trial studies supporting its efficacy. Bond (2004) examined data from four studies of the conversion from day treatment program to supported employment and nine randomized controlled trials comparing supported employment to a variety of alternative approaches. The four conversion studies represented six conversion sites with 317 consumers in supported employment and three comparison sites with 184 consumers in day treatment. Bond reported an average threefold increase in employment rate (from 12% to 38%) for the conversion group and virtually no change for the day treatment group (from 13% to 15%) between the pre–post time periods of the studies. For the experimental studies, the comparison was between relatively new supported employment programs with traditional vocational services. Bond indicated that these randomized controlled studies have shown there is a 20–40% increase in the competitive employment rate when using supported employment services versus other vocational programs. The average employment rate for consumers with mental illness in supported employment was 56% compared to 19% in traditional vocational programs. Bond reported a large effect size of 0.85 by weighting each study equally. Supported employment also was found to be effective for consumers from racial and ethnic minority backgrounds. Mueser et al. (2004) conducted a randomized controlled study in the inner city of Hartford, CT. They compared three approaches to VR for severe mental illness: the IPS model of supported employment, a psychosocial rehabilitation (PSR) program, and standard vocational services. They randomly assigned unemployed consumers with mental illness who are predominantly African American (46%) and Latino (30%) to IPS, PSR, or standard services and followed them for 2 years. Consumers in IPS achieved significantly better employment outcomes than clients in PSR and standard services, including more competitive work (73.9% vs. 18.2% vs. 27.5%, respectively) and any paid work (73.9% vs. 34.8% vs. 53.6%, respectively).

FUTURE RESEARCH DIRECTIONS

It is clear that medical, behavioral, and social sciences research has been used to inform rehabilitation counseling practice. Nevertheless, the lack of strong theory-driven research and empirical evidence to inform assessment, planning, and intervention in the rehabilitation process has been one of the most recurring and frequent criticisms of rehabilitation counseling research (Berkowitz et al., 1975; Chan et al., 2003). Current rehabilitation practices have been characterized by some scholars as "experience-based," "eminence-based," or "habit-based" (Law, 2002). In addition, rehabilitation research is frequently nonexperimental or quasi-experimental in nature (Bolton, 2004). The lack of randomized controlled trials is seen as a major barrier to the successful implementation of evidence-based practice in rehabilitation (Chwalisz & Chan, 2008). To fully adopt an evidence-based approach in rehabilitation, Dunn and Elliott (2008) proposed that the field needs to: (1) embrace a comprehensive theory-driven research agenda, (2) validate effective interventions based on this research agenda, and (3) facilitate the provision of empirically supported interventions based on the research evidence.

Chan et al. (2010) suggested that the evidence-based practice movement may present a window of opportunity for rehabilitation counseling to promote and support a systematic agenda for theory-driven rehabilitation research. The use of scientific evidence derived from theory-driven research to inform rehabilitation counseling practice could improve employment rates and quality of employment outcomes for people with significant disabilities. However, the complex nature of rehabilitation both in service delivery and population makes process and outcome research challenging (Johnston, Stineman, & Velozo, 1997). Specifically, rehabilitation encompasses a broad scope of services, spans along the medical-vocational rehabilitation continuum from hospital care to community based services, and is provided through an array of disciplines (e.g., rehabilitation medicine, social work, and rehabilitation counseling) for individuals with diverse and complex impairments and disabilities. The process typically involves a range of personal and environmental processes and the interactions thereof, making it difficult to determine what aspects of service delivery contribute to what outcome. Chan, Tarvydas, et al. (2009) advocated that the World Health Organization (WHO) *International Classification of Functioning, Disability, and Health* (ICF) model can be used as a rehabilitation framework for conceptualizing and determining medical and VR assessment, planning, and service needs and to provide evidence-based services for people with chronic illness and disability. They underscored that the ICF model can also be used to develop a systematic research agenda to develop and validate evidence-based practices for VR.

Specifically, the ICF paradigm is structured around the three broad components: (1) body functions and structure, (2) activity (related to tasks and actions by an individual) and participation (involvement in a life situation), and (3) individual characteristics and environmental factors. Functioning and disability

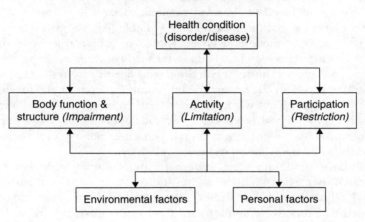

FIGURE 18.2
The World Health Organization ICF Model

are viewed as a complex interaction between the health condition of the individual and the contextual factors of the environment, as well as personal factors. The emphasis of the ICF is on function rather than condition or disease and is designed to be relevant across cultures as well as age groups and genders, making it highly appropriate for heterogeneous populations. Key constructs and how they interact to affect full inclusion, health status, and quality of life of people with chronic illness and disability are depicted in Figure 18.2.

The ICF model has been embraced by many health care and rehabilitation health researchers, and the voluminous research generated by these health researchers can also be invaluable for rehabilitation counselors. The research agenda of rehabilitation counseling researchers should focus on conducting systematic research to validate relationships among constructs in the ICF model and how these constructs uniquely contribute and interact with each other to affect full inclusion and participation of people with disabilities in the community as well as employment, health condition, and quality of life (Chan, Keegan, et al., 2009). This type of research agenda will contribute significantly to the availability of best evidence, which will influence rehabilitation counseling practice. Specifically, randomized controlled trials conducted to validate ICF-guided interventions can be used to improve functioning, increase activity levels, maximize individual character strengths, modify the environment (e.g., employer attitudes), encourage full participation in the community, promote physical health and mental health well-being, and increase employment opportunities for people with disabilities, especially those from subpopulations with the lowest employment outcomes.

Research questions involving moderators address when or for whom a variable most strongly predicts or causes an outcome variable, whereas mediators establish how or why one variable predicts or causes an outcome variable

(Frazier, Tix, & Barron, 2004). A mediator provides information about the underlying mechanisms for change, whereas a moderator effect is basically an interaction whereby the effect of an independent variable (e.g., treatment) differs at different levels of another independent variable (e.g., severity). Importantly, testing mediator and moderator effects should be a high priority in the rehabilitation counseling research agenda, which will further promote the use of evidence-based practice in the field. Similar to health care research, the study of moderator effects in VR research is important, as what works for European American clients may not work for individuals from diverse racial and ethnic minority backgrounds; what works for men may not work for women; and what works for individuals with sensory impairments may not work for persons with psychiatric disabilities (Chan, Tarvydas, et al., 2009).

Similarly, moderators are extremely important in other key areas of VR research. For example, in studying the role of resiliency factors in psychosocial adjustment to disability, future research can examine whether the adjustment process is similar or different for persons with sudden onset versus chronic conditions. Therefore, it is very important for rehabilitation researchers to expend more research efforts to test moderator effects of race, gender, disability type, health status, and immunity (e.g., social support, coping skills, and resilience) and vulnerability factors (e.g., stress). For theory or model building, it is equally important to study the mediator effect (i.e., the underlying mechanisms of change) in order to better design effective interventions (Hoyt, Imel, & Chan, 2008). An increased emphasis on testing mediator and moderator variables in the VR research paradigm is needed in order to develop effective model-driven, culturally sensitive and evidence-based VR interventions for individuals with disabilities in the 21st century (Chan, Tarvydas, et al., 2009).

CONCLUSION

In conclusion, incorporating research-based knowledge into rehabilitation counseling practice, to ensure that people with disabilities receive empirically validated assessment, intervention, and consultation services, is particularly relevant in today's era of accountability, research utilization, and evidence-based practice (Chan et al., 2010; Chan, Keegan, et al., 2009; Chronister et al., 2008; Law, 2002). As a conceptual framework or philosophy, evidence-based practice advocates that every rehabilitation and health professional should have an interest in delivering the best possible services to their customers—based, whenever possible, on the best clinical practices available from the strongest research evidence. VR researchers and practitioners must develop a strong focus on theory development, empirical evidence, and clinical application. Within the context of evidence-based practice, Dunn and Elliott (2008) argue for the primacy of theory and its place in rehabilitation research. Advocacy for the development of theory-driven research programs that embrace methodological pluralism will advance new theory and produce meaningful research programs that inform practice in VR service delivery. The development of a systematic research agenda and conducting meaningful theory-driven research and intervention research will generate new knowledge and accumulate high-quality evidence, enhancing the ability of rehabilitation counselors to truly engage in evidence-based practice to improve employment outcomes and quality of life of people with disabilities.

CONTENT REVIEW QUESTIONS

- How did the evidence-based practice approach to health care service delivery evolve within the United States?
- What are the main conceptual bases of evidence-based practice?
- How can rehabilitation counselors become more effective practitioners within the framework of evidence-based practice?
- Which evidence-based methodologies and concepts are crucial in improving rehabilitation counselors' knowledge of evidence-based practice and research utilization?
- How can the evidence-based decision-making process be illustrated?
- Describe a hierarchical framework that emphasizes the importance of randomized controlled trials/experimental studies.
- What is the gold standard for best scientific evidence in evidence-based medicine? How does it apply to rehabilitation counseling?
- Which elements can be considered as barriers in promoting the application of evidence based in rehabilitation counseling?
- Describe empirically supported strategy interventions in rehabilitation counseling.
- How can the field of rehabilitation counseling apply, support, and advance theory-driven research?
- Discuss how the World Health Organization ICF can be used to guide the development of a systematic research agenda in rehabilitation counseling?

ACKNOWLEDGMENTS

The contents of this chapter were developed with support through the Rehabilitation Research and Training Center on Effective Vocational Rehabilitation Service Delivery Practices established at both the University of Wisconsin-Madison and the University of Wisconsin-Stout under a grant from the Department of Education, National Institute on Disability and Rehabilitation Research (NIDRR) grant number PR# H133B100034. However, the contents do not necessarily represent the policy of the U.S. Department of Education, and endorsement by the Federal Government should not be assumed.

REFERENCES

American Psychological Association. (2005). *Policy statement on evidence-based practice in psychology*. Retrieved from http://www.apa.org/practice/resources/evidence/evidence-based-statement.pdf

Berkowitz, M., Englander, V., Rubin, J., & Worrall, J. D. (1975). *An evaluation of policy-related research*. New York, NY: Praeger.

Berkowitz, M., Englander, V., Rubin, J., & Worrall, J. D. (1976). A summary of "An evaluation of policy-related research." *Rehabilitation Counseling Bulletin, 20,* 29–45.

Bezyak, J. L., Kubota, C., & Rosenthal, D. (2010). Evidence-based practice in rehabilitation counseling: Perceptions and practices. *Rehabilitation Education, 24,* 85–96.

Bolton, B. (2004). Counseling and rehabilitation outcomes. In F. Chan, N. L. Berven, & K. R. Thomas (Eds.), *Counseling theories and techniques for rehabilitation health professionals* (pp. 444–465). New York, NY: Springer.

Bolton, B., & Akridge, R. L. (1995). A meta-analysis of skills training programs for rehabilitation clients. *Rehabilitation Counseling Bulletin, 38,* 262–273.

Bond, G. R. (2004). Supported employment: Evidence for an evidence-based practice. *Psychiatric Rehabilitation Journal, 27,* 345–359.

Borenstein, M., Hedges, L. V., Higgins, J. P. T., & Rothstein, H. R. (2009). *Introduction to meta-analysis*. New York, NY: Wiley.

Chambless, D. L., & Hollon, S. D. (1998). Defining empirically supported therapies. *Journal of Consulting & Clinical Psychology, 66*(1), 7.

Chan, F., Bezyak, J., Romero-Ramirez, M., Chiu, C. Y., Sung, C. & Fujikawa, M. (2010). Concepts, challenges, barriers, and opportunities related to evidence-based practice in rehabilitation counseling. *Rehabilitation Education, 24,* 179-190.

Chan, F., Keegan, J., Sung, C., Drout, M., Pai, C. H., Anderson, E., & McLain, N. (2009). The World Health Organization ICF model as a framework for assessing vocational rehabilitation outcomes. *Journal of Rehabilitation Administration, 33,* 91–112.

Chan, F., Miller, S., Pruett, S., Lee, G., & Chou, C. (2003). Research. In D. Maki & T. Riggar (Eds.), *Handbook of rehabilitation counseling* (pp. 159–170). New York, NY: Springer.

Chan, F., Rosenthal, D. A., & Pruett, S. (2008). Evidence-based practice in the provision of rehabilitation services. *Journal of Rehabilitation, 74*(2), 3–5.

Chan, F., Shaw, L., McMahon, B. T., Koch, L., & Strauser, D. (1997). A model for enhancing consumer-counselor working relationships in rehabilitation. *Rehabilitation Counseling Bulletin, 41,* 122–137.

Chan, F., Tarvydas, V., Blalock, K., Strauser, D., & Atkins, B. J. (2009). Unifying and elevating rehabilitation counseling through model-driven, diversity-sensitive evidence-based practice. *Rehabilitation Counseling Bulletin, 52,* 114–119.

Chronister, J. A., Cardoso, E., Lee, G. K., Chan, F., & Leahy, M. J. (2005). Evidence-based practice in case management. In F. Chan, M. Leahy, & J. Saunders (Eds.), *Case management for rehabilitation health professionals* (Vol. 2, pp. 369–387). Osage Beach, MO: Aspen Professional Services.

Chronister, J. A., Chan, F., Cardoso, E., Lynch, R. T., & Rosenthal, D. A. (2008). The evidence-based practice movement in healthcare: Implications for rehabilitation. *Journal of Rehabilitation, 74*(2), 6–15.

Chwalisz, K., & Chan, F. (2008). Methodological advances and issues in rehabilitation psychology: Moving forward on the cutting edge. *Rehabilitation Psychology, 53,* 251–253.

Chwalisz, K., Shah, S. R., & Hand, K. M. (2008). Facilitating rigorous qualitative research in rehabilitation psychology. *Rehabilitation Psychology, 53*(3), 387–399. doi:10.1037/a0012998

Cohen, J. (1988). *Statistical power analysis for the behavioral sciences* (2nd ed.). Hillsdale, NJ: Erlbaum.

DePalma, J. A. (2002). Proposing an evidence-based policy process. *Nursing Administration Quarterly, 26*(4), 55–61.

Dilk, M. N., & Bond, G. R. (1996). Meta-analytic evaluation of skills training research for individuals with severe mental illness. *Journal of Consulting and Clinical Psychology, 64,* 1337–1346.

Drake, R., Merrens, M., & Lynde, D. (Eds.). (2005). *Evidence-based mental health practice: A textbook.* New York, NY: W.W. Norton.

Dunn, D. S., & Elliott, T. R. (2008). The place and promise of theory in rehabilitation psychology. *Rehabilitation Psychology, 53,* 254–267.

Durlak, J. A. (1995). *School-based prevention programs for children and adolescents.* Thousand Oaks, CA: Sage.

Dutta, A., Gervey, R., Chan, F., Chou, C., & Ditchman, N. (2008). Vocational rehabilitation services and employment outcomes for people with disabilities: A United States study. *Journal of Occupational Rehabilitation, 18*(4), 326–334. doi:10.1007/s10926-008-9154-z

Frazier, P. A., Tix, A. P., & Barron, K. E. (2004). Testing moderator and mediator effects in counseling psychology research. *Journal of Counseling Psychology, 51,* 115–134.

Graham, I., Logan, J., Harrison, M., Straus, S., Tetroe, J., Caswell, W., . . . Robinson, N. (2006). Lost in knowledge translation: Time for a map? *Journal of Continuing Education in the Health Professions, 26*(1), 13–24. Hedges, L. V. (1981). Distribution theory for Glass's estimator of effect size and related estimators. *Journal of Educational Statistics, 6,* 107 -128.

Hedges, L. V. (1981). Distribution theory for Glass's estimator of effect size and related estimators. Journal of Educational Statistics, 6, 107–128.

Hedges, L. V., & Olkin, I. (1985). *Statistical methods for meta-analysis.* Orlando, FL: Academic Press.

Hettema, J., Steele, J., & Miller, W. R. (2005). Motivational interviewing. *Annual Review of Clinical Psychology, 1*(1), 91–111.

Holm, M. (2000). Our mandate for the new millennium: Evidence-based practice–the 2000 Eleanor Clarke Slagle Lecture. *American Journal of Occupational Therapy, 54*(6), 575–585.

Horvath, A. O., & Symonds, B. D. (1991). Relation between working alliance and outcome in psychotherapy: A meta-analysis. *Journal of Counseling Psychology, 38,* 139-149.

Horvath, A. O., Del Re, A., Flückiger, C., & Symonds, D. (2011). Alliance in individual psychotherapy. In J. C. Norcross (Ed.), *Psychotherapy relationships that work* (2nd ed.). New York, NY: Oxford University Press.

Hoyt, W. T., Imel, Z. E., & Chan, F. (2008). Multiple regression and correlation techniques: Recent controversies and best practices. *Rehabilitation Psychology, 53*(3), 321–339. doi:10.1037/a0013021

Huffcut, A. I., Conway, J. M., Roth, P. L., & Stone, N. J. (2001). Identification and meta-analytic assessment of psychological constructs measured in employment interviews. *Journal of Applied Psychology, 86,* 897–913.

Johnston, M. V., Stineman, M., & Velozo, C. A. (1997). Outcome research in medical rehabilitation: Foundations from the past and directions for the future. In M. J. Fuhrer (Ed.), *Assessing medical rehabilitation practices: The promise of outcomes research.* Baltimore, MD: Paul H. Brookes.

Kosciulek, J. F., & Szymanski, E. M. (1993). Statistical power analysis of rehabilitation counseling research. *Rehabilitation Counseling Bulletin, 36,* 212–219.

Law, M. (2002). *Evidence-based rehabilitation: A guide to practice.* Thorofare, NJ: SLACK Incorporated.

Leahy, M., Chan, F., & Saunders, J. (2003). A work behavior analysis of contemporary rehabilitation counseling practices. *Rehabilitation Counseling Bulletin, 46,* 66–81.

Lundahl, B., Kunz, C., Brownell, C., Tollefson, D., & Burke, B. (2010). A meta-analysis of motivational interviewing: Twenty-five years of empirical studies. *Research on Social Work Practice, 20*(2), 137–160. doi:10.1177/1049731509347850

Lustig, D. C., Strauser, D. R., Rice, N. D., & Rucker, T. F. (2002). The relationship between working alliance and rehabilitation outcomes. *Rehabilitation Counseling Bulletin, 46,* 24–32.

Mueser, K. T., Clark, R. E., Haines, M., Drake, R. E., McHugo, G. J., Bond, G., . . . Swain, K. (2004). The Hartford study of supported employment for persons with severe mental illness. *Journal of Consulting and Clinical Psychology, 72*(3), 479–490. doi:10.1037/0022-006X.72.3.479

Nathan, P., & Gorman, J. (1998). *A guide to treatments that work.* New York, NY: Oxford University Press.

National Center for the Dissemination of Disability Research. (2006). Overview of International Literature on Knowledge Translation. *FOCUS: A Technical Brief, 14,* 1–6.

Parker, R. M., & Hensen, C. E. (1981). *Rehabilitation counseling: Foundations, consumers, and service delivery.* Boston, MA: Allyn & Bacon.

Pruett, S. R., Swett, E. A., Chan, F., Rosenthal, D. A., & Lee, G. K. (2008). Empirical evidence supporting the effectiveness of vocational rehabilitation. *Journal of Rehabilitation, 74*(2), 56–63.

Rubin, S., Chan, F., & Thomas, D. (2003). Assessing changes in life skills and quality of life resulting from rehabilitation services. *Journal of Rehabilitation, 69*(3), 4–9.

Rubin, S. E., & Rice, J. M. (1986). Quality and relevance of rehabilitation research: A critique and recommendations. *Rehabilitation Counseling Bulletin, 30,* 33–42.

Sackett, D. L., Rosenberg, W. M. C., Gray, J. A. M., Haynes, R. B., & Richardson, W. S. (1996). Evidence-based medicine: What it is and what it isn't. *British Medical Journal, 312,* 71–72.

Schlosser, R. W. (2006). The role of systematic reviews in evidence-based practice, research, and development. *FOCUS: A Technical Brief, 15,* 1–4.

Schmidt, F. L., & Hunter, J. E. (2003). Meta-analysis. In J. A. Schinka & W. F. Velicer (Eds.), *Handbook of psychology (Vol. 2): Research methods in psychology* (pp. 533–554). Hoboken, NJ: John Wiley & Sons.

Smith, M. L., & Glass, G. V. (1977). Meta-analysis of psychotherapy outcome studies. *American Psychologist, 32*(9), 752–760. doi:10.1037/0003-066X.32.9.752

Smith, M. L., Glass, G. V., & Miller, T. I. (1980). *The benefits of psychotherapy.* Baltimore, MD: The Johns Hopkins University Press.

Straus, S. E., Tetroe, J., & Graham, I. D. (2009). Knowledge to action: What is and what it isn't. In S. E. Straus, J. Tetroe, & I. D. Graham (Eds.), *Knowledge translation in health care: Moving from evidence to practice* (pp. 3–12). Chichester, UK: Wiley-Blackwell.

Sudsawad, P. (2007). *Knowledge translation: Introduction to models, strategies, and measures.* Austin, TX: Southwest Educational Development Laboratory, National Center for the Dissemination of Disability Research.

Thirty-Third Institute on Rehabilitation Issues. (2008). *Evidence based practices: Improving employment outcomes for people with significant disabilities.* Hot Springs, AK: University of Arkansas Rehabilitation Continuing Education Center.

Tucker, J., & Reed, G. (2008). Evidentiary pluralism as a strategy for research and evidence-based practice in rehabilitation psychology. *Rehabilitation Psychology, 53*(3), 279–293.

U.S. Government Accountability Office. (2005). *Vocational rehabilitation: Better measures and monitoring could improve the performance of the VR program* (GAO-05-865). Washington, DC: Author.

Wagner, C. C., & McMahon, B. T. (2004). Motivational interviewing and rehabilitation counseling practice. *Rehabilitation Counseling Bulletin, 47,* 152–161.

Walker, B. B., Seay, S. J., Solomon, A. C., & Spring, B. (2006). Treating chronic migraine headaches: An evidence-based practice approach. *Journal of Clinical Psychology, 62*(11), 1367–1378. doi:10.1002/jclp.20316

Wampold, B. E. (1997). Methodological problems in identifying efficacious psychotherapies. *Psychotherapy Research, 7*(1), 21–43.

Wampold, B. E. (2001). *The great psychotherapy debate.* Mahwah, NJ: Lawrence Erlbaum Associates.

19

Technology

Mary Barros-Bailey

LEARNING OBJECTIVES

After reading this chapter, you should be able to:

■ Survey the main areas to consider in the use of technology within and supportive of each party within the client–counselor relationship.
■ Discuss behavioral and competency issues and assessment as these apply to technology.
■ Describe the Three-Step Assessment Process when evaluating assistive technology needs and provide basic tools and resources to meet those needs.

In 2005, the Rehabilitation Counseling Consortium was organized through efforts of the Commission on Rehabilitation Counselor Certification (CRCC). The Consortium arrived at a definition of rehabilitation counseling, which states that it is a:

> group of professionally prepared and credentialed counselors with specialized knowledge, skills and attitudes who work collaboratively in a professional relationship with persons with disabilities to achieve their personal, social, psychological and vocational goals. These professionals adhere to the Rehabilitation Counseling *Code of Professional Ethics for Rehabilitation Counselors* and practice with the Rehabilitation Counseling Scope of Practice in order to ensure the provision of qualified services to consumers. The profession is supported by organizations and institutions whose purposes are to promote and develop the profession. (Rehabilitation Counseling Consortium, 2005a)

The Rehabilitation Counseling Consortium went on to define the rehabilitation counselor as someone ". . . who possesses the specialized knowledge, skills, and attitudes needed to collaborate in a professional relationship with people who have disabilities to achieve their personal, social, psychological, and vocational goals" (Rehabilitation Counseling Consortium, 2005b). Central and inherent to both definitions is the importance of the therapeutic relationship—that is, the client–counselor relationship in rehabilitation counseling. It is this relationship that prominently leads the expectations of behaviors, responsibilities, and competencies stated or implied in the first section of the *Code of Professional Ethics for Rehabilitation Counselors* (CRCC, 2010), *The Counseling Relationship*, that will serve as the rubric for examining the use of technology in rehabilitation counseling.

This chapter addresses technology as it impacts, enhances, or inhibits the very core of the work of the rehabilitation counselor and rehabilitation counseling from the perspective of the client that of the counselor. Technology is, after all, a tool that has become part of our personal and professional lives. First, the prevalence of technology is explored in American society in general, and then specific to people with disabilities. Next, behavioral issues associated with technology are examined. Third, general technological competence for the counselor and client is addressed. Finally, knowledge of assistive technology, which is an obvious and important competency for the rehabilitation counselor to possess, is described and assessment tools are discussed that may be beneficial to this process.

TECHNOLOGY USAGE IN THE UNITED STATES

The General Public

Imagine a public place, any public place—the airport, a coffee shop, the library, a classroom, or some other location. How many people have cellular phones? If it is an average crowd in the United States, likely close to 90% will have these phones; of these people, over 70% of adults will probably be using them to text an average of 10 times per day and nearly 90% of teenagers will use them for the same reason about 50 times per day (Pew Internet, 2010). Although cell phones are the most common electronic gadget used by Americans for all sorts of activities from the Pew Research activity form calling, to texting, to taking pictures and other uses, the Pew Research Center estimates that in 2010, 59% of Americans owned desktop computers, 52% had laptop computers, 47% possessed MP3 players, 29% had downloaded podcasts (although the word was first used only in 2004 per the Merriam-Webster Online, 2010), 42% used game consoles, 5% read e-books on readers, and 4% owned tablet computers. These gadgets and technology have infused our society with a new lexicon that has changed the way we learn, teach, entertain, recreate, shop, relate to others, maintain records, and perform many more activities in our lives. Gadgets have changed the manner in which clients may approach or perform basic activities of daily living or instrumental activities of daily living. Understanding and effectively using technology in the counseling process is important to both parties involved in the client–counseling relationship, and the support and delivery systems in which that relationship occurs.

People With Disabilities

Comparable statistics were sought for people with disabilities for these technologies, but were difficult to locate. The National Telecommunications and Information Administration (NTIA) regularly reports on the use of computer and Internet technology for people with disabilities. In 2010, it noted that:

> Only half of all households (51%) headed by someone with a disability had an Internet user, compared to the majority of households (81%) headed by someone without a disability. Only four out of ten households (43%) headed by someone with a disability subscribed to Internet services at home, compared to seven out of ten households (73%) where the householder has no disability. Broadband Internet subscription at home showed a similar pattern (38% compared to 68%). (NTIA, p. 31)

Some of the reasons assumed by the NTIA to cause the disparity in the statistics were that the population of people with disabilities were on the average of lower socioeconomic standing, were older, had lower educational attainment, and resided more frequently in rural America.

An earlier study by the NTIA (2004) identified the following disability populations having the greatest Internet and computer usage:

1. Deaf or severe hearing impairment, 72.1%
2. Difficulty leaving home, 67.8%
3. Difficulty typing, 64.4%
4. Difficulty walking, 64.2%
5. Blind or severe vision impairment, 63.7%
6. Multiple disabilities, 58.9%
7. None of these disabilities, 71%

For people with disabilities not engaging in the workforce, who most likely would be part of the rehabilitation counselor's caseload, Internet usage was noted by NTIA (2004) to be the following:

1. Deaf or severe hearing impairment, 47.9%
2. Blind or severe vision impairment, 40%
3. Difficulty typing, 34.3%
4. Difficulty walking, 33.1%
5. Multiple disabilities, 27.9%
6. Difficulty leaving home, 26.1%
7. None of these disabilities, 52.5%

Studies on the use of computers and the Internet by people with disabilities are not conclusive, and some seem contradictory. The Rural Institute (2006) reviewed the various data regarding the use of the Internet by people with disabilities and confirmed them to be contradictory data. Furthermore, they posited that because there are several barriers to Internet and computer access by people with disabilities, it is likely that the digital divide indeed exists between those with and without disabilities. These perceived barriers to Internet access are indicated to be the following: (1) cost of adapted hardware and software; (2) limited locations for Internet access; (3) unavailable workplace Internet access due to the low rate of employment for people with disabilities; and, (4) inaccessible web sites for people using assistive technology (Rural Institute, 2006). Studies regarding technology use by people with disabilities demonstrate a rift between the access of the general public to the Internet and that of people with disabilities caused by those disabilities; however, those with disabilities can realize some of the greatest educational, recreational, and lifestyle gains with the use of this medium (Barros-Bailey, Aguilar, & Burks, 2000).

Advances in technology that engage more senses than before its invention allow the general public to more efficiently and effectively use it; access to it is of tremendous benefit to people with disabilities. For example, voice-activated telephone systems require the ability for such a system to receive verbal input from people of all ages, using different tones, accents, and pitches. These systems allow research and development efforts to hone the efficiency of the technology for those who might articulate differently because of voice function that might be altered because of a disability. Phone applications extend voice activation to gadgets that previously might not be so readily accessible. As the cost of research and development could be justified because of the commercial benefit of such research efforts, ultimately the technology is made more accessible to people with disabilities.

TECHNOLOGY AND BEHAVIOR

Shetchman and Horowitz (2003) tested the assumption that people interact the same with computers as in live communication. They found that when people thought they were interacting with a computer and not an individual, people used less effort in their communication behavior. That is, people act differently when they are using technology, particularly in the online environment, than when they are in face-to-face or telephonic interactions. The immediacy of Internet communication draws upon people's impulsivity (Caplan, 2002; Davis, Flett, & Besser, 2002; Suler, 2004). While this impulsivity has been documented in research studies for nearly a decade, more recent reports (Goleman, 2007) are identifying the neurological causes of the phenomenon. Goleman (2007) explains that in the interaction with a computer there is the absence of cues from body language and other sensory stimuli to assist in decoding communication. Therefore,

> if we are typing while agitated, the absence of information on how the other person is responding makes the prefrontal circuitry for discretion more likely to fail. Our emotional impulses disinhibited, we type some infelicitous message and hit "send" before a more sober second thought lends us to hit "discard." (Goleman, 2007, p. 12)

Beyond the lack of cues, the immediacy of the decoding process when information is received through one of the gadgets and the resulting response fails to allow time to serve as a mitigation or check and balance to the impulsivity.

When it comes to the use of much of this new and emerging technology, impulsive responses are the norm rather than the exception. Understanding this phenomenon is important in the client–counselor relationship to interpret and improve communication. In short, less communication effort coupled with impulsivity in online interaction may lead to a kind of mindless communication resulting in potential behaviors that would otherwise be considered improper in more traditional forms of communication used in counseling practice (e.g., face-to-face or even telephone counseling).

Being aware that communication happens differently with the use of technology is an important point of discussion between the client and the counselor so that the technological medium becomes a facilitator rather than a barrier within the client–counseling relationship. This awareness also helps guard against misinterpretation of the intent, tone, or other content of a message received and immediate reaction to it that might lead the interaction in a direction never originally intended. Because technology not only facilitates the interaction, but also records it, there is documentation of the interaction that either or both parties may regret and it may possibly be saved over a variety of servers.

For nearly two decades, the first two rules cited by Shea and Shea (1994) regarding online conduct—called netiquette—are: Rule (1) remember to be human and Rule (2) behave in the same way online as in real life. Shea and Shea (2006) posit that the reason for these rules comes from people sometimes forgetting that when they communicate using a computer there is a person at the other end of the hardware connection, not another innate object; therefore, the same standard for human behavior is expected, although "some people think that a lower standard of ethics or personal behavior is acceptable in cyberspace" (Shea & Shea, 2006, p. 1). The remaining netiquette rules are as follows:

Rule 3: Know where you are in cyberspace
Rule 4: Respect other people's time and bandwidth
Rule 5: Make yourself look good online
Rule 6: Share expert knowledge
Rule 7: Help keep flame wars under control
Rule 8: Respect other people's privacy
Rule 9: Don't abuse your power
Rule 10: Be forgiving of other people's mistakes

In rehabilitation counseling, the "mindless communication" dynamic is demonstrated through an example of how someone may communicate differently online than in person. Counselors may find that some clients disclose more about themselves and circumstances using technology than in a face-to-face session. Or, there might be expectations as to how often or quickly technology is used and responses are made by a counselor. Not only it is important that counselors and clients are aware of the pitfalls that may occur with the use of technology, the discussion should also include boundary setting regarding its use. Examples of boundaries may include what kinds of interactions are allowable with the use of the technology, when or how often the technology is used, and any other expectation with respect to its use.

TECHNOLOGICAL COMPETENCY

Computer and Internet competency assessment tools provide objective measures that could be used to assess not only the competency of clients, but also that of practitioners (Brasley, 2006; Hobbs, 2002; Jiang, Chen, & Chen, 2004). They could serve as a starting point for identifying not only the kinds of technological competencies a client or counselor possesses, but also psychometrically driven assessment tools that could help determine the training needs for counselors and clients. Many assessments exist that could be used. The Buros Institute (http://buros.unl.edu/buros/jsp/search.jsp) provides a source for identifying such measures. Some examples are discussed in this chapter.

Barros-Bailey (2007) found that rehabilitation counselors had difficulty with the expectation that they might be responsible for assessing their client's technological competencies. Perhaps this may be because rehabilitation counselors themselves may feel inadequate in their own technological competencies in order to be responsible for evaluating that of their clients. In the Barros-Bailey study, respondents commented on the impact of the Internet and computers on counselor education and competency. These competency issues not only involved the need for increased exposure to ethical use of the media, but also technical aspects and literacy updates for counselors. Some counselors seemed to take issue with aspects of their professional code of ethics (CRCC, 2010) requiring them to verify a client's ability to use computers. This was best summarized by one counselor who stated, "I think it would be patronizing to assume [clients] are not competent and need to be verified," and another added, "To the best of my knowledge there is no reliable way to determine who should or should not be using a computer based on competence." Overall, comments from respondents reflected a desire that the codes of ethics should be general and not specific, with several rehabilitation counselors displaying a bit of disbelief about the scope of their responsibilities expected in these codes with respect to assessing client competency (e.g., "Some of the questions you asked regarding client's Internet use appear inappropriate for counselors to be ethically responsible for.").

Technology is emerging at such an accelerated rate that it has outstripped our development of and knowledge about assessment instruments, tools, and methods to measure competencies regarding its use. But, in fact, there are ways to measure these competencies. The *Technology and Internet Assessment* (Ealy, n.d.), *New Technology Tests: Computer Rules* (NFER-Nelson Publishing Co., Ltd., n.d.), and *New Technology Tests: Computer Commands* (NFER-Nelson Publishing Co., Ltd., n.d.) are examples of normed instruments that test basic computer and/or Internet skills of clients or professionals. The *Technology and Internet Assessment* (Ealy, n.d.), for example, assesses basic competencies that could be beneficial to the counseling process through its various features: use of technology, specific computer skills, acquisition of technical knowledge, basic Internet knowledge, Internet information skills, adapting to technological change, impact of technology, and ethics in technology. These kinds of assessments could be used to test a counselor's basic level of computer/Internet literacy and help determine areas for further education and training. Or, rehabilitation counselors could include these kinds of tests in a client's vocational testing battery to help identify the client's ability to use technology or potential need for training. A more basic method of assessing competency of the client may be through a structured list of questions integrated into the intake form or as part of the vocational diagnostic interview and counseling process that provide the rehabilitation counselor with a screener as to the client's technical competencies.

Graduate and continuing education programs could focus on assisting rehabilitation counselors in developing and understanding basic technological skills involved in the *process* and *application* of technology. Individual assessment classes could integrate the use of instruments or methods to assess technological competence as part of the individualized assessment. For example, problematic use of the Internet (PUI) (Caplan, 2002, 2005; Davis et al., 2002; Goleman, 2007; Meerkerk, Van Den Eijnden, & Garretsen, 2006) may be an area of awareness that needs to be integrated into the training of counselors. A body of research is emerging regarding PUI, and assessment instruments to help counselors in measuring this phenomenon have been developed in the last decade like the On-line Cognition Scale (Davis et al., 2002) or the Generalized Problematic Internet Use Scale (Caplan, 2002). These assessment tools may provide useful information for counselors to understand their own behavior with the use of technology, or that of their clients, and subsequently to control issues that may arise from that behavior. The importance of Internet behavior awareness competencies is an emerging area that lags far behind the awareness of hardware and software issues in the use of technology. However, it is one of the areas where counselors and clients may potentially lack the most knowledge but may be able to control the most.

ASSISTIVE TECHNOLOGY

A formal and legal definition of assistive technology has been part of the American vernacular for over two decades. In short, assistive technology is any low or high technology that might be used by an individual with disabilities to perform functions in a way that might otherwise be difficult or impossible. Important to the definition is the concept of low and high technology. What is the difference? Typically, low technology is that which includes materials or other processes that might have existed prior to the Industrial Revolution. That is, using a block of wood to prop up a computer monitor for better position and accommodation of the hardware at a worksite would be an example of low technology because that block of wood existed before the Industrial Revolution and is easily and readily obtained at a very low cost. An example of high technology might be an auditory reader of e-mail received through a smartphone for someone who might be visually impaired or blind. What is important is the use and purpose of the technology, not whether it is low or high technology.

This section discusses the reasons why assistive technology might be important in the accommodation process. Further, issues of accessibility will be explored, and ideas for assessing assistive technology needs will be offered.

Why Accommodate?

Barros-Bailey (2010) identified seven reasons why accommodation and assistive technology needs should be considered. These include the following:

1. Improving morale, self-worth, and self-concept
2. Preventing injury
3. Creating good will
4. The benefit may far outweigh the cost and assist others in the client's workplace, home, and social environments
5. Attracting, hiring, training, or serving all people regardless of their function
6. Increasing productivity
7. Complying with the law

Although much of the literature regarding the use of assistive technology and accommodation seems to be responsive to the enforcement needs and requirements of legal mandates, this should be the last consideration in the list of why accommodation and the use of assistive technology may be important within the rehabilitation process. The impact on individuals and those around them should drive the decision.

Accessibility

The concept of assistive technology presumes that it facilitates access by those who otherwise would not have such an opportunity without its existence. Access is one of the standards within the CRCC code of ethics (2010) to which rehabilitation counselors are held accountable with the use of computers and/or the Internet. With the use of online technologies, a way to measure access is through the capacity of the person with a disability to use the hardware and software sufficient to complete the needed tasks of communication and the entry and retrieval of data. In other words, it is the universal access of the electronic media that becomes important to consider in the client's ability not only to communicate with the rehabilitation counselor and potentially other members of the team, but also to participate in services (e.g., assessment and job search) from which he or she may be prevented if electronic universal barriers exist.

Although the law should be the last reason why someone should consider accommodation and assistive technology, the law itself provides societal standards that are considered mandatory within that society. Often, these standards also provide the threshold of expected accessibility. Computer and electronic accessibility standards have been adopted at the national level under the auspices of the Americans with Disabilities Act (ADA; Patrick, 1996; Waddell, 1998) and Section 508 of the Rehabilitation Act as amended in 1998 (Access Board, 2000a, 2000b). Internationally, the online accessibility standard set by W3C has three priority levels constituting higher accessibility thresholds than Section 508 in the United States. For the international Priority 1 level, the Web content developer *must* satisfy the checkpoint of accessibility; for Priority 2, the content *should* be satisfied; and, for Priority 3, the developer *may* include this checkpoint in development (www.w3c.org/TR/WCAG10).

In 2008, the Americans with Disabilities Amendments Act clarified some of the intentions of Congress regarding the original intent and objectives of the Americans with Disabilities Act from nearly two decades previously. The amendment contained the following updates or provisions to the ADA:

1. The basic three-part definition of disability stayed the same.
2. "Substantially limits" will not have as high of a standard.
3. "Mitigating measures" will not be considered.
4. "Major life activities" will be expanded to include bodily functions.
5. "Episodic and remission limitations" will be considered as if active.
6. The definition for "regarded as having a disability" will be very broad with no substantially limits requirements.

These Acts provide legal guidelines that should help facilitate low technology as well as software and hardware universal access for people with disabilities. A variety of free online diagnostic tools, such as cynthiasays™ (International Center for Disability Resources on the Internet and Internet Society Disability and Special Needs Chapter, 2003; Kasday, 2000) and Wave™ (webaim, 2010), could assist in determining web site accessibility based on national and international standards. What these tools do not check for, however, is the assessment of the gap between the activity and the level of function of an individual. The rest of this section provides some tools to assist with that gap evaluation.

Three-Step Assessment Process

Barros-Bailey (2010) identified a three-step assessment process for the consideration of accommodation and the use of assistive technology.

Step 1: Assess Work Demands

Rehabilitation counselors need to know what the demands of the work entail. That is, what are the physical, mental, and/or cognitive demands of work that the individual's residual function could be mapped against? The best tool to assess work demands is the job analysis. Many job analyses formats use constructs derived from the *Revised Handbook for Analyzing Jobs* (U.S. Department of Labor, 1991b) that were the job rating standards upon which the *Dictionary of Occupational Titles* (DOT; U.S. Department of Labor, 1991a) occupations were classified. Yet these standards are often insufficient to measure the demands of work within the disability context, and they do not contain constructs allowing for the mental and cognitive demands of work (Occupational Information Development Advisory Panel [OIDAP], 2009, 2010). O*NET is the database developed by the U.S. Department of Labor in 1998 to replace the DOT. The database was developed for workforce development purposes, not for disability assessment. The O*NET does not use constructs, descriptors, scales, and measures to capture work demands that are well suited to map against human function as is needed in working with people with disabilities (OIDAP, 2009, 2010). Therefore, DOT constructs such as those defining strength demands (e.g., sedentary, light, medium, heavy, and very heavy) continue to be used in many public and private disability systems until an alternative occupational information system is developed that could be more appropriately applied in disability assessment (Barros-Bailey, 2010). Efforts under way by the Social Security Administration (OIDAP, 2009, 2010) have the potential of establishing physical, mental, and cognitive work demand constructs, and corresponding appropriate scales applicable to human function, which could be used by rehabilitation counselors in their job analysis forms to better assess the demands of work in this phase of the three-step assessment process.

Until better work demand standards that tie to human function are developed, some sources have attempted to develop assessment tools and instruments to properly assess work demands in order to facilitate the evaluation and development of a plan to meet the individual's needs. King County in Seattle, Washington, developed the King County Job Analysis Bank available free online that provides a variety of job analysis formats to evaluate the demands of work from many perspectives such as cognitive, behavioral, exposure sensitivity, hearing, hand, physical, and so on (http://www.kingcounty.gov/employees/HumanResources/services/jobanalysis/resources.aspx). It is important that the job analysis instrument uses methods of measurement and observation on the job that provide a comprehensive assessment of what the work requires so that changes in the workplace could be best understood with the context of the residual function of the individual. A job analysis assessment tool used in any evaluation should consider the purpose for which it is being used so that it will contain the correct measures to collect the data from the job setting that provide the best match against information available about the client's functional levels.

Step 2: Evaluate Physical, Mental, and Cognitive Function

Evaluating the capacities of the individual is the corresponding part of the three-step analysis. This information is triangulated from a variety of different sources: the diagnostic vocational interview, functional capacities obtained from qualified professionals (e.g., rehabilitation audiology, neuro-ophthalmology, orthopedics) using a variety of assessment tools (e.g., functional capacity evaluations, neuropsychological batteries, audiology exams).

Place the words "assistive technology assessment checklist" into any search engine and a variety of tools will immediately become available, free and in different formats. However, the categories most of these tools are organized around consider the need, purpose, and assessment of the accommodation needs of an individual. Typically, there are 11 functional areas in most assessment tools:

1. Seating, positioning, and mobility
2. Communication
3. Computer access
4. Motor aspects of writing
5. Composition of written material
6. Reading
7. Mathematics
8. Organization
9. Recreation and leisure
10. Vision
11. Hearing

Classifying the individual's function into these categories is useful for considering what resources might be available to accommodate the work to a client's functional level.

Step 3: Perform a Gap Analysis

Many of the assistive technology checklists provide ideas and resources to consider tailoring the assistive technology assessment vis-à-vis the needs of an individual. Becoming familiar with these areas provides a rubric for rehabilitation counselors when interviewing a client, structuring an assessment, and developing a rehabilitation plan to meet the client's needs. Ultimately, the assessment of work demands and of the individual's residual functions should be based on human function so that the terminology and constructs are more readily matched and an assessment of the gap between the person's needs and work activity are determined.

The development of a rehabilitation plan using appropriate assistive technology is best served by a common language. There are multiple resources available to clients, counselors, and the public to identify sources of assistive technology. The U.S. Department of Labor's Office of Disability Employment Policy provides the Job Accommodation Network (JAN) and access to free consultation, assessment tools, and databank of resources. The Searchable Online Accommodation Resource (SOAR) is a database that contains thousands of potential low and high technology solutions. JAN provides free online or telephone support by qualified specialists to assist clients or counselors to troubleshoot problems and develop options for accommodation needs. JAN's web site includes a variety of other resources such as publications by disability, occupation, product or service, topic, or in alternative languages.

Locally, assistive technology projects provide directed assessments and services, professional expertise, training, lending libraries, computer laboratories, and more to help identify the best interventions to include in the rehabilitation plan to facilitate access and inclusion of people with disabilities in the workplace. These federally funded programs by the Technology-Related Assistance for Individuals with Disabilities Act provide local communities with free or low-cost access to technical specialists who could assist with the evaluation and accommodation alternatives to meet the needs of people with disabilities.

CONCLUSION

Technology has always been part of the client–counselor relationship, whether part of the first known counseling methods used over 100 years ago with Frank Parsons—the first known counselor—using quills and paper, or today involving texting, voice over the Internet protocol (voIp, such as Skype) for distance face-to-face sessions, or other forms of high technology communication. Low and high technology media are important to supporting and building the client–counselor relationship. Current and emerging high technologies should be used to support and not hinder the counseling process.

This chapter examined technology usage in the United States as it pertains to the general public and particular to people with disabilities with a variety of impairments. The evolution of communication gadgets that facilitate human interaction and storage quickly, synchronously, or asynchronously has created a new dynamic to how people communicate and affect behavior. In fact, in 1998, an international peer-review journal—*CyberPsychology, Behavior, and Social Networking* (Mary Ann Liebert, Inc. Publishers)—was created to capture scholarly articles about the behavior of those communicating in cyberspace. Rehabilitation counselors and the programs educating these professionals need to integrate awareness and understanding of the different behaviors (e.g., impulsivity) resulting from the use of common technology as part of developing technological competence. A variety of resources were discussed that could assist in assessment of competencies of clients and counselors and in developing training programs to meet competency needs. Finally, literature regarding technology in rehabilitation counseling would be deficient if it did not include a discussion regarding assistive technology. Therefore, this chapter provided a justification as to the reasons accommodation and the use of assistive technology is important, the last of which is the fact that it is the law. Determining accessibility and assistive technology needs a three-step process—the evaluation of work activity, an assessment of the individual's function, and a gap analysis of the residual human function to the demands of work. Assistive technology could potentially mitigate barriers and facilitate inclusion of individuals into settings and environments they could otherwise not access.

The challenge of writing any chapter about technology is that as soon as a book is published, new forms of technology have emerged. Therefore, the attempt in this chapter was to focus on essential concepts to consider in the use of technology in the client–counselor relationship, methods of assessment and evaluation, and resources of where to seek information should technology change tomorrow, as it likely will.

CONTENT REVIEW QUESTIONS

- When using technology in the client–counselor relationship, why is awareness of how technology can affect the relationship important? What considerations and expected behaviors or boundaries need to be set within the relationship so that technology could assist and not inhibit the therapeutic process?
- How can rehabilitation counselors be assessed or assess clients' technological competencies? Why is assessment of these competencies important?
- Discuss how you would assess your own technological competencies with respect to behavioral or technological needs. How would you find standards specific to your area of practice or desired area of practice that might identify the minimum level of competency? How about the standards for clients and their desired areas of practice?
- Identify a hypothetical case and apply the three-step assessment process and outline an assistive technology plan. How do you go about including the variables in the job analysis tool? How can you best capture the work demands data to map to functional information about the client?
- What resources exist to help professionals and clients with assistive technology? How can you empower clients to access assistive technology resources over their work lives or life spans?

REFERENCES

Access Board. (2000a). *Standards for electronic and information technology: An overview.* Retrieved from http://www.access-board.gov/sec508/summary.htm

Access Board. (2000b). *Electronic and information technology accessibility standards: Final rule (Federal Register No. 36 CFR Part 1194).* Washington, DC: National Archives and Records Administration.

Access Board. (2008). *ADA Amendment Act of 2008.* Retrieved from http://www.access-board .gov/about/laws/ada-amendments.htm

Barros-Bailey, M. (2007). *Internet and computer ethics for public sector rehabilitation counselors: A mixed methods study.* Doctoral dissertation. University of Idaho. Available from Pro-Quest Dissertations and Theses database (UMI No. 3265569).

Barros-Bailey, M. (2010). *Forensic and non-forensic systems where the dictionary of occupational titles is the primary source of occupational information.* Boise, ID: Intermountain Vocational Services.

Barros-Bailey, M. (2010, October 15). *Assistive technology in the accommodations process.* Idaho Business Leadership Network 2010 Conference, Boise, ID.

Barros-Bailey, M., Aguilar, P. G., & Burks, M. R. (2000). Creating an accessible Internet. *OnTheInternet.* Retrieved from http://www.isoc.org/oti/articles/0200/barros.html

Brasley, S. S. (2006, May). Building and using a tool to assess info and tech literacy. *Computers in Libraries, 6–7,* 44–48.

Caplan, S. E. (2002). Problematic Internet use and psychosocial well-being: Development of a theory-based cognitive-behavioral measurement instrument. *Computers in Human Behavior, 18,* 553–575.

Caplan, S. E. (2005). A social skill account of problematic Internet use. *Journal of Communication,* 721–736.

Commission on Rehabilitation Counselor Certification. (2010). *Code of professional ethics for rehabilitation counselors.* Retrieved from http://www.crccertification.com

Davis, R. A., Flett, G. L., & Besser, A. (2002). Validation of a new scale for measuring problematic Internet use: Implications for pre-employment screening. *CyberPsychology & Behavior, 5*(4), 331–345.

Ealy, M. (n.d.). *Technology and internet assessment.* Clearwater, FL: H & H Publishing.

Economics and Statistics Administration, National Telecommunications and Information Administration, U.S. Department of Commerce. (2004, September). *A nation online.* Washington, DC: Author.

Economics and Statistics Administration, National Telecommunications and Information Administration, U.S. Department of Commerce. (2010, November). *Exploring the digital nation: Home broadband Internet adoption in the United States.* Washington, DC: Author.

Goleman, D. (2007). Flame first, think later: New clues to e-mail misbehavior. *New York Times,* Retrieved from www.nytimes.com

HiSoftware ©, International Center for Disability Resources on the Internet and Internet Society Disability and Special Needs Chapter. (2003). *Cynthia Says™.* Retrieved from www.cynthiasays.com

Hobbs, S. D. (2002). Measuring nurses' computer competency: An analysis of published instruments. *Computers, Informatics, Nursing, 20*(2), 63–73.

Jiang, W. W., Chen, W., & Chen, Y. C. (2004). Important computer competencies for the nursing profession. *Journal of Nursing Research, 12*(3), 213–225.

Kasday, L. R. (2000, June 28–July 2). *A tool to help human judgment of Webpage accessibility.* Paper presented at the RESNA 2000. Orlando, FL.

Meerkerk, G., Van Den Eijnden, R. J. J. M., & Garretsen, H. F. L. (2006). Predicting compulsive Internet use: It's all about sex! *CyberPsychology & Behavior, 9*(1), 95–103.

Merriam-Webster Online. (2010). Retrieved from http://www.merriam-webster.com/

NFER-Nelson Publishing. (n.d.). *New technology tests: Computer commands.* London, UK: Author.

Occupational Information Development Advisory Panel. (2009). *Content model and classification recommendations for the Social Security occupational information system.* Baltimore, MD: Social Security Administration.

Occupational Information Development Advisory Panel. (2010). *OIDAP findings report: A review of the National Academy of Sciences report entitled a database for a changing economy: Review of the occupational information network (O*NET).* Baltimore, MD: Social Security Administration.

Patrick, D. L. (1996, September 9). *Letter to the honorable Tom Harkin.* Washington, DC: Assistant Attorney General, U.S. Department of Justice, Civil Rights Division.

Pew Research Center, Internet & American Life Project. (2010, September 2). *Cell phones and American adults.* Retrieved from http://pewinternet.org

Pew Research Center, Internet & American Life Project. (2010, August 9–September 13). *Tracking survey.* Retrieved from http://www.pewinternet.org/

Rehabilitation Counseling Consortium. (2005a). *Rehabilitation counseling definition.* Schaumburg, IL: Commission on Rehabilitation Counselor Certification.

Rehabilitation Counseling Consortium. (2005b). *Rehabilitation counselor definition*. Schaumburg, IL: Commission on Rehabilitation Counselor Certification.

Rural Institute. (2006). *Disability and the digital divide: Comparing surveys and disability data*. Retrieved from http://rtc.ruralinstitute.umt.edu/TelCom/Divide.htm

Shea, V., & Shea, C. (1994). *Netiquette*. Retrieved from http://www.albion.com/netiquette/corerules.html

Shea, V., & Shea, C. (2006). *Netiquette*. San Rafael, CA: Albion.com

Shetchman, N., & Horowitz, L. M. (2003). *Media inequality in conversation: How people behave differently when interacting with computers and people*. Retrieved from http://citeseerx.ist.psu.edu/

Suler, J. (2004). The online disinhibition effect. *CyberPsychology & Behavior, 7*(3), 321–326.

U.S. Department of Labor. (1991a). *Dictionary of occupational titles*. Washington, DC: Author.

U.S. Department of Labor. (1991b). *Revised handbook for analyzing jobs*. Washington, DC: Author.

Waddell, C. D. (1998, June 17). *Applying the ADA to the Internet: A Web accessibility standard*. Paper presented at the In Pursuit ... A Blueprint for Disability Law and Policy Conference for the American Bar Association. Retrieved from http://people.rit.edu/easi/law/weblaw1.htm

WAVE. (2010). Retrieved from http://wave.webaim.org/

W3C. (2010). Retrieved from www.w3c.org/TR/WCAG10

20

Clinical Supervision

James T. Herbert

LEARNING OBJECTIVES

After reading this chapter, you should be able to:

■ Differentiate the meaning and process of administrative supervision from that of clinical supervision.
■ Understand the knowledge needed to work as an effective clinical supervisor and the desired attributes of an effective supervisor.
■ Examine two supervision models, peer consultation and triadic supervision, which offer potential for use in rehabilitation counseling practice.
■ Review a theoretical model that describes the transition process from working as a counselor to becoming an effective clinical supervisor.
■ Revaluate the use of clinical supervision as the preferred term for professional practice.

Within rehabilitation counseling practice, there are two complementary aspects of supervision. Administrative supervision is the first aspect and it is the one that most rehabilitation counselor supervisors perceive competence. Clinical supervision is the second aspect that most supervisors, at least those within the public vocational rehabilitation program, perceive limited competence (Herbert & Trusty, 2006). Administrative supervision relates to the documentation of vocational rehabilitation efficiency and effectiveness of client services provided. As such, it is more retrospective where the focus often involves a review of how each counselor contributes to overall agency outcomes and complies with established work policies. For example, administrative supervision may focus on counselor performance measures such as the length of time between an initial referral for client services and an approved individualized written rehabilitation plan was completed, the number of clients who are competitively employed as a result of vocational rehabilitation services, the amount of case dollar expenditures for a given client within a particular time frame, and level of client satisfaction with services from data collected by the rehabilitation agency or facility. These indicators pertain to service efficiency and effectiveness that have a clear agency focus and are influenced by individual counselor performance.

Although administrative supervision often involves client case reviews and the documentation used to evaluate client progress, it also has a broader scope that concerns general work behavior of the counselor as well. As a result, supervisors may address counselor work behavior associated with attendance, tardiness, relationships with coworkers and supervisors, written and verbal skills, ability to effectively handle job-related stressors and initiative. In addition, administrative supervision tends to occur at prescribed time intervals (e.g., quarterly or yearly evaluations) and often includes written documentation to monitor changes in counselor work performance. These evaluations are used largely as evidence for decisions about job tenure as well as consideration for salary increases. Even though these appraisals are necessary for evaluating work performance as well as identifying areas needing improvement, they do not specifically address a critical part of rehabilitation counseling practice—the relationship between counselor and client and how this relationship affects rehabilitation outcomes.

Examination of the client–counselor relationship used to address client concerns and to facilitate positive change represents the crux of clinical supervision. Applied to rehabilitation counseling practice, clinical supervision refers to an evaluative yet supportive relationship between counselor and supervisor where the focus centers on the counselor–client relationship (Herbert, 2004a, 2004b). For example, clinical supervision may examine counselor attitudes toward specific clientele such as persons with substance abuse problems, ex-offenders with disabilities, and clients who have different ethnic or cultural backgrounds than the counselor. Clinical supervision may also help counselors develop more effective ways to introduce positive confrontation with a client in order to facilitate employment and independent living or teach counselors how to listen more empathically when client concerns are not as acutely expressed during an intake interview. As a third example, clinical supervision may help counselors address professional burnout and what might be done to re-engage them so they can work more effectively with their clients.

As implied in each of these examples, the supervisory relationship involves what some authorities (e.g., Bordin, 1983) have described as a working alliance. This alliance is one where there is mutual agreement as to the goals of supervision and one where throughout the supervisory process, the clinical supervisor provides constructive feedback to improve counselor performance so that acceptable standards of practice are followed (Herbert, 2009). Feedback provided by the clinical supervisor requires some observation of client–counselor interaction through either live or delayed methods (i.e., electronic recording) of counseling sessions and/or case review where the counselor discusses problems or concerns in working with particular clients. These methods allow the supervisor to understand how the counselor perceives the client, what factors obstruct the rehabilitation process, and how the counselor believes they should be addressed (Brislin & Herbert, 2009). The clinical supervisor can offer other strategies through constructive feedback that may help the counselor work through problems with a given client. It should be noted, however, that research to support how the supervisory alliance contributes to counselor self-efficacy is both limited and mixed. Some studies indicate that the supervisory alliance is unrelated (Ladany, Ellis, & Friedlander, 1999) while others (e.g., Efstation, Patton, & Kardash, 1990) indicate a positive relationship exists. More recently, evidence by Lorenz (2009) found that the combined effect of the supervisory working alliance, supervisory style, and supervisor behavior were predictive of counselor self-efficacy for graduate students completing their counseling practicum. In her study, supervisory style or the manner by which supervisors use different approaches given supervisee needs (see Friedlander & Ward, 1984) was measured on three dimensions: attractive (i.e., supportive, friendly, open, flexible), interpersonally sensitive (i.e., relationship-invested, therapeutically perceptive), and task oriented (i.e., goal-oriented, structured). Although the supervisory style construct was predictive of counselors'-in-training beliefs regarding their capability to perform counseling tasks, it was not clear as to whether one type of supervisory style was more influential than another in contributing to furthering counseling skill development.

It is also important to note that the construct of supervisory style has different dimensions and operational definitions that have been noted in the literature. For example, Heron (1990) proposed that supervision styles vary on two dimensions: authoritative or facilitative. Authoritative styles are characterized by supervisors who are more prescriptive (offering advice, giving explicit instruction), informative (sharing knowledge), and confrontational (challenging counselor beliefs and attitudes). Facilitative styles include supervisors who are more cathartic, catalytic (encouraging counselor to be reflective and self-directed), and supportive (confirming counselor's values and worth as a skilled helper). Other conceptualizations describing supervisory style have been proposed by Bernard (1979), Holloway (1995), and Shanfield and Gil (1985) that readers may wish to review. Interestingly, despite the theoretical underpinning that a supervisor's style is based on individual supervisee needs, an earlier literature review by Spence, Wilson, Kavanagh, Strong, and Worrall (2001) indicates that supervisors do not appreciably alter their supervisory style. These authors as well as others (e.g., Reese et al., 2009) conclude that despite the list of recommendations for promoting effective supervisory behaviors, styles, and working alliance that are all intended to improve counselor skill development, there is little empirical evidence to support these claims. Despite this lack of evidence, it is noteworthy to mention that some evidence exists that effective clinical supervision contributes to occupational well-being and reducing turnover among counselors working in substance-abuse treatment settings (Knudsen, Ducharme, & Roman, 2008). Whether similar benefits extend to rehabilitation counselors in other employment settings is not known, however.

While administrative and clinical supervision share common activities that include evaluating, leading, organizing, planning, and staffing (Crimando, 2004), as applied to clinical supervision, these activities are directed toward examining the client–counselor relationship and how the counselor addresses client needs to facilitate the rehabilitation process. From this perspective, rehabilitation counselor supervisors must not only be competent counselors themselves but also possess sufficient knowledge and skills to develop and sustain a style that results in an effective working alliance with counselors they supervise. Further, while an attempt to distinguish between the two supervisory domains has been articulated, in rehabilitation counseling practice, they often interface. An earlier model by Schultz, Copple, and Ososkie (1999) and subsequent refinement by Schultz (2008) describing a tripartite model of supervision provides a useful context for describing these supervisory functions within rehabilitation counseling practice. Accordingly, although the supervisory relationship addresses administrative, educational, and clinical components, the fundamental aspect in this relationship concerns the supervisory working alliance between counselor and supervisor. This alliance is largely influenced by how the power differential between supervisor and counselor is manifested and what types of power (coercive, expert, legitimate, referent, and reward) are exercised. In some cases, this differential may reward counselor behavior through verbal praise or other means (reward power), demonstrate competence or expertise to a given problem (expert power), and recognize that the counselor and supervisor perceive similarity on a given supervisory issue that is addressed during supervision (referent power), or because of the existing nature of each person's position, the supervisor may have a right to intervene directly in order to protect client interests (legitimate power). In other less constructive situations, the supervisor may use power through punishment such as making condescending or insensitive remarks (coercive power). Schultz also notes that the power differential manifested within the supervisory relationship is influenced by the organizational culture that exists in each rehabilitation work setting. In settings where counselor empowerment, teamwork, and continuous quality improvement are emphasized, rehabilitation counselors are more likely to find these features more conducive to supporting the organization's mission.

KNOWLEDGE AND DESIRED ATTRIBUTES IN A CLINICAL SUPERVISOR

Theilsen and Leahy (2001) developed the first scale in rehabilitation counseling practice to assess knowledge and skills required to work as a clinical supervisor. Their scale, the *Rehabilitation Counseling Supervision Inventory*, identified six domains which included ethical and legal issues, supervision and counseling theories and models, intervention techniques and methods to address supervisee (counselor) training needs, evaluation and assessment techniques used in supervision, rehabilitation counseling knowledge, and the supervisory relationship.

It is interesting to note that relative to all of the domains measured, the supervisory relationship, while still perceived as being of moderately high importance, was also the domain with the lowest rated mean. Given the importance of the supervisor–counselor relationship that is often described in the clinical supervision literature (e.g., Stebnicki, 1998), it is surprising that this domain was not rated higher in terms of its perceived importance to work as an effective clinical supervisor. The study also found that degree level, employment setting (e.g., general hospitals, private proprietary settings, state vocational rehabilitation agency, universities), gender, job title (e.g., administrators, counselors, educators, and supervisors), and training in clinical supervision resulted in perceived differences in importance across the six domains. Thus, knowledge and skill sets needed to work as an effective clinical supervisor are influenced by a variety of demographic and situational variables. Finally, it was reported that the majority of certified rehabilitation counselors who participated in the study supported the establishment of specific experience and training requirements in order to provide clinical supervision. Paradoxical to this finding, the Commission on Rehabilitation Counselor Certification actually established an adjunct designation in clinical supervision in July of 1999 but, due to lack of interest, the credential was dropped in December of 2002 (S. Stark, personal communication, September 28, 2010). This type of certification is recognized in several other counseling fields, however, including the specialties of addictions (Addiction Professionals Certification Board), marriage and family therapy (Association for Marriage and Family Therapists), and mental-health counseling (National Board for Certified Counselors) (Herbert, 2009).

While having relevant knowledge regarding clinical supervision is necessary, it is not sufficient in order to work as an effective supervisor. When asked about what qualities rehabilitation counselors prefer in a clinical supervisor, research by Herbert (2004c) found that rehabilitation counselors in the state vocational rehabilitation program have four basic preferences. First, supervisors must be accessible. Counselors have a clear preference for supervisors who are easy to approach and can engage others effectively to address their concerns. Second, supervisors must be available when problems arise. While having regularly scheduled supervisory meetings communicates that supervision is an important part of one's professional development, supervisors must develop some plan when the counselor has concerns that come up unexpectedly. Third, supervisors must be capable. Because supervisors have worked as counselors themselves, they bring with them important experience that can benefit other counselors, particularly new counselors who often simply want to know, "What should I do in this situation?" Supervisors must also understand that the developmental needs of a new rehabilitation counselor, who often requires a more structure and problem-solving orientation, are different from those of an experienced counselor who might prefer a collegial style of supervision (Herbert & Trusty, 2006). Fourth and finally, supervisors must be flexible and, when appropriate, use humor effectively. Working with persons with disabilities can be a challenging work. Having a supervisor who is inviting, has an effective sense of humor, and can engage counselors about their professional concerns is fundamental to good clinical supervision. Conversely, negative qualities associated with ineffective supervision found by Herbert (2004c) included such behaviors as being disinterested, showing lack of respect, demonstrating poor listening skills (talking too much or too little), arguing or using relationship power as a way to manipulate the counselor, being intolerant of differences, failing to clarify expectations, and being unprepared for the supervision session. These reported behaviors obviously should be avoided as part of clinical supervision practice (Magnuson, Wilcoxon, & Norem, 2000).

Although these supervisor attributes are ones associated with effective and less effective supervision, one fundamental aspect is that because of its evaluative nature, clinical supervision invites conflict (Mueller & Kell, 1972). Consequently, the skill involved in managing conflict by the clinical supervisor will often contribute to not only how supervision is perceived but also how the counselor manages conflict within the client–counseling relationship (Nelson, Barnes, Evans, & Triggiano, 2008). In their effort to provide guidelines in managing supervisory conflict Nelson et al. (2008) interviewed 12 supervisors (counselors, psychologists, and social workers) who were viewed by their peers as being excellent clinical supervisors. Using a qualitative research design, they identified supervisor attitudes and attributes deemed critical in resolving conflict, supervisor reactions to conflicts, and strategies in working through conflicts. From this analysis, the researchers learned that although effective supervisors do not enjoy conflict, they reframe it as something that should be embraced rather than avoided. While conflict during supervision can produce a host of feelings, many supervisors also noted that it provided an opportunity to grow professionally. Their supervisory experiences indicate that when supervisors are perceived as genuine, patient, humble, vulnerable, and transparent (i.e., "disclose their own anxieties and shortcomings") and perceive supervisee anxiety as an opportunity for professional growth, there is less chance for supervisory conflict. When conflicts occur, supervisors were more likely to attribute it to situations when goals and expectations of clinical supervision were not clear and/or mutually agreed upon. This understanding was particularly critical during the initial stage of the supervisory relationship. In fact, clarifying expectations was viewed as "one of the most dependable strategies" to reducing potential conflicts. Supervisors also used a self-coaching technique where they would remind themselves that conflict is a "natural part of the process" and something not to take personally. When necessary, supervisors should also consult with other supervisors when experiencing particularly challenging supervision conflicts. If needed, bringing in another supervisor to observe the supervision session may assist in resolving counselor–supervisor conflicts.

Having clarified differences between administrative and clinical supervision and reviewing knowledge areas and personal attributes required to work effectively as a clinical supervisor, we now examine a basic problem in rehabilitation counseling practice. Despite the need for clinical supervision, it is a practice that does not regularly occur as part of one's professional development. Major obstacles to account for this problem are associated with having insufficient time and training on how to provide clinical supervision (Schultz, Ososkie, Fried, Nelson, & Bardos, 2002) as well as lack of administrative support (Herbert, 2004c). As a result, clinical supervision within rehabilitation counseling practice is an irregular and individualized practice at best. Further complicating this problem is the fact that there remains an entrenched group of rehabilitation counselors and supervisors who perceive little need for changing the status quo. In the next section, this issue and what can be done to address this problem are explored further.

USING PEER CONSULTATION AND TRIADIC MODELS OF CLINICAL SUPERVISION

Although a basic goal of clinical supervision is to assist counselors to work more effectively, the fact remains that there are rehabilitation counselors who do not desire it and, if available, do not want it. Sadly, in this situation, it is often true that many of these counselors are the same persons who could benefit from clinical supervision the most. Within rehabilitation counseling practice, this situation seems particularly evident among experienced counselors who have had limited or no clinical supervision as part of their professional development. When asked about clinical supervision preferences, it is clear that these counselors want to be left alone (Schultz et al., 2002). From their perspective, good clinical supervision is equivalent to no supervision. This situation, which has been found in both the public vocational rehabilitation (e.g., Herbert, 2004c) and proprietary rehabilitation settings (King, 2009), presents difficult challenges for the supervisor who wants to initiate clinical supervision. Although there may be a host of individual reasons for not pursuing clinical supervision, the one unifying aspect is that this reluctance is often based on cognitive distortions regarding one's belief to work as an effective counselor, an understanding of the counseling process and the counseling profession. These distortions may be formed during initial practicum and internship experiences during graduate school that continue into one's professional career (Howard, Inman, & Altman, 2006).

In terms of resistance to clinical supervision on the part of rehabilitation counselors, there are several options available to the clinical supervisor: (1) implement clinical supervision as part of case management or administrative supervision and, in effect, develop a "blended" supervision approach, (2) secure support from higher administrative personnel within the agency or facility and institute a policy that it becomes a required part of each counselor's professional development, (3) initiate a peer consultation model, or (4) implement a "hybrid" triadic supervision model. As the first two options may be more procedural in nature and the latter two may be more unfamiliar to many rehabilitation counselors, the next section will examine the use of peer consultation and triadic supervision models. We will also look at a new application of peer supervision through distance education technology.

**COGNITIVE DISTORTION STATEMENTS
FOR AVOIDING CLINICAL SUPERVISION**

Examples of false beliefs that counselors use to avoid seeking clinical supervision include:

- "If there is something I can improve as a counselor, my client will let me know."
- "I can become a better rehabilitation counselor by listening to my own taped counseling sessions or reviewing case file information myself."
- "I have worked as a counselor for 10 years and never had a 'clinical supervisor'—why do I need one now?"

Although listening to clients regarding the manner and effectiveness of counseling services and reviewing prior client-counselor sessions are helpful tools in promoting counselor development, by themselves they are insufficient. Counselors, particularly new counselors, often require an outside perspective that provides insight into client–counselor interactions. Examining counselor reasons for the manner and content of such exchanges can lead to a better understanding of counselor issues that may interfere with client progress. For example, consider this client statement made in the initial intake interview: "I am not sure that you can help me. I mean what do you know about life from sitting in a wheelchair?" Depending on a counselor's theoretical orientation, skill level, and established client rapport, the rehabilitation counselor may respond in a variety of ways such as the following:

Response 1: "Well, you're right, I don't know what it is like but that doesn't mean that I haven't had my own challenges in life. Would it help if I share some of my experiences so you might feel more comfortable working with me?"

Response 2: "So, maybe you're thinking, 'How can I be of any help to you since I am not a wheelchair user myself'?"

Response 3: "Can you tell me more about what life is like for you sitting in a wheelchair?"

Response 4: "Would you prefer working with a counselor who also has a similar type of lived experience as you?"

Response 5: "I am wondering if what you are saying is a way to tell me that maybe you are not ready for vocational rehabilitation services?"

Perhaps none of these responses resonate with you but as a clinical supervisor an examination of client–counselor interactions provides valuable insight about counselor intentions. For instance, the first response suggests that perhaps the counselor is feeling a bit threatened by the client and believes that sharing some personal experience may convince the client that he/she understands something about life challenges and, in effect, is qualified

-continued

to work with the client. The second response places the emphasis directly on the client–counselor relationship and provides an opportunity to explore this relationship. The third response places the focus on learning more about the client's worldview with an implied invitation that there is something to learn here. The fourth response indicates that the counselor is essentially in agreement with the client and offers to assist by referring the client to a counselor who may have a similar lived experience. The reason for wanting to transfer the client, however, may be motivated more by counselor anxiety. The final response provides an interpretation of the client statement with a hypothesis as to what it means as far as receiving services. This interpretation may or may not be conducive in further developing the client–counselor relationship. Each of these responses provides an opportunity for the clinical supervisor to examine: (1) counselor intentions and motivations as it pertains to client interactions, (2) how these intentions addressed or did not address client needs, (3) how responses were consistent with the counseling orientation held by the counselor, and (4) feelings and thoughts about how this statement impacted the counselor and, to some extent, the client. Clinical supervision provides a forum to explore these aspects so that professional growth results in and hopefully improves client outcomes.

Peer Consultation

Peer consultation allows counselors to provide multiple perspectives to assist other counselors to work more effectively with their clients (Granello, Kindsvatter, Granello, Underfer-Babalis, & Moorhead, 2008). An early description of a supervision peer group model was proposed by Borders (1991). She believed that the model could be used with counselors of various skill levels. Using this approach, one of first tasks requires each group member to be assigned a role to play when providing feedback to the counselor requesting the consultation. This assigned role may be from the perspective of the client, the counselor, or some other person identified as important (e.g., employer, family member). Group members can also be asked to explore various aspects within a role. For example, one person assigned to a counselor role could view the tape from a person-centered approach; another member could view the segment from a cognitive-behavioral approach. Within a counseling orientation, role assignment could be broken down further as one counselor focuses on nonverbal behavior while another counselor concentrates on the level and effectiveness of empathic responses the counselor made during the taped session. These assigned roles are ones determined by the presenting counselor or other peer group member prior to the actual consultation. After this procedural aspect is completed, the counselor wanting consultation provides a brief (5 minute) presentation that describes client concerns, the counselor–client relationship, and other relevant information to provide a context for other peer counselors to understand the reason for consultation. The counselor also has several questions for peer group members to consider as they review a client–counselor videotape segment of the session (e.g., "Are there better ways I could have confronted this client about missing the psychological testing appointment?"). As the counseling session segment is viewed, peer group members are asked to stay in their prescribed roles, as they review the client–counselor segment and provide feedback to the counselor wanting consultation. Borders believes that by staying in their prescribed roles, any feedback given to the counselor seeking consultation will not be perceived as threatening. To further enhance the intentionality of providing supportive feedback, Borders recommends that the counselor not discuss any aspect of the tape and simply listen to peer feedback. By following this guideline, defensive comments and digressions are minimized. It is the job of the group facilitator to ensure that these procedural elements are followed and that effective group process occurs.

Building on this model, Lassiter, Napolitano, Culbreth, and Ng (2008) addressed peer group supervision from a multicultural perspective. Using the same format described earlier, group members would address diversity elements and cultural contexts of the counselor. These aspects consider issues that pertain to age, disability status, gender, sexual identity, power, oppression, and privilege related to ethnicity/race. Using the role assignment procedure, examples of questions to promote multicultural awareness include the following:

> How might this client view the counselor, given the counselor's style and cultural context in comparison with the client's context? What role does culture play in the way the counselor relates to this client? How would issues of trust and rapport be different if the counselor and client were from similar cultural backgrounds? What strategies might the counselor apply to improve the working alliance with this client? What impact might intervention strategies have on this client given the cultural context of both the counselor and the client? (pp. 168–169)

Lassiter et al. (2008) believe that it is important that the supervisor or group facilitator provide an environment that promotes multicultural awareness, knowledge, and skills. In order to do so, the supervisor must set expectations that include multicultural perspectives by providing opportunities for reflection (e.g., asking peers to keep a supervision journal where they write about influences of power, privilege, and oppression within the counseling relationship). Diversifying group membership will also promote discussion of cultural issues such as those pertaining to age, disability, ethnicity/race, gender, and sexual orientation. Lassiter et al. believe that the group supervisor must also model acceptance, introspection, openness, and respect for peer group members so that group members feel safe to provide honest feedback and make mistakes without recrimination. Appropriate self-disclosure regarding one's biases and stereotypes and discussion of one's cultural values are indicative of effective multicultural supervision practices and one that should be used in performance evaluation (Robertson, 2006). Implementing these recommendations to enhance multicultural competence as part of clinical supervision not only produces this effect but also increases the probability of positive engagement among group members (Kaduvettoor, O'Shaughnessy, Mori, Beverly, Weatherford, & Ladany, 2009). Readers interested in learning about other indicators of multicultural competence may want to review seminal papers such as the one produced by Sue, Arrendondo, and McDavis (1992). In terms of developing greater awareness of multicultural issues within rehabilitation counseling practice, there are several textbooks available that may be helpful (e.g., Balcazar, Suarez-Balcazar, Taylor-Ritzler, & Keys, 2010; Leung, Flowers, Talley, & Sanderson, 2007).

Triadic Supervision

Triadic supervision has two different meanings as described in the counselor supervision literature. On the one hand, it is a method used when there are usually two counselors or counselor trainees who are supervised by one clinical supervisor. This method can be used as an adjunct or alternative to individual supervision (Hein & Lawson, 2008). On the other hand, it is a process of supervision where three participants are each assigned a specific role during supervision. Developed by Charles Spice in 1976, the need for a different method of supervision emerged because of the recognition that many beginning counselors are resistant to supervision because of initial negative experiences. Accordingly, supervision must be delivered in a positive manner using other peers without the reliance on sophisticated equipment such as audio/video recording. Spice believed that once supervisees become skilled in the fundamental aspects of supervision, they could then "synthesize these processes into their own unique supervisory styles" (p. 1). He also contended that effective supervision occurs only when participants are skilled in the process of critical evaluation. In order to develop this process, triadic supervision involves assigning each person one of three roles: supervisee, commentator, and facilitator. These roles are rotated throughout the supervision process. Because supervision involves a critical analysis of a counselor's competence, it has the potential for being "destructive and painful." Recognizing this potential outcome, in the first session of triadic supervision the commentator is required to focus on things that the supervisee (counselor) has done well and then examine things that might be improved. This analysis is conducted before all three members meet to review the first counseling session or segment that has been audio- or videotaped. If no counseling samples are available to evaluate, then a case review method could be used during supervision. The shortcoming of this format, however, is that one does not have the opportunity to review client–counselor interaction and, as a result, counselors' reports of what transpired are filtered from this perspective (Herbert, 2004b).

The actual process of triadic supervision begins with the supervisee providing a summary of the counseling session that includes a description of the client, identified client concerns, counselor goals or feelings about the counseling session, and related issues that the supervisee would like to discuss. These issues are most likely centered around the reason(s) for wanting the consultation. After this introduction, the commentator shares whatever significant points he/she wishes to address. The supervisee, in turn, responds to these points. During this exchange, the facilitator focuses on the process between commentator and supervisee with regard to (1) instances where one or the other person is inaccurately perceived, (2) clarification of feelings, (3) points during supervision when digression occurs, and (4) parallel process (meaning what occurs between supervisee and commentator is similar to what happens between supervisee and client).

Using the framework proposed by Spice (1976) and incorporating the format of triadic supervision, a hybrid model for counselors not initially seeking clinical supervision could be developed. In this model, there would be two supervisors, the person responsible for conducting clinical supervision ("regular" supervisor) and the experienced (but reluctant) counselor who would serve as a "peer supervisor." Initially, the peer supervisor would assume the role of commentator and eventually facilitate the process as described previously. In this way, the reluctant counselor is placed in a new and perhaps more comfortable paradigm. As a peer supervisor, the experienced (and initially reluctant) counselor is now placed in a role of engaging another counselor to focus on client–counselor concerns. At the same time, this arrangement allows the peer supervisor an opportunity to observe how the regular clinical supervisor conducts supervision. Consistent with social learning theory (Bandura, 1977), this hybrid approach allows the peer supervisor to observe how supervision can be conducted in a different manner and, in time, benefit both the counselor and the new peer supervisor. This model does, however, introduce a new challenge for the regular clinical supervisor in terms of managing relationship dynamics. The clinical supervisor must have a clear focus, remain involved, and provide support for two persons rather than one (Hein & Lawson, 2008).

Although Spice's model was proposed nearly 35 years ago, there is virtually no research that examined the efficacy of this method on improving counselor skills. An exception is a study by Lawson, Hein, and Stuart (2009) who investigated the use of triadic supervision (doctoral students under the supervision of a faculty member) among six master's level counselors. In this qualitative study, two supervisees were paired with a supervisor. Using open-ended interview questions to investigate the impact of this approach, the investigators identified five major outcomes. First, counselor-supervisees expressed that triadic supervision decreased the amount of time available to examine issues regarding their own counseling work. Second, supervisees recognized that in order for this method to work effectively, compatibility among all three members involved was critical. Compatibility referred to variables such as counseling style, prior work experience, and communication style. This perception led supervisees who felt compatible to express greater comfort during supervision, openness, and trust within the triad. Third, most participants valued the feedback from their peer and believed it was genuine. In some instances, however, participants were reluctant to provide honest feedback for fear of hurting the other counselor's feelings. In certain instances, this avoidance of critical feedback created situations where neither counselor wanted to provide negative feedback to the other counselor. Fourth, participants valued their counseling partner as someone who could offer a different and valuable perspective independent of the supervisor. Fifth, most counselors viewed their peer as offering an additional source of support beyond what the supervisor provided. For many, this support validated their own worth as counselors and could often be experienced through simple eye contact with one another.

Finally, there have been comparison studies that purport that both triadic and traditional individual supervision formats are comparable in counselor skill development (Nguyen, 2004) as well as producing an effective working alliance between supervisor and supervisee (Newgent, Davis, & Farley, 2005). However, the empirical literature on comparative evaluation effectiveness is very limited (Lyman, 2010). Given its potential to reduce anxiety in counselor supervisees, particularly in individuals who are unlikely to seek out clinical supervision, both format and method of triad supervision offer options for rehabilitation counselor supervisors.

Peer Supervision Through Distance Education

Before leaving the topic of peer supervision methods, the provision of instruction through online or distance education is an increasing application within rehabilitation counselor education (Gilbride & Stensrud, 1999). This technology within a peer supervision model not only provides consultation to counselors in addressing client issues and related concerns but also has additional features of providing support without any time restrictions for counselors who may be geographically isolated, offers the possibility of providing virtual feedback almost instantaneously and, for some counselors, may be a more preferred way of communicating (Yeh et al. 2008). For example, using an alias designation, persons who feel awkward expressing themselves in a typical face-to-face peer supervision group may feel more comfortable in web-based bulletin board discussions. This feature may encourage counselors to talk more easily about current or past failures, mistakes, or situations when they were unsure how to proceed (Yeh et al., 2008). In addition to these advantages, Stebnicki and Glover (2001) cite that electronic communication or e-supervision as a complement to traditional clinical supervision provides increased time for processing and clarifying thoughts and a greater monitoring capacity for supervisors. Further, with advances in digital technology that allow rehabilitation counselors to make high-quality audio and video recordings in any setting, it is now possible to document client–counselor sessions that can be shared within peer group or individual clinical supervision applications (Byrne & Hartley, 2010).

Although studies are emerging regarding the effectiveness of online supervision, there appears to be supportive evidence for its use in counseling practice. For example, in an exploratory study of online peer supervision with counselors-in-training, Yeh et al. (2008) found after examining frequency and content of peer supervision online comments that the online peer support group "has the potential to not only offer support to new counselors, but to also facilitate change over time" (p. 2900). In a qualitative study of several students completing a rehabilitation counseling practicum, Graf and Stebnicki (2002) found from the process of documenting and analyzing email messages that students went through a developmental process as counselors. Initially, student-counselors focused on trying to better understand the nature of their clients' disabilities and behaving in a way that clients would approve of them and connect with them within the counseling relationship. The relationship with their onsite supervisors evolved from initial admiration with a strong need for approval that eventuated by the end of practicum to viewing this person more critically and perhaps more accurately as someone with expertise but also having fallibilities.

Making the Transition From Counselor to Supervisor

An inherent problem that continues to exist in the counseling field is a long-held belief that counselors promoted to supervisory positions do not require any specialized training in clinical supervision. This situation is problematic for several reasons, chief among them being that it is unethical to provide services without appropriate training. An increasing number of counselors recognize the importance of having clinical supervision training (Bernard & Goodyear, 1998). Despite these problems, studies examining rehabilitation counseling supervisory practices have uniformly found that it is a role that most supervisors report knowing how to perform effectively but have little or no formal training (Herbert, 2004c; Herbert & Trusty, 2006; King, 2009; Schultz et al., 2002). Extrapolating from these studies, it seems that a major criterion used for appointment as a supervisor was that these individuals performed well as counselors and, as a result, were deemed worthy of promotion by administrative personnel. Such practice, though, continues the fallacy that "counseling skills can be transferred to the supervision relationship, and supervisors can model the behaviors of their own supervisors" (Baker, Exum, & Tyler, 2002, p. 15). This transition from practicing counselor to clinical supervisor can be difficult and brings unique challenges as one negotiates the role shift from counselor to supervisor (Herbert, 1997).

In making the transition from counselor to supervisor, Stoltenberg, McNeill, and Delworth (1998) described an Integrated Development Model where supervisors go through a sequence of four levels. Level 1 supervisors are either "highly anxious or somewhat naïve," motivated to doing the "right" thing or tend to be dualistic in their thinking as to what is appropriate or not appropriate as applied to counseling practice. These supervisors tend to provide a great deal of structure and nurturance when working with counselor-supervisees. As they learn more about the nuances of providing clinical supervision, they experience increasing levels of confusion and conflict that are more typical of Level 2 supervisors. These responses can result in fluctuating interest for providing clinical supervision, particularly when their supervision is questioned or not valued by the counselors they supervise. Because clinical supervisors are theoretically "master counselors" themselves, the transition period for a Level 2 supervisor tends to be short because they often rely on their own skills as a counselor in order to gain insight about problems they are experiencing. Obtaining consultation from another supervisor functioning at the next level of supervision may also facilitate this transition. At Level 3, supervisors have stable interest for providing clinical supervision, have settled into their roles as supervisors, and have a good understanding of their strengths relative to supervisees with whom they work better. They are comfortable with the evaluation process involved in supervision and make a balanced assessment of counselor–supervisee performance levels. Eventually, these supervisors may reach the final developmental level—Level 3 Integrated. At this level these individuals are considered "master supervisors" who are equally adept at working with counselors at various levels of development and counselor orientations. Perhaps not surprisingly, these individuals are also considered master therapists and, as such, they have a clear understanding about personal issues that impact counselor roles and effectiveness.

As implied earlier, length of work experience is unrelated to professional growth as a supervisor; the reason being that without specific training, supervisors are likely to repeat the same mistakes (Worthington, 1987). As noted by Granello et al. (2008), what is needed to promote developmental change is for the person to make "a cognitive shift from thinking like a counselor (e.g., focusing on client dynamics) to thinking like a supervisor (e.g., focusing on the counselor's educational needs)" (p. 34). This process requires the supervisor to think more critically in ways to assist the counselor–supervisee to become a more effective counselor. Granello et al., quoting an earlier work by Watkins (1995), list several self-critical questions that supervisors should be asking:

> What did I do in that supervisory hour? Why did I do that? How did I help my supervisee? How did I hinder my supervisee? Are my supervisory interventions becoming more effective? If so, how and why? If not, why? (p. 34)

Although these types of self-examination questions can provide insight, Stoltenberg et al. (1998) contend that finding answers to these questions also necessitates consultation from other supervisors in order to obtain multiple perspectives. It is also argued that engaging in this process should be part of life-long learning and, in doing so, it provides not only therapeutic benefit for the supervisor but an additional assurance of legal protection against negligence.

While proposals have been made to develop clinical supervision competence, for the most part, these pre-professional training courses are geared at the doctoral level rather than at the master's level (Herbert & Bieschke, 2000). Rehabilitation counselor education programs are designed to train counselor practitioners and, with each cycle of new accreditation standards, the curriculum requirements seem to be increasingly burgeoning. As a result, it is understandable that coursework in clinical supervision may be perceived as something needed but not critical. Yet, it is often the case that many rehabilitation counselors in the short period of several years will be asked to provide clinical supervision to other counselors. In addition, some educators purport that supervision training should be a part of graduate work because it will help these students to have a clearer understanding of the supervision process and perhaps improve supervision services for those who assume this role in the future (e.g., Bahrick, Russell, & Salmi, 1991). Certainly, without any formal training or mentoring from their own supervisors, it is difficult to assume that the same counselors who are promoted to supervisors will suddenly emerge with the skills necessary to further develop another counselor's competence. Recommendations for clinical supervision training are something that has been called for over 30 years (e.g., Bernard, 1979); yet surprisingly, there have been few research studies that have examined the effectiveness of such training. Although the need for the development and evaluation of clinical supervision training has been a recommendation repeated in the rehabilitation counseling literature (Herbert, 2009), to date there seems to be no research available that has examined its efficacy. This status is one that typifies the general counselor supervision literature as well with a few exceptions (e.g., McMahon & Simons, 2004).

FINAL THOUGHT

Although I have made an effort to differentiate the focus and nature of administrative and clinical supervision, I suspect that part of the confusion among counselors is that it is often the case that supervisors typically function in both roles (Herbert & Trusty, 2006; Tromski-Klingshirn & Davis, 2007), and the distinction is lost in actual practice. Perhaps, as a profession, we should develop a term other than "clinical supervision." While this term is used in various counseling, psychology, and allied health fields, and is used in this chapter, my experience in working with other rehabilitation counselors in the field is that the term is not only unfamiliar to them but, to some extent, it seems inconsistent with rehabilitation philosophy and the ideals that we promote in our everyday interactions with the people we serve. To demonstrate this point, if I were to ask, "What terms, images, and/or feelings do you associate with the word 'clinical'?" If you are like many rehabilitation counselors whom I have worked with over the years and you were asked this question, I would expect to hear terms that reflect pathology, science, testing, or medical images. In terms of affective responses, persons often associate feelings like "detached," "cold," or "analytical" with the term "clinical." Given these common word associations, it may partially explain why there is some reluctance to receiving clinical supervision, particularly among experienced vocational rehabilitation counselors who work in the public rehabilitation program (Herbert, 2004c). Clearly, medical models, pathology, and being detached from the people with whom we work with are not ideals to which we subscribe to as part of rehabilitation counseling practice. Consequently, I would advocate that in the future we use a different and perhaps more accurate term— rehabilitation counseling supervision. While simple, the intended emphasis is on counseling as a specific activity central to rehabilitation practice. I am not sure whether this term will replace clinical supervision as the preferred term; perhaps it would only further blur the two aspects of supervision that were discussed in the beginning of the chapter. It does, however, mirror our professional identity as rehabilitation counselors and ultimately what each of us should be doing to ensure that competent and ethical practice occurs when working with people with disabilities.

CONTENT REVIEW QUESTIONS

- What are basic differences between administrative and clinical supervision?
- If you worked effectively as a rehabilitation counselor, does this experience alone necessarily prepare you to work as an effective clinical supervisor? Why or why not?
- What knowledge areas and supervisor attributes are needed to work effectively as a rehabilitation counselor supervisor?
- What reasons explain why more rehabilitation counselors and supervisors are not receptive to clinical supervision?
- What is meant by peer supervision and triadic supervision? How might each of these models be used with counselors who are less receptive to clinical supervision?
- How does one incorporate multicultural aspects as part of clinical supervision?
- What advantages might exist for online peer supervision?
- Explain developmental challenges that rehabilitation counselors who are promoted to supervisory positions may experience as they pertain to clinical supervision.
- Should the term "clinical supervision" be retained as a preferred term in rehabilitation counseling practice? Why or why not?

REFERENCES

Bahrick, A. S., Russell, R. K., & Salmi, S. W. (1991). The effects of role induction on trainees' perceptions of supervision. *Journal of Counseling & Development, 69,* 434–438.

Baker, S. B., Exum, H. A., & Tyler, R. E. (2002). The developmental process of clinical supervisors in training: An investigation of the supervisor complexity model. *Counselor Education and Supervision, 42,* 15–30.

Balcazar, F. E., Suarez-Balcazar, Y., Taylor-Ritzler, T., & Keys, C. B. (Eds.). (2010). *Race, culture and disability: Rehabilitation science and practice.* Sudbury, MA: Jones and Bartlett.

Bandura, A. (1977). *Social learning theory.* New York, NY: General Learning Press.

Bernard, J. M. (1979). Supervisory training: A discrimination model. *Counselor Education and Supervision, 19,* 60–68.

Bernard, J. M., & Goodyear, R. K. (1998). *Fundamentals of clinical supervision* (2nd ed.). Boston, MA: Allyn & Bacon.

Borders, L. D. (1991). A systematic approach to peer group supervision. *Journal of Counseling & Development, 69,* 248–252.

Bordin, E. S. (1983). A working alliance based model of supervision. *The Counseling Psychologist, 11*(1), 35–42.

Brislin, D. C., & Herbert, J. T. (2009). Clinical supervision for developing counselors. In I. Marini & M. Stebnicki (Eds.), *The professional counselor's desk reference* (pp. 39–48). New York, NY: Springer.

Byrne, A. M., & Hartley, M. T. (2010). Digital technology in the 21st century: Considerations for clinical supervision in rehabilitation education. *Rehabilitation Education, 24,* 57–68.

Crimando, W. (2004). Administration, management, and supervision. In T. F. Riggar & D. R. Maki (Eds.), *Handbook of rehabilitation counseling* (pp. 305–317). New York, NY: Springer.

Efstation, J. F., Patton, M. J., & Kardash, C. M. *Psychology, 37,* 322–329.

Friedlander, M. L., & Ward, L. G. (1984). Development and validation of the supervisory styles inventory. *Journal of Counseling Psychology, 31,* 541–557.

Gilbride, D., & Stensrud, R. (1999). Expanding our horizons: Using the internet in rehabilitation education. *Rehabilitation Education, 13,* 219–229.

Graf, N. M., & Stebnicki, M. A. (2002). Using e-mail for clinical supervision in practicum: A qualitative analysis. *Journal of Rehabilitation, 68*(3), 41–49.

Granello, D. H., Kindsvatter, A., Granello, P. F., Underfer-Babalis, J., & Moorhead, H. J. H. (2008). Multiple perspectives in supervision: Using a peer consultation model to enhance supervisor development. *Counselor Education and Supervision, 48,* 32–47.

Hein, S., & Lawson, G. (2008). Triadic supervision and its impact on the role of the supervisor: A qualitative examination of supervisors' perspectives. *Counselor Education and Supervision, 48,* 16–31.

Herbert, J. T. (1997). Quality assurance: Administration and supervision. In D. R. Maki & T. F. Riggar (Eds.), *Rehabilitation counseling: Profession and practice* (pp. 246–258). New York, NY: Springer.

Herbert, J. T. (2004a). Clinical supervision. In D. R. Maki & T. F. Riggar (Eds.), *Handbook of rehabilitation counseling* (2nd ed., pp. 305–317). New York, NY: Springer.

Herbert, J. T. (2004b). Clinical supervision in rehabilitation counseling settings. In F. Chan, N. L. Berven, & K. R. Thomas (Eds.), *Counseling theories and techniques for rehabilitation health professionals* (pp. 510–533). New York, NY: Springer.

Herbert, J. T. (2004c). Qualitative analysis of clinical supervision within the public vocational rehabilitation program. *Journal of Rehabilitation Administration, 28,* 51–74.

Herbert, J. T. (2009, October). *Clinical supervision of master's level state VR counselors: A training model.* Paper presented at the meeting of the National Council on Rehabilitation Education, Rehabilitation Services Administration, and Council of State Administrators of Vocational Rehabilitation National Training Conference on Rehabilitation Education, Washington, DC.

Herbert, J. T., & Bieschke, K. J. (2000). A didactic course in clinical supervision. *Rehabilitation Education, 14,* 187–198.

Herbert, J. T., & Trusty, J. (2006). Clinical supervision practices and satisfaction within the public vocational rehabilitation program. *Rehabilitation Counseling Bulletin, 49,* 66–80.

Heron, J. (1990). *Helping the client: A creative practical guide.* London, UK: Sage.

Holloway, E. L. (1995). *Clinical supervision: A systems approach.* Thousand Oaks, CA: Sage.

Howard, E. E., Inman, A. G., & Altman, A. (2006). Critical incidents among novice counselor trainees. *Counselor Education and Supervision, 46,* 88–102.

Kaduvettoor, A., O'Shaughnessy, T., Mori, Y., Beverly, C., III., Weatherford, R. D., & Ladany, N. (2009). Helpful and hindering multicultural events in group supervision:

Climate and multicultural competence. *The Counseling Psychologist, 37,* 786–820. doi:10.1177/0011000009333984

King, C. L., (2009). *Rehabilitation counselor supervision in the private sector: An examination of the long term disability setting.* Unpublished doctoral dissertation, Boston University, Boston, MA.

Knudsen, H. K., Ducharme, L. J., & Roman, P. M. (2008). Clinical supervision, emotional exhaustion, and turnover intention: A study of substance abuse treatment counselors in NIDA's clinical trials network. *Journal of Substance Abuse Treatment, 35,* 387–395. doi:110.1016/j.jsat.2008.02.003

Ladany, N., Ellis, M. V., & Friedlander, M. L. (1999). The supervisory working alliance, trainee self-efficacy, and satisfaction. *Journal of Counseling and Development, 77,* 447–455.

Lassiter, P. S., Napolitano, L., Culbreth, J. R., & Ng, K. M. (2008). Developing multicultural competence using the structured peer group supervision model. *Counselor Education and Supervision, 47,* 164–178.

Lawson, G., Hein, S. F., & Stuart, C. L. (2009). A qualitative investigation of supervisees' experiences of triadic supervision. *Journal of Counseling & Development, 87,* 449–457.

Leung, P., Flowers, C. R., Talley, W. B., & Sanderson, P. R. (2007). *Multicultural issues in rehabilitation and allied health.* Linn Creek, MO: Aspen Professional Services.

Lorenz, D. C. (2009). *Counseling self-efficacy in practicum students: Contributions of supervision* (Doctoral dissertation, Publication No. 3380959). Retrieved from ProQuest Dissertations & Theses.

Lyman, S. R. (2010) *Triadic supervision in CACREP accredited counselor education programs: Current practices and rationale.* (Doctoral dissertation). Available from ProQuest Dissertations and Theses database. (UMI No. 2026813951)

Magnuson, S., Wilcoxon, S. A., & Norem, K. (2000). A profile of lousy supervision: Experienced counselors' perspectives. *Counselor Education and Supervision, 39,* 189–202.

McMahon, M., & Simons, R. (2004). Supervision training for professional counselors: An exploratory study. *Counselor Education & Supervision, 43,* 301–309.

Mueller, W. J., & Kell, B. L. (1972). *Coping with conflict: Supervising counselors and psychotherapists.* New York, NY: Appleton-Century-Crofts.

Nelson, M. L., Barnes, K. L., Evans, A. L., & Triggiano, P. J. (2008). Working with conflict in clinical supervision: Wise supervisors' perspectives. *Journal of Counseling Psychology, 55,* 172–184.

Newgent, R. A., Davis, H., Jr., & Farley, R. C. (2005). Perceptions of individual, triadic, and group models of supervision: A pilot study. *The Clinical Supervisor, 23,* 65–79.

Nguyen, T. V. (2004). A comparison of individual supervision and triadic supervision. *Dissertation Abstracts International, 64*(09), 3204A.

Reese, R. L., Usher, E. L., Bowman, D. C., Norsworthy, L. A., Halstead, J. L., Rowlands, S. R., ... Chisholm, R. R. (2009). Using client feedback in psychotherapy training: An analysis of its influence on supervision and counselor self-efficacy. *Training and Education in Professional Psychology, 3,* 157–168.

Robertson, S. L. (2006). Multicultural supervision: Focusing on performance appraisals. *Journal of Rehabilitation Administration, 30,* 189–202.

Schultz, J. C., (2008). The tripartite model of supervision for rehabilitation counselors. *Journal of Applied Rehabilitation Counseling, 39*(1), 36–41

Schultz, J. C., Copple, B. A., & Ososkie, J. N. (1999). An integrative model for supervision in rehabilitation counseling. *Rehabilitation Education, 13,* 323–334.

Schultz, J. C., Ososkie, J. N., Fried, J. H., Nelson, R. E., & Bardos, A. N. (2002). Clinical supervision in public rehabilitation counseling settings. *Rehabilitation Counseling Bulletin, 45,* 213–222.

Shanfield, S. B., & Gill, D. (1985). Styles of psychotherapy supervision. *Journal of Psychiatric Education, 9,* 225–232.

Spence, S. H., Wilson, J., Kavanagh, D., Strong, J., & Worrall, L. (2001). Clinical supervision in four mental health professions: A review of the evidence. *Behaviour Change, 18,* 135–155.

Spice, C. G., Jr. (1976). *Training professionals to anticipate the challenges of the future A leader's guide to the triadic model of supervision.* Retrieved from ERIC Document Reproduction Services (Accession No. ED 126 396).

Stebnicki, M. A. (1998). Clinical supervision in rehabilitation counseling. *Rehabilitation Education, 12,* 137–159.

Stebnicki, M. A., & Glover, N. M. (2001). E-supervision as a complementary approach to traditional face-to-face clinical supervision in rehabilitation counseling: Problems and solutions. *Rehabilitation Education, 15,* 283–293.

Stoltenberg, C. D., McNeill, B., & Delworth, U. (1998). *IDM supervision: An integrated developmental model for supervising counselors and therapists.* San Francisco, CA: Jossey-Bass.

Sue, D. W., Arrendondo, P., & McDavis, R. J. (1992). Multicultural competencies and standards: A call to the profession. *Journal of Multicultural Counseling and Development, 20,* 64–88.

Theilsen, V. A., & Leahy, M. J. (2001). Essential knowledge and skills for effective clinical supervision in rehabilitation counseling. *Rehabilitation Counseling Bulletin, 44,* 196–208.

Tromski-Klingshirn, D. M., & Davis, T. E. (2007). Supervisees' perceptions of their clinical supervision: A study of the dual role of clinical and administrative supervisor. *Counselor Education and Supervision, 46,* 294–304.

Watkins, C. E., Jr. (1995). Researching psychotherapy supervision development: Four key considerations. *The Clinical Supervisor, 13,* 111–118.

Worthington, E. L., Jr. (1987). Changes in supervision as counselors and supervisors gain experience: A review. *Professional Psychology: Research and Practice, 18,* 189–208.

Yeh, C. J., Chang, T., Chaing, L., Drost, C. M., Spelliscy, D., Carter, R. T., … Chang, Y. (2008). Development, content, process and outcome of an online peer supervision group for counselor trainees. *Computers in Human Behavior, 24,* 2889–2903.

Acronyms for Common Terms in Rehabilitation Counseling

BY CATEGORIES

SELECTED ORGANIZATIONS

ACA American Counseling Association

Subdivisions of the ACA

ARCA American Rehabilitation Counseling Association
IAMFC International Association for Marriage and Family Counseling
NRA National Rehabilitation Association

Subdivisions of the NRA

NAMRC National Association of Multicultural Rehabilitation Concerns (Formerly: National Association of Non-White Workers [NANRW])
NRCA National Rehabilitation Counseling Association
RCEA Rehabilitation Counselor and Educators Association

OTHER ORGANIZATIONS

AAMFT American Association for Marital and Family Therapy
ACCD American Coalition of Citizens with Disabilities
ADAPT American Disabled for Adaptive Public Transportation
ADARA Professionals Networking for Excellence in Service Delivery with Individuals who are Deaf or Hard of Hearing (formerly: American Deafness and Rehabilitation Association)
AERA American Educational Research Association
AMCHA American Mental Health Counseling Association
APA American Psychological Association
ARC Alliance for Rehabilitation Counseling
IARP International Association of Rehabilitation Professionals
IRI Institute on Rehabilitation Issues
NCME National Council on Measurement in Education
NCRE National Council on Rehabilitation Education
PNHP Physicians for a National Health Program
RESNA Rehabilitation Engineering and Assistive Technology Society of North America
UN United Nations

Specialized Agencies of the UN/Acronyms

CRPD Convention on the Rights of Persons with Disabilities
CSDH Commission on Social Determinants of Health
ICD International Classification of Disease
ICF International Classification of Functioning, Disability, and Health

ICF-CY	Children and Youth Version of the International Classification of Functioning, Disability, and Health
ICFDH-2	International Classification of Functioning, Disability, and Health; Beta-2
ICIDH	International Classification of Impairments, Disabilities and Handicaps
ILO	International Labour Organization
MDG	Millennium Development Goals
UNDP	United Nations Development Programme
UNESCO	United Nations Educational, Scientific and Cultural Organization
UNICEF	United Nations International Children's Emergency Fund
WHO	World Health Organization

CERTIFICATION BODIES/CREDENTIALS

AASCB	American Association of State Counseling Boards
APCB	Addiction Professionals Certification Board
CFT	Certified Family Therapist
CRC	Certified Rehabilitation Counselor
CRCC	Commission on Rehabilitation Counselor Certification
LPC	Licensed Professional Counselor
NBCC	National Board for Certified Counselors
NCA	National Credentialing Academy

ACCREDITATION BODIES

CACREP	Council for Accreditation of Counseling and Related Educational Programs
CHEA	Council for Higher Education Accreditation
CORE	Council on Rehabilitation Education
COPA	Council on Postsecondary Accreditation
CORPA	Commission on Recognition of Postsecondary Accreditation (formerly: Council on Postsecondary Accreditation [COPA])

GOVERNMENTAL/LEGISLATIVE

ACTKIT	Assertive Community Treatment Knowledge Informing Transformation
ADA	Americans with Disabilities Act
CAP	Client Assistance Program
CFR	Code of Federal Regulations
CIL or ILC	Center of Independent Living
DBTAC	Disability and Business Technical Assistance Center
DCS	Department of Correctional Services
DHS	Department of Human Services
DOL	Department of Labor
DOT	Dictionary of Occupational Titles
DRRP	Disability and Rehabilitation Research Program
EEOC	Equal Employment Opportunity Commission
EN	Employment Network
FMLA	Family and Medical Leave Act
GAO	Government Accountability Office
GINA	Genetic Information Nondiscrimination Act
HIPAA	Health Insurance Portability and Accountability Act
HITECH	Health Information Technology for Economic and Clinical Health Act
HUD	Housing and Urban Development
IPE	Individual Plan of Employment (Formerly: Individualized Written Rehabilitation Plan [IWRP])
JAN	Job Accommodation Network
NCD	National Council on Disability

NCDDR   National Center for the Dissemination of Disability Research
NIDRR   National Institute on Disability and Rehabilitation Research
NTIA   National Telecommunications and Information Administration
OCR   Office of Civil Rights
OIDAP   Occupational Information Development Advisory Panel
OIS   Occupational Information System
OSERS   Office of Special Education and Rehabilitation
PHI   Protected Health Information
RRTC   Rehabilitation Research and Training Center
RSA   Rehabilitation Services Administration
SAMHSA   Substance Abuse and Mental Health Services Administration
SSA   Social Security Administration
SSDI   Social Security Disability Insurance
SSI   Supplemental Security Income
TWWIIA   Ticket to Work and Work Incentives Improvement Act
USERRA   Uniformed Services Employment and Reemployment Rights Act
VOIP   Voice Over the Internet Protocol
WIA   Workforce Investment Act

CANADIAN ACRONYMS

CARP   Canadian Association of Rehabilitation Professionals
CCRC   Canadian Certified Rehabilitation Counselor

MISCELLANEOUS

AT   Assistive Technology
CBR   Community-Based Rehabilitation
DALY   Disability-Adjusted Life Year
DPO   Disabled Peoples' Organization
DSM   Diagnostic and Statistical Manual
DSM-IV-TR   Diagnostic and Statistical Manual of Mental Disorders, 4th Edition, Text Revision
GATB   General Aptitude Test Battery
GDP   Gross Domestic Product
GRE   Graduate Record Examination
HMO   Health Maintenance Organization
HRQOL   Health-Related Quality of Life
IDM   Integrated Development Model
INCOME   Imaging, iNforming, Choosing, Obtaining, Maintaining, and Exiting
IPS   Individual Placement and Support
IRT   Item Response Theory
JTI   Job Task Inventory
MHID   Multiple Heritage Identity Development
MID   Minority Identity Development
MVS   My Vocational Situation
NGO   Non-governmental organization
PDO   People with Disability Organization
POS   Point of Service
PPO   Preferred Provider Organization
PSR   Psychosocial Rehabilitation
PUI   Problematic Use of the Internet
PWD   Persons with Disability
QOL   Quality of Life
R/CID   Racial/Cultural Identity Development
RC   Rehabilitation Counselor

RCE	Rehabilitation Counselor Education
RIASEC	Realistic, Investigate, Artistic, Social, Enterprising, and Conventional
SAT	Scholastic Aptitude Test
SCID-I	Structured Clinical Interview for DSM-IV Axis I Disorders
SDS	Self-directed Search
SSN	Social Safety Net
TSA	Transferable Skills Assessment
VR	Vocational Rehabilitation
W3C WAI	World Wide Web Consortium Web Accessibility Initiative

ALPHABETICALLY

AAMFT	American Association for Marital and Family Therapy
AASCB	American Association of State Counseling Boards
ACA	American Counseling Association
ACCD	American Coalition of Citizens with Disabilities
ACTKIT	Assertive Community Treatment Knowledge Informing Transformation
ADA	Americans with Disabilities Act
ADAPT	American Disabled for Adaptive Public Transportation
ADARA	Professionals Networking for Excellence in Service Delivery with Individuals who are Deaf or Hard of Hearing (formerly: American Deafness And Rehabilitation Association)
AERA	American Educational Research Association
AMCHA	American Mental Health Counseling Association
APA	American Psychological Association
APCB	Addiction Professionals Certification Board
ARC	Alliance for Rehabilitation Counseling
ARCA	American Rehabilitation Counseling Association
AT	Assistive Technology
CACREP	Council for Accreditation of Counseling and Related Educational Programs
CAP	Client Assistance Program
CARP	Canadian Association of Rehabilitation Professionals
CBR	Community-Based Rehabilitation
CCRC	Canadian Certified Rehabilitation Counselor
CFR	Code of Federal Regulations
CFT	Certified Family Therapist
CHEA	Council for Higher Education Accreditation
CIL or ILC	Center of Independent Living
COPA	Council on Postsecondary Accreditation
CORE	Council on Rehabilitation Education
CORPA	Commission on Recognition of Postsecondary Accreditation (formerly: Council on Postsecondary Accreditation [COPA])
CRC	Certified Rehabilitation Counselor
CRCC	Commission on Rehabilitation Counselor Certification
CRPD	Convention on the Rights of Persons with Disabilities
CSDH	Commission on Social Determinants of Health
DALY	Disability-Adjusted Life Year
DBTAC	Disability and Business Technical Assistance Center
DCS	Department of Correctional Services
DHS	Department of Human Services
DOL	Department of Labor

DOT	Dictionary of Occupational Titles
DPO	Disabled Peoples' Organization
DRRP	Disability and Rehabilitation Research Program
DSM	Diagnostic and Statistical Manual
DSM-IV-TR	Diagnostic and Statistical Manual of Mental Disorders, 4th Edition, Text Revision
EEOC	Equal Employment Opportunity Commission
EN	Employment Network
FMLA	Family and Medical Leave Act
GAO	Government Accountability Office
GATB	General Aptitude Test Battery
GDP	Gross Domestic Product
GINA	Genetic Information Nondiscrimination Act
GRE	Graduate Record Examination
HIPAA	Health Insurance Portability and Accountability Act
HITECH	Health Information Technology for Economic and Clinical Health Act
HMO	Health Maintenance Organization
HRQOL	Health-Related Quality of Life
HUD	Housing and Urban Development
IAMFC	International Association for Marriage and Family Counseling
IARP	International Association of Rehabilitation Professionals
ICD	International Classification of Disease
ICF	International Classification of Functioning, Disability, and Health
ICF-CY	Children and Youth Version of the International Classification of Functioning, Disability, and Health
ICFDH-2	International Classification of Functioning, Disability, and Health; Beta-2
ICIDH	International Classification of Impairments, Disabilities and Handicaps
IDM	Integrated Development Model
ILO	International Labour Organization
INCOME	Imaging, iNforming, Choosing, Obtaining, Maintaining, and Exiting
IPE	Individual Plan of Employment (Formerly: Individualized Written Rehabilitation Plan [IWRP])
IPS	Individual Placement and Support
IRI	Institute on Rehabilitation Issues
IRT	Item Response Theory
JAN	Job Accommodation Network
JTI	Job Task Inventory
LPC	Licensed Professional Counselor
MDG	Millennium Development Goals
MHID	Multiple Heritage Identity Development
MID	Minority Identity Development
MVS	My Vocational Situation
NAMRC	National Association of Multicultural Rehabilitation Concerns (Formerly: National Association of Non-White Workers [NANRW])
NBCC	National Board for Certified Counselors
NCA	National Credentialing Academy
NCD	National Council on Disability
NCDDR	National Center for the Dissemination of Disability Research
NCME	National Council on Measurement in Education
NCRE	National Council on Rehabilitation Education
NGO	Non-governmental organization
NIDRR	National Institute on Disability and Rehabilitation Research
NRA	National Rehabilitation Association

NRCA	National Rehabilitation Counseling Association
NTIA	National Telecommunications and Information Administration
OCR	Office of Civil Rights
OIDAP	Occupational Information Development Advisory Panel
OIS	Occupational Information System
OSERS	Office of Special Education and Rehabilitation
PDO	People with Disability Organization
PHI	Protected Health Information
PNHP	Physicians for a National Health Program
POS	Point of Service
PPO	Preferred Provider Organization
PSR	Psychosocial Rehabilitation
PUI	Problematic Use of the Internet
PWD	Persons with Disability
QOL	Quality of Life
R/CID	Racial/Cultural Identity Development
RC	Rehabilitation Counselor
RCE	Rehabilitation Counselor Education
RCEA	Rehabilitation Counselor and Educators Association
RESNA	Rehabilitation Engineering and Assistive Technology Society of North America
RIASEC	Realistic, Investigate, Artistic, Social, Enterprising, and Conventional
RRTC	Rehabilitation Research and Training Center
RSA	Rehabilitation Services Administration
SAMHSA	Substance Abuse and Mental Health Services Administration
SAT	Scholastic Aptitude Test
SCID-I	Structured Clinical Interview for DSM-IV Axis I Disorders
SDS	Self-directed Search
SSA	Social Security Administration
SSDI	Social Security Disability Insurance
SSI	Supplemental Security Income
SSN	Social Safety Net
TSA	Transferable Skills Assessment
TWWIIA	Ticket to Work and Work Incentives Improvement Act
UN	United Nations
UNDP	United Nations Development Programme
UNESCO	United Nations Educational, Scientific and Cultural Organization
UNICEF	United Nations International Children's Emergency Fund
USERRA	Uniformed Services Employment and Reemployment Rights Act
VOIP	Voice Over the Internet Protocol
VR	Vocational Rehabilitation
W3C WAI	World Wide Web Consortium Web Accessibility Initiative
WHO	World Health Organization
WIA	Workforce Investment Act

B

Scope of Practice for Rehabilitation Counseling

ASSUMPTIONS

- The Scope of Practice Statement identifies knowledge and skills required for the provision of effective rehabilitation counseling services to persons with physical, mental, developmental, cognitive, and emotional disabilities as embodied in the standards of the profession's credentialing organizations.

- Several rehabilitation disciplines and related processes (e.g., vocational evaluation, job development and job placement, work adjustment, and case management) are tied to the central field of rehabilitation counseling. The field of rehabilitation counseling is a specialty within the rehabilitation profession with counseling at its core, and is differentiated from other related counseling fields.

- The professional scope of rehabilitation counseling practice is also differentiated from an individual scope of practice, which may overlap, but is more specialized than the professional scope. An individual scope of practice is based on one's own knowledge of the abilities and skills that have been gained through a program of education and professional experience. A person is ethically bound to limit his/her practice to that individual scope of practice.

UNDERLYING VALUES

- Facilitation of independence, integration, and inclusion of people with disabilities in employment and the community.
- Belief in the dignity and worth of all people.
- Commitment to a sense of equal justice based on a model of accommodation to provide and equalize the opportunities to participate in all rights and privileges available to all people and a commitment to supporting persons with disabilities in advocacy activities to achieve this status and empower themselves.
- Emphasis on the holistic nature of human function, which is procedurally facilitated by the utilization of techniques such as:
  - interdisciplinary teamwork;
  - counseling to assist in maintaining a holistic perspective; and
  - a commitment to considering individuals within the context of their family systems and communities.
- Recognition of the importance of focusing on the assets of the person.
- Commitment to models of service delivery that emphasize integrated, comprehensive services, which are mutually planned by the consumer and the rehabilitation counselor.

Scope of Practice Statement

Rehabilitation counseling is a systematic process that assists persons with physical, mental, developmental, cognitive, and emotional disabilities to achieve their personal, career, and independent living goals in the most integrated setting possible through the application of the counseling process. The counseling process involves communication, goal setting, and beneficial growth or change through self-advocacy, psychological, vocational, social, and behavioral interventions. The specific techniques and modalities utilized within this rehabilitation counseling process may include, but are not limited to:

- assessment and appraisal;
- diagnosis and treatment planning;
- career (vocational) counseling;
- individual and group counseling treatment interventions focused on facilitating adjustments to the medical and psychosocial impact of disability;
- case management, referral, and service coordination;
- program evaluation and research;
- interventions to remove environmental, employment, and attitudinal barriers;
- consultation services among multiple parties and regulatory systems;
- job analysis, job development, and placement services, including assistance with employment and job accommodations; and
- the provision of consultation about and access to rehabilitation technology.

Selected Definitions

The following definitions are provided to increase the understanding of certain key terms and concepts used in the Scope of Practice Statement for Rehabilitation Counseling.

Appraisal

Selecting, administering, scoring, and interpreting instruments designed to assess an individual's aptitudes, abilities, achievements, interests, personal characteristics, disabilities, and mental, emotional, or behavioral disorders, as well as the use of methods and techniques for understanding human behavior in relation to coping with, adapting to, or changing life situations.

Diagnosis and Treatment Planning

Assessing, analyzing, and providing diagnostic descriptions of mental, emotional, or behavioral conditions or disabilities; exploring possible solutions; and developing and implementing a treatment plan for mental, emotional, and psychosocial adjustment or development. Diagnosis and treatment planning shall not be construed to permit the performance of any act that rehabilitation counselors are not educated and trained to perform.

Counseling Treatment Intervention

The application of cognitive, affective, behavioral, and systemic counseling strategies includes developmental, wellness, pathologic, and multicultural principles of human behavior. Such interventions are specifically implemented in the context of a professional counseling relationship and may include, but are not limited to: appraisal; individual, group, marriage, and family counseling and psychotherapy; the diagnostic description and treatment of persons with mental, emotional, and behavioral disorders or disabilities; guidance and consulting to facilitate normal growth and development, including educational and career development; the utilization of functional assessments and career counseling for persons requesting assistance in adjusting to a disability or handicapping condition; referrals; consulting; and research.

Referral
Evaluating and identifying the needs of a client to determine the advisability of referrals to other specialists, advising the client of such judgments, and communicating as requested or deemed appropriate to such referral sources.

Case Management
A systematic process merging counseling and managerial concepts and skills through the application of techniques derived from intuitive and researched methods, thereby advancing efficient and effective decision making for functional control of self, client, setting, and other relevant factors for anchoring a proactive practice. In case management, the counselor's role is focused on interviewing, counseling, planning rehabilitation programs, coordinating services, interacting with significant others, placing clients and following-up with them, monitoring progress, and solving problems.

Program Evaluation
The effort to determine what changes occur as a result of a planned program by comparing actual changes (results) with desired changes (stated goals), and by identifying the degree to which the activity (planned program) is responsible for those changes.

Research
A systematic effort to collect, analyze, and interpret quantitative or qualitative data that describe how social characteristics, behavior, emotions, cognition, disabilities, mental disorders, and interpersonal transactions among individuals and organizations interact.

Consultation
The application of scientific principles and procedures in counseling and human development to provide assistance in understanding and solving current or potential problems that the consultee may have in relation to a third party, be it an individual, group, or organization.

C

Code of Professional Ethics
for Rehabilitation Counselors

PREAMBLE

Rehabilitation counselors provide services within the Scope of Practice for Rehabilitation Counseling. They demonstrate beliefs, attitudes, knowledge, and skills to provide competent counseling services and to work collaboratively with diverse groups of individuals, including clients, as well as with programs, institutions, employers, and service delivery systems, and provide both direct (e.g., counseling) and indirect (e.g., case review and feasibility evaluation) services. Regardless of the specific tasks, work settings, or technology used, rehabilitation counselors demonstrate adherence to ethical standards and ensure that the standards are vigorously enforced. The Code of Professional Ethics for Rehabilitation Counselors, henceforth referred to as the Code, is designed to provide guidance for the ethical practice of rehabilitation counselors.

The primary obligation of rehabilitation counselors is to clients, defined as individuals with or directly affected by a disability, functional limitation(s), or medical condition and who receive services from rehabilitation counselors. In some settings, clients may be referred to by other terms such as, but not limited to, consumers and service recipients. Rehabilitation counseling services may be provided to individuals other than those with disabilities. Rehabilitation counselors do not have clients in a forensic setting. The subjects of the objective and unbiased evaluations are evaluees. In all instances, the primary obligation remains to clients or evaluees and adherence to the Code is required.

The basic objectives of the Code are to: (1) promote public welfare by specifying ethical behavior expected of rehabilitation counselors, (2) establish principles that define ethical behavior and best practices of rehabilitation counselors, (3) serve as an ethical guide designed to assist rehabilitation counselors in constructing a professional course of action that best serves those utilizing rehabilitation services, and (4) serve as the basis for the processing of alleged Code violations by certified rehabilitation counselors.

Rehabilitation counselors are committed to facilitating the personal, social, and economic independence of individuals with disabilities. In fulfilling this commitment, rehabilitation counselors recognize diversity and embrace a cultural approach in support of the worth, dignity, potential, and uniqueness of individuals with disabilities within their social and cultural context. They look to professional values as an important way of living

Adopted in June 2009 by the Commission on Rehabilitation Counselor Certification for its Certified Rehabilitation Counselors. This Code is effective as of January 1, 2010.

Developed and Administered by the Commission on Rehabilitation Counselor Certification (CRCC®) 1699 East Woodfield Road, Suite 300 Schaumburg, IL 60173 (847) 944-1325 http://www.crccertification.com

out an ethical commitment. The primary values that serve as a foundation for this Code include a commitment to:

- respecting human rights and dignity;
- ensuring the integrity of all professional relationships;
- acting to alleviate personal distress and suffering;
- enhancing the quality of professional knowledge and its application to increase professional and personal effectiveness;
- appreciating the diversity of human experience and culture; and
- advocating for the fair and adequate provision of services.

These values inform principles. They represent one important way of expressing a general ethical commitment that becomes more precisely defined and action oriented when expressed as a principle. The fundamental spirit of caring and respect with which the Code is written is based upon six principles of ethical behavior:

Autonomy: To respect the rights of clients to be self-governing within their social and cultural framework.
Beneficence: To do good to others; to promote the well-being of clients.
Fidelity: To be faithful; to keep promises and honor the trust placed in rehabilitation counselors.
Justice: To be fair in the treatment of all clients; to provide appropriate services to all.
Nonmaleficence: To do no harm to others.
Veracity: To be honest.

Although the Code provides guidance for ethical practice, it is impossible to address every possible ethical dilemma that rehabilitation counselors may face. When faced with ethical dilemmas that are difficult to resolve, rehabilitation counselors are expected to engage in a carefully considered ethical decision-making process. Reasonable differences of opinion can and do exist among rehabilitation counselors with respect to the ways in which values, ethical principles, and ethical standards would be applied when they conflict. While there is no specific ethical decision-making model that is most effective, rehabilitation counselors are expected to be familiar with and apply a credible model of decision making that can bear public scrutiny. Rehabilitation counselors are aware that seeking consultation and/or supervision is an important part of ethical decision making.

The Enforceable Standards within the Code are the exacting standards intended to provide guidance in specific circumstances and serve as the basis for processing complaints initiated against certified rehabilitation counselors.

Each Enforceable Standard is not meant to be interpreted in isolation. Instead, it is important for rehabilitation counselors to interpret standards in conjunction with other related standards in various sections of the Code. A brief glossary is located after Section L to provide readers with a concise description of some of the terms used in the C.

ENFORCEABLE STANDARDS OF ETHICAL PRACTICE
Section A: The Counseling Relationship
A.1. Welfare of Those Served by Rehabilitation Counselors
a. *Primary Responsibility*. The primary responsibility of rehabilitation counselors is to respect the dignity and to promote the welfare of clients. Clients are defined as individuals with, or directly affected by a disability, functional limitation(s) or medical condition

and who receive services from rehabilitation counselors. At times, rehabilitation counseling services may be provided to individuals other than those with a disability. In all instances, the primary obligation of rehabilitation counselors is to promote the welfare of their clients.

b. Rehabilitation and Counseling Plans. Rehabilitation counselors and clients work jointly in devising and revising integrated, individual, and mutually agreed upon rehabilitation and counseling plans that offer a reasonable promise of success and are consistent with the abilities and circumstances of clients. Rehabilitation counselors and clients regularly review rehabilitation and counseling plans to assess continued viability and effectiveness.

c. Employment Needs. Rehabilitation counselors work with clients to consider employment consistent with the overall abilities, functional capabilities and limitations, general temperament, interest and aptitude patterns, social skills, education, general qualifications, transferable skills, and other relevant characteristics and needs of clients. They assist in the placement of clients in available positions that are consistent with the interest, culture, and the welfare of clients and/or employers.

d. Autonomy. Rehabilitation counselors respect the rights of clients to make decisions on their own behalf. On decisions that may limit or diminish the autonomy of clients, decision making on behalf of clients is taken only after careful deliberation. They advocate for the resumption of responsibility by clients as quickly as possible.

A.2. Respecting Diversity
a. Respecting Culture. Rehabilitation counselors demonstrate respect for the cultural background of clients in developing and implementing rehabilitation and treatment plans, and providing and adapting interventions.

b. Nondiscrimination. Rehabilitation counselors do not condone or engage in discrimination based on age, color, race, national origin, culture, disability, ethnicity, gender, gender identity, religion/spirituality, sexual orientation, marital status/partnership, language preference, socioeconomic status, or any basis proscribed by law.

A.3. Client Rights in the Counseling Relationship
a. Professional Disclosure Statement. Rehabilitation counselors have an obligation to review with clients orally, in writing, and in a manner that best accommodates any of their limitation, the rights and responsibilities of both rehabilitation counselors and clients. Disclosure at the outset of the counseling relationship should minimally include: (1) the qualifications, credentials, and relevant experience of the rehabilitation counselor, (2) purposes, goals, techniques, limitations, and the nature of potential risks and benefits of services, (3) frequency and length of services, (4) confidentiality and limitations regarding confidentiality (including how a supervisor and/or treatment team professional is involved), (5) contingencies for continuation of services upon the incapacitation or death of the rehabilitation counselor, (6) fees and billing arrangements, (7) record preservation and release policies, (8) risks associated with electronic communication; and (9) legal issues affecting services. Rehabilitation counselors recognize that disclosure of these issues may need to be reiterated or expanded upon throughout the counseling relationship, and/or disclosure related to other matters may be required depending on the nature of services provided and matters that arise during the rehabilitation counseling relationship.

b. Informed Consent.   Rehabilitation counselors recognize that clients have the freedom to choose whether to enter into or remain in a rehabilitation counseling relationship. They respect the rights of clients to participate in ongoing rehabilitation counseling planning and to make decisions to refuse any services or modality changes, while also ensuring that clients are advised of the consequences of such refusal. Rehabilitation counselors recognize that clients need information to make an informed decision regarding services and that professional disclosure is required for informed consent to be an ongoing part of the rehabilitation counseling process. They appropriately document discussions of disclosure and informed consent throughout the rehabilitation counseling relationship.

c. Developmental and Cultural Sensitivity.   Rehabilitation counselors communicate information in ways that are both developmentally and culturally appropriate. Rehabilitation counselors provide services (e.g., arranging for a qualified interpreter or translator) when necessary to ensure comprehension by clients. In collaboration with clients, rehabilitation counselors consider cultural implications of informed consent procedures and, when possible, rehabilitation counselors adjust their practices accordingly.

d. Inability to Give Consent.   When counseling minors or persons unable to give voluntary consent, rehabilitation counselors seek the assent of clients and include clients in decision making as appropriate. Rehabilitation counselors recognize the need to balance the ethical rights of clients to make choices, the mental or legal capacity of clients to give consent or assent, and parental, guardian, or familial legal rights and responsibilities to protect clients and make decisions on behalf of clients.

e. Support Network Involvement.   Rehabilitation counselors recognize that support by others may be important to clients. They consider enlisting the support, understanding, and involvement of others (e.g., religious/spiritual/community leaders, family members, friends, and guardians) as resources, when appropriate, with consent from clients.

A.4. Avoiding Harm and Value Imposition
a. Avoiding Harm.   Rehabilitation counselors act to avoid harming clients, trainees, supervisees, and research participants, and to minimize or to remedy unavoidable or unanticipated harm.

b. Personal Values.   Rehabilitation counselors are aware of their values, attitudes, beliefs, and behaviors and avoid imposing values that are inconsistent with rehabilitation counseling goals.

A.5. Roles and Relationships With Clients
a. Prohibition of Sexual or Romantic Relationships With Current Clients.   Sexual or romantic rehabilitation counselor–client interactions or relationships with current clients, their romantic partners, or their immediate family members are prohibited.

b. Sexual or Romantic Rehabilitations With Former Clients.   Sexual or romantic rehabilitation counselor–client interactions or relationships with former clients, their romantic partners, or their immediate family members are prohibited for a period of 5 years following the last professional contact. Even after 5 years, rehabilitation counselors give careful consideration to the potential for sexual or romantic relationships to cause harm to former clients. In cases of potential exploitation and/or harm, rehabilitation counselors avoid entering such interactions or relationships.

c. Prohibition of Sexual or Romantic Relationships With Certain Former Clients.   If clients have a history of physical, emotional, or sexual abuse or if clients have ever been diagnosed with any form of psychosis or personality disorder, mental retardation, marked cognitive impairment, or if clients are likely to remain in need of therapy due to the intensity or chronicity of a problem, rehabilitation counselors do not engage in sexual activities or sexual contact with former clients, regardless of the length of time elapsed since termination of the client relationship.

d. Nonprofessional Interactions or Relationships Other Than Sexual or Romantic Interactions or Relationships.   Rehabilitation counselors avoid nonprofessional relationships with clients, former clients, their romantic partners, or their immediate family members, except when such interactions are potentially beneficial to clients or former clients. In cases where nonprofessional interactions may be potentially beneficial to clients or former clients, rehabilitation counselors must document in case records, prior to interactions (when feasible), the rationale for such interactions, the potential benefits, and anticipated consequences for the clients or former clients and other involved parties. Such interactions are initiated with appropriate consent from clients and are time limited (e.g., extended free-standing friendships are prohibited) or context specific (e.g., constrained to an organizational or community setting). When unintentional harm occurs to clients or former clients, or to other involved parties, due to nonprofessional interactions, rehabilitation counselors must show evidence of an attempt to remedy such harm. Examples of potentially beneficial interactions include, but are not limited to, attending a formal ceremony (e.g., a wedding/commitment ceremony or graduation); purchasing a service or product provided by clients or former clients (excepting unrestricted bartering); hospital visits to ill family members; or mutual membership in professional associations, organizations, or communities.

e. Counseling Relationships With Former Romantic Partners Prohibited.   Rehabilitation counselors do not provide counseling services to individuals with whom they have had a prior sexual or romantic relationship.

f. Role Changes in the Professional Relationship.   When rehabilitation counselors change roles from the original or most recent contracted relationship, they obtain informed consent from clients or evaluees and explain the right to refuse services related to the change. Examples of role changes include: (1) changing from individual to group, relationship, or family counseling or vice versa, (2) changing from a forensic to a primary care role or vice versa, (3) changing from a nonforensic evaluative role to a rehabilitation or therapeutic role or vice versa, (4) changing from a rehabilitation counselor to a researcher role (e.g., enlisting clients as research participants) or vice versa, and (5) changing from a rehabilitation counselor to a mediator role or vice versa. The clients or evaluees must be fully informed of any anticipated consequences (e.g., financial, legal, personal, or therapeutic) due to a role change by the rehabilitation counselor.

g. Receiving Gifts.   Rehabilitation counselors understand the challenges of accepting gifts from clients and recognize that in some cultures, small gifts are a token of respect and gratitude. When determining whether to accept gifts from clients, rehabilitation counselors take into account the cultural or community practice, therapeutic relationship, the monetary value of gifts, the motivation of the client for giving gifts, and the motivation of the rehabilitation counselor for accepting or declining gifts.

A.6. Multiple Clients

When rehabilitation counselors agree to provide counseling services to two or more persons who have a relationship (e.g., husband/wife; parent/child), rehabilitation counselors clarify at the outset which person is, or which persons are, to be served and the nature of the relationship rehabilitation counselors have with each involved person. If it becomes apparent that rehabilitation counselors may be called upon to perform potentially conflicting roles, rehabilitation counselors clarify, adjust, or withdraw from roles appropriately.

A.7. Group Work

a. Screening.   Rehabilitation counselors screen prospective group counseling/therapy participants. To the extent possible, rehabilitation counselors select members whose needs and goals are compatible with goals of the group, who do not impede the group process, and whose well-being is not jeopardized by the group experience.

b. Protecting Clients.   In a group setting, rehabilitation counselors take reasonable precautions to protect clients from harm or trauma.

A.8. Termination and Referral

a. Abandonment Prohibited.   Rehabilitation counselors do not abandon or neglect clients in counseling. They assist in making appropriate arrangements for the continuation of services when necessary (e.g., during interruptions such as vacations, illness, and following termination).

b. Initial Determination of Inability to Assist Clients.   If rehabilitation counselors determine that they are unable to be of professional assistance to clients, they avoid entering such counseling relationships.

c. Appropriate Termination and Referral.   Rehabilitation counselors terminate counseling relationships when it becomes reasonably apparent that clients no longer need assistance, are not likely to benefit, or are being harmed by continued counseling. They may terminate counseling when in jeopardy of harm by clients or other persons with whom clients have a relationship, or when clients do not pay agreed-upon fees. They provide pretermination counseling and recommend other clinically and culturally appropriate service sources when necessary.

d. Appropriate Transfer of Services.   When rehabilitation counselors transfer or refer clients to other practitioners, they ensure that appropriate counseling and administrative processes are completed in a timely manner and that open communication is maintained with both clients and practitioners. Rehabilitation counselors prepare and disseminate, to identified colleagues or records custodian, a plan for the transfer of clients and files in the case of their incapacitation, death, or termination of practice.

A.9. End-of-Life Care for Terminally Ill Clients

a. Quality of Care.   Rehabilitation counselors take measures that enable clients to: (1) obtain high-quality end-of-life care for their physical, emotional, social, and spiritual needs, (2) exercise the highest degree of self-determination possible, (3) be given every opportunity possible to engage in informed decision making regarding their end-of-life care, and (4) receive complete and adequate assessment regarding their ability to make competent, rational decisions on their own behalf from mental health professionals who are experienced in end-of-life care practice.

b. Rehabilitation Counselor Competence, Choice, and Referral.   Rehabilitation counselors may choose to work or not to work with terminally ill clients who wish to explore their end-of-life options. They provide appropriate referral information if they are not competent to address such concerns.

c. Confidentiality.   Rehabilitation counselors who provide services to terminally ill individuals who are considering hastening their own deaths have the option of breaking or not breaking confidentiality on this matter, depending on applicable laws and the specific circumstances of the situation and after seeking consultation or supervision from appropriate professional and legal parties.

Section B: Confidentiality, Privileged Communication, and Privacy

B.1. Respecting Client Rights
a. Cultural Diversity Considerations.   Rehabilitation counselors maintain beliefs, attitudes, knowledge, and skills regarding cultural meanings of confidentiality and privacy. They hold ongoing discussions with clients as to how, when, and with whom information is to be shared.

b. Respect for Privacy.   Rehabilitation counselors respect privacy rights of clients. They solicit private information from clients only when it is beneficial to the counseling process.

c. Respect for Confidentiality.   Rehabilitation counselors do not share confidential information without consent from clients or without sound legal or ethical justification.

d. Explanation of Limitations.   At initiation and throughout the counseling process, rehabilitation counselors inform clients of the limitations of confidentiality and seek to identify foreseeable situations in which confidentiality must be breached.

B.2. Exceptions
a. Danger and Legal Requirements.   The general requirement that rehabilitation counselors keep information confidential does not apply when disclosure is required to protect clients or identified others from serious and foreseeable harm, or when legal requirements demand that confidential information must be revealed. Rehabilitation counselors consult with other professionals when in doubt as to the validity of an exception.

b. Contagious, Life-Threatening Diseases.   When clients disclose that they have a disease commonly known to be both communicable and life threatening, rehabilitation counselors may be justified in disclosing information to identifiable third parties, if they are known to be at demonstrable and high risk of contracting the disease. Prior to making a disclosure, rehabilitation counselors confirm that there is such a diagnosis and assess the intent of clients to inform the third parties about their disease or to engage in any behaviors that may be harmful to identifiable third parties.

c. Court-Ordered Disclosure.   When subpoenaed to release confidential or privileged information without permission from clients, rehabilitation counselors obtain written, informed consent from clients or take steps to prohibit the disclosure or have it limited as narrowly as possible due to potential harm to clients or the counseling relationship. Whenever reasonable, rehabilitation counselors obtain a court directive to clarify the nature and extent of the response to a subpoena.

d. Minimal Disclosure.   When circumstances require the disclosure of confidential information, only essential information is revealed.

B.3. Information Shared With Others
a. Work Environment.   Rehabilitation counselors make every effort to ensure that privacy and confidentiality of clients is maintained by employees, supervisees, students, clerical assistants, and volunteers.

b. Professional Collaboration.   If rehabilitation of clients involves the sharing of their information among team members, clients are advised of this fact and are informed of the team's existence and composition. Rehabilitation counselors carefully consider implications for clients in extending confidential information if participating in their service teams.

c. Clients Served by Others.   When rehabilitation counselors learn that clients have an ongoing professional relationship with another rehabilitation counselor or treating professional, they request release from clients to inform the other professionals and strive to establish a positive and collaborative professional relationship. File review, second-opinion services, and other indirect services are not considered an ongoing professional relationship.

d. Client Assistants.   When clients are accompanied by an individual providing assistance to clients (e.g., interpreter and personal care assistant), rehabilitation counselors ensure that the assistant is apprised of the need to maintain and document confidentiality. At all times, clients retain the right to decide who can be present as client assistants.

e. Confidential Settings.   Rehabilitation counselors discuss confidential information only in offices or settings in which they can reasonably ensure the privacy of clients.

f. Third-Party Payers.   Rehabilitation counselors disclose information to third-party payers only when clients have authorized such disclosure, unless otherwise required by law or statute.

g. Deceased Clients.   Rehabilitation counselors protect the confidentiality of deceased clients, consistent with legal requirements and agency policies.

B.4. Groups and Families
a. Group Work.   In group work, rehabilitation counselors clearly explain the importance and parameters of confidentiality for the specific group being entered.

b. Couples and Family Counseling.   In couples and family counseling, rehabilitation counselors clearly define who are the clients and discuss expectations and limitations of confidentiality. Rehabilitation counselors seek agreement and document in writing such agreement among all involved parties having capacity to give consent concerning each individual's right to confidentiality. They clearly define whether they share or do not share information with family members that is privately, individually communicated to rehabilitation counselors.

B.5. Responsibility to Minors or Clients Lacking Capacity to Consent
a. Responsibility to Clients.   When counseling minor clients or adult clients who lack the capacity to give voluntary, informed consent, rehabilitation counselors protect the confidentiality of information received in the counseling relationship as specified by national or local laws, written policies, and applicable ethical standards.

b. Responsibility to Parents and Legal Guardians.   Rehabilitation counselors inform parents and legal guardians about their role and the confidential nature of the counseling relationship. They are sensitive to the cultural diversity of families and respect the inherent rights and responsibilities of parents/guardians over the welfare of their children/charges according to law. They work to establish, as appropriate, collaborative relationships with parents/guardians to best serve clients.

c. Release of Confidential Information.   When minor clients or adult clients lack the capacity to give voluntary consent to release confidential information, rehabilitation counselors seek permission from parents or legal guardians to disclose information. In such instances, rehabilitation counselors inform clients consistent with their level of understanding and take culturally appropriate measures to safeguard the confidentiality of clients.

B.6. Records
a. Requirement of Records.   Rehabilitation counselors include sufficient and timely documentation in the records of their clients to facilitate the delivery and continuity of needed services. They take reasonable steps to ensure that documentation in records accurately reflects progress and services provided to clients. If errors are made in records, rehabilitation counselors take steps to properly note the correction of such errors according to agency or institutional policies.

b. Confidentiality of Records.   Rehabilitation counselors ensure that records are kept in a secure location and that only authorized persons have access to records.

c. Client Access.   Rehabilitation counselors recognize that counseling records are kept for the benefit of clients and therefore provide access to records and copies of records when requested by clients, unless prohibited by law. In instances where the records contain information that may be sensitive, confusing, or detrimental to clients, rehabilitation counselors have a responsibility to educate clients regarding such information. In situations involving multiple clients, access to records is limited to those parts of records that do not include confidential information related to other clients. When rehabilitation counselors are in possession of records from others sources, they refer clients back to the original source.

d. Disclosure or Transfer.   Unless exceptions to confidentiality exist, rehabilitation counselors obtain written permission from clients to disclose or transfer records to legitimate third parties. Steps are taken to ensure that recipients of counseling records are sensitive to their confidential nature.

e. Storage and Disposal After Termination.   Rehabilitation counselors store the records of their clients following termination of services to ensure reasonable future access, maintain records in accordance with national or local statutes governing records, and dispose of records and other sensitive materials in a manner that protects the confidentiality of clients.

f. Reasonable Precautions.   Rehabilitation counselors take reasonable precautions to protect the confidentiality of clients in the event of disaster or termination of practice, incapacity, or death of the rehabilitation counselor.

B.7. Consultation
a. Agreements.   When acting as consultants, rehabilitation counselors seek agreement among parties involved concerning each individual's right to confidentiality, the obligation of each individual to preserve confidential information, and the limits of confidentiality of information shared by others.

b. Respect for Privacy.   Rehabilitation counselors discuss information obtained in consultation only with persons directly involved with the case. Written and oral reports presented by rehabilitation counselors contain only data germane to the purposes of the consultation, and every effort is made to protect the identity of clients and to avoid undue invasion of privacy.

c. Disclosure of Confidential Information.   When consulting with colleagues, rehabilitation counselors do not disclose confidential information that reasonably could lead to the identification of clients or other persons or organizations with which they have a confidential relationship unless they have obtained the prior consent of the persons or organizations or the disclosure cannot be avoided. They disclose information only to the extent necessary to achieve the purpose of the consultation.

Section C: Advocacy and Accessibility

C.1. Advocacy

a. Attitudinal Barriers.   In direct service with clients, rehabilitation counselors address attitudinal barriers, including stereotyping and discrimination, toward individuals with disabilities. They increase their own awareness and sensitivity to individuals with disabilities.

b. Advocacy.   Rehabilitation counselors provide clients with appropriate information to facilitate their self-advocacy actions whenever possible. They work with clients to help them understand their rights and responsibilities, speak for themselves, make decisions, and contribute to society. When appropriate and with the consent of clients, rehabilitation counselors act as advocates on behalf of clients at the local, regional, and/or national levels.

c. Advocacy in Own Agency and With Cooperating Agencies.   Rehabilitation counselors remain aware of actions taken by their own and cooperating agencies on behalf of clients and act as advocates for clients who cannot advocate for themselves to ensure effective service delivery.

d. Advocacy and Confidentiality.   Rehabilitation counselors obtain the consent of clients prior to engaging in advocacy efforts on behalf of specific, identifiable clients to improve the provision of services and to work toward removal of systemic barriers or obstacles that inhibit access, growth, and development of clients.

e. Areas of Knowledge and Competency.   Rehabilitation counselors are knowledgeable about local, regional, and national systems and laws, and how they affect access to employment, education, transportation, housing, financial benefits, and medical services for people with disabilities. They obtain sufficient training in these systems in order to advocate effectively for clients and/or to facilitate self-advocacy of clients in these areas.

f. Knowledge of Benefit Systems.   Rehabilitation counselors are aware that disability benefit systems directly affect the quality of life of clients. They provide accurate and timely information or appropriate resources and referrals for these benefits.

C.2. Accessibility

a. Counseling Practice.   Rehabilitation counselors facilitate the provision of necessary accommodations, including physically and programmatically accessible facilities and services to individuals with disabilities.

b. Barriers to Access.   Rehabilitation counselors collaborate with clients and/or others to identify barriers based on the functional limitations of clients. They communicate information on barriers to public and private authorities to facilitate removal of barriers to access.

c. Referral Accessibility.   Prior to referring clients to a program, facility, or employment setting, rehabilitation counselors assist clients in ensuring that these are appropriately accessible, and do not engage in discrimination based on age, color, race, national origin, culture, disability, ethnicity, gender, gender identity, religion/spirituality, sexual orientation, marital status/partnership, language preference, socioeconomic status, or any basis proscribed by law.

Section D: Professional Responsibility

D.1. Professional Competence
a. Boundaries of Competence.   Rehabilitation counselors practice only within the boundaries of their competence, based on their education, training, supervised experience, professional credentials, and appropriate professional experience. They demonstrate beliefs, attitudes, knowledge, and skills pertinent to working with diverse client populations. They do not misrepresent their role or competence to clients.

b. New Specialty Areas of Practice.   Rehabilitation counselors practice in specialty areas new to them only after having obtained appropriate education, training, and supervised experience. While developing skills in new specialty areas, rehabilitation counselors take steps to ensure the competence of their work and to protect clients from possible harm.

c. Qualified for Employment.   Rehabilitation counselors accept employment for positions for which they are qualified by education, training, supervised experience, professional credentials, and appropriate professional experience. They hire individuals for rehabilitation counseling positions who are qualified and competent for those positions.

d. Monitor Effectiveness.   Rehabilitation counselors continually monitor their effectiveness as professionals and take steps to improve when necessary. They take reasonable steps to seek peer supervision as needed to evaluate their efficacy as rehabilitation counselors.

e. Continuing Education.   Rehabilitation counselors recognize the need for continuing education to acquire and maintain a reasonable level of awareness of current scientific and professional information in their fields of activity. They take steps to maintain competence in the skills they use, are open to new procedures, and keep current with the diverse populations and specific populations with whom they work.

D.2. Cultural Competence/Diversity
a. Interventions.   Rehabilitation counselors develop and adapt interventions and services to incorporate consideration of cultural perspective of clients and recognition of barriers external to clients that may interfere with achieving effective rehabilitation outcomes.

b. Nondiscrimination.   Rehabilitation counselors do not discriminate against clients, students, employees, supervisees, or research participants in a manner that has a negative effect on these persons.

D.3. Functional Competence
a. Impairment.   Rehabilitation counselors are alert to the signs of impairment from their own physical, mental, or emotional problems, and refrain from offering or providing professional services when such impairment is likely to harm clients or others.

They seek assistance for problems that reach the level of professional impairment, and, if necessary, limit, suspend, or terminate their professional responsibilities until such time it is determined that they may safely resume their work. Rehabilitation counselors assist colleagues or supervisors in recognizing their own professional impairment and provide consultation and assistance when warranted with colleagues or supervisors showing signs of impairment and intervene as appropriate to prevent harm to clients.

b. Disaster Preparation and Response.   Rehabilitation counselors make reasonable efforts to plan for facilitating continued services for clients in the event that rehabilitation counseling services are interrupted by disaster, such as acts of violence, terrorism, or a natural disaster.

D.4. Professional Credentials

a. Accurate Representation.   Rehabilitation counselors claim or imply only professional qualifications actually completed and correct any known misrepresentations of their qualifications by others. They truthfully represent the qualifications of their professional colleagues. They clearly distinguish between accredited and nonaccredited degrees, paid and volunteer work experience, and accurately describe their continuing education and specialized training.

b. Credentials.   Rehabilitation counselors claim only licenses or certifications that are current and in good standing.

c. Educational Degrees.   Rehabilitation counselors clearly differentiate between earned and honorary degrees.

d. Implying Doctoral-Level Competence.   Rehabilitation counselors refer to themselves as "doctor" in a counseling context only when their doctorate is in counseling or a closely related field from an accredited university.

D.5. Responsibility to the Public and Other Professionals

a. Sexual Harassment.   Rehabilitation counselors do not condone or participate in sexual harassment.

b. Reports to Third Parties.   Rehabilitation counselors are accurate, honest, and objective in reporting their professional activities and judgments to appropriate third parties, including courts, health insurance companies, those who are the recipients of evaluation reports, and others.

c. Media Presentations.   When rehabilitation counselors provide advice or comment by means of public lectures, demonstrations, radio or television programs, prerecorded tapes, technology-based applications, printed articles, mailed materials, or other media, they take reasonable precautions to ensure that: (1) the statements are based on appropriate professional counseling literature and practice, (2) the statements are otherwise consistent with the Code, and (3) the recipients of the information are not encouraged to infer that a professional rehabilitation counseling relationship has been established.

d. Exploitation of Others.   Rehabilitation counselors do not exploit others in their professional relationships to seek or receive unjustified personal gains, sexual favors, unfair advantages, or unearned goods or services.

e. Conflict of Interest.   Rehabilitation counselors recognize that their own personal values, moral beliefs, or personal and professional relationships may interfere with their ability to practice competently. Under such circumstances, they are obligated to decline participation or to limit their assistance in a manner consistent with professional obligations.

f. Veracity.   Rehabilitation counselors do not engage in any act or omission of a dishonest, deceitful, or fraudulent nature in the conduct of their professional activities.

g. Disparaging Remarks.   Rehabilitation counselors do not disparage individuals or groups of individuals.

h. Personal Public Statements.   When making personal statements in a public context, rehabilitation counselors clarify that they are speaking from their personal perspective and not on behalf of all rehabilitation counselors, the profession, or any professional organizations with which they may be affiliated.

D.6. Scientific Bases for Interventions

a. Techniques/Procedures/Modalities.   Rehabilitation counselors use techniques/procedures/modalities that are grounded in theory and/or have an empirical or scientific foundation. When using techniques/procedures/modalities that are not grounded in theory and/or do not have an empirical or scientific foundation, rehabilitation counselors define the techniques/procedures/modalities as unproven or developing. They explain the potential risks and ethical considerations of using such techniques/procedures/modalities and take steps to protect clients from possible harm.

b. Credible Resources.   Rehabilitation counselors ensure that the resources used or accessed in counseling are credible and valid (e.g., Internet link and books used in bibliotherapy).

Section E: Relationships With Other Professionals

E.1. Relationships With Colleagues, Employers, and Employees

a. Cultural Competency Considerations.   Rehabilitation counselors maintain beliefs, attitudes, knowledge, and skills regarding their interactions with people across cultures. They are respectful of approaches to counseling services that differ from their own and of traditions and practices of other professional groups with which they work.

b. Questionable Conditions.   Rehabilitation counselors alert their employers to conditions or inappropriate policies or practices that may be potentially disruptive or damaging to the professional responsibilities of rehabilitation counselors or that may limit their effectiveness. In those instances where rehabilitation counselors are critical of policies, they attempt to affect changes in such policies or procedures through constructive action within the organization. Such action may include referral to appropriate certification, accreditation, or licensure organizations, or voluntary termination of employment.

c. Employer Policies.   The acceptance of employment in an agency or institution implies that rehabilitation counselors are in agreement with its general policies and principles. They strive to reach agreement with employers as to acceptable standards of conduct that allow changes in employer policies conducive to the growth and development of clients.

d. Protection From Punitive Action.   Rehabilitation counselors take care not to harass or dismiss employees who have acted in a responsible and ethical manner to expose inappropriate employer policies or practices.

e. Personnel Selection and Assignment.   Rehabilitation counselors select competent staff and assign responsibilities compatible with their skills and experiences.

f. Discrimination.   Rehabilitation counselors, as either employers or employees, engage in fair practices with regard to hiring, promoting, and training.

E.2. Consultation

a. Consultation as an Option.   Rehabilitation counselors may choose to consult with professionally competent persons about their clients. In choosing consultants, rehabilitation counselors avoid placing consultants in a conflict of interest situation that precludes the consultant from being a proper party to the efforts of rehabilitation counselors to help clients. If rehabilitation counselors are engaged in a work setting that compromises this consultation standard, they consult with other professionals whenever possible to consider justifiable alternatives.

b. Consultant Competency.   Rehabilitation counselors take reasonable steps to ensure that they have the appropriate resources and competencies when providing consultation services. They provide appropriate referral resources when requested or needed.

c. Informed Consent in Consultation.   When providing consultation, rehabilitation counselors have an obligation to review, in writing and verbally, the rights and responsibilities of both rehabilitation counselors and consultees. Rehabilitation counselors use clear and understandable language to inform all parties involved about the purpose of the services to be provided, relevant costs, potential risks and benefits, and the limits of confidentiality. Working in conjunction with the consultees, rehabilitation counselors attempt to develop a clear definition of the problem, goals for change, and predicted consequences of interventions that are culturally responsive and appropriate to the needs of consultees.

E.3. Agency and Team Relationships

a. Clients as Team Member.   Rehabilitation counselors ensure that clients and/or their legally recognized representatives are afforded the opportunity for full participation in decisions related to the services they receive. Only those with a need to know are allowed access to the information of clients, and only then upon a properly executed release of information request or upon receipt of a court order.

b. Interdisciplinary Teamwork.   Rehabilitation counselors who are members of interdisciplinary teams delivering multifaceted services to clients must keep the focus on how to serve clients best. They participate in and contribute to decisions that affect the well-being of clients by drawing on the perspectives, values, and experiences of the counseling profession and those of colleagues from other disciplines.

c. Communication.   Rehabilitation counselors ensure that there is fair and mutual understanding of rehabilitation plans by all parties cooperating in the rehabilitation of clients.

d. Establishing Professional and Ethical Obligations.   Rehabilitation counselors who are members of interdisciplinary teams clarify professional and ethical obligations of the team as a whole and of its individual members. They implement team decisions in rehabilitation plans and procedures, even when not personally agreeing with such decisions, unless these decisions breach the Code. When team decisions raise ethical concerns, rehabilitation counselors first attempt to resolve the concerns within the team. If they cannot reach resolution among team members, rehabilitation counselors consider other approaches to address their concerns consistent with the well-being of clients.

e. Reports.   Rehabilitation counselors secure from other specialists appropriate reports and evaluations when such reports are essential for rehabilitation planning and/or service delivery.

Section F: Forensic and Indirect Services

F.1. Client or Evaluee Rights
a. Primary Obligations.   Rehabilitation counselors produce unbiased, objective opinions and findings that can be substantiated by information and methodologies appropriate to the evaluation, which may include examination of individuals, research, and/or review of records. They form opinions based on their professional knowledge and expertise that can be supported by the data gathered in evaluations. They define the limits of their opinions or testimony, especially when an examination of individuals has not been conducted. Rehabilitation counselors acting as expert witnesses generate written documentation, either in the form of case notes or a report, as to their involvement and/or conclusions.

b. Informed Consent.   Individuals being evaluated are informed in writing that the relationship is for the purpose of an evaluation and that a report of findings may be produced. Written consent for evaluations are obtained from those being evaluated or the individuals' legal representatives/guardians unless: (1) there is a clinical or cultural reason that this is not **possible;** (2) **a court or legal** jurisdiction orders evaluations to be conducted without the written consent of individuals being evaluated; and/or (3) deceased evaluees are the subject of evaluations. If written consent is not obtained, rehabilitation counselors document verbal consent and the reasons why obtaining written consent was not possible. When minors or vulnerable adults are evaluated, informed consent is obtained from parents or guardians.

c. Dual Roles.   Rehabilitation counselors do not evaluate current or former clients for forensic purposes except under the conditions noted in A.5.f. or government statute. Likewise, rehabilitation counselors do not provide direct services to evaluees whom they have previously provided forensic services in the past except under the conditions noted in A.5.f. or government statute. In a forensic setting, rehabilitation counselors who are engaged as expert witnesses have no clients. The persons who are the subject of objective and unbiased evaluations are considered to be evaluees.

d. Indirect Service Provision.   Rehabilitation counselors who are employed by third parties as case consultants or expert witnesses, and who engage in communication with clients or evaluees, fully disclose to individuals (and/or their designees) the role of the rehabilitation counselor and limits of the relationship. Communication includes all forms of written or oral interactions. When there is no intent to provide rehabilitation counseling services directly to clients or evaluees and when there is no in-person meeting or other communication, disclosure by rehabilitation counselors is not required.

e. Confidentiality.   When rehabilitation counselors are required by law, employers' policies, or extraordinary circumstances to serve in more than one role in judicial or administrative proceedings, they clarify role expectations and the parameters of confidentiality with their colleagues and with evaluees.

F.2. Rehabilitation Counselor Forensic Competency and Conduct

a. Objectivity.   Rehabilitation counselors are aware of the standards governing their roles in performing forensic activities. They are aware of the occasionally competing demands placed upon them by these standards and the requirements of the legal system, and attempt to resolve these conflicts by making known their commitment to this Code and taking steps to resolve conflicts in a responsible manner.

b. Qualification to Provide Expert Testimony.   Rehabilitation counselors have an obligation to present to the court, regarding specific matters to which they testify, the boundaries of their competence, the factual bases (knowledge, skill, experience, training, and education) for their qualifications as an expert, and the relevance of those factual bases to their qualifications as an expert on the specific matters at issue.

c. Avoid Potentially Harmful Relationships.   Rehabilitation counselors who provide forensic evaluations avoid potentially harmful professional or personal relationships with individuals being evaluated, family members, romantic partners, and close friends of individuals they are evaluating. There may be circumstances, however, where not entering into professional or personal relationships is potentially more detrimental than providing services. When such is the case, rehabilitation counselors perform and document a risk assessment via use of an ethical decision-making model in order to arrive at an informed decision.

d. Conflict of Interest.   Rehabilitation counselors recognize that their own personal values, moral beliefs, or personal and professional relationships with parties to a legal proceeding may interfere with their ability to practice competently. Under such circumstances, rehabilitation counselors are obligated to decline participation or to limit their assistance in a manner consistent with professional obligations.

e. Validity of Resources Consulted.   Rehabilitation counselors ensure that the resources used or accessed in supporting opinions are credible and valid.

f. Foundation of Knowledge.   Because of their special status as persons qualified as experts to the court, rehabilitation counselors have an obligation to maintain current knowledge of scientific, professional, and legal developments within their area of claimed competence. They are obligated also to use that knowledge, consistent with accepted clinical and scientific standards, in selected data collection methods and procedures for evaluation, treatment, consultation, or scholarly/empirical investigations.

g. Duty to Confirm Information.   Where circumstances reasonably permit, rehabilitation counselors seek to obtain independent and personal verification of data relied upon as part of their professional services to the court or to parties to the legal proceedings.

h. Critique of Opposing Work Product.   When evaluating or commenting upon the professional work products or qualifications of other experts or parties to legal proceedings, rehabilitation counselors represent their professional disagreements with reference to a fair and accurate evaluation of the data, theories, standards, and opinions of other experts or parties.

F.3. Forensic Practices

a. Case Acceptance and Independent Opinion.   Although all rehabilitation counselors have the discretionary right to accept retention in any case or proceed within their area(s) of expertise, they decline involvement in any case when asked to take or support predetermined positions, assume invalid representation of facts, alter their methodology or process without foundation or compelling reasons, or where there are ethical concerns about the nature of the requested assignments.

b. Termination and Assignment Transfer.   If necessary to withdraw from a case after having been retained, rehabilitation counselors make reasonable efforts to assist evaluees and/ or referral sources in locating another rehabilitation counselor to take over the assignment.

F.4. Forensic Business Practices
a. Payments and Outcome.   Rehabilitation counselors do not enter into financial commitments that may compromise the quality of their services or otherwise raise questions as to their credibility. They neither give nor receive commissions, rebates, contingency or referral fees, gifts, or any other form of remuneration when accepting cases or referring evaluees for professional services. Although liens should be avoided, they are sometimes standard practice in particular trial settings. Payment is never contingent on outcome or awards.

b. Fee Disputes.   Should fee disputes arise during the course of evaluating cases and prior to trial, rehabilitation counselors have the ability to discontinue their involvement in cases as long as no harm comes to evaluees.

Section G: Evaluation, Assessment, and Interpretation

G.1. Informed Consent
a. Explanation to Clients.   Prior to assessment, rehabilitation counselors explain the nature and purposes of assessment and the specific use of results by potential recipients. The explanation is given in the language and/or developmental level of clients (or other legally authorized persons on behalf of clients), unless an explicit exception has been agreed upon in advance. Rehabilitation counselors consider personal or cultural context of clients, the level of their understanding of the results, and the impact of the results on clients. Regardless of whether scoring and interpretation are completed by rehabilitation counselors, by assistants, or by computer or other outside services, rehabilitation counselors take reasonable steps to ensure that appropriate explanations are given to clients.

b. Recipients of Results.   Rehabilitation counselors consider the welfare of clients, explicit understandings, and prior agreements in determining who receives the assessment results. They include accurate and appropriate interpretations with any release of individual or group assessment results. Issues of cultural diversity, when present, are taken into consideration when providing interpretations and releasing information.

G.2. Release of Information to Competent Professionals
a. Misuse of Results.   Rehabilitation counselors do not misuse assessment results, including test results and interpretations, and take reasonable steps to prevent the misuse of such by others.

b. Release of Data to Qualified Professionals.   Rehabilitation counselors release assessment data in which clients are identified only with the consent of clients or their legal representatives, or court order. Such data is released only to professionals recognized as qualified to interpret the data.

G.3. Proper Diagnosis of Mental Disorders

a. Proper Diagnosis.   If within their professional and individual scope of practice, rehabilitation counselors take special care to provide proper diagnosis of mental disorders. Assessment techniques (including personal interviews) used to determine care of clients (e.g., focus of treatment, types of treatment, or recommended follow-up) are carefully selected and appropriately used.

b. Cultural Sensitivity.   Rehabilitation counselors recognize that culture affects the manner in which the disorders of clients are defined. The socioeconomic and cultural experiences of clients are considered when diagnosing.

c. Historical and Social Prejudices in Diagnosis and the Diagnosis of Pathology.   Rehabilitation counselors recognize historical and social prejudices in the misdiagnosis and pathologizing of certain individuals and groups. They may refrain from making and/or reporting a diagnosis if they believe it would cause harm to clients or others.

G.4. Competence to Use and Interpret Tests

a. Limits of Competence.   Rehabilitation counselors utilize only those testing and assessment services for which they have been trained and are competent. They take reasonable measures to ensure the proper use of psychological and career assessment techniques by persons under their supervision. The requirement to develop this competency applies regardless of whether tests are administered through standard or technology-based methods.

b. Appropriate Use.   Rehabilitation counselors are responsible for the appropriate applications, scoring, interpretations, and use of assessment instruments relevant to the needs of clients, whether they score and interpret such assessments themselves or use technology or other services. Generally, new instruments are used within 1 year of publication, unless rehabilitation counselors document a valid reason why the normative data from previous versions are more applicable to clients.

c. Recommendations Based on Results.   Rehabilitation counselors are responsible for recommendations involving individuals that are based on assessment results, and have a thorough understanding of educational, psychological, and career measurements, including validation criteria, assessment research, and guidelines for assessment development and use. In addition to test results, rehabilitation counselors consider other factors present in the client's situation (e.g., disability or cultural factors) before making any recommendations, when relevant.

d. Accurate Information.   Rehabilitation counselors provide accurate information and avoid false claims or misconceptions when making statements about assessment instruments or techniques. Special efforts are made to avoid utilizing test results to make inappropriate diagnoses or inferences.

G.5. Test Selection

a. Appropriateness of Instruments.   Rehabilitation counselors carefully consider the validity, reliability, psychometric limitations, and appropriateness of instruments when selecting tests for use in given situations or with particular clients.

b. Referral Information.   If clients are referred to a third party for assessment, rehabilitation counselors provide specific referral questions and sufficient objective data about clients to ensure that appropriate assessment instruments are utilized.

c. Culturally Diverse Populations.   Rehabilitation counselors are cautious when selecting assessments for use with individuals from culturally diverse populations to avoid the use of instruments that lack appropriate psychometric properties for those client populations.

G.6. Conditions of Test Administration

a. Administration Conditions.   Rehabilitation counselors administer assessments under the same conditions that were established in the standardized development of the instrument. When assessments are not administered under standard conditions, as may be necessary to accommodate clients with disabilities, or when unusual behavior or irregularities occur during the administration, those conditions are noted in interpretation, and the results may be designated as invalid or of questionable validity.

b. Technological Administration.   When using technology or electronic methods to administer assessments, rehabilitation counselors should ensure that the instruments are functioning properly and provide accurate results.

c. Unsupervised Test-Taking.   Rehabilitation counselors do not permit unsupervised or inadequately supervised use of tests or assessments unless the tests or assessments are designed, intended, and validated for self-administration and/or scoring.

G.7. Test Scoring and Interpretation

a. Reporting Reservations.   In reporting assessment results, rehabilitation counselors indicate any reservations that exist regarding validity or reliability because of the circumstances of the assessments or the inappropriateness of the norms for persons tested.

b. Cultural Diversity Issues in Assessment.   Rehabilitation counselors use with caution assessment techniques that were normed on populations other than that of the client. They recognize the effects of age, color, race, national origin, culture, disability, ethnicity, gender, gender identity, religion/spirituality, sexual orientation, marital status/partnership, language preference, socioeconomic status, or any basis proscribed by law on test administrations and interpretations, and place test results in proper perspective with other relevant factors.

c. Research Instruments.   Rehabilitation counselors exercise caution when interpreting the results of research instruments not having sufficient technical data to support respondent results. The specific purposes for the use of such instruments are stated explicitly to examinees.

G.8. Assessment Considerations

a. Assessment Security.   Rehabilitation counselors maintain the integrity and security of tests and other assessment techniques consistent with legal and contractual obligations. They do not appropriate, reproduce, or modify published assessments or parts thereof without acknowledgment and permission from the publisher.

b. Obsolete Assessment and Outdated Results.   Rehabilitation counselors do not use data or results from assessments that are obsolete or outdated. They make every effort to prevent the misuse of obsolete measures and assessment data by others.

c. Assessment Construction.   Rehabilitation counselors use established scientific procedures, relevant standards, and current professional knowledge for assessment design in the development, publication, and utilization of educational and psychological assessment techniques.

Section H: Teaching, Supervision, and Training

H.1. Rehabilitation Counselor Supervision and Client Welfare
a. Client Welfare. Rehabilitation counselor supervisors meet regularly with supervisees to review case notes, samples of clinical work, or live observations in order to ensure the welfare of clients. Supervisees have a responsibility to understand and follow the Code.

b. Rehabilitation Counselor Credentials. Rehabilitation counselor supervisors work to ensure that clients are aware of the qualifications of the supervisees who render services to clients.

c. Informed Consent and Client Rights. Rehabilitation counselor supervisors make supervisees aware of the rights of clients including the protection of their privacy and confidentiality in the counseling relationship. Supervisees provide clients with professional disclosure information and inform them of how the supervision process influences the limits of confidentiality. Supervisees make clients aware of who has access to records of the counseling relationship and how these records are used.

H.2. Rehabilitation Counselor Supervision Competence
a. Supervisor Preparation. Rehabilitation counselors who offer supervision services regularly pursue continuing education activities, including both counseling and supervision topics and skills.

b. Cultural Diversity in Rehabilitation Counselor Supervision. Rehabilitation counselor supervisors are aware of and address the role of cultural diversity in the supervisory relationship.

H.3. Roles and Relationships With Supervisees or Trainees
a. Relationship Boundaries With Supervisees or Trainees. Rehabilitation counselor supervisors or educators clearly define and maintain ethical professional, personal, and social relationships with their supervisees or trainees. Rehabilitation counselor supervisors or educators avoid nonprofessional relationships with current supervisees or trainees. If rehabilitation counselor supervisors or educators must assume other professional roles (e.g., clinical and/or administrative supervisors, instructors) with supervisees or trainees, they work to minimize potential conflicts and explain to supervisees or trainees the expectations and responsibilities associated with each role. They do not engage in any form of nonprofessional interactions that may compromise the supervisory relationship.

b. Sexual or Romantic Relationships. Rehabilitation counselors do not engage in sexual or romantic interactions or relationships with current supervisees or trainees.

c. Exploitative Relationships. Rehabilitation counselors do not engage in exploitative relationships with individuals with whom they have supervisory, evaluative, or instructional control or authority.

d. Sexual Harassment. Rehabilitation counselor supervisors or educators do not condone or subject supervisees or trainees to sexual harassment.

e. Relationships With Former Supervisees or Trainees. Rehabilitation counselor supervisors or educators are aware of the power differential in their relationships with supervisees or trainees. Rehabilitation counselor supervisors or educators foster open discussions with former supervisees or trainees when considering engaging in a social, sexual, or other intimate relationships. Rehabilitation counselor supervisors or educators discuss with the former supervisees or trainees how their former relationship may affect the change in relationship.

f. Nonprofessional Relationships.   Rehabilitation counselor supervisors or educators avoid nonprofessional or ongoing professional relationships with supervisees or trainees in which there is a risk of potential harm to supervisees or trainees or that may compromise the training experience or grades assigned. In addition, rehabilitation counselor supervisors or educators do not accept any form of professional services, fees, commissions, reimbursement, or remuneration from a site for supervisee or trainee placements.

g. Close Relatives and Friends.   Rehabilitation counselor supervisors or educators avoid accepting close relatives, romantic partners, or friends as supervisees or trainees. When such circumstances cannot be avoided, rehabilitation counselor supervisors or educators utilize a formal review mechanism.

h. Potentially Beneficial Relationships.   Rehabilitation counselor supervisors or educators are aware of the power differential in their relationships with supervisees or trainees. If they believe that nonprofessional relationships with supervisees or trainees may be potentially beneficial to supervisees or trainees, they take precautions similar to those taken by rehabilitation counselors when working with clients. Examples of potentially beneficial interactions or relationships include attending a formal ceremony, hospital visits, providing support during a stressful event, or mutual membership in professional associations, organizations, or communities. Rehabilitation counselor supervisors or educators engage in open discussions with supervisees or trainees when they consider entering into relationships with them outside of their role as clinical and/or administrative supervisors. Before engaging in nonprofessional relationships, rehabilitation counselor supervisors or educators discuss the rationale for such interactions, potential benefits or drawbacks, and anticipated consequences with supervisees or trainees. Rehabilitation counselor supervisors or educators clarify the specific nature and limitations of the additional role(s) they have with supervisees or trainees. Nonprofessional relationships with supervisees or trainees are time limited or context specific and initiated with their consent.

H.4. Rehabilitation Counselor Supervisor Responsibilities

a. Disclosure and Informed Consent for Supervision.   Rehabilitation counselor supervisors provide professional disclosure that, at a minimum, is consistent with the jurisdiction in which they practice. They are responsible for incorporating into their supervision the principles of informed consent. They inform supervisees of the policies and procedures to which they are to adhere and the mechanisms for due process appeal of individual supervisory actions.

b. Emergencies and Absences.   Rehabilitation counselor supervisors establish and communicate to supervisees the procedures for contacting them or, in their absence, alternative on-call supervisors to assist in handling crises.

c. Standards for Rehabilitation Counselor Supervisees.   Rehabilitation counselor supervisors make their supervisees aware of professional and ethical standards and legal responsibilities. Rehabilitation counselor supervisors of post-degree rehabilitation counselors encourage these rehabilitation counselors to adhere to professional standards of practice.

d. Resolving Differences.   When cultural, ethical, or professional issues are crucial to the viability of the supervisory relationship, both parties make efforts to resolve differences.

When termination is warranted, rehabilitation counselor supervisors make appropriate referrals to possible alternative supervisors.

H.5. Rehabilitation Counselor Supervisor Evaluation, Remediation, and Endorsement

a. Evaluation.   Rehabilitation counselor supervisors or educators clearly state to supervisees or trainees, prior to and throughout the training program, the levels of competency expected, appraisal methods, and timing of evaluations for both didactic and clinical competencies. Rehabilitation counselor supervisors or educators document and provide supervisees or trainees ongoing performance appraisal and evaluation feedback.

b. Limitations.   Throughout ongoing evaluation and appraisal, rehabilitation counselor supervisors or educators are aware of and address the inability of some supervisees or trainees to achieve, improve, or maintain counseling competencies. Rehabilitation counselor supervisors or educators: (1) assist supervisees or trainees in securing remedial assistance when needed, (2) seek professional consultation and document their decision to dismiss or refer supervisees or trainees for assistance, (3) ensure that supervisees or trainees have recourse in a timely manner to address decisions that require them to seek assistance or to dismiss them, and (4) provide supervisees or trainees with due process according to organizational policies and procedures.

c. Counseling for Supervisees.   Rehabilitation counselor supervisors or educators address interpersonal competencies of supervisees or trainees in terms of the impact of these issues on clients, supervisory relationships, and professional functioning. With the exception of brief interventions to address situational distress, or as part of educational activities, rehabilitation counselor supervisors or educators do not provide counseling services to supervisees or trainees. If supervisees or trainees request counseling or if counseling is required as part of a remediation process, rehabilitation counselor supervisors or educators provide them with referrals.

d. Endorsement.   Rehabilitation counselor supervisors or educators endorse supervisees or trainees for certification, licensure, employment, or completion of academic or training programs based on satisfactory progress and observations while under supervision or training. Regardless of qualifications, supervisors or educators do not endorse supervisees or trainees whom they believe to be impaired in any way that would interfere with the performance of the duties associated with the endorsement.

H.6. Responsibilities of Rehabilitation Counselor Educators

a. Rehabilitation Counselor Educators.   Rehabilitation counselor educators who are responsible for developing, implementing, and supervising educational programs are skilled as teachers and practitioners. They are knowledgeable regarding the ethical, legal, and regulatory aspects of the profession, are skilled in applying that knowledge, and make students aware of their responsibilities. Rehabilitation counselor educators conduct rehabilitation counselor education and training programs in an ethical manner and serve as role models for professional behavior.

b. Infusing Cultural Diversity.   Rehabilitation counselor educators infuse material related to cultural diversity into all courses and workshops for the development of professional rehabilitation counselors.

c. Integration of Study and Practice.   Rehabilitation counselor educators establish education and training programs that integrate academic study and supervised practice.

d. Teaching Ethics.   Rehabilitation counselor educators make students aware of their ethical responsibilities, standards of the profession, and the ethical responsibilities of students to the profession. They infuse ethical considerations throughout the curriculum.

e. Peer Relationships.   Rehabilitation counselor educators make every effort to ensure that the rights of peers are not compromised when students lead counseling groups or provide clinical supervision. They take steps to ensure that students understand they have the same ethical obligations as rehabilitation counselor educators, trainers, and supervisors.

f. Innovative Techniques/Procedures/Modalities.   When rehabilitation counselor educators teach counseling techniques/procedures/modalities that are innovative, without an empirical foundation or a well-grounded theoretical foundation, they define the counseling techniques/procedures/modalities as unproven or developing and explain to students the potential risks and ethical considerations of using such techniques/procedures/modalities.

g. Field Placements.   Rehabilitation counselor educators develop clear policies within their training programs regarding field placement and other clinical experiences. They provide clearly stated roles and responsibilities for students, site supervisors, and program supervisors. They confirm that site supervisors are qualified to provide supervision and inform site supervisors of their professional and ethical responsibilities in this role.

h. Professional Disclosure.   Before initiating counseling services, rehabilitation counselors-in-training disclose their status as students and explain how this status affects the limits of confidentiality. Rehabilitation counselor educators ensure that clients at field placement are aware of the services rendered and the qualifications of the students and supervisees rendering those services. Students obtain permission from clients before they use any information concerning the counseling relationship in the training process.

H.7. Student Welfare
a. Orientation.   Rehabilitation counselor educators recognize that orientation is a developmental process that continues throughout the educational and clinical training of students. They have an ethical responsibility to provide enough information to prospective or current students about program expectations for them to make informed decisions about entering into and continuing in a program.

b. Self-growth Experiences.   Rehabilitation counselor education programs delineate requirements for self-disclosure as part of self-growth experiences in their admission and program materials. Rehabilitation counselor educators use professional judgment when designing training experiences they conduct that require student self-growth or self-disclosure. Students are made aware of the ramifications their self-disclosure may have when rehabilitation counselors whose primary role as teachers, trainers, or supervisors require acting on ethical obligations to the profession. Evaluative components of experiential training experiences explicitly delineate predetermined academic standards that are separate and do not depend on the level of self-disclosure of students. As a condition to remain in the program, rehabilitation counselor educators may require that students seek professional help to address any personal concerns that may be affecting their competency.

H.8. Cultural Diversity Competence in Rehabilitation Counselor Education Programs and Training Programs
a. Diversity.   Rehabilitation counselor educators actively attempt to recruit and retain a diverse faculty and student body. They demonstrate commitment to cultural diversity competence by recognizing and valuing diverse cultures and types of abilities faculty and students bring to the training experience. They provide appropriate accommodations as required to enhance and support the well-being and performance of students.

b. Cultural Diversity Competence.   Rehabilitation counselor educators actively infuse cultural diversity competency into their training and supervision practices. They actively educate trainees to develop and maintain beliefs, attitudes, knowledge, and skills necessary for competent practice with people across cultures.

Section I: Research and Publication

I.1. Research Responsibilities
a. Use of Human Participants.   Rehabilitation counselors plan, design, conduct, and report research in a manner that reflects cultural sensitivity, is culturally appropriate, and is consistent with pertinent ethical principles, laws, host institutional regulations, and scientific standards governing research with human participants. They seek consultation when appropriate.

b. Deviation From Standard Practices.   Rehabilitation counselors seek consultation and observe stringent safeguards to protect the rights of research participants when a research problem suggests a deviation from standard acceptable practices.

c. Precautions to Avoid Injury.   Rehabilitation counselors who conduct research with human participants are responsible for the welfare of participants throughout the research process and take reasonable precautions to avoid causing injurious psychological, emotional, physical, or social effects to participants.

d. Principal Researcher Responsibility.   The ultimate responsibility for ethical research practice lies with principal researchers. All others involved in the research activities share ethical obligations and responsibilities for their own actions.

e. Minimal Interference.   Rehabilitation counselors take precautions to avoid causing disruption in the lives of research participants that may result from their involvement in research.

I.2. Informed Consent and Disclosure
a. Informed Consent in Research.   Individuals have the right to consent to become research participants. In seeking consent, rehabilitation counselors use language that: (1) accurately explains the purpose and procedures to be followed, (2) identifies any procedures that are experimental or relatively untried, (3) describes any attendant discomforts and risks, (4) describes any benefits or changes in individuals or organizations that might be reasonably expected, (5) discloses appropriate alternative procedures that would be advantageous for participants, (6) offers to answer any inquiries concerning the procedures, (7) describes any limitations on confidentiality, (8) describes formats and potential target audiences for the dissemination of research findings, and (9) instructs participants that they are free to withdraw their consent and to discontinue participation in the project at any time without penalty.

b. Deception.   Rehabilitation counselors do not conduct research involving deception unless alternative procedures are not feasible. If such deception has the potential to cause physical or emotional harm to research participants, the research is not conducted, regardless of prospective value. When the methodological requirements of a study necessitate concealment or deception, the investigator explains the reasons for this action as soon as possible during the debriefing.

c. Voluntary Participation.   Participation in research is typically voluntary and without any penalty for refusal to participate. Involuntary participation is appropriate only when it can be demonstrated that participation has no harmful effects on participants and is essential to the research.

d. Confidentiality of Information.   Information obtained about participants during the course of research is confidential. When the possibility exists that others may obtain access to such information, ethical research practice requires that the possibility, together with the plans for protecting confidentiality, be explained to participants as part of the procedures for obtaining informed consent.

e. Individuals Not Capable of Giving Informed Consent.   When individuals are not capable of giving informed consent, rehabilitation counselors provide an appropriate explanation to and obtain agreement for participation and appropriate consent from a legally authorized person.

f. Commitments to Participants.   Rehabilitation counselors take reasonable measures to honor all commitments to research participants.

g. Explanations After Data Collection.   After data is collected, rehabilitation counselors provide participants with full clarification of the nature of the study to remove any misconceptions participants might have regarding the research. Where scientific or human values justify delaying or withholding information, rehabilitation counselors take reasonable measures to avoid causing harm.

h. Agreement of Contributors.   Rehabilitation counselors who conduct joint research establish agreements in advance regarding allocation of tasks, publication credit, and types of acknowledgment received, and incur an obligation to cooperate as agreed.

i. Informing Sponsors.   Rehabilitation counselors inform sponsors, institutions, and publication channels regarding research procedures and outcomes. They ensure that appropriate bodies and authorities are given pertinent information and acknowledgment.

I.3. Reporting Results
a. Accurate Results.   Rehabilitation counselors plan, conduct, and report research accurately. They provide thorough discussions of the limitations of their data and alternative hypotheses. They do not engage in misleading or fraudulent research, distort data, misrepresent data, or deliberately bias their results. They explicitly mention all variables and conditions known to the investigator(s) that may have affected the outcome of studies or interpretations of data. They describe the extent to which results are applicable for diverse populations.

b. Obligation to Report Unfavorable Results.   Rehabilitation counselors report the results of any research of professional value. Results that reflect unfavorably on institutions, programs, services, prevailing opinions, or vested interests are not withheld.

c. Identity of Participants.   Rehabilitation counselors who supply data, aid in the research of another person, report research results, or make original data available, take due care to disguise the identity of respective participants in the absence of specific authorization from the participants to do otherwise. In situations where participants self-identify their involvement in research studies, researchers take active steps to ensure that data is adapted/changed to protect the identities and welfare of all parties and that discussion of results does not cause harm to participants.

d. Reporting Errors.   If rehabilitation counselors discover significant errors in their published research, they take reasonable steps to correct such errors in a correction erratum or through other appropriate publication means.

e. Replication Studies.   Rehabilitation counselors are obligated to make available sufficient original research data to qualified professionals who may wish to replicate the study.

I.4. Publications and Presentations
a. Recognizing Contributions.   When conducting and reporting research, rehabilitation counselors are familiar with and give recognition to previous work on the topic, observe copyright laws, and give full credit to those to whom credit is due.

b. Contributors.   Rehabilitation counselors give credit through joint authorship, acknowledgment, footnote statements, or other appropriate means to those who have contributed significantly to research or concept development in accordance with such contributions. Principal contributors are listed first and minor technical or professional contributions are acknowledged in notes or introductory statements.

c. Student Research.   For articles that are substantially based on students' course papers, projects, dissertations or theses of students, and for which students have been the primary contributors, they are listed as principal authors.

d. Duplicate Submission.   Rehabilitation counselors submit manuscripts for consideration to only one journal at a time. Manuscripts that are published in whole or in substantial part in another journal or published work are not submitted for publication without acknowledgment and permission from the previous publication.

e. Professional Review.   Rehabilitation counselors who review material submitted for publication, research, or other scholarly purposes respect the confidentiality and proprietary rights of those who submitted it. They use care to make publication decisions based on valid and defensible standards. They review article submissions in a timely manner and based on their scope and competency in research methodologies. Rehabilitation counselors who serve as reviewers at the request of editors or publishers make every effort to review only materials that are within their scope of competency and use care to avoid personal biases.

f. Plagiarism.   Rehabilitation counselors do not plagiarize, that is, they do not present another person's work as their own work.

g. Review/Republication of Data or Ideas.   Rehabilitation counselors fully acknowledge and make editorial reviewers aware of prior publication of ideas or data where such ideas or data are submitted for review or publication.

h. Nonprofessional Relationships.   Rehabilitation counselors avoid nonprofessional relationships with research participants when research involves intensive or extensive interaction. When a nonprofessional interaction between researchers and research participants may be potentially beneficial, researchers must document, prior to the interaction (when feasible), the rationale for such interactions, the potential benefits, and anticipated consequences for research participants. Such interactions are initiated with appropriate consent of research participants. Where unintentional harm occurs to research participants due to nonprofessional interactions, researchers must show evidence of an attempt to remedy such harm.

i. Sexual or Romantic Relationships With Research Participants. Rehabilitation counselors do not engage in sexual or romantic rehabilitation counselor–research participant interactions or initiate relationships with current research participants.

j. Sexual Harassment and Research Participants. Rehabilitation counselors do not condone or subject research participants to sexual harassment.

I.5. Confidentiality

a. Institutional Approval. When institutional review board approval is required, rehabilitation counselors provide accurate information about their research proposals and obtain approval prior to conducting their research. They conduct research in accordance with the approved research protocol.

b. Adherence to Guidelines. Rehabilitation counselors are responsible for understanding and adhering to national, local, agency, or institutional policies or applicable guidelines regarding confidentiality in their research practices.

c. Confidentiality of Information Obtained in Research. Violations of participants' privacy and confidentiality are risks of participation in research involving human participants. Investigators maintain all research records in a secure manner. They explain to participants the risks of violations of privacy and confidentiality and disclose to participants any limits of confidentiality that reasonably can be expected.

d. Disclosure of Research Information. Rehabilitation counselors do not disclose confidential information that reasonably could lead to the identification of research participants unless they have obtained the prior consent of participants. Use of data derived from counseling relationships for purposes of training, research, or publication are confined to content that are disguised to ensure the anonymity of the individuals involved.

e. Agreement for Identification. Rehabilitation counselors identify clients, students, or research participants in a presentation or publication only when it has been reviewed by those clients, students, or research participants and they have agreed to its presentation or publication.

Section J: Technology and Distance Counseling

J.1. Behavior and Identification

a. Application and Competence. Rehabilitation counselors are held to the same level of expected behavior and competence as defined by the Code regardless of the technology used (e.g., cellular phones, email, facsimile, video, audio, audiovisual) or its application (e.g., assessment, research, and data storage).

b. Problematic Use of the Internet. Rehabilitation counselors are aware of behavioral differences with the use of the Internet, and/or methods of electronic communication, and how these may impact the counseling process.

c. Potential Misunderstandings.   Rehabilitation counselors educate clients on how to prevent and address potential misunderstandings arising from the lack of visual cues and voice intonations when communicating electronically.

J.2. Accessibility

a. Determining Client Capabilities.   When providing technology-assisted services, rehabilitation counselors determine that clients are functionally and linguistically capable of using the application and that the technology is appropriate for the needs of clients. Rehabilitation counselors verify that clients understand the purpose and operation of technology applications and follow-up with clients to correct possible misconceptions, discover appropriate use, and assess subsequent steps.

b. Accessing Technology.   Based on functional, linguistic, or cultural needs of clients, rehabilitation counselors guide clients in obtaining reasonable access to pertinent applications when providing technology-assisted services.

J.3. Confidentiality, Informed Consent, and Security

a. Confidentiality and Informed Consent.   Rehabilitation counselors ensure that clients are provided sufficient information to adequately address and explain the limits of: (1) technology used in the counseling process in general, (2) ensuring and maintaining complete confidentiality of client information transmitted through electronic means, (3) a colleague, supervisor, and an employee, such as an information technology (IT) administrator or paraprofessional staff, who might have authorized or unauthorized access to electronic transmissions, (4) an authorized or unauthorized user including a family member and fellow employee who has access to any technology the client may use in the counseling process, (5) pertinent legal rights and limitations governing the practice of a profession over jurisdictional boundaries, (6) record maintenance and retention policies, (7) technology failure, unavailability, or crisis contact procedures, and (8) protecting client information during the counseling process and at the termination of services.

b. Transmitting Confidential Information.   Rehabilitation counselors take precautions to ensure the confidentiality of information transmitted through the use of computers, email, facsimile machines, telephones, voicemail, answering machines, and other technology.

c. Security.   Rehabilitation counselors: (1) use encrypted and/or password-protected Internet sites and/or email communications to help ensure confidentiality when possible and take other reasonable precautions to ensure the confidentiality of information transmitted through the use of computers, email, facsimiles, telephones, voicemail, answering machines, or other technology, (2) notify clients of the inability to use encryption or password protection, the hazards of not using these security measures, and (3) limit transmissions to general communications that are not specific to clients, and/or use nondescript identifiers.

d. Imposters.   In situations where it is difficult to verify the identity of rehabilitation counselors, clients, their guardians, and/or team members, rehabilitation counselors: (1) address imposter concerns, such as using code words, numbers, graphics, or other nondescript identifiers and (2) establish methods for verifying identities.

J.4. Technology-Assisted Assessment   Rehabilitation counselors using technology-assisted test interpretations abide by the ethical standards for the use of such assessments regardless of administration, scoring, interpretation, or reporting method and ensure that persons under their supervision are aware of these standards.

J.5. Consultation Groups   When participating in electronic professional consultation or consultation groups (e.g., social networks, listservs, blogs, online courses, supervision, and interdisciplinary teams), rehabilitation counselors: (1) establish and/or adhere to the group's norms promoting behavior that is consistent with ethical standards and (2) limit disclosure of confidential information.

J.6. Records, Data Storage, and Disposal

a. Records Management.   Rehabilitation counselors are aware that electronic messages are considered to be part of the records of clients. Since electronic records are preserved, rehabilitation counselors inform clients of the retention method and period, of who has access to the records, and how the records are destroyed.

b. Permission to Record.   Rehabilitation counselors obtain permission from clients prior to recording sessions through electronic or other means.

c. Permission to Observe.   Rehabilitation counselors obtain permission from clients prior to observing counseling sessions, reviewing session transcripts, and/or listening to or viewing recordings of sessions with supervisors, faculty, peers, or others within the training environment.

J.7. Legal

a. Ethical/Legal Review.   Rehabilitation counselors review pertinent legal and ethical codes for possible violations emanating from the practice of distance counseling and/or supervision.

b. Laws and Statutes.   Rehabilitation counselors ensure that the use of technology does not violate the laws of any local, regional, national, or international entity, observe all relevant statutes, and seek business, legal, and technical assistance when using technology in such a manner.

J.8. Advertising

a. Online Presence.   Rehabilitation counselors maintaining sites on the Internet do so based on the advertising, accessibility, and cultural provisions of the Code. The Internet site is regularly maintained and includes avenues for communication with rehabilitation counselors.

b. Veracity of Electronic Information.   Rehabilitation counselors assist clients in determining the validity and reliability of information found on the Internet and/or other technology applications.

J.9. Research and Publication

a. Informed Consent.   Rehabilitation counselors are aware of the limits of technology-based research with regards to privacy, confidentiality, participant identities, venues used, accuracy, and/or dissemination. They inform participants of those limitations whenever possible, and make provisions to safeguard the collection, dissemination, and storage of data collected.

b. Intellectual Property.   When rehabilitation counselors possess intellectual property of people or entities (e.g., audio, visual, or written historical or electronic media), they take reasonable precautions to protect the technological dissemination of that information through disclosure, informed consent, password protection, encryption, copyright, or other security/intellectual property protection means.

J.10. Rehabilitation Counselor Unavailability
a. Technological Failure. Rehabilitation counselors explain to clients the possibility of technology failure and provide an alternative means of communication.

b. Unavailability. Rehabilitation counselors provide clients with instructions for contacting them when they are unavailable through technological means.

c. Crisis Contact. Rehabilitation counselors provide referral information for at least one agency or rehabilitation counselor-on-call for purposes of crisis intervention for clients within their geographical region.

J.11. Distance Counseling Credential Disclosure
Rehabilitation counselors practicing through Internet sites provide information to clients regarding applicable certification boards and/or licensure bodies to facilitate client rights and protection and to address ethical concerns.

J.12. Distance Counseling Relationships
a. Benefits and Limitations. Rehabilitation counselors inform clients of the benefits and limitations of using technology applications in the counseling process and in business procedures. Such technologies include, but are not limited to, computer hardware and/or software, telephones, the Internet and other audio and/or video communication, assessment, research, or data storage devices or media.

b. Inappropriate Applications. When technology-assisted distance counseling services are deemed inappropriate by rehabilitation counselors or clients, rehabilitation counselors pursue services face-to-face or by other means.

c. Boundaries. Rehabilitation counselors discuss and establish boundaries with clients, family members, service providers, and/or team members regarding the appropriate use and/or application of technology and the limits of its use within the counseling relationship.

J.13. Distance Counseling Security and Business Practices
a. Self-description. Rehabilitation counselors practicing through Internet sites provide information about themselves (e.g., ethnicity and gender) as would be available if the counseling were to take place face to face.

b. Internet Sites. Rehabilitation counselors practicing through Internet sites: (1) obtain the written consent of legal guardians or other authorized legal representatives prior to rendering services in the event clients are minor children, adults who are legally incompetent, or adults incapable of giving informed consent and (2) strive to provide translation and interpretation capabilities for clients who have a different primary language while also addressing the imperfect nature of such translations or interpretations.

c. Business Practices. As part of the process of establishing informed consent, rehabilitation counselors: (1) discuss time zone differences, local customs, and cultural or language differences that might impact service delivery and (2) educate clients when technology-assisted distance counseling services are not covered by insurance.

J.14. Distance Group Counseling
When participating in distance group counseling, rehabilitation counselors: (1) establish and/or adhere to the group's norms promoting behavior that is consistent with ethical standards and (2) limit disclosure of confidential information.

J.15. Teaching, Supervision, and Training at a Distance
Rehabilitation counselors, educators, supervisors, or trainers working with trainees or supervisees at a distance disclose to trainees or supervisees the limits of technology in conducting distance teaching, supervision, and training.

Section K: Business Practices

K.1. Advertising and Soliciting Clients
a. Accurate Advertising.   When advertising or otherwise representing their services to the public, rehabilitation counselors identify their credentials in an accurate manner that is not false, misleading, deceptive, or fraudulent.

b. Testimonials.   Rehabilitation counselors who use testimonials do not solicit them from current clients or former clients or any other persons who may be vulnerable to undue influence.

c. Statements by Others.   Rehabilitation counselors make reasonable efforts to ensure that statements made by others about them or the profession are accurate.

d. Recruiting Through Employment.   Rehabilitation counselors do not use their places of employment or institutional affiliations to recruit or gain clients, supervisees, or consultees for their private practice.

e. Products and Training Advertisements.   Rehabilitation counselors who develop products related to their profession or conduct workshops or training events ensure that the advertisements concerning these products or events are accurate and disclose adequate information for clients to make informed choices.

f. Promoting to Those Served.   Rehabilitation counselors do not use counseling, teaching, training, or supervisory relationships to promote their products or training events in a manner that is deceptive or would exert undue influence on individuals who may be vulnerable. Rehabilitation counselor educators may adopt textbooks they have authored for appropriate instructional purposes.

K.2. Client Records
a. Appropriate Documentation.   Rehabilitation counselors establish and maintain documentation consistent with agency policy that accurately, sufficiently, and in a timely manner reflects the services provided and that identifies who provided the services. If case notes need to be altered, it is done in a manner that preserves the original notes and is accompanied by the date of change, information that identifies who made the change, and the rationale for the change.

b. Privacy.   Documentation generated by rehabilitation counselors protects the privacy of clients to the extent that it is possible and includes only relevant or appropriate counseling information.

c. Records Maintenance.   Rehabilitation counselors maintain records necessary for rendering professional services to clients and as required by applicable laws, regulations, or agency/institution procedures. Subsequent to file closure, records are maintained for the number of years consistent with jurisdictional requirements or for longer periods during which maintenance of such records is necessary or helpful to provide reasonably anticipated future services to clients. After that time, records are destroyed in a manner assuring preservation of confidentiality.

K.3. Fees, Bartering, and Billing

a. Establishing Fees.   In establishing fees for professional counseling services, rehabilitation counselors consider the financial status and locality of clients. In the event that the established fee structure is inappropriate for clients, rehabilitation counselors assist clients in attempting to find comparable services of acceptable cost.

b. Advance Understanding of Fees.   Prior to entering the counseling relationship, rehabilitation counselors clearly explain to clients all financial arrangements related to professional services. If rehabilitation counselors intend to use collection agencies or take legal measures to collect fees from clients who do not pay for services as agreed upon, they first inform clients of intended actions and offer clients the opportunity to make payment.

c. Referral Fees.   Rehabilitation counselors do not give or receive commissions, rebates, or any other form of remuneration when referring clients for professional services.

d. Withholding Records for Nonpayment.   Rehabilitation counselors may not withhold records under their control that are requested and needed for the emergency treatment of clients solely because payment has not been received.

e. Bartering Discouraged.   Rehabilitation counselors ordinarily refrain from accepting goods or services from clients in return for rehabilitation counseling services because such arrangements create inherent potential for conflicts, exploitation, and distortion of the professional relationship. Rehabilitation counselors participate in bartering only if the relationship is not exploitative or harmful to clients, if clients request it, if a clear written contract is established, and if such arrangements are an accepted practice in the community or culture of clients.

f. Billing Records.   Rehabilitation counselors establish and maintain billing records that are confidential and accurately reflect the services provided, the time engaged in the activity, and that clearly identify who provided the services.

K.4. Termination

Rehabilitation counselors in fee-for-service relationships may terminate services with clients due to nonpayment of fees under the following conditions: (1) clients were informed of payment responsibilities and the effects of nonpayment or the termination of payment by third parties and (2) clients do not pose an imminent danger to self or others. As appropriate, rehabilitation counselors refer clients to other qualified professionals to address issues unresolved at the time of termination.

Section L: Resolving Ethical Issues

L.1. Knowledge of CRCC Standards

Rehabilitation counselors are responsible for reading, understanding, and following the Code, and seeking clarification of any standard that is not understood. Lack of knowledge or misunderstanding of an ethical responsibility is not a defense against a charge of unethical conduct.

L.2. Application of Standards

a. Decision-Making Models and Skills.   Rehabilitation counselors must be prepared to recognize underlying ethical principles and conflicts among competing interests, as well as to apply appropriate decision-making models and skills to resolve dilemmas and act ethically.

b. Addressing Unethical Behavior.   Rehabilitation counselors expect colleagues to adhere to the Code. When rehabilitation counselors possess knowledge that raises doubt as to whether another rehabilitation counselor is acting in an ethical manner, they take appropriate action.

c. Conflicts Between Ethics and Laws.   Rehabilitation counselors obey the laws and statutes of the legal jurisdiction in which they practice unless there is a conflict with the Code. If ethical responsibilities conflict with laws, regulations, or other governing legal authorities, rehabilitation counselors make known their commitment to the Code and take steps to resolve conflicts. If conflicts cannot be resolved by such means, rehabilitation counselors may adhere to the requirements of law, regulations, or other governing legal authorities.

d. Knowledge of Related Codes of Ethics.   Rehabilitation counselors understand applicable ethics codes from other professional organizations or from certification and licensure bodies of which they are members. They are aware that the Code forms the basis for CRCC disciplinary actions, and understand that if there is a discrepancy between codes they are held to the CRCC standards.

e. Consultation.   When uncertain as to whether particular situations or courses of action may be in violation of the Code, rehabilitation counselors consult with other professionals who are knowledgeable about ethics, with supervisors, colleagues, and/or with appropriate authorities, such as CRCC, licensure boards, or legal counsel.

f. Organization Conflicts.   If the demands of organizations with which rehabilitation counselors are affiliated pose a conflict with the Code, rehabilitation counselors specify the nature of such conflicts and express to their supervisors or other responsible officials their commitment to the Code. When possible, rehabilitation counselors work toward change within organizations to allow full adherence to the Code. In doing so, they address any confidentiality issues.

L.3. Suspected Violations

a. Informal Resolution.   When rehabilitation counselors have reason to believe that another rehabilitation counselor is violating or has violated an ethical standard, they attempt first to resolve the issue informally with the other rehabilitation counselor if feasible, provided such action does not violate confidentiality rights that may be involved.

b. Reporting Ethical Violations.   When an informal resolution is not appropriate or feasible, or if an apparent violation has substantially harmed or is likely to substantially harm persons or organizations and is not appropriate for informal resolution or is not resolved properly, rehabilitation counselors take further action appropriate to the situation. Such action might include referral to local or national committees on professional ethics, voluntary national certification bodies, licensure boards, or appropriate institutional authorities. This standard does not apply when an intervention would violate confidentiality rights (e.g., when clients refuse to allow information or statements to be shared) or when rehabilitation counselors have been retained to review the work of another rehabilitation counselor whose professional conduct is in question by a regulatory agency.

c. Unwarranted Complaints.   Rehabilitation counselors do not initiate, participate in, or encourage the filing of ethics complaints that are made with reckless disregard or willful ignorance of facts that would disprove the allegation, or are intended to harm rehabilitation counselors rather than to protect clients or the public.

L.4. Cooperation With Ethics Committees
Rehabilitation counselors assist in the process of enforcing the Code. They cooperate with requests, proceedings, and requirements of the CRCC Ethics Committee or ethics committees of other duly constituted associations or boards having jurisdiction over those charged with a violation. They are familiar with the Guidelines and Procedures for Processing Complaints and use it as a reference for assisting in the enforcement of the Code.

L.5. Unfair Discrimination Against Complainants and Respondents
Rehabilitation counselors do not deny individuals services, employment, advancement, admission to academic or other programs, tenure, or promotions based solely upon their having made or their being the subject of an ethics complaint. This does not preclude taking action based upon the outcome of such proceedings when rehabilitation counselors are found to be in violation of ethical standards.

Index

American Rehabilitation Counseling
Association, 27, 43, 205, 251, 345
Americans with Disabilities Act (1990),
46, 51, 63, 73, 87, 314, 421. *See
also* Disability; and Workers'
Compensation
ability to work, 64–65
and accommodation, 65
and direct threat, 66
disability, definition of, 64
vs. Family and Medical Leave Act,
68–69
and medical testing, 66–67
and provision for confidentiality, 68
state laws, 67
"undue hardship," doctrine of, 65–66
Americans with Disabilities Act
Amendments Act (ADAAA,
2008), 87
AMHCA. *See* American Mental Health
Counseling Association
ARC. *See* Alliance for Rehabilitation
Counseling
ARCA. *See* American Rehabilitation
Counseling Association
Assertive Community Treatment
Knowledge Informing
Transformation (ACT KIT), 401
Assessment, 221, 232, 327–328, 418, 419
behavioral, 223
and bias, 226–227
decision making, 227–232
definition, 213
disability determination, 230–232
ecological, 223–224
functional, 224
and information interpretation, 225
interviews and types, 218–221
organizing information, 225–226
and performance indicators, 216, 221
process, 216
real environment, 223–224
reliability and validity in, 217
standard tests and inventories for,
221–222
standardization in, 217
treatment and case service plans,
229–230

use of simulation in, 222–224
work samples, use in, 222
and working model development,
226, 231
Assistive technology. *See* Technology,
assistive
Association for Play Therapy, 27–28
Association for Specialists in Group
Work, 345
Attitude, 95, 114, 115, 151, 171, 260, 350,
382, 430

Bandura's social cognitive theory, 324
Behavior, 92–94, 95, 124
Bio-medical model, 148
Biopsychosocial, 168, 233, 261, 392
Boulder Conference (1949), 22, 23

CACREP. *See* Council for Accreditation of
Counseling and Related Educational
Programs
Campbell Collaboration, 393, 396
Career development, theories, 324. *See also*
INCOME framework
importance of, 318–319
social cognitive career theory, 322
Super's life-span and life-space theory,
319–320
Case advocacy, 303
Case management, 3, 10, 98–99, 198
advocacy in, 290–291
and alternative service organizations,
289–290
areas covered, 99
assertive client and good fit, issues in,
279–280
client-centered paradigm, 274–275, 276,
278, 285–287, 289
and community counseling,
286–288
and consonance, 277–279
consumer-driven paradigm, 276–277,
281, 285
and counseling career, 291–292
definition, 270
diversification of, 269, 270

Disability culture
    as a lived experience, 155–156
    purpose of, 154
    and "Ugly Laws," 154
Disability prevention
    primary prevention, 88, 89
    secondary prevention, 89
    tertiary prevention, 89
Disability Rights Community. *See also*
        Disability; Disability Culture;
        Disability Studies; and Independent
        Living Movement
    and cross-disability identification, 149
    and language usage, 157
    and nonprofit organization, role of, 159
    purpose of, 148
    rehabilitation knowledge, issues with,
        158–159
    and social model, 148, 156
Disability rights movement, 49, 51
Disability studies, 152–154
Disability Studies Quarterly, 152
Discrimination, 63, 65, 73, 76, 157, 376
Disease model. *See* Bio-medical model

Ecological adaptation model, 93–96,
        94, 104
Ecological assessment, 223–224
Ecological model, 89, 90–93, 90, 168
Economic model. *See* Functional
        Limitations model
Educators, 3, 5, 10, 30, 41, 46, 47, 48, 52,
        86, 444
Empathy fatigue, 251
"Employment Network,"72
Employment, supported, 328–329
Empowerment, 31, 46, 49, 51, 85, 168, 215,
        289, 302, 303, 304
Environmental identity, 320
Environmental normative standards, 94
Ethics, 25, 199, 230, 371
    clinical standards, 340–341, 341
    decision making models, characteristics
        of, 348–349
    definition, 342
    education, 345
    ethical counseling, components of, 340

ethical dilemma, 253, 350, 355, 357, 363
external regulatory standards, 340, 341,
        342, 346–347
governance processes, 342–347, 344
internal standards, 340, 341
vs. law, 342
mandatory *vs.* aspirational, 343, 344, 345
principles and practices, 354
and professional organizations,
        344, 344–347
professional standards structure, 341, 347
Tarvydas' integrative decision making
        model, 349–358
violation and sanction, 343
Ethnorehabilitation, 175
Eugenics, 119
Evidence-based medicine/practice
    and ICF model, 407
    importance of, 392
    and knowledge translation,
        399–402
    meta-analysis in, 396–398
    philosophy of, 392
    PICO format, 393
    questioning, importance in, 393
    randomized clinical trials and levels,
        394–395
    research utilization issues, 395–402
    resources for, 393, 400–402
    and vocational rehabilitation in
        interventions, 404–405

Family, 132, 134
    as caregivers, 137–138
    challenges faced by, 136–137
    disability and importance of family,
        135–136
    employment and community living,
        139–140
    rehabilitation process, adaptation to,
        138–139
    and relationship networks, 134–135
    therapists, 140–144
Family and Medical Leave Act, (FMLA,
        1993), 68–69
    vs. Americans with Disabilities Act,
        68–69

Paternalism, 40
Patient Protection and Affordable Care Act
    (ACA, 2010), 126
Peer consultation, 437–439
    and distance education, advantages
        in, 441
    e-supervision and counseling practice,
        441–442
People with disabilities, 43, 50, 93, 114, 119,
        126, 149, 154, 168, 174, 250, 254, 256,
        259, 264, 318, 323, 327, 407, 415–416
Personal identity, 320
Physicians for a National Health
        Program, 127
Practice laws, 27
Principle analysis, 354, 362
Problematic Use of Internet (PUI), 419
Psychiatric rehabilitation, 9, 284, 405
Psychologists, counseling, 22–23
Psychology, 6, 22, 26, 88, 172
Psychomedical model, 90, 131–132
Psychotherapy, 402
PsycINFO, 393, 396
The *Publication Manual of the American
        Psychological Association* (2010), 86

Quality of Life (QOL), 86, 96, 97, 181,
        271, 339

Racial/Cultural Identity Development
        Model (R/CID)
    conformity stage, 381
    dissonance stage, 382
    importance of, 381
    integrative awareness stage, 382–383
    introspection stage, 382
    purpose, 381
    resistance and immersion stage, 382
RCEA. *See* Rehabilitation Counselor and
        Educators Association
Rehabilitation, 3–6, 9, 95, 97, 99, 139, 140,
        174, 193, 202, 242, 252, 274, 284, 298,
        392, 394, 395
    community-based, 180–181
    concept, 83, 96–97
    counseling models, 89–96

counselor development, 101–104
counselor functions, 98, 99
definition, 84, 96
disabilities and career counseling,
        326–330
insurance, 11, 52
potential, 96
psychiatric, 9, 100, 405
service delivery systems, 98–100
vocational, 10, 41, 50– 52, 62–63, 96, 194
    systemic theory of, 132–133, 134, 145
Rehabilitation Act (1920), 41
Rehabilitation Act (1973), 46, 51, 62–63
    Amendments (1973), 46, 50, 88, 149
    Amendments (1978), 51
    Amendments (1986), 46, 51, 150
    Amendments (1992), 46, 48, 51
    Amendments (1998), 46, 51, 328, 421
Rehabilitation Counseling Consortium,
        4, 44, 194
*Rehabilitation Counseling Supervision
        Inventory*, 432
Rehabilitation Counselor and Educators
        Association, 44
Rehabilitation Counselor Education
        (RCE), 242
"Rehabilitation Counselor Preparation," 47
Rehabilitation counselors, 193, 202, 228,
        230, 232, 259, 299, 306, 314, 316–318,
        321, 326, 347, 349, 375, 379, 394–395,
        418, 435, 443. *See also* Advocacy;
        Assessment; Case management; and
        Counseling, rehabilitation
    community-based rehabilitation,
        180–181
    core skills and the skilled helper model
        stages, 244–245
    and counseling process, 195
    and counseling relationship, 244
    definition, 171, 194, 413–414
    disabilities and career counseling, 167,
        326–330
    education and training issues, 47–48,
        203–204, 242
    evidence-based approach, 198,
        200–201
    functions, 195, 215, 246, 259
    guidelines for, 261–264